Also by Meryle Secrest

DUVEEN

DUVEEN

A Life in Art

MERYLE SECREST

ALFRED A. KNOPF　　　NEW YORK　2004

THIS IS A BORZOI BOOK
PUBLISHED BY ALFRED A. KNOPF

Copyright © 2004 by Meryle Secrest Beveridge
All rights reserved under International and Pan-American
Copyright Conventions. Published in the United States
by Alfred A. Knopf, a division of Random House, Inc., New York,
and simultaneously in Canada by Random House of Canada,
Limited, Toronto. Distributed by Random House, Inc., New York.
www.aaknopf.com

Knopf, Borzoi Books, and the colophon are registered trademarks
of Random House, Inc.

Library of Congress Catalogue-in-Publication Data
Secrest, Meryle.
Duveen : a life in art / by Meryle Secrest.
p.   cm.
Includes bibliographical references and index.
ISBN 0-375-41042-2 (alk. paper)
1. Duveen, Joseph Duveen, Baron, 1869–1939.
2. Art dealers—England—Biography.   I. Title.

N8660.D82S43 2004
709'.2—dc22
[B]   2004046521

Manufactured in the United States of America
Published September 22, 2004
Reprinted Once
Third Printing, December 2004

For Gillian

They do not know that they seek only the chase
and not the quarry.

—*Blaise Pascal*

Contents

Illustrations

Preface and Acknowledgments

The archives of Duveen Brothers, art dealers in London, Paris, and New York, have long been legendary. This massive compendium of information about paintings, sculpture, furnishings, and objets d'art, comprising almost six hundred boxes of material and spanning more than a century, had, it has been said, more secrets hidden within it about the undercover world of buying and selling Old Masters than any other single source of information. Very few people had ever seen this archive, and its contents were locked away at the Metropolitan Museum of Art in New York for decades. But then the decision was made to pass the whole archive along to the Getty Research Institute for the History of Art and the Humanities in Los Angeles. It was put on microfilm and has been made available for study for the first time.

I had heard about the fabulous Duveen Archive when I began work on a biography of Bernard Berenson in 1976. Since Berenson had served as Duveen's expert on Italian Renaissance art, I was eager to see the archive, but was refused permission. I made a vow then that if the archive was ever made public, and I was still alive, I would be first in the queue. Well, I'm still here, and I have had the happy privilege of perusing its contents as the microfilm became available. As I thought, it was worth the wait.

The archive begins in 1876 and ends in 1981. However, the bulk of the letters, cables, photo albums, ledgers, sales books, stock books, manuscripts, and newspaper clippings is centered around the great years of roughly 1905 until 1939, just before World War II. These were the years when Joseph Duveen, later Lord Duveen of Millbank, son of the founder of Duveen Brothers, was buying works of art by Old Masters and selling them to American collectors such as Andrew Mellon, Jules S. Bache, Henry Clay Frick, J. P. Morgan, Henry E. and Arabella Huntington, S. H. Kress, P. A. B. and Joseph Widener, William Randolph Hearst, Marjorie Merriweather Post, and a host of lesser lights. One approaches such an archive with caution, knowing the traditional secretiveness of the art dealing world and the tendency of those donating to public repositories to do a thorough vetting of the material beforehand. Part of the importance of the

Duveen Archive is that this does not seem to have happened. The last owner of Duveen Brothers, Edward Fowles, evidently decided that the firm had nothing to hide, or that if it did, such shocks to collective sensibilities could be dealt with, given the right historical distance.

What does the archive contain? This book is an attempt to show some of the findings. It is also an attempt to deal with the question of Duveen's reputation, which has suffered since his own time, when he was a member of the British upper class, on countless committees, showered with honors and tiptoed around by the art-world press. What has to be understood in any assessment of Duveen's reputation is that most of the time, he was not doing the actual buying. He stayed in New York. The chases for merchandise in London, Paris, Vienna, Berlin, Prague, Milan, and elsewhere were being conducted by his brothers, Edward and Ernest, of the London branch, and Fowles and Armand Lowengard, of the Paris. These four extremely knowledgeable, energetic, and cautious men were well aware that they could not allow their lucrative businesses in Grafton Street (London) and the Place Vendôme (Paris), not to mention Fifth Avenue, to be threatened by sales of fakes.

So they bought extremely carefully and at the top of the market, which was a kind of guarantee that the Old Master in question would turn out to be "right," as they termed it. They were resourceful and hard to fool, and never minded telling Duveen off, a circumstance that he, curiously, meekly accepted. They acted as a brake on his impulsive decisions and exuberant willingness to sell, along with those exaggerations which came naturally to him but that filled them with foreboding. In effect, they proposed and Duveen, in New York, shuffled the index cards and decided which millionaire was going to be the new owner, *before they bought.* It was axiomatic that no new owner meant no purchase. Even when Duveen was making one of his masterstrokes and buying huge collections, as he did fairly often, he had a pretty shrewd idea who the new owners would be and, as in the sales from the Rodolphe Kann Collection, invariably had made his money back with interest before he had written the check. Their job was to stop Joe from making mistakes. Given the cavalier attention to condition that pertained in the 1920s, the wild and woolly market, and Duveen's characteristic rashness, that Duveen Brothers maintained its reputation has to be considered an achievement. The one problem the four men were never quite able to resolve was Bernard Berenson, for reasons that will become clear.

Sadly, a great many people who might have contributed substantially to this book are no longer with us: Kenneth Clark, the great British art historian; Francis Haskell, professor of the history of art at Oxford University; Sir Ellis Waterhouse; Professor Meyer Schapiro; Sir Harold Acton; Sir Geoffrey Agnew; Sir John Pope-Hennessy; Jean Gimpel; David Carritt; John Walker and J. Carter Brown, former directors of the National Gallery of Art in Washington; and Jean Fowles, widow of Edward. I have found myself referring to notes I made twenty-seven years ago when I interviewed these men and women for my biography *Being Bernard Berenson* (1979). Even so, some questions that I longed to ask will have to remain unanswered.

There are unanswered questions about the Demotte affair (chapter 11) that resisted determined efforts to uncover the truth. Was Émile Boutron, the forger of old French stone bas reliefs, who supposedly killed himself, actually murdered to silence him? There was an official inquiry in 1923, but all attempts to find the files in French records led to a dead end. Was Georges Demotte, the Belgian art dealer who employed Boutron, accidentally killed in a hunting accident that same year, or was that death more than a coincidence? Again, attempts to reach the truth were unsuccessful. My research assistant, Aude Pivin, was told by the Louvre that there was a file that presumably contained important information, but since a retired *conservateur* was writing a book about Demotte, she could not examine it. It seems officials at the Louvre believe Demotte's death "was no accident."

Fortunately I was able to make contact with members of Duveen's family, who were most helpful: Ricky Duveen, from the Hangjas side of the family; Anthony H. C. Duveen, son of Joe's brother Henry; and Clive Duveen, grandson of Joe's brother Louis. Raymond Duveen, son of Joe's brother Edward, and his wife, Pamela, gave me a delicious lunch and shared photographs and reminiscences. Benjamin, son of Joe's brother Benjamin, and his wife, Annetta, entertained me overnight in their Port Chester, New York, home, and gave me vital information, as did Annetta's son Charles. I am grateful to them all. I am also indebted to Roger Jenkins, the television and radio producer, who has long been interested in Duveen's life, and who entertained me in his charming village home near Cirencester, let me peruse his Duveen files, and gave me copies of interviews he made with Duveen's daughter, the late Dolly Burns; her husband, Bryan; and the late Sir John Foster. I cannot thank him enough.

Friends of Dolly Burns who were named to administer her two charitable trusts welcomed me warmly and gave me much help and advice. The biographer Janet Morgan, Lady Balfour of Burleigh, was kindness itself; she of course knew exactly what I needed to know and took a lively interest in the discoveries I was making. She and her husband entertained my husband and me royally at their Scottish mansion on several occasions. Besides being an accomplished writer and a fine cook, she makes the best cake in the world. Alan Bevis, Dolly Burns's former solicitor, gave me lunch at the Oxford and Cambridge Club and passed along an album of tributes Dolly Burns had gathered following her father's death, as well as family photographs. Christopher Campbell, another friend of the well-known hostess, was also enormously helpful. Robert Skidelsky, Maynard Keynes's biographer, shares my interest in people and had some insightful observations to make about Dolly Burns and her circle. Thanks to their interest, the Dolly Burns Charitable Trusts awarded me a grant to support the considerable research that has been involved in this undertaking, particularly the lists of Duveen paintings, sculpture, furnishings, and so on at the back of the book. I must mention here the particular help of the art historian Megan Smith, who not only provided me with endless details but made a special study of the Duveen paintings at the Metropolitan which has been invaluable.

I am indebted to the Getty Research Institute, and in particular Wim de Wit, head of Special Collections and Visual Resources, for his enthusiastic support of this project. Similarly, Mark Henderson, reference librarian; Jocelyn Gibbs, head of cataloguing; Dr. JoAnne Paradise, senior collections curator; and John Walsh, former director of the Getty Museum, gave me information, counsel, and vitally needed encouragement. I am also indebted to the Getty Research Institute for a travel grant to pursue my studies there.

Staff members of the National Gallery of Art in Washington took endless pains to answer my requests for information. I am particularly grateful to Maygene Daniels, head of the archives, who found some wonderful oral histories; Nancy Yeide and Ann Halpern of the curatorial files; Lemia Douma, head of reference services; Deborah Ziska, chief of press and information; Faya Causey, head of academic programs; Ann Hoenigswald, painting conservator; and Dodge Thompson, chief of exhibitions, for their help and counsel. I am also most grateful to Susan Roeper, librarian at the Sterling and Francine Clark Art Institute in Williamstown, Massachusetts, who helped me so much when I was working on the Duveen material in the institute's files; to Michael Ann Holly, head of academic programs, and Darby English, as well as Michael Conforti, director, and his wife, Licia. My thanks also go to Liana Paredes Arend, curator for Western European art at Hillwood Museum, the former home of Marjorie Merriweather Post, for her interest and help, and to Samuel Sachs II, director of the Frick Collection, for similar interest and help.

Michael Findlay, director of Acquavella in New York, read this manuscript and gave me much advice and encouragement. I am also grateful for the kindly counsel of Frank Herrmann, as well as Richard Kingzett, the distinguished associate director of Agnew's on Old Bond Street, and John Partridge, of Partridge Fine Arts in New Bond Street. Others to whom I owe warm thanks are Barbara Dawson Aikens, chief of collections processing, Archives of American Art; Rupert Allason; John M. Andrews; Bonnie Angelo; Timothy Bathurst of Artemis; Dr. Charles Avery, Sir Jack Baer, Martin Bailey; A. J. Baker, the Honorable Daniel and Ruth Boorstin; David Bull; Aniello Bianco, managing director, Chadbourne and Parke; Jack Chapman; Stephen J. Conrad; Marisa Keller, archivist, Corcoran Gallery of Art; Andrew Decker; Irene Dennis; Robin Moore Ede; David Ellis-Jones, Wildenstein; Richard Feigen; Martin Gayford, art critic, *Daily Telegraph;* René Gimpel, Gimpel Fils; Marco Grassi; Isabelle Grey; Nuño Vassallo e Silva, deputy director, Fundação Calouste Gulbenkian, Lisbon; Leslie Morris, curator, Houghton Library, Harvard; Thomas Hoving; Andrew Hunt of Amadeo Design; Shelley M. Bennett, curator, Huntington Library and Art Collections; Lawrence Jeppson; Philip Kopper; Ian F. Locke; DeCourcy McIntosh, executive director, Frick Art and Historical Center, Pittsburgh; Brian Masters; Evelyn Nef; Bruce Abrams, County Clerk's Office, New York Supreme Court; Sara Campbell, senior curator, Norton Simon Museum; Dr. Marilyn Perry, director, the Samuel Kress Foundation; John Richardson; Franklin W. Robinson, director, Herbert F. Johnson Museum of Art, Cornell University; Professor William St. Clair; Dr. Naomi Sawelson-Gorse; Peyton Skipwith, deputy managing editor, Fine Art Society; John Saumarez Smith; Clarissa Post; Sothebys; Professor Peter Stansky; Lawrence Steigrad; Sir Roy Strong; David Thompson; Sir Christopher White; Marion Whitehorn; Christopher Wright; and Mme. Lilian Ziegel.

A project like this is, as Alistair Cooke used to say, like going down Grand Canyon on a mule, a good thing to *have* done. For all those who held my hand and cheered me onward, I have special thanks: my agent, Lynn Nesbit, in New York; my former agent, Murray Pollinger, in London; my patient and indulgent husband, Thomas Beveridge; and my editor for the past sixteen years, Victoria Wilson. There really is no one like her.

—Meryle Secrest

DUVEEN FAMILY GENEALOGY

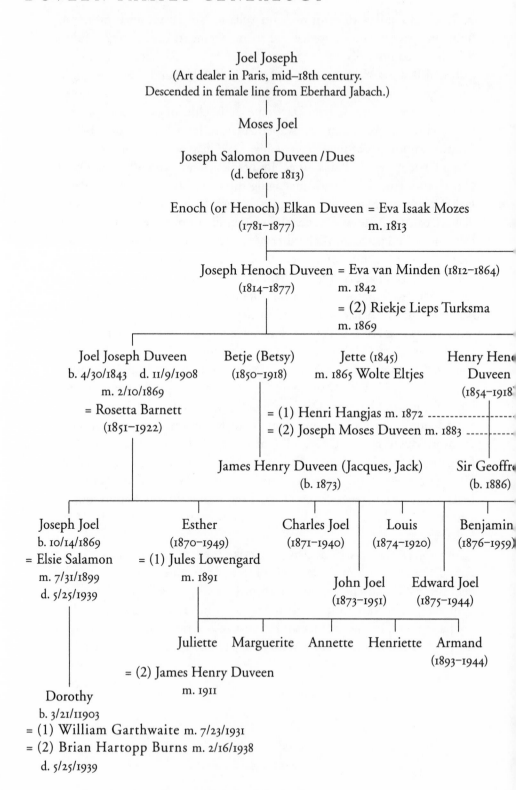

Joel Joseph
(Art dealer in Paris, mid–18th century.
Descended in female line from Eberhard Jabach.)

Moses Joel

Joseph Salomon Duveen / Dues
(d. before 1813)

Enoch (or Henoch) Elkan Duveen = Eva Isaak Mozes
(1781-1877)   m. 1813

Joseph Henoch Duveen = Eva van Minden (1812-1864)
(1814-1877)   m. 1842

= (2) Riekje Lieps Turksma
m. 1869

Joel Joseph Duveen
b. 4/30/1843 d. 11/9/1908
m. 2/10/1869
= Rosetta Barnett
(1851-1922)

Betje (Betsy)
(1850-1918)

Jette (1845)
m. 1865 Wolte Eltjes

Henry Henc
Duveen
(1854-1918

= (1) Henri Hangjas m. 1872 ------------------
= (2) Joseph Moses Duveen m. 1883 -----------

James Henry Duveen (Jacques, Jack)
(b. 1873)

Sir Geoffr
(b. 1886)

Joseph Joel
b. 10/14/1869
= Elsie Salamon
m. 7/31/1899
d. 5/25/1939

Esther
(1870-1949)
= (1) Jules Lowengard
m. 1891

Charles Joel
(1871-1940)

Louis
(1874-1920)

Benjamin
(1876-1959)

John Joel
(1873-1951)

Edward Joel
(1875-1944)

Juliette Marguerite Annette Henriette Armand
(1893-1944)

= (2) James Henry Duveen
m. 1911

Dorothy
b. 3/21/11903
= (1) William Garthwaite m. 7/23/1931
= (2) Brian Hartopp Burns m. 2/16/1938
d. 5/25/1939

Compiled from a genealogy in
The Rise of the House of Duveen
by James Henry Duveen and con-
temporary sources

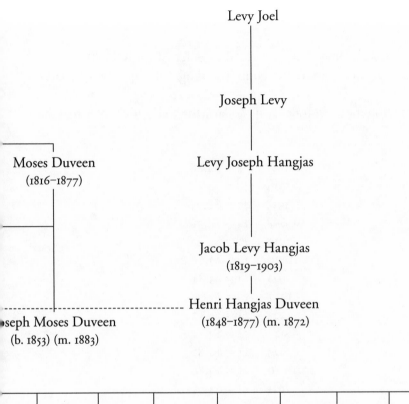

Levy Joel

Joseph Levy

Moses Duveen
(1816–1877)

Levy Joseph Hangjas

Jacob Levy Hangjas
(1819–1903)

Henri Hangjas Duveen
(1848–1877) (m. 1872)

seph Moses Duveen
(b. 1853) (m. 1883)

Albert Joel
(1877–1882)

Henry Joel
(1878–1963)

Annette Evalina
(1879–1954)

Bertrand Joel
(1882–?)

Ernest
(1883–1959)

Evaline
(1884–1976)

Joseph Edgar
(dates unknown)
b. 1885?)

Florence
(1886–1978)
= René Gimpel
(m. 1912)

A Note on Exchange Rates

Since, in Duveen's time, London was the center of the Old Master art market, sales prices are quoted in pounds sterling. (One guinea = £1 and 1 shilling.)

For contemporary equivalents in dollars, the following tables may be helpful:

1913	£1 = $4.86
1914	£1 = $4.92
1915	£1 = $4.75
1916–8	£1 = $4.76
1919	£1 = $4.42
1920	£1 = $3.66
1921	£1 = $3.84
1922	£1 = $4.42
1923	£1 = $4.57
1924	£1 = $4.41
1925	£1 = $4.82
1926–30	£1 = $4.86
1931	£1 = $4.53
1932	£1 = $3.50
1933	£1 = $4.23
1934	£1 = $5.03
1935	£1 = $4.90
1936	£1 = $4.97
1937	£1 = $4.94
1938	£1 = $4.88
1939	£1 = $4.43

—Source: *Banking and Monetary Statistics, 1914–1941*, United States Federal Reserve

DUVEEN

Chapter One

THE CHASE

IT IS GENERALLY AGREED THAT, of the select band of women enter-prising enough to be called collectors in the nineteenth century, Lady Charlotte Schreiber won hands down. Possessed of considerable means, dauntless energy, and the zest for the chase which is the natural prerequisite for the making of great collections, Lady Charlotte knew no barriers when it came to her own quarry. These included lace, fans, and playing cards, and, above all, ceramics. She loved china with a passion in the days when hardly anyone knew enough to recognize Chelsea, Bow, Worcester, and Derby, or cared, leaving such treasures to be picked up in any old junk shop for derisory sums. The more she collected, in those halcyon days of the 1860s and 1870s, the more enthralled she became by the chase. As her son Montague Guest wrote, "She hunted high and low, through England and abroad; France, Holland, Germany, Spain, Italy, Turkey, all were ran-sacked; she left no stone unturned, no difficulty, discomfort, fatigue, or hardship of travel daunted her, or turned her from her purpose, and she would come back, after weeks on the Continent . . . rich with the fruits of her expeditions."

No doubt she benefited from those tips by anonymous scouts that fig-ure so largely in such narratives. On one occasion she learned that there were some wonderful pieces of china for sale in a tiny farmhouse miles from any town or railway. In the pursuit of such hidden treasure a collector needed to be infinitely ready to conjure up any means of transportation available. There is an eyewitness account of this particular hunt, so typical of Lady Charlotte's enterprise, by someone who had also received a tip, per-haps from the same source. He, too, was hot on the trail, which involved an

Joseph Duveen's father, Joel, as a young
entrepreneur. Date unknown

inordinately slow and lengthy journey by train. As this hunter neared the
quarry he observed a passenger coach on a road parallel to the tracks coming toward him. The fly roared past at breakneck speed, but he managed to
catch a glimpse of a certain indomitable face. He knew, before he reached
his destination, that he had arrived too late.

The disappointed buyer was Joel Joseph Duveen, a man who, it must
be said, was her equal in terms of energy, dash, and devil-may-care determination. It is sometimes thought that his son Joseph Duveen, the most
spectacular art dealer the world has ever known, appeared in all his singularity from a back street in the Yorkshire town of Hull. This convenient fiction glides over the fact that the future Lord Duveen was in all essential
respects modeled after his equally formidable father. Here was a man who,
in the best Horatio Alger tradition, began from nothing, coming from
nowhere, and at the end of a scintillating career, as Sir Joseph Duveen, was
dining with aristocrats and on intimate terms with kings, rich, successful,
and feared. To take charge of an establishment that has risen to the heights
of Old Bond Street is not quite the same as having reached there in the first
place; but that is another part of the story.

The riddle of Joseph Duveen starts with the story of his father, and in both men one sees characteristics that were to imprint these personalities on their age; men who, like Isambard Kingdom Brunel, for instance, but metaphorically, threw bridges across chasms and hollowed out mountains to reach their goals. An early photograph of Joel Joseph shows a wide, high-cheeked face, one ear dextrously cocked, as if awaiting the latest rumor, a fussily trimmed beard and mustache, broad, flat, pudgy hands and the insouciant air of a man who will leap up in a second and dash out of the door. The expression is alert and good-natured, optimistic; and there is something about the smile that suggests someone not only prepared to challenge authority but used to discovering, as Alice did in Wonderland, that most barriers built by custom and snobbery are nothing but packs of cards.

It is true that Joel Joseph was self-made, but to say that he came from nowhere is perhaps not quite the case. Looking down the Duveen lineage one finds generational mirrors refracting ever fainter reflections of collectors and dealers in furniture, porcelains, tapestries, and Old Master paintings. Jacques Duveen, who later took the name of Jack, wrote a valuable account of the Duveen family origins and the early life of Joel Joseph, based on conversations he had with his uncle in the years before the latter's death in 1908; he called it *The Rise of the House of Duveen*. Jack claimed to have traced the family pedigree back to the seventeenth-century Du Vesnes (hence, Duveen), who were related to Eberhard Jabach. This head of a family of wealthy merchant bankers was a Sephardic Jew who moved from Spain to France during one of the early persecutions. He was well enough known to have been painted by Sir Anthony van Dyck and Charles le Brun, and was a distinguished art collector, one of the principal buyers at the sale of the collection of the ill-fated Charles I (1600–1649), another exemplary patron of the arts, particularly Italian painting. Jack Duveen wrote in *Art Treasures and Intrigue*, "The tradition is that when [Jabach] returned from the sale he entered Paris at the head of a convoy of wagons loaded with artistic conquests, like a Roman victor at the head of a triumphal procession." Even Jabach's considerable resources were not limitless, and when he, a few years later, was obliged to sell 110 of his best paintings to Louis XIV (1638–1715), the collection formed the nucleus of what would become the Louvre. Among the most famous works were three incomparable paintings by Giorgione: *Rustic Concert, Holy Family with St. Catherine,* and *St. Sebastian and Donor;* Titian's *Christ at Emmaus, Entombment, Jupiter and Antiope,* and *Mistress;* Correggio's *Antiope;* and Caravaggio's *Death of Mary:* acknowledged masterpieces of the Italian Renaissance. All the glory that such names conjured up became synonymous with a fabulous past, and the name of Duveen, so carelessly corrupted from the aristocratic Du Vesne, a constant noble reminder of what had been lost.

During the French Revolution one of Jabach's descendants, Henoch Elkan Duveen, emigrated from Paris to Holland, where, in 1810, he took over a small iron foundry in Meppel. Joel later told A. C. R. Carter that his grandfather had been an army contractor for horses and their equipment to the King of Saxony. So the legend began that Joel had begun life as a blacksmith's apprentice, and in fact he is listed as such in the Meppel registry, according to a Dutch chronicler of the Duveen family. Joel's father, Joseph Henoch Duveen (Henoch Elkan's son), was more than a blacksmith, however. The same account notes that he was a manufacturer of stoves and heaters, specializing in iron safes fitted with secret locks. A smithy was attached to the foundry and Joel claimed to have learned how to make horseshoes as part of a lengthy apprenticeship while being groomed for a future in manufacturing. Starting them young and making them proficient in every aspect of the business became one of his maxims when the time came to train his own sons.

One of Henoch Elkan's cousins, Levy Joseph—the names are confusing, since they recur down through the generations, with hardly any alteration—also fled from France during the same period and somehow assumed the surname of Hangjas, no one knows quite how. He established a branch of the family which carried on the tradition of trading in antiques, setting himself up in business in The Hague. The two branches remained in contact, and there was more than one intermarriage between first cousins. One male member of the Hangjas branch even assumed the name of Duveen when he married one of the Duveen girls.

Managing an ironworks would seem something of a departure from the inherited family passion, but even that had a precedent. Jack Duveen wrote that his grandfather Jacob Levy Hangjas, Levy Joseph's son, dealt in old metals as well as running a wholesale business in antiques and had a warehouse and wharf on the river Spaarne for the dismantling of steamships. Joel's father had also dealt in antiques before he took over the ironworks and passed that business on to one of his daughters, a girl who married the Ridder (Chevalier) van Esso, or Essoo. To give a business to a girl was unusual in those days. Girls were more often moved around like pawns in the game of tightening family connections or consolidating spheres of influence, a game at which art dealers excelled, like minor principalities. None played it better than the Duveens, the Hangjas branch in particular. Several Hangjas girls married leading art dealers of the day: De Maan, Van Schaak, and a man named Levy Fresco, said to have owned the gallery that served as the model for Dickens's novel *The Old Curiosity Shop.* By such prudent methods intricate chains of association were forged that could have satisfying consequences.

Joel Joseph Duveen, born in Meppel on April 30, 1843, was named for the great-great-great-grandfather who was descended on the female line from Eberhard Jabach. No doubt that significant point was impressed on him at an early age, and if he showed any talent for the antique business, there was no shortage of teachers. Jack Duveen relates that Joel was indeed a willing pupil under the tutelage of his aunt, the one who had married the Ridder van Esso. Her specialty is not described, but it would have been axiomatic that a Dutch dealer would have a sophisticated knowledge of ceramics. He or she would know, in the case of old Delft polychrome pottery, then becoming increasingly scarce and prized, that a Paris firm was making a clever profit from nice copies. He would learn about the confusing marks separating genuine old silver from its mundane, therefore modern, facsimiles. He would have to know how Oriental porcelain, called Oost Indiesch in Holland, had been made, so that he could instantly recognize the genuine and rare from its many counterfeits. He would have studied those hieroglyphics adorning the bases of vases and ornaments and learned to decipher their significance. He would be able to tell when a piece of china had been repaired or tampered with, no matter how delicate the hairline of evidence. Similarly, he would know where to look for those minute clues verifying antique Chippendale from virtually identical reproductions. Thanks to intensive training, he could discern an Old Master beneath layers of discolored varnish and defacing restorations and be equally able to spot a fake, no matter how persuasively painted in the ateliers of Rome and Paris. He would be able to make a discovery at an auction and then know how to conceal that fact by a show of indifference. The first imperative was that he could not be fooled and the second, that he learn to dissemble, hiding his real feelings; perhaps the most important lesson of all.

As for the chase itself, the feints, subterfuges, and stratagems, the deceits, intrigues, and double dealings, learning all that took a lifetime. Such knowledge was never written down, but learned by rote like great epic poems until a student could predict every move, giving that extra negotiating advantage that makes all the difference. He would also have become an aesthete, because any dealer who wanted to attract wealthy clients had to have a collector's instinct. The curious fact was that most of them did. The Duveens either had or developed superb memories and an uncanny ability to spot hidden treasures. They called it the Duveen eye.

Joel's future seemed assured, but then there was a family tragedy. In his irresistible biography of Duveen, published in 1951, the playwright S. N. Behrman has demoted Joseph Henoch Duveen to a blacksmith and describes his wife as a simple farm woman with a penchant for collecting bits of cheap Delft. This picturesque version of events is the probable reason why Jack Duveen was moved to write his own account in 1957. He writes that Joel's mother, Eva van Minden of Zwolle, was no ignorant country girl but the well-educated daughter of an East India merchant. She appears not to have had the least interest in collecting, but inspired her son with her love of books and music and made sure he was properly educated. Joel was her firstborn; then came two daughters, Jette and Betje (Betsy), Jack's future mother, and finally Henoch (Henry), born in 1855 and twelve years Joel's junior. Eva Duveen was beautiful and cultivated but physically fragile, and an invalid for the final years of her life, dying at the age of fifty-two on August 20, 1864. Her parting words to her firstborn, then aged twenty-one, were to look after his sisters and nine-year-old brother and care for his father. This last piece of advice turned out to be prescient because, after Eva's death, Joseph turned to drink for consolation, dangerously neglecting his business affairs. Joel had been trained to take charge, and suddenly the full burden of managing the ironworks had fallen on him. His efforts failed, largely due to his inexperience of the ways of the world. He had neglected to grease the palm of a government inspector, and a lucrative contract was revoked as a result, effectively bankrupting the firm.

Jack Duveen makes no mention of recriminations between father and son, but these seem likely, even inevitable. Besides, Joel was hardly a boy anymore. Duveens, who began working as early as sixteen or seventeen, were expected to be making their mark by their early twenties. Joel had been given a major responsibility and had made a mess of it. He had to leave home—the sooner, the better. It is charming to think of him setting out for England with boxes of his mother's Delft under his arm, as Behrman narrates. The prosaic truth, according to Jack Duveen, is that an uncle gave him a letter of introduction to some wholesale importers of Dutch produce in Hull on the North Sea named Doumouriez and Gotschalk. Leaving his father and younger sisters and brother behind, he sailed for England in 1866 and was hired as a lowly apprentice—an indignity for someone his age—at the minuscule sum of fifteen shillings a week.

To remain in such a job would be intolerable for any Duveen, and for the moment Joel had the extra handicap of knowing almost no English. He soon gravitated to the company of an old Dutch foreman named Jan. Joel told Jack, "Even he did not speak English properly but his Frisian was not so far removed from the Yorkshire Anglo-Saxon. However, in a few minutes we became very friendly, and he offered to give me a few hours that evening to show me the stock." Joel noticed there were a large number of smoked hams in the warehouse that Doumouriez and Gotschalk had deemed too poor to sell. He suggested that the merchandise be soaked in brine to improve its appearance and then put up for auction, an idea that apparently had not occurred to anyone. It was gratefully accepted.

One day Jan hinted that dirty work was afoot in the office. Somehow the suppliers of Doumouriez and Gotschalk were becoming known to their competitors, along with the names of their customers. As a result they were losing business; something had to be done. Showing that initiative and enterprise that were such marked aspects of his character, Duveen sprang into action. When the next shipment of imports arrived on the docks early one morning, Duveen was there—as a spy. As he watched, one of the office clerks was seen making lists of the Dutch sources (names on the labels that were always removed before being forwarded) and passing them along to another young man, who rewarded him with a tip. Duveen told his employers, who confronted the culprit. He confessed, and Joel's salary was smartly increased to three pounds a week.

Then came Joel's finest hour. It was clear to him that Doumouriez and Gotschalk, while possessing an excellent reputation for reliability and honest dealing, lacked that get-up-and-go that he was uniquely favored by providence to provide. Thanks to the treachery of a clerk, they had lost considerable business; well, he was the man to get it back for them. If they would give him a week in Holland, he had a scheme not only to recover their former suppliers but to increase their numbers and get better wholesale prices into the bargain. Such an idea struck them as the maddest folly. But, on the other hand, what did they have to lose? They must have realized that they had found an unusually gifted salesman. There was only one problem, Gotschalk said. It happened to be a Saturday, and there was no boat running from Holland that day. It was too late to catch the Harwich boat, and nothing went out on a Sunday, meaning that Joel would not arrive in Holland until Monday night at the earliest. There was really no pressing reason why he should not start work on Tuesday morning instead of Monday; but Duveen, with the failure of his father's business still vivid in his mind, had something to prove. If Doumouriez and Gotschalk would give him their price lists, he would guarantee to get across somehow that very day, that afternoon.

As soon as he had the precious lists, he packed and ran down to the docks. There he had the good luck to find a Dutch fishing smack just

about to sail for Harlingen, a Frisian port on the Zuider Zee. The crossing
was stormy, but a day later they arrived none the worse. He had not lost a
working second. A few days afterwards Joel returned to Hull "with a fine
collection of offers at prices that would enable the firm to make good profits while beating all competitors . . . in price and quality." It was a kind of
dry run for all the maneuvering that would come later. He topped this by
opening new markets for Doumouriez and Gotschalk in Liverpool and
Manchester, and every time he succeeded, his income rose. By the end of
the year, instead of fifteen shillings a week he was earning fifteen pounds, a
staggering sum in those days. He had become the best-paid employee in
the Hull produce business. Even his father was impressed.

It is tempting to think of Joel Joseph Duveen in terms one would use
for a strategist, someone who by virtue of superior daring and decisive
action achieves victory. As Napoleon said, "L'audace, l'audace, et toujours
l'audace!" and the comparison with that genius is tempting. Being bested
by a woman like Lady Charlotte Schreiber was a story Joel could conde-
scend to tell, because it happened so seldom. Like many men of energy and
vision, he tended to be impatient and demanding in personal relationships.
But at that stage of his life he had not yet developed the suspiciousness,
amounting to paranoia, that would mar his final years. He was too trust-
ing, naïve almost. That willingness to look on the bright side had led to the
collapse of his father's business, and now it would bring him up short
again. After trying, and failing, to become a partner in the firm of Doumouriez and Gotschalk, he set himself up in partnership with a Dutch
acquaintance to go into the Dutch produce business on his own. He had
energy and vision, but he had taken at face value his partner's assurances
that the necessary capital would be forthcoming. In fact there was no
money, and the threat of bankruptcy loomed again. Chalk up one more
failure for Joel Joseph. After the predictable upheaval—and Duveen's
explosions of rage would become legendary—he stomped out.

THE DUTCH CHRONICLER of the Duveen family in Meppel believed
that before he left for England, Joel Joseph had spent some months living
with his aunt Reina in Zwolle and had been a great asset in her husband's
antique shop. And so, after his experiments with an ironworks and the
wholesale produce business, it seemed inevitable that Joel should turn his
attention as ancestral habit and inclination would suggest and start thinking seriously about antiques.

One of his English friends was Barney Barnett, the son of a Hull jeweler and brother of a girl, Rosetta, whom Joel was taking out. Joel suggested that he and Barney take a trip to Holland. As soon as they arrived he went straight to the home of his uncle Jaap, Jacob Levy Hangjas (Jack's future grandfather), who was living with his wife, Anna, in a beautiful seventeenth-century corner house in Haarlem. They stayed for dinner and admired the rooms filled with valuable antique furniture, crystal, silver, paintings, and tapestries. The dining room in particular had cabinets full of prize Oost Indiesch porcelain. Throughout the meal young Barnett kept looking longingly at these trophies of the hunt, and as soon as they were alone, he asked Joel whether he thought "Oom" Jaap might part with any of them. He was sure he had a hot market for them in Hull.

Joel was confident those particular items were not for sale, but he knew where there were others, because his uncle was a wholesale dealer in art. As ever alert to a promising business deal, Joel said, "Look here, Barney, if you can sell these things like hot cakes, jewellers and antique dealers all over England could do the same." Instead of buying a single case, why didn't they buy a dozen cases between them and sell them around the area? Barney was doubtful but allowed himself to be carried along by his friend's enthusiasm.

Once they entered Oom Jaap's warehouse and saw the size of the opportunity, Joel's ambitions soared into the stratosphere. Here were hundreds upon thousands of pretty little cups and saucers, some in matching sets of a dozen, for sale at tenpence each. They ended up buying the lot, as well as a further group of old Delft jars that were slightly more expensive: one shilling and threepence each. The total bill, payable in three months, was just over two hundred pounds ($1,000).

Joel took examples back with him, and by the time he returned home, taking a roundabout route by way of Leeds, Manchester, Liverpool, and Chester, he had sold them all—even before the goods arrived in Hull. Between them, Joel and Barney made more than a thousand pounds' ($5,000) profit. Jack Duveen wrote, "From then onwards the two young partners travelled regularly through Holland accompanied by my father who, although only twenty years old at the time, was already a great expert with a good knowledge of the Continental markets." He was referring to Henri Hangjas, Oom Jaap's son, who later married Joel's sister Betsy and took the Duveen name.

Jack Duveen does not describe the moment when Joel Joseph Duveen and Barney Barnett opened their own establishment, but it must have come about with that first successful raid on Oom Jaap's warehouse. From no particular career, Joel suddenly had a start in the antique business, a

new partner, and bright prospects. With Henri Hangjas as advisor, someone on whom he could rely because he was in the family, all Joel had to do
was listen carefully and then find the money—and Oom Jaap was willing
to lend. It was almost too easy. At first the firm of Barnett and Duveen
hedged their bets, looking for cheap items that would involve modest capital investments and pay off in quick sales, like the cups and saucers. But
Henri was always pushing them to widen their horizons and start dealing
in something really attractive. After three successful forays into Holland,
they had amassed a capital of five thousand pounds ($25,000), and Henri
decided they were ready for the next step in their education.

Boas-Berg of Amsterdam, who had a store on the Kalverstraat, was considered the greatest art dealer of his day. He was also known as touchy and
temperamental, and nothing he had for sale was cheap. Joel recalled that
he, Barney Barnett, and Henri Hangjas were passing Boas-Berg's window
one day when their attention was taken by some china vases they could see
lining the walls of the interior. They were Nankin porcelain of the *lange
lyzen* type, a name given by seventeenth-century Dutch importers to a particular design of graceful figures in Nankin blue painted on a dazzling
white ground. The vases came in sets of five, and there must have been
dozens of such sets, tightly packed on shelves around the room. In a flash,
Joel's mind was made up. "It was the first time that I felt this irresistible
urge to buy," he told Jack Duveen. "Old Boas-Berg saw my look, and
remarked, 'Yes, they are very good,' and then added, 'The only blue-and-
white I have ever bought.' " Duveen told the owner he would like some
sets and asked how much he wanted for the perfect ones. "Perfect ones! Do
you think I deal in damaged pots?" the old man roared, and Duveen had to
do some fast explaining. After he repeated his question he was told the
price was sixty pounds per set.

Joel glanced towards Henri; Henri approved. At once he began walking
along the shelves, picking out his merchandise. He would take this one,
and this one, and this one, he said, instinctively selecting the vases with the
deepest and most lustrous blues. When he got to the tenth, Boas-Berg,
completely unnerved by such crude wholesale methods, shouted, "Stop! I
won't sell any more today!" Having bargained the price down to fifty
pounds a set, Joel wrote a check and received a receipt, but noted that
when they left, Boas-Berg refused to shake hands. The idea that someone
who had just made a large sale should feel ill-used was unique to Joel
Duveen's experience, but, as he said, Boas-Berg "loved his stock better than
money."

Barney Barnett was predictably horrified at this costly adventure, but

Henri was sure it was the best piece of business Joel had ever done. Henri had once found a fine set which he bought for the same price (fifty pounds, or $250) and sold in London for a hundred and fifty pounds. He congratulated Joel on his uncanny ability to select the best examples. Joel was all for collecting the merchandise then and there. Barney thought he was mad. Asking for delivery before the check had cleared would surely antagonize Boas-Berg even further. But Henri was willing to try, and while he returned to make their case, Joel rented a sitting room in the hotel in which they were staying. Henri returned victorious and they sat down to a meal later that day surrounded by fifty glorious Nankin vases. Joel observed, "It was a very clear day and I have never forgotten the sight of those lovely blues lighting up that large room." When the sets arrived in Hull, they sold for two hundred and fifty pounds each, almost as fast as they could be unpacked. It was another triumph for the team of Barnett, Duveen, and Hangjas.

After that, the boys from Hull were ready to buy anything Henri suggested, as he guided them through the ever murkier waters of fine Nankin, famille verte, famille rose, and famille noire. The quality was rising steadily, but the prices were going up even faster—those Dutch dealers knew what they had. Henri thought they might do better in Belgium, where, after all, they had the advantage of being able to signal each other in Dutch, a language so seldom spoken elsewhere, it amounted to a private code. They bought a few fine pieces in Antwerp, Brussels, Ghent, and Bruges and were on the point of returning to London when Henri received a telegram from his father: RETURN IMMEDIATELY HAWTHORN. Whatever did that mean? Joel wanted to know. Henri could hardly contain his excitement: His father was referring to the rarest and most perfect of all Nankin porcelain, the hawthorn jars. They just managed to make the Brussels-Amsterdam express, arriving in Haarlem early that afternoon. Oom Jaap was waiting for them at the station. He had learned that a baron whom everyone knew as Dolle Piet (Mad Pete), who had a country house between Haarlem and Leyden, was prepared to sell a hawthorn ginger jar of the very finest blue. A dealer in Leyden had already offered a thousand gulden for the jar (eighty-eight pounds, or $440), but the baron would not make up his mind until Henri had seen it.

Jack Duveen wrote: "Joel Duveen, who never allowed the grass to grow under his feet, chartered the fastest pair of horses in Haarlem and drove the whole party to the large mansion. The Baron received them at the head of the grand outer stairway, and invited them all to come first into the library for a drink . . . but Henri begged him to let them see the [jar] while the light was still good. The Baron had [it] brought in, and then my uncle beheld the most beautiful 'jewel' he had ever seen . . ." A hawthorn vase from the K'ang-hsi period, known to Victorian dealers as a ginger jar, is noted for its poetic tracery of cherry blossoms on a deep-blue, lustrous ground, and it is the quality of this blue that is especially prized. The legend is that a nameless Chinese artist had been inspired to make the vase by the sight of cherry blossoms floating on the Blue River (the Yangtze) in late spring, "the reflection of the azure sky in the dark ice [making] for them a deep, crackled background. It was a sight to wrench the heart of an artist with ecstasy." For years the artist tried vainly to produce the exact shade of blue. The kiln was either too hot and the blue too black, or too cool, causing the blue to fade to gray. Encouraged by his emperor, the artist began to experiment with a particularly rare and beautiful cobalt, imported from an Arab merchant. Further disappointments followed until the day that he opened his kiln to discover that the impossible had been achieved: "There in front of him lay vases of deep yet translucent blue that had the almost miraculous quality of a marbled waviness," Jack Duveen wrote. "The colour seemed to throb, just as the sunlit sky had made to throb those blue reflections on the ice floe. The white prunus sprays, nervously drawn on this palpitating blue, had an effect almost of lightning." And now Henri, Oom Jaap, Barney, and Joel were standing in the presence of a flawless example of the hawthorn jar and the moment when this vision of loveliness had been achieved.

Showing that decisiveness which was such a conspicuous aspect of his character, Joel immediately started to bargain. He knew, thanks to Henri, that the offer of a thousand gulden was far too small, since a vase of that quality had to be worth three hundred to four hundred pounds ($1,500–$2,000). He would offer five thousand gulden, cash down. The baron at first thought he was joking, but when Duveen sat down and began to count out the money his expression changed. He was all for having them stay to dinner but Joel, taking no chances, wanted to be off with his prize, and they left half an hour later. Henri was thrilled with the purchase, but Barney and Oom Jaap were sure he had paid two thousand gulden too much. They would be lucky to make a hundred pounds' profit, in their view. Henri was the only one convinced Joel had not made a mistake.

There was only one problem. Duveen knew that he did not have a customer in the north of England who could pay such a large sum for a single piece of Chinese porcelain. He obviously had to sell it in London, but to whom? Henri, with his surprising contacts, came to the rescue. He knew an artist named Henry Grego, who was a friend of James Orrock's, then the greatest living collector of fine Chinese porcelain. In those days when nothing happened without an introduction, Henri proposed to introduce Joel to Grego, who would then take them to meet Orrock for a small personal consideration, the standard operating procedure. Joel and Barney practically leapt aboard the next train for London, and once they had been introduced to Grego, the three of them took a taxi to Orrock's apartment, where they were cordially received.

The moment to unveil the treasure had arrived. "My God!" Orrock exclaimed. He took up the jar and carried it over to the window. He turned it this way and that. He tried it under various lights. He "absolutely gloated" over it, Joel Duveen recalled. Then he abruptly asked, "How much?" The price, Duveen said without turning a hair, was twelve hundred pounds. Sold. Grego received a hundred pounds for his trouble, and Henri, who presumably could have sold the jar himself, got a hundred and twenty pounds, leaving a nice little profit of one hundred and seventy pounds each for Joel and his partner. That particular hawthorn ginger jar is now in the Victoria and Albert Museum.

The hawthorn ginger jar sale was, in a sense, Duveen's undoing. Just thinking about all the rich men in London who would pay thousands for the right piece of merchandise made him feel limp. Why was he bothering with tenpenny cups in the backwater of Hull when every instinct told him he was destined for greater things? But Barnett, cautious where Joel was reckless, and content with small rewards, would not consider leaving Hull. Besides, even Joel had to concede that he needed to know about much more than Oost Indiesch porcelain if he was to succeed in that competitive world. He was ready for a new line and thought he had found it with old Dutch oak cabinets, which were practically worthless in Holland but fetched a nice penny in the British market, so he began to import them by the dozen. Then a further opportunity presented itself.

In December of 1868 Duveen was traveling in an old-fashioned stagecoach with Henri Hangjas through the Achterhock (Back Corner) of Gelderland. They had gone there to look at some family porcelain in a large country house near Ruurloo, not far from the German border, but on their arrival, had discovered the goods had been sold to another family member for a derisory sum, "a tenth of what I would have given," Joel recalled with some indignation. They had approached the new owner as a matter of course, but there was nothing doing. So they were on their way back to Haarlem, and Duveen had started to doze off when Henri, that font of surprising information, shook him and asked him whether he would be interested in some first-quality Beauvais tapestries. Of course he would, said the future Tapestry King (as he came to be called), but what were Beauvais tapestries? They were not far from Slangenburg, one of the biggest medieval castles in Holland, owned by the Count von der Goltz, and the word was out that a complete wall covering of tapestries might be for sale. These had been created in Beauvais from designs of the Flemish painter Charles-Antoine Coypel and showed scenes from the story of Don Quixote. If the owner was willing to sell, they would fetch a fortune in the Paris market.

By then Duveen was wide awake, because valuable tapestries fetching high prices were just the kind of merchandise he wanted. At Zelham, a village about five miles from Slangenburg, they alighted at the inn and were able to hire a post-chaise, as Duveen recalled, "one of those beautifully painted old shays, drawn by a racing trotter." He took charge of the reins, and thanks to a blessedly smooth road, they reached the castle in about twenty minutes. Since they had the benefit of an introduction from an antiquarian in Utrecht, they were courteously received. The Count was happy to show them his roomful of the Don Quixote tapestries, vibrant figures on the palest of yellow grounds with glorious borders. And now the young man who had started out by ordering used furniture in cartloads, like so many sides of beef, was fast metamorphosing into someone who appreciated what he was seeing and whose ambition was becoming the superfine. He called it "my usual fever for possession." Once the urge had him in its grip, it was useless for an owner to protest that such beauty was not for sale. Duveen simply translated it into his own language, which meant that he should be offering more money. When, in this particular case, it dawned on him that the owner actually meant what he said, Duveen was a man whose ambition had been deferred, not deterred. (He finally acquired the tapestries not once, but twice, and the second time around he paid double, perhaps to demonstrate that it was useless to deny a Duveen.)

It was dark by the time they returned to their horse and carriage. As they were turning out of the drive a man loomed out of the darkness and the horse reared up in fright. He was a servant who worked at the castle and had some information to sell. After agreeing on the price, the man told Joel and Henri that a family in Arnhem owned furniture upholstered with the same Don Quixote tapestries they so much admired. He gave them an address; they went to the house the next morning. This time they were in luck. The owner and his sister really did need to sell and they had, indeed, inherited furniture from Slangenburg that they would be happy to show. As the dust covers were removed one by one, Duveen stared in astonishment: two large and two small settees, six bergères (low, wide easy chairs), six large armchairs, and twelve single chairs, all richly gilt, carved in the Louis XV style and upholstered with the famous Beauvais tapestries. More and more beauties were unwrapped, each more exquisite than the last: two screens, identically carved in Louis XV style and covered with Don Quixote scenes; a pair of commodes in Louis XV with rich ormolu mounts, by Caffieri, and another pair in Louis XVI by Jean-Henri Riesener, with ormolu mounts by Pierre Gouthière. There was a small escritoire and chiffonier, also by Riesener. There were delicate occasional tables and a bonheur-du-jour (lady's writing and dressing table) in matching lacquers with more ormolu mounts by Gouthière. There were two large cabinets and two small bookcases with tambour sliding doors in the form of richly bound books, all by David Roentgen.

Duveen said, "Most of the pieces were signed by their makers, but at that time I knew practically nothing about French furniture, and I only found out about their tremendous importance when I began to deal regularly in the finest pieces; but I was nevertheless stunned by our find." Henri said he had never seen furniture of that quality outside museums and palaces. He was sure the collection must be worth double the asking price of thirty thousand gulden. The urgent question became, how were they to afford this heavenly treasure trove, since buy it they must? Henri was willing to put up a third, but they had nothing like enough money with them. The owner finally agreed on a down payment of four thousand gulden and also agreed to let the partners remove the furniture with the understanding that he would accompany them as far as Haarlem, where they would borrow the balance from Henri's father. For Joel had already learned an absolute rule about his business, which was that you never gave a seller a chance to change his mind, or a rival a chance to outbid you. Somehow or other you took the goods with you.

Leaving with vans full of delicate furniture presented a certain obstacle in this case but one that, as usual, called forth all of Duveen's resourcefulness. Fortunately for him, Arnhem was a major railway center, and he was able to hire two special cars to be added to the next fast train for Amsterdam. "In less than two hours I had everything in two old-fashioned removal vans. The men worked for double wages, and a few minutes before our train left for Amsterdam the three of us were on it, the furniture travelling behind us." However, once they arrived in Haarlem, they were chagrined to discover that Oom Jaap had gone to Brussels. Between them, he and Henri could only raise a further eight thousand gulden, leaving a large balance outstanding. Again, Henri came to the rescue, managing to borrow the remainder from an old friend of his father's, and the owner was paid in full.

As fast as they had bought the furniture, they had to get rid of it, because too much money was at stake. The pair took their prize straight to Paris, and were obliged to accept an offer of £8,000 ($40,000) for the lot, much to Henri's disgust. Joel later learned that the collection's true value was closer to £40,000. Still, they had paid off their debt and made a profit; split three ways, the net worked out at just over £1,800 each, less expenses. There was enough, Duveen decided early in 1869, to pay for a nice wedding.

He had been engaged for some time to Barney's sister Rosetta, but her family had refused to sanction their marriage until his financial prospects were brighter. Rosetta, slim, dark-haired, and not conventionally pretty, had, to judge from an early photograph, a sharp-featured, knowing little face. She would always remain in the background of his life, supplying the oasis of calm that her dashing, high-spirited, and impatient husband needed. She, too, had a salesman's instincts. A. C. R. Carter related that, fairly soon after their marriage, Joel returned home one day with two hundred English silver lever watches. His wife thought a bit and then recalled that dozens of sailors were about to descend upon the port of Hull the next day and would be passing right by their window. Carter wrote, "She contrived with much industry and patience to have the . . . watches showing the same time when the sailors went by. The sight of two hundred watches agreeing about the time was a spectacle probably never seen before or since . . . The sailors were quick to discern the phenomenon, and not a watch remained unsold." Rosetta became skilled in book-keeping for her husband (some claimed double entry), in a beautiful copperplate hand.

They were married in a synagogue in Kingston upon Hull on February 10, 1869. He was twenty-five, and she, at age twenty-three, may or may not have known that she was one month pregnant with the future Lord Duveen. As a wedding present, her father gave them three hundred pounds.

Chapter Two

BOND STREET

J OSEPH JOEL DUVEEN was born over his parents' shop at 45 English Street in Hull on October 14, 1869. For the next several years children followed in monotonous succession at roughly thirteen-month intervals. Esther was born on September 7, 1870. Next came Charles, on December 21, 1871; John, on January 13, 1873; Louis, on February 21, 1874; Edward, on March 20, 1875; and Benjamin, on September 7, 1876. Joel had become a British subject by then—one of his sons thought he did so when he was twenty, but this must have come later, perhaps around the time of his marriage—and any grandiose plans for a move to London had to give way before the prosaic reality of yet another mouth to feed.

In an effort to improve profit margins the firm of Barnett and Duveen had begun to look at more expensive Dutch merchandise, ebony-and-palissandre wood cabinets of the Dutch Palladian period that furnished the very grand houses built by East India merchants of the seventeenth century. To do this required the cooperation of a specialist in that field. Joel went to The Hague and made a profitable agreement with a rich dealer, who offered him a year's credit to leave the buying to him, i.e., not become a rival for that particular market. For once Joel, who positively enjoyed competing, saw the logic of the arrangement. The contract worked so well that for the next thirty years, Joel was able to import high-quality Dutch antiques and objets d'art.

Barnett and Duveen had also begun the wholesale importation of Dutch *staande* (standing) clocks, forerunners of the majestic English grandfather clock. The best of them, Jack Duveen wrote, "had a clever mechanical movement of ships or other scenes as part of the dial, as well as

Family photograph of Joel and Rosetta Duveen with nine of their children,
c. 1882. Joseph is in the back row, standing, with arms crossed; his sister
Esther is seated at his feet. The boys wear the caps, jackets, waistcoats,
and ties of Brighton College, a boarding school for boys.
The other children in the picture are not identified.

a carillon of from twelve to twenty-four tunes," and sometimes fetched as
much as two hundred pounds. Clocks and cabinets formed the upper end
of their wares, and Oom Jaap's stream of cheap cups and saucers kept the
ready money coming in. Toward the end of 1871, as Rosetta, with two small
children to care for, was expecting a third, Joel's sister Betsy came to live
with them. She had been unhappy at home ever since her father had
remarried, to a woman who plainly thought she and her brother Henry
Joseph unduly complicated her life and had done her best to make them
miserable. Having his sister move in was a great help to Joel, both at home

and at work, where all those crates of old Chinese porcelain had to be dealt with somehow. Betsy made herself useful matching up the thousands of cups and saucers and then overseeing the unpacking and repacking of fragile items by the girls her brother had begun to employ. She left a year later to marry Henri, but since he obligingly became a Duveen, she kept her maiden name. Betsy, of course, could not have made a better choice of husband as far as her brother was concerned.

With the Hangjas-Duveen network thus cemented, Joel Duveen was more impatient than ever to strike out for London. But he had to wait until 1876, when a graceful dissolution of the partnership presented itself. Barney's father wanted to retire and hoped his son would take over his business. Would Joel agree? The idea was heaven sent and Joel was even more pleased to learn that Henri also wanted to expand to London. Joel took the next train to the metropolis and met Henri there, where he offered him a one-third partnership in the business. Henri would do the buying in Europe and Joel, the selling in London. Since this arrangement took natural advantage of the activities each liked best, the whole matter was agreed upon in less than an hour. Then Henri happened to mention that Joel's younger brother, Henry Henoch, then aged twenty-one and still unhappy at home, was running around with a "wild set" in Amsterdam, as Jack described it. He needed someone to take him in hand. Why not send him to America on their behalf? Joel said expansively. They needed a new market, and his assignment would be to find wealthy clients and forge alliances with American dealers. At no point were young Henry's inclinations even considered and as it turned out, he most particularly did not want to leave Holland. He had fallen in love with Henri's sister, Jeannette, then just sixteen, and was talking about eloping. Why the family that had tolerated a marriage between Betsy and Henri, who were cousins, should balk at another marriage between cousins is a mystery, but they did. Perhaps Jeannette was considered much too young—in an age when girls married at seventeen—or perhaps there is some other reason which has not survived. At any rate, they were united in their opposition. Joel rushed to Amsterdam, swept his brother up in his wake, and transferred him briefly to Hull. There Henry, whose knowledge of Oriental porcelain was not bad, was given a three-day crash course in the business. He was given a tour of the premises and its contents and sat in on talks with customers. Joel lectured and expounded and made young Henry take notes. Then Henry was shipped off to Boston.

Joel had ordered new stationery, printed "J. J. Duveen, Importer of Antique China, Silver and Works of Art, Late Barnett and Duveen," and was all for moving to London then and there. He had decided to open his doors on Oxford Street between Oxford Circus and Marble Arch, then as now one of the prime shopping areas of the city. That came to nothing; no doubt the rents scared him off. Then he and Henri looked at an equally desirable area, Bond Street; but again, what they could afford was far too small to accommodate their needs. They left for Paris, having come to no decision. Joel Duveen, always looking for ways to exploit family contacts, knew that the Hangjas branch had built up a good relationship with the Lowengard family in Paris, which only sold high-class French furniture and tapestries. For their part the Lowengards, headed by the venerable Jules, were looking for a London outlet, since London was the center of the antiques trade. They soon had an amicable agreement by which Lowengards would choose some of their best items and send them to London once suitable premises had been found.

Arrangements were formalized late in 1876, but the promised London partnership never took place. Returning from Spain early in 1877, Henri and his wife were traveling from Leyden to The Hague one evening in an open carriage when a thunderstorm broke and they were drenched. Henri took a chill. This developed into typhoid, presumably contracted during his Spanish visit, and he never recovered. He died at the age of twenty-nine, leaving Betsy with four young children, including Jack, and expecting a fifth. Although the family was against it, Betsy courageously set up in business herself and managed to provide for her five small children. Joel's plan to open in London's West End was, for the moment, still a dream. He found more modest quarters in Soho, where the son of the architect Richard Norman Shaw remembered going to look at some old German paneling. Shaw recalled, "In the yard we found the future Lady Duveen peeling potatoes, and two of their sons making mud-pies in the gutter."

One of these could have been Joseph Joel. Almost nothing is known about his childhood, but something may be deduced from the fact that he was barely a year old when his mother's attention had to be transferred to Esther; only two when Charles arrived; and just three years old when John appeared. Sibling rivalry can have no more fertile ground, and Rosetta, torn between the kitchen and her duties in her husband's business, can hardly be blamed if she thought first about feeding her children and worried later (if at all) about their psychological well-being. During a period of seventeen years she had a total of fifteen children. Benjamin, in 1876, was followed by Albert Joel in 1877; Henry, in 1878; Annette, in 1879; Bertrand, in 1882; Ernest, in 1883; Eveline, in 1884; Joseph Edgar, (circa 1885); and Florence, in 1886. Albert Joel died at the age of five, and Bertrand and

Joseph Edgar also died in childhood (dates unknown). Given that this still left four daughters and eight sons, Joseph Duveen's later determination to have no Duveens succeed him seems almost inevitable.

Joel was doing well financially, but the demands of a continually growing family cast into doubt the idea that he and Rosetta could afford much household help, certainly to begin with. It is clear that Esther, as oldest girl, was pressed into service as mother's helper when she was quite young, because when she went to get married her mother insisted that Betsy's daughter Evaline be sent to run the household, since after giving birth to fifteen children, Rosetta said, she was too delicate to look after them herself. One solution that did present itself was to send the boys away to boarding school.

Joel later said he was bringing his boys up to "behave like gentlemen," and Brighton College, the all-boys school to which Joe was sent, which admitted its first pupil in 1847, was small enough to provide a thorough grounding in English, history, mathematics, geography, and science; it also taught Latin, Greek, French, and German. Some of the famous Old Brightonians include the Antarctic explorer Sir Vivian Fuchs; the actors George Sanders and Sir Michael Horden; and the artist Sir Edward Poynter. The senior school admitted boys aged fourteen to nineteen; but Joseph evidently left after two or three years to join his father's business. He always complained about that. To go to Oxford University was his dearest wish, but his father insisted, because there were too many others to educate. It is certainly true that his younger brothers had educational opportunities denied Joseph. Ben and Henry, his juniors by eight and nine years respectively, went to the Belgian École Moyenne de l'État at Hal in 1888, and when they did not do well there (neither of them spoke a word of French or Flemish), they were transferred to a school outside Paris, so that their doting father could visit them during his weekly trips to the French capital. By then Joe had been working in the business for two years.

Joseph Duveen said that he remembered several artists coming to his father's gallery when he was a youngster, usually to borrow accessories that would act as backdrops for their paintings. There were Sir Luke Fildes, who had a real eye for decorative effect, and Val Prinsep, who would often choose ornate, somewhat vulgar Italian brocades that could be depended upon to make a splash in the backgrounds of his work. Then there was Sir John Millais, who always chose the best and most tasteful of his father's tapestries. In those days, Millais was Joe's idol, and he especially loved that artist's painting of his daughter Margaret as Pomona, gathering apples in an orchard. From an early age painting and sculpture interested him much more than the furniture, tapestry, and porcelain in which his father specialized. He often went on buying trips with his father and, one day, setting out on his own, found an old painting of a family group. He bore it home in triumph, certain that he had discovered a Gainsborough. When his mother was particularly derisive he vowed that one day he would bring her the most famous Gainsborough in the world.

THAT HENRY JOSEPH DUVEEN (always called Uncle Henry to distinguish him from the other Henrys in the family) should be willing to leave the love of his life and be shipped off to America with only the most rudimentary idea of what he was supposed to do, is a mystery. The answer has to lie somewhere in the peculiarities of his temperament, and family solidarity. For Uncle Henry would become a collector of rare stamps, and his collection would be worth a fortune, indicating an acquisitive mind, an ability to discriminate, the willingness to pore over microscopic details, and perseverance—the attributes of a scholar rather than a builder of fortunes. In fact he is always described as modest and retiring, the kind of man one slowly comes to know and trust, rather than someone who immediately demolishes doubt by the force of his personality. Like all Duveens he had a natural appreciation of the beautiful and rare allied with a retentive memory. He also had a quality that was of great value in his calling. One hates to call it deviousness; call it a talent for finding his way around in an alien environment. In a photograph, he is almost hugging himself with private amusement, that of a man who relishes outsmarting the opposition.

Leaving Jeannette behind is harder to explain. He appeared resigned to his older brother's dictates. He knew the importance of the success of the joint enterprise and how that outweighed all other considerations. And he was hardly being set adrift. His assignment in Boston was to make contact with the Koopman brothers, sons of a Duveen mother, and also wholesale importers of Dutch art. Having met them, he did his best to persuade the Koopmans to become business partners but the offer was coolly received. News of Joel's competitive inclinations had, perhaps, reached them; at any rate, after a few weeks Henry moved on to New York, where news of the death of Henri Hangjas Duveen reached him. He was homesick and miserable so far from his family. At the same time he could not help being encouraged by what he was discovering. He wrote on March 7, 1877, "I like Amerika very well. It is a first class money making country, it is a fine rich country, it beats England in everything, you will be astonished what it is like, it is A one." The repetitive emphasis on the money to be made had its predictable effect on Joel. He gave instructions by cable that Henry was to find a shop or warehouse in New York in which to show the goods he was shipping over by the next White Star steamer.

Joel had selected some choice bits of Delft and Chinese porcelain, fine English and Dutch silver and handsome pieces of Dutch furniture that, he reasoned, would be attractive to the heirs of the original settlers in New Amsterdam. There were some good seventeenth- and eighteenth-century portraits and, finally, some decorative Flemish and French tapestries and Louis XIV and Louis XV furniture. All of these items had been chosen with great care and although some sold quickly, things were not happening fast enough to suit Joel. So he booked passage on the new White Star line *Britannic* and prepared to leave London for his first trip to America. Then at the last moment an even more marvellous piece of merchandise fell into his lap.

Henry had written several times to ask for Gobelin tapestries. A day before Joel was due to embark, a titled Englishwoman offered him four large Gobelin panels, some as wide as twenty feet, in an almost perfect state of preservation. The largest had designs by Boucher and all the backgrounds were in the delicate damassé yellow of the Don Quixote tapestries. The price was £12,000 and Joel promptly wrote a check on an overdrawn account. The tapestries had to get to New York. He knew he could sell them for a fabulous price.

Joel did not have time to ship the tapestries on ahead, so he took them along as personal luggage. All went well until he reached customs in New York, where awkward questions were asked; but Henry "knew how to get over troubles with the officials there," Joel said, without elaborating.

When he reached the business premises Henry had rented in John Street in lower Manhattan, he was horrified. The neighborhood was dreadful, "our beautiful stock was badly placed and badly lit, and the windows were not good enough for an old-clothes shop." The crucial importance of choosing the best possible framework for the picture was a lesson Henry had yet to learn. Within a week, Joel had moved them to handsomer quarters in Maiden Lane. "Of course the cost took even my breath away," Joel said, "but I knew only too well that trying to do things on the cheap meant ruin." Unfortunately, making the move absorbed all the profits Joel had hoped to take back to London to cover his £12,000 overdraft. He needed a rich client fast and Henry thought he had just the man. This particular San Francisco railway millionaire (probably C. P. Huntington) was an habitué of the great European palaces and museums and, as Henry knew, difficult

The corner of Broadway and Nineteenth Street, where the young
and struggling Duveen Brothers set up one of their shops in the 1870s

to please. The brothers sent out their invitation and waited. When the
great man finally arrived, Henry conducted him on a personal tour, showing him the most ethereal pieces of Chinese porcelain, the finest handmade
examples of French furniture, and the rarest Persian rugs. The client merely
yawned.

Joel realized the time had come to give Henry a lesson in salesmanship.
On a pretext, Henry bowed out and Joel took over. He had something
exquisite, something superfine to show the client, but unfortunately it was
not for sale. The client must give his word not to tell anyone that he had
seen it. The client agreed readily enough. Joel then took him upstairs and
drew a curtain to reveal the first Gobelin tapestry, intoning its royal origins. As he unveiled the panels one after another he realized that, at last, he
had caught his fish. So when the client asked the price, Joel smoothly
deflected the question. The set was not for sale. The more he declined, the
more furious the client became. Finally, almost stamping with rage, the
man insisted on knowing the price. He would pay $175,000. No, said Joel
in a masterstroke. He was asking for $150,000, and that is all he would

take. He sold the tapestries, covered his $60,000 overdraft, and made a loyal client. Inflaming a client with the rage to buy by refusing to sell would be one of his son's specialties.

From the start Joel realized that having Henry permanently in New York gave him a unique competitive advantage. American dealers usually went to Europe to buy during their slack season (April to October), but then they had to hope that it would all sell during the autumn and winter, or they were left with money tied up in stock. Because of the high New York rents and associated expenses, Jack Duveen wrote, even prosperous firms could be ruined in a matter of months. In the case of Duveen, all Henry needed to do was cable for what he wanted and, a few days later, it would be on a boat for New York, since it was either already in London or easily available on the French, Dutch, and Belgian markets. The method worked so well that by the late 1890s, every autumn the London branch sent the New York branch almost three hundred cases a week, for something like six weeks: everything from Oriental and Dresden china, tapestries, rugs, velvets, and embroideries to silver and old leather. And Henry, not, Joel thought, one of nature's salesmen, was developing his own style. A few years after the successful establishment of J. J. Duveen in New York, Henry was closing the gallery when he saw a man staring into the window, as if on the point of entering. It was a Saturday night in 1882, and Henry was on his way home, but the stranger seemed so entranced and simultaneously apologetic at arriving late that Henry invited him inside. The visitor soon revealed himself as a neophyte collector, eager to be enlightened. Uncle Henry was charmed. They walked around the gallery for the better part of an hour, and in the end the visitor bought a pair of inexpensive enameled Chinese vases. He wanted to come back again some Saturday night after he had closed his own store. There was another friendly visit, and this time the visitor spent slightly more money. Each time he returned, he bought more expensive items, which finally ran into the hundreds of thousands of dollars. He was Henry's first wealthy client, and one of his best: the department-store owner Benjamin Altman. Uncle Henry had successfully launched Duveen Brothers on their meteoric New York career.

FINDING RICH CLIENTS: This was the clue to any successful business, and Joel Duveen was just as eager to move into the higher realms in London as he was in New York; but there remained the small matter of the right address. He still had his heart set on Oxford Street, and in 1879 an opportunity presented itself when he heard by accident that Messrs. Phillips, who specialized in English porcelain and pottery, were preparing to let a part of their too-spacious premises at 181 Oxford Street, an ideal location two doors west of the Pantheon. He was there like a shot and came away with a signed agreement a few hours later. He was to have a small shopfront on the ground floor and part of the upper floors in which to display his larger items. He then paid a visit to Messrs Lowengard in Paris, who had already provided him with some choice examples of high-style furniture and tapestries for the American market. This time Duveen was buying for a select group of rich English merchants and industrialists, so he was looking for decorative objects rather than items of specialized interest. He bought £40,000 worth of merchandise from the Lowengards, who then took him on an extended tour of the Paris market. Among the further items Joel selected were seven pairs of Chinese "mandarin" vases once used for *lampadaires,* or lamps, each seven or eight feet tall, which had been favored by the great bronze artists of the Louis XV and Louis XVI periods. The choice of objects reflected Duveen's growing appreciation of beauty and value as well as his calculated awareness that each item had to be guaranteed to sell, because the bills would come due two or three months later.

There was no question that Bond Street had larger and more important stocks of French furniture than he did, but "his Oriental porcelain surpassed everything ever seen before in London," Jack Duveen wrote. Then there were the tapestries. Since those first ignorant days, Duveen had acquired a knowledge that, by general agreement, made him a master of that sub-specialty. "He had brought over the finest and rarest kinds of Gothic, Renaissance and eighteenth-century periods and felt certain that the great private buyers would . . . come to him." This, in a lifetime of shrewd merchandising, was a major error. Not only did he run into some heavy sales resistance—great buyers preferring, no doubt, to patronize grand old names—but he had aroused the hostility of his competitors, who did not care to have their territories poached upon. Perhaps this was when Duveen learned the poisonous value of whispering campaigns, the method both he and his son would use to good effect themselves. He was going too far too fast. Jack Duveen wrote that the other dealers spoke disparagingly about his wares to their own clients and ridiculed his "crazy" prices, or damned with faint praise, and that "this stabbing in the back nearly ruined him." Duveen spent sleepless nights worrying about the bills that were coming due on his fine French furniture and priceless tapestry collection. He visited every dealer and, as a last resort, offered his wares to those few who could afford them, "but it was no use. Most of them were sarcastically sorry for him." Finally he had to meet his obligations and was still short the immense sum of £500. One night as he was tossing and turning, Rosetta, who he had assumed was asleep, asked him what was wrong. "Of course I denied that I was worrying," Joel recalled, "but she told me not to lie to her because she was quite sure I was badly troubled. In the end I had to tell her." Without a word, Rosetta arose and returned with £220 in cash that she had saved from the housekeeping, plus her favorite pair of pearl earrings, for which she thought he could probably get £300. Joel was on the point of refusing when she said in a stern voice, "Duveen!" He remarked to Jack, "My boy, I knew of old that when she said this it was the last warning before a very bad storm. So I gave in; but I vowed one day I would cover her with diamonds."

Then, as luck would have it, the very next day life presented the great salesman with a way out. As he was crossing Oxford Circus he ran into an old client from Hull, Arthur Wilson, a wealthy shipowner. Although Duveen knew that Wilson's house in Hull was completely furnished and, in particular, that he did not care for the French style, his predicament made him desperate. He proposed that if Wilson would just come and see what he had, he would sell at bargain-basement prices. Wilson laughed and replied that he was having cash flow problems of his own. He had bought a big house in Mayfair for £30,000 that his wife disliked so much she would not go inside. He had been obliged to buy an even bigger house for more money and now he could not sell the first house. He jokingly said that if Duveen would sell his house, he would buy Duveen's furnishings. Was he serious? It seemed he was. Duveen said he would guarantee to sell his house in a week. How did he intend to do that? Duveen did not know, but he would think of something. They shook hands on the deal and Duveen went to work. That very day, he had all the big London agents working on the sale of the Mayfair house at double commission. As he had promised, it was sold within a week. Wilson kept his part of the bargain. Duveen said, "When he saw my stock he could not resist its beauties, and he bought far more than he had promised . . . The decoration and furnishing of Mr. Wilson's house was the finest advertisement I could have had, and his rich friends almost fell over each other to get beautiful objects, too." Including the Chinese *lampadaires*.

Duveen was becoming an interior decorator almost despite himself. Like all Duveens, he was passionately interested in the surroundings against which his vases, desks, mirrors, and tapestries were going to be shown. He was not the first, nor would he be the last, to rebel against the suffocating and funereal conformity of Victorian bad taste, which naturally put him at odds with fashionable architects of the day. Jack Duveen wrote:

> He . . . greatly admired the Dutch and Flemish Renaissance styles. With the help of Teunissen of the Hague, and Moens of Brussels, he was able to buy many old wall panellings of the sixteenth and seventeenth centuries, which he used for the decoration of the large dining rooms of the great houses of London and the country in that long, prosperous period that ended with the first World War.
>
> This decorating entailed a great deal of supervision, work that in itself was not remunerative; but, as the clients were only too glad to profit from Duveen's innate taste, they usually bought all their furniture, tapestries, pictures and porcelains from him. Within a few years Joel Duveen was the most sought-after decorator in London . . .

Then another opportunity presented itself. One night in 1883, four years after Duveen's arrival in Oxford Street, there was a fire at Messrs Phillips. The fire did not spread to the Duveen side of the building, but the facade was so weakened that it had to be demolished and rebuilt. Seizing the opportunity, Duveen went about designing a more prominent show window for the ground floor and a semicircular window for the second (European first) floor. This news was greeted with alarm by Messrs. Phillips and its architect, a Mr. Cookshott, who objected that a big bay window on the second floor would ruin the look of his façade and set the whole town talking. This, Duveen said, was exactly what he wanted. The architect hemmed and hawed and finally thought he had a plan to make the window less of an eyesore by dividing it into sections. He assured Duveen that these would be so small as to be hardly noticeable.

Work was beginning a few days later when Duveen made a surprise visit to the site. Cookshott had prepared a wooden model of the show window to scale and was looking it over when Duveen burst into the room with a roar. Cookshott said, "Before I could interfere he made a rush at the woodwork and kicked it to pieces. 'You call this almost invisible?' he bellowed at me." Duveen got his way and the terrible window, brilliantly lit at night, was put into service. Duveen gave a place of honor to a Louis XV lacquer-and-ormolu commode, on top of which were a large gilt clock and matching candelabra. As backdrop, he had a four-panel screen decorated with scenes by Watteau. The effect was the height of elegance and went some distance to mollifying the architect: "This man whom I had looked upon as a brutal ignoramus had exquisite taste." Messrs. Phillips had nothing to complain about, either, because the surreal effect in a dim, gaslit street, of a brightly lit window hanging, as it seemed, in space, stopped traffic. The fame of "The Duveen Lighthouse" even reached Buckingham Palace, and the Prince and Princess of Wales (the future Edward VII and Queen Alexandra) decided they must pay a visit. Duveen was in his element as he gave them a personal tour, stopping from time to time to expound upon a choice specimen. The princess very much admired a Louis XV sofa, covered with a particularly handsome piece of Gobelin tapestry. She sank down upon it with a sigh of pleasure. It was so comfortable. Might she ask the price? Duveen said it had been sold that morning for fifteen thousand pounds. "Goodness! I daren't sit on so much wealth!" the princess said, and got up in a hurry.

To have captured the attention of the royal family would seem to have achieved all that life had to offer. But the more Duveen sold the more problems he had with money. This paradoxical state of affairs could be explained by the exigencies of his particular temperament. Pulling off a big sale simply encouraged him to think in ever more ambitious terms. He would immediately want to gamble on the next piece of Gobelin, the next suite of furniture (said to have belonged to Marie Antoinette), or the next absolutely unique, not-to-be-equalled, piece of Oriental porcelain. But therein lay his downfall since, as has been noted, the credit between dealers was short term, two or three months at most. Bills came due rather quickly, but the problem was that a generous credit system pertained between dealer and buyer. The richer the client, the more compliant the terms, two years being not unusual. The client got to enjoy the goods for months on end, and peremptory returns were not unheard of, given Duveen's usual guarantee that he would take anything back, less 10 percent. Thanks to this kind of revolving door, the price usually went up accordingly, but occasionally he had to take a loss. True, on the whole, more and more money came in, but he never felt rich, and in the meantime Duveen had an overdraft. Confrontations with bank managers became routine. One story, perhaps apocryphal, concerns a manager who has just learned that Duveen has exceeded his overdraft limit for the umpteenth time and summons his assistant in a rage. "William," he calls out, "bring all the money from the safe and hand it over to Duveen. He thinks he has the right to all of it!" His son Joseph inherited, and even improved upon, this curious pattern, leading one to assume that both men periodically had to place themselves and their whole futures in jeopardy so as to feel the thrill that comes from once more snatching victory from the jaws of ruin.

Joel's habitual money troubles caused great problems for his younger brother in New York, who disliked roller-coaster rides. After the daily telegram begging for money, Henry would set out on the distasteful task of calling in the bills, a particularly bad move with people who could afford to pay up but did not care to be reminded of it. Some took permanent offense, and Henry would end up feeling acutely embarrassed and blaming Joel. After he married Dora Falcke in 1884, a feeling grew that a married man with a successful New York business should not have to continue to take orders from his brother. A kind of rivalry sprang up between the two branches. Sides were being taken pro and con by their friends. Then there were Henry's very nice contacts in the New York Customs House to consider. Antagonizing people like that was just not good business for Joel Duveen. Things reached such a pass that neither brother would speak to the other, and the edifice of J. J. Duveen was headed for total collapse.

Finally, in 1887, Betsy Duveen, who by this time had remarried (to another cousin, Joseph M. Duveen) and was running a successful antique business in Amsterdam, decided something must be done. As it happened, both men were in Holland in 1890 on separate buying trips. She invited them to dinner and each accepted, not knowing that the other would be there. Uncle Henry came early, as was his wont; Joel, as usual, was late. They were already seated at table when he burst into the room.

Jack wrote, "I shall never forget that scene. Uncle Joel called out, 'What's this?' Uncle Henry jumped up and, looking furiously at my mother, said: 'This is a mean trick, Betsy!'

"For a few painful seconds the . . . brothers glared at each other, and then my mother said: 'I am not going to have you two fools quarrelling any longer,' and, addressing her eight-years-older brother, she said: 'Here, Joel, sit down next to me. You are right, I did arrange this, and Henry knew no more about it than you did.' "

Joel took a step toward the table, but in a moment he had walked over to Henry and they were hugging each other. That was the end of the fight, signaling Joel's realization that making Henry a partner was long overdue. Sweeping the table clear, Joel immediately began to make grand plans for the future of Duveen Brothers in New York. They would move to even better quarters, in the Union Square area, where he had always wanted to be. They would open with a splash.

They immediately headed for Paris and the Lowengards, choosing delectable pieces of French furniture and a special set of three French tapestries, *Comédies de Voltaire,* after paintings by Boucher. London was turned upside down for choice English silver, and the finest things from Oxford Street were earmarked for export. Then, just as they were about to embark for New York, in a curious echo of what had happened before, another last-minute telegram arrived, this time from a leading dealer in Antwerp.

By then Joel and Henry were used to encountering superb suites of Louis XV furniture but even they had to concede that this one, in the height of the Louis XV style, was particularly fine. Two outsize sofas, six single chairs, eight armchairs, firescreens, stools and bergères were all covered in silk tapestry on a grayish-white ground representing *Scènes d'Enfant* by the Louis XV court painter François Boucher. The suite of furniture had been commissioned by Louis XV's mistress, the Marquise de Pompadour, who had decreed that the Manufacture Royale des Gobelin should never make another one like it. It was known, however, that Jacques Neilson, head of one of the weaving departments, had secretly made several copies. This was one of them and in a much better state of preservation than the

Duveen Brothers at the turn of the century, moving slowly uptown and upscale to larger premises at Fifth Avenue and Thirty-first Street

One of the New York showrooms of Duveen Brothers in the early years; the
emphasis is on coats of armor, bronzes, stained glass, and oriental carpets.

Pompadour original. It had come from the Hungarian castle of an Austrian
nobleman, who wanted £20,000 for it. Duveen paid up and worried later.
He knew it was perfect for New York.

Arriving in New York Duveen assumed his other role of decorator and
plunged into the happy task of making his new Union Square premises at
Broadway and Eighteenth Street fit for the glories they were about to display. (Duveen Brothers would remain at this address for the next twenty
years.) Moving partitions around and creating big enough shop windows
was the boring part. What he really liked was choosing the right background effects. When he decided that the city could not provide fabrics
exquisite enough to suit his prizes, he contacted Carlhian & Beaumetz of
Paris, explaining precisely what he wanted, and received a cable gratifyingly soon to say that the bolts of fabric were being shipped on the next
steamer. Meantime, another overdraft deadline was looming, so Joel
decided he would have to sell the Pompadour suite before it was ready to

be shown to best advantage. He had chosen just the right French gray silk but since it had not arrived, some *Comédies de Molière* tapestries would have to do. To his surprise the total result was not as muddled as he had feared. The time had come to set the trap. By now Joel was accustomed to using hotel porters as de facto spies—another habit his son would elevate to an art form—and learned that the same Californian who had bought their four Gobelin panels was back in town. Joel was going to make him buy the Pompadour suite! He was so confident. Henry hated to disillusion him.

Next day Joel Duveen called upon the San Francisco railway millionaire, who was quite happy to see him, his royal tapestries having been much admired on his native soil. Joel then told him the history of the suite and confided his overdraft problems. The client came to look at the furniture and suddenly barked at Joel, "Young man, if you'll sell it cheaply I'll buy it now and pay before I leave the room!" Joel told him he wanted $150,000 in cash with a guarantee to buy it back in two years with a 10 percent profit to the buyer. The client took out his checkbook then and there. Duveen picked up the check with satisfaction. He then asked casually whether the client had noticed the very beautiful tapestries on the wall illustrating the *Comédies de Molière*. No he had not, the client said, heading for the door, "and you are not going to make me take them, too."

THE SUCCESS OF the New York branch—by 1895, they reached a profit of £500,000—inspired Joel Duveen to aim once more at the summit of achievement in London: Bond Street. In 1893 he happened to be passing a coach entrance leading to a courtyard in Old Bond Street when he encountered the owner of a building in the courtyard. He was moving, and his suite of rooms was for sale. Was Duveen interested? When Duveen objected that the only access to the business would be through the coach entrance, the owner said he had an option on an adjoining building that fronted the street. Duveen, now interested, asked the price, but it was much too high. Walking back to Oxford Street, he began to wonder whether the situation was exactly as described. Some discreet inquiries revealed that there was no option on the Old Bond Street address, but it *was* for sale. Duveen bought that building first and, in due course, acquired the courtyard property as a storage area at a far more reasonable price. After the antiques business, buying property in London was so much easier, almost restful. Duveen "owned a housing estate at Sutton, a brick works at Cheam . . . a row of shops in Finchley Road and the freeholds of 67 and 68

New Bond Street," Edward Fowles, last owner of Duveen Brothers, wrote. He also bought Gloucester House, former home of the Duke of Cambridge, which stood at the corner of Piccadilly and Park Lane. That stately home met the fate of so many other great London houses when Duveen tore it down to make way for an undistinguished apartment building.

Fowles has left a detailed description of the premises at 21 Old Bond Street, where he went to work as a lowly assistant to the receptionist at the tender age of thirteen. His assignment was to take the early shift before the receptionist, who was also caretaker at Duveen's Hampstead home, arrived. Fowles would appear bright and early at eight-thirty along with the porters, whose job was to spread fresh sand on the cobbled courtyard (livery sand, it was called) in preparation for the arrival of the first carriage. The sand was carefully raked over after each carriage had departed, and "woe to the employee who dared to leave the imprint of his boot in livery sand!" Fowles wrote.

Fowles's job, if he saw someone looking in the window, was to rush to the door, urge the visitor inside, and size him up. He learned to make instant judgments: "A man with a fur coat and a great big stick and a top hat was looking for an advertisement." But if he saw someone coming in wearing "a crumpled-up coat with his scarf hanging down to the ground and a top hat that hadn't been polished for a week that was probably a Rothschild or a Rockefeller." Taking the measure of his man was fairly crucial, because it was his responsibility to operate one of the three foot bells which would summon either "one of the young Duveens" or the great Duveen himself.

One of the galleries on the ground floor held rotating exhibitions, and the second was full of glass cases containing all manner of odds and ends: porcelains, glass, silver, old locks, fancy keys, and the like. More important porcelains were displayed on the floor above, and the top-floor gallery, which had a glass roof, contained Joel's collection of extremely fine tapestries. There were two small rooms leading from the ground-floor gallery. One was a sitting room in which deals were concluded, usually to the accompaniment of afternoon tea. The other was devoted to pictures. Joel had hung an exhibition of eighteenth-century French masters to open his gallery in 1893, but it was not much of a success. Still, he had brought over some other French paintings by Boucher, Largillière, Watteau, and Fragonard, and hung them in his tiny room. The paintings came from Lowengard.

By 1890, Joel's ties with the firm of Lowengard in Paris were so cordial, and he had benefited in so many ways from all that the business relationship offered, that there was only one thing left to do. That was, to cement their association with a marriage. This was becoming a distinct possibility. Joel and Rosetta's oldest daughter, Esther, was of age, as charming as she was beautiful, and one of the Lowengard heirs, Jacques Jules, had taken notice. There were two or three things wrong with this idea. First of all, Lowengard was at least twenty years Esther's senior. This could hardly be considered a serious objection since he had so much to offer her in the way of an elegant lifestyle. True, Esther did not love him but she liked him well enough. The main problem was that she had fallen in love with her first cousin Jack, her junior by three years. Joel had acted as Jack's legal guardian since his father's death and was enormously fond of his nephew. But, sentiment aside, what could Jack offer Esther? He was barely eighteen. There was the problem of first cousins marrying—well, Betsy, Jack's mother, was now married to a first cousin, Joseph M., and their children had turned out fine, but one never knew. Adolescent love affairs were notoriously fleeting. In the meantime there was Lowengard, with all that such a union meant for the future of Duveen Brothers. After a struggle, Esther consented and she and Jacques Jules were married in the spring of 1891. Jack swore he would never marry anyone else and was true to his word. He waited twenty years, and when Lowengard finally died, he married Esther (in 1911).

So many beautiful weddings were celebrated once Joel and Rosetta moved into the grandest house of all, The Elms, standing on three acres with an uninterrupted view over Hampstead Heath. There had been a building on this site since the second half of the seventeenth century, when something called Mother Huff's Tea Rooms was a popular attraction. The site was far too choice to be wasted, and Mother Huff's gave way to the residence of Lord Erskine, Lord Chancellor, who built a house there early in the nineteenth century. Successive owners enlarged upon it, always expanding sideways to take advantage of the glorious views over London. Drawing room was added to drawing room until there were five reception rooms, plus plentiful bedrooms above, a conservatory, stables, a coach house, gardens, and verandas. Further embellishments were made by the Hodgson family, principally by J. E. Hodgson, a professor of painting at the Royal Academy when Joel Duveen acquired the house in 1894. This first-class artistic provenance would have been enough of a lure for Joel Duveen; but the house's curious façade, containing elements of Dutch architecture in its gabled roof line as well as Gothic Revival in its window treatments, must have exercised a nostalgic allure for him, too, while adding that element of grandeur a self-made man finds irresistible.

One entered off Spaniards Road, down a driveway to the caretaker's

Imposing façade of The Elms in 1895, the spacious mansion to which Joel Duveen brought his wife and twelve children, with a rear view over Hampstead Heath

Gathering of the clan in June 1902, when Annette, third from left, married a diamond merchant, Montague Nathan Abrahams. The bridesmaid at far left is not identified. In the back row, left to right: Louis Duveen; the bridegroom; Charles; Edward; Uncle Henry; Ernest; unidentified; Henry; unidentified; Joel; Joseph; Benjamin; unidentified; Jack; Geoffrey; and John Duveen. In the front, seated left to right, Mrs. Louis Duveen; the bride; Esther (Mrs. Jules Lowengard); two unidentified ladies; Rosetta, the matriarch; Uncle Henry's wife; Elsie, Joseph's wife; Eva; and Florence, standing. The photograph appears to be a composite, but the setting is clearly the rear façade of The Elms.

A typical interior: Dutch paneling and Louis XV furniture

The dining room of The Elms, large enough to accommodate all the
big and little Duveens and assorted spouses

cottage, through gates embellished with Duveen's monogram, and pulled up in front of a semicircular stone portico. Just outside the front door, Duveen placed a charming stone sculpture of three lightly clad children playing with a goose, which is still there. The interiors contained elaborate Gothic paneling, enlivened by some Art Nouveau bas reliefs, and baronial ceilings. There was also a library and a dining room large enough (thirty feet square) to accommodate the most lavish of Duveen family gatherings.*

When the marriage was celebrated between Annette Duveen and Captain Montague Nathan "Harry" Abrahams, her first husband, in 1902, the whole family gathered for a photograph in the garden with the house in the background. Joel, in morning dress, looked most distinguished as he stood behind his seated wife. A matronly Rosetta, in a plumed hat, and with tiers of frills descending from her capacious waistline, was by far the most prominent member of the group in an outfit that, if not actually covered in pearls, as Joel had once promised, certainly accorded her pride of place. The bride and groom, arrayed in mere wedding finery, were relegated to stage right. Everyone knew to whom the credit belonged for this splendidly elevated position towering over the great metropolis, with its own grounds, stables, and staff, and what an achievement The Elms represented. It was perhaps a moment of complete happiness for this curious and gifted man, and he made the most of it. Duveen kept a stable of twenty horses and liked nothing better than to drive the considerable distance from rural Hampstead to 21 Old Bond Street in a four-in-hand. Seeing him roaring down Old Bond Street and pulling into the courtyard was a fine sight, Fowles recalled, even if the proud owner too often got stuck in a traffic jam.

Despite all the warnings he received (Joel Duveen must never see him idle, so he must always be dusting or rubbing a bronze when the great man appeared), Fowles found Duveen an indulgent employer. Every summer Duveen and his wife gave a garden party for their employees at The Elms, and there was always a vast tent liberally equipped with scrumptious refreshments and plenty of beer on tap. The guests were invited to take part in games and Joel would join them. He particularly liked the sack races, and would fall about, laughing so hard that everyone else reached the finish line long before he did.

*The Elms was for sale in 1999 for £10 million.

Chapter Three

LADY LOUISA MANNERS

ALL JOEL'S BOYS GREW UP learning about the business. It was part of Joel's philosophy that they should not think themselves too grand for work, and when it came to learning how to buy and sell they could not do better than to emulate his example. As he told the young Fowles, "Go out in the morning and visit the dealers and auction sales. In that way you will . . . find out what is on the market." He had started as an apprentice and so should they, and Joseph Duveen was quite proud of the fact that he had been put to work wrapping pieces of art and had even learned how to build packing cases. Four of the oldest boys: Joseph, Charles, Louis, and Edward, were given a particularly concentrated education by their father, and they were each quick-witted and eager, but from the start there was something about the firstborn that set him apart. A photograph of Joseph Duveen taken, perhaps, when he was in his twenties, is notable for the anticipation that shines from his blue eyes; he meets the photographer's camera with a gaze so frank and full of a buoyant zest for life that anyone would find him irresistible. Joel was no exception, because Joe was made a partner in 1890, when he was twenty-one.

One indication that Joe, like his cousin Jack, was soon motivated by the thrill of making an exciting discovery is given in an account he wrote in about 1910 of an incident that took place twenty years before, around 1890. He wrote that his father had received a letter from Lady Henry Somerset indicating that she had some tapestry overdoors for sale and asking him if he would like to come and see them. Joel took Joe along to the stately home, Eastnor Castle, Malvern, in the Midlands, and sat in on the discus-

Duveen in young manhood, hopeful,
eager, and on his way

sions about the terms of the sale. The bargaining was protracted, so young
Joe decided to make an informal tour of the building. Being, as he modestly described himself, somewhat inquisitive, he began opening doors,
and came upon a huge, beautifully paneled salon that, to his practiced eye,
had obviously once held some large tapestries. He asked Her Ladyship
whether this was true, and she conceded that it was. The room had once
held a set of Boucher panels, but they had been sold to a Mr. Kann of Paris.
Joel Duveen said it was very sad that she had not approached him about
these tapestries, because he was an acknowledged expert on the subject,
which was perfectly true. About a decade later, when Joe and Joel were
invited to visit the Kann Collection in Paris, they at last saw the celebrated
Boucher tapestries. Joel recalled their visit to Eastnor Castle and, no doubt,
his chagrin at not having been allowed to buy them. Rodolphe Kann
replied, "Well, Duveen, you will never get them now."

He was wrong.

IN EXPLAINING THE RISE of the house of Duveen, S. N. Behrman made the felicitous comment that Duveen's whole career was based on the observation that Europe had plenty of art and America had plenty of money: simple, but also simplistic. Nothing would have persuaded titled Europeans, and particularly the British landed aristocracy, to part with their family heirlooms had there not been a catastrophic change of fortune in the final years of the nineteenth century. As late as the 1870s, something like seven thousand families in England, Scotland, Ireland, and Wales among them owned four-fifths of the land of the British Isles. A select few, some two hundred and fifty "territorial magnates"—as David Cannadine calls them in *The Decline and Fall of the British Aristocracy*—each owned more than 30,000 acres and had 30,000 pounds a year to their names, a fortune in those days. An even more select group owned at least two country houses apiece, as well as great houses in London in all the best areas: Park Lane, Mayfair, Belgravia, and Grosvenor Square. Families like the Buccleuchs, the Derbys, the Devonshires, and the Bedfords, with incomes of 75,000 pounds a year, "sometimes had more country houses than they knew what to do with and . . . possessed private art collections almost without rival in the world," Cannadine writes. In the face of such wealth, the idea that anyone would need to sell anything seems derisory; and in fact, before 1882 hardly any part of a noble inheritance ever came up for auction. But then, in the 1880s, disaster struck. Millions of acres of grain were being planted on what had been prairie lands in the American West, as well as in Canada, Argentina, Australia, and New Zealand, and this fact, combined with railways and refrigerated ships, led to a huge global glut of grain and meat produce that lasted until the 1930s. Prices of European agricultural products fell dramatically, providing yet one more example of what happens when cheap goods from overseas overwhelm a market. In the prosperous and protected mid-Victorian years, domestic wheat sold for fifty to fifty-five shillings a quarter; but in the 1880s and 1890s the flood from overseas forced prices down to twenty-seven shillings, reaching a calamitous low of twenty-two shillings and ten pence, or less than half their former price, by 1894. Since rents were the income-earning staple of the landed aristocracy, incomes fell accordingly, but fixed expenditures still had to be met.

Paintings and sculptures that had adorned stately corridors for centuries were being put on view in auction rooms, if not for the masses, for the educated classes, for the first time in living memories. A whole new generation of hangers-on: scouts and runners they were called, small-time dealers, distant relatives, or minor cousins, suddenly acquired a wonderful new source of income ferreting out works that were or might be coming up for sale, no matter how emphatic the owners' denials. In 1882 the Duke of Hamilton caused a sensation by selling the entire contents of his palace: everything from furniture and glass to paintings and sculpture, and realized the record-breaking sum of almost £400,000 (roughly $200,000 at the time).

There was another, even more spectacular sale by the impoverished Duke of Marlborough, who parted with some of his most important paintings in the years 1884–1885. Two of his greatest treasures, a Raphael Madonna and a Van Dyck of Charles I on horseback, went to London's National Gallery. But the remaining Old Masters, including marvelous works by Rembrandt, Rubens, Holbein, Van Dyck, and Breughel, were privately sold. The duke wanted £367,500 for eleven of his pictures but only realized £223,000. That, as Gerald Reitlinger observed in *The Economics of Taste,* was nevertheless "something beyond all precedent in 1884–1885."

At the same time, from the late 1870s to the First World War, American "squillionaires," as Bernard Berenson called them, with vast fortunes from railways, mining, iron, and steel, were building themselves palaces and represented a theoretically limitless market for just the kinds of treasures that wealthy Europeans had accumulated for centuries. In *Mr. Clemens and Mark Twain* Justin Kaplan has painted a vivid portrait of the burst of energy and money that was reshaping New York City in particular in the years after the Civil War. He wrote that to be in New York then

> was to be at the scrambling center of American life. Six years of war and peace had made it a city of extremes and contradictions, where the best and the worst, the highest and the lowest, existed side by side in sunshine and shadow, in splendor and squalor. The white marble palace of A. T. Stewart, the merchant prince who vied with William B. Astor for the title of richest man in the city, rose in Italianate grandeur over the shanties behind Fifth Avenue . . . Prosperous crowds and a tremendous traffic of vehicles surged along Broadway, directed by the elite of the police force. But in the Five Points section of the lower East Side, home of ragpickers, prostitutes, new immigrants, and the desperate poor, crime reached a level

of such frequency and violence that the police were afraid even to patrol.

The rich, retreating ever further north on Fifth Avenue away from the painful sights and smells of the starving, were raiding Europe for its costliest treasures. J. Pierpont Morgan, the great financier, was an early client of Duveen Brothers, buying all kinds of trinkets from them for his wife, Adelaide, such as "Chelsea porcelains, Dresden candlesticks, a silver lamp bracket, a green velvet embroidered coverlet, antique Italian gilt and carved wooden candlesticks, and a Louis XIII armchair."

Like Isabella Stewart Gardner in Boston, Morgan was one of the few wealthy Americans to appreciate Old Master paintings. He was well aware that Raphael was the most admired name in the United States, since that master of the Italian Renaissance represented, to American artists and architects, the supreme moral and aesthetic ideal. Yet there was only one example of that artist's work in America, his portrait of Tommaso Inghirami, bought by Mrs. Gardner at the urging of her advisor, Berenson, in 1898. Two weeks after buying a portrait by Gainsborough of the Duchess of Devonshire, Morgan acquired an early Raphael altarpiece, the *Colonna Madonna,* painted in 1504–05 for the convent of Sant' Antonio of Padua in Perugia. That some experts considered the work bland and boring was beside the point. It was a Raphael; it was a Madonna, after all; and the price Morgan paid was extraordinary: two million francs ($400,000).

If Americans bought paintings, their tastes were limited to the *paysage intime* works of the Barbizon school painters like Jean-Désiré-Gustave Courbet and Jean-François Millet, or depressingly predictable French academic painters such as Pierre-Auguste Cot and Henri-Alexandre-Georges Regnault. American museums were in their infancy, and there was the further pitfall, for a dealer negotiating in dollars, of the dollar's erratic fluctuations, in contrast to the solid gold pound and louis d'or. Still, the drift was toward New York, as Jacques Seligmann's Paris firm realized. The Duveens had established an early bridgehead, but they were not the first. Knoedler & Company set up shop in 1846, and such firms as Durand-Ruel and Gimpel & Wildenstein followed. As Seligmann's son, Germain Seligman (who dropped the final *n* from the family name), suggested, collectors of that period had every kind of instinct but aesthetic. Buying and selling they understood; but why a Van Dyck, or even a Raphael, should be superior to a canvas by salon painters with all those hyphenated names was a subject beyond their ken, almost beyond their imaginings. Enter the experts, European museum officials with expertise in a special field, who were happy to give their opinions free of charge, at first. (As the demand for expertise grew, so did their financial expectations.) There were even sub-specialties of experts, like Bernard Berenson and Robert Langton Douglas, who inhabited a kind of netherworld in which they negotiated sales of works of art for a percentage of the profit and then provided the necessary testimonials, for another percentage, of course. But more visible by far was the dealer, with a shopfront on some of the most exclusive streets of London, Paris, and New York. One could buy from him secure in his knowledge, taste, and guidance; he alone could point the buyer toward the best investment. Jacques Seligmann also understood another important aspect of high finance. Captains of industry did not deal with minor func-tionaries. Big men who entered New York art galleries wanted to encounter other big men. It was a nice distinction, one that would occur to Joseph Duveen quite soon. Furthermore, when they bought they were not buying works of art but Durand-Ruels, Knoedlers, Wildensteins, and Seligmanns. So Jacques Seligmann believed. Joseph Duveen had other ideas. In time, the only name that would count would be Duveen's.

IN THE OLD DAYS Joel Duveen liked to fill his pockets full of cash and, with his wife Rosetta, take the night train from London to Paris. That way he could arrive in Paris bright and early at 6:15 a.m. without wasting any time in a bed. He would hire a four-wheeler and go on a concentrated buy-ing spree, usually getting a discount for cash, and not wasting time eating, either—his wife would have brought sandwiches with them. While Rosetta kept the accounts Joel would be giving the driver directions to the next stop. They would return home that same night; "a long trip of nine hours each way," Edward Fowles wrote in *Memories of Duveen Brothers,* "broken by customs inspections and channel crossings." On one of those long and tiring trips, Joel Duveen got into a heated argument with a sta-tionmaster and attacked him with his gold malacca cane. He was charged with assault, and it must have taken all of Rosetta's charm and tact to extri-cate him.

Like many men accustomed to having almost limitless reserves of energy, Joel gave himself no quarter as he aged. Shortly after Esther's wed-ding in 1891, Joel charged off to Newcastle on the overnight Scottish Express to visit one of his clients, Lord Durham. He worked all the next day and returned on the overnight train to London. There was a blizzard and he caught a cold during the journey. Rosetta was all in favor of his staying home, but Joel would have none of it; he had an urgent business matter in Brussels. Since he was determined to go on traveling she thought she and their sixteen-year-old son, Louis, had better go with him.

An influenza epidemic was in full force and by the time they arrived at the Grand Hotel in Brussels, all three of them had caught the flu. Rosetta and Louis were prostrate; Joel was even more seriously ill. Two Belgian doctors were summoned but they seemed powerless to help, so Rosetta sent a telegram to Joel's sister Betsy begging her to come at once. She and Jack had barely enough time to pack a suitcase before catching the overnight Paris Express.

They arrived in Joel's elegant, overheated bedroom to find the invalid in the care of a large and incompetent nurse, loudly proclaiming that his last hour had come. She was dismissed immediately. The invalid took a grateful look at his sister and breathed, "I am saved!" A telegram had also been dispatched to Sir Andrew Clarke, Queen Victoria's favorite doctor, who replied that he would arrive by night steamer. "The immediate effect," Jack wrote, "was that uncle became less agitated and for the first time after two sleepless nights was able to get some sleep between the agonizing spells of coughing."

The distinguished specialist, who had arrived with an entourage (his wife, his wife's maid, and his own valet), thoroughly examined the patient and told Betsy that Joel was suffering from double pneumonia and that only the most devoted nursing could save him. After some anxious days when there seemed to be no improvement, Joel's temperature dropped, and the pains in his chest slowly disappeared. Rosetta and Louis were on the mend, and after three weeks Joel was allowed to sit up and receive some visitors. It had taken that long to get him back on his feet.

Joel was only forty-seven, but physically he was never the same. From then on, his nephew said, he had to leave England every autumn and remain away until the following Easter, traveling to Rome, Naples, Palermo, Cairo, and the French Riviera. In other words, he was out of the office for a crucial six months of every year. Someone had to replace him. By the time Fowles arrived in Old Bond Street in 1899, Joe and Louis were in firm control.

As Edward Fowles said, among the Duveen sons, Joseph and Charles shared their father's temperament: resourceful, dynamic, and mercurial. The other surviving sons: John, Henry, Edward, Louis, Ernest, and Ben, were calmer and more level-headed, qualities of heart and mind that were certainly useful in that volatile household, although when it came to selling, they were often at a psychological disadvantage. Fowles recalled that for a time, Duveen Brothers maintained a small branch in Newport, Rhode Island. Since this resort was teeming with the idle rich every summer, it seemed an excellent ploy to send young, handsome John to manage affairs. But then, Uncle Henry discovered young John was spending far too much time lounging away the afternoon at tea parties and far too little selling paintings. He was summarily dismissed.

Joseph, the oldest, was gradually putting the stamp of his own personality on the firm. Although his father had always dressed appropriately, his fine careless manner was bound to give his clothes a certain lived-in look. His son never made that mistake. He absolutely demanded perfection from his staff—receptionists wore frock coats and striped trousers, and even the clerks had to wear tails—and he himself set the standard. His own costume was a perfectly tailored suit, a silk shirt with large, starched white cuffs (thoughtfully provided for penciling notes), a four-inch double collar, a handsome tie adorned with a single perfect tie pin, and a soft felt hat, as faultless as it was unvarying. Fowles wrote that, at the end of his life, Joe's shirtmaker refused to make double collars any longer, "and thus ended a tradition which must have lasted for almost half a century."

One never could tell what Joe's mood would be. One moment his eyes would be alive with mischief, and the next, he would have retreated behind an imperious silence that the young Fowles found quite unsettling. Joe's younger brothers and sisters were just as wary. "It was [Joe's] habit to give the younger members of the family pocket money before they returned to school, and they would often approach me to act as their intermediary. If I succeeded in bearding the lion in his den, it meant that he was in a good enough humor to receive them." On the other hand, all of them bore the brunt of their father's unpredictable moods. Joe recalled that when they sat down to dinner at their Oxford Street quarters, Joel would begin the meal with the words, "Let no one speak unless I ask a question." This image of a whole family plunged into gloom is contradicted by another comment, this one from Rosetta, that her sons and husband were absolutely forbidden to talk business at dinner. No doubt so much depended on what Joel had sold that day, how good business looked, and how he felt. It was true that Duveen senior's tolerance for slow-wittedness and perceived inefficiency in his sons was notoriously low. Joel noticed one day, Fowles wrote, that a delivery van was standing idle and that Joseph's dilatory behavior seemed to be the cause. He was after him with a roar, brandishing the familiar gold malacca cane. Fowles does not record whether the cane met its target or whether Joe was let off with a box on the ears.

What Joel would have found unsupportable in his son, perhaps, were reflections of his own qualities of impulsiveness and of making instant wrong decisions. What he doubtless loved about him were all the signs and portents that here was a Duveen worthy of the name: one with a retentive memory, an instinctive eye for quality, a gift of persuasion, and a boyish eagerness, even effervescence, that captivated everyone. All of Joel's own qualities: the fierce competitiveness, the drive for ever more ambitious goals, the impatience, intolerance, warmth, and aesthetic sensitivity, were mirrored in this firstborn. But was he *too* competitive? Was there a frantic quality to this need to excel that would take young Joe down blind alleys, making mistakes the firm could ill afford? He was clever, but was he ready?

A famous incident illustrates the youthful hubris that gave Joel reason for such concern. There are varying accounts, but it seems generally agreed that J. P. Morgan was in London on one occasion when Uncle Henry was also visiting Old Bond Street. Joseph Duveen asked his uncle for permission to try his hand at a bulk sale to the great collector. He would include six beauties in a tray of thirty portrait miniatures and get Morgan to buy the whole lot. Morgan examined the group with care and asked the price for all thirty. Joe was triumphant, but he had reckoned without Morgan's superior tactical skills. Morgan perused the group one more time. Then he slipped the six best miniatures into his pocket, divided the total price by thirty and multiplied by six. That was the price he intended to pay. Of course, Duveen could have demurred; but it was J. P. Morgan, after all. Jean Strouse, author of *Morgan: American Financier,* wrote: "Uncle Henry smiled. 'Joe,' he said, 'you're only a boy. It takes a man to deal with Morgan.' "

Sculpture was never Duveen's strong point, which was not entirely his fault. The history of sculpture is full of stories about exquisite forgeries that have fooled even the experts and are exhibited as genuine for decades in some of the best museums. Very seldom does the reverse apply, but it did at least once in the case of Duveen Brothers. Fowles recalled that one day an old man pushed a wheelbarrow into their courtyard with a huge block of stone inside it that turned out to be a marble statue of the Virgin and Child. Both Louis and Joe were summoned, and they decided it was interesting enough to buy for the price asked, which was a little less than fourteen pounds ($60). The brownish marble piece was subsequently judged to be by the celebrated Florentine sculptor Antonio Rossellino, was bought by Morgan, and is now at the Metropolitan Museum. As Fowles wrote, "This lucky speculation had an unfortunate effect on Joseph Duveen: he began to look round for other similar sculptures to buy." Finding an Italian marble Madonna for sale, he put down $10,000. It had been owned by the

Baron Rothschild and should have been without flaw. Unfortunately, it was a forgery by one of the world's cleverest sculptors, Giovanni Bastianini (1830–1868). The Madonna was finally shipped to Paris where it sold for a few hundred francs.

The boy would not listen. He was reckless. He thought he knew it all. He spent the company's money disastrously. The list could go on and on. And yet . . . there was something very ingenious about him, as even his father had to admit.

Joel had recently bought a set of seven Beauvais tapestries of scenes of country life from the Château Gatelier in the Loire. Although not by the great Boucher himself, the tapestries had similar enchantments: mythological pastoral scenes in which shepherdesses, frivolous and irresistible, disported themselves on swings amid cascades of flowers. Joel also knew that he probably had a client for some of the tapestries, R. W. Hudson, who had made a fortune persuading housewives to buy Sunlight soap. Hudson was building a town house for himself in London and a neo-Gothic mansion in Buckinghamshire, and was bound to like something. While his father was away in the south of France, Joseph Duveen cleared the top-floor gallery and built a set of rooms so that the prospective client could see exactly how these tapestries would look in his new house. The preparation took months, and when the day arrived to invite the client to the gallery, Joel, who had by then returned, insisted on conducting the sale himself. All seven tapestries were sold. It was hurtful not to be allowed to conduct the actual sale, but on the other hand, Joseph had reminded the old wholesale salesman that one could sell in bulk in a retail market if one set the stage properly.

Of course, the importance of creating the proper background was something Joel hardly needed to be taught, but it was one of the first lessons his son applied with even greater flair than his father had done. All those mind-numbing trips to Paris, jumping on and off the night train, making exhausting rounds to the dealers and then jumping back on again, at which Joel excelled, had been taken over by Joe. He was the one who now went to Paris every weekend during the summer to attend the big auction sales and spot the winners. Originally, Duveen Brothers had kept a small establishment in Paris at the corner of the rue de la Paix and the rue des Petits Champs, but that was closed in 1897 and the stock sold at auction in London. So every summer Joe took up residence in a hotel suite in the Place Vendôme which, from a business point of view, was not a bad place, either.

That particular summer he scored another decorating coup. Senator William Clark, who had made a fortune in copper mines in Montana and became a successful politician, was ambitious to add his idea of domiciliary grandeur to that being displayed in the Fifth Avenue palaces of Mrs. William Astor and Cornelius Vanderbilt II. Clark, who was a Francophile, engaged the services of Henri Deglane, who had built the huge and florid Grand Palais in Paris, for a site he had bought at Fifth Avenue and Seventy-seventh Street. The resulting edifice was nine storeys high and contained more than a hundred rooms. It took seventeen years to build and the cost was between $5 million and $7 million, which supposedly made it the most expensive mansion in New York at the time.

The second floor, or piano nobile, contained a hall thirty-six feet high, with white marble walls and Breche violette marble columns; a dining room; a conservatory; and a vast main picture gallery. Other galleries on this floor displayed the owner's vast collection of tapestries, rugs, lace, Old Master drawings and paintings, eighteenth-century English portraits, and the predictable group of paintings from the Barbizon school. The grand salon in the southwest corner of the house was designed in white and gold and contained paneling and a ceiling mural from the Hôtel de Clermont, a private residence on the rue de Varenne in the exclusive Faubourg St-Germain area of Paris. In short, the vast edifice simply begged to be adorned by those masterminds at Duveen Brothers, who could always deliver the best, for a price.

Somehow or other—the record is vague on this point—Joe acquired a detailed knowledge of the interior, right down to the placement of the electric chandeliers. Then he commissioned a plaster maquette of the building, complete in every Duveen detail—carpets, tapestries, furniture, furnishings, the lot. The maquette cost $20,000; but there is something about seeing one's house in doll-size dimensions that is irresistible, particularly when the presentation takes place in a hotel suite in the Place Vendôme. Senator Clark proceeded to place a gratifying number of orders. Joe might be hotheaded and rash; but on the other hand, he had this ability to take infinite pains, which was particularly useful to all those millionaires overwhelmed with petty detail. And to have intimate knowledge of a rich man's house was the kind of training of the eye that pays continual dividends. Edith Standen, secretary to the collection assembled by P. A. B. and Joseph Widener, recalled that Duveen could describe with complete accuracy, not just a set of five Chinese vases on a noble lord's mantelpiece, but their outlines in detail, along with their provenances. As Bernard Berenson, who would be such a seminal influence on Duveen, wrote, "We must look and look and look till we live in the painting and for a fleeting moment become identified with it. If we do not succeed in loving what through the ages has been loved, it is useless to lie ourselves into believing that we do. A good rough test is whether we feel that it is reconciling us with life."

Selling to Senator Clark provided Joe with a further lesson in how to deal with wealthy collectors. In 1911 Duveen learned from Charles Wakefield Mori, a small Parisian dealer, that Clark, who had been traveling in Italy, had fallen in love with a statue by the eighteenth-century Italian sculptor Antonio Canova of Pauline Bonaparte Borghese as Venus, which he had seen in the Galleria Borghese in Rome. Might Duveen Brothers know of another fine Canova marble? Duveen thought a bit and then remembered that the Hope Venus, a contemporary copy by Canova that had been created for Thomas Hope of Deepdene, was still gracing that mansion. The owner might be persuaded to part with it for $25,000. The word came back from Mori that this would not do at all. To price such a work at a measly $25,000 would lead his client to assume that it was not important. If Duveen wanted Clark to buy the marble, he must give it an important price. Duveen raised the price to a preposterous $110,000, and got it. Learning how to ask for too much money was one of those influences on a young man's thought processes that leaves a permanent mark.

Taking care of the very rich and exalted, their needs, interests, tastes, and whims, extended even to Buckingham Palace. As Duke of York, the future George V, with his wife, Princess Mary of Teck, often visited Duveen Brothers. The duke, a passionate collector of postage stamps, became friendly with Uncle Henry, who, as has been noted, was similarly afflicted. The Prince of Wales also extended his patronage, and when, following Queen Victoria's death in 1901, he became Edward VII, almost his first act was to call in Duveen Brothers, this time in their secondary role as decorators. Something had to be done about the lugubrious Victorian decor and ghastly tartan hangings which had contributed to his gloom as heir apparent. Fowles was dispatched with yards of Duveen's beautiful old silks and velvets to camouflage the tartans and cover up the upholstery, but quietly thought it would take a great deal more than these stopgap measures to improve the look of Buckingham Palace.

Summoned to supply tapestries and rugs for the coronation ceremonies in Westminster Abbey in 1902, the firm also commissioned six coronation chairs, made to order in Paris, and was able to borrow a Gothic tapestry in gold thread that had belonged to Cardinal Mazarin, which was hung above the altar during the ceremonies. (Morgan had bought the tapestry from the

Duveens for $500,000, in a sale contested by Jacques Seligmann, who claimed a half-share of the profit, but that is another story.) To have his firm figure so prominently in this august event gave Joel even more social cachet and catapulted his firstborn into the limelight as perhaps no other event could have done. It was their good luck that their taste for eighteenth-century French was one that the new monarch also shared. Before long, owners of great London houses were looking with disfavor on their own Victoriana and turning to the delicately refined interiors as exemplified by the galleries of Duveen Brothers. The firm was busier than ever.

SINCE JOSEPH DUVEEN's career would be so closely linked with Old Master paintings, drawings, and sculpture, that it took him so long to put Duveen Brothers on the right course is curious. It was perfectly clear to him, if only from the price Morgan had paid for his Raphael, that great works by Raphael, Titian, Leonardo, Reynolds, Turner, Gainsborough, and Watteau were just begging to become Duveens. The opportunities were limitless, but getting his father to see what they were missing was another story.

It was not that Joel Duveen did not know and appreciate Old Masters. The trouble was, he knew when he was being fooled. The infamous collection of Dom Marcello Mazzarenti that was bought in 1902 by Henry Walters of Baltimore for $1 million (because it supposedly contained eight Raphaels and six Titians, not to mention works by almost every other great artist one could think of) had been seen by Joel Duveen in Rome at Easter of 1898. He had contemptuously dismissed it. As he knew, the chances of buying what a work purported to be were roughly analogous to picking up a nugget of gold on the Bond Street sidewalk.

Joel would have known that the Great Master invariably ran a school. It was a paint factory, a business proposition. The results could be, and often were, accepted as by the master if they bore his signature even though they might, in fact, be the work of apprentices. To add to the confusion, such paint factories routinely turned out large numbers of copies. Writing to Sir Dudley Carlton in 1618, Peter Paul Rubens said, "As this reproduction is not yet quite completed I am going to retouch it throughout myself. So it can pass for an original if necessary." Of other copies by his apprentices, Rubens wrote, "I have retouched them to such an effect that they can hardly be distinguished from the original . . . they are perfect miracles at the price."

In addition, paintings that have existed in a perfectly preserved state for five hundred years, Italian Renaissance works in particular, are so rare as to be almost nonexistent. Most have been retouched, some so extensively that, were the additions removed, only a fragment of the original would remain. As for deliberate deceptions, those are limited only by the ingenuity of the human mind and the promise of profit. One of the delightful stories told by Francis Henry Taylor in his book on the history of art collecting, *The Taste of Angels,* has to do with the days before World War II, during Mussolini's reign, when an American tourist bought a Titian in Florence. Warned that heavy export duties would be inevitable, the owner had a restorer cover the work with a heavy coat of protective varnish and then paint a modern landscape on the surface. The painting sailed through customs and arrived in Paris. There another restorer set to work returning the painting to its original condition. "The artist worked for several weeks: first disappeared the modern landscape and then appeared the Titian. He kept on cleaning, not satisfied with what he found, until, finally, beneath it, hard up against the very canvas itself, was a portrait of Mussolini."

The story is probably apocryphal, but there was nothing imaginary about the professional schools that sprang into being as art market prices rose. Some of them were so specialized that teams of artists might be employed, each an expert in one tiny aspect of a particular master's work. Then there were bravura artists like Malatesta, working in Modena, who claimed to be able to render a Titian in that master's own brushstrokes. In Siena, the painter G. F. Ioni (or Joni), who was also a gilder and restorer, took a slightly different approach, manufacturing original designs of Italian quattrocento paintings, many of which found their way into museum collections. Part of Ioni's genius lay in his ability to give his Madonnas faces that perfectly accorded with the way his age thought they ought to look. Such an illusion passes quickly, and Ioni's fake Madonnas are clear enough to spot nowadays from the vacuous stares they exhibit. Being deceived by what is in plain sight is a phenomenon not just limited to paintings.

Prosperous forgers imply corruption among dealers, and it was known that rich Americans in particular, not just Walters but collectors like P. A. B. Widener, Theodore Davis, John G. Johnson, and even the great J. P. Morgan, had been hoodwinked. The certificates of authenticity were always reassuring even though they might be so equivocal as to be worthy of Machiavelli. When Fowles challenged Wilhelm von Bode, director of the Kaiser Friedrich Museum in Berlin and the "archimandrite" of German expertise, about a certificate he had given for a Petrus Christus Madonna that the former did not think could be genuine, Bode just laughed. "You don't understand the intricacies of the German language," he said. "After a brief description of the subject, I say, in fact, 'I have never seen a Petrus Christus like this . . .' " At the same time the intrigues of the market were, and have always been, closely guarded secrets. If a client asked too many pointed questions, he might be told that "if dealers were to make their private dealings publicly known, they might as well go out of business right away, because no client would ever trust them." Such an admission hardly inspires confidence. An American journalist, writing to his editor in New York, concluded with exasperation, "The impression you get when you have been to see half a dozen dealers is that the whole business is crooked and rotten and the information you get from [them] is not of any great value."

There were ways around the problem for a prominent dealer like Joel Duveen with a reputation worth defending. As his son would have been the first to point out, Americans with big houses and no ancestors to speak of were perfectly willing to adopt, and plenty of aristocrats had portraits of eighteenth-century ancestors for sale, with gilt-edged provenances. As a

Lady Louisa Manners: the portrait by John Hoppner
that began Duveen's career, and for which he paid
a punishing price at auction

safe proposition this could hardly be safer, especially if there was also a collector ready to buy. Then, in June 1901, an opportunity presented itself in the form of an auction at Robinson and Fisher's of a painting of a lady, Lady Louisa Manners, by John Hoppner. Fowles was set the task of inquiring whether Benjamin Altman would like Duveen's to bid for the painting on his behalf. Mr. Altman replied that he would.

Lady Louisa, wearing a straw bonnet under the chin and gloves to show she is out for a country walk, is seen in three-quarter face in front of one of those romantic glades so favored by eighteenth-century English portraitists. She was born in 1747, the elder daughter of Lionel Murray, third Earl of Dysart. She married John Manners, a member of Parliament from Grantham Grange, county Lincoln; succeeded her brother Wilbraham, fifth Earl of Dysart, as Countess of Dysart; and died in 1840 at the great age of ninety-three. Her aristocratic pedigree, in other words, was impeccable. But from a collector's point of view, she was hardly the kind of ancestor one would want on the walls, being stocky, with a generous bosom surging out of a flimsy bodice, and flat, blunt features that spoke of a daughter of the soil rather than a lady of high degree. One would have expected the great Duveen Brothers to go to battle for a portrait by Sir Joshua Reynolds or Sir Thomas Lawrence rather than by Hoppner, a facile imitator of both styles; and whereas Reynolds and Lawrence have a dazzling gift of suggesting depths of romantic charm in their sitters, Hoppner's vision of Lady Louisa is thoroughly pedestrian and bland. What Duveen Brothers, or rather, Joe, saw in the painting, has mystified everyone since. Still, for some reason, he wanted her and thought the painting was as good as sold.

The art critic A. C. R. Carter, who knew both Duveens, recalled that day in June 1901 when Joseph braved the auction market for Old Master paintings. As Carter wrote, Joseph said he was determined to make his name in that field. His father had his doubts but had agreed to support his son. Once again, Joel was not prepared to let Joe do the bidding. This may have had less to do with Joe's inexperience than with Joel's suspicion that Joe was about to be thoroughly shaken up by other dealers. Duveen Brothers already knew that the great house of Agnew's looked upon the idea of their entering the big picture market with intense disfavor. It fell to the house of Charles and Asher Wertheimer of Bond Street to apply the stiletti. Carter wrote of Joel Duveen and Wertheimer, "As it happened, the affair was a duel between them from beginning to end. At 14,000 guineas Wertheimer was in front. 'Pounds?' queried his wily rival to gain time. 'No. Guineas,' was the auctioneer's reply. Then after a pause Duveen senior said, 'Fifty!' and the contest had its triumphant climax." The total price (a guinea being worth 21 shillings) was £14,752, the auction record at the time for any English picture and the price Duveen Brothers was made to pay for entry into the club.

Not surprisingly, once the painting was shipped to New York Mr. Altman did not like it, and the Bond Street office had to take it back. It was finally sold to Herbert, the first Baron Michelham, no doubt at a loss. Never mind; the incident had shown that Duveens had money, means, and determination, and that Joel would stand behind his boy (even if he might suspect that he was wrong.)*

It did not take Joseph Duveen long to learn every trick of the trade in the auction rooms, and he rather enjoyed the chance to turn the tables on his tormentors. When, in 1905, a K'ang-hsi porcelain vase, once picked up in Wardour Street for 12s. 6d., came up for sale, Duveen let it be known that he was going to buy it. After the news was leaked, a competitor decided he was going to give Joe a run for his money. He bid the vase up to £5,900 in the confident expectation that Joe would cap it with a bid of £6,000, as seemed inevitable. "At 5,900, however, Duveen rapped out, 'Finished.' " It was some years before the unwilling victor could find a new buyer for the vase." As they said in the auction rooms, Duveen had dropped it on his toes.

In 1928 Duveen was offered the chance to buy back the Hoppner in 1928, along with Romney's *Lady Forbes*. The price was £45,000 for both, but he willingly paid more for the Romney alone not to have to buy the Hoppner, explaining, "Don't want buy Manners. I hate it."

Chapter Four

THE RAJAH'S PEARL

OR A MAN WHO WOULD LIVE IN A SWIRL of public events and controversies, consorting with great men on two continents, always in the news in one way or another, much about the life of Joseph Duveen is nevertheless obscure. Introduce any topic under the sun and he would regale you with anecdotes and opinions; stray into the realm of life beyond the office or what he and his wife had discussed that morning and silence descended. Private letters or diaries which might have given some insight into the man himself are not to be found. Somewhere along the line someone, perhaps Joseph Duveen himself, decided to draw a veil, and so no one knows exactly why he acted as he did when the time came for him to choose a wife. All that is known is that in 1899 he became engaged to the daughter of Isaac Lewis, a South African gold millionaire. Being Joseph Duveen, the festivities attendant upon the wedding were lavish and prolonged. The family gathered from afar, among them Uncle Henry and his wife, Dora. They brought with them a friend, a demure nineteen-year-old named Elsie Salamon, whose own fortune must be considered trifling when compared with the one that Miss Lewis was bringing to her marriage. Miss Salamon began to appear at the prenuptial parties and met the groom in the usual way. The results showed Joseph Duveen at his most inconsistent and inspired. Not only did he decline to marry Miss Lewis but he married Miss Salamon instead.

Not very much more is known about Elsie Salamon. One knows that her father, Sol, was in the business of tobacco, although whether he grew it or traded in it is not clear. One knows that she, as one of three beautiful sisters, was used to a comfortable life; but how she grew up, her interests,

Elsie Salamon, aged eighteen, in the summer of 1899,
when she married Joseph Duveen

hopes, and dreams, are a mystery. A photograph of her, perhaps taken the
year of their marriage, shows a girl with a mass of dark hair, wide-set eyes,
a pretty mouth, a heart-shaped face, and an air of languorous gracefulness.
Her perfectly chosen gown, of a heavy silk, draped becomingly around her
slender waist, her pearl choker and necklace, and the huge ring she wears
speak of a girl who is aware of her charms and prepared for her station in
life. There is also a certain guarded look about her eyes suggestive of someone who is not particularly at ease in a large group and has learned to mask
her feelings. Sir John Foster, who met her in later years, considered her
beautiful but unapproachable. "She just said yes and no." Kenneth Clark
contributed a more telling anecdote about her, following a visit to
Duveen's palatial New York apartment in the 1920s. Dinner was served on

a legendary Sèvres service in blue and gold that had been made for Empress Catherine of Russia. When the future Lord Clark complimented Duveen upon it, and said what a privilege it had been to use it, Duveen replied, "Sèvres service? Nothing. Eat off it every day." Elsie's response to the same comment was, "Yes, it is nice. And we don't get it out every day, I can tell you. The last time we used it was for Mr. Ramsay MacDonald."

Certain people seemed fated to play a certain kind of role in Joe's life. In the face of his outrageous overstatements, they quietly insisted upon the truth. In the face of his mountainous ambition, they imparted the impression that they had nothing to prove. If he wanted center stage, they were endlessly prepared to admire from the sidelines. And when the party was over and he had left the room awash with crumpled bits of paper and smoldering cigar ends, they moved around picking up the pieces. Rosetta played such a role in Joel's life, and this was the one, perhaps, that Elsie was destined to play in Joseph's. It was true that Edward Fowles, who had the same forthright responses as Elsie's, was one of the few people in whom Duveen ever confided. And if Joe told Elsie, as he did Edward, about some of the great disappointments of his life, and how emotionally insecure he felt, he could do so with complete confidence, knowing that she kept her secrets.

They were married in the New West End Synagogue on July 31, 1899, with Joe's uncles Barney Barnett and Henry Duveen acting as witnesses. The bride had moved to her father-in-law's house, The Elms, in Hampstead, and Fowles wrote that the wedding breakfast took place at Claridge's, "the most modern and luxurious of London's great hotels." They went to Paris for their honeymoon so that Elsie could acquire an appropriate wardrobe. When thirty trunks of clothes subsequently arrived, her husband "swallowed hard," but never mind. His wife was a sight to behold, as King Edward VII, a connoisseur of the field, would be quick to appreciate. They went to New York that autumn, and Joseph Duveen's clients "vied with each other to have the handsome Duveen couple adorn their boxes at the opera, and add prestige to their dinner parties," Fowles wrote. Their first and only child, Dorothy Rose, always called Dolly, was born four years later (in 1903) at their house in Fitzjohn's Avenue, Hampstead.

As many men do who live in uncertainty, at home Joseph Duveen wanted an exact and unvarying routine. He drank little wine and no spirits, never ate red meat, and would declare himself satisfied with cold chicken and fruit at lunch and half a dozen plover eggs and a bird for dinner. He rose at regular hours, and unless he was out at night, which he usually was, was in bed by 11 p.m. Of course he always wore the very best clothes. He insisted on traveling first-class and staying in the best hotels, but, as with Berenson (who shared the same taste for luxury once abroad), this could have had as much to do with the need to be seen in the smartest places. Duveen genuinely loved fast cars. His chauffeur was once charged with driving too fast up Broadway (he was caught at 237th Street in the Bronx). The man explained that his client, who was in the car at the time, knew they were exceeding the speed limit but urged him on. The chauffeur was fined thirty dollars, which no doubt Duveen paid.

Duveen concentrated the attention some men give to wines on tobacco, which was another weakness. Although he was never photographed with a cigarette in hand, he was a chain smoker and particularly fond of fine Havana cigars. In matters of food he resembled his father, who was always too busy to eat, and Joe once told a young staff member that when he was his age, he only had time to eat lunch on Sundays. Duveen's quietly abstemious habits seem curiously at odds with his flamboyant public personality, which could have been deployed at least partially, in an effort to stand out in a noisy crowd. He had an actor's instincts; some said, Fowles wrote, that he had developed an infectious laugh in conscious imitation of another dealer who could mow down the opposition by the calculated use of this particular asset. Calculated or not, his clients found the laugh, and him, irresistible.

By the time he reached adulthood Duveen's self-protective measures had been well honed in the rough-and-tumble of family life. Not only did he positively seem to enjoy being the butt of a joke, but he never took offense, and his ability to hide what he might be thinking and feeling had been developed to a fine art. He could also give as good as he got. There is an anecdote that gives a remarkable insight into Duveen's thought processes. He told Fowles that, shortly after he and Elsie were married, they went to the races. His horse came in a winner and he made the elementary mistake of brandishing his ticket triumphantly in the air. In a flash, someone had snatched it and made off with it through the crowd. With the help of a policeman Duveen caught the culprit, but although the man's pockets were thoroughly searched, the ticket had disappeared. The policeman explained to Duveen in a kindly way that the thief would have passed it on to an accomplice immediately. It was a lesson Duveen never forgot. When, years later, on a train journey to Russia, he had a picnic lunch but no knife, he stole one from a station restaurant and planted it in the pocket of his nephew Armand Lowengard. Armand did not seem to mind, and they all had a good lunch.

He was, one writer observed, "an extraordinary character—a unique mixture of arrogance and humility, of shrewdness and simplicity, of modesty and extreme ostentation." What he was like in the hothouse emotional atmosphere of marriage can only be guessed. As his first biographer noted, Duveen paid absolutely no attention to his own money, and if his valet had forgotten to provide for the day's financial needs with some small change—like royalty, he preferred to carry little or none—would claim to be completely helpless. By contrast, Elsie, like her mother-in-law, was very sharp about the daily accounts and was known to terrorize the tradesmen. Duveen had an incorrigible habit of clapping his hands when he needed people, one that doubtless was humored at the office but might have been less kindly regarded at home. He, like his father, suffered from what Sir Winston Churchill called "black dog" days when, if obliged to say something, he would make everyone sorry that he had. These derelictions were more than compensated for by a genuine interest in others and acts of generous impulse that Elsie might think rash. The extent of Duveen's paternal instincts can be gathered from the fact that he loved babies and would peer into carriages to exclaim over the adorableness of the infant and declare he had never seen such a beauty.

His daughter, the late Dolly Burns, said, "We lived on the corner of what used to be called Norfolk Street and Park Lane, up near Marble Arch; the house is still there. There was a garden in front overlooking Hyde Park. On one side of the street was my father's house and on the other side, Uncle Henry's. This was in the days when they had buses pulled by horses. I remember that. And also my mother had beautiful black horses with a Victoria." She recalled that once when they were on holiday in a hotel by the sea she did not want to go into the water because it was too cold. Her father summoned a waiter to bring a kettle of hot water. Duveen then poured the hot water into the sea and invited her to try again. She went in perfectly happily. She adored her father, and in their curious way, one guesses that Joe and Elsie were a devoted pair. In the early photographs of them that have survived, they are always close together.

JOEL DUVEEN HAD A 50 PERCENT interest in Duveen Brothers. Uncle Henry, as junior partner, held 35 percent, and Joe, as one of the heirs apparent, had only 15 percent. In such circumstances it was fortunate for Duveen that Uncle Henry was usually a safe three thousand miles away and that his father took such leisurely winter vacations (he was sometimes away for seven months of a year); without these factors it is unlikely that he would have had as free a hand as he did in the early years of the twentieth century. As it was, he began to act as if the whole business belonged to him years before it would. One could hardly quibble since, Fowles reported, by 1902 business at Duveen Brothers had tripled in five years. It would seem logical to wish to remodel the premises. (This conclusion was reached once Joel was safely off on a trip around the world.) Out went the plaster walls and in came fine French oak paneling which one is not surprised to learn was made to order in Paris. Instead of something that looked like the inside of a shop, the entrance hall was transformed into a beautifully appointed living room hung with pictures, in which a fire burned invitingly for much of the winter and, given the English climate, the spring and autumn as well. That newfangled gadget, the telephone, made its appearance. Members of the staff were housed in offices. Gone were those myriad examples of virtu so dear to Joel's heart, along with the display cases that contained them. In came objects guaranteed to have much bigger price tags, and tapestries displayed so as to inspire a client with the idea that he needed several at once.

Joe had even grander visions in mind. The fact that Duveen Brothers no longer had a branch in Paris and was reduced to doing business from a hotel in the Place Vendôme hardly accorded with his idea of adequate surroundings, even if the hotel was the Ritz. He had always found eighteenth-century French architecture the height of elegance, and as he knew, the magnificent Place Vendôme, the large almost-square on the Right Bank which gives onto the fashionable rue St-Honoré, just a stone's throw from the Tuileries and the Louvre, epitomized all that was meant by Parisian taste and refinement. Chopin died at number 12 in 1849, and the architect of the Place Vendôme, Jules Hardouin-Mansart, built himself a magnificent private house behind one of the square's eighty-foot-high façades. By the time Duveen was there, it would have been inhabited by one famous jeweler after another. The house of Mauboussin established itself there in 1827, Cartier arrived in 1847, and Boucheron in 1893. Chaumet, the imperial jeweler, would move its collection of diadems inherited from its founder, Marie-Etienne Nitot, to the Place Vendôme in 1907. No aggregation of the most costly objects the human imagination could devise could be better suited as a background for the wonders teeming in Duveen's imagination. All that remained was to find suitable accommodation. Beginning in 1903, Duveen had a standing order with a French real-estate agent to find quarters in the Place Vendôme. Nothing came of it.

The ground floor of the fine buildings on the place is faced with arches, behind which are courtyards and further shops and offices. On one of his trips to Paris Duveen insisted on taking a personal walking tour with his

agent and inspecting each courtyard in turn. Arriving at number 20, Place
Vendôme, then occupied by the furriers Bechoff-David, Duveen discovered some disused stables behind the arches. Bechoff-David were
persuaded to grant a sub-lease, the dilapidations were removed, and construction began. Duveen engaged the services of René Sargent, possibly
because he had already built a bank for J. P. Morgan elsewhere on the place;
the Trianon Palace Hotel at Versailles was another example of his work.
The idea of the Petit Trianon, that sober town house in the neoclassical
style that Louis XIV had built for Madame de Pompadour in 1762, was
suddenly the height of fashion. Moïse Camondo, head of a family of Jewish bankers, the "Rothschilds of the East," who admired the arts of eighteenth-century France even more fervently than Duveen did, would insist
on having *his* Petit Trianon at 63, rue de Monceau. (His house was built in
1911 and is now the Musée Nissim de Camondo.) In Duveen's case, a
gallery inside a courtyard presented a slight disadvantage, which he
attempted to overcome by having red and white marble installed in the
courtyard so that one could hardly miss it. One entered a stately hall with,

The lovely little Duveen Brothers gallery,
tucked away (at left) in a courtyard
just off the Place Vendôme, Paris

on one side, a staircase in white stone, covered with a handwoven Savonnerie carpet in pale gray. The main reception room, on the other, was dominated by an antique marble chimney piece and its walls covered, in the
French fashion, with fabric: a handsome red damask.

No description of the interior furnishings has come down to us, but it
is possible to imagine them, like those of Camondo's own Petit Trianon, as
the best examples of Louis XV and Louis XVI that money could buy:
"couches, armchairs, screens, sketches of the hunts of Louis XV by Jean-
Baptiste Oudry, round tables, oval tables, tables to be set in corners, tiny
desks, sewing tables, rolltop desks, chests of drawers—all fashioned from
the rarest woods, signed by the greatest masters and decorated with porcelain inlays or gilt bronze details or composed of marquetry made from
pearwood, rosewood, sycamore, and boxwood," as Edmund White wrote
in *The Flaneur*. To add to the fairy-tale effect, perhaps in imitation of his
father's Oxford Street windows, Duveen decreed that the stairwell leading
to the upper floors should be ablaze with light. Unfortunately, as Fowles
recalled, the building used so much electricity that, despite the heavy-duty
cables that had been installed, the lights were always going out and the firm
had to employ a full-time electrician. There was the other small problem
that the only way to get to the basement was via an outside entrance; an
objection Duveen would no doubt have dismissed with "Details, details"
and a wave of his hand. He could be maddening.

One thinks again of the engineer Isambard Kingdom Brunel, son of
another distinguished engineer, who all his life remained in the thrall of
the impossible. Having inherited, from his father, the goal of building a
tunnel under the Thames, he got more than halfway across and had two
celebratory dinners in the tunnel before the shield holding the water in
check gave way, and corpses of workmen had to be fished out of the water.
As Kenneth Clark wrote in *Civilisation,* "That was the way with Brunel's
designs: they were so bold that shareholders were frightened and with-
drew—sometimes, I am bound to say, with reason." The Thames tunnel
was finished nevertheless and Brunel went on to build the Great Western
Railway. Clark wrote, "Every bridge and every tunnel was a drama,
demanding incredible feats of imagination, energy and persuasion, and
producing works of great splendour." He could have said the same about
Duveen.

BY THAT MYSTERIOUS ALCHEMY that transforms high-achieving men
into philanthropists, Joel Duveen was now thinking about his legacy, and

the Sir Henry Irving sale in December 1905 first gave him the idea. It seems that the actor-manager had made a large collection of portraits of actors immortalized by their roles, among which two paintings stood out. The first was a portrait by James McNeill Whistler of the great Irving himself in his role as Philip II of Spain in Tennyson's *Queen Mary*. This was bought by Charles Freer, founder of the Freer Gallery of Art in Washington, a great admirer of Whistler's, for 4,800 guineas. The second was a portrait of Ellen Terry crowning herself as Lady Macbeth by John Singer Sargent. This should have sold for a high price, but on the day of the sale the bidding stopped at 1,200 guineas and the painting was withdrawn. Hearing a whisper to the effect that the Sargent was about to be sold to an American, Joseph put the idea in his father's head that he should buy Ellen Terry's portrait for the nation. He did, and it now has a place of honor at the Tate Gallery in Millbank.

Then a further opportunity for philanthropy presented itself. The Tate owned a handsome collection of paintings by the man Kenneth Clark called "far the greatest painter that England has ever produced": Joseph Mallord William Turner. Most of his works were, however, in storage at the senior institution, the National Gallery in Trafalgar Square. It was clear that new exhibition space was needed, and Joel undertook to provide five rooms on the main floor, with others below. It really was a handsome gift, and one suspects that the choice of Turner may have had as much to do with the son as with the father. In years to come Joseph Duveen would be a frequent visitor to the Turner rooms at the Tate. He would stand for hours in front of one particular painting, *Bridge and Tower,* now called *The Ponte Delle Torri, Spoleto.* This shimmering view of what may be a ruined Roman aqueduct in the middle distance, with a sun blanching its color to the palest of grays, has been rendered in insubstantial and floating planes of color that take it beyond the purely picturesque into realms of the imagination. That Duveen should be transfixed by such a vision in which emotion has been transformed into pure color, suggests not only a sophisticated taste but a surprising delicacy of feeling, however well hidden. For, as Duveen said, "If I owned that picture I should want nothing else in the world."

OTHER ASPECTS OF JOEL DUVEEN'S LEGACY were, at this stage in his life, giving him far more cause for concern. As far as the future of his daughters went, the main thing was to get them suitably married. After her original rebellion Esther had married Jacques Jules Lowengard happily enough, and they had three daughters: Juliette, Marguerite, and Annette Henriette, as well as a son, Armand, born in 1893, who would become vitally important in the Duveen scheme of things. Annette Duveen's marriage to Harry Abrahams, a diamond merchant, must have struck Joel as perfectly satisfactory. The problem came with Eveline, always called Eva. Sir John Foster said, "Eva was a very attractive woman and when she announced she was going to marry Arthur Cecil Abrahams, who wasn't so important in the Jewish hierarchy, her father, who was an old tyrant, wouldn't have it." Sir John called him "meshugge," or crazy. " 'Out of the house!' he said. So she left and the youngest daughter, Florrie, packed up and went with her!" Eva and Arthur were married in 1904. Arthur Abrahams went on to become a stockbroker and the head of British Red Cross in World War II. He was knighted in 1942, so Eva became Lady Abrahams, which would have mollified Joel. When the time came to write his will, Florrie's insurrection was evidently much on her father's mind. There are heavy references to the importance of her choosing the right husband and hints of the financial penalties awaiting her if her fiancé is not approved by

Joel Duveen in later years,
wealthy and formidable

the family. In 1912, four years after her father's death, Florrie married René Gimpel, the well-known Parisian art dealer, and a very respectable choice indeed.

Although only in his early sixties, the great founder of the house of Duveen would have been aware that his influence, along with his ability to deal with the atmosphere of constant crisis and intrigue, was in decline. A photograph taken later in life is instructive in the clues it provides to his state of mind. Joel Duveen was still physically trim and cuts a dashing figure in a frock coat, its lapels trimmed in black silk, a polka-dotted waistcoat, high collar, and dark tie. But the heady confidence and zest of his youth have given way to a cold stare, that of a man defensively prepared for the worst.

Joel Duveen was also wearing a pearl tie pin, an affectation his son mimicked. Among Joel's proudest possessions was a particularly lustrous, rare, and valuable black pearl. He had worn it one afternoon when visiting his uncle Jacob Levi Hangjas ("Ooom Jaap") and the old antique dealer had recognized it and claimed to know its provenance. According to him, the pearl had come from a rajah who gave it to a sea captain's wife. Its history was romantic and bloody; somehow it had ended up in Holland, and Joel, unknowing, had bought it. Perhaps that rajah's pearl had assumed a particular significance in his life. He was still head of the firm, and the pearl was the symbol as well as the amulet.

Having drummed the idea of competition into the heads of his sons from an early age, Joel Duveen could hardly be surprised to discover that he had raised eager, impatient, and contentious young men. Although they would present a united front to the world (and the usefulness of family connections had been demonstrated over and over again), if pushed far enough more than one son was ready to rebel, not just against another brother but against his father as well. Charles, who was only two years younger than Joe, had the Duveen eye, in his case for furniture and porcelain. He had been sent to help Uncle Henry in New York when he was only sixteen and was by far the most serious contender with Joe for the leading role in the firm. Unfortunately he also had the Duveen quicksilver temperament, by turns expansive and argumentative, as well as a tendency to lose money, and was not on particularly good terms with Uncle Henry. John, as has been noted, had an indolent charm that did not impress Uncle Henry, either. Louis, who tended to stammer when nervous, presented a more interesting case; quiet and scholarly, he showed a marked aptitude and would become the firm's expert on the Italian Renaissance. Edward was another Duveen son with a fine instinct for, and appreciation of, paint-

Charles Duveen, who fought with brother Joseph
and dropped his last name, for a price

ing and sculpture as well as architecture and decor, and a well-developed
business sense. Then there were Benjamin, Henry, and Ernest, the three
youngest, all of them potential contenders.

The situation was doubtless exacerbated by the fact that Joe had par-
layed his 15 percent into a dominant role in Duveen Brothers, at least in
London. He was being aided and abetted far too often by Uncle Henry
(who had never quite forgiven Joe for relegating him to the permanent role
of junior partner). There was also the undeniable fact that Joe had made a
brilliant beginning and was taking Duveen Brothers to an ever more com-

Top left: Louis Duveen; *top right:* Edward Duveen

Bottom left: Benjamin Duveen; *bottom right:* Uncle Henry

manding position in the art market. It was perhaps no accident that Joe's moment of greatest triumph threatened to tear Duveen Brothers apart.

RODOLPHE KANN, a prosperous banker, was an associate of Cecil Rhodes and Otto Beit who had made a fabulous fortune in the diamond and gold mines of South Africa. Along with his brother Maurice, Kann began to collect paintings, sculpture, and objets d'art in 1880 and did so with such single-minded concentration that by the time he died twenty-five years later, he owned, by general agreement, the finest private galleries in Paris and among the finest in Europe. Like all collectors, he sought the exquisite and rare. Such was his judgment, aided by the omnipresent Wilhelm von Bode, that he succeeded, whether they were early works by masters in Italy and the Netherlands or selections by eighteenth-century French painters, including Watteau and Fragonard. He collected Franz Hals, Vermeer, and Van Dyck and all manner of furniture and objets, including bottles, boxes, commodes, Chinese figurines, ivory and Renaissance bronzes, Louis XV ormolu candelabra, statuettes, plates, clocks, tables, pot stands, screens, and vases. He owned the Boucher tapestries from Lady Henry Somerset that Joel had coveted a decade before. The glories of his collection, however, were ten Rembrandts, a number that would be impossible for any collector to assemble today and that was remarkable even in that epoch. They included Rembrandt's enchanting portrait of his son Titus and *Aristotle Contemplating the Bust of Homer,* which are now at the Metropolitan Museum of Art in New York, along with twenty other paintings from the Kann Collection.

Although Kann's collection was never open to the public, he was generous with his permission for visitors with the right connections and often lent his paintings under the pseudonym of Monsieur X. As a result, his collection was well known, and when he died in 1905 the news spread fast. René Gimpel, Florrie's future husband, and his partner, Nathan Wildenstein, took options on the paintings, which they sold for a high price to Duveen Brothers once Joe and Uncle Henry had arranged the financing for the spectacular $4.2 million sale. It was, without doubt, one of the most successful coups anyone had seen and the biggest success of Joseph Duveen's career.

There was one small problem: No one had bothered to tell Joel Duveen that these negotiations were taking place. Jack Duveen, his favorite nephew, was in charge of his family's relatively small gallery in Liverpool, named for his stepfather, Joseph M. Duveen. At Easter of 1907 he was summoned to join his uncle, who was staying at the Hermitage in Monte Carlo. The journey took three days, and upon his arrival he discovered that his uncle had found out about the sale. He was beside himself with rage. Joel Duveen said, "They wanted to conclude this business without even consulting me. Just as if I didn't count any more. They want to push me out of the active lead of the business with this great coup."

When Jack's family firm moved from The Hague to Liverpool some years earlier, Joel had been generous, helping them establish credit in their new location and even passing along furniture and bedding. Although Jack does not mention it in his book, it would seem that he had a particular reason to visit his uncle that Easter. The family needed further credit and in fact he had been sent to ask his uncle if he would act as guarantor for loans to the gallery of seven thousand pounds. This was readily granted, which might be one reason why Jack decided to act as peacemaker for this particular contretemps. Why not go to Paris yourself, he told his uncle, "take the lead and show them that yours is still the master-brain." Joel was delighted at the boldness of the idea and took the train to Paris. Jack described in detail Joel's visit to the Kann galleries a few days later, his initial doubts and the degrees by which his uncle was persuaded that the Rembrandts, which he thought would only interest museums, would be very attractive to American collectors. There were the Boucher tapestries too, of course. As Jack describes it, Joel finally said, "Jack, my boy, we must insist on having the whole collection, pictures included!" As for Joe Duveen, he recalled that once the sale was completed, his father turned to him and his brothers, gesturing toward the Boucher tapestries, and said, "Boys, there is our savings bank."

News of this colossal transaction—the description of the Rodolphe Kann Collection filled four large folio volumes—hit the London and Paris art worlds on August 7, 1907. A. C. R. Carter, art critic of the *Daily Telegraph,* who broke the story, wrote, "French commentators agreed that Paris itself had not been so much startled by any tidings since the day when it was announced that the Pitt diamond had been bought by the Regent Duke for the boy-King Louis Quinze at the huge sum of two and a half million francs."

Once Joel had persuaded himself that buying the Kann Collection was his idea, every instinct told him to be forgiving, and he had a particular reason for not wanting to aggravate any family tensions just then. He had been diagnosed with glomerulonephritis, then called Bright's disease, a disease of the kidneys which could have been brought about by a streptococcal throat infection. Acute nephritis, which includes blood in the urine, puffiness of the face and ankles, uremia and high blood pressure, is mainly a disease of childhood; its outlook is particularly bleak in adults. In Joel Duveen's case it was slow but persistent, and by the summer of 1906 he took a doctor everywhere he traveled.

Nevertheless, the fact that Joe and Henry had been conspiring to buy the Kann Collection without consulting him left Joel with the nasty feeling that they wanted to remove him from office. This, as Edward Fowles relates, was perfectly true. That he must set up on his own in Paris—with Uncle Henry in the background, of course—had been fixed in Joe's mind for the last two or three years and was the secret reason why he had built the Petit Trianon in the Place Vendôme. He and Henry were in perfect agreement. Uncle Henry would dissolve his partnership with Joel and between them they would simply bypass London altogether. Once Joel had recovered from the sense of betrayal such a defection had aroused, he was ready with a counterproposal. He knew that his son Charles was deter-mined to go into business, and given their temperaments, there was no chance of a happy partnership with Joe. Joe did, however, have someone Charles wanted: an able young assistant named H. F. Dawson, who was financially independent, made an excellent impression, and had a very good eye. To Joe's indignation, Joel arranged matters so that this valuable employee should leave Duveen Brothers and go into partnership with Charles in a gallery in Brook Street under the latter's name. Joel proposed to incorporate himself in this new company, along with John and Edward, who was also trading under his own name on Bond Street. Thanks to the capital Joel could bring, there would be no shortage of ready cash for hand-some new quarters in London, Paris, and New York, possibly Buenos Aires as well. Then Joel invited Jack to join them. Jack wrote, "I should have to give up my very prosperous business in Liverpool but I had always looked upon my uncle as a father, and I accepted without hesitation."

Lawyers were engaged, and a head-on collision seemed inevitable. Then something happened. Perhaps Rosetta, with her gift for calming the excitable temperaments of her husband and son, stepped in at the crucial moment, as she had done so many times before. No matter how successful they were, three or four fragmented businesses working at cross purposes could not possibly be as effective as the same group working toward a single aim under a united leadership. It was a question of *mishpocheh,* family unity and family loyalty. Joel had not worked all his life, building a network of family interrelationships and marital alliances, only to have his oldest son destroy this fabric of associations, assembled with so much patient care. At the eleventh hour, both sides retreated, and a new agreement was hammered out in October 1907. Joe got almost everything he wanted, in return for concessions that his brothers wanted. Charles received an annual stipend and agreed to drop his surname and trade as C. J. Charles (later, Charles of London). Edward was probably also compensated in a similar way. While in business for himself he, too, dropped his last name, and would later join Duveen Brothers, running the London office. John had already retired from the company the year before. Joe's terms, that no other brother be given a partnership, were accepted. Fowles wrote that although all the brothers received regular allowances and were technically honorary directors, Henry and John, for instance, were not expected to show their noses in Bond Street. Ernest, Louis, and Benjamin all entered the firm as salaried employees for varying periods and proved themselves to be extremely valuable assets in London, Paris, and New York. Jack was out in the cold.

Fowles wrote that Joel "was deeply grieved that Uncle Henry had seen fit to consider deserting him, but he did not realise himself how ill he was. I felt a great deal of sympathy for both sides in the affair." The settlement, which Joel's faction had naturally opposed, led to permanently bruised feelings. There was no reason why one brother should take sole command when others were just as resourceful, efficient, and enterprising. What is more, as will be seen, Joseph Duveen always seemed to manage to have every last penny tied up in stock, so that although someone always seemed ready to sue for his share, no one quite could. Doubtless no one was prepared to concede that between talent and genius is a wide gulf. Given his exceptional gifts Joseph Duveen was right to insist on his position of eminence, and in terms of his emotional health it was essential that he confront his father. As his only child, Dolly Burns, was aware, everyone else seemed completely cowed by her grandfather, but not her father.

One likes to think that some sort of reconciliation scene took place between Joel and his firstborn reminiscent of that moment when, estranged from Henry, Joel encountered him at dinner in their sister's house and tearfully embraced him. The indications are that the eventual settlement pleased him as much as it must have pleased Joe and that it simply served to formalize the actual state of affairs. It is true that the Duveens' other great purchase of that period, which took place in the summer of 1906, went through without a hint of a disagreement even though Joseph Duveen was making all the decisions.

IN THE DAYS BEFORE WORLD WAR I Berlin rivaled London and Paris as a center of art, its collectors being in the market for French Impressionists and Old Masters. In the latter category Wilhelm von Bode, with his high forehead, deeply ridged lines around his thin mouth, and pince-nez, was the ruling authority, imposing his will like a ringmaster in a circus, with a pyrotechnical display of hauteur. After he became director general of the Kaiser Friedrich Museum in 1905 Bode's reputation was so enhanced and his influence so commanding that any collector who did not intend to let the Kaiser Friedrich inherit had a lot to answer for.

Of the group of cultured Jewish merchants of taste who were buying Old Masters, none was more justly celebrated than Oscar Hainauer, a banker who was Berlin representative of the Paris Rothschilds. He had diligently studied the collections in the great European museums and no doubt benefited still further from regular visits to the great Rothschild mansions in Paris. Then he bought the perfectly chosen art collection of another banker and formed the ambition that nothing should enter his own doors unless it was the best. Bode, who praised sparingly, spoke of Hainauer's "extraordinarily fine taste and keen eye," and it was true. Whatever Hainauer acquired—whether European tapestries, Oriental rugs of the fifteenth and sixteenth centuries, Italian Renaissance paintings, Netherlandish school paintings, sculptures in marble, bronze and terra cotta by such Renaissance masters as Donatello and Rossellino, or pieces of jewelry by Renaissance goldsmiths—was outstanding.

Hainauer did not live long enough to enjoy his collection; he died in 1894, two years after his retirement. He had bought with such a free hand and maintained such a handsome establishment that Bode could be forgiven for thinking that the collection would one day be given to his museum. In fact, as a way of sealing the deal, Bode had prepared a catalogue. Still, the widow Hainauer could not make up her mind. Jack Duveen wrote, "[Hainauer's] widow became increasingly perturbed by the threatening political atmosphere and the growing anti-Semitic spirit that the Prussian aristocracy showed even at court." She confided in Bode, explaining that she could not afford to give the collection to the museum; she had to sell it. Bode acted fast. He offered the modest sum of 1,250,000 marks for the whole collection and threatened the widow with the Kaiser's displeasure should she refuse him. Bode took the further precaution of ensuring that none of the other Berlin dealers would offer more than the museum. Everyone knew the figure was derisory. Hainauer himself had warned his wife that she must not sell for less than 3,000,000 marks. She did not know what to do.

When a hugely important collection is for sale, the stage fills rapidly with characters who have a more or less direct interest in seeing that a piece of the pie comes to them. Such a person materialized in the form of God-frey von Kopp, an Austrian aristocrat of dubious reputation who is said to have once "sold" Trajan's Column to a gullible American. After leaving Vienna in a hurry—there was some scandal or other—Kopp appeared in Paris, where he set himself up as an art dealer. He also persuaded the widow Hainauer he could get twice what Bode offered and that she should leave it all up to him.

As it happened, that summer of 1906 Bode was on an extended trip to London and the Berlin coast was clear. Kopp then approached Joseph Duveen. Would Duveen Brothers care to buy? Joseph Duveen, with the prospect of a $4.2 million sale already in the works, did not hesitate. In buying the Rodolphe Kann and Oscar Hainauer collections (he added to the list later by buying selectively from the smaller Maurice Kann collection), he was following good business practice. When a painting is put up for auction and a dealer buys, since the sales price is known the dealer's profit will be circumscribed by whatever the client considers reasonable. But when a dealer buys a collection the value of the piece of sculpture or painting is whatever he says it is, and how much he calculates he has paid for each item remains a trade secret. Just the same, at the moment when his star was on the ascendant, Joseph Duveen was already deeply in debt, and only his Uncle Henry's and his father's business contacts saved him. These were extensive. Lord Farquhar, the London banker, who was also a great friend of Edward VII, supported Joel, as did Sir Samuel Scott of Scott's Bank, where Joel kept his accounts. When Scott's Bank merged with Parr's, Lord Farquhar headed that bank too, which was most convenient. Joseph Duveen further arranged for an overdraft on the London-Liverpool Bank of six million dollars, which turned out to be a lifetime commitment on the bank's part. Thanks to Uncle Henry, there were also the Morgan banks in New York, among others; whatever he did—and he was always pushing the limits—Joseph Duveen never ran out of money. Buying the Hainauer Collection must have looked to him as one more way to consolidate his position as the family's dominant figure. Less than four hours after Kopp arrived in his London office, Joseph Duveen was on the train for Berlin.

Since Duveen was on good terms with Bode and consulted him frequently, coaxing the Hainauer Collection out from under his nose would take some doing; and at the start, the interview with widow Hainauer went badly. She was torn between her need to make the best possible sale and her fear of antagonizing Bode and the Kaiser; she seemed almost paralyzed with indecision. Using the irrefutable logic of the marketplace, Duveen offered her 4 million marks, more than three times what Bode was offering. This seemed only to agonize her further. Could she have two days to think it over? Duveen by now was well schooled. She must either accept or reject. She accepted. One does not know how quickly Duveen spirited the collection out of Berlin. One only knows that by the time Bode heard the bad news, and railed at the widow Hainauer (as the Kaiser railed at Bode), it would have been too late. Jack Duveen wrote that Kopp took the immense commission of sixteen thousand pounds. This he spent that same summer, traveling through Europe with a harem of pretty girls. Whatever was left over was dropped at the roulette tables in Monte Carlo.

The Hainauer Collection began to repay its investment almost as soon as it arrived in London. Benjamin Altman, P. A. B. Widener, and J. P. Morgan needed no persuading and snapped up the magnificent Italian Renaissance sculptures for a total of $5 million. In other words, Duveen Brothers immediately realized a profit of nearly $4 million. The catalogues of the even larger Kann Collection were eagerly studied and secret sales were made even before the collection was officially bought in the summer of 1907. Morgan bought Ghirlandaio's portrait of Giovanna Tornabuoni, along with such trifles as two wings of a triptych by Memling and works by some minor Dutch and Flemish masters for a total of $1 million. Altman grandly bought four of the Rembrandts, including the enchanting portrait of Titus, along with a Vermeer and some sculptures, for a paltry $500,000. Arabella Huntington, widow of the railway magnate Collis P. Huntington, was furnishing a house in Paris and bought most of the fine furniture and the gem of the collection, Rembrandt's *Aristotle,* for $2.5 million. The Kann Collection sales price was also covered in short order. Meanwhile, the firm retained a huge quantity of lesser trinkets which furnished its galleries in London, Paris, and New York and formed much of the Duveen inventory for years.

AFTER HE HAD GONE to such lengths to reduce his brothers to the role of disinterested spectators and buy off brothers Charles and Edward, when he discovered that competition was coming from a new direction, Joseph's reaction may be imagined. It seems that Jack Duveen's business in Liverpool was not quite as flourishing as described, because even before the settlement was reached which shut him out of any future Duveen company, he had decided to set up shop in London. He arrived early in 1906 and took rooms upstairs in an old Georgian mansion at 38 Dover Street, around the corner from Old Bond Street.

From Joseph Duveen's point of view it was bad enough that Jack was setting up in London as a Duveen. What made things intolerable was that Jack was still using his stepfather's name of Joseph M. Duveen, even though he had bought his parents out some time before. Joe wrote a letter to Jack that has not survived, in effect asking him to trade under his legal name of Jacques. Jack wrote a polite reply in which he said that since J. M. Duveen & Son had been in business since 1883, to change the name would be to give up all the goodwill that the firm had built up over the years. He said he had been reluctant to establish himself in London, knowing how his relatives were likely to feel. Now he had no choice. His business had been built on cheap imports from Holland, which were no longer cheap, and his North of England clients had stopped buying. He had to look for a wider market. He had no desire to compete and fervently hoped they would all remain on good terms.

Jack's own enterprise was so modest in comparison with Duveen Brothers' mighty undertaking that he could be forgiven for thinking they were overreacting. There is a consistent undertone running through the lawsuit that eventually followed. Here is sister Betsy, who lost her husband when she was only in her twenties, pluckily carrying on the business, and now here is her clever son, precociously memorizing all the Chinese characters on Oost Indiesch porcelain. All of this is happening under the benevolent eye of Joel Duveen, who takes Betsy's family under his wing and is a second father to Jack. It has always been a case of the senior Duveen providing for Betsy's struggling family. No doubt Jack thought this would always be the case, but he had reckoned without his cousin Joseph.

To trade under his own name when he owned the firm seems like a reasonable request, and why Jack refused to do so is hard to understand. The fact was that he did refuse, and in doing so, made an enemy. Writing as James Henry Duveen, Jack's two books, *Secrets of an Art Dealer* and *Art Treasures and Intrigue,* describe at length the dirty tricks of the art world, so one might expect that he would be ready for anything Joe might throw at him; but the fact was that he was not. He claimed to have been told by his uncle Joel that Joe was going to punish him by taking his two best clients, Sir William Bennett, the leading surgeon in London, and W. H. Lever, later Lord Leverhulme, away from him. Since extracting clients from other dealers was child's play for Joe Duveen, one is perfectly willing to believe he tried, as Jack Duveen claims, to spoil several sales to Lever and Bennett. In a righteous fury, Jack Duveen decided to confront his tormentor head-on and moved to 9 Old Bond Street in 1908, a few doors away from Duveen Brothers.

Testimony at Jack Duveen's suit for slander against his cousin in 1910 reveals that, if the situation was muddled while he had rooms in Dover Street, with letters, invitations, and even checks going to his firm instead of Duveen Brothers, it deteriorated still further once J. M. Duveen & Son were in business in Bond Street. Uncle Joel, who had not minded having Jack set up shop in Dover Street, and had asked Charles to lend him eight large display cases, had quite another reaction once his favorite nephew was on his doorstep. Joseph Duveen testified, "I think my father was more angry even than I. He was wild about it; in fact I had very rarely seen him so angry about anything." The seven thousand pounds in loan guarantees were immediately withdrawn. Two months later Uncle Joel took the extraordinary step of changing his name from Joel Joseph to Joseph Joel. No mention of this was made when Jack's lawsuit was eventually heard— Jack claimed he had been vilified and Joe admitted to having called him "an ungrateful scoundrel"—but the cause and effect is clear enough. There is no question that Jack stood to benefit from being another Bond Street Duveen, but he also stood to lose if business directed to his Joseph M. somehow ended up at the doors of the better-known Joseph J., not to mention his son, the other Joseph J. Joel also cut Jack and his mother out of his will. (After the trial was heard, the presiding judge wondered why the action had ever been brought and awarded Jack one farthing damages. He had to pay his own legal fees of five thousand pounds.

IN THE MIDDLE OF THE FAMILY UPROAR, on August 5, 1907, Joe had ordered Edward Fowles to go to Paris to take charge of the Kann Collection. Fowles was only twenty-two and felt far too young for such responsibility, but Joe did not dare to send a brother just then, and so Fowles was elected. Joe promised he would be there a week; Fowles stayed for the next thirty-two years. His immediate responsibilities were huge: taking care of the objects, arranging for cleaning and transportation and also overseeing the building of the Petit Trianon, which opened the following May. Duveen, too, spent much of the autumn in Paris, giving his address as 51, avenue d'Iéna and making frequent trips back to London as the family dispute was being resolved. That address happened to be the Kann mansion, a handsome building surrounding an inner courtyard at the corner of the rue Auguste Vacquerie and the avenue d'Iéna. There was a similarly grand mansion next door belonging to Rodolphe Kann's brother Maurice. When connecting doors were opened, the second floors of both mansions made a single immense gallery in which the Kann Collections were on display. That year of 1907, *le monde entier* came to see the collection before it was dispersed: Calouste Gulbenkian, Elsie de Wolfe, the Rothschilds, Arabella Huntington, Bernard Berenson, Lord and Lady Michelham, Mr. and Mrs. Ralph Curtis, Mrs. Henry Goldman, Sir Martin Conway, Madame Louis de Errazuriz—the list is a long one, since they trooped past for six months, until March of 1908. Joseph Duveen was, naturally, a frequent visitor, according to the Rodolphe Kann guest book. His energies were for once fully occupied, taking care of the Kann and Hainauer acquisitions, building the new Paris gallery, and arranging for the new Turner wing at the Tate. When his father was knighted in the summer of 1908 he received a thousand letters and telegrams, all of which Joe answered. Or so he claimed. Knighthood was an extraordinary accomplishment for the man who began as a penniless immigrant in Hull all those years before, but it came very late. Joel was given a private audience by King Edward VII, and when he feebly tried to kneel for the honor the king checked him with a smile.

Fowles recalled that Sir Joseph arrived in Paris that summer to visit the newly opened gallery and could barely walk up the few front steps, even with the assistance of his male nurse. "It was depressing to see this man, formerly so full of life and energy, reduced to such a condition," he wrote. It is hard to avoid conjecturing that the family quarrel further weakened the patient's defenses. Eventually his mind was wandering, and in his muddled state he sometimes seemed overwhelmed by suspicion. The smallest incident might lead to a crisis. When he made his final trip to the south of France that autumn of 1908, Sir Joseph was put on the train by his brother, Henry, but then the train began to move, and the patient became so agitated by the fact that Henry was still in the compartment that his doctor had to pull the emergency cord. Keeping a doctor became almost impossible. When one doctor said he could not stand it any longer, Joseph Duveen bribed him handsomely to stay. (He was paid six thousand pounds.) Early in November 1908, Joseph, in Paris, was summoned to Hyères. The end was near. Fowles wrote, "I had realized that in spite of their quarrels and bickerings over business matters, he was deeply attached to his father."

Sir Joseph died on November 9, 1908. He did not live to see the opening of the Turner wing, which took place in 1910; nor could he have predicted the heights to which Duveen Brothers would soar in the future. He had, however, left his affairs in good order, making a will as late as September of that year. His children received their share of the family fortune even if (thanks to Joe) they would have a hard time cashing it in. Rosetta was well cared for and continued to live at The Elms for another fourteen years. The boys were settled on their various paths, and three of the girls were

Rosetta Duveen at the turn of the century,
covered with the jewels and furs her husband
had promised her years before

married off; as noted, Florrie, the youngest, would be married a few years later. Sir Joseph had decided which of the boys should get his personal effects—Louis, for some unexplained reason, did not receive a keepsake. Charles was given his three pearl studs. John had his large dressing case with silver gilt fittings. Edward had his repeater watch and three pairs of cufflinks. Benjamin received his small dressing case, and Henry, his beaver-lined coat. Florrie had five hundred pounds put aside for her future trousseau and a small white heart-shaped pin to use as a pendant. Various nieces, nephews, cousins, and Dutch relatives were mentioned in the will, as were some old employees at 21 Old Bond Street. On condition that he passed on to Ernest the tie pin that his father had given him during his life-time, Joseph Joel, the firstborn, inherited the rajah's pearl.

Chapter Five

THE SOUND OF A SELL

'Twas whispered by Fry, it was muttered by Dell
And at Holmes for a space was permitted to dwell
And B.B. heard faintly
The sound of a sell.

—"A Christmas Attribution," circa 1910

A MONG THE LEGIONS of cunning, expert, and devious men who influenced Joseph Duveen apart from his father Joel, a little French dealer was high on the list. Nathan Wildenstein, who came from Alsace and was eighteen years Joseph Duveen's senior, told his grandson Daniel that he was an only child and his father a Sephardic rabbi who had died the day Nathan was born. Much later Daniel learned that, far from dying the day of his son's birth, Nathan's father lived for almost thirty years longer and was not a rabbi, and that the Wildensteins were Ashkenazic Jews from Eastern Europe rather than Sephardic Jews from Spain and Portugal. Most of all, Nathan Wildenstein was not an only child but the oldest of seven, with three other brothers and three sisters in the family.

As Daniel Wildenstein relates in his book *Marchands d'Art* his grandfather's ancestors had been horse traders for almost two hundred years, with all the expertise that implies. They knew how to spot a good horse and, equally, how to sell as a healthy specimen an animal that would be dead in three days. This ability to observe the smallest signs and portents in horse flesh that others might not notice transferred itself effortlessly to the equally arcane subject of discriminating between paintings, although the choice of métier came about almost by accident. It seems that after the Prussians entered Alsace and that French province became German in 1871, the inhabitants were given a stark choice: to leave and stay French or remain and learn German. Nathan panicked and left, while the rest of his family stayed. To have a single member defect in this way struck his parents as unforgivable. Everyone stayed or everyone left, but one did not, under any circumstances, break up the family. The rupture was so bitter that it was as if he had never been born, which perhaps accounts for Wildenstein's fanciful inventions about his origins, his deviousness and equivocations. He seemed to care only for "la belle France" and visiting the Louvre.

He was by nature an exceptional salesman. Daniel Wildenstein wrote, "He had it in the blood. He knew how to operate, detect people's tastes, their longings, their desires, with an infallible intuitive sense." One day one of his clients asked him if he would sell some paintings for her and he did not hesitate, despite the fact that he knew absolutely nothing about art. He learned fast. By the time Joseph Duveen was a force in the art market, Nathan Wildenstein had become a partner of René Gimpel's, from another Alsatian family that also defected in 1871, and whose firm, Gimpel et Fils at 57, rue la Boétie, was highly regarded in Paris and elsewhere.

Daniel Wildenstein claimed that Joseph Duveen often said, "If I had never known your grandfather, I would never be where I am today," and it may well have been true. Nathan Wildenstein's appearance was far from prepossessing. In youth he had a wide, engaging smile, but as he aged the lines in his face stiffened into something closer to a grimace and his exquisitely tailored clothes could not disguise his round shoulders and sunken chest. His manner, to judge from his letters, was icily polite; he did everything by stealth, and he was *exigéant,* as the French say; exacting, hard to please. All that experience with horseflesh gave him the necessary training in deceptive salesmanship and the half-answer that conceals the truth. But he was an essential figure; Duveen had to deal with him, if only because he was Gimpel's partner, and in 1912 Gimpel married Duveen's sister Florrie. In a way, sparring with Wildenstein was good practice for whatever the art market had in store; as with tennis, when playing with a master one was bound to improve one's game. Not that Joseph Duveen needed much more schooling by the time he was engaging in hand-to-hand combat with Wildenstein. One of the more amusing aspects of the courtroom battle he waged with Cousin Jack over the latter's arrival in Bond Street is the extent to which Duveen managed to frustrate the judge and opposing lawyers by his obfuscatory behavior. First, he talked very fast—a lifelong trait—and second, he absolutely, positively refused to give a straight yes or no. He played with the idea. He danced around it. He pirouetted and ducked and sidestepped with such finesse that Mr. Justice Ridley finally said in exasperation: "I wish you would not talk so much. It is extremely difficult to take your evidence." Overwhelming one's adversary with words while saying nothing is an art, and Duveen no doubt enjoyed using that accomplishment with Wildenstein as much as Wildenstein enjoyed exacting ever further concessions. Daniel Wildenstein referred to the shouting matches that would take place when each man suspected the other of being after the same painting. Having exhausted their repertoire of scatological insults, Duveen and Wildenstein would finally call a truce and agree to buy it jointly.

This was evidently the case with the Rodolphe and Maurice Kann sales. Wildenstein had the advantage, since he was on good terms with Maurice Kann, the surviving brother, no mean collector himself, as well as Maurice's son Édouard, who was Rodolphe's heir. So far so good; but the Gimpel and Wildenstein partnership could not possibly raise the huge sums needed to finance the sales of either collection—and Jack Duveen thought the Rodolphe Kann Collection had been vastly overpriced—and neither did they have American millionaire clients. By taking an option on the Rodolphe Kann Collection Gimpel and Wildenstein ensured they would benefit handsomely from the Duveen sale, and Wildenstein took the further precaution of requiring a commission for any sale he himself arranged. Both men had actually leased the Rodolphe Kann mansion for some months while sales were underway. It was so much simpler just to leave all the objects handsomely displayed in their accustomed places at 51, avenue d'Iéna, which explains Duveen's grandiloquent announcement of Rodolphe Kann's address as his own during the months that the collection was on view. However, Duveen was still dependent on Wildenstein as the man on the spot, and Wildenstein took full advantage of that fact as he wrung his stringent terms from Duveen Brothers.

By 1909 the two men were flirting with the idea of acquiring the Maurice Kann Collection as well, or rather, parts of it. Since Duveen's galleries and storage areas were already jammed to overflowing with the myriad objets from the Kann and Hainauer collections that had not yet been sold, he did not particularly want to take on another complete collection. There were some marvelous things and some mediocre things. The trick was going to be how to buy the marvelous things he could sell at once and avoid the mediocre things that were going to clutter up the premises for years. But there was a further hurdle to surmount. To be on the safe side, they wanted to find out how much of a market there was for the marvelous things before they committed themselves.

Deciding how to accomplish this feat of legerdemain absorbed

Duveen's attention in the summer of 1909. There was a promising client, Baron Edmund de Rothschild, from the English branch of that famous banking family, not the major Rothschild collector, but certainly a contender. The baron had been in to see him in London twice that week, Joseph Duveen wrote to Nathan Wildenstein on July 21, 1909. He wanted two Guardi pictures from the Maurice Kann Collection and the "Boucher room," a reference to eight painted panels, *The Arts and Sciences,* created for Madame de Pompadour's library in the chateau of Crécy, one of the gems of the collection. The challenge was how to get the baron inside the building without asking Kann's permission. Duveen wrote, "It would look as if you or we had sent him for the purpose of choosing things before we actually purchased [them]; and that would of course spoil our purchase. As you know, Kann is a very sharp man!" Somehow, the baron had to be smuggled into the house while Kann was out. Did Wildenstein think that Monsieur Fischer (perhaps Kann's butler) would let them in and then be discreet about it? Wildenstein replied almost at once that Kann was away and Fischer was amenable; the coast was clear. Duveen, emphasizing there would be something in it for him, urged Wildenstein to get Rothschild to buy the large Cuyp and the snuff boxes the collector admired in addition to the two small Guardis and the Boucher room. He thought the latter ought to sell for two million francs ($400,000). In other words, the baron must be persuaded to want what Duveen thought he ought to buy, an attitude toward his clients that was becoming steadily refined, even in those early days.

The Rothschild visit was all arranged. The baron and Wildenstein arrived at the appointed hour, but, to the latter's horror, Monsieur Fischer was not there. He had chosen that moment to go to the country. Showing the determination and dash so characteristic of his personality, Wildenstein was off in a flash, tracking the errant gatekeeper to his lair and strong-arming him back to Paris, presumably while Rothschild waited outside the door of the Kann mansion, tapping his foot. All ended well. The baron liked several things, although he resisted all of Wildenstein's ministrations to take the Cuyp. He yearned for one of the Rembrandts, which Duveen had told Wildenstein he must not sell, since he was saving it for someone else. The baron wondered how the Boucher panels would fit in his house. In other words, it was quite a successful visit.

Duveen was all for taking the next train to Paris and buying the items they had selected at the lowest possible price, of course. But Wildenstein's next letter was not encouraging. He had paid a visit to the collector and learned that Kann did not want to sell the cream of his collection to

Duveen. Kann was sure the sale would be widely publicized—he was right about that—and that would reduce the value of the remainder. So he was asking a fantastic price for the things Duveen wanted. The only solution was to demur and wait for Kann to see reason. Wildenstein rather thought that would happen in the autumn. If Duveen played his cards right, he could "easily" make a profit of 75 percent. From subsequent correspondence it is clear that the deal with Kann was finally accomplished to the satisfaction of all concerned, and included four outstanding Rembrandts, the large Cuyp landscape that had once belonged to Count Boni de Castellane, a pair of fine portraits by Frans Hals, a quantity of eighteenth-century French gold boxes that Duveen thought he could easily sell, and the Boucher panels. This feathery, light-hearted series of paintings of children engaged in grown-up occupations such as fishing, hunting, poetry, and painting, a favorite conceit of the eighteenth century, did not go to the baron after all. They ended up gracing the boudoir of Mrs. Henry Clay Frick at 1 East Seventieth Street in New York, where they can be seen to this day.

Isabella Stewart Gardner,
Berenson's patron, in 1906

ISABELLA STEWART GARDNER, a flamboyant socialite who began collecting European art for her museum, Fenway Court, after she inherited nearly $2 million from her father in 1891, wrote to Berenson in 1897 that she had just returned from Paris. There she had seen some wonderful paintings, "bought by those Jews, Kann, and Gustave Dreyfus." She continued, "They have had great luck and have packed up and walked off with the things they bought in Italy. Don't you think the best way to do is that. Put the Giorgione in a trunk and presto! Do you fancy they realize how their behaviour appears to an Anglo-Saxon?" That piece of vituperation, freely expressed to someone with whom she was on affectionate terms, could only mean that the lady did not know to whom she was writing, which was not altogether her fault. In fact Berenson was a Litvak, a Jew from Lithuania, whose family had emigrated to Boston in 1875, when he was ten years old. His father, Alter Valvrojenski, the new Albert Berenson, became a peddler, tramping up to New Hampshire and Maine, and his mother took in lodgers. Meanwhile Bernhard, the firstborn, who was precociously clever, was admitted to Boston Latin School, traditionally the entry to Harvard University, and then Harvard itself. He subsequently gained the attention of Mrs. Gardner, who helped send him to Europe after he graduated, and he evolved, by degrees, into her expert on the Italian Renaissance. He was the one who single-handedly acquired many of the major holdings that now grace Fenway Court, that elegant replica of a Venetian Renaissance palace, the Isabella Stewart Gardner Museum.

Since Berenson was baptized when he was an adolescent into the Episcopal Church by Phillips Brooks, minister of Trinity Church, Boston, he could be forgiven for thinking of himself as a New England Episcopalian; that he also claimed (to Mrs. Gardner) that they both had common Stuart ancestors is harder to excuse. The fact that he had, in fact, been born a Jew was not generally known until World War II, and if he suffered from the casual anti-Semitism voiced by his benefactor, he did not show it.

However, given the commonplace way in which such sentiments were being voiced by ordinary decent-minded people at the turn of the century, it is not too surprising that Berenson should choose to disguise his origins, and only surprising that Duveen made no point of avoiding the issue. There were, of course, the marked differences in their early family backgrounds. B.B., from a painfully poor family, would naturally conceal anything that would impede his goal of becoming "a true gentleman," as he expressed it. By contrast, Duveen, as son of one of the nouveau riche, accustomed to handsome and elegant surroundings, naturally identified with the wealthy and titled clients whom he met in his father's Bond Street gallery. Some of his best clients were Jews, as were many of the art dealers with whom he had daily contact. An accident of birth had shielded him from much of the buffeting to which Berenson had been subjected in the slums of Boston. If he encountered prejudice, he seems to have sailed right past it. Berenson, who was for years at the financial mercy of his skittish and unpredictable benefactor, could not afford that luxury.

By the time Duveen and Berenson joined forces in 1906, the former had established himself as the dominant dealer in Bond Street and was a force to be reckoned with in Paris and New York. Now his ambition soared into the ether: he wanted to straddle the international art market like a colossus. Whatever impulses in that direction could be traced to subconscious needs, the methods of achieving that goal were consciously and deliberately set. By then Duveen was well aware that Italian Renaissance paintings, which would become one of his main stocks in trade, were the most speculative of all merchandise. Whereas eighteenth-century English portraits usually came with impeccable pedigrees, and even early Flemish paintings, the Van Eycks and Memlings, had been guarded as precious objects and were consequently never retouched, Italian thirteenth-to-fifteenth-century paintings were in ruins and unsigned. As has been noted, the market in fakes was another quagmire, along with the gullibility of collectors with more money than sense. Even the great J. P. Morgan himself had been fooled. He actually managed to believe that the bronze doors from the cathedral at Bologna were for sale. He then paid a fast-talking Italian nobleman for them. Rather later, he discovered his mistake. Stings like that always seemed to be happening, and Duveen was well aware of how little it would take to put his own reputation in jeopardy.

At first, he had given the task of scouting for Italian paintings to Walter Dowdeswell, member of an old-established firm of London picture dealers. Dowdeswell showed up in Florence wearing full evening dress, along with a top hat and d'Orsay cape, which was his first mistake, and then compounded his error by being unable to outguess his superior adversaries among the legions of slick dealers and fraudulent counts. What Duveen needed was someone with all the tricks that only time and bitter experience has taught, someone with an impeccable reputation. Berenson, it seemed, had become that man. Long before he turned to picture dealing, Berenson had established his reputation by his famous "lists," i.e., an exhaustive catalogue of Italian Renaissance paintings in public and private hands, to which he had given authors (such paintings being notoriously unsigned)

Bernard Berenson, photographed in 1910 while
staying at Beaulieu with Ralph Curtis

according to a novel method he had developed from the theories of Giovanni Morelli and of Crowe and Cavalcaselle (the latter authors had produced a six-volume history of Italian painting in 1864–66).

Berenson, whose forays into the art market had been limited to whatever sales he could negotiate for Mrs. Gardner, was now an active dealer
although just a gentleman scholar in the eyes of the world. He had even
usurped the position held by Wilhelm von Bode, which took some doing.

Manipulating the prickly sensibilities of this tiny, contentious "true
gentleman," by now well established in a Florentine villa with squadrons of

servants and Mary, his bluestocking, Quaker wife, was just another skill that Duveen set himself to mastering. Perhaps he knew, or soon guessed, that B.B. had an overriding ambition. It was one that had taken vague shape in the 1890s, soon after he began to advise Mrs. Gardner in his role as dealer-expert, continued to gather momentum after he bought his house, i Tatti, in Settignano outside Florence, in 1907, and became an *idée fixe* during World War I. He wanted to leave his villa (sometimes described as a picture gallery with library attached), to Harvard, his alma mater. This, since he and Mary had no children, would be his legacy. It is hard to avoid the suspicion that this goal, as grandiose in its way as any Duveen envisioned, colored everything that followed. In any event, when Duveen offered Berenson a profit-sharing arrangement in 1912 (Berenson was to receive a percentage of the profits from the sale of any painting he authenticated), B.B. and Mary accepted with alacrity. She wrote gleefully, "Bernhard went to Duveens. They were most flattering, and if ⅒ of what they say is true, a future of affluence lies before us!" Mary Berenson became an important part of the sales business, often sent by her husband to inspect a likely piece of merchandise and give a preliminary opinion. Whenever a particularly handsome sale resulted, luxurious visions danced in her head: "motor-trips, house-furnishings, B.B.'s *oggetti* [objets], opera-boxes(!) and so on." In later years Berenson would complain that all his wife thought about was sending money back to England for her daughters by her first marriage, Ray and Karin Costelloe. For his part, B.B. ordered more books for the library and dreamed about Harvard.

ONE OF THE PAINTINGS Isabella Stewart Gardner wanted from the Kann Collection was *Portrait of a Man* by Andrea del Castagno. The work, which depicts an animated-looking figure wearing a rich red garment, is characteristic of the fifteenth-century Florentine, who was noted for the vigor and monumentality of his compositions. That there was something mesmerizing about the portrait, with its clean lines and almost confrontational pose, could not be denied, and B.B. used his choicest adjectives when he wrote to Mrs. Gardner ("the grandest surviving work of one of the greatest figures in Italian art," "an overwhelming masterpiece"). There was, however, a slight problem. Duveen's purchase of the Kann Collection had been made possible because J. P. Morgan wanted his pick of the thirty best pictures and had thrown in $2 million to make sure he got it. One of the pictures he wanted was *Portrait of a Man*. But that had already been promised to Mrs. Gardner. What was Duveen to do? He did not want to antagonize Mrs. Gardner, and he could certainly not afford to antagonize Morgan. While Duveen temporized, B.B., who saw the chances of a Kann sale slipping away, turned on the superlatives to describe another portrait, *A Woman in Green and Crimson* by Antonio Pollaiuolo. It was even better than the Castagno, "the most vigorous, the most plastic, the most characterfull in existence . . . jewel-like in its glory." B.B.'s tastes in pictures tended to be austere; his wife thought the painting positively hideous. Since he eventually downgraded the painting himself, giving it the humiliating label of "Florentine" in his posthumous final lists (1963), the conclusion that the painting was inferior to the Castagno on artistic, not to mention pecuniary, terms is clear. But B.B. was determined to have Mrs. Gardner buy something. Duveen had previously offered the painting to Benjamin Altman, usually the docile customer of Uncle Henry. But for once Altman refused to buy, explaining that he could not bring himself to own a work by a painter whose name he could not pronounce. Mrs. Gardner, with no such reservations, bought it.

So the Castagno went to Morgan in the end, as Duveen knew it would. One of the accomplishments of Uncle Henry that had made him such an asset to Duveen Brothers was the quiet, steady way he had made inroads into the ranks of those collectors with infinite resources, with J. P. Morgan heading the list. Morgan, as they knew, was single-mindedly set upon acquiring the rarest and best. One of the first examples of such complete dedication, from Duveen Brothers' point of view, was the affair of the C. T. Garland collection of oriental porcelain. Generally acknowledged to be one of the finest collections in existence, it included an exquisite red-hawthorn-on-black-ground specimen that Joel had bought in 1891 from George Salting, the other great collector of oriental porcelain, for £1,500. The same baluster-shaped beaker was valued at £30,000 some twenty-five years later. Garland's collection was largely the work of Uncle Henry, who had guided the great collector as he hoarded his treasures and who estimated that by the turn of the century, Garland had bought £180,000 of merchandise from him. When Garland died, the collection was on loan to the Metropolitan Museum of Art in New York and was returned to Duveen Brothers to be sold. It soon was, and a chance meeting was responsible.

Edward Fowles recalled how, in June of 1899, he met J. P. Morgan for the first time. Morgan had entered the Bond Street gallery in search of Uncle Henry, who had not yet arrived. Although he did not know exactly what Morgan looked like, Fowles could hardly mistake him for anyone else, thanks to a peculiar facial feature which, according to a popular

J. Pierpont Morgan aboard the *Corsair*,
watching the Yale/Harvard boat race
in the summer of 1910

schoolboy rhyme of the time, announced his arrival blocks away. The
extravagant deformation of his nose (caused by a skin disease called rhino-
phyma, which caused it to swell and turn a ghastly blue) required a strong
stomach. Jack Duveen had had an instantaneous reaction. He wrote, "I
had heard of a disfigurement but what I saw upset me so thoroughly that
for a moment I could not utter a word. If I did not gasp I must have
changed color. Mr. Morgan noticed this, and his small, piercing eyes transfixed me with a malicious stare . . . when at last I managed to open my
mouth I could produce only a raucous cough."

Fowles managed to stammer out that Uncle Henry was expected
shortly, and Morgan went home. The minute Uncle Henry appeared,

Fowles told him the news, and Henry ran off in the direction of Morgan's house. When he came back an hour later, he had sold the Garland collection. To add to the triumph, Morgan wanted even more of the rarest and best added to it by Duveen Brothers. Fowles's budding career took a sharp upward turn and Duveen Brothers basked once more in that happy circumstance by which valuable objects keep returning for resale, with increased profits each time around. After Morgan's death, when the Garland collection came back yet again, Duveen Brothers paid $3 million for it.

Since male collectors were, more often than not, curiously unprepossessing men—pallid gray business figures who got lost in crowds—Morgan's appearance set him apart, to say the least. Understanding the Morgan psyche became one of the first challenges in Joseph Duveen's long and successful campaign to separate wealthy men from at least a part of their fortunes. One of the favorite maxims of this financier, the organizing force behind General Electric, U.S. Steel, and vast railroad empires, as well as America's de facto central banker for decades, was, "A man always has two reasons for the things he does: a good reason—and the real reason." Yet, when asked why he had acted in a certain way, he would reply, "I thought it was the thing to do." This is where Uncle Henry came in, because "cachet" was Uncle Henry's favorite word. Cachet was what you wanted after you had bought your Bouguereaus and Meissoniers. Cachet meant living appropriately, in the manner of men of style. Cultivated Europeans had their town houses and country seats, their wives, mistresses, motor cars, horses, and hounds. And they had their collections, inherited from centuries of discriminating ancestors. This marked them. To own what they had once owned put self-made men on a par with heirs to kingdoms, which in a way they were. If it was the thing to admire early printed books, maps, portrait miniatures, watches, clocks, and the like, as seen in the royal collection in Windsor, Morgan would study that collection. He also noted with care which painters were admired by Sir Richard Wallace, a renowned British collector, which furniture, which tapestries, which porcelains and bronzes. He, too, would acquire them—it was the thing to do.

His biographer Jean Strouse noted that Morgan bought with almost compulsive fervor, rather like William Randolph Hearst in later years, who stored up stockroom after stockroom of unopened crates. Coming upon a bill for a bust of the infant Hercules, attributed to Michelangelo, Morgan drew a blank. Where was it now? he asked his librarian, Belle da Costa Greene. It was in his library, she replied, "and faces you when sitting in your chair. It has been there about a year." When his collection eventually went on view at the Metropolitan, it totaled 4,100 works of art that included 550 enamels, 260 Renaissance bronzes, nearly 700 pieces of porcelain from the eighteenth century, 39 tapestries, 900 miniatures, and over 50 European paintings.

That exhibition was delayed until after Morgan's death partly because of a set of circumstances that pertained during his collecting period. In 1897 the new Revenue Act had imposed a 20 percent tariff on imported works of art. (Books and manuscripts were exempt.) A year later the Trea-

An undated portrait of Uncle Henry, the devious,
clever brains of the New York branch in the
years before World War I

sury charged Mrs. Gardner with a bill for $200,000 duty on $1 million worth of objects she had imported that year. It brought to an instant halt her fervor for collecting and acted as a horrid example to those other collectors who thought they too would like to import beautiful European objects to America. For his part, Morgan kept his harem in London, partly at his home in Princes Gate or on loan to museums, sensibly refusing to add to his nation's coffers in this ruinous fashion.

Uncle Henry had long ago worked out a different solution, which he put into action the first time Joel went to America and was threatened with duties on the four large Gobelin panels with Boucher designs that he was bringing with him. That danger was averted because Henry "knew how to get over troubles with the officials there," Joel said then. Whether it meant bribes passing hands or imaginative smuggling, one senses Henry was up to anything. As Mary Berenson wrote of him, "He is a wonderful genial old rogue—the best salesman in the world." Despite everything Uncle Henry could do, however, there would be periodic attempts to reform on the part of customs officials and someone would start asking pointed questions. The questions became so awkward at one period that Joel decided he had better go to New York himself and clear matters up. He sailed there in 1887 with Rosetta and sixteen-year-old Esther. On arrival the three of them were subjected to an embarrassing personal search and even more search-

A cartoon from *Puck* magazine depicting J. Pierpont Morgan, whose unlimited budget has a magnetic attraction for all the treasures of Europe

ing questions. Still, for the most part Uncle Henry managed to keep the wheels turning smoothly, and by 1909 he had wangled the ultimate insider's job: as appraiser to U.S. Customs on imported works of art. As such, Uncle Henry naturally tended to think that works imported by other dealers were superior to his own humble offerings, and priced them accordingly.

This patient maneuvering on Uncle Henry's part, so characteristic of his habitual modus operandi, put the firm of Duveen Brothers in as advantageous a position as it was ever likely to have so long as the U.S. government pursued its wrong-headed course of taxing European antiques. But pressure was building for a repeal. J. P. Morgan, who kept on buying, was running out of places to put his treasures and had dropped the rather large hint that they might end up in the Metropolitan. Or they might not, but in the meantime the Revenue Act was very seriously displeasing Mr. Morgan. So in 1909 Congress amended the act to provide a duty-free exemption for works of art more than one hundred years old. That was more like it. Mr. Morgan was happy again, and so were European dealers like Duveen who had been obliged to take self-protective measures in the cause of Art. Now they could be perfectly aboveboard about them.

Such was the sanguine atmosphere in 1910, or so it seemed to Uncle Henry in New York, capably assisted by Joe's brother Benjamin, and to Joseph in London, helped by the resourceful Louis. But then disaster struck. It seemed that for years there were two sets of sales books for New York, ones prepared for the prying eyes of customs officials, and the real sales books, kept for safety in London. Now that the laws had been changed, Joseph Duveen, making one of his few miscalculations, thought the coast was clear and the time had come to have the actual sales books sent to New York. He took the necessary precaution of having them placed in a strong room, of course, but it seems that was not enough. The story is that one of the employees at Duveen Brothers in New York had tangled with either brother Benjamin or Joe Duveen himself—the accounts conflict—and decided to take his revenge. The U.S. government was on the prowl for cases of smuggling that predated 1909 and offering a reward of 10 percent of the moneys recovered for information leading to an arrest. The employee just happened to know a barber who knew the ropes. Between them they worked out the way they would blow the whistle on Duveen Brothers. The employee "worked diligently during evenings and weekends on the books"—presumably the real ones that Duveen had imprudently allowed to enter New York—"and sent the results to the United States Customs Bureau."

On October 18, 1910, the U.S. government made a raid on the Duveen Galleries at Fifth Avenue and Thirty-first Street and seized $1 million worth of imported antiques and paintings, claiming unpaid customs duties variously described as from $2 million to $10 million. Benjamin Duveen went to jail and was released only after he posted a $50,000 bond. As for poor Uncle Henry, helplessly sailing toward New York on the SS *Lusitania,* he was arrested before he could set foot on U.S. soil. The government subsequently claimed that he was traveling along with a valuable carpet, taken from a fourteenth-century sultan's tomb, that was worth at least $15,000, according to an independent appraiser. Uncle Henry had papers valuing it at a mere $1,500. He, too, was released on bail ($75,000).

Ten percent of $2 million is $200,000, so the anonymous employee and his accomplice stood to make a fortune from the result of their enterprise. But for Duveen Brothers the arrests were humiliating. Work had already begun on construction of a new gallery at Fifth Avenue and Fifty-sixth Street. (Duveen Brothers had a forty-year lease on the lot.) That had to be postponed, and no other business could be conducted during the fourteen months that the case was being fought out in court. Uncle Henry felt the shame of the suit particularly. Fowles wrote that he felt "he would never again be able to show his face in the United States."

Joe, who was made of sterner stuff, was all for going into battle and made his first connection with Louis Levy, of the firm Stanchfield and Levy (later Chadbourne, Stanchfield and Levy), who with his partner would represent Duveen Brothers in all of its American litigations to come. What made the arrests even more annoying was that "everyone knew," as was claimed in the lawsuits, that customs officials had been perfectly willing to turn blind eyes to smuggling with only token efforts to intervene. It was a kind of sport that was played everywhere. P. A. B. Widener and his son Joseph were supposed to have smuggled two famous Van Dyck portraits out of Italy in a false exhaust pipe. Elia Volpi, a well-known Italian dealer, offered Fowles two handsome Titian portraits of the Spilimberg sisters that are now at the National Gallery in Washington. From the cracks that had developed Fowles concluded the paintings must have been rolled up and smuggled in, and that someone spent quite a bit of time attempting to paint out the cracks. Then there was the day when the Wideners shipped a huge crate, something like ten feet by six, to the Petit Trianon gallery in the Place Vendôme, where it was waiting in the courtyard when Joseph Widener arrived. Once opened, it revealed an enormous bust of the senior Widener. The son impatiently demanded that the bust be destroyed at once. A small packing case was retrieved from the ruins. This turned out to contain a terra-cotta figure which Joseph Widener proudly announced was a Michelangelo. Uncle Henry looked it over carefully. Then he remarked, to Widener's instant chagrin, that he hoped Widener had not paid too much for it. That was another problem. Italian dealers were just as delighted to smuggle a fake work out of the country as a real one, all in the cause of adding further uncertainty to the proceedings.

The U.S. government was very interested in what might have been hidden inside various pieces of furniture that had made their way to the galleries at Fifth Avenue and Thirty-first Street over the years. U.S. District Attorney Wise worked himself into a fine fury of indignation as he described in court the ways in which Duveen Brothers had defrauded the U.S. government out of its rightful customs duties. He said, "When a cabinet, Louis XVI, or Louis XV, came into this port, what happened? Entered as a manufacture of wood or some such classification as that. In the drawer of that cabinet, articles of immense value were sealed up, not declared on the invoice, not covered by the entry." There would be separate instructions in the mail telling the New York office what to look for and also containing an alibi letter. That letter would state that something, a tapestry or an objet, had been included by mistake and requesting its return. Of course, Wise said, no returns were ever made, and in the meantime valuable imports, such as tapestries worth hundreds of thousands of dollars, entered the country duty-free.

Joe and Louis Duveen, who were named in the civil suit but not actually required to appear, handsomely volunteered to stand trial and were each fined $10,000. The *New York Times* reported that they paid with four new $5,000 bills. The civil suit was settled when Stanchfield and Levy managed to whittle down the government's claim for $10 million, or even $2 million, to $1.2 million—a huge sum nevertheless.

There remained the problem of Uncle Henry, who, District Attorney Wise said, should serve a prison term. The argument was that he had committed a criminal act; and it was true that the government was getting prison terms for other men who had committed the crimes of smuggling in things like sugar, figs, cheese, laces, harps, cigars, and even women's dresses. One sentence was for five years. Why should Uncle Henry be exempt, just because he was now sixty, and his firm had already paid a huge fine? As the government hesitated, Uncle Henry, who had escaped to London, pleaded ill health, and in fact he *was* ill. He had "hardening of the arteries" and had contracted Bright's disease, the ailment that had felled his brother and that would kill him, too. What was to be done about Uncle Henry?

Chapter Six

LIVING WITH CACHET

T HE IDEA THAT SOMETHING HAD TO BE DONE about Uncle
Henry had reached the highest levels. The First National Bank, one
of three financial institutions in New York considered so powerful that
they were called "the Trio," had loaned the money to pay the $1.2 million
fine, against bills outstanding to Duveen Brothers, notably paintings sold
to Benjamin Altman that had not been paid for. The other two banks considered part of the Trio were the National City Bank and J. P. Morgan &
Co. That Morgan might have put in a friendly word for Uncle Henry at
First National Bank was beyond doubt. After hearing that poor Uncle
Henry had been arrested on board the *Lusitania* and had spent the night in
jail, Morgan and Altman immediately advanced the $75,000 bail required
to get him out.

The backdoor manipulations of J. P. Morgan & Co. could be discerned
dispensing checks and moving funds around for the greater good of Uncle
Henry. So when Judge Martin, in May 1911, let Uncle Henry off with cautionary words and a fine of $15,000, it is not hard to suspect that some-
where in the dim recesses of New York politics lurked a connection
between Martin and the great financier. District Attorney Wise was so
exasperated that he quit the case. The *New York Times* pointedly wondered
why a Syrian who smuggled in a harp got seven months while Uncle
Henry, who smuggled in millions of dollars' worth of merchandise, was
tenderly released. The judge attempted to defend himself. Uncle Henry's
physical condition had reached such a state in the judge's eyes that he was
practically dying (he lived for another eight years), and how could you lock
up a man like that? Besides, the judge said, when good men find out they

can cheat the government, and everyone else is doing it, can it really be their fault? Morgan could not have made the point better himself.

Uncle Henry could hold his head up again and his impetuous nephew Joseph could start building his New York gallery at Fifth Avenue and Fifty-sixth Street, liberally dispensing another $1 million of other people's money. At the end of his life Frank Lloyd Wright, knowing that he only had this one chance at scandalizing New York, built a round building (the Guggenheim Museum) on flat-fronted Fifth Avenue. In the same way, Duveen knew he had only this one opportunity to make an impression and intended to make the most of it. He hired René Sargent, the architect who had designed his Petit Trianon in the Place Vendôme, to create another counterfeit. This one was modeled after the Ministry of Marine Building in the Place de la Concorde, designed by Louis XV's architect, Jacques-Ange Gabriel. Duveen could not have known how many Mies van der Rohe modernist, and even brutalist, skyscrapers would come to inhabit that handsome avenue. He was working against brownstone modestly han-

720 Fifth Avenue at Fifty-sixth Street in 1912, when the imposing New York branch of Duveen Brothers was built. The modest windows fronting on the avenue are displaying some Chinese porcelain, and the firm's name is engraved in very small letters on either side of the main door.

dled; and his importation of eighteenth-century notions of grandeur and elegance, carried out in a creamy white stone, was startling enough.

One entered the building on the Fifth Avenue side, through a door discreetly set back inside an arched frame, and beneath a second-storey colonnade of pillars handsomely garlanded and crowned with a pediment. Directly below this was a bas relief of what might have been Neptune's wife holding a shield, but was more likely to be some kind of suitably arcane reference to the goddess of art. The *New York Times* reported that there were no display windows, but a contemporary photograph attests that there was one on either side of the front door, although each was so discreet one could be forgiven for having missed it. On the stones flanking each side of the door were the small carved words DUVEEN BROTHERS. Shilling cups and saucers had, by an astonishing leap of pure salesmanship, led to this. One forgets, said John Partridge, chairman of the Bond Street firm that had many amicable dealings with Duveen in the past, that great establishments were once run quite differently. There was none of this nonsense about big picture windows revealing their treasures to unworthy eyes. "There would be a butler in front who greeted people and directed the

Interior decor at 720 Fifth Avenue; Duveen's tastes have gravitated to all things eighteenth-century and French.

client to whomever he wanted to see and it was all a very graceful way of doing things," he said. "It was all stage-managed for the very rich."

As for the interiors, with their pedestals of rare woods supporting exquisite oriental porcelains, their bombé cabinets, gilt and satin Louis XV armchairs, and Savonnerie carpets, their tapestries and carved wooden panels, these were all any wealthy man could aspire to emulate in a lifetime of learning how to live with cachet. No contemporary descriptions have come down to us, but 720 Fifth Avenue must have caused a stir when it opened in 1912; and perhaps its splendid atmosphere, in a lifetime of living in splendid quarters, was the deciding factor for Joseph Duveen. After all, Uncle Henry was not the man he had been even though, his confidence restored, he had taken to patrolling the outer perimeter of the building with cane at the ready, practically daring anyone to strike a match on those immaculate walls. Shortly after the building opened, Joseph Duveen changed course. Instead of frequent forays to New York from London and Paris, he would go into reverse and make frequent trips to London and Paris from New York. It made eminent sense for the firm's topnotch salesman.

If Kenneth Clark is to be believed, Joe Duveen also began to turn his highly developed marketing skills into something approaching a magic trick. According to Clark, who visited the New York gallery in the 1920s, there were only six small showrooms. (The stately size of the four-storey building argues against this.) Whatever the actual number one entered, according to Clark, a series of rooms, each covered in a different color velvet, with velvet-lined cupboards and velvet-covered easels. The visitor proceeded from one room to the next by a circuitous route, "and when one returned to the first room the position of the easel had been changed, so that one didn't know that one was back at square one till one had done the circuit several times." Each time there was a different painting on display, calling forth fulminations of ecstasy from the great Duveen himself, who would occasionally be overcome with emotion and have to sit down. Clark had noticed upon entering the hall that it contained a baroque figure of the Virgin and Child. Duveen said it was rubbish, but Clark rather admired it. Duveen added he would sell it for practically nothing, leading the art historian to conclude that it had probably been bought as a Bernini and discovered not as billed. "Although I recognised that this was a sort of bribe, I accepted, because he could never have sold it without a name."

Duveen always had generous instincts, especially if he thought someone deserved to be helped. Paul Sachs, a young banker who became a Harvard art historian, recalled that at the height of the 1907 Wall Street panic—one of the preludes to the great stock market crash of 1929—a print dealer had offered him a group of Rembrandt drawings from a collection he knew well, that of Marsden J. Perry. The price was an irresistible $10,000. Sachs was working all day and could not get to see the prints until the evening, at which point someone else had snapped them up; that someone was, of course, Duveen. Duveen kept the prints for twenty years, finally selling them for a profit of $50,000. Being Duveen, he had it in the back of his mind that Sachs had narrowly missed the prize, and kept a few prints aside for him. Sachs bought them gratefully and gave them to the Fogg Museum at Harvard.

THE MAGNANIMOUS REPEAL OF CUSTOMS duty on works of art had led to the predictable consequences. International art firms like Gimpel & Wildenstein, Knoedler, Seligmann, Glaenzer, and Kleinberger had converged on this irresistible market full of new millionaires bent on acquiring instant culture. And certain fin-de-siècle artists whose works had been in high demand were losing favor. Such a shift in emphasis was clear at the New York auction in 1910 of the collection of the late C. T. Yerkes, a streetcar magnate whose Fifth Avenue mansion had been adorned with rugs, tapestries, and sculptures as well as a desirable collection of Old Masters along with the usual assortment of fluff. The collection was good enough that when the American Art Association announced the auction, Duveen Brothers jumped in and offered a nice round sum—$1.25 million—for the whole thing. The AAA declined.

Wesley Towner, in *The Elegant Auctioneers,* has left a vivid picture of that unseasonably warm evening in April of 1910 when the first group of paintings came up for auction in Mendelssohn Hall. There were "Olympian gentlemen with side whiskers and big financial voices" and "ladies in hobble skirts restricting their steps to a snail's pace, long-waisted ladies with boas made of song birds' feathers, heavy ladies drooping with chenille tassels, their feet pinched into long, slender shoes with Louis XV wooden heels." But the essence of the crowd, its backbone, as it were, were the dealers from New York, London, and Paris, wearing dark, wrinkled suits and inscrutable expressions, who could make or break the sale. While some wretchedly insignificant pictures took high prices, there were artists like Meissonier whose star was on the decline: Yerkes had paid $13,500 for his *Reconnaissance,* which only brought $5,300. Edward Burne-Jones, high priest of the Pre-Raphaelites, whose painting *The Princess Led to the Dragon,* Yerkes had bought for $12,500 a decade before, fetched a mere $2,050.

On the other hand, buyers were fighting for newly chic Corots. *Morning* went to Howard McCormick for $52,100; and Uncle Henry, representing Duveen Brothers, paid $80,500 for *The Fisherman,* as well as a further $60,500 for Troyon's *Going to Market.*

All this was but a prelude to the real fight of the evening, over Turner's *Rockets and Blue Lights.* It was known that Yerkes had perversely paid about $78,000 for this masterpiece, which was quite out of step with American tastes. This was before Joseph Duveen, that Turner aficionado, had decided that Americans *should* like it. Bids started at $50,000 and soared upward. Towner wrote, "Not a feather stirred, not a substantial breath was drawn, until the dreamlike seascape . . . had fallen to Duveen's at $129,000, far and away the highest price—for the moment at least—a picture had ever brought at public sale in the United States." Before the Yerkes sale, rumors had been circulating that the principal dealers were conspiring to run a knockout, which would have had the predictably disastrous effect on prices. If this was true, Uncle Henry broke from the pack almost at once, nobly handing out tens of thousands which had to be topped. He was in high spirits that spring of 1910, six months before the customs duties scandals. When he noticed that Harry Payne Whitney and his wife, Gertrude, née Vanderbilt, were bidding in twenty-five-dollar increments for two Guardi panels they fancied, Uncle Henry decided the spectacle of two millionaires doling out pocket money was too shameful to be borne, besides being bad for business. So when another, larger Guardi, which the Whitneys also wanted, came up for sale, he decided to teach them a lesson. For every ten-dollar bill the Whitneys were willing to gamble, he slapped down five hundred. Pretty soon the Guardi panel, which they had no doubt hoped to pick up for a trifling sum, was up to $17,000. At this point Harry Payne Whitney, unable to bear the suspense any longer, bid $20,000. "Duveen, simulating despair at such incontestable munificence, shook his head," and the hammer fell. "Whitney stood up in his place. 'You made me pay for that,' he said, wagging his finger roguishly at Duveen as the audience burst into laughter."

Uncle Henry had mastered all the tricks and could do it with such impishness that losers did not mind, even when a piece of goods had been "dropped on their toes," as the saying went. But occasionally even he was bested in what looked like the deal of a lifetime. This one began promisingly in Paris in September 1913. Louis Benois of St. Petersburg, imperial architect to the Russian court, arrived at the Petit Trianon, Place Vendôme, accompanied by his wife and carrying a small parcel. In it was a Madonna and Child which the Benois couple claimed was an unknown Leonardo. If true, this would be one of the most valuable paintings, if not the most valuable, that Duveen Brothers had ever acquired. Berenson, who had only seen photographs of the work, happened to be visiting Paris and was summoned. He examined the Benois Madonna and was convinced, which is not to say that he liked what he saw. He wrote later, "I found myself confronted by a young woman with a bald forehead and puffed cheek, a toothless smile, blear eyes, and furrowed throat. The uncanny anile apparition plays with a child who looks like a hollow mask fixed on inflated body and limbs."

This jaundiced description could be attributed to Berenson's general dislike of Leonardo's work, but whether he liked it or not was superfluous as far as Joe was concerned. Duveen Brothers immediately offered a down payment and signed a contract to buy the painting for $1 million. There was a slight catch. Tsar Nicholas II, who knew about the painting, wanted an option to buy by a certain date. Duveen Brothers, confident that royalty would not exert such a clause (royals almost never did), courteously agreed. Time ticked away and the Leonardo seemed practically theirs when, at the eleventh hour, the tsar played his card. The Benois Madonna went to the Hermitage and Duveen Brothers lost their great coup. The newspaper coverage was pretty good, all the same. The sales price, at $1.5 million, set new records.

That Duveen Brothers was beginning to think in terms of a million dollars showed not only the extent of their financial backing but the huge prices collectors were starting to pay. In *The Economics of Taste,* Gerald Reitlinger called 1913 "the most lavish in all the recorded annals of art history," with the great Italian paintings, in particular, making a spectacular showing. Mary Emery of Cincinnati paid £60,000 for the Augsburg *Portrait of Philip II* by Titian. Hugh Lane, the owner of that painting, also sold Titian's *Man in a Red Cap* to Henry Clay Frick for £50,000. (The painting was on its way to Frick in 1915 when Lane went down with the *Lusitania*.) Sir Herbert Cook had also paid serious money in 1913 for Titian's portrait of Caterina Cornaro, although he bought it as a Giorgione—the more valuable name. Some Italian Renaissance masters were even more of a draw in those halcyon years; Benjamin Altman was about to give Duveen £103,300 for *The Holy Family* by Mantegna, a painting Duveen had bought at auction in Berlin for a mere £29,500, when his death in October 1913 negated the sale. Those immediate prewar years were, not surprisingly, thrilling ones for Duveen. Frick, who was not exactly the all-around exclusive property of Duveen Brothers that Joe would have preferred, had consented to buy from them a handsome Gainsborough portrait of the Honorable Frances Duncombe, for $400,000.

The portrait shows this daughter of a West Country aristocrat in a powdered wig and the tight bodice and hooped skirt of the Van Dyck period. Her blue satin sleeves are slashed to reveal lace like thistledown concealed beneath. Her wide blue skirt has been looped back in artistic folds to reveal a delicate underskirt of exquisite ivory satin decorated, like the overskirt, with rows of pearls, and her hat, of the same soft blue, has a rakish feather. She is looking to her right with a pretty little tilt of the chin, as if she has just heard the rustle of a bird in the enchanted landscape in which she finds herself. The whole portrait speaks of the dash and brio, not to mention mesmerizing artistry of costume, deportment, perfectly arranged porcelain hands and delicately pointed foot, that made Gainsborough so rightly fashionable as a portrait painter. The Honorable Frances Duncombe was housed for a while at J. P. Morgan's home in Princes Gate, but for some curious reason he never got to like her, and in 1911 Frick gratefully took her in.

Gainsboroughs of any period were in high demand, and so were paintings by Frans Hals, always a reliable crowd pleaser. Duveen bought that artist's portrait of himself, his wife, and their children for $400,000, and it eventually went to the Thyssen collection.

Then there was the portrait *The Count-Duke of Olivares* by Diego Velázquez, also one of the first "big" pictures Duveen bought (in August 1909). As Edward Fowles recalled, Arabella Huntington wanted to please her son, Archer, who was a patron of the Hispanic Society of America. True to form, Duveen, who now had a buyer, went straight to the owner, Colonel Holford, who owned Dorchester House in London, on the site of what is now the Dorchester Hotel. Holford took half a million dollars and Arabella Huntington, who gave the painting straightaway to the Hispanic Society in her son's name, paid $600,000. That should have made for a handsome profit, but Edward Fowles explained that this was not necessarily the case.

He recalled that Max Bruhl, a noted financier, once went to Duveen to point out the error of his ways. Bruhl said, "Look here, Mr. Duveen, this is what you sold to Mr. Frick. You had to pay cash and borrow money at six percent to pay for it," but Frick could take his time about paying and sometimes gave Duveen shares in lieu of cash. Bruhl argued, "You're not making any money out of it at all." Fowles added, "But you know, the strange thing was Duveen didn't mind that. He loved the bigness of it all." It must have been acutely mortifying for Duveen in those years that one of the biggest sales of all, Rembrandt's *The Mill*, did not go through his hands. Duveen had sold Altman three Rembrandt portraits from the Rodolphe Kann Collection for £50,000 each (the actual total in 1909 was

£155,000), but this single Rembrandt brought £103,300, just two years later. It went from Lord Lansdowne via the dealer Arthur J. Sulley to P. A. B. Widener and is now at the National Gallery of Art in Washington.

There is no doubt, however, that Duveen had a large role to play in these escalating prices. Not only was he making adroit use of the competitive spirit between Frick, Altman, and Huntington to lift the prices of Velázquez, Rembrandt, and Gainsborough into the realms of fantasy, but he was also creating brand-new markets for such (formerly) modestly priced eighteenth-century portraitists as Lawrence, Raeburn, Romney, and Hoppner. As the money began to pour in—$13 million in sales in Paris in 1909 alone—Duveen's ambitions lurched ever further upward. The Petit

The great collector Otto H. Kahn on a Palm Beach, Florida, golf course in 1934. Like many wealthy bankers and collectors of art, he was surprisingly short.

Trianon, though perfect in its way, had upper-floor glass-roofed picture galleries that looked better on paper than they proved to be in practice, since adjacent buildings spoiled the light, and was already too small. Duveen commandeered a building behind it that fronted on the rue St.-Honoré, to give them more space for offices, and a second adjoining building to contain new, more spacious exhibition rooms. (He took the precaution of negotiating for this particular building under an assumed name, to keep the price down.) Pretty soon there was ample exhibition space, a new strong room, an elevator, a library, and all manner of storage space. For the moment even Duveen was satisfied.

Millionaires and their wives were appearing from all directions, with overwhelming urges to buy paintings by fifteenth-century Italians whose names they had barely been able to pronounce a week before. It was perfectly amazing how many of them turned out to be bankers. Otto Kahn, for instance, was a leading partner in the investment banking firm of Kuhn, Loeb and Company, a railroad financier and chief benefactor of the Metropolitan Opera for years, earning him the sobriquet of "the Great Ottokahn." A photograph of Kahn and his diminutive wife, Adelaide, in the library of their palatial Fifth Avenue mansion shows her gazing at a distant painting on an easel by the Flemish master Joachim Patinir. Her husband, comfortably seated beside the marble fireplace, contemplates a portrait by Rembrandt hanging over the mantel, sumptuously framed. Being innocents abroad in the great game, Otto and Addie, as she liked to be called, knew less than nothing about the Italians, which did not stop them from finding the subject alluring, particularly when B.B. was whispering sweet nothings into their ears. In the late spring of 1913 B.B. thought he had discovered a new *Madonna and Child with Saints* by Benedetto Bonfigli. The intermediary was "Baron" Michele Lazzaroni, an Italian with whom Berenson often dealt. What Berenson must have known, and the diminutive Addie quite certainly did not, was that Lazzaroni was a particularly unscrupulous customer in that quintessentially unscrupulous world. The faces of the Virgin, the Child, and two fetching angels had been repainted in what became known as "the Lazzaroni manner." No hint of this is suggested in Berenson's letter of recommendation to Louis Duveen, which calls the picture "a perfect fairy-tale of sentiment and colour." Mrs. Kahn paid $25,000 for it, and Duveen made his usual handsome profit—the price had been 40,000 francs, or $8,000. But the Bonfigli was a bad bargain; years later, when Mrs. Kahn decided to sell it, Duveens would only offer her $15,000, and everyone agreed the Lazzaroni repaint had to come off.

The "Small Cowper Madonna" by Raphael

A pretty little painting by a minor fifteenth-century Perugian artist of a Virgin offering a peach to a Child paled in comparison with the great name of the sixteenth-century painter from Urbino Raffaello Sanzio, or Raphael. One of the glories of Panshanger, the Cowper family seat in Hertfordshire, was a Raphael Madonna and Child known as the Panshanger Raphael or the Small Cowper Madonna, to distinguish it from a larger Raphael in the same collection. In 1913 the Small Cowper Madonna was for sale, and it was entrancing. The mother, her wide eyes and delicately modeled nose and chin framed by a simple braid of blond hair, sits in a classical landscape, holding her naked baby, a blond of perhaps six or seven months old, on one arm. The baby cradles his mother's neck and is looking serenely toward some distant prospect. The modeling, contours, and subtle composition, with its lovely floating line and subdued color, repeat the feeling of tranquil enclosure, the perfect and beautiful union of Mother and Child that is characteristic of Raphael's work. It is, despite its hackneyed subject, a portrait of great distinctiveness; one feels these are real people, not just abstractions. The Madonna and Child was one of Raphael's favorite subjects, and he painted it over and over again, with great sensitivity and originality, but none has ever surpassed the Small Cowper Madonna in its atmosphere of almost haunting tenderness. When Raphael painted it, he was only twenty-two years old.

The painting was rightly considered one of the glories of the Cowper collection, which by 1913 had already been plundered alarmingly. So when it was learned that the Small Cowper Madonna had been sold to Duveen Brothers for considerably more than $500,000, the protests began to build. It was said that Duveen Brothers had found an American buyer, Benjamin Altman, and that devoted art lover had agreed to buy the work for $750,000. Again, Altman's death put paid to hopes for that sale. Such a price would have been spectacular, but the alternative was not bad; Duveen lined up P. A. B. Widener, who was willing to pay almost as much: $700,000. Duveen personally accompanied the prize to New York on the White Star *Olympic*. He arrived on January 21, 1914, and announced the sale three weeks later.

If there had been rumblings of alarm in London when Rembrandt's *The Mill* left British shores in 1911, this time there was open revolt. The *Times,* that forum for distinguished protest, was bombarded with letters, including one from Baron Rothschild. Lady Desborough, who had been chiefly involved in the negotiations for the sale on behalf of the heirs, was roundly criticized and, in turn, was furious with Joseph Duveen for crowing about his marvelous coup. Others wanted to know what was wrong with the National Gallery in London for letting such a masterpiece slip away. Lady Desborough had very fairly offered the Raphael to the nation first, at the reasonable asking price of £70,000, and the trustees had lamely countered that they had only £5,000 a year to spend. Besides, they had plenty of Raphaels. Sir Claude Phillips, art critic and collector, who had just retired as keeper of the Wallace Collection, was particularly indignant. "That the Desborough collection should lose," he said, "and the nation fail to secure so exquisite a thing as this Panshanger Raphael is a catastrophe that we should not cease to deplore, though it is one among the many that of late years we have been compelled to suffer. The blows of this kind follow one another with such regularity and at such short intervals that they must in the long run harden those upon whom they descend." The National Gallery owned many beautiful Raphaels, but "no Madonna of a beauty so suave or so characteristic of the Urbinate in his profoundly interesting time of transition." (The painting did go to a National Gallery eventually—the one in Washington, D.C.)

ONE OF THE MAJOR REASONS why American millionaire collectors needed personal advisors is so obvious that it has all but been forgotten: In the days of Altman, Frick, Huntington, and Morgan, there were almost no illustrations. As Francis Haskell remarks in his essay on Altman in the Metropolitan Museum *Journal,* "Well-illustrated books and sale catalogues were still comparatively rare, and crossing the Atlantic took time." Sir Jack Baer, recently retired as chairman of Hazlitt, Gooden and Fox of London, added that this was true for decades. "If you think that when I started, and my career doesn't go back all that far" (he was speaking of the 1940s) "how few illustrated books there were. For instance, there were big books about Gainsborough but the only illustrations looked like mezzotints. My firm goes back to 1880 and there is a complete set of Christies and Sothebys catalogues, as well as other catalogues from the 1920s. Very few had any illustrations and these were very poor." Art experts, even dealers, were a necessary evil, not only because they had seen the objects at first hand but because they had, to give Henry Duveen as an example, built up their expertise from decades of study. The fact that, where price was concerned, the interests of dealers obviously ran counter to those of their clients, could not be helped. Dealers naturally guarded ferociously whatever photographs they could assemble and constantly begged for more from within their own networks. The mere request for a photograph, in the world of art dealing, set off alarms, tipping off the owner (or the competition), and prices would rise accordingly. One of Duveen's skills became his devious ability to extract such information from under the noses of his adversaries, leaving them none the wiser. So the client was, in the decades before sophisticated photographic techniques and mass publication, at the mercy of his expert or dealer, even one with as educated a taste and suspicious a mind as Benjamin Altman.

This extraordinarily successful self-made man, who began with his brother as a clerk in the dry-goods business and ended up founding a large department store at Fifth Avenue and Thirty-fourth Street, was a liberal employer who was among the first to provide lunch, rest, and medical ser-

Benjamin Altman, painted by
Ellen Emmet Rand in 1914

vices for his employees. A lifelong bachelor, he was thrifty, personally modest and retiring. Attempts to determine what motivated Altman to become
a collector have largely come up with a blank. Unlike Morgan, he showed
no particular interest in visiting museums or collections, nor was he
inclined to display his wealth and position by invitations to visit his Fifth
Avenue gallery—designed as part of the house on the Rodolphe Kann
model. The quiet way in which he would slip in and out of his own department store, almost unnoticed, extended to the manner of his acquisitions.
These should take place silently, by stealth, and the tendency of Joseph
Duveen to call in the press and boast about the price he had just extracted
from some reluctant millionaire would madden and infuriate him. A couple of years after Henry Duveen's very public contretemps with U.S. Customs, which once more offended Altman's code of *omertà,* there was
another crisis.

Altman's art gallery in his Fifth Avenue apartment

The reason involved one of two paintings Altman had just bought from Duveen Brothers: a full-length portrait of Philip IV by Velázquez and a full-length portrait of that monarch's minister the Count-Duke of Olivares. Altman paid $1 million for both paintings, and all would have been well (the portrait of Philip IV, at least, had an impeccable provenance from the Villahermosa Palace in Madrid) except for one nagging detail. The fact that Duveen had earlier sold another Velázquez portrait of the Count-Duke of Olivares to Arabella Huntington somehow came to light. No doubt helpful reporters reminded their readers that the Huntington painting was supposed to have been "the only full-length portrait" that Velázquez ever executed. It sounds exactly like the kind of thing Duveen would say, painting himself into a corner as usual, and it was rather left to his diplomatic second-in-command, Edward Fowles, to find a way out. Fowles pointed out right away that the portraits were not identical because the sitter faced in different directions, but there was no getting around the fact that, after proclaiming the uniqueness of Huntington's full-length portrait, Duveen had belatedly turned up two more full-length ones. Nasty suspicions were raised that perhaps the new *Count-Duke of Olivares* was not by Velázquez after all. It is hard to know which offended Altman more: the doubts raised about his painting or that awful publicity. He wrote to Uncle Henry, "I stood by you in your hour of trouble, alone!" (which was not quite true) ". . . interviewing newspaper men and stopping certain insinuating remarks made by private parties, as well as art dealers, and emphasizing to everybody my high opinion of you and your firm . . . Do I not *desire* [sic] *some* consideration for all this?" His pleas were in vain. Duveen Brothers had to find a way out, and soon. The diplomatic solution concocted, presumably not by Fowles, was that the new discovery was a replica of the Huntington version, begun by Velázquez and finished by an assistant. There are so-called weasel clauses in real-estate contracts, and no doubt this explanation was an art-dealing equivalent, one that would satisfy the sellers if not the buyer. Altman decided to keep the splendidly authenticated Philip IV, which is now at the Metropolitan Museum of Art, and return his version of the Duke. After several years' delay, that painting went to the Museu de Arte, São Paulo, Brazil.

However cautious Altman's purchases were—and he knew that he could always send a painting back—when it came to Italian paintings, he was at a real disadvantage, along with everyone else. Since nobody knew anything about them except Bode and Berenson, collectors had to lean helplessly on one or the other; and, naturally enough, the reputation of the latter began to grow by leaps and bounds once he and Duveen joined forces. Very soon after their famous partnership began, in about 1910, Altman began buying Italian Renaissance paintings.

At first, all went well. Altman bought an exquisite small portrait of a young boy, thought to be Federigo Gonzaga, and painted for his mother, Isabella d'Este, by Francesco Francia, that is now at the Metropolitan Museum. He also bought another masterpiece, this one by Botticelli, *The Last Communion of Saint Jerome*, in tempera and gold on wood, now also at the Metropolitan. But then came less happy purchases. He bought a Filippino Lippi Madonna and Child, now at the Metropolitan, which today is tentatively ascribed to Raffaellino del Garbo, a minor artist. Altman's *Madonna and Child* by Verrocchio, at the same museum, has been similarly demoted to "workshop of." As for the *Madonna and Child* by Sebastiano Mainardi (also now at the Metropolitan), although it is still considered to be by that artist, it came from the Paris collection of the Baron Michele Lazzaroni. One cannot help wondering whether, when Altman bought the portrait *Filippo Archinto, Archbishop of Milan*, then ascribed to Titian, in 1913, he had been told about a nearly identical portrait by Titian which had been bought by the Philadelphia collector John G. Johnson four years earlier. (It is now at the Philadelphia Museum of Art.) In that version, the sitter is shown seated behind a transparent curtain, which besides being a technical tour de force, is thought to represent the fact that the archbishop was repeatedly prevented from actually taking up his position. It may be that the Metropolitan Museum version, the one Altman bought, came first, or vice versa; no one really knows. But when the two are compared, there is no doubt that Philadelphia's is the more masterful work. The one Altman was persuaded to buy is now thought to be either "workshop of" Titian or by Leandro Bassano, definitely a lesser light in a famous family of peasant painters living in a mountain village some thirty miles outside Venice.

Then there was a famous wreck of a picture, *Portrait of a Man,* sometimes called *Ariosto,* which Altman bought in 1913, at the end of his life.

Portrait of a Man (Ariosto) by Titian, which Altman
bought as a Giorgione on Berenson's advice

Since paintings by Giorgione are few and far between, and since an early Giorgione is almost impossible to tell from an early Titian, opinions are always ricocheting between the two painters, opinions of art historians, that is. When it comes to dealers, the rarer the better, so Giorgione is always the label that gets slapped on, as it did in this case. Berenson wrote helpfully that he was ready to stake his reputation on the painting's being a Giorgione. This was curious, because when he saw the painting in 1895 at the famous loan exhibition of Venetian art at the New Gallery in London (before he was working for anybody), he thought it was "a work by the young Titian, or else only a copy of such a work, the copy by Polidoro Lanzani." Berenson's youthful doubt may have been colored by his awareness that another male portrait sometimes called *Ariosto,* this one actually signed by Titian, was at the National Gallery of Art in London. The poses are identical, but the London portrait, Kenneth Clark wrote, is "one of the most perfect early solutions of life-size portraiture." It shows the vigor and sureness of touch that the Altman version conspicuously lacks; the latter looks positively anemic by comparison. As well it should, since the Altman painting has been cut down and so mistreated, its surface thin and abraded, that, as one expert wrote, "an attribution to either Giorgione or Titian is altogether hypothetical."

Berenson had the right to change his mind, but he never explained why a painting he said was in a state of "deplorably bad preservation" in 1895 became, seventeen or eighteen years later, in a "miraculously fine state." Francis Haskell wrote, "Visitors to the Metropolitan who ponder over this problem as they gaze at this sad, but still moving, ghost of a picture may be interested to know that Altman himself was not too happy about it." A year before he died, Altman told Henry Duveen that he had hung the Giorgione in his gallery and was studying it earnestly. He sincerely hoped he would get to like it. (The painting is now labeled as by "a Giorgionesque painter.")

Altman died on October 7, 1913, his death a great blow to the House of Duveen. Thanks to Uncle Henry, Altman had refined his passion for oriental porcelain and studied catalogues with as much close attention to detail as did his mentor, that lover of recondite information. Before definitely buying a piece, Altman would immerse it in water for days so that any flaws or breakages, however cleverly disguised, would slowly reveal themselves. Once having made a purchase, he and Uncle Henry would sit down together and experience something close to a joint intoxication as they gloated over and stroked their latest treasure. If he had never bought anything else, Altman's collection of porcelains would have ensured him a kind of immortality, thanks to Uncle Henry.

But the old campaigners in so many art-dealing wars had become much more to each other. They consulted, argued, commiserated, and celebrated each other's achievements. As Uncle Henry was helping to oversee the building of the Duveen Brothers establishment on Fifth Avenue in 1912, Altman was engaged in enlarging his own premises. He took such an interest in the progress of Duveen Brothers' new structure that in one of his letters to Uncle Henry he called it "our" building. He was a dear friend, and what could not have made his death any easier was the avidity with which he was buying that year of 1913. Just four months before he died, in June of 1913, Altman launched himself on one of his greatest purchases. This was another enchanting Rembrandt, *The Toilet of Bathsheba,* a painting Jack Duveen had seen years earlier, in 1888. It was then owned by Baron Steengracht, who, like Rodolphe Kann in Paris, had allowed so many visitors to see his collection that it was one of the chief tourist spots in The Hague.

The baron died in 1912 and the collection came up for auction in Paris the following summer. *Bathsheba,* signed and dated 1643 by Rembrandt, was painted a few months after he had lost Saskia, the wife he idolized. She died after giving birth to their fourth child and the painting was thought to have been executed in her memory. Like Rembrandt's better-known *Bathsheba* at the Louvre, the Steengracht nude has that quality of tender, almost aching intimacy which characterizes Rembrandt's paintings of fallible and vulnerable womankind. Altman was predictably smitten, and Uncle Henry was dispatched to the Salle Georges Petit to make the winning bid. Altman had been warned that the painting would fetch at least £30,000 and probably more. Henry Duveen bought it for £44,000, and when the gavel fell, he whispered to Jack Duveen, "I don't think I could have stopped bidding." They were all ecstatic, and Altman must have felt the same way, but his cable was, like the man himself, understated to the last. He wrote: MANY THANKS VERY HAPPY KINDEST REGARDS TO ALL ALTMAN.

Altman died of kidney disease at the age of seventy-three, but not before ensuring that his collection, then worth a spectacular $20 million, would go to the Metropolitan Museum of Art. Although it was never to include the Small Cowper Madonna, in addition to the priceless collection of porcelains, the Rembrandts, Vermeers, de Hooches, Hobbemas, Cuyps, and the like, there were also a portrait of Lucas van Uffel by Anthony Van Dyck; *Wheatfields* by Jacob Van Ruisdael; *Christ and the Pilgrims of*

Emmaus by Velázquez; the sixteenth-century Florentine "Rospigliosi Cup" in gold, enamel, and pearls; Luca della Robbia's *Madonna and Child with Scroll;* Clodion's sculpture *Bacchus and a Nymph;* and endless other treasures. Galleries at the Metropolitan are named for its great benefactor, but the department store that also bore his name has closed its doors forever.

THE NOTION THAT COLLECTING PORTRAITS from the British Golden Age was already the thing to do had been set in motion, not by the landed aristocrats, but by the newly rich: industrialists and manufacturers intent on improving their social status with beautiful houses and a discreetly bought title thrown into the bargain. There was, for instance, Edward Cecil Guinness, who became Earl of Iveagh. His brewing company profits were put to good use in assembling a spectacular collection of British portraiture during the 1880s and 1890s. According to a history of Agnew's, the young Joseph Duveen found out that his father was selling Spanish leather screens to Guinness at a moment when Agnew's was selling him paintings worth thousands of pounds, and this was what made him determined to go into paintings. It may be true, but one guesses that Joe Duveen would hardly have needed the point underlined at a moment when the market for Old Masters was exploding. Guinness bought Kenwood, an exquisite eighteenth-century house standing in its own grounds in Hampstead, near London, the better to house his treasures. The collector Baron Ferdinand de Rothschild built Waddesdon Manor in Buckinghamshire and, with his penchant for amazingly florid interiors, proceeded to gild his own lily with all that taste and money could devise. A vogue for the eighteenth century: its architecture, design, and costume, if not its manners and ideals, was the latest fashion. Malcolm Warner wrote, "Contemporary British artists found a ready market for paintings that looked back romantically to eighteenth-century life—scenes featuring young women in mob-caps, 'souvenirs' of Reynolds and Gainsborough, illustrations to Oliver Goldsmith's *The Vicar of Wakefield.*"

The portraits and scenes they coveted seemed to breathe a different air. These were human beings in an Arcadian world in which, at last, people were at liberty to follow their cherished pursuits, surrounded by idyllic landscapes, dressed in silks and satins, and accompanied by elegant companions thinking beautiful thoughts. In such an atmosphere of wish fulfillment there is no past or future. There are no profit-and-loss statements; money itself has ceased to be important, because it has bought everything that matters. So many feelings were bound up in what might seem simply a coarse and gluttonous need to acquire. There was the kind of warm glow that follows any purchase—one thinks of Henry Duveen seated with Altman, both of them drinking in the sight of the newest acquisition—along with so much nostalgia for a life the new collectors never knew existed; and a need, hardly buried, to disassociate themselves from the brutal struggle that had made it all possible.

So beautiful paintings went to very grand houses like Kenwood, with its Robert Adam double-cube-shaped library, its neo-Palladian gilded columns, and its exquisite mirrored recesses; and Waddesdon Manor, modeled after the Château de Chambord. The Old Masters left the huge London houses, which might have looked like Chesterfield House, with its extravagant first-floor ballroom in rococo gilt and marble; or 60 Knightsbridge, with its colonnaded gallery; or Ashburnham House, with its Charles II staircase; or Spencer House, with its Great Room designed by James Stuart in 1759. The paintings found new homes in Senator William Clark's Fifth Avenue mansion, perhaps; or the Du Barry Room in the Frick, with its view over Central Park; or the double-and-quadruple-hung art gallery in William B. Astor's Fifth Avenue mansion. There was very little to choose between the grandeur of the European examples and their American counterparts glistening with crystal, silver, satins, and gilt; and that was the idea.

Altman and Frick might be considered the prototypical American millionaires: rough diamonds without education and polish who slowly matured into, if not aesthetes, at least respectable members of society and distinguished philanthropists. Perhaps the quintessential example of such a transformation, however, was Henry Edwards Huntington of California. He was the nephew and business associate of an even more ruthless and unscrupulous relative, Collis P. Huntington, who had built railroads from the Atlantic to the Pacific in the 1860s. After his uncle's death in 1900, H.E.H., as he was called, not only inherited a third of his uncle's vast estate, money he used to build electric streetcars in suburban Los Angeles, but eventually his wife as well, the unlovely but highly civilized Arabella.

H.E.H. was, as Jacques Seligmann recalled, a giant of a man, well over six feet. He had a military bearing and the kind of rough-hewn looks one finds in such captains of industry, especially in the wild and woolly West. He had begun life as a log roller, had graduated to selling hardware in one of his uncle's stores, and before long was helping to run a railroad. In that regard, Seligmann recalled, H.E.H. once related how he had broken a strike. He arrived at a small station one day to find his men refusing to work and declaring that no train was going to leave the station. H.E.H., who was only twenty but wise to the ways of the world, pulled out a pair of shotguns and waved them in the air. He was going to drive the train out himself, and "the first s.o.b. who tries to stop me is a dead man." By then, H.E.H. was old and ill, but echoes of the same fiery resolve were still in evidence as his voice rose and his eyes flashed. He continued, "And I got on the engine and took that blankety-blank train out of the station!"

Much as one would like to give Duveen credit for the molding of this rough-hewn specimen, one has to concede that the largest influence on his life has to have been Arabella Huntington. When they were married in 1913—H.E.H. divorced his first wife to marry her—she was likely to have been sixty-three, although accounts differ, giving her age as sometimes fifty-seven and sometimes sixty. In any event she was almost completely blind as well as overweight. In her youth she had been elegant in a clearcut, studious kind of way; there was something romantic and passionate about her. She seems to have had little formal education but learned to speak French fluently. After the death of Collis P., which left her one of the wealthiest women in the world, she devoted herself to filling up her enormous house on Fifty-seventh Street at Fifth Avenue with treasures. (The house was on the site now occupied by Tiffany & Co.) There were also her other houses in Throgs Neck, the Adirondacks, San Francisco, and Paris to furnish and refurnish. She then devoted herself to art. Since Duveen Brothers was just down the street, it stood to reason that the fortunes of that institution and those of Arabella and her future husband, H.E.H., would become happily linked. For Duveen, it was almost like having a bottomless pit of money. The Huntingtons would buy from Duveen on terms, making yearly installments and putting up railroad stock as collateral. That kind of income source was all that Duveen needed to keep his own credit line in good repair. The Huntington checks would come in and whenever the books seemed in danger of balancing, Joseph Duveen would uncover another marvel which his favorite clients simply had to have. In the years between 1908 and 1917, H.E.H. and Arabella between them spent over $21 million. It is hard to think of a cozier business arrangement.

Arabella began by assembling a major collection of eighteenth-century French decorative art, about which Duveen, it must be said, was an acknowledged expert. Arabella had met the Duveens before their showplace on Fifth Avenue was ever built, in 1907, when she was taken to view the Rodolphe Kann Collection in Paris. In addition to the famous Rembrandt *Aristotle Contemplating the Bust of Homer,* she bought several other

Above: Mrs. Arabella
Huntington, an
unflattering portrait
by Oswald Birley

Right: Henry E.
Huntington, a
companion por-
trait by Oswald
Birley

paintings, including the *Madonna and Child* by Roger van der Weyden that now hangs in the Huntington Library and Art Collections in San Marino, California.

When Edward Fowles met her, he was startled to discover that she was suffering from an advanced stage of glaucoma, which did not prevent her from seeing fine details through a kind of mist. He wrote, "Sometimes she would remove the heavy glasses and throw her head back so that her fine complexion and beautiful teeth could be admired." She had recently bought an enormous house at 2, rue de l'Élysée, on the corner of the avenue Gabriel on the Right Bank, which had belonged to Baron Hirsch. Its main attraction was a vast second-floor room paneled in plate-glass mirrors. Mrs. Huntington naturally wanted to remove all the plate glass and replace it with huge tapestries, which, to no surprise, Duveen would be charmed to find for "Madam," as he always called her.

In the summer of 1907 he wrote to tell her that, since she left Paris, he had made three visits to the rue de l'Élysée to oversee her renovations and redecorations. Following his father's pattern, he had taken the overnight train from London, arriving in Paris at six in the morning, spent all day and all night at the house, and returned to London on Sunday by the afternoon train. He was happy to report that he had found just the right tables for the salon, "not 'genuine fakes' as you sometimes humorously say!" he wrote.

The Kann Collection was being dismantled. "The few [objects] that you left which were not quite fine enough have been dispersed amongst some celebrated people in Paris and New York, who have had to content themselves with the leavings." Such shameless flattery must have been welcome to someone who had felt the lash of social disapproval while she was married to Collis P. Huntington, a universally detested man. Whatever her social status, in the realm of the arts Arabella reigned serene. Her future husband, H.E.H., had always loved books, but his taste in art had been confined to nineteenth-century French Barbizon and Academic Salon painting, interspersed with cheap prints. But by 1911, a good two years before he and Arabella were united, he had been talked into buying three Gainsboroughs for the considerable sum of $775,000. And that was just the beginning.

By that technique of flattering attention to detail which was such a part of Duveen's ability to woo his customers the Huntingtons gradually allowed him to take command of their restorers, workmen, managers, and lawyers as well. He was so willing to take endless pains, not to mention risk and expense: he was forever "sending down" Old Masters from New York to San Marino, a journey of three thousand miles, to see if they could get to like them. It is said he even made the arrangements for their wedding in Paris. This is not to say the Huntingtons did not occasionally rebel, as may be inferred from Arabella's reference to "genuine fakes." And Edward Fowles recalled that H.E.H. came to the Place Vendôme one morning for a chat, just in time to hear Duveen working himself up into a frenzy of admiration for a new London acquisition. H.E.H. interrupted him. " 'Wait a minute . . .' H.E.H. exclaimed, rising to his feet," Fowles wrote. " 'I will give you the works.' Waving his arms, he shouted at me, 'The greatest picture I have ever owned! It's simply stupendous,' in mimicry of Joe's sales talk. He sat down again, laughing uproariously." Duveen stopped talking.

Chapter Seven

"SPY MANIA"

ONE OF THE FASCINATING CHARACTERS on the fringes of Duveen's life was Calouste Sarkis Gulbenkian, an Armenian who had made a fortune in oil. Gulbenkian was devoted to a magnificent art collection which he called his "harem" and kept sequestered in his Parisian *hôtel particulier* at 51, avenue d'Iéna. The collection should have gone to the National Gallery in London, but, according to Kenneth Clark and Edward Fowles, the government bungled it and it went instead to Portugal. One sees him as a match for Duveen in suspiciousness, a trait of character that had made him rich. His specialty of being especially wary of the fine print and his admonition to check, check, and double-check became so lodged in Clark's mind that it became a family maxim. But the fact that in business he trusted no one for long made Gulbenkian a prickly proposition for Joseph Duveen, who, as long as he was not engaging in a business duel of wits, was the soul of bonhomie. His solution was to keep a certain distance and leave the overtures up to Gulbenkian. He had good reason; if he had something to sell, Gulbenkian always knew exactly how much Duveen wanted him to buy it, and the more psychological pressure he felt, the more maddening he became. Gulby, as they called him, pulled the same trick on everyone, that is to say, seeming full of interest until the dealer closed in for the kill, at which point he would find a thousand reasons for backing away. He bargained relentlessly, giving the shameless explanation that he was just a small collector with modest funds. But even when a painting, a piece of furniture, or a gold box was bought, Gulby was ruthless about returning it at the slightest pretext. His response became so unvarying that Duveen Brothers had to retreat from their original policy of

A rare photograph of Calouste Gulbenkian, taken in the 1930s
as he waited for friends at Lisbon Airport with his secretary,
Mme. Jeanne Theys. Gulbenkian, with a fortune estimated
between £300 million and £400 million, was once
considered the world's richest man.

a money-back guarantee and write a special contract just for him to limit
his options.

Gulbenkian's purchases from Duveen were largely limited to furniture
and such esoterica as oriental manuscripts and china. Much of the time he
preferred to scout for his own paintings, using his usual subterranean
methods. He was always extremely well informed. On one occasion Gulbenkian told Arthur Ruck, a London dealer whom Duveen often used as
an intermediary, about a rumor he had heard that Sir Herbert Cook might
sell some paintings. Since the Cook collection was well known and
included one of Rembrandt's incomparable portraits of his son Titus, this
was very big news, if true. Ruck, who was on friendly terms with Cook,
might have acted in Gulbenkian's behalf but told Duveen instead. (Since

Gulbenkian's penny-pinching ways were famous, Ruck must have reasoned that Duveen's commissions would be more generous.) Duveen's response may be assumed. Ruck was given the job of "working" the pictures—a curiously interesting term, still used in espionage.

Ruck was unsuccessful, so Duveen turned to a relative of Cook's, who expressed confidence in being able to get whatever Duveen wanted. Unfortunately, said relative was penniless and needed something on account. One way or another, Duveen Brothers ended up paying him an annual stipend for several years even though no business resulted. The paintings, including the Rembrandt *Titus,* continued not to be for sale long after Duveen left this world. *Titus* was finally put up for auction at Christie's in 1965. It was bought by Norton Simon for the then record price of £798,000 and is one of the pearls of the Norton Simon Collection in Pasadena, California. It is said that the great collector was doing the bidding himself and had arranged a set of signals in advance for continuing to bid or declining, depending on whether he stood up or sat down. In the heat of the moment he stood up when he should have sat down, or vice versa, and lost the painting; that is, until the auctioneer agreed to reopen the bidding.

Duveen would never have used such clumsy methods. In the days when he personally still went to the big sales, every move was calculated to make him as inconspicuous as possible, inconspicuous, that is, to all but the auctioneer. That man was trained to know by the shake of Duveen's head or the blink of an eye by just how much Duveen was willing to raise the bidding. His satisfaction when he reached his goal was equally nuanced; he would sit back, rub his cheek, and close his eyes.

One example of the ways in which Duveen and Gulbenkian danced around each other was occasioned by the Bischoffsheim sale at Christie's in May 1926. Henry Louis Bischoffsheim, from an old French Jewish banking family, was a connoisseur of art, and when it was learned that paintings and furnishings from his London house were going on the market, Duveen's top men—his brothers Ernest and Edward in London, and Armand Lowengard and Edward Fowles in Paris—went on high alert. Among the paintings by Boucher, Gainsborough, Frans Hals, Romney, Reynolds, and Hoppner were a pair of oval portraits of a boy and a girl by François-Hubert Drouais, *Portrait of a Queen of Spain* by Antonio Mor, and a full-length portrait of a member of the French court by the eighteenth-century painter Jean-Marc Nattier.

Detailed reports from London and Paris were being relayed in April to New York almost by the hour. The Boucher was decorative, but they thought it only a larger version of another Boucher on the same subject and not as well handled. The Gainsborough *Portrait of Mrs. Minet* was from his best period, but the sitter was middle-aged, fat, and plain and they thought some radical retouching would be needed to make her saleable. The Mor was likely to command a high price despite the lady's unpromising features. The Romney, a portrait of Lady Lushington, was horribly dirty and had bitumen cracks, but they thought it would clean up beautifully and then be worth much more, if they could get it for seven thousand or eight thousand pounds. The Hoppner *Portrait of Honorable Leicester Stanhope,* a boy with a dog, was absolutely out. The boy's expression was most unpleasant, and even the dog turned them off. They liked the two oval children's portraits by Drouais, but the fact that the one of the boy was much better might cause some technical problems during the bidding. The chef d'oeuvre was obviously the Nattier. This was on a far more lavish scale than most English full-length portraits. The details were exquisite, and the sitter, the Duc de Penthièvre, had such an air of manliness and confident energy that one could hardly believe this same painter specialized in head-and-shoulders studies of vapid young women.

Duveen, in New York, loved the idea of the pair of Drouais, which went so well with eighteenth-century French furniture. He agreed the large Nattier was splendid, but was sure he could not sell it unless, as they rather hoped, Gulbenkian wanted it. Edward and Ernest were ordered to find out exactly what Gulbenkian wanted. A few days later the reply came that Gulbenkian did indeed want the Nattier. He had tried desperately to find out the minimum price and said that different London dealers had quoted sums between six thousand and ten thousand pounds. Gulbenkian was sure Duveens would make him pay through the nose so that they could crow about it in the papers. (There was a newspaper strike just then, but never mind.) On the contrary, he was told, it was his fault if the pictures he wanted fetched high prices. He insisted on asking everyone's opinion, so dealers would naturally bid against each other for the painting in the hope of selling it to him later. He was told the bidding could go as high as fifteen thousand pounds. After Duveens insisted on a firm order, Gulbenkian agreed, with an interesting caveat: the lower the price eventually obtained, the higher the commission he would pay.

Duveen took a half-share on the pair of Drouais with another dealer prepared to pay up to twelve thousand pounds. So the financing was in place; but he sensed a lack of enthusiasm for the idea, which worried him. He wanted Edward and Ernest to tell him honestly whether the paintings were worth buying. Duveen had been given a broad hint from Agnew's that they wanted the only better Drouais, and since that painting was likely to come up first, the bidding might be high, which meant that the second painting's price might become artificially inflated. Edward and Ernest must think it through. If they bought the boy, they had to go for the girl, no matter what. On the other hand, if they did not get the boy, he did not want the girl. The best solution would be to get Christie's to sell them as a single lot.

The great day came and went. The first casualty was the Romney, which went for too much, they thought. They had succeeded in getting the Drouais paintings offered as a pair, but then the bidding became suspiciously heated and the final price was 13,000 guineas, over their limit. But Lot 70, the Nattier, closed at a surprising 11,500 guineas, or slightly more than 12,000 pounds, which must have satisfied even Gulbenkian. It only remained to find out who had outbid them on the two Drouais. Duveen, who had been questioning London repeatedly, grumbled that extracting information from them was worse than a trip to the dentist's. He finally learned that the new owner was René Gimpel, his brother-in-law, acting in half-shares with Daniel Wildenstein. Somehow Gimpel and Wildenstein must have found out Duveen was after the pair of Drouais. Joe was perfectly delighted that the paintings had been dropped on their toes.

SOME YEARS BEFORE it became a feather in one's cap to say one had beaten Duveen out of a picture, the great man had perfected the art to which every dealer aspired, that is, to know where all the great paintings were. That was not so difficult in the days when aristocrats, awakened to the possibilities, were thinking of selling and all those Americans were buying. The owner of a stately home would invite a prominent dealer to see certain pictures—seldom all of them, of course—which he might one day be persuaded to sell. These fishing expeditions were useful for everyone. The owner might get an opinion on what the painting was worth, which he could sometimes do by naming an astronomical sum, thereby goading the dealer into naming another. The dealer came away with some possibilities filed away in his mind for future reference.

Since the deliberations of Duveen's scouts were only meant for internal use, they are remarkably candid and, incidentally, demonstrate the extent to which the paintings that subsequently came to American collections reflected the taste of Joseph Duveen. More accurately, they showed his perspicacity in promoting the right kind of art. Offered a portrait by Bartolomeo Veneto, Duveen refused it because the subject was ugly and had a horrible nose. He cautioned Paris, "We had enough trouble getting rid of the Raphael." He was referring to the portrait *Giuliano de Medici, Duke of Nemours,* from the Oscar Huldschinsky collection, which Duveen tried to sell to Andrew Mellon and persuaded the great financier and art lover to hang in his house. Mellon sent it back because "the man has an evil face." Duveen sold it to Jules Bache and it is now at the Metropolitan, with the attribution "after Raphael." As for another portrait, of a bearded man by Titian, Bache turned it down because the man was bald.

It was the same story when Walter Dowdeswell and Silva White, who was Duveen's expert on furniture and objets, went to inspect some Old Masters and miscellaneous furnishings in the collection of Sir Philip Grey-Egerton. Dowdeswell thought the portrait by Thomas Lawrence of a lady in a white dress was glorious, but since the sitter was not very pretty it was not worth their time. This search for pretty people was repeated endlessly. Captain Ernest Duveen and Edward Fowles went to the dealer Spinks to look at a Reynolds owned by a member of the Hertford family and described in detail a bust portrait of a boy in a yellow jacket, green cloak, and wide lace collar. They felt bound to note that Duveen had seen the painting and did not like it because it was too small and the boy had a rather "podgy" face. After looking at a pair of portraits by Gainsborough of Lord and Lady Grosvenor at the Duke of Westminster's, Fowles and Lowengard thought the one of the lady desirable, if "a little tight" in handling, but disqualified the male sitter, calling him "ugly" and "rat-faced."

The same was true for the Reynolds small painting of Elizabeth, Countess of Sutherland, owned by the Duke of Sutherland, which Ruck went to see with Ernest Duveen. The portrait was admittedly exquisite, but they thought there was something severe about the lady's youthful good looks. She might be worth having, but only at a bargain price. The duke had several other portraits of this same ancestor. Hoppner had painted her, again in three-quarter-face, in a white dress, against a charming sylvan scene; but again she seemed too stiff, almost censorious. This was not the kind of adopted ancestor you wanted to have staring down at your New York dinner parties. She was recommended only if the price was right. Ruck and Duveen added, almost as an afterthought, that of course the picture was very fine.

These references to a fine picture with a regrettable subject extended to sculpture and tapestries as well. When looking at the collections owned by Lord Savile at Rufford Abbey, White and Dowdeswell spent some time describing a sixteenth-century Flemish tapestry panel, some eight feet high by eighteen feet wide, the subject being the Crucifixion. While the thirty figures in the scene, in their crimson and blue brocades, were very handsome, and the floral backgrounds fresh and decorative, they were disinclined to buy. It was true it was a very fine tapestry but the subject was a bit depressing. Another tapestry owned by Lord Savile was even less to their taste. There were birds and animals of the chase in the foreground, with two falconers in the middle distance crossing a bridge. The whole thing was most indelicately handled and not right for Duveen Brothers.

Much of the business of traveling the length and breadth of Britain to look at aristocratic treasures went to Ernest and Edward Duveen, or trusted scouts like Dowdeswell, Ruck, and White; but Duveen was also on the hunt whenever he was in England. A Mr. Maguire from Ireland called at their Grafton Street premises early one summer and escorted Edward Duveen to the premises of W. A. Holder, a highly regarded restorer who worked for Duveen Brothers and also the National Gallery in London. Holder wanted them to see a Drouais, this time a single painting of two small children. Knowing Duveen's fondness for that artist, Edward arranged to have the painting sent over to Claridge's, where Duveen always stayed whenever he was in town. Duveen, however, found the painting too dark, and Holder was bound to concede that it would not lighten up much after cleaning.

On another occasion, Captain Ernest and Sir Joseph went to Elvaston Castle, Derby, the seat of Lord Harrington, to inspect four portraits said to be by Hoppner, all of children. Duveen had to concede that they were charming but fussed about the fact that, although supposedly boys, they all looked like girls. He took particular exception to a portrait of a child patting a dog, which he thought unsaleable, and suspected that the Hoppner painting known as *The Drummer Boy* was probably by Reynolds.

They all liked to make attributions and would do so, one suspects, on general principles. Ernest Duveen, looking at *Lady Castlereagh* by Lawrence, tentatively suggested the painting could not be genuine because the face had "no feeling or power." Duveen was breathtakingly confident in his ability to pronounce on the authenticity of a work, as in 1918 when he was taken to see a painting owned by Sir William Savage. The book noted, "In Mr. Joseph's opinion the picture is by Holbein." He would make equally grand statements about Van Dycks, Velázquezes, Rembrandts, and even paintings said to be by Titian and/or Giorgione during the periods when these artists were virtually indistinguishable. The only time he showed distinct signs of being out of his depth was when faced with something from the Italian Renaissance, and that was what Berenson was for. In fairness to him, Duveen's eye was, as has been noted, exceptionally keen, and years of daily exposure were bound to have refined his ability to perceive an artist's signature; braggadocio did the rest.

One wonders how much attention he ever paid to the beguiling alterations and amendations of clever restorers, or how much he cared. Certainly, every time a painting was assessed there was always the automatic expectation that the old varnish would be stripped and a nice new coat applied. Damaged paintings would also be sent to the restorer's shop, and W. A. Holder, it was said, had a positive gift for "mending without repainting," as Sir Charles Holmes, a former director of the National Gallery, claimed in *Self and Partners.* That is as may be, but Holmes certainly was guilty of what would now be considered major damage when, at the suggestion of Duveen Brothers, Holder turned the oval portrait of Lady Horatio Waldegrave by Gainsborough into a rectangle. Armand Lowengard suggested it, Duveen agreed, and the painting was bought for £20,000 plus 10 percent commission.

There were also instances in which the owners, perhaps for calculated reasons, asked Duveen's emissaries to look at paintings hung so high up on a wall that proper viewing was impossible. On one occasion, the light was so bad Duveen's men had to view the works with flashlights. Anything could turn them off about a painting, not just an unpleasant expression. It was too monochromatic; not interesting enough; the dog was wrong; the man's legs were crossed or the woman's hand was awkwardly painted. A painting could not be too large or too small. What they were looking for was the big, important picture, and this insistence on buying at the top of the market no doubt saved Duveen Brothers from gambling on many marginally interesting paintings that might turn out to be copies, "school of," or outright forgeries. Besides, when the portrait was important enough, it somehow jumped across the chasm of prettiness and landed firmly on the side of greatness, whatever its physiognomic shortcomings. Lady Louisa Manners ought to have been in that category, and no doubt Joel Duveen persuaded himself of this when he backed his son's disastrous bid for that unhappy work. But it was soon clear that a Thomas Gainsborough painting that swam into Duveen's orbit in 1909 most definitely was.

This was a portrait of Karl Friedrich Abel, a virtuoso performer on the viola da gamba and noted composer. Gainsborough, whose thrilling evocations of society women in the grand manner transported them into something approaching divine status, almost kept Duveen Brothers in business at times. Whatever the economic conditions, a young and beautiful and titled girl whom Gainsborough had painted was sure to make a conquest. Karl Friedrich Abel was hardly in that category. The German-born musician had the blunt, square features of a town parson or city clerk; and by the time Gainsborough had painted him he was stout enough (a contemporary claimed) to have housed twin boys under his waistcoat.

None of that mattered in this instance. Abel's spirited and elegant compositions, it was agreed, had "brought about a total revolution in our musical taste," a contemporary wrote. Gainsborough, for whom music was almost as important as painting, was a close friend of Abel's and sketched him repeatedly. His affectionate regard is evident in every brushstroke. The composer, a viola da gamba resting against his leg, is seated at a table, about to start on a new composition—an allegro movement, we are told. His head is slightly cocked and his blue eyes gaze into the distance as he summons his inner voices. He is, as described, heavily built, but by no means commonplace. His satin waistcoat is streaked with gold highlights, which are repeated on the brown braided and tasseled jacket he wears, and one sees in the lining a flash of that vibrant blue which was Gainsborough's trademark. The patient white dog at the sitter's feet, the blaze of crimson on the upholstered chair, and the sweep of emerald and turquoise in the background curtain make the portrait not only more colorful than many of Gainsborough's works, but add just that dash and flair that distinguished the composer's style, as well as the artist's.

When Gainsborough exhibited the work at the Royal Academy in London in 1777, one critic called it "the finest modern portrait we remember to have seen." Queen Charlotte acquired it after Abel's death a decade later, and it passed through a number of distinguished collections before being bought by Agnew's in 1897. At the end of the nineteenth century the painting's value was still fairly modest. In 1897 Sir Ronald Sutherland Gower paid £1,260 for it. Buying from Agnew's took a leap of faith on Duveen's part because, despite his lifelong rule to sell first and buy later, he did not then have a likely customer, nor would he for five years. He sold the painting in 1914 to the New York railroad owner George Jay Gould, and his faith in it was finally rewarded when it came back into his hands in 1925. This time around the picture went to Henry E. Huntington, who paid $290,000 for it.

When Duveen fell in love, he fell hard. Grace Dalrymple, the tall, handsome daughter of a Scottish lawyer, was painted at least twice by Gainsborough. In one full-length portrait she is seen in profile gliding into a room, aged about twenty-four, wearing a fashionable gray wig in the high-dressed Marie Antoinette style and an exquisite gold brocaded gown, cut daringly low to show a snowy bosom. Some time after marrying Sir John Elliott, a wealthy doctor some eighteen years her senior, "Dally the

Grace Dalrymple Elliott, one of the portraits by Thomas
Gainsborough that Duveen could not resist

Tall" embarked on a series of liaisons, including one with the Prince of
Wales. She stated that her baby daughter was the result of that union. She
had an exciting visit to France during the Revolution, claiming to have
been imprisoned four times, and then had another affair or three with
French noblemen before ending her life quietly in the Ville d'Avray near
Paris.

Obviously Grace Dalrymple Elliott, with her emphatic brows, high
coloring, perfect mouth, and cascading curls, was an adventurer after
Duveen's heart. The portrait that captivated him showed her head and
shoulders, gazing dreamily toward the viewer, wearing something low-cut
and white with splashes of Gainsborough blue. The half-smile and the
slight tilt of the head give her a languorous appeal, and it is easy to see why
he was smitten. He had seen her at Welbeck Abbey, seat of the Duke of
Portland, as early as 1922 and thought then she might be worth five thou-

sand pounds. Nothing came of that visit, and several years went by before
the duke was ready to talk prices. Unfortunately the value of the painting,
in the duke's eyes, had galloped ahead at such a pace that the lady was now
worth fifty thousand pounds, according to him. He was willing to entertain the idea of forty thousand. Determined as Duveen was ("We must
have her," he privately told his staff), he bravely faced the duke down. Even
at forty thousand he was not a buyer. There matters stood until, in 1930,
Duveen saw his darling again and was even more determined to have her.
How much he paid for her is unclear, but this time she was his. Since the
portrait of Mrs. Elliott did not sell until 1946, some years after Duveen's
death, it is tempting to think that he could not bear to part with her and
hung her, as is likely, in his New York quarters. (The painting is now at the
Frick.)

IN THE DAYS WHEN JOEL DUVEEN was beginning to feel the cold
wind of his oldest son's ambitions, the main source of his own spy network
was a hotel or apartment concierge. Tips discreetly distributed paid divi-
dends when it could be learned, for instance, that a collector had just
arrived at a hotel, that someone had taken a large apartment in a *joli
quartier,* or that a rival dealer had been seen entering the premises of a
client Joel considered "his." Things went even better when the concierge in
question had been persuaded to confide in one dealer and cut out the rest,
although this could get expensive. When the price was too high, Joel had to
be prepared to be spied upon, in which case he delivered his telegrams to
the post office rather than to the concierge and kept a sharp eye on whoever
was emptying his wastepaper basket. He was staying at a hotel when his
suspicions about being deceived by Henry and Joseph had reached their
height. He had been using a desk in the main salon and suddenly noticed
that a maid of a relative, also staying at the hotel, was about to make off
with the basket into which he had tossed some letters. He stopped her, of
course. Whom was she working for? He did not know, but he had his suspicions. At the same period Joel did his best to warn Jack Duveen about the
dirty tricks his own son was capable of. Jack scoffed; he would like to see
Joe try to ruin him. Uncle Joel responded, "My boy, you don't know Joe."

To have one's own father suspect one capable of anything is disturbing,
even if the general verdict about Joe had a certain melancholic charm for
that family of reflexively competitive men. That is not to say that Joe was
always successful. Robert Langton Douglas, a connoisseur, museum official, and sometime dealer, testified for Duveen during a trial and happened

to mention that he knew of a Leonardo da Vinci in private hands in Ireland. Duveen jumped to his feet and was "stabbing the air with his forefinger as if bidding for it. 'I must have it,' he cried across the court, but the witness smiled and shook his head.

"During the first recess, Sir Joseph made his way inside the court rail to Mr. Langton Douglas and said, 'My dear fellow, you really must tell me where it is, right away.'

" 'Ah-h-h,' said his expert, 'we shall see.' "

Perhaps no nice sale resulted, and then again, perhaps it did, and Langton Douglas received his usual finder's fee. That was Duveen: he was inured to arguments that would have deterred lesser men.

On another occasion, having found someone he thought would be a first-rate agent in the pursuit of some Old Masters owned by the Duke of Devonshire, Duveen was off and running and bombarded the agent with letters and telegrams long after it became clear that the duke would not sell. His agent, who stood to make a handsome commission and was as anxious as anybody to get the paintings, could not convince Duveen that there was nothing doing. Duveen was, he wrote, a perfect genius at banging his head against a stone wall. But as Duveen would have reasoned, if a man says he can get it and then suddenly cannot get it, something must have happened. Perhaps another dealer has begun poaching on his turf? Perhaps the agent has fallen from favor in the duke's eyes, in which case he must be replaced? His mind, ever alert to subtlety and nuance, was not well equipped to accept the obvious.

Still, Duveen's assessment of a given situation seldom overestimated the duplicitous possibilities in that world of feints, counterthrusts, false clues, intrigues, and betrayal. In the high-stakes game of art dealing one of his natural assets was his ability to bedazzle; and in the Edwardian and late Edwardian worlds in which he moved, in which "devotion to the superficial was a code of behavior and proof of social superiority," it was particularly useful. His naturally sharp verbal reflexes had been honed to mimic the high-toned, brittle badinage used in the best circles. With Oscar Wilde, he would have believed one should treat all the trivial things in life seriously and vice versa, or would have acted as if he did, and he kept his ambitions to himself. But there was something about him that transcended artifice. To be amusing and convivial was intrinsic to his naturally buoyant outlook on life. Because he was always happily willing to poke fun at himself, a most un-English trait, he disarmed his critics and made those who would have liked to keep him at bay shrug their shoulders in helpless laughter.

"Capable of anything": Joseph Duveen in the 1920s

Sir Charles Holmes recalled that when he was editor of the *Burlington Magazine,* Duveen came to see him. He had just bought a huge new collection—it might have been the Kann—and proposed buying a complete issue of the magazine in order to celebrate that fact. Holmes had a difficult time explaining that, as the expression went, "it just isn't done." He wrote, "The mere pressure of his determination and enthusiasm was difficult to resist, indeed I found his energy quite fascinating . . . and when I finally said 'No,' it was said with more qualification than our custom was." That particular mixture of "bravura and independence," as Kenneth Clark wrote, was infectious, "and when he was present everyone behaved as if they had had a couple of drinks."

Duveen's flow of conversation was particularly useful when dealing with American millionaires like Andrew Mellon, who doled out phrases as parsimoniously as pocket change, and he always had a new anecdote. One of the charming stories told by S. N. Behrman concerns a religious painting being considered by "an extremely respectable High Church duke." According to Behrman, Agnew's had it for sale and the duke was contemplating its purchase. He made the mistake of asking Duveen what he thought about it. "Very nice, my dear fellow, very nice," Duveen replied. "But I suppose you are aware those cherubs are homosexual." Back it went to Agnew's. When the same painting came into Duveen's hands some time later, the cherubs were restored to full heterosexual status.

A slightly different version of the same story is told by Sir John Foster, who was close to the Duveen family in the 1930s. He said that Duveen's only important client during the Depression was Anna Thomson Dodge (Mrs. Horace Dodge), who was settling her husband's estate in the auto industry just before the 1929 collapse of the stock market and made a fortune. "So she went on buying pictures. I think she was in Dearborn or Detroit, and she sees this rather lovely fifteenth-century Italian picture from Colnaghi's. So Joe, instead of saying it's a copy, or a fake, said, 'It's a lovely picture but I wouldn't have it on my walls.' She wants to know why not. He replies, 'Because the relationship of the artist with the models for those puttis was so disgusting. I always remember that relationship.' So she whistled it back to Colnaghi's, who couldn't sue, couldn't do anything!"

Duveen spoke in bursts, seldom requiring an answer, and when in the middle of a sale knew exactly when to advance, when to retreat, and, on exotically rare occasions, when to say nothing. For all his apparent impulsiveness he was a careful judge of character. Still there was, in some essential way, something childlike about him, thought René Gimpel, who was never a child. When Duveen asked naïvely what people thought of him and his firm, Gimpel answered they thought he was a great salesman and had all the most beautiful pieces. Duveen said, "They are right, don't you think?"

He had the American ability to seem at home wherever he went. As Josephine Tey wrote of one of her characters, "He travelled like royalty and was given almost diplomatic privileges; he was dressed by the world's best tailors and had acquired the social tricks of the world's best people; in everything but essence he was the well-bred man of the world." But if you met him in America, where he was very grand, you would not recognize him in British social circles, where he played the fool, according to Kenneth Clark. He had the actor's need to live up to other people's expectations, perhaps because he always felt himself to be an outsider.

Mary Berenson, who was an astute judge of character, had a sneaking fondness for Duveen and loved his visits. "It's like drinking champagne," she would say, and Berenson, who disliked him, would answer, "More like gin." Still, she wondered how, in a society in which modesty and understatement were de rigueur, the British could stand Duveen's compulsive boasting. He had that in common with Henry Oppenheimer, an "old-style" Jewish collector from Kenneth Clark's early career, who would congratulate himself mournfully about how much something had cost him. Similarly, even events which might give one pause for rueful reflection left hardly a mark on Duveen. After the ruinous customs case of 1910, whenever Duveen was twitted on the subject, he would point out, quite reasonably and with much satisfaction, that no dealer had ever paid such a huge fine before. In the summer of 1923 Duveen, whom she always called "Jo," came to visit Mary Berenson in Chilling, and she confided that she and her

Nicky Mariano, Berenson's amanuensis, in 1947

husband had settled a considerable sum on Nicky Mariano, Berenson's indispensable secretary and confidante. She wrote to her husband, "He got up and shook my hand and said, 'It's the best investment you ever made. She's a wonderful person.' And he beamed all over when I said it was because of him we could do it. I think it really attached him to us humanly . . ." She called him a "cockatoucan."

As JOHN PARTRIDGE KNEW, Duveen thought nothing of "helping" his clients find well-trained staffs. Chauffeurs and butlers were his specialty. It was his business to know what his clients were thinking once comfortably tucked into the back seats of their automobiles. It was his business to know who came and went, what the collector said and what he was about to buy or sell. Regular payments were a part of this networking, meticulously recorded, as someone working at the Fifth Avenue library once discovered. Almost as soon as Duveen was awake, a secretary would appear with breakfast and piles of newspapers, already marked up. The political situation, international exchange rates, interest rates, the court circular, birthdays, anniversaries, and deaths came in for his scrutiny. Duveen always wanted to be up to date about the lives of those he was cultivating and was fussy about the kinds of flowers he wanted sent if someone was in the hospital, or had a birthday, or got engaged, or was embarking on a transatlantic liner. He spent a fortune on Christmas presents, not always wisely. One recipient noted that his son, aged fifteen, had received a rocking horse.

Such largesse, Behrman wrote, was not limited to clients and their staffs, but shone all around him: to "critics, museum directors, restorers, architects, decorators, and servants of all grades, including deck stewards on ships. Accustomed to doing things *en prince,* he scattered largesse, often for no specific purpose but with a touching faith in the emotion of gratitude." That Duveen's generosity stemmed from his innocent delight in giving people pleasure: well, that was part of it, perhaps. But one suspects he also planned to make them dependent on him. By means of constant small courtesies and attentions he would insinuate himself into their lives. They would turn to him constantly. They must be unable to function without him. To a surprising degree, this became true, because he was so alert to their needs and knew how to get things done. He bought their cigars and chose the colors for their grand salons and found the brocades and chandeliers and boiseries. He got them tickets on steamships and invitations to stately homes and Buckingham Palace garden parties. He arranged for seats to sold-out plays and planned itineraries and even, it was said, was matchmaker for one or two advantageous marriages. Duveen could do anything, but that was because he thought of everything.

To those who lived through it, the high summer of 1914 looked like any other summer. True, the great powers were engaged in an arms race, but no one thought that out of the ordinary. King George V visited Paris to the accompaniment of some elaborate parades and dinners, and the French president, Raymond Poincaré, visiting the tsar, found himself fêted and toasted with even greater ceremony. The assassination at Sarajevo of Archduke Francis Ferdinand and his wife on June 28, 1914, was

Edward Fowles at his desk in the Place Vendôme in 1927

a distant curiosity that barely seeped into the general consciousness. The newspapers were reassuring. "There is no ground for anxiety as to war," the London *Times* reported. Dolly Duveen, then aged eleven, said in later years, "Daddy was sure there wouldn't be a war."

Duveen just then was engaged in some very nice pieces of business. Among them were sales of several paintings to Mr. and Mrs. E. T. Stotesbury of Philadelphia, who were picking out the choicest treasures from among the handsome wares on display inside the new "Merchant Marine" building at 720 Fifth Avenue. Another wealthy Philadelphian, P. A. B. Widener, was lavishing even more money on his own splendid interiors, buying marble busts, tapestries, Persian rugs, vases, tables, figurines, sofas, armchairs, folding screens, inlaid writing tables, picture frames, and much else for the staggering total of $756,073.29. By then Widener and his son Joseph (his son George having perished on the *Titanic* in 1912), had already paid out a princely sum for Raphael's Small Cowper Madonna, and they had paid once more when it was delivered in January 1914. According to Edward Fowles, the costs of cleaning, framing, and insurance, along with the usual percentage to the arranger of the deal, amounted to a further $65,000.

That summer Duveen, his wife, and his daughter were in Evian "taking the cure." Fowles was in a hot and lazy, almost deserted Paris while his wife and eighteen-month-old daughter were enjoying the ocean breezes at Ambleteuse, a beach resort near Boulogne. No one could have known that the assassination of the archduke and his wife would set such a ghastly chain of events in motion, and with such speed. Austria-Hungary declared war on Serbia on July 28, 1914. Serbia appealed to Russia, which began to mobilize. On August 1, Germany declared war on Russia, and a day after that, German troops marched on France. Three days after that, Germany invaded Belgium, at which point England entered the war. In just one month, huge and impersonal forces had convened to set a world war in motion.

Knowing what was going to happen before it did had been a point of pride for Duveen, his first line of defense in the cause of protecting Duveen Brothers. But this time the alarm came not from him, but from Uncle Henry. Fowles wrote, "I was just leaving for home when, to my surprise, Uncle Henry walked in. 'You're just the man I am looking for, Eddie,' he exclaimed. . . . 'All the German waiters left the hotel at Vittel last night. The Germans are mobilising: there's going to be a war'!" It was the Quatorze Juillet and Duveen Brothers had, as it turned out, just two weeks to get their most valuable objects, their paintings and sculpture, shipped to London from Le Havre. Fowles described the scene as men from Chenue, the Paris shipping company used by all the artists and museums, appeared in full force and packed up the paintings and then the porcelain and ornaments. Precious tapestries were removed from chairs and sofas and used to wrap up vases, and fragile objets were packed in shipments small enough to travel as hand luggage on the trains to London. They were going to make it, but only just. Fowles recalled that one of the gems of the collection, Boucher's famous set of painted panels *The Arts and Sciences,* left by the last train to London.

Fowles's wife and baby, traveling by a circuitous route from the coast, took twenty-four hours to make the relatively short journey back to Paris and their apartment on the rue Miromesnil. Duveen arrived from Evian a few days later. He was not very communicative about how they had got there, Fowles wrote. Dolly was more enlightening. It appeared that, taking his usual prompt action, Duveen, who had a car in Evian, bought up all the available gasoline and hid it in the garden of the hotel. The obvious plan was to drive back to Paris, but this idea was for some reason abandoned. Then Duveen discovered that a client of his, R. W. Hudson, a wealthy soap manufacturer, had somehow arranged for a special train to

Paris. Naturally, he and his wife and daughter, and presumably a chauffeur and maid or two, were soon comfortably installed in the same plush quarters. Once in Paris, they moved into the Crillon, and Dolly remembers seeing French soldiers being taken off in taxis to fight in the Battle of the Marne.

Duveen had two immediate concerns. The first was to get Elsie and Dolly shipped off safely to London. Dolly said, "Mother and I and a maid set off in a taxicab to Cherbourg. I remember soldiers stopping us along the way to examine our passports. Then we got on a boat and had to sleep on the floor. Somehow, we made it to London. Mother stayed in London to wait for Daddy and I was sent on to New York with a maid." What the Duveens had not realized was that the White Slave Traffic Act of 1911 had made it illegal for anyone to cross a state line, or enter the United States, with a young girl unless he or she had the necessary papers. Her chaperone, of course, had no such signed permission from Dolly's parents. Dolly said, "I was on the old *Mauretania* and was kept on board. They told me I was either going to Ellis Island or back to England, but somebody saved me"—presumably Daddy, pulling strings again—"and after eight hours I was allowed to go on to my boarding school in Connecticut."

Duveen's second concern was the fate of the Huntingtons. They were in France for the summer, staying in a house they had just rented, the Château Beauregard near Versailles. The house, which stood in an extensive park, pleased them for different reasons. H.E.H., who was a nature lover, according to Fowles, loved to stroll in the rambling gardens with their lush green lawns and mature trees. Arabella tackled the huge project of furnishing the chateau's vast rooms with her usual zest; seven truckloads of furniture and paintings were shipped six thousand miles from California to accomplish this objective. (Some years later, Duveen Brothers would be saddled with the task of sending them all back.) No doubt both of them found a certain aspect of the chateau irresistible. In the early seventeenth century it had been decorated with over three hundred identically sized portraits of eminent historical figures, lined up row on row around the walls of its picture gallery like postage stamps. Wherever they looked, men in ruffled collars and ecclesiastical robes looked solemnly back.

In the annoying way of furnishings, some tables, chairs, and other miscellany could not be made to fit their new spaces, so that meant more anxious investigations of Duveen's stock, with the latter only too ready to oblige. Arabella and her bridegroom seem to have taken little notice of the gathering storm at first. (In any event, America was still neutral.) But then her son, Archer, and daughter-in-law, Helen, were arrested. They were traveling in Europe that summer and had arrived in Nuremberg. Archer Huntington was a student of topography and always traveled with a quantity of maps. He was also said to resemble "a certain Russian grand duke." Since Germany and Russia were at war by then, things looked black indeed. But the senior Huntingtons contacted a friend in Paris, who contacted a U.S. minister in Brussels, who contacted President Wilson's secretary. The doors of their prison cells were opened and Archer and Helen were soon safely in London.

Once they were installed at Claridge's, Archer and Helen's next concern was to get the senior Huntingtons out of the Château Beauregard. This proved to be difficult. First, Arabella and H.E.H. had only just arrived. Second, they had hired thirty-two servants. (There were thirteen inside and nineteen outdoors.) Third, they wanted to make a trip to Germany. They stubbornly set off, but once they reached Nancy they were persuaded to turn around by an American who, presumably, told them they were advancing straight into the front lines. Returning to the chateau they were involuntary hosts to a company of French troops, who behaved impeccably but requisitioned their only car.

After some further persuasion Arabella finally consented to retire to London. "It took three days to pack her thirty-five trunks," Henry Huntington's biographer, James Thorpe, wrote, "and two motorbuses to transport the trunks to the railway station." The next issue was how to get them to Le Havre. For Duveen, this was almost easy. The British ambassador, Sir Austin Lee, owed him a favor, so the ambassador's personal car was put at their disposal. Arriving at Le Havre, they found the docks jammed with British citizens, all of them trying to get home. The Huntingtons, being Americans, did not qualify. But they had arrived in such style, and Duveen was with them. Persuading recalcitrant officials to bend the rules was child's play to him. Pretty soon the Huntingtons had the necessary *laissez-passer* and were installed in a comfortable stateroom although not, one supposes, surrounded by their thirty-five trunks. It was quite a trick, and they were exceedingly grateful to Duveen, if not his forever.

ONE OF THE MOST CURIOUS ASPECTS of this period of Duveen's life has to do with a public statement he made at the outbreak of World War I. He told the *Daily Telegraph* of London (probably its art critic, A. C. R. Carter, who was almost the official mouthpiece for Duveen Brothers) that the company planned to close its London office and concentrate on its activities in New York and Paris. The announcement was made on July 22, one week after Uncle Henry and Edward Fowles began frantically packing up the Paris office and sending paintings to London by every train. That he should publicly be claiming to do something that was not true—the Paris office barely functioned for the next four years, while the London office continued on merrily—is inexplicable, unless somehow connected with larger events. And, in fact, the realization that Europe was about to be plunged into war would lead to the biggest panic on Wall Street since that of 1907. There was already an industrial recession in the U.S., and the idea that transatlantic trade would dry up and worsen the problem spread like wildfire. In *The House of Morgan,* Ron Chernow wrote, "After the czar mobilized over a million Russian troops on July 29, all the European markets shut down. As overseas investors rushed to liquidate securities through New York, the Stock Exchange took its steepest one-day dive since the 1907 panic."

That crisis, as Duveen well knew, had been resolved almost singlehandedly by J. Pierpont Morgan in the face of official helplessness. To keep abreast of national and international events had become almost second-nature to Duveen, if only to guess which currencies would be up and which down in the constantly risky business of buying and selling across borders. The elder J. P. Morgan was dead, but his son, J.P. Jr., always called Jack, shared with Duveen the view, in officially neutral America, that Germany was the aggressor and that every effort should be made to arm the Allies, as Britain and France were called, so they could defend themselves. Attractive loans began to be made by the House of Morgan to companies willing to join in the de facto war effort, something that Germany, along with isolationist politicians and German sympathizers, was quick to protest. "A dual myth was being born—that the Morgans were stooges of the British crown and that their money was drenched in blood," Chernow wrote. Showing which side he was on, Duveen joined the debate by making a public show of confidence in continued trade with France.

THE IDEA THAT SPIES WERE EVERYWHERE was not confined to wealthy Americans traveling in Germany who looked like Russian grand dukes and carried suspicious numbers of maps. In Italy, Bernard and Mary Berenson went on an innocent motoring trip to study the painters of the Marche and were arrested on suspicion of being Germans; a mob attacked their car and almost destroyed it. It was Berenson's first experience of what he called "spymania." In the U.S., the realization that the country, with its fledgling army and rudimentary coastal defenses, might be vulnerable to enemy attack, however unlikely, began to stir. The youthful Secret Service knew that the British had eight hundred spies in New York alone, and the Germans perhaps an equal number, but the combined forces of military and naval intelligence, along with the service, could only muster ten men to work in counterespionage. The Secret Service began to believe that the Kaiser wanted to force the U.S. into a war he was sure of winning. Submarines, so the scenario went, would be brought in to support a landing by the German navy, and New York itself would be starved into submission in a matter of days or weeks.

How realistic this assessment was is another matter. The Secret Service knew that German agents, in a supposedly neutral country, were working to propagandize, agitate, foment strikes, disrupt shipments of munitions, cut off supplies of liquid chlorine (used in making poison gas), acquire newspapers and airplane factories, plant bombs, and sabotage the war effort in all kinds of creative ways. One of the most famous agents was Franz von Papen, then military attaché to the German embassy, who would become vice-chancellor of the German Republic, German ambassador to Austria, and an important member of the Nazi Party. Dr. Heinrich Albert, a privy councilor of the German Empire during the Kaiser's regime, later secretary of the treasury, was considered even more dangerous. By 1915 he was already in the U.S., ostensibly as an official of the Hamburg-American Steamship Line at 45 Broadway. Only a few government officials had any idea of the ambitious scope of the German counterespionage. Some plots, however, were beginning to be uncovered.

One of the first, in the spring of 1915, was quickly unmasked. The goal of Franz von Rintelen, a Berlin banker and expert in sabotage, was to disrupt U.S. shipments by planting bombs which would explode once the merchant vessels were in open waters. Huge amounts of money were involved. The Secret Service learned that between half a million and a million dollars had been sent from Germany over a four-month period. In the short time he was at large, Rintelen managed to plant bombs in thirty-five merchant ships and foment a strike at the Remington arms plant in Bridgeport, Connecticut. He was picked up by the British in August 1915, as he landed in England, before he could do much harm. But the discovery of the Rintelen plot underscored what Henry and Joseph Duveen must have known, i.e., that Atlantic travel was becoming increasingly risky, and not just because of the new German U-boats with their deadly torpedoes. Perhaps, as they traveled back and forth to London, the Duveens also knew that munitions were being shipped in supposedly neutral passenger liners. It is even possible that crates being sent by Duveen Brothers to London contained more than their seemingly innocuous cargoes of paintings and furniture.

One of those passenger ships was the 31,500-ton SS *Lusitania.* Owned by the Cunard White Star Line, the *Lusitania* was only seven years old and one of the most comfortable and elegant of the Cunard boats, if not the biggest and fastest; she carried two thousand passengers and crew. The *Lusitania* was scheduled to make a routine transatlantic crossing to England in the spring of 1915 when George Sylvester Viereck, editor and publisher of *The Fatherland,* a newspaper based in New York, and another undercover German agent, received some serious news. He learned that the *Lusitania* was scheduled to be torpedoed. Since the ocean liner had been built with loans from the British government on the understanding that it could be turned to military uses if necessary, this made a certain kind of sense, although the boat was patently still in civilian service. What bothered Viereck were the political repercussions if any Americans were on board. He telephoned Dr. Albert. If Americans were to lose their lives, he said, nothing could keep the United States out of the war. He, at least, did not appear to welcome a simultaneous war with the U.S. His concerns were brushed aside. Carl Schimmel, one of Papen's aides, boasted that he had planted a "cigar" full of TNT in the bowels of the ship.

As the boat was nearing the Irish coast on May 7, 1915, the U-boat attacked. Some 1,195 people lost their lives, including 128 Americans. Were there munitions in the hold which blew up when the torpedo hit? Was there a "cigar" of TNT aboard? The German U-boat captain claimed to have only used one torpedo but to have heard two explosions. No one quite knew what had caused so much damage. It seemed clear, however, whether or not civilians were hapless hostages to military hardware, the Germans were in earnest about their war of terrorism. The sinking of the *Lusitania* was a catastrophic, catalytic event.

Chapter Eight

THE FAY CASE

D UVEEN WAS ALWAYS ANGLING after the great collector Henry Clay Frick, who, for perverse reasons, bought most of his works of art from Knoedler. With patience and tenacity he had laid his long-term plans even as Frick deigned to buy a bronze here and a Gainsborough there. As he waited, Duveen took the measure of his man.

Frick once said that railroads were the Rembrandts of investment. One would have thought it was therefore a mere leap of the imagination for a director of the U.S. Steel Corporation and investor in railroads to move from the magical sight of a train barreling full steam ahead to the one contained within a picture frame on a wall. It was not. Frick's idea of paradise was listening to an organist playing "The Rosary" and "Silver Threads Among the Gold" while he perused the latest edition of the *Saturday Evening Post.* Perhaps Duveen, stretching for a reason Frick could appreciate, had tried the ultimate argument, i.e., the sensible nature of the investment. No really big man wants anything less than a gilt-edged security, and buying an Old Master had the advantage of low maintenance; Duveen would have argued low risk as well. (However, a specialist on art theft for Interpol once exclaimed that the hardest part about his job was bringing his agents up to speed on art history. Most of them would not have recognized a stolen Old Master if it stepped off the wall and bit them.) Perhaps the argument was tried on Frick. If so, it made no impression.

Frick had never bought antique furnishings or tasteful objets from anyone, and it showed. He always said he never would. But by 1915 he was building a glorious mansion on upper Fifth Avenue and at last needed something to put in it, lots of things. He finally thought of Duveen. Natu-

Henry Clay Frick, a portrait by John Christian Johansen

rally Duveen was embarrassingly eager to oblige. The only problem was that Duveen sold beautiful things—by his own admission—and Frick only bought junk. How could the old collector, whom Gimpel described as a man with eyes of solid steel, be made to see reason? Well, there was the whole question of cachet again, and finally the argument looked like a winner.

When the Morgan art—paintings and sculpture, bronzes, enamels, porcelains, and miniatures—went on view as a loan exhibition at the Metropolitan Museum of Art in 1913, one of its great prizes was the "Fragonard Room." This referred to fourteen panels by Jean-Honoré Fragonard called *Romans d'amour et de la jeunesse,* executed at the height of his extravagantly idealized, light, airy style. The idea was that some of these panels would

Right: The Pursuit from Fragonard's *Romans d'Amour* series at the Frick Collection

Below: A Frick Collection interior: the Fragonard Room

grace the new pavilion in Madame Du Barry's garden at Louveciennes which Louis XV was building for her. She, however, took a dislike to them for some reason, and they remained with the artist until his death in 1806. Eventually they were acquired by Agnew's, which sold them to J. Pierpont Morgan, who paid $350,000 for them in 1898, already a hefty price, and then was faced with what to do with them. A room must be specially designed. That was where Duveen came in. He chose the panelings for Morgan's house at Prince's Gate in London, and no doubt supplied every detail of the room's furnishings as well. When the Fragonard panels were removed to their temporary quarters in New York, even the thought of dismounting them seemed sacrilegious, so woodwork and cornices from Prince's Gate went with them.

No doubt the museum had hoped that the semi-permanence of the installation would be its own argument for a subsequent gift, but it was not to be. Morgan, teetering on the edge of giving the whole collection to the museum, naturally wanted his munificence to be adequately recognized. In short, he wanted a Morgan Wing. He thought the Metropolitan Museum of Art should find the money for that. Decision makers at the museum were sure Mr. Morgan could afford to provide a wing as well. It was an impasse, only settled after Morgan's death in 1913 when his will left the problem up to his son. Jack Morgan looked over his inheritance and decided the art collection had to go.

René Gimpel recalled that his brother-in-law happened to be visiting the museum one Sunday and drifted into the Fragonard Room. To his surprise, Duveen saw Knoedler and his associates studying the panels intently. It came over him in a flash that Knoedler was going to sell the room to Frick. Next morning he raced around to Morgan's and asked the price; it was $1,250,000. Duveen made a faint effort to bargain. He would give them $1 million cash. The answer was "Take it or leave it." Duveen took it. He then asked Jack Morgan if he would kindly telephone Mr. Frick to relay the news that the Fragonard Room now belonged to Joseph Duveen and that Duveen was willing to sell it to him, at cost.

It was a brilliant stroke. Duveen did not have to waste any time convincing the collector of the Fragonard Room's superior merits. These went without saying; the panels were installed in a great museum. He did not have to bring up the idea of cachet; J. Pierpont Morgan's name was a gilt-edged guarantee. He did not even have to suggest that he, Joseph Duveen, should supervise the installation. He was obviously the one man equipped to handle the delicate art of displaying the Fragonards in an appropriate setting. It was also a stroke of genius, psychologically speaking. Frick was getting the Fragonards free—free of the middleman's percentage, that is. They were almost bargains. Nothing could have been better calculated to warm at least the edges of this businessman's heart. A month later, Sir Charles Allom, the architect, had been engaged to remodel one of Frick's new rooms, pushing out walls and relocating doors and windows so as to properly house the beauties. Of course, Duveen personally supervised the installation at every stage. He commissioned the paneling, and when it came back from Paris, was startled to see that the maker, De Cour, had let the idea of an installation for a millionaire go to his head. Curlicues and arabesques sprouted as far as the eye could see, liberally splashed with gold leaf. He had eclipsed even the Fragonards. Duveen sent the paneling back.

The Metropolitan Museum of Art had seriously bungled matters, but they did get some rather good pieces in the end. In the meantime Duveen Brothers was in the glorious ascendant, not just with Frick but with Jack Morgan as well. When Duveen captured the Fragonard Room he had already, a mere ten days before, bought the famous Morgan porcelains, some fourteen hundred specimens, for a record-breaking $3 million. Incorporated into the Morgan group, which Uncle Henry had helped embellish, was the original C. T. Garland collection of oriental porcelain, which Duveen Brothers had sold him. There were even echoes of the fine discriminating eye of Joel Duveen, who had bought his red-hawthorn-on-black-ground specimen from George Salting in 1891. The Morgan porcelains had, as it were, been baptized from the early days by Duveen Brothers, and it stood to reason that the firm should be offered the chance to buy them back again, at escalating prices, of course. There is no record of a bidding war. Jack Morgan appears to have approached Joe Duveen informally, although no correspondence to this effect has survived. Duveen, of course, knew exactly who was going to start buying some of his choicest pieces. Frick was entirely agreeable. Whatever Herculean efforts had been needed to persuade Frick to leave matters of taste entirely in Duveen's hands had succeeded.

Among the heavenly stools, chairs, tables, vases, andirons, consoles, candlesticks, bread baskets, urns, jardinières, caskets, clocks, commodes—paintings and sculpture as well—that made their way into the Frick mansion in the next few years, one Gainsborough deserves a particular mention. Duveen's eminence as a master of interior decor had imprinted itself on Frick's awareness. But he continued to cling to the idea that Knoedler's were the only people to deal with when it came to buying important pictures. This state of affairs could not be allowed to continue. As S. N. Behrman tells it, Duveen went to dine with Frick one evening and managed to wring

The Mall in St. James's Park by Thomas Gainsborough

from him the reluctant admission that he wanted a certain picture, which he did not name, and was not sure of getting it from Knoedler's.

That Frick's taste was now educated to want Old Masters instead of kitsch was the good news. The bad news was that he was not buying through Duveen's. Using his superb espionage network, Duveen found out via London that a very great painting was about to be sold to Knoedler by a certain aristocrat who lived in Wiltshire. Duveen fired off instructions. His man must take the first train down, give the owner a thousand pounds as a binder, and then offer to outbid anyone else for the painting. It was Gainsborough's *Mall in St. James's Park.*

The picture, unlike anything else Gainsborough ever painted, depicts several groups of fashionably dressed women taking a stroll through a wooded landscape. From the placement of the groups and their sidelong glances it is clear the air is full of chatter, even backbiting, yet the sameness of their doll-like features is puzzling. Is this meant to be Woman with a capital W—there is only one man in the painting—engaged in frivolous gossip and assessing the competition? Is there some larger moral to be drawn about human blindness to the beauties of nature? For nature, in this painting, is very beautiful indeed. Great swags of branches lean over the gossiping crowds, their feathery leaves in tawny golds and blue-greens; there is a cow to be seen somewhere and a hint of open fields beyond. As one of the artist's late works, it was considered a fascinating exercise of dreamlike beauty, more remarkable than Watteau's *Embarquement pour Cythère*. An eye schooled to appreciate Fragonard would snap it up in a minute.

As Behrman tells it, the next time Duveen dined with Frick he found the collector deeply depressed. Ferreting out the truth was child's play: Frick had lost his *Mall*. Duveen lived for moments like these. Why hadn't Mr. Frick told him he wanted this painting? Duveen had already bought it. Mr. Frick must understand he had only to ask Duveen for anything he wanted and Duveen would get it. Duveen nobly added that he would sell it at cost: $250,000. Knoedler could probably have bought it for less, but that was not the point. Frick had been taught a lesson, in the nicest possible way.

That is the story as Behrman tells it, and very nice it is too. The problem is that it did not happen quite that way. A front-page story in the *New York Times* describing the sale says that *Mall* was acquired from Thomas Agnew & Sons, meaning that this art dealer had won the bidding war. Agnew's, which did not have a New York office, would often sell paintings to Duveen's when Duveen had an American buyer, although Henry Duveen energetically denied there was anyone in mind. This means that there was no Duveen emissary dispatched from London on the first train, no cash down, and no open check. Joseph Duveen had probably contacted Agnew's and taken half-shares on the picture, which Agnew's had won after fighting it out with Knoedler.

Whatever the truth of the matter, Behrman was probably right in suggesting that an incident of some kind turned Frick in Duveen's direction in the final years of his life. One of Duveen's favorite plays was an English comedy called *A Pair of Spectacles* by Sydney Grindy, with Sir John Hare in the leading role. As he leaves for the office one morning, the central character picks up the wrong pair of spectacles and, as a result, takes one pratfall after another. At this point Duveen would draw the gentle moral: it was his role in life to provide his clients with the right pair of spectacles, so that they could properly appreciate what he was selling them. He would laugh and laugh about that.

There were more sumptuous sales to be made from the Morgan collection as the months went by, Renaissance bronzes, Limoges enamels, and majolica ware among them. In every case Duveen Brothers benefited from the cozy relationship that had been built up between father and son. J. Pierpont's practical-minded heir was an Anglophile, spending up to six months a year in England. He and Duveen were united in their detestation of Germany and their determination to win the war. Jack Morgan was, at the same time, aware of the dangers. In the past there had been a blackmail attempt, and there were always streams of abusive letters from people who were convinced they had been defrauded by him, his bank, or both.

By July of 1915 the firm of J. P. Morgan & Co. had handled $500 million worth of war contracts on behalf of the British and French governments, and the threats had become more menacing. One letter to Thomas Lamont, an officer of the bank, said, "My dear Mr. Lamont—Your death doom is marked by your activity for the British war loan, which will deal death to my brothers on the battlefield in Germany. It shall be a distinct pleasure for me to puncture your black heart with lead some time in the distant future." Jack Morgan must have feared that it would be only a matter of time before someone tried to kill him.

That attempt came in the summer of 1915, two months after the sinking of the *Lusitania*. It was the Fourth of July holiday weekend. Frank Holt was, to all appearances, as decorous and upright a member of society as one could wish. Tall, slender, and scholarly, of German-American parentage, he taught German at Cornell University. He was married, about forty years old, and, as it turned out, perfectly prepared to die in the cause of stopping the U.S. from aiding the war effort against Germany. To that end he traveled to Washington, and on the Friday afternoon of July 2 he took a public tour of the Senate and surreptitiously planted a powerful bomb in the reception hall adjoining Vice President Thomas Marshall's private office. It was just about four o'clock. Holt took a berth on the overnight train to New York and had the satisfaction of hearing, while the train was still in the station, the sound of a huge explosion coming from the Capitol.

By Saturday morning he had arrived at Jack Morgan's sixty-acre country estate on the coast of Long Island near Glen Cove. The Morgans had several guests staying for the weekend, among them the British ambassador, Sir Cecil Spring-Rice, and his wife. They were eating breakfast as the doorbell rang. It was Holt, demanding to see Morgan. When the butler refused to let him in, Holt pulled two revolvers out of his pocket and rushed through the door—it was learned later that he was also carrying a stick of dynamite. The butler immediately raised the alarm. The Morgans, in another part of the house, ran up the back stairs and along the landing,

J. P. ("Jack") Morgan Jr. in 1923

just in time to find Holt making his way up the front stairs, shouting, "Now, Mr. Morgan, I have got you!"

Without hesitation Morgan's wife, Jessie, threw herself on Holt. As he struggled to get away from her, Jack Morgan crashed on top of him. Morgan, who weighed about 220 pounds, knocked the slighter man to the floor, fighting to get one of the guns out of Holt's hand. Two shots had already been fired and Morgan discovered only later that he had been hit by them both. One entered his groin and lodged near the base of his spinal column. The second went straight through his right thigh. Neither wound, as it turned out, was life-threatening. Holt still had another weapon in his left hand, which was pinned under Morgan's body, and he was struggling to free it, but before that happened Jessie Morgan had descended on him again and she and the children's nurse had wrenched it away from him. As Holt continued to resist, the butler brought down a heavy lump of coal smartly on his head, which ended the matter. The fight had only lasted a matter of minutes. Three days later Jack Morgan was doing well, according to his son Junius. He wanted to go downstairs and work at his desk, but his family would not let him. That was the day Holt slipped out of his cell in Nassau County Jail and threw himself to his death onto a concrete floor twenty feet below. It was determined later that he was actually Erich Muenter, a former Harvard instructor suspected of poisoning his wife with arsenic in Cambridge in 1906.

The *New York Times* wrote, "The attempted assassination of so prominent an American as Mr. Morgan . . . can have no other effect than that of turning public opinion against Germany and her cause." But more was to come. Before he died Holt had sent a letter to his wife claiming that two ships, the *Saxonia* of the Cunard Line and the *Philadelphia* of the American Line, which left New York on Saturday July 3, would blow up in mid-Atlantic on the seventh, if his calculations were correct. The lady told the authorities. Both boats were searched and all the cargo accounted for. Bombs on ships were on everyone's mind. Four British freighters that had been loaded from the South Brooklyn piers in April and May were belatedly found to have had bombs in their cargo. These were not discovered until the ships were unloaded in Le Havre; luckily none of them had gone off. It seemed as if Holt's threat had been baseless. But then, on the afternoon of July 7, the day he had predicted, another ocean liner blew up at sea, the *Minnehaha,* owned by the Atlantic Transport line. An explosion in hold number 3 shook the vessel from stem to stern, stunning some members of the crew and throwing others into the air. The explosion left no doubt in anyone's mind that this was the boat Holt had really been talking about. No one thought he could have done all this by himself. He had to have had accomplices.

WALL STREET WAS AT LAST aware of the danger presented by crazed professors willing to assassinate bankers on the wrong side of the European conflict. Everyone seemed to be hiring bodyguards, although, the *New York Times* observed, Mr. William Rockefeller and Mr. John D. Rockefeller Jr. had been seen walking unaccompanied down Wall Street, the way they always did. It was true that the Morgan bank was taking precautions. Plain-clothes men were on duty inside the bank and out, and customers with business for the Allies were escorted to the doors of taxis and sent safely on their way. Nothing happening in the months that followed would have made those men in prominent positions feel any easier. Bombs continued to be found on ships—seventeen by the autumn of 1915. There were outbreaks of strikes in munitions factories, factory fires and explosions, passport frauds, and by October there was another assassination attempt, this one on Franklin R. Voorhees, a Chicago broker in war materials.

There was surely no danger to Joseph and Henry Duveen as owners of an establishment devoted to the innocent pursuit of art. Or was there? It was the moment for the appearance of a curious figure whom no one could ever explain. He was Bertram Boggis, an English merchant seaman who had left his calling in January 1915 because, according to him, he did not fancy being blown up by U-boats. He was on the New York waterfront doing odd jobs when he saw an advertisement by Duveen Brothers for a warehouse porter. There was a queue of applicants, and, according to Colin Simpson in *Artful Partners,* Boggis kept being rejected and returning to the end of the line to start all over again. Boggis: the very name suggested a bulldog manner. Duveen dressed him up in a doorman's uniform complete with gold braid and instructed him to preside over the entrance hall of the Fifth Avenue building. Concealed in the coat's capacious outlines were a gun and a marlinespike, a naval accessory which he presumably knew how to use. Boggis proceeded to make himself useful in so many ways that he inherited, not just a small part of Duveen Brothers after his master died, but the utterly undeserved reputation of being knowledgeable about art.

That year of 1915, Duveen Brothers began to keep a scrapbook. Thanks to Joseph Duveen's passion for organization, Duveen Brothers was building a library and a handsome archive into which carbons of letters and new correspondence were constantly being filed. On occasion Duveen would keep scrapbooks, although these were very few and usually limited to legal suits. It seems odd, therefore, that in 1915 he would keep a scrapbook about a particular German plot to blow up American ships. It was called the Fay case.

So far bombs had been smuggled aboard boats with mixed results. Robert Fay, a lieutenant in the Imperial German Army, was an expert electrician and chemist with a new idea. Instead of smuggling a bomb on board, he would build a mine that could be attached to the rudder of a ship. As the ship began to move, a bronze cord attached to a rachet would gradually be pulled away and two firing pins released to explode the TNT within. As designed, the mine would not go off until the ship was in deep water. It was, in a sense, even better than a torpedo, which might miss its target. The hapless ship would be carrying its own destruction and no one on board could prevent it.

Robert Fay made his way to New York under a pseudonym and bought a thirty-two-foot motorboat, essential if he was to experiment with the right kind of clamps for his underwater bombs. He and his brother-in-law, Walter Schultz, a mechanical draftsman, set up an experimental laboratory in Grantwood, New Jersey, and began to negotiate for raw materials, using $30,000 in hand. They had established a quiet connection with a pro-German munitions broker in New York, and the goods started to roll in: dynamite, TNT, fulminate cans, fuses, cartridges, and the like. Obviously they needed recruits, and other men began to join the conspiracy. There were Paul Daeche, a young German, who did some of the actual buying; Dr. Herbert Kienzle, an inventor and engineer; Paul Seibe, another sympathizer; and Max Breitung, secretary and treasurer of the Oil Well Supply Company.

All this was happening in the summer of 1915 just after the assassination attempt on Morgan by Holt (alias Muenter), whom Fay reportedly knew. He also knew Rintelen. He was taking every precaution to escape notice, and the curious fact is that from the first Fay and friends seem to have been intently watched; spies were spying on the spies. According to a Secret Service report on counterespionage written twenty years later, the Fay ring was discovered before it could do much damage because a certain Contesse de Beckendorf, who was "close" to the munitions broker, tipped off the Secret Service "in a fit of jealous pique." According to newspaper reports, someone else was already keeping the service fully informed: he was Paul Seibe, who, it turned out, was a double agent. On October 25, 1915, Fay's room in an apartment house on Fifth Street, Weehawken, was raided and found to contain eight sticks of dynamite, more than eighty pounds of TNT, and eight completed bombs. Fay and Schultz were tracked to a wood near Grantwood, and arrested. Fay readily confessed, which made people suspicious, particularly when his brother-in-law said cheerfully, "It looks like twenty years, doesn't it?" The *New York Times* wrote, "And the police are now asking why it is that the prisoners gave up so easily . . ."

As for Max Breitung, the young oil well executive, he readily revealed he had met Paul Daeche on an Atlantic crossing and had given him some advice about buying copper and other kinds of metals without once suspecting any nefarious intent. He was a cousin of his employer, E. N. Breitung, head of the banking firm of that name, a wealthy mining engineer and real-estate developer. He presented himself to the authorities early in November and was released on $25,000 bail.

E. N. Breitung came to his cousin's defense. He said he had heard a rumor that the conspiracy had been an English plot and that Robert Fay was actually a British or French agent.

This raises a number of interesting questions, even though Fay was tried and convicted. Shortly after his incarceration in the Atlanta federal prison in 1916, Fay and another prisoner made a well-planned escape. Fay was not found until the end of the war, when he turned up in Spain. Even if, as was widely believed, Fay was a genuine German agent, his plot was known almost as soon as it was hatched; and if Duveen was privy to the secret, it was for a very good reason. The second Lord Esher, a good friend of his, now a member of the British Imperial War Council, had asked Duveen if he could borrow some unused office space in Paris for military purposes. Duveen of course agreed. The military body in question was the Army Intelligence Corps. Fowles wrote, "In less than no time our fine offices which overlooked the Marché St. Honoré were occupied by a very busy military staff." This is the link, and would explain the intentness with which Duveen followed every twist and turn of the case, as it came to light that autumn of 1915. Interestingly, Max Breitung was absolved of any wrongdoing. His lawyer in the case was John Stanchfield, one of Duveen's team of lawyers.

That the British had an urgent interest in getting the U.S. into the war against Germany goes without saying. It is clear that the policy of conciliation toward Germany being conducted by President Wilson was arousing opposition. The election campaign of 1916 was coming up, and even though Wilson would win by a narrow margin, it seemed evident that American neutrality would have to end, if only because of repeated German attacks on neutral American ships. In fact, the struggles of 1915 have to be seen against the backdrop of the equally intense battle being waged for American public opinion and the future of Europe. A certain sense of his role on the world stage seemed to take hold of Duveen's imagination at this pivotal moment. On the one hand he began to labor under the innocent delusion that his every pronouncement was being sought and pondered over by princes. That was the regrettable part. On the other hand, this sense of responsibility would show itself more and more as, in the next two decades, he began to display acts of generosity unequaled by any other dealer in his sometimes grubby world. Duveen the megalomaniac and Duveen the great patron of art battled it out and somehow coexisted.

DUVEEN WAS USUALLY EMBROILED in a lawsuit, and it is tempting to think that these costly and time-consuming battles of wits took place because a side of his nature positively relished them. It was an extension of that competition for first place that had been the leitmotif of his life. Part of it must also be ascribed to his fondness for hyperbole. A work of art was not only the most divine object he had ever seen (like babies) or the most execrable, ridiculous, shameful, hateful, and obviously false piece of work he had ever seen in his life. One wonders which gave him most pleasure: flaunting a provocative opinion or rescuing himself from a hair-raising situation with dramatic last-minute reprieves. Like Frank Lloyd Wright, he specialized in triumphantly surmounting the obstacles that he had placed in his own path.

That first lawsuit in which he won his Pyrrhic victory against Jack Duveen (or lost it, depending on one's viewpoint) was a forerunner of all the other victories and defeats he suffered in his career of costly legal wranglings. There was, it is true, a small tussle between Duveen Brothers and a certain Mrs. Charlotte Springer, who sued to recover what she claimed was $20,000 due on a commission involving the sale of tapestries owned by the King of Spain to the late J. Pierpont Morgan. That was a trifling affair, made interesting only by the lady's determined efforts. After three attempts, Mrs. Springer finally lost when the Appellate Division of the New York State Supreme Court rejected her arguments in the summer of 1916. There would always be middlemen and -women who believed money was owed, and most of them went away because the burden of proof was on them. Dealers who claimed other dealers were denigrating their goods had a similar dilemma. Everybody knew, as Jack Duveen ceaselessly pointed out, that the quickest way to dispose of a rival was to claim he was selling a fake or, as it was politely termed, a "modern copy." This was equally hard to answer, which was why it was such a popular accusation on both sides of the Atlantic, and a dealer would have to be really outraged to retaliate, knowing how hard it was to prove a negative.

It is no surprise that, in his all-out campaign to win over Frick and annihilate the competition, Joseph Duveen should try this trick on one of the dealers Frick had graced with his patronage. He was Edgar Gorer, a successful dealer in antiques and objets, with galleries on Bond Street and Fifth Avenue. In the early summer of 1915, he brought suit against Joseph and Henry Duveen, claiming they had "practically destroyed" his trade with Frick and other rich men by means of this time-honored expedient. His complaint made the front page of the *New York Times,* perhaps because he was suing for $575,000 in damages. Gorer claimed that earlier in the year, he had tried to sell Frick a valuable antique Chinese vase from the K'ang-hsi period but that Joe Duveen told Frick and his wife it was a modern copy. The dealer, Duveen claimed, had been hoodwinked. His uncle quietly backed him up.

To have a junior Duveen, with an admittedly sketchy knowledge of oriental porcelain, slap down an outrageous assertion was one thing. To have a senior, with decades of specialized knowledge behind him, make the same claim was quite another. If Uncle Henry thought something was fishy, he was probably right. But Gorer, who had seen Duveen, by then, starting to make big sales to Frick, was fighting for his commercial life. In the battle to monopolize a big client's confidence, he could not afford to ignore either Duveen. He had to win.

The announcement of the suit was made on May 7, 1915. That was the day Edgar Gorer was crossing the Atlantic on the *Lusitania* and the very day it was torpedoed. Gorer lost his life. It would not be the last time that fate had saved Duveen from an awkward and expensive confrontation but then, like Frank Lloyd Wright, he seemed to live a charmed life.*

A painting by George Romney, *The Kemble Sisters,* which was bought by Henry E. Huntington in 1913, presented a more challenging case. The portrait of two sisters depicted them strolling through what might be a stagy, stormy landscape—or maybe they were clouds. At any rate they were identified as the actress and author Fanny Kemble, member of a famous theatrical family, and her even more illustrious sister, the actress Mrs. Siddons. The painting was bought, not from Duveen, but from Lewis and Simmons, art dealers in New Bond Street with a branch on Fifth Avenue, for £20,000. Lewis and Simmons had acquired the work from a picture dealer in King Street, St. James's, who had paid 361 guineas (£379) for it in a knockout. It was then described as by Sir Joshua Reynolds, and Lewis and Simmons had bought it for considerably more than 361 guineas but certainly less than £20,000.

Reynolds was a pretty good name, but for some reason Lewis and Simmons decided to rebaptize the painting as by Romney. They had found, in Romney's appointment book, two references in 1776 and 1777 to sittings with "the ladies." Although no names were given the dealers decided these must be the Kemble sisters, and were positive enough about their belief to give Huntington some gilt-edged guarantees. Sometime later Huntington hung the picture in his rooms in the Metropolitan Club in New York and was heard boasting about his new Romney. In due course Duveen made his usual confident assertion that the picture could not possibly be by Rom-

---

*The *Lusitania* was carrying several prominent members of the art world. Others who died were Sir Hugh Lane, the newly appointed director of the National Gallery of Ireland; Charles F. Fowles, of Scott and Fowles, and his wife; and Gerald Letts, the London dealer. Frank Partridge was rescued from the water hours after the boat sank.

ney. He did not actually call it a fake. His argument, advanced with his usual bubbling good humor and conviction, was enough for Huntington. In 1917 Lewis and Simmons refused to take the painting back and Huntington brought suit.

One can predict Duveen's argument in cases of this kind. He might not have the expert knowledge to positively assert that a work was, or was not, by a certain Old Master. He could feel it in his bones. There was something about the aura presented by a painting, perhaps. Or his instinct, refined by

A painting bought by Henry E. Huntington in 1913
as *The Kemble Sisters* by Sir Joshua Reynolds, which
turned out to be of the Waldegrave sisters and by the
lesser-known painter Ozias Humphrey

decades of studying paintings, might be more like it. For there was no other way to educate the eye except, as Berenson said, to look and look until you had trained yourself to appreciate subtleties that escaped all but the keenest of observers. In the case of *The Kemble Sisters,* such an argument might be mere sophistry. Perhaps Duveen, with his expert spy network, had discovered how modest the painting's provenance was and how unlikely the Lewis and Simmons argument that it had to be a Romney. He could safely cast doubt on such a claim. Yet even if he did know the painting's sales history, one suspects that he also used the argument of his own eye when he went to inspect the portrait at the Metropolitan Club. As devious as he was capable of being, it is clear that he became an authority on authorship, particularly where eighteenth-century English portraiture was concerned. He might just be right.

Since in this case the client was suing, Duveen was in no immediate danger of having a lawsuit land on him. Still, just to be on the safe side, he made it his business to see that the lawyer representing H.E.H. was his own lawyer, Louis Levy. Every time the plaintiff's lawyers attempted to point out that Huntington had brought his suit because of Duveen, Mr. Levy was ready to jump in with an objection—in the interests of fairness, of course.

Huntington readily conceded at the trial that he was not an expert on art. What he wanted, and had begun to buy in quantity, were English portraits in the grand manner, and the Romney *Kemble Sisters* seemed suitably grand. One, presumably Mrs. Siddons, is in profile, her right arm raised as if pointing prophetically toward their glorious future. The other, presumably Fanny, is in the foreground, pausing in her stride to strike a fetching pose, her left hand resting just below her waist. The rocky path, the scanty, low-cut dresses, and the billowing capes are all dramatic enough. But the classically Greek features have the vapid and unlikely look of all such feminine ideals of beauty down through the ages; to stamp his sitters with such stereotyped expressions is the kind of mistake no great artist would make. Romney's portrait of Lady Broughton, now at the Huntington Museum in San Marino, who is also seen out walking in some Thespian-like scenery, which is close in feeling, shows a vivacity and singularity, not to mention masterful handling of detail and finish, absent from the so-called Kemble work. It seems almost painted by numbers.

The arguments were heard by Mr. Justice Darling, by general agreement as elegant and artistically well-informed a judge as anyone could wish. As the days rolled on, one expert after another was called in to express his absolute confidence, amounting to a conviction, that the joint portrait had to be a Romney, countered by all the other experts who expressed their absolute confidence, amounting to etc., that the portrait could not possibly be by Romney. The argument was rapidly deteriorating into name calling and the kind of impasse in which nobody, on whichever side of the argument, likes to be embroiled.

Then came the eleventh-hour save. It would appear, according to Behrman, that Duveen had taken the precaution of checking up on the story of the portrait as told by Lewis and Simmons. Behrman's version usually flatters the Duveen position, that it was his foresight, his clever anticipation of the truth of a matter, that won through in the end. It therefore should be approached with caution, knowing just how often Duveen was really saved by a piece of dumb luck.

The luck in this case came in the form of a small-time scout named Vickers, who had worked in the art world all his life and was then almost eighty. He recalled that in his youth, he had been told by an old London picture dealer that Horace Walpole, the English politician and man of letters, had grandnieces named Maria and Horatia Waldegrave. A painter of miniatures by the name of Ozias Humphry had asked Walpole if he might paint the two beauties. Walpole gave his consent but did not actually commission the work. Humphry was delighted with the result and perhaps the ladies were too, but Walpole did not like the painting and would not buy it.

This put an entirely different light on the matter. If it could be shown that the sitters were not the famous Kemble sisters but the less famous Waldegrave ones, and that the painter was a minor miniaturist who had painted a portrait nobody wanted, Duveen was off the hook. But Duveen's really clever idea (according to Behrman) was to check up on the movements of the Kemble sisters on the days when they were supposed to have been sitting for Romney. It was learned that Mrs. Siddons was playing in Birmingham (a playbill was found attesting to this fact) and Miss Kemble was abroad—in France. According to a more sober account, lawyers on both sides were involved in the sleuthing, which was only completed on the very last day of the trial. What actually clinched the matter, according to Barnett Hollander in *The International Law of Art*, was the discovery in the library of the Royal Academy of a sketch, signed by Humphry, which was plainly a preliminary study for the picture. The defense collapsed. Huntington got his money back, plus interest, plus £10,000 in costs. Duveen picked up all sorts of laurels for his prescience and absolutely infallible eye. As for the inglorious Humphry portrait, Gerald Reitlinger noted that in 1944 it was sold for sixty-three pounds.

IN THE SCRAMBLE FOR INSTANT ANCESTORS continually being fostered by all those American "squillionaires," Gainsborough reigned supreme, but there were times when Sir Thomas Lawrence and even the Scottish painter Henry Raeburn were swept along in the general American pandemonium. Romney, whom René Gimpel dismissed as a dreadfully bad painter—he was probably right—continued to take their fancy, particularly if more of his works had the name Emma Hamilton attached, and even if they did not. His portrait of Anne de la Pole came up at auction in the Oppenheim sale at Christie's in 1913, and Duveen made the winning bid of £41,370 ($243,600). He sold it that year to the first Baron Michelham; the painting is now at the Boston Museum of Fine Arts. Romney's portrait *Miss Penelope Lee-Acton,* from the collection of Lord de Saumarez, sold for the equally handsome sum of £45,000, or $225,000, and made its way to Henry E. Huntington in 1916. The stratospheric prices being obtained consolidated Duveen's steady climb to the absolute pinnacle of the international market in Old Masters, war or no war.

Then there were the Italian Renaissance paintings Berenson was unearthing and the continuing sell-offs of the Morgan collections. Duveen had the most of the best, which did not prevent his restless search for more and better yet. For several years he had been following the status of a collection of fine French furniture assembled by a well-known collector, a Monsieur Chabrières-Arlès of Paris and Lyons: 250 items, mostly French and Italian Renaissance furniture and furnishings by the greatest artisans in Lyon. Edward Fowles, in Paris, was given the responsibility of negotiating and completed it successfully; Duveens paid $1.5 million. The irreplaceable objects, most of museum quality, were crated and shipped to New York, where they arrived safely despite the German submarines.

The very fact that Duveen Brothers were paying such huge sums was having a reinforcing effect on the market. Works of certain artists must be priceless, because Joseph Duveen thought so. Voices like Gimpel's who actually dared to question the relative merits of paintings were drowned out in the general clamor to find out how Duveen did it. This had its good and its bad aspects. Duveen no longer needed to convince his clients of anything. On the other hand, as he would learn to his cost, paintings that came back on the market with his provenance had to be supported, no matter what their real worth, and no matter what the cost to the firm, in the essential business of maintaining the Duveen illusion.

The very idea, however, that a work might ever be worth less than it had, would have seemed preposterous in those prosperous days. Duveen Brothers could look toward the future with confidence. The United States was about to enter the war at last; a British victory had been ensured. Money was rolling in. Flushed with success, Duveen made the predictable shift of direction: he began to look for a way to give money away. One of the surprising aspects of this infinitely surprising personality is the muted thread that runs beneath everything he said and did: he really loved art. Not just Turner, or the Old Masters; his determination to learn absolutely everything about his world had turned him at an early stage toward modern art. In the years before his father gave Sargent's *Ellen Terry as Lady Macbeth* (1905) to the Tate, Duveen began attending the summer and autumn exhibitions of the New English Art Club, then held in a small one-room gallery off the Egyptian Hall, Piccadilly. The British equivalent of the Salon des Réfusés in Paris, the New English Art Club, founded in 1888, was reacting against the salon orthodoxies of the Royal Academy and the work of painters like James Sant, Frederick Goodall, Lawrence Alma-Tadema, Cadogan Cowper, and J. W. Waterhouse.

These, and other completely forgotten artists, were, in 1901, delivering their variations on historical and/or mythological subjects, set pieces such as Benjamin Constant's idealized portrait of Queen Victoria or exotica like *Snake Charmer, Cairo* by Frederick Goodall. By contrast, a new generation of young painters such as Wilson Steer, Walter Sickert, Roger Fry, Muirhead Bone, and William Orpen were turning, as did members of the Ashcan school in the U.S. at about the same time, to real studies of real people in real situations. The work was fresh, vivid, arresting, and for the most part unbought.

Duveen found this shocking. He personally knew of Englishmen with incomes of £4,000 a year who did not have a single original painting in the house. Something must be done. Obviously the British public needed educating. It was a logical extension of the role he had assumed: part salesman, part parent, part teacher, part public scold. He wrote, "These people have got to be educated, and the best way of educating them is by exhibitions which have catalogues with the prices of the exhibits marked in plain figures." The next-best way was through museum exhibitions. There too, as perhaps he knew already, a stubborn right not to know pervaded the highest circles. As Frances Spalding observed in her history of the Tate, in 1918 the distinguished director of the National Gallery, C. J. Holmes, refused to buy a Cézanne even though he had a special government grant and came back from Paris with the money unspent. It was clear that, if the British were ignorant about their own artists, they were even more ignorant about the great waves of thought sweeping the Continent and artists like Van Gogh, Manet, Monet, Sisley, Renoir, and all the others. Duveen intended to act.

When Joel Duveen had given his Turner wing on two floors to the Tate, and there was no money for a linking staircase, Joseph Duveen provided it. He found money in 1915 to redecorate some of the rooms and more money for the proper display of Turner's *Liber Studiorum*. In 1919 he presented Gauguin's *Faa Iheihe* (1898) to the Tate. He paid for a new mosaic pavement by Boris Anrep to replace an original pink terrazzo pavement that was damaged during a Zeppelin raid. He established a small yearly fund for the purchase of watercolors and drawings. But it was his offer in 1915 to pay for a set of modern foreign galleries that marked him as a major contributor to the Tate. He would eventually pledge £30,000, a very large gift in those days, to build four new galleries and attach another room specifically to honor the American artist John Singer Sargent. Green marble doorways, brown silk wall coverings, painted and gilt ceilings, walnut seats, and marble-bordered parquet floors further added to the cost. He donated three more paintings: Sargent's oil study for *Madame Gautreau,* Augustus John's *Madame Suggia,* and Sargent's *Claude Monet Painting at the Edge of a Wood.* The Tate had to put something in all those nice empty rooms. In 1925, thanks to the new Courtauld Fund, they graciously accepted works by Van Gogh, Degas, Utrillo, Seurat, and even Cézanne. When the new rooms were finally opened in 1926 the trustees resisted all of Duveen's blandishments and declined to hang a portrait of his father or install a bust of Duveen himself. But they did consent to some large elaborate lettering over the main doorway naming the donor, executed by the talented Eric Gill, which pleased him well enough.

THE FIRM WAS IMMENSELY PROSPEROUS and rapidly getting richer—in 1920 its net profits were an amazing $710,032—but there were periodic rumblings beneath the surface to remind Duveen that he still had siblings with powerful interests willing, if necessary, to make life nasty and expensive. First of all his younger brother Louis, who had been educated at Oxford and was playing a pivotal role in the London house, took it into his head to break away. He wanted his brother Ernest, the firm's London expert on the Italian Renaissance, to join him, and approached Fowles to become a third partner. Louis was always thought of as delicate and stammered when he was nervous. Fowles was not at all sure about his business acumen, but Ernest was a different matter. Fowles's opinion of Ernest had been influenced by Uncle Henry, who always said that the younger Duveens were "all lazy and not workers." But he came to think that Ernest was very astute, if not the cleverest of them all.

If Ernest were part of the equation, Fowles must have reasoned, this would be an interesting proposition. However, just then Ernest was in France, a captain in the fledgling British Flying Corps (later the Royal Air Force). Louis had been excused from service. Edward, or Eddie, then thirty-nine, joined up and was given a lieutenant's commission but was discharged two years later on the grounds of ill health: asthma, emphysema, neurasthenia, and a heart condition. Eddie had, like his brothers, a flair for beautiful things. Jack Duveen recalled how, when Eddie was just a schoolboy, he found a Delft pottery replica of a fabulous Chinese animal made by Adriaan Pijnacker, one of the greatest Delft potters. Eddie bought it in a shop in Soho for two shillings and sixpence, something like fifty cents, and Jack sold it in Amsterdam for £125 ($625).

After starting in business under the name of Hamilton & Co. (because Joe would not let him trade as a Duveen), Eddie subsequently set up shop in his own name before joining Duveen Brothers as a director, presumably around the time of his discharge from the army in 1916. While Ernest and Louis played the principal roles as scouts, Eddie kept the day-to-day business affairs going in the London office, which soon moved to 4 Grafton Street around the corner from Bond Street. With the loss of Ernest, his presence there was essential. Fowles had been drafted, which annoyed him as "the vast majority of critics, dealers and museum officials seemed immune," including, of course, Joseph Duveen.

Louis's idea hinged on Ernest (presumably Edward was not interested), who was having adventures of his own. In the summer of 1916 he was flying over the German lines at a height of eight thousand feet when his engine failed and he had to jump for his life. He fell, unconscious but not badly hurt, just inside the British lines.

The confrontation rapidly became as rancorous as the one that almost destroyed the family firm ten years before. By the summer of 1917 all communication between Louis in London and Uncle Henry and Joe in New York had stopped, and Joe was particularly upset that Ernest had sided against him. The complaint was made to Lockett Agnew, grandson of Thomas Agnew, who had founded the firm in 1817 and with whom Duveen Brothers had made many satisfactory sales over the years. By then Louis and Ernest had lost their bid to buy Duveen Brothers from Joe and Uncle Henry, but they had received a cash settlement and approached Agnew's in an apparent attempt to cut out the New York office.

Lockett Agnew who, as Joe Duveen's senior by a decade, was something of an elder statesman in their world, replied he would be happy to negotiate but would only take a 25 percent interest, instead of the usual half, and would be bound to offer the other 25 percent to Duveen Brothers in New York. Agnew had been hearing a great deal about the "internal eruptions," he told Joe, and agreed that Louis was very bitter about what had happened. He wrote, "I have told him that what he says to me he must say to no one else, that I am going to forget all about it, and that quarrelling amongst families is a fatal error and an ugly spectacle, and that everything ought to be arranged amicably." This eminently sane advice appeared to have had its effect. At any rate, Louis changed his mind and retired quite happily, as Edward Fowles had suspected he would. (He died in 1920 at the age of forty-six.)

Ernest settled his differences with Joe and returned to the firm. Benjamin was already in New York, and in 1919 Armand Lowengard made his appearance. This nephew, Esther's son, would turn out to be one of Duveen's most valuable employees. He was studying at Oxford but left at the outbreak of war to enlist in the French army. He was badly treated as a German prisoner and received a severe wound which continued to trouble him. These harrowing experiences for a man barely in his twenties (he was born in 1893) left him with an understandable sense of outrage that would erupt at the most inconvenient moments. The second the conversation turned in the right direction Armand would insist on disrobing to display his scar, which was located, as Edward Fowles delicately put it, in the region of the lower back. Fowles wrote, "He did this in Alec Waugh's presence once, and in due course poor Armand's 'little trait' appeared in the novel, *Island in the Sun.*" Lowengard was no businessman, but he had a kind of genius for recognizing quality in art and would become indispensable in Paris.

With Ernest and Edward in London, along with the reliable Silva White, Duveen Brothers was patching itself back together even before Lowengard joined the firm. But in June 1917, just as matters seemed to be on the mend, Uncle Henry had a stroke. His health had been poor ever since the disastrous customs suit, and it soon became obvious he would never get better. Like his brother before him, he was visibly shrinking. Even though the main work of the New York house had been conducted by Joe for several years, the fact is that Uncle Henry's contacts, expertise, and hard-earned business acumen were priceless assets. His death in 1919 threw the firm's future into doubt once more. It did not help that Frick had just died and had, at the eleventh hour, returned $1 million worth of mer-

The newly knighted Sir Joseph and Lady Duveen in 1919

chandise that he had been about to purchase. Duveen knew he would have to negotiate for Uncle Henry's share of the business with his only son, Geoffrey, then a lieutenant in the British Army, and a huge financial reorganization went on for the next two or three years.

Balanced against this was the fact that business had never been better. The Huntingtons in particular, who had been making noises about leaving their estate with its books and art collection to the nation for years, had started to take themselves seriously and created the Huntington Library, Art Gallery and Botanical Gardens in San Marino in August of that year. Duveen could now appeal (and did), not just to their fancy for eighteenth-century British paintings, but to their need to "balance" their collection with whatever he could think of. Besides, he liked Geoffrey and no doubt took to heart Lockett Agnew's advice, offering the latter some very generous terms. These were accepted and, at long last, Duveen was uncontested master of all he surveyed. He also received a signal honor: he was knighted. Colin Agnew, Lockett's nephew, wrote in the summer of 1919 to congratulate him upon the honor: He could not think of anyone who deserved it more.

Chapter Nine

THE CHASE CONTINUES

T HE DECADE OF THE 1920S was the high point of Duveen's spectacular career, ample reward for all those years of patient negotiation, family crises, financial disappointments and reversals. Times were changing and Duveen was changing with them. He was too human not to continue taking his usual cock-of-the-walk pleasure in each new acquisition and the prices which continued to soar, it would seem, endlessly upward. But his triumphs were increasingly shaded, as he reached the age of fifty, by presentiments of the future, just as his clients were beginning to take account of their own lives and their legacies. He had appreciated the lengths J. P. Morgan took in assembling an art collection which he tried to give to the nation. Altman had already given his treasures away. The terms of the will left by Frick bequeathed his Fifth Avenue mansion to a board of trustees which was instructed to make it a center for the study of art. He had watched the idea of the public good creeping by degrees over H. E. Huntington and his spendthrift, generous, fastidiously perceptive wife. Many, if not most, of the collections being assembled by his American clients seemed destined to end up in the public's hands. Duveen's sales techniques would adjust to the new realities, but, in fairness to him, this was not the whole story. He genuinely shared his clients' pleasure in giving, and that made him, if not original, highly unusual.

Besides, there were so many wonderful things to sell and so many opportunities to insert other schools of paintings into collections that the fledgling benefactors might never have heard of. The race to get there first was, if anything, picking up speed, and Duveen Brothers were always on the move.

Even before the war Mary Berenson had remarked upon their break-neck pace. She wrote in 1913: "Ernest, the youngest partner, went from Paris to London on Monday." (An all-day trip by train and channel steamer.) "On Tuesday night, to Edinburgh." (An all-night trip.) "Back to London on Wednesday night, crossed to Paris Thursday, started for Florence Friday and starts back to Paris today, Sunday. Not all the riches of the Orient would tempt me to lead such a life. And he doesn't sleep on trains!" She was from an older generation for whom travel was considered arduous, uncertain, and expensive and undertaken with frequent pauses for rest in between. To see Ernest shuttling between Florence and Edinburgh would have seemed against the natural order of things. There was something almost grotesque about all that haste. Her comment underscores the extent to which Duveen goaded his scouts in London and Paris, firing off commands by the hour (his hand, presumably, resting on a European timetable) and doodling on the latest cable.

Duveen, in a most uncharacteristic setting, on the beach at the Lido in Venice. Daughter Dorothy is sitting beside him; an American friend, Mr. Heilbut, is at top right and Dorothy's cousin Claude is seated below him. Claude, one of Louis's children, later became His Honour Judge Duveen.

Almost any sale, if dangled enticingly enough, could arouse his instinct for the chase. On Monday, April 4, 1921, he received a cable from the Paris office saying that a rich and prominent Viennese industrialist had just died, and asking whether he was interested in buying two Boucher pictures from the late collector's holdings. These had been acquired from Duveen Brothers in 1896. Duveen had offered four thousand pounds for them in 1909. Was he still interested?

A day later, on Tuesday, April 5, Duveen replied in code from New York that these were the best examples of Boucher's work extant and he had to have them. These, he told Fowles, were just the kind of "great things" he was constantly talking about and worth ten thousand pounds at least. Fowles should be leaving for Vienna at once. Unfortunately, as Duveen knew, Fowles was stuck in Paris because other business was hanging fire. On the other hand, if Fowles were to cable his acceptance, the nephew who made the offer might take this evidence of Duveen's willingness to buy to sell them to someone else. The only thing to do was to send Armand out by the next train, hinting that a sale might be in the offing. Duveen wanted an immediate reply from Fowles. Fowles cabled the next day that Armand was leaving for Vienna immediately and that he quite agreed with Duveen that this was the best course. A week later, Fowles was free to go to Vienna to join Lowengard. Duveen ordered Fowles to take enough money to pay for the Bouchers and bring them back with him. The business about a Romney that was also for sale was not so pressing. He did not want the Bouchers to be lost, because he was "crazy" about them.

By April 20 the Bouchers had been captured for four thousand pounds. Duveen was anxious. Had Fowles given them a deposit? Did they have anything in writing? There were export formalities to be considered. Did Fowles think this was going to be difficult? Duveen needed reassurances.

A day later Fowles, who was back in Paris, told Duveen he had not paid a deposit and had nothing in writing. Their contact was the Norwegian consul and a very rich man. He was selling only because he wanted to build up funds in his Swiss bank account. No one wanted Austrian kroner, as the money was devaluing by the hour and, in April 1921, scarcely worth the paper it was printed on. There was the further complication of a permit from the Austrian government, which was imposing 12.5 percent export taxes and insisting that money from any sales remain in the country. The only solution was to have a private agreement with the consul that, for official purposes, the Bouchers would be sold for a thousand pounds, to be paid in kroner, whilst the balance of the money would go into the Swiss bank account. Naturally the client did not want this in writing.

Duveen was not happy. He thought Armand should go back to Vienna and hover about until the Bouchers were placed in his hands. He wrote, "If Wildenstein hears of these 2 Bouchers you will absolutely lose them and it is ridiculous to reason otherwise." Armand stayed home anyway, and the pictures arrived six or seven weeks later, on June 7. They badly needed cleaning but would look marvelous. This made Duveen nervous. How marvelous? How were they framed? How *should* they be framed? Much anxious questioning followed before he was satisfied that his jewels would be displayed to their best advantage. He was appeased, if momentarily. There was always another crisis.

BY THEN DUVEEN WAS HABITUALLY DEALING in six-figure sales, and so the amount of time and energy expended on the purchase of two Bouchers, however attractive, when the profit was so marginal, is curious. It illustrates, if illustration were needed, the aesthetic nature of his response to a challenge as well as its compulsive aspects. If one thought of him as superficial and easily distracted, one would be wrong. Behind the bombast was a cool head plotting to reach goals that could be long-term and might never materialize. The contrast between the gentlemanly atmosphere in the grand old firm of Thomas Agnew & Sons and the manner of the upstart Duveens is instructive. While Lockett and his cousins Colin and Gerald Agnew were perfectly positioned to take advantage of whatever deals came to their door—and their contacts with the British aristocracy were legendary—they were less likely to take aggressive advantage of deals that might be on the distant horizon or bid for the big pictures that might make their fortunes or bankrupt them. Besides, they were gentlemen with gentlemanly lives. Duveen was always ahead because he had no other life. Home, wife, daughter, family, hobbies: other interests were subservient to the one compelling interest of his life. As Mary Berenson also noticed on that visit of the Duveens in 1913, "We talked politely on various topics for the first half hour—and then I broached the selling of pictures, and a loud sigh of satisfaction went up to the ceiling, and we settled in to a thoroughly congenial topic."

Too, Duveen had the edge because he did not mind the gamble, in fact positively relished it. A case in point is the Holford Collection, which came up for sale in the 1920s. It consisted of a few very good pictures and some less interesting ones. The trustees naturally wanted to sell the whole collection. Duveen naturally wanted to take the best and leave the rest. It was an impasse, so he amiably suggested that the collection be sold at auction and recommended Messrs Christie, Manson and Woods. But, as he wrote to Sir Alec Martin, its chief auctioneer, he had already told the trustees they stood to make far more from individual sales than by auction and he was so sure he was right that he had a bet with the principal trustee that the whole collection would not fetch half a million pounds. It was a very disadvantageous one to him personally. If it fetched less than that, he would win a hundred pounds. But if it fetched more, Duveen would pay out a thousand pounds. Duveen wrote, "Privately, however, I do not think it will fetch more than 300,000 pounds, and then everything would depend on me, how I felt, particularly perhaps, in regard to my stomach." That elliptical comment does at least point to the idea that Duveen, so confident on the surface, ever prepared to outplot and outmaneuver his competitors in the game of high stakes, was paying a certain price. What made the task so taxing was the uncertainty of the outcome, the last-minute delays and disappointments, and the jockeying for position that could sometimes drag out for a decade or more. It was enough to give anyone a stomach ache.

DESPITE OCCASIONAL SETBACKS the years after World War I are a long success story of pictures fought for and won, sometimes against great odds. In 1919 alone, he acquired Rembrandt's portrait of Flora, now at the Metropolitan; a triptych by Cimabue depicting Christ, St. Peter, and St. James, from the Comtesse de Brousillon; two Frans Hals portraits; a marble bust of Louis XV by Lemoyne; a Terbourg; Falconet and Clodion sculptures; and Chinese and French porcelains. Descriptions of sales that year alone take up thirty pages in the Duveen books.

One of the Romneys Henry and Arabella Huntington had come to own during World War I is a painting of Penelope Lee-Acton. The young woman, a minister's daughter, is wearing a close-fitting white silk dress and a towering straw hat trimmed with an enormous silk bow. She is poised before a gentle landscape with the sun setting in the distance. Her head, turned to look away from the viewer, her casually linked hands, and her pensive look seem designed to reflect the mood of her recent marriage—her husband, Nathaniel Lee-Acton, was a widower whose first wife, Susannah, had recently died, and in fact Romney had also painted her. The pale, slim figure, the setting sun, the dark arch of trees, and the golds and mauves of the fields beyond are curiously elegiac, as if neither the husband nor his new wife dared to hope for too much happiness. The painting's emotional impact was quite striking, and it was a great coup for Duveen when he bought it from Agnew's for $225,000 just as the Germans were advancing on Paris. He had Frick in mind, but Frick would not buy. Naturally he immediately thought of the Huntingtons, who were then in Throgs Neck, New York, visiting one of their houses. Whether he sent them a photograph or the actual painting is not known, but in the summer of 1915 it was clear that they did not like it, either, perhaps finding something too sad and droopy about it—after all, they were newlyweds themselves. Using the method that he would often employ successfully with certain recalcitrant buyers, Duveen began to argue strenuously. He as good as told them that they *had* to like it. How could they not? It was the best Romney in existence. (This was a distinct overstatement.) He had paid more money for it than any other Romney, he said, which was likely. Then he even did something awful and unthinkable, from a dealer's point of view: he told them how much he had paid for it. He practically sent them a notarized copy of the sale. They succumbed and bought it a year later, probably at cost.

Duveen had far less trouble with another Romney, one of two he bought at the Duke of Hamilton sale at Christie's in November 1919, presumably because it had an imprimatur from Hamilton Palace itself. The Huntingtons did not take one of the Romneys, a portrait of Lord Courtenay, which Duveen bought for the modest sum of 16,000 guineas. But they were enchanted by a much more expensive Romney, *The Beckford Children*. Duveen paid in excess of $260,000 for it but obviously did not cite that figure to the Huntingtons, who bought the painting for more than $350,000.

That the Huntingtons should prefer this enchanting picture of two little girls in white dresses posed against a landscape that bears more than a passing resemblance to the one in the Penelope Lee-Acton picture is not surprising. They have rosy cheeks, pink lips, and curly hair, and are chubby, in common with so many idealized portraits of children in the eighteenth and nineteenth centuries. But as in so many portraits, their air of infant well-being belies a cruel reality. Their father, William Beckford of Fonthill Abbey, Wiltshire, was one of the richest men in England, having inherited a vast West Indian sugar fortune, but also one of the most eccentric and feckless. A committed homosexual, he had been dragooned into marriage by his formidable mother, who chose his bride: Lady Margaret Gordon, the pretty, good-natured blond niece of her friend Lady Euphemia Stewart. Lady Margaret appears to have perceived the true state of affairs and accepted him on his own terms; the relationship was affectionate, even close. But then she conceived, miscarried, and delivered a dead son, which put a strain on the marriage. There were further tensions when Beckford's predilection for boys began to be rumored and a peerage, which would have made him Baron Beckford of Fonthill, was withdrawn. His wife stayed with him loyally through the resulting scandal and bore a second child, their first daughter, Maria, in 1785. A second girl, Susan Euphemia, was born a year later; her mother died in agony of puerperal fever two weeks later. The daughters, who were cared for by their paternal grandmother, were fairly well ignored and slightingly treated by their father, who once said, "Why should I trouble myself more about them than about any other two young women I might happen to meet with?" That comment was made a year before Maria died in Bath in 1818 at the age of thirty-three. Still, Beckford liked Romney's work and it was a pretty painting.

The Wideners, another interesting American family of self-made men, this time from Philadelphia, were being cultivated with the same loving care Duveen was lavishing on the Huntingtons. P. A. B. Widener, the founder, born in 1834, began life as a butcher's boy. Unlike Joel Duveen, he stayed in the wholesale meat-packing business, and by the time of the Civil War he had built up his business and enough political contacts to win a contract to supply mutton to Union troops within ten miles of Philadelphia. In common with Joel Duveen, P. A. B. (always known as Peter) knew enough to know what he did not know, and cultivated the finer things in life with all the single-minded zeal he brought to his business affairs. By the turn of the century Widener had the same clever idea that H.E.H. had, i.e., that the suburbs needed attention. He switched from perishables to moving people around on streetcars and made an even bigger fortune. He had been collecting high art from about the 1880s and was grand enough to be painted by John Singer Sargent in 1902. But perhaps his most notable achievement was the construction of a vast palatial limestone mansion, Lynnewood Hall, on a three-hundred-acre estate in suburban Philadelphia (Elkins Park), worthy of an earl and a great deal more ostentatious than many English country houses. The entrance, with its vast portico supported by Corinthian columns, dominated the façade. This was bordered on either side by extensive residential wings with high-ceilinged, beautifully proportioned rooms stacked one behind the other in a classic enfilade. A third wing, directly behind the columned entrance, was reserved for art, and that was even grander, as befits a collection that would one day rival any assembled by all those other self-made men. Even the servants were grand. The butler never spoke to the housekeeper directly but sent her messages via the footmen; she replied by way of the housemaids.

The staff, naturally, was enormous, somewhat reduced during the Depression, when the owner was obliged to economize and fire six of the two dozen gardeners.

Uncle Henry, that clever and patient man, had put his foot in the door of the Widener façade as early as 1909. He began courting, not the great P.A.B. himself, or even his aesthetically minded son Joseph, but a nephew, George, confusingly given the same name as another son of P.A.B.'s, the one who was lost when the *Titanic* went down in 1912. The nephew George lived on happily for many years, buying art. He and Henry were great friends, shown by the unguarded detail with which the latter described his physical problems in the years before he died. They both loved orientalia, and George bought a long list of porcelains in 1919 to the tune of $300,000–$400,000. He also bought furnishings, tables, majolica, and paintings and entrusted to Duveen Brothers the kinds of fussy little repairs of pedestals and lampshades that they were almost masochistically willing to undertake. When George thought it might be nice to have his wife painted by Sir William Orpen (in 1920), Joseph Duveen, who had inherited him, airily arranged it.

By then Joseph had put his own foot in the door in the cause of embellishing the already spectacular art collection being assembled by the Wideners. Something about Duveen's willingness to go anywhere any time and expend any amount of energy to get something must have struck an answering chord in P.A.B., who died in 1915, and Joseph, who would outlive Duveen. Perhaps because of the early fakes they bought, Joseph Widener's goal, like that of Isabella Stewart Gardner and Arabella Huntington, became to demand the very best example of an artist's work. This saved Widener from pressure when Duveen was trying to sell something doubtful, but it also made him vulnerable when a really choice specimen swam into view, like the Small Cowper Madonna by Raphael, which he bought in 1914. A fifteenth-century bronze incense burner fashioned by Il Riccio of Padua, which went on sale in New York in 1916, was another example. Its previous home, the Davanzati Palace in Florence, with its columns, its opulent alcoves, its imposing staircases and vast ceilings of gilded wood, equaled anything Lynnewood Hall had to offer, and perhaps that was part of its charm. At any rate Duveen bought it at auction for $66,000, and one can be sure that Joseph Widener paid considerably more than that.

Still, the Wideners' list of purchases from Duveen Brothers: the furniture, porcelains, carpets, bijouterie, and the like, was less significant than Duveen would have liked. When rare and valuable things were bought, they tended to come through Uncle Henry, such as a unique yellow square Chinese vase that Joseph Widener acquired on the former's advice early in 1916. There was a reason for that. Five years earlier, P. A. B. Widener had bought a Limoges enamel plaque from Armand Lowengard's family firm in Paris. Although Duveen had complete confidence that the plaque was genuine—and he had the further assurance of Armand's almost infallible eye—the fact was that nasty rumors had begun to circulate about the plaque almost as soon as it was bought. Jacques Seligmann, who had no love for Duveen, said that he had seen the plaque before it went to Lowengard. The man who brought it to him claimed he had made it and more or less hinted there were more where that one came from. This was becoming Duveen's problem because by then, the senior Lowengard having died, he was a trustee of the Lowengard estate. It happened that W. R. Valentiner, an art expert who was cataloguing the Widener collection, would not accept the plaque as genuine. The situation was not made any easier by Duveen, who had rashly said he would refund the money and then backed away from the idea and, instead, summoned a raft of experts, all willing to contradict Valentiner. Widener returned the plaque, but still Joseph Duveen would not give a refund. Widener could have sued, but a long-drawn-out lawsuit would have been the certain consequence and, in any case, he could hardly expect to reclaim money from Duveen Brothers. What he wanted was a quiet little exchange, and Joseph Duveen would not give him one. Meanwhile, Uncle Henry was fretting about the matter, and the Wideners were discovering that while they loved the uncle, the nephew set their teeth on edge.

So matters stood for some years, one of the rare occasions on which Duveen let his personal feelings get in the way of his business interests. But when Henry died in 1919, something had to be done. It made no sense to let a trifling matter of twenty thousand dollars—the cost of the plaque—come between Duveen Brothers and the handsome sales that the Wideners potentially represented. So, belatedly, Joseph Duveen wrote Joseph Widener a humble-pie letter in which he said he would be happy to let him have some hundred or so bronze medals from the Hainauer Collection as a fair compensation. Widener replied that he had not very much wanted the medals but only some kind of return on the money expended. He would be glad to look at them again. In the meantime he was happy that the disagreement had been settled amicably, because he knew how much it had worried Uncle Henry. He ended up accepting the offer. A couple of weeks later, Joseph Duveen wrote to say he was about to sail for England and could not dream of leaving the country without coming to see Joseph Widener. No doubt he was kindly received.

As he would for any client, Duveen often wrote letters of introduction on their behalf whenever they wanted to see a collection in private hands. At the end of World War I he wrote to Joseph Widener asking him whether a young collector named Carl Hamilton might be allowed to call on him and see his collection. Duveen described him as a dear friend and "great amateur." Since Duveen tended to ascribe to his clients and friends the sometimes hypothetical qualities he also gave his wares, the description must be viewed with caution. At that stage Hamilton might be considered an amateur in artistic matters, but there was nothing great about him. His inexperience, if that is the word, would eventually metamorphose into the kind of cunning that would defeat even as masterful a tactician as Sir Joseph Duveen. As Jean Fowles, Edward Fowles's widow, once said, "Edward thought Hamilton was an operator and didn't trust him. But Joe always had a great weakness for a crook."

From the very beginning Hamilton appeared to be self-invented as well as extraordinarily determined. Like Emma Hamilton, that equally ruthless self-promoter, who emerged from lowly circumstances to consort with princes, Carl Hamilton's origins are obscure. The late Alice de Lamar, who knew him well, called him "a waif of uncertain origin, an orphan child." He sometimes liked to say his mother took in washing and his father was a drunk, but that could have been self-dramatization. His real name was unknown; it was always said that "he invented the name of Hamilton for himself because he liked the sound of it." Even as a boy his powers of persuasion were advanced. He somehow came to the attention of Mrs. E. H. Harriman, wife of an American railroad executive and mother of Averell, the future ambassador to Great Britain and Russia and governor of New York. She took Hamilton up with enthusiasm, helping him to get a scholarship to Andover and later sending him to Yale University, where, presumably, he picked up the manners and polish that would be so useful later. At Yale, he was already an entrepreneur of some skill, running a clothes-pressing service for students. As Alice de Lamar tells it, while still at Yale he legally adopted an Italian boy, also an orphan, then aged five, whom he named Gordon and who also went to Andover and Yale. She wrote, "Though dutiful and grateful to Carl, Gordon was glad to be away from him and no longer dependent, for Carl was an embarrassment because he was actually a well-meaning 'crackpot.' Carl was afflicted with a mental illness one can politely call 'folie de grandeur.' After he discovered Art, he sincerely believed he was destined to become one of the greatest collectors."

When she met him in 1921, Carl was twenty-nine and Gordon about fifteen. Alice de Lamar does not mention that certain friends of hers, including B.B. and his wife, Mary, who loved to meddle in other people's lives, were promoting a match between her and Hamilton. The friends presumably knew more about Hamilton's spendthrift habits than she did; they also knew that she was an heiress to an immense fortune. She, being a lesbian, as well as astute and unsentimental, would have nothing to do with such a preposterous idea. But one way or another she saw a great deal of him, and was aware that he had made a fortunate investment in coconut oil and soap, which due to wartime shortages had increased in value. Hamilton cashed in at the top of the market and made the first of many purchases from Duveen.

De Lamar thought Duveen took him up partly because of his links with the well-placed Harrimans. Such a young man needed an appropriate setting, and so Duveen chose a New York apartment at 270 Park Avenue. The building, in French Renaissance revival style, was about ten storeys high, with its own inner courtyard and spacious floor plans for a discriminating clientele. The fourteen-room Hamilton apartment was redecorated to Duveen's specifications and probably furnished by him as well. There were sand-finish walls (backgrounds for the paintings to come), antique Persian rugs, parchment lampshades, fine Italian antique furniture, Florentine brocade hangings, and everything in the best of taste. Dr. Lamar added, "I wouldn't put it past Duveen to have run an account at the florists as well, for there were always fresh flowers in the vases."

Like many American entrepreneurs, Hamilton had a curiously pious attitude toward life. David Alan Brown, curator of the National Gallery of Art in Washington, who organized a Berenson exhibition in 1979, believed Hamilton had originally intended to become a missionary and was attracted, with "almost Victorian enthusiasm," to art's spiritual aspects. At any rate, what Hamilton wanted were Italian Renaissance paintings, and B.B. and Mary were only too happy to oblige. In 1919, when it was offered to Hamilton through Duveen, Berenson gave a certificate of authentication for Andrea Mantegna's *Judith and Holofernes*. However, in 1902, when it had been owned by Lord Pembroke, Berenson wrote it was the work of someone in Mantegna's school and not by the master himself. (It is now at the National Gallery of Art as by Mantegna.)

Many of Berenson's attributions for Hamilton's collection, if not this one, seem curiously ill advised. There was, for instance, his attribution to Piero della Francesca of *Crucifixion,* which was smuggled out of Italy in 1915, hidden in a custom-made cavity behind a worthless religious scene painted on a heavy piece of wood. Again, Berenson managed to convince himself that it was the genuine article, and the painting would be one of the reasons for a bitter fight between Hamilton and Duveen at the end of Duveen's life. One painting acquired by Hamilton about which there is no doubt is *Feast of the Gods,* then thought to be by Bellini and now ascribed to Bellini and Titian, but it did not come from Duveen. The seller was a prominent London dealer, Arthur J. Sulley. This annoyed Duveen very much. In the first place, the recommendation had been made by Berenson, and Duveen was outraged that Berenson would be working for another dealer when he had signed an exclusive contract with Duveen Brothers. That contract was due to expire; and anticipating a noisy session Duveen, who had invited Berenson to his Paris apartment, took the precaution of placing mattresses against all the doors. Berenson's subtle mind somehow picked up the thought at the eleventh hour. He changed the meeting's venue to Duveen's Paris office. This defused the situation, and the meeting went smoothly, because, Fowles said, they needed each other.

Hamilton was a different matter. To learn that a client had bought from another dealer sent Duveen's reflexes into their usual overdrive. This kind of behavior could not be allowed. He began to woo Hamilton with single-minded zeal, and that collector was only too willing to be the focus of Duveen's undivided attentions. One painting after another swam into Hamilton's orbit and was snapped up. It must have taken time for Duveen to realize whom he was dealing with. Of the fifty-five paintings that, at one time or another, Hamilton supposedly "bought" from Duveen, only four were actually paid for, and the Mantegna *Judith and Holofernes* was not one of them.

In short, Hamilton was running a kind of de facto art gallery without having invested a penny, while Duveen continued to pay interest on the bank loans with which he had financed the paintings in the first place. This was one of those curious business arrangements which always struck outsiders as self-defeating if they knew about them, which much of the time they did not. The Berensons, who stayed at Hamilton's apartment in the winter of 1920, claimed not to know that Hamilton's wares had not been paid for. The claim is disingenuous, since all of Hamilton's paintings were in Berenson's "parish," as he termed it, and since he received a percentage of the profits, he learned from his Duveen statements that they had not actually been sold. It is clear that everyone involved in this bizarre situation accepted the proposition that Hamilton would be moving in the right social circles and sooner or later someone would want to buy a painting; he would take the usual commission. That, at any rate, was the plan. Years later Duveen would say with disgust that every time he raised the subject, Hamilton would say he was about to conclude a sensational sale, but he never did.

In the light of what happened later, Duveen was almost embarrassingly duped by Hamilton; but so, curiously enough, was Berenson. One of the famous stories in that regard concerns yet another painting now at the National Gallery in Washington, *St. John in the Desert* by Domenico Veneziano. Both Berensons had been charmed by Hamilton, finding "something exhilarating, infectious and intoxicating about this American Bacchus." Alice de Lamar always thought Mary was in love with Hamilton but Mary was hardly deceived, having already noticed his dislike of nude women and his distinct preference for handsome young men, on the canvas or off it. Still, she and B.B. saw, or thought they saw, all kinds of financial prospects and decided to give Hamilton a present: a small painting in which the young St. John, wearing nothing but a cloak and a halo, is seen in an icy landscape. It was a handsome gift, but thought to be a fairly minor work by the fifteenth-century Italian painter Pesellino. Some time later the young American art historian Richard Offner became convinced it was by the much more famous Florentine painter Veneziano, and Berenson belatedly agreed.

To lose such a painting out of misguided kindness was very bad luck for Berenson, who was always looking for ways to improve his bank account, and dumb luck for Hamilton, who could not have known what he had been given. It was all part of what seemed Hamilton's run of good fortune in those heady days just after the First World War, luck that was to change so dramatically in later years. Alice de Lamar wrote, "If Carl's traits could be considered 'manic depressive,' then one only saw the eternal manic phase."

WILLIAM SALOMON, a wealthy banker, was another collector who turned out to be a great deal less promising than originally billed. Exactly when he swam into Duveen's orbit is unclear—accounts vary—but what is evident is that he took up Duveen Brothers, or vice versa, at the end of World War I. He proved himself to be a man in a great hurry, having conceived the ambition of making his house a center for the study of art, on the Frick model. The problem was that there was nothing much to study, which was what made him so interesting. Salomon was not only buying in job lots, like Carl Hamilton, but sending letters tinged with shades of anxiety. Clever collectors, of course, never make this elementary mistake, knowing that it is practically an open invitation for the seller to unload paintings he usually has to present in the most flattering light in order to sell them at all.

The first set of six, all Italian Renaissance paintings authenticated by B.B., for which Duveen Brothers had paid $145,000, went to Salomon for $650,000. Then Salomon bought a second set of six, along with a Titian portrait, some authenticated by B.B. and others by a Dr. O. Siren. There was another nice profit to Duveen Brothers, for a total of $1.1 million. They were all paid for, which was a gratifying aspect of these sales. The problem was that several of the paintings had doubtful attributions, to put it mildly, a problem that was compounded in 1919, that year when almost everything went wrong, by the collector's untimely death. His will suggested that his heirs either establish a center for the study of art or give the paintings away. These suggestions struck nobody as a good idea, so in 1923 Salomon's entire collection, housed at his former residence, 1020 Fifth Avenue, was put up for auction, but not by Duveen Brothers. Sir Joseph was faced, either with the humiliating possibility that his paintings would be sold for less than his own estimations, or buying them himself. This he elected to do, and it cost him $1 million, just about what he had received for them four years before.

One of the big problems in the Salomon collection was a portrait of a man in a red cap which Siren had optimistically authenticated to Botticelli and was now under siege. Fowles was dispatched to Florence by Duveen, under protest (he wrote that he never could resist Duveen's "wonderful, large blue eyes"), to try to "winkle" an attribution to Botticelli out of B.B. Fowles was sure it was hopeless. He knew B.B. was angry because Siren had been called in to make some of the authentications. Fowles just knew B.B. would punish Joe by refusing to give him what he wanted. That was true at first. Nicky Mariano, Berenson's longtime secretary and longtime mistress, wrote in *Forty Years with Berenson* that B.B. "refused categorically in spite of the financial advantage." Fowles added that Nicky forgot one small detail. After the predicted explosion by B.B., she came to Fowles quietly and told him that the moment to get what he wanted was at hand. B.B. meekly dictated a letter to the effect that the portrait was an unusually late work of Botticelli's, and then signed it.

In any event the Botticelli label did not convince anyone for long, even

Duveen. A few days after the Salomon sale, in January 1923, Duveen was writing to Arabella Huntington recommending that she buy six of the Salomon paintings, including the Botticelli, which he now downgraded to Jacopo del Sellaio, a minor figure. He was quite frank about his advice. Some of the fifteen paintings he described were too small, or in bad condition, or not very interesting, or not worthy of her. He actually condemned two of them. The Vincenzo Catena *Madonna and Child with Saints* was no good, a polite way of saying it was probably a fake. The Della Gatta *Portrait of a Young Lady as Lucrezia* was "dreadful." Mrs. Huntington may have bought the Bernardino dei Conti *Portrait of a Lady* and one other work. Two of the Salomons went to John R. Thompson of Chicago and another to Mrs. Duke of Newport. Philip Lehman bought Francia's *Virgin and Child with St. Jerome and St. Francis,* a painting now at the Metropolitan. Two were never sold during Joseph Duveen's lifetime. The fate of the Botticelli/del Sellaio is unknown.

Salomon had been the kind of collector who judged a future purchase by how well it would fit on a particular wall and never traveled without a folding ruler. Philip Lehman, of Lehman Brothers, the New York bankers, was made of sterner stuff. This fastidious collector had arrived on the scene early, buying from the Kann Collection in 1908, and with extreme care. His emphasis was always on Old Masters, but early in the 1920s his taste threatened to take a disastrous turn. It appears that one of his favorite paintings, which had hung in his dining room for many years, was a fulllength portrait by Claude Monet of the artist's wife, titled *The Japanese Fan.* No doubt on one of his many invitations to dine with Lehman Duveen had ample time to consider the dangerous shift of interest that the Monet represented. You could not, however, argue a man out of what he liked. The main thing was to get him to like something else more. One day Duveen, in Paris, appeared at the Place Vendôme with Lehman, who was staying with him at the Ritz. A particularly fine fifteenth-century French Gothic tapestry from the De Cour collection was brought out to be admired. It showed a prince, or some other *grand seigneur,* in the act of going on a hunt. A *grand seigneur* was certainly more to be desired as the focus of interest at a dinner party than an artist's wife, no matter how charming. The tapestry went up and *The Japanese Fan* came down. Since (for business reasons) Joseph Duveen never sold a French Impressionist painting if he could help it, the Monet disappeared into his storage rooms for the next thirty years.

One of the nice things about bankers was that they always came up with the money eventually, even if they did exact stringent terms, and

Duveen, as has been noted, cultivated bankers as clients. Henry Goldman, a banker with an office and residence on Fifth Avenue, was another customer who could be relied upon to like Italian Renaissance paintings and buy uncritically. In the early 1920s he bought a painting, the dead Christ mourned by his mother (variously titled *The Entombment* and *Deposition*) with an enthusiastic recommendation from B.B. that it was a Fra Angelico, a very valuable attribution indeed. The painting (which found its way to the Kress Collection and the National Gallery of Art) had been transferred from wood to canvas. That was fairly commonly done, but the extent of the restoration was something else again, enough to cast doubt on the optimistic Fra Angelico label. It is now considered to be by a far lesser artist, once again, Jacopo del Sellaio, and even this is doubtful. At $250,000, it was an expensive mistake for Goldman.

As for Clarence Mackay, "the Atlantic cable and telegraph tycoon," he and his wife lived on a suitably grand scale with a house on East Seventy-fifth Street and a mansion, which Jacques Seligmann called a chateau, in Roslyn, Long Island. He bought from Duveen—and by 1936 would have run up over half a million dollars in debts that he could not pay—but for the most part, his collection came from Seligmann. Speaking of Mackay's choices, the late London art dealer and connoisseur David Carritt, who knew the collection well, said that if Mackay had made an occasional bad mistake it did not matter, because he bought "fabulously" and had "some heavenly pictures."

Among the heavenly pictures Mackay bought and eventually needed to sell were seven scenes from the life of St. Francis, *St. Francis and the Poor Knight,* by the fifteenth-century Sienese artist Stefano di Giovanni, called Sassetta. These panels were part of a larger composition painted for the high altarpiece of the Church of San Francesco in San Sepolcro. Berenson owned the central panel, a full-length portrait of St. Francis, and Kenneth Clark had always admired it. So when, in the 1930s, Clark became director of the National Gallery in London and learned that Mackay was in financial difficulties, he made inquiries. Mackay had reportedly bought his panels for half a million dollars—a sale on paper only. Clark estimated that Duveen had paid about $150,000 for them and that $175,000 was a fair price, it being the Depression and the price of Old Masters at an historic low. Interestingly, Duveen by then was a member of the National Gallery's board of trustees, a clear conflict of interest to which the board was somehow blind.

Clark sent repeated letters and telegrams to Mackay but received no reply. His lack of success was reported at a subsequent board meeting,

Kenneth Clark, photographed
in Vienna in 1937

attended by Duveen. " 'Of course he hasn't answered,' [Duveen] said, with his most expansive smile; 'he never saw the letter.' 'Nor the telegrams?' 'Of course not! I know Mr. Mackay's butler.' " Clark wrote, "That a trustee of the Gallery should have bribed a vendor's butler not to show him our offer was a bit thick . . ." The order went out that another telegram should be sent, which actually reached Mackay, and the panels went to the National Gallery.

Why Duveen should have interposed himself between Mackay and this particular sale is curious, especially when the latter owed him money that he presumably wanted back. If his goal, as seems likely, was to demonstrate that nothing would be done without his permission, or commission, it was the rashest possible display of power, given the circumstances, and one that would come back to haunt him.

Then there was Jules Bache, whom Edward Fowles referred to as "Julie," a stockbroker who had a house on the avenue d'Iéna and came into the Duveen fold through Armand Lowengard's father, Jules. He, too, went broke during the Depression, putting Duveen in the tiresome position of being asked to resell paintings for which he had already received at least one handsome commission. (This continual recycling, of course, did not always present him with the delicate and vexing issues surrounding the Salomon sale.) There were John D. Rockefeller Jr., who was buying from Duveen by 1919, and the enigmatic Andrew Mellon, the financier, who would figure so largely in Duveen's future fortunes. There were the fabulous Stotesburys, tucked away in Whitemarsh Hall, their Chestnut Hill, Philadelphia, estate. They were such good customers that Duveen commissioned Douglas Chandor, a London society portraitist, to execute a pastel portrait of Mrs. Stotesbury. The whole affair took place in such secrecy that, it was claimed, neither Stotesbury knew about it until the portrait was unveiled as a Christmas present. Given Duveen's relish for conspiracy and undercover activities, this, unlikely though it may seem, is perfectly possible.

The conflicting interests of these collectors and other prime targets for Duveen's solicitude could be guaranteed to keep sales brisk and prices gratifyingly high. In the autumn of 1921, there were almost weekly shipments from Paris and London to New York, and monthly bulletins about his activities in the papers. In April, he was looking at a Rubens. That same month he bought Titian's *Portrait of Giorgio Cornaro* (also called *The Man with the Falcon*), owned by Dr. Edward Simon, for $300,000, and no clue in the newspaper report about which collector he had in mind. In June,

Jules S. Bache

Duveen bought the historic sixteenth-century harness that had been made for the second Earl of Pembroke. It came from Wilton House, Salisbury, where the poet Sir Philip Sidney wrote *Arcadia,* and Duveen paid close to $100,000 for it. He acquired *Portrait of a Man* by Frans Hals from the collection of Count Maurice Zamoyski, the Polish ambassador to France, and sold it to John McCormack, the Irish-born tenor and opera star, for $150,000. He had cause to be proud of all these acquisitions. But then, that autumn of 1921, came the most spectacular sale of all.

Chapter Ten

THE BLUE BOY

O NE OF THE CHARMING STORIES in Behrman's book about Duveen has to do with a painting that is second only to da Vinci's *Mona Lisa* in its almost universal appeal. According to Behrman, Duveen happened to be traveling on the *Aquitania* with H.E.H. and Arabella Huntington in the summer of 1921. The Huntingtons had taken a complete suite of rooms, all of them decorated with copies of Gainsborough's paintings. One of them was *The Blue Boy*, famous almost since the first day it was exhibited in 1770 and the image of choice with which to adorn everything from biscuit boxes, highball glasses, and playing cards ever since.

Seeing the handsome portrait of this particular boy in his dining room, Huntington was moved to inquire, "Who's the boy in the blue suit?" Duveen of course knew the answer; all the answers. To have H.E.H. express an interest was tantamount to a command; the rest followed inexorably.

It is a delightful story, with just enough truth to keep it interesting. No doubt *The Blue Boy* was hanging in facsimile in his dining room on the *Aquitania,* and no doubt H.E.H. did express an interest in having Duveen acquire it for him. But the idea that he had never seen the painting before is a canard. He had known it, longed for it, tried to buy it, and collected prints of it for twenty years. It is much more likely that he had mooned over it with the look of a collector who knows that such a work can never be acquired, even with a blank check.

As for Duveen, the idea that buying *The Blue Boy* represented the summit of all any dealer could attain in this world was hardly a new one. Everyone knew that the Duke of Westminster and his family had owned the painting for over a century and that its credentials were impeccable. Berenson had tried to acquire it for Isabella Stewart Gardner in 1896. He wrote, "You know that Gainsborough is one of the world's painters, and you know that *The Blue Boy* is his masterpiece. So of course you must have it. Indeed I advise you to borrow, to do anything, but to get that picture." But the price was $150,000, and she was unwilling to throw away her fortune on a single work, no matter how great. Duveen claimed that his father had tried to buy it in 1900 for £50,000, a figure that was refused, and that he himself had doubled the offer a decade later, with no success either. All kinds of *Blue Boys* were on the market and selling for respectable sums even when it was clear that they could not be genuine. Gimpel noted in 1918 that a fake *Blue Boy* had been knocked down at the Hearn sale in New York for more than $32,000. He commented sourly, "It's harder to sell a genuine painting." Duveen's brother Louis had been offered another *Blue Boy* at the home of Sir J. Robinson of Hyde Park Terrace in 1919. The entry was made in the Scouts Book for that year, where it was recorded without comment.

More to the point, as Duveen's correspondence with Colin Agnew shows, he had been negotiating through Agnew's to buy the Duke of Westminster's Gainsborough for two years. So the idea was hardly extemporaneous in that summer of 1921. That Duveen had put it in Huntington's mind is much more likely—he might even have booked the Gainsborough Suite for him—but the credit, in this case, goes to Agnew's. They had the contact, but Duveen had the client, and what a client!

As Edward Fowles pointed out, Huntington had already tried to buy the painting directly from the Duke of Westminster without success. "He didn't realize that, with a man like [that] you couldn't go to him and say, 'Your picture is worth $300,000.' It didn't mean anything to him whatsoever. Duveen was clever enough to go along and say, 'I'll give you £200,000 for those three pictures.'" Fowles was referring to the fact that Huntington had admired almost as fervently another Westminster painting, which he also knew well: *Mrs. Siddons as the Tragic Muse* by Sir Joshua Reynolds. As Duveen was aware, for years both paintings hung opposite each other in the duke's drawing room at Grosvenor House, London. Duveen also knew that punitive 60 percent taxation was having its effect even on the man popularly known as the richest peer in England, and the duke had put the Reynolds up for auction at Christie's some eighteen months before. Although he was advised to keep his reserve price to £40,000, the duke had insisted on £60,000; the closest bid was £50,000, and the duke had withdrawn the painting. Nevertheless, he wanted to be rid of it, and to make an offer that included the Reynolds was a brilliant stroke on Duveen's part. Duveen also threw in Gainsborough's *The Cottage Door,* one of many versions of the rustic idyll the artist painted during his lifetime and arguably the best. Speaking of Duveen's offer, Fowles said, "That was a sound that meant something to the Duke. It was a round sum. And it worked."

Fowles was on the scene that day in Paris in the autumn of 1921 when Huntington was formally offered the painting. He said, "Duveen had a large desk in his room and it was arranged with three blotters with pads and pencils, and so on. Duveen sat in the middle, Huntington on the right and I sat on the left. Duveen did an awful lot of talking and Huntington said *not a word.* I felt very nervous and I could see Duveen perspiring. And then Huntington said, 'Well, goodbye, Duveen. Maybe I'll see you in a day or two.' " Duveen had to wait with as much equanimity as he could summon until a letter arrived from the Château de Beauregard confirming that Huntington was buying *The Blue Boy* for $728,800, payable in six-month bills. Duveen bought the three paintings for $800,000 and sold them for just over $1 million. The profit was respectable and the publicity priceless.

Jonathan Buttall, the boy in the picture, who was born in 1752, was the son of a prosperous ironmonger who sold his goods in Greek Street, Soho. Gainsborough knew the family, shared the adolescent boy's love of books and music, and their friendship deepened as the latter reached manhood. From contemporary accounts, Buttall appears to have been courtly and amiable, with the kind of imperturbable manner that Gainsborough, who was much more mercurial, valued in his friends; at any rate, he specifically requested that Buttall attend his funeral. (The painter died in 1788.) There is X-ray evidence that the artist had executed another painting underneath, since the lower part of a man's face is just identifiable at the top of the canvas. Scholars have therefore concluded that this could not have been a commissioned portrait, or the artist would have used a fresh canvas. It had been thought for years that Gainsborough was trying to disprove the theory of his rival Reynolds that paintings ought to be executed in warm, mellow colors. Gainsborough, it was said, used cool blues to show it could be done. However, Reynolds's manifesto postdates *The Blue Boy* by some years, which rather refutes this argument.

What seems more plausible is that Gainsborough was at the height of his admiration for Van Dyck when the portrait was painted in Bath. There was a huge vogue for Van Dyck's portraiture at the time. Fashionable ladies and gentlemen were wearing seventeenth-century costumes to masquerade balls, and students at Harrow wore them when they took part in archery competitions. Silver filigree lace, gold braid, exquisite silks, cascading

Jonathan Buttall: The Blue Boy by Thomas Gainsborough

satins shot with highlights—these were the very latest style. Gainsborough evidently had such dress-up costumes as part of his artistic stock in trade, because the Van Dyck costume Jonathan Buttall is wearing can be identified on other sitters in other paintings, a one-size-fits-all fancy dress. Gainsborough evidently loved the conceit of an old-fashioned look on a thoroughly modern boy. He adored the color and furthermore, there seems to be a direct parallel between his portrait of Jonathan Buttall and Van Dyck's portrait, a century before, of the seven-year-old George Villiers, second Duke of Buckingham, who also stands in the same pose but with the opposite elbow raised and leg thrust forward. That young man's father had been murdered shortly before, and by perhaps no coincidence, Jonathan Buttall had recently lost his father (in 1768). Perhaps Gainsborough saw himself as a substitute father; perhaps he thought that this was the right moment to celebrate the coming of age of Jonathan, who would have been about sixteen. The life-size portrait was for Jonathan but it was also for himself: as one writer put it, a "jeu d'esprit."

Paintings in oils are very forgiving and hide all kinds of wrong turns. Gainsborough had originally painted a dog in the lower-right-hand corner and had gone to some lengths to finish off its fluffy coat before apparently deciding that it would not do. (This, too, was discovered only recently.) The dog has disappeared behind a pile of rocks, in the foreground of a quickly sketched, barely suggested hillside, vanishing into massed trees and an overcast sky tinged with menacing grays and blues.

The sitter stands facing the viewer and his expression, somewhere between a gaze and a smile, manages to convey the carefree candor of childhood just before it gives way to a sobering awareness of manhood and responsibilities assumed. That poignant moment when adolescents are hovering between two worlds was one Gainsborough understood and painted with great delicacy and finesse, as can be seen from an even more ambivalent portrait, that of Elizabeth Linley at age fourteen with her brother Thomas, aged twelve. Youth on the edge of an uncertain future— one sees it in the haunted gaze of Elizabeth Linley, and in *The Blue Boy*, in the chaotic menace in the background and the elaborate finery behind which a boy is hiding.

As for the Gainsborough blue that so preoccupied Duveen, it is, of course, not just blue but an intricate blending of many blues. There are indigo, lapis, cobalt, slate, turquoise, cream and even charcoal, all painted in overlapping transparent glazes, using the confident, slashing brush-strokes that were Gainsborough's unique trademark. In a tribute to the painter written after his death, Sir Joshua Reynolds wrote, "All those odd scratches and marks which, on a close examination, are so observ-able . . . and which even to experienced painters appear rather the effect of accident than design: this chaos, this uncouth and shapeless appearance, by a kind of magic, at a certain distance assumes form." *The Blue Boy* has been so familiarized by constant repetition that, like a landscape seen too often, its effect has dulled the senses, and it really takes time to see what a master-piece it is. One can then appreciate the exquisite modeling of the straight nose, the high forehead, the soft child's mouth, and the enigma of the brown eyes. Somehow the painter has achieved a masterful effect that is all the more miraculous for being subtle and understated. That this portrait is as compelling nowadays as it was two centuries ago has to mean that it has captured something basic to the human experience.

Mrs. Siddons as the Tragic Muse by Sir Joshua Reynolds

Mrs. Siddons as the Tragic Muse is as mannered and artful as *The Blue Boy* is evanescent and artless. In contrast to Gainsborough, who increasingly worked toward the fleeting impression that the sitter will dissolve and vanish in an instant, Reynolds strove to make his figures as rounded and solid as paint and imagination could devise. The great actress, who achieved a well-earned reputation for her ability to move an audience to tears, is seated on a throne, her face pale and troubled, one hand raised as if she is momentarily pausing for thought. The extremely naturalistic, even daring, portrayal of her as an ordinary human being caught in a great human dilemma (the title of the painting is an allusion to Melpomene, the Greek muse of tragedy) must have struck her contemporaries as startling and novel. Gainsborough's own portrait of her as a lady of fashion has all of his dash and glamour but is much less interesting. The Reynolds study, with its gorgeous deep browns and fawns and dull oranges, its sense of heavy, discreetly opulent fabrics, its command of gesture and its unguarded nakedness of expression, has to be seen as one of the most revealing portraits of an actress ever executed. No wonder it appealed to Duveen, who loved everything about the theatre. To think that he was safeguarding the future of such a painting must have given him particular pleasure in light of his father's gift, to the Tate, of *Ellen Terry as Lady Macbeth.* This sale would have a particular significance for him, and it was not the only one.

IT IS HARD TO BELIEVE NOWADAYS, but when Duveen bought *The Blue Boy* in 1921 the boy's costume was not blue but green. Repeated coats of discolored varnish—that mellow golden glow so admired in the nineteenth century—had turned the color from a scintillating blue to a murky green. Almost the first statement Duveen made when he took charge of the work was to announce that he would wipe away the accretion of decades. The delicate task was undertaken by the reliable W. A. Holder, and Duveen sent periodic reports to California as they were relayed from London. On December 1, 1921, Holder had begun to clean half of the arm, which was gray with filth. The beautiful blue was emerging. Holder did not think any restoration would be needed. Five days later, on December 6, the accumulated varnish and dirt was gone and the result was a revelation. None of the shimmering blues seemed to have been lost in the process, and once it was finished the critics were silenced. The *New York Times* commented, "In its renewed youth and beauty, with the glorious original blue, there are many who are now saying that *The Blue Boy* is not only the finest English painting but perhaps the world's most beautiful picture."

Now that *The Blue Boy* was more beautiful than ever, the reaction might be predicted: why did it have to leave England? As soon as the sale to Huntington had been finalized, Duveen sent him a secret cable begging him not to make it public for the time being. He said that he was about to have an audience with King George V and thought he knew why. His Majesty would certainly want to know why the painting could not be kept in England. According to newspaper reports, several "important British galleries"—not identified—were subsequently offered the chance to buy but could not, "in these hard times, find the large sum required to purchase this particular picture."

On January 3, 1922, Duveen cabled Huntington that the painting had gone on exhibit in the large English Room of London's National Gallery with Gainsborough's portrait of Mrs. Siddons on one side and his exquisite, unfinished portrait of his daughters chasing a butterfly on the other. (The National Gallery acquired this painting for the measly sum of £3,349 a year later.) A wooden barrier protected *The Blue Boy* and guards were in constant attendance as the gallery jammed with visitors, the men removing their hats as a mark of respect. There was a huge queue outside in Trafalgar Square as the weeks went by, and further queues inside, waiting to enter room 25. Street sellers worked the lines, selling cheap reproductions, and ninety thousand visitors came to see it during the month. As the time grew shorter the tone of the daily press reports grew sharper. "Why should the painting go to America, of all places?" Even Cole Porter wrote a song about it, "The Blue Boy Blues," in which the painting was viewing with apprehension its transfer from "the gilded galleries of Park Lane" to the ruffianly frontiers of the American West. No wonder, the song went, the Blue Boy was becoming "bluer and bluer."

There were demonstrations in Trafalgar Square, and when the final whistle blew at four o'clock on January 25, one writer commented that "it seemed more like the farewell cry of an Atlantic liner." The guards, sensing the mood, gave the crowds ten more minutes before ushering out the last stragglers. That was the moment when Sir Charles Holmes, director of the gallery, made his grand gesture. He wrote on the back of the canvas, "Au revoir, C.H." What was he thinking? He must have known the painting would never come back.

Elaborate precautions were being taken for *The Blue Boy*'s journey of six thousand miles. It was removed from its frame and the stretchers on the reverse were reinforced. A box, specially constructed so that nothing touched any of the surfaces, kept the painting firmly in position. This was then packed inside a steel box which was itself enclosed in a waterproof, iron-bound box. Since the painting's dimensions were six feet by four, this was a sizable undertaking. Meanwhile Huntington was said to be planning to build a room in which the great picture would be enshrined, "a worthy setting for this noble painting."

Another three-week exhibition followed in the Duveen Galleries in New York. More crowds came to see *The Blue Boy*, and the press was ecstatic. The portrait continued its triumphal progress from the doors of

720 Fifth Avenue to Grand Central Station, where a private stateroom had been reserved on the transcontinental express. More guards had been hired, and since the possibility of theft or mutilation during the five-day trip was very real, Sir Joseph himself was on the train. All three paintings reached Los Angeles safely on March 22. He had asked the Huntingtons for their advice about hotels and was gratified to be invited to stay at their San Marino Ranch outside Los Angeles. To have captured *The Blue Boy* was a coup de théâtre. To have transported it safely to California, given all the possible pitfalls, was a miracle. Duveen was now the most famous art dealer in the world.

Shortly before *The Blue Boy* left for California, it made a trip to Hampstead. All those years ago, when Joe had brought home a painting he naively thought was a Gainsborough, he had told his mother that he would one day bring her the most famous Gainsborough in the world. By 1922 Rosetta, who had outlived her husband by fourteen years, was ailing and confined to her bed in The Elms, with its splendid views out over the heath. But she was well enough to be visited and when the full glory of the portrait was revealed, one can imagine her smile. As Duveen used to say, "Nobody knows how much I owe to the grit of my Yorkshire mother." She died on June 25, 1922.

BOYS OF VARIOUS COLORS WERE IRRESISTIBLE to the spirit of the age and, naturally enough, Duveen was always trying to repeat his triumph, even if no painting could ever surpass *The Blue Boy* in the rarefied heights of desirability. Even Gainsborough himself had never equaled it, although his painting of Master Nicholls, an even more appealing youngster dressed fetchingly in a Van Dyck costume of shimmering pink (*The Pink Boy*), is its nearest equivalent. But where *The Blue Boy* is calm and at ease, *The Pink Boy* seems simpering and mannered.* But another boy of greater charm looked more promising. He was Charles William Lambton, *The Red Boy,* by Sir Thomas Lawrence, an enchanting vision of a youth, perhaps aged ten or twelve, in a white ruffled collar and deep red suit, reclining against a background of sepia rocks. The boy had originally been given a yellow outfit, but his father reminded the artist that he had been

*Its execution—a foot awkwardly turned out, an arm wrongly foreshortened—is unworthy of the master; and in any event the painting was out of reach, being owned by Baron Ferdinand de Rothschild. (It now is owned by the National Trust at Waddesdon Manor, Buckinghamshire.)

given the sobriquet of "the Yellow Dandy," and there was even a derisory song to that effect. The color must be changed, so Lawrence overpainted the yellow with crimson, allowing flashes of the undercoat to be glimpsed as highlights for the costume. The painting of the boy, whose face is almost too pretty and whose pose trembles on the verge of self-consciousness, is nevertheless a classic example of the eighteenth-century version of a child genius. (It was also nicknamed *The Young Byron.*) Although the painting never left Lambton Castle, it was extremely well known through reproductions, and, in fact, copies of it had been for sale to the Trafalgar Square queues as they waited to see *The Blue Boy.* This might have given its owner, the Earl of Durham, an idea. At any rate, there were periodic rumors that it was about to be sold, which Duveen monitored through his Agnew contacts.

In 1929 the rumors became more serious, and Duveen began an energetic pursuit. If anyone was going to have *The Red Boy,* it must be he. He waited anxiously while various intermediaries began negotiating with the Earl of Durham early in 1929. The earl signified his commitment to sell but his price took everyone's breath away: £200,000. In other words, he knew what Duveen had paid for *The Blue Boy* and had set his sights accordingly. There was no question that Master Lambton was, in his way, just as appealing as Master Buttall, and the prices of Lawrence's paintings were strong. Still, the relative fame of paintings is something else, and the earl was gently told, or perhaps not so gently, that his painting was worth about forty thousand pounds. Another argument advanced, that even the most famous Titian or Giorgione in the world would not reach that sum, would have been less compelling. From the earl's point of view, he knew the value of what he had and was prepared to hold out for it. From the point of view of Duveen Brothers, *The Red Boy* was no bargain. So matters stood for the next three years.

Then, in 1932, as the Depression took hold, the owner finally decided to put the contents of Lambton Castle up for auction. Included in the sale was *The Red Boy.* He had bowed to the realities of the world after the crash. Obviously he could not ask the same price. He would halve it. He put a reserve of £100,000 on *The Red Boy* and there were no takers.

ANOTHER *RED BOY,* this time by Goya, was a happier proposition. It was owned by the wife of Henri Bernstein, a French playwright, who was the son of a rich Jewish businessman of Polish stock; his mother was the daughter of a New York banker. He owned an enchanting portrait of a little boy, *Don Manuel Osorio Manrique de Zúñiga,* or *The Red Boy.* This was one of a series of portraits of members of the Count of Altamira's family which the artist painted between 1785 and 1788, i.e., contemporaneously with the Gainsborough. The boy is four years old, with wide brown eyes, a rosebud mouth, and a mop of hair. He is holding a string attached to the leg of a magpie, who seems sublimely indifferent to the staring eyes of a pair of crouching cats in the background. The boy's rich red costume, which looks to be of velvet, his wide silvery sash, tied with a huge bow, his pretty little satin shoes, decorated with more bows, and his air of innocent bemusement make this one of Goya's most playful and endearing works. But, oddly enough, the painting, which is now at the Metropolitan Museum of Art, was considered of far less consequence than a Gainsborough or a Reynolds and taken so casually by its owner that he used it as a prop for a new play, *La Galerie des Glaces,* which starred Charles Boyer. It was definitely worthy of Duveen Brothers. Duveen's moment came one night in 1924 when Bernstein needed cash urgently to cover a serious gambling debt. Fowles came up with the money on short notice and the painting changed hands. (It was allowed to stay as a theatrical prop for the run of the play.) The price was something like $135,000, and Duveen sold it to Jules Bache for double that. (The Behrman story that Bache's son-in-law, Gilbert Miller, a theatrical producer, got Duveen to reduce that price has been disproved.) One hates to think how much Goya's *Red Boy* would fetch on today's market.

APPEALING BOYS AND TOMBOYISH GIRLS continued to make their way through the Duveen showrooms in the years that followed. Since Duveen, in common with most of the big international dealers, had weeded out fat-faced boys and homely girls, one could depend on the ones for sale to be more or less irresistible. Still, one has to say that a particular girl is perhaps the most appealing and adorable of them all. She is also another example of a child with a tragic background. So many eighteenth-century children died young, or were rejected by their parents, or were assumed to be ready for the trials of adulthood at far too young an age.

Pinkie, as she was called, was descended from a long line of Barretts, successful sugar and rum merchants and landholders in Jamaica since the seventeenth century. Her full name was Sarah Goodin Barrett Moulton, daughter of Elizabeth Barrett and Charles Moulton. She was born on one of the Barrett estates, Little River, St. James's, Jamaica, in the spring of 1783 and named for her mother's younger sister, Sarah, who had died two years

Sarah Goodin Barrett Moulton: Pinkie
by Sir Thomas Lawrence

before at the age of seven. Her mother and father appear to have separated when she was five or six. She had three younger brothers: Edward, born in 1785, Samuel, born in 1787, and George, born in 1789. In common with other Jamaican families, Elizabeth Barrett Moulton took it for granted that the children must be sent to England to complete their educations, although the ages at which they were dispatched seem astonishingly young. In 1792, when Pinkie was nine, Edward seven, and Samuel five, they sailed to England across perilous seas—England and France were at war the following year—a six-week trip, and with no possible idea of whether they would ever see their mother or Jamaica again. Along with other Jamaican emigré children they were enrolled in Mrs. Fenwick's School at Flint House, Greenwich.

There is no record of the effect this triple bereavement had on their mother, Elizabeth Barrett Moulton. All that is known is that Pinkie's grandmother, Judith Barrett, who had lost a Sarah of her own, felt the loss severely. A year after Pinkie's departure she wrote to her niece in London, "I become every day more desirous to see my dear little Pinky; but as I cannot gratify myself with the Original I must beg the favor of You to have her picture drawn at full Length by one of the best Masters." Thomas Lawrence, a brilliant young artist who had just been appointed Painter in Ordinary to the King and elected to the Royal Academy, was the obvious choice. Pinkie sat for her portrait in 1794, when she was eleven. In September of that year she came down with a bad cold and was just recovering from that when one of her brothers contracted whooping cough. Presumably, she caught it too. At any rate, she died at Greenwich on April 23, 1795, when she was just twelve years old. She was buried in the parish churchyard of St. Alfege, Greenwich, on April 30, a day before her portrait went on view at the Royal Academy. Her brother George, who was not yet three when she and her brothers left Jamaica, was already dead. Samuel died at the age of twenty-seven. Edward Barrett Moulton lived the longest, until 1857, and became the father of Elizabeth Barrett Browning, the poet. Pinkie was the aunt she only knew from a painting.

Pinkie, a vision in white and pink, is silhouetted against a bright blue sky studded with clouds. Her grandmother had asked that she be painted "in an easy Careless attitude," i.e., informally, and the painter appears to have chosen to depict her in the act of a dance step. She turns toward the viewer, her right arm tucked behind her back and her left hand raised across her chest, one small foot pointed forward, as if she had just finished a pirouette. The idea of movement is heightened by her filmy skirt, which is billowing out behind her, and the loose pink ribbons on her satin bonnet, which are trailing over her shoulder. She stares at the viewer, and there is something about her heart-shaped face, with its stubborn chin, that has nothing of the child about it, although at the age of eleven she could hardly be called an adolescent, much less a young woman. Nevertheless there is a hint of precocious maturity in the outlining of a leg beneath the filmy skirt and the budding shape of her breasts that gives the painting its curious ambivalence; she seems to be half girl, half woman, poised between two worlds in the manner of Jonathan Buttall in *The Blue Boy*. Finally, there is the landscape behind Pinkie, or rather the lack of it. She is poised on the crest of a hill with the horizon far beneath her, those immense, strange lands into which she has been exiled. There she stands, with her pretty pirouette and staring eyes, mistress of all she surveys, in precocious and rebellious isolation.

DUVEEN SOLD *PINKIE* TWICE. In the early days, some of his best clients were Herbert Stern, the first Baron Michelham, president of the London merchant bankers Herbert Stern & Co., and his pretty young wife, Aimée Geraldine Bradshaw Stern, who lived in Arlington House, London. They also owned a country estate, Strawberry Hill in Middlesex, and a large apartment on the rue Nitot near the Place des États-Unis. The Michelhams, who rapidly became important clients, had been introduced by a good friend of Ernest's, Captain Jefferson Davis Cohn, who was the manager of a large racing stable. Fowles recalled that Ernest and Joe took to Captain Cohn at once, and indeed he was influential in throwing some very nice business their way, since the Michelhams bought on a grand scale: furniture, objets, carpets, tapestries, and paintings, and also began to lean on Duveen Brothers for everything from advice on plumbing to the precise placement of their new treasures. This was just the kind of helplessness Duveen found so appealing and for which he was willing to be endlessly accommodating. Fowles regarded Cohn with a slightly more jaundiced eye, if only because he took a cut of 15 percent for every item that the Michelhams bought from Duveen Brothers. Fowles thought that most ungentlemanly.

In those days just before World War I, the Michelhams had been charmed by *Pinkie,* and bought it from Duveen in 1910 for the relatively modest price of £60,900. Since, as Fowles wrote, the Michelhams were such important clients, they accustomed themselves rapidly to Duveen's seductive terms and were sometimes quite huffy about the little matter of bills outstanding. When Michelham died in 1919, Duveen Brothers was owed $6 million, and the convoluted process by which that bill was eventually paid is a story in itself. Finding herself quite short of cash in 1923, Baroness Michelham decided to auction off the contents of Strawberry Hill with the advice and counsel of Captain Jefferson Davis Cohn. Rather soon after that she found it necessary to sell Arlington House and its handsome contents. It was known that the collection included not only *Pinkie,* but *Anne de la Pole,* the portrait by Romney that Duveen had sold to the Michelhams in 1913; two fine Boucher panels; a brace of Lawrences, Romneys, and Hoppners; and a huge selection of quite valuable furniture. It also included *Lady Louisa Manners* by Hoppner, which had been such an expensive mistake in 1901 and which Duveen had sold to Michelham at a loss. Someone would have to buy that back quietly, so as to maintain the fiction of ever-escalating prices. That person (or persons) would have to be someone no one would suspect. Jack Stern, one of Michelham's two sons, and Captain Cohn were very willing (at 15 percent) to be those people. A quiet little deal was struck by which Duveen Brothers acted as agents for the estate, meaning that the firm would have first refusal on whatever Stern and Cohn "bought." Duveen Brothers could later sell, with no fanfare, the paintings they did not want to be seen buying.

The sale was one of the sensations of the autumn season and made the front page of the *New York Times* in November 1926. "Today, as soon as the doors opened a crowd collected," the paper reported. "It soon filled every available inch of space of the auction room at the Michelham mansion, 20 Arlington Street, just off Piccadilly.

"The first lots were knocked down at very low prices, one Romney realizing less than $1,000. After more low figures—one painting, by an unknown artist, was knocked down at one guinea amid roars of laughter—things suddenly warmed up." Two panels by Boucher, a pastoral scene called *La Fontaine d'Amour* and men and women with birdcages, *La Pipée aux Oiseaux,* were bought in by Cohn for £47,250. They went in 1935 to Anna Thomson Dodge of Detroit and are now at the Getty. Acting through the same intermediary, Duveen also again bought Romney's *Anne de la Pole,* which went for 44,000 guineas. Duveen bought the portrait of Miss Catherine Tatton by Gainsborough which was painted for her father, the Reverend William Tatton, rector of Rotherfield, Sussex, and prebendary of Canterbury Cathedral, another work he had previously sold to Lord Michelham. He paid 44,000 guineas for that as well. (The painting went to Andrew Mellon and is now at the National Gallery.) Romney's *Lady Elizabeth Forbes* also went through Cohn and fetched £24,000. *Lady Louisa Manners* was knocked down for £18,900.

Such was the mood of the sale that even Romneys considered to have doubtful provenances, such as *The Children of Captain Little,* went for a respectable 21,000 guineas. (The painting is still considered a Romney and is at the Detroit Institute of Fine Arts.) Another Romney, *Lady Hamilton as Ambassadress* (also known as *Emma Hamilton on Her Wedding Day*), was supposedly the last portrait of that lady painted by Romney before her lover, Charles Greville, handed her over to become the bride of his uncle,

Sir William Hamilton. The painting is hardly the best in Romney's long and slavish chronicling of his favorite model, but even that went for 40,000 guineas in the Michelham sale, ostensibly to Cohn.

The most famous painting in the sale, *Pinkie,* went to Duveen Brothers for 74,000 guineas, or $377,000, which the auctioneer said was the highest price ever paid for a picture at public auction anywhere in the world. H. E. Huntington bought it for about £90,000, or $439,000.

The sale, the London office cabled to Duveen in New York on November 25, 1926, had been a huge success, despite their original doubts about it. The papers were full of the story and the publicity had been priceless. Gerald Agnew had been especially delighted by the high prices, and he, along with the other dealers, said that Duveen Brothers had saved the day. Duveen was particularly interested in the fate of another Gainsborough, *Master John Heathcote,* which he had sold to the Michelhams in 1913 via Agnew's. The painting, of a toddler wearing the kind of girl's outfit that baby boys wore in those days, was executed for the child's parents as a special favor by the artist because all their other children had died in an epidemic. The boy is holding a tiny bouquet of flowers and, in the other hand, a hat appropriately trimmed with a black feather. Duveen always said he hated it, so Ernest Duveen was surprised that he would suddenly show an interest in the work. Duveen did not care for the portrait enough to do much about it for the next few months. By then he thought he had a buyer, the governor of Massachusetts, Alvan Tufts Fuller, but he acted too late; Fuller had already approached Cohn directly.

All of Duveen's competitive instincts surfaced immediately. He did not particularly want to sell the picture, but he was determined that the governor should come to heel. The idea that he could have some fun frustrating Captain Cohn also might have appealed to him. He told the Paris office to "try to upset the business . . . so that Fuller must come to me." A cry of anguish went up from Paris. It was much too late. The sale was as good as made. There were more words to this effect which Duveen brushed aside. All he wanted to know was what Fuller would have to pay to buy the painting from Cohn. That turned out to be £43,000. It was a simple matter to undercut Cohn, and so Duveen offered it to Fuller for £40,000. There was a fierce cable from Cohn: CONSIDER YOUR INTERFERENCE IMPERTINENT UNWARRANTABLE, but it was too late. There was nothing he could do, since all the paintings and furniture bought in on Duveen's orders were stored at the Place Vendôme. The picture was soon on its way to Boston and is now at the National Gallery of Art in Washington.

Chapter Eleven

THE DEMOTTE AFFAIR

Accord ing to a French monthly magazine, British court circles were deeply concerned about the mental health of the reigning monarch, George V. It seems he had been found running up and down Piccadilly one day, his hat on the back of his head and his hands in the armholes of his waistcoat, shouting, "I am Sir Joseph Duveen! I am Sir Joseph Duveen!"

Despite this jeering comment, Duveen might be forgiven, after the triumphant sales of *The Blue Boy* and *Pinkie,* for believing that the King of England was having delusions of grandeur about *him*. There was no doubt about his eminence. There seemed no limits to the coups de théâtre he could pull off, and also no question about the new enemies he was making in the international art world. As usual when feeling overconfident, Duveen was making statements made to order for those who were itching to pull him off his pedestal. That year of 1923 was remarkable for some major gaffes, ones that would have far-reaching consequences.

The first mistake began logically enough. Michael Dreicer, a wealthy jeweler and well-known collector, had died, and the executors of his will, the Fifth Avenue Bank of New York, asked Duveen Brothers to appraise his collection. The firm was often hired in cases of this kind and was usually also engaged to sell the works for a percentage, or they might buy some of the choicest pieces outright. So far, so good; but then Duveen arrived at a statue of a seated Virgin and Child in champlevé enameled bronze that Dreicer bought as a thirteenth-century work with a provenance back to Isabella of Spain. He paid a lot of money for it, $14,000, shortly before he died, on the usual terms, i.e., an installment plan. The first third had been paid but the rest of the bill was outstanding. Presumably Theodore Hetzler, who was president of the bank, did not particularly want to make a further cash outlay for an object he was planning to sell and expected the dealer to take it back. Duveen readily admitted that he had business interests with this bank, although he did not describe them; for the purposes of understanding the hidden agendum one may assume that the bank's interests and his own were identical. In his opinion Sir Joseph said that the work was "not genuine." No aspersions were cast on the esteemed colleague who had sold it to Dreicer. But the word was out. The statue was a fake.

One likes to think that if Uncle Henry had still been alive, none of this would have happened. Duveen had no business acting as an expert in the highly specialized world of medieval champlevé, even if he was the most famous art dealer in the world. But with Uncle Henry's passing there was no one in New York to rein in Joe and Ernest; Armand and Edward were too far away. Besides, Hetzler must have thought (as Duveen undoubtedly did) that after a few pointed questions the dealer would be glad to take the statue back, no questions asked. They must have been astounded when the seller, Georges Joseph Demotte, sued for slander and half a million dollars.

For his part, Duveen had his own reasons for suspecting Demotte. Demotte was a Belgian-born dealer with galleries in Paris on the rue de Berri and in New York at 8 East Fifty-seventh Street, literally around the corner from Duveen Brothers. For some years Demotte had been one of the leading dealers in the flourishing business of selling medieval objects to American collectors and institutions. As Elizabeth Bradford Smith wrote in *Medieval Art in America,* "France, the richest and most highly populated country in Europe during the twelfth and thirteenth centuries, had erected literally thousands of churches during these years and had richly endowed them with sculptures, stained glass, tapestries and liturgical objects. The secularization of monasteries and the seizing of church property by the state as a result of the French Revolution had, in a sense, 'liberated' a great many works of art belonging to the church."

In the years before 1906 it was perfectly legal to approach the curé of a small village church and persuade him to part with some object of devotion that he, in any case, thought worth almost nothing. An acceptable copy would do just as well, and this was usually part of the bargain. That object, passing through the hands of middlemen and small dealers, reaching a Paris dealer like Demotte and then finding its way to an American collection, appreciated in value by leaps and bounds. As a result, a statue that went for nothing in rural France could achieve stratospheric prices once it hit the international big time. In short order there was a perfectly wonderful opportunity for some curious characters. One of them was Gilbert Romeuf.

Duveen, who had sold such items in cooperation with Demotte and Gimpel, knew Romeuf well, as did Fowles. Like most such characters, Romeuf seemed to have no past, although a saber wound on his right cheek was indicative of something interesting. Since had had an almost encyclopedic knowledge of the French countryside, what mattered was what he knew and when. Duveen had several dealings with him. Fowles recalled that one such piece of business involved an ornamented silver bust of St. Martin that had been owned by a village church in the Limoges district since the thirteenth century and was sold to J. P. Morgan. A copy was provided for the church. Some years later that copy found its way to the London art market and was offered to the firm of Durlacher Brothers in New Bond Street. The Paris dealer who had it for sale was not very happy to learn from Durlacher that the bust was not, as they say, "right." This dealer subsequently joined forces with "a Belgian dealer"—perhaps Demotte—to sue the church for fraud and Romeuf as well, who had brokered both sales. Fowles wrote, "Romeuf proved to be a nimble witness: when asked whether he had sold the original bust, he replied that he had sold five or six of them and could not testify that any particular one was the original."

Romeuf is sometimes described as Duveen's agent, and perhaps he was for a time; but Duveen soon decided that he was a thoroughly tricky customer. The subject in question was a painting of the crucifixion by Fra Angelico owned by a French aristocrat that came up in 1916 and that Romeuf led Duveen to believe was for sale. After querying Berenson and receiving a telegram in reply to the effect that the painting was "ideal" and he should buy it, Duveen appears to have pondered the matter. The evidence is the telegram itself, which has been adorned with the kind of geometric doodles Duveen invariably made when in doubt. Romeuf was the intermediary, and he led them a merry chase. The family was about to sell; or could not quite sell yet. The owner was at sea with the navy and could not be reached. The offer must be improved. The more Romeuf explained, the more suspicious Duveen became. So did the Paris office. "We cannot make out whether this is a gigantic bluff on Romeuf's part," Fowles wrote after a month of delays, "but he makes rendez-vous from day to day, none of which have been kept." Then the Paris office, always loath to show its hand, decided to approach the family directly. The owners said that

Romeuf had tried every possible ruse, including engaging the assistance of their priest, to get them to sell their painting. They had repeatedly told him it was not for sale. They meant it. The whole thing had been a monumental waste of time.

The flourishing market in medieval works of art finally spurred the French government to take action. In 1906 a law was enacted that gave the government power to take over church property. Since much of the property in question was inside churches that were always left open, the law was a joke. It did, however, mean that sales of religious objects were no longer free and easy but would have to be conducted with the kind of absolute secrecy an art dealer counts on in a clandestine world. That Demotte should be anxious not to have his assertions about his wares examined too closely seems logical. According to him, the champlevé Virgin and Child came from the collection of Prince Antonio d'Orléans, Duke of Galliera, uncle of the King of Spain, and therefore the royal collection. According to tradition, he said, Queen Isabella had valued it so highly that she had a niche installed on the saddle of her horse so that she could take it wherever she went. To suggest otherwise was to impugn his reputation. Demotte seemed particularly incensed at the comment Duveen made to another dealer that he was so convinced the statue was a fake, he was willing to spend $500,000 to prove it. That, presumably, gave Demotte his idea about the precise sum in reparation owed him by Duveen. As for Duveen, he was, at that point, negotiating for items from the Brauer Collection in Paris that included Italian Renaissance busts, bas reliefs, fourteenth-century French ivories, and some small Italian bronzes, and one of his chief competitors was Demotte. As the correspondence makes clear, Duveen considered Demotte a confounded nuisance, and the feeling was cordially returned.

Demotte was, in his way, as rashly assertive as Duveen was. As it would transpire, he had even more to lose. René Gimpel related the kind of story Demotte liked to tell, having to do with the way he would travel through the French countryside rescuing bits of broken masonry and fragments of statuary from ignorant peasants whose single perverse aim in life was to destroy them. To hear Demotte talk he had, over and over again, saved precious historical artifacts out of sheer generosity of spirit.

Demotte was one of the principal exporters but not the only one. The American sculptor-turned-art-dealer George Gray Barnard was even more efficient at transferring these undervalued relics from French shores to American ones. Barnard shipped over something like six hundred works of art before 1911; belated French protests about such "pillage" led to a second law in 1913 tightening controls over exports deemed to be historical monuments. Despite these controls, Barnard continued to buy and sell. So did Demotte; the miracle is that he went unchallenged for so long, that is, until the affair of the champlevé Virgin and Child.

Duveen's conclusions about the statue had been reached a year before the lawsuit was filed. To his credit, he wrote memos to his Paris staff asking them to find evidence to back up his opinion. The reply from that office was interesting, if inconclusive. There was a general belief that he was right. The old dealer Gouvert, now dead, whose son was still in the business, had been a clever forger and had specialized in twelfth-century Limoges. When his son saw the photographs, the reply was that the work was too clumsy to have been done by Gouvert: the ultimate insult. Others in the shady world of fakes and forgeries explained that no one person would have made a statue of this kind. Some anonymous craftsman would have done the chasing and another the enameling, so that the work could never be traced. Meantime, Paris was trying to make contact with the statue's presumed former owner, Prince Antonio d'Orléans. The prince, who also styled himself Prince Antoine de Bourbon, was supposed to have accused a lady friend of stealing some of his jewelry. Paris concluded that the man was a shady customer and "no better than a runner," i.e., the lowest of the low in the hierarchy of art dealing.

A month later, Paris was even more convinced the work was false. There was something mannered and fussy about it, which made them think it might be by a Belgian, the one who made the so-called Byzantine book cover that another dealer had bought. Or perhaps it was from the atelier of a well-known Spanish ring. Once the lawsuit was filed, Duveen renewed his efforts to prove his point. He brought in two experts on champlevé enamel and then claimed, on a flimsy pretext, that their guarded remarks supported his position. He consulted an expert in metallurgy, again with unsatisfactory results. He was still willing to spend a vast sum to prove the statue "wrong," although the figure kept dwindling. Soon it was $100,000 instead of $500,000, and before long he dropped the idea altogether. In the meantime Jean Vigouroux, former manager of Demotte's New York gallery, who had his own fight brewing with Demotte, wrote to tell Duveen he was absolutely right about the statue. Demotte had sold dozens of fakes. Vigouroux knew the man who had made this one and would be charmed to join forces with Duveen in the fight against Demotte. Evidently he wanted to claim the reward; but by then Duveen was not sure he wanted to give one.

While Armand, in Paris, was being asked by his "affectionate uncle" to look at the scrapbooks in the Bibliothèque des Arts Décoratifs to see whether he could find a model for the Demotte Virgin, another scandal was about to emerge, involving a different kind of fake. Again, the trail led back to Demotte.

On May 22, 1923, just six days after Demotte sued Duveen for slander, the front page of *Le Matin* contained an article called "A Miracle at the Louvre." The subject was two twelfth-century full-length stone bas reliefs of kings which had been found in a garden adjoining the ruins of the Church of Notre-Dame-de-la-Couldre in Parthenay. The elongated, almost exaggeratedly protracted figures, wearing crowns, their feet bare, had been sold to the Louvre by Demotte in 1914, along with another bas relief of some shepherds that had also once adorned the same church; these, to judge from their dazzled expressions, have just been told of Christ's birth.

The only problem was that the writer of the article (not identified, but clearly a specialist) had found engravings of the same bas reliefs in books published half a century before. In those books the kings had no legs at all but were broken torsos lying on the ground. As for the shepherds, they had no heads, no beards, and no arms. What a miracle, the writer commented ironically: Some dead statues had been "born again."

This delicious scandal blew the minor matter of a squabble between two dealers right off the front pages. The possibility that someone with inside knowledge was citing chapter and verse about doctored statues inside the hallowed halls of the Louvre was too good to miss, even if the name of the merchant actually involved had not yet been made public. Furthermore, there were two more Parthenay kings in America. These had been sold to Isabella Stewart Gardner at the same time, with an enthusiastic recommendation from Berenson. That was strange, since B.B. liked to say he "never baptized outside his own parish," and this had to be the first time he had ever claimed expertise in medieval French statuary. These, too, had miraculously restored torsos and legs, a fact that B.B. had failed to mention.

Next day, the papers were full of explanations about the curious Parthenay kings. It was simple, Paul Vitry, curator of the department of medieval sculpture at the Louvre, said. In the decades since the broken statuary was discovered, in 1843 and 1876, many more pieces had been recovered and been added to the kings and the shepherds. Vitry said the fragments had been lovingly gathered together by the nuns of Chavagne at Parthenay. A skilled workman "dressed the wounds"—his quaint term—and reassembled the bas reliefs in their original glory. There was no miracle, even at the Louvre.

Two thirteenth-century French medieval sculptures which
Isabella Stewart Gardner bought through Berenson as the
genuine article. They turned out to have fake torsos and legs.

This explanation was disputed by Mlle J. Guilhaud, owner of what had
been the convent of Chavagne. She recalled that she had seen the twelfth-
century torsos being taken away but she had never seen anyone come looking for bits and pieces of legs, a version that was emphatically seconded by
her neighbor, a local archeologist and collector. The anonymous writer for
Le Matin brought up a stylistic argument concerning the fact that the
kings had bare feet. Christ and his Apostles might be depicted barefoot,

but the idea that kings of that period would be similarly unshod was non-sense. Fortunately, forgers who might have an artistic gift invariably knew nothing about historical accuracy, which made their work easy to spot, he wrote.

That day, Fowles's letter from Paris was full of the story, confirming the suspicions of the mysterious writer for *Le Matin*. It was clear that vital areas, like legs and feet and even heads and arms, had been replaced in a wholesale manner. Parisians were talking about nothing else. No one knew who was behind the campaign to discredit the Louvre and, by implication, Demotte, but Jean Vigouroux was suspected. The gossip was that he was being aided and abetted by Duveen, which would give Demotte's lawyers all kinds of interesting talking points. It was vital that Duveen have nothing to do with Vigouroux.

There was more. Questions were being raised about other figures that came from Demotte in 1909 and were now in the Louvre. They were two so-called warriors, sixteenth-century bas reliefs from the Château de Mogneville in the village of Contrisson (Meuse). At least one of them looked suspicious, but since the château had been completely destroyed during the Revolution the trail seemed to have dried up. But then Maître Braye, a member of the Bar-le-Duc archeological society, discovered that one of the reliefs had been defaced by small boys, who used it as a target for their stones, and all that was left was the man's calf and slipper. As for the other, the oldest inhabitants of the village said it had never been a warrior, but "some personage of mythology who flourished a trident." The authorities could ignore the scandal no longer. On May 28, a week after *Le Matin* had launched its series of revelations, the public prosecutor for the Seine district began an investigation.

That May of 1923, every day seemed to bring sensational charges. Almost as soon as an inquiry was announced, the authorities were confronted with the news (no news to anyone in the business for decades) that gangs of art thieves were making off with statuary taken from churches. If, in the old days, the whole thing was done in a sportsmanlike way, with a polite request to the priest and money changing hands, the new crowd was no longer bothering with such niceties. Objects vanished and copies reappeared some time afterwards. The originals were swallowed up by the international art market. There was only one copy or, to judge from Romeuf, there were any number of copies. Some lucky collector bought the original. A thirteenth-century statue of a Virgin and Child from the Île de France school had mysteriously disappeared. It was said to have been snatched from the church of St.-Sauveur-sur-École by a band of men in a car, only to be returned some time later. The copy was almost perfect and the only way it had been identified was by a close examination of the head, which had been repaired in the original and was now in perfect condition.

Then a new witness stepped forward. It seemed that an Italian workman, a molder and patina maker named Pierre Belli, who lived in the Paris suburbs, had confessed that he himself had extracted the Virgin and Child from the church, taken a mold of it, and replaced the original with his replica. According to the smalltime Paris antique dealer who bought it, the statue was in hard stone and had a rather interesting polychrome texture. However, it was in bad condition. The head was broken. The Virgin's left arm, which held the Child, had been redone in plaster, and one of her wrists, also broken off, had been replaced with a piece of wood. Faced with such detailed testimony from knowledgeable witnesses, the abbé at the church of St. Sauveur-sur-École had no recourse but to confess that he had sold the statue and replaced it with a copy, which he did with as good a grace as he could muster. The abbé had been paid 2,500 francs for the statue. The workman's fee was 1,000 francs. The Paris antique dealer sold it for 14,000 francs to a Belgian who specialized in, etc. etc. The trail led back once again to Demotte. As for the American client, that was rumored to be W. K. Vanderbilt, and the price paid, 400,000 francs.

Paris writers pointed out that a dealer engaged in the repair and manufacture of medieval statuary was running a large operation. He had to have scouts. He needed vans and garages. He had to rent studios where copyists could be employed discreetly. Vigouroux, who kept popping in and out of these investigations, claimed to know the sculptor employed to make the Parthenay kings, the warrior bas reliefs, and any number of other choice items for Demotte. So did a French expert in Gothic sculpture named Cornillon, who said he had repeatedly warned the Louvre about the trade in faked and heavily restored sculpture, but had been ignored. The trouble was, the sculptor in question was dead.

EVERYONE AGREED THAT EMILE BOUTRON, the chief sculptor at Demotte's nine-room atelier in Montparnasse on the rue Dutot, had an inspired eye. Like the legendary fakers of any age, he seemed to have mastered more than the necessary techniques to make even an exact copy, detail by detail, as described in contemporary sources, but could fashion original designs that would look as if they had come from the medieval imagination. This ability to repair, amend, alter, and invent anew made him extremely valuable. And in this case he had the necessary knowledge not to make historical errors. His widow claimed that the Parthenay kings were given bare feet not because of any mistake on his part—he had originally sculpted them in armor—but because Demotte insisted. Boutron was happy enough with the work he was doing. He would rather work steady hours and pick up a paycheck than have to worry about selling what he had made. What happened to his *navets,* or "turnips," as he called them—slang for a bad painting, or daub—was no concern of his. Just the same, he happened to visit the Louvre one afternoon and came back home with the surprising news that his own work was on exhibit there. He told his wife, "Our patron must be pretty confident to have such cheek as to stick things like that in the Louvre."

On reflection, however, it was quite a compliment. There was no getting around that. Some time afterward he began to talk about that fact, discreetly or indiscreetly. "M. de Stoecklin, who was a friend of Boutron's . . . told how Boutron once bragged to him that he was the only living sculptor to have his works in the Louvre. He bet De Stoecklin a dinner that he couldn't tell the real from the fake in any of his work."

His wife was proud of the fact that her husband's work had been accepted by public museums in France and abroad; it was a testament to his stature as an artist. Just the same, she was concerned about the risks he was running. He seemed sublimely unaware that he knew too much and that that made him dangerous, as far as certain people were concerned. Just exactly when he did begin to fear for his life is not clear. But he told one sculptor working in the studio, "I am rather worried. I am afraid they want to silence me."

On the morning of April 9, 1920, he was working as usual. He was alone in his studio. Other workers in adjoining rooms heard the sound of his hammer and chisel going steadily until about midday. Suddenly there was a shot. They raced into the room and found him on the floor, with blood all around him and splattering his work. He had been shot in the head; the bullet had lodged in his brain. On one side was a chisel; there was a revolver on the other. He was rushed to the Hospital Necker and died there some hours later without regaining consciousness.

Despite the fact that all accounts say Boutron was alone at the time, a fellow worker testified at the inquest that he had seen the sculptor kill himself. The case was closed, although there were some curious aspects. To begin with, whether Boutron was, or was not, alone, never seems to have been cleared up. Secondly the wound, if self-inflicted, took place in a strange way, from the right rear, behind the ear. That a man would attempt to hold a gun in this position seemed implausible, particularly given the heavy revolver he was using. Third, Demotte's hostility to Boutron and his wife was marked, as she discovered the next day when she went to the studio, nominally in her husband's name. She said, "I was refused admittance and the same happened on other days when I went to claim what was due me of my husband's belongings and take a look at his accounts. I was convinced then that his death was not suicide. I asked for an enquiry, but I was refused." She also said that the day after her husband's death, Demotte warned her not to ask any questions, "because I don't owe you anything, and don't forget that you are poor and I am rich."

The widow Boutron had remained silent for three years. But now Demotte was on the defensive and she wanted her questions answered. She asked that the case be reopened, and her request was granted. An official inquiry into the circumstances of her husband's death was ordered on July 10, 1923. Madame Boutron made another sensational charge. She said that the sculptor in whom her husband had confided—no name was given— "was ready to give evidence in my behalf but he also died mysteriously some weeks ago in the same studio. He was found dead at the foot of a ladder and it was believed that he had fallen and killed himself. This time I hope that the truth will be discovered."

Would a talented forger who believed he was about to be unmasked decide to commit suicide? Or would his employer, hearing that he was starting to boast about his prowess, decide he knew too much? The death of Boutron has never been satisfactorily explained. The inquiry his widow asked for was apparently closed for lack of evidence; there is no trace of it in the official records. Descriptions of the circumstances surrounding his death come from brief reports in the French newspapers and the *New York Times*. Colin Simpson's book *Artful Partners* has a fuller account, but from sources that have not been located, and the book has no notes. According to this information, the gun used was a cavalry model with a nine-inch barrel, its butt inlaid in silver with the monogram GR. Simpson writes that Fowles easily identified these initials as belonging to Gilbert Romeuf. That someone like Romeuf would willingly leave behind incriminating evidence seems highly unlikely. On the other hand, if the gun was planted, why was this obvious clue ignored? Some of these questions could presumably be answered in the archives of the Louvre, which has kept a secret file on the Demotte case for the past eighty years. This writer's representative was, however, denied access.

The Simpson chronology cites June 9, 1923, as the date of Boutron's death, i.e., during the height of the investigations, which makes a better story but is contradicted by the actual date: April 9, 1920. Other details in

Simpson's account have inaccurate dates or wrong spellings ("Vigouroux" is misspelled throughout, as is the name of the examining magistrate, M. Ameline, and Boutron's first name is given as "Henri"). Furthermore, there are no records about the reopened inquiry in the Seine court archives. All that has been found are the archives in the Hospital Necker and the official cause of death: "Fracture du crâne par balle de revolver."

IF DEMOTTE HAD NEVER brought his action for slander against Duveen, none of this would probably have been discovered. The irony of his dilemma was that his most active antagonist that summer of 1923 was Vigouroux. With or without Duveen's help, Vigouroux was on the attack. It was clear that other Paris dealers had been waiting for years to go after what they must have seen as Demotte's reckless tactics. Cornillon, the expert in Gothic art who was also a dealer, opened the attack on the American front, claiming that fabricated sculpture had been sold to American collectors and even the Metropolitan Museum of Art in New York. He asserted that 20 percent of the Gothic art in that museum was a fake. "I know every important piece in it that passed through the dealer in question is faked, or fabricated, from a fragment of the original statue." Two days later Vigouroux, who had managed Demotte's New York gallery for twenty years, jumped in with claims of his own, stating that he could cite chapter and verse. He said that he himself had sold many of these items in good faith before realizing how extensive the deception was. He claimed that at least twenty pieces in the Metropolitan were either faked or restored, and that of a hundred pieces bought by John D. Rockefeller some years before, three-quarters were spurious. American collectors, he said, had been "stuck for tens of millions of dollars by unscrupulous dealers, of which my former employer was the chief." Demotte responded appropriately by suing him. He claimed Vigouroux had pocketed money he was owed while he was his New York manager. It was not the first time Demotte had gone on the attack. Two years before he claimed that Vigouroux had defrauded him out of $3,000 over the sale of some Persian manuscripts and actually had him arrested in Paris. Vigouroux was released when the manuscripts were found in a safe in New York.

Meantime, the Metropolitan issued statements to the effect that its collections did not contain any fakes. René Gimpel and George Gray Barnard expressed a similar confidence in the genuineness of American collections. Only Henry Walters of Baltimore, a vice president of the Metropolitan, was willing to admit he had been deceived. He said, "I have an art collection and I keep a special case into which I put pieces which I discover to be spurious." He now had something like thirty false pieces in the case, for a total value of $100,000. If a collector as experienced and wary as Walters had been cheated out of large sums of money, could it really be true that no one else in America had been stung? He said, "The growth of museums is so rapid in America and the danger of spurious art so constant that the Metropolitan is considering starting a school for training museum directors."

Walters's comments were some indication of the naiveté, or complacency, with which Americans were buying works of art in general, and medieval statuary in particular. What percentage of "amendations" made a statue more or less authentic? Speaking only of its financial value, Edouard Jonas, president of the Art Dealers' Syndicate of Paris, spelled out a table of declining values, depending on how much had been restored. The value went down by 25 percent if the head was restored. Restored limbs meant an even greater decrease, 33 percent. Restored feet were not a serious problem. Any other restoration brought the price down by 10 percent. He continued, "Any case of a sale where the existence of more than ten per cent restoration has not been stated is flagrant dishonesty. It is obtaining money under false pretenses." The French were more or less aware, but the American market hardly seemed to care. It was back to the old problem: i.e., that skillful forgers fabricated an ideal, in the 1920s, of the way medieval sculpture ought to look. They had mirrored that image so perfectly that contemporary viewers were blind to the deception and might even prefer it. But in any case, sculptures were being manhandled as recklessly as paintings. They seemed to be considered as extra-large bits of decorative atmosphere or be incorporated, say, into a Spanish cloister, which was what Mrs. Gardner did with her Gothic kings from Parthenay.

Then there was the case of another pair of thirteenth-century French kings, life-size statues in carved stone, which supposedly came from the Abbée de Montieres, St. Jean, Côte d'Or. They had been bought by Demotte in the Manzi sale of 1919, and by the 1930s they were being exhibited in Duveen's Fifth Avenue galleries. James Rorimer, the Metropolitan's expert in Gothic sculpture, repeatedly went to see them and wanted to buy them but just knew something was wrong. Paul Sachs recalled that Rorimer finally asked permission to examine the statues with one of the new X-ray machines and Duveen agreed. Rorimer was able to demonstrate that the statue's heads had been switched and several other creative alterations and amendations had been made. No doubt he got a reduction in the $80,000 price tag. The heads were returned to their rightful owners and the sale was made. Duveen's only comment, to an associate, was, "You'd better get two of those machines."

By the early summer of 1923 Fowles, writing sensible letters from Paris, and Louis Levy, in New York, were beginning to exert some sort of control over their wayward leader. While Fowles politely suggested and cautioned, Levy took a more direct approach, apparently exasperated beyond endurance by his client's stubborn ability to keep his own hot water at a rolling boil. For the fact is that Duveen was itching to get into the fight. Henry Walters's remarks about the fakes he himself had bought seemed to signal, to Duveen, a kind of admission that Cornillon and Vigouroux had identified actual fakes in the Metropolitan Museum of Art. Wouldn't it be a good idea, Duveen wrote, if he made a statement about how welcome an investigation would be? He did at least have the sense to ask Levy. The answer was "No!" There was another issue involving what Duveen considered a provocative statement by Demotte's lawyer John Quinn in yesterday's papers. Didn't Mr. Levy think it was the perfect moment to inform Quinn that if he wanted a fight, he could have it, "and that pretty sharply"? The answer was another emphatic "No!" There was a handwritten note in the margin: "You are to say nothing and do nothing. If you depart from this advice I can be of no help to you!"

Duveen had to have known that Levy, his indispensable ally in so many fights, was too valuable to lose. He had to content himself with a dignified statement in reply to the suit for slander in which he reiterated his confidence in Demotte's honesty as a dealer along with his lack of confidence in that statue in particular. If he had hoped for backing in the trade, he was not getting it. The Bond Street dealers, a cable from his London office said, thought he had just made unnecessary trouble for himself. Why was he giving opinions on other people's merchandise anyway? He had a positive genius for getting himself into untenable positions. Ordinary people thought he was doing it out of "spite." Perhaps they were not far wrong.

WHILE THE ACCUSATIONS and denials proceeded at a lively pace, Duveen had plenty of other affairs on his mind. He bought a Holbein in Austria for £40,000 and paid an equally handsome price for a Frans Hals owned by Lord Spencer. There were a Mantegna and also a newly discovered Vermeer, a large portrait of a young man that had turned up in Paris. Duveen paid ten thousand or twelve thousand pounds for it and sold it to Bache. Gimpel thought it was a dreadful picture, certainly not a Vermeer, and it is not among the Bache paintings that were subsequently given to the Metropolitan. But the great excitement of May 1923 was the sale of the Brownlow collection, a superior group of Old Masters that had been owned by the late Adelbert Wellington, third Earl of Brownlow. Duveen had been following that affair closely and had approached the earl's executors about four paintings in which he was particularly interested: a Van Dyck, *Anton Triest, Burgomaster of Ghent;* Albert Cuyp's *The River Maas at Dordrecht;* a Cima in a wonderful state of preservation; and an attractive Bellini. In fact, Duveen Brothers was offered the four paintings for £50,000, which seemed excessive. They turned the offer down. That, as it transpired, was a mistake.

Duveen had reckoned without the competitive spirit of Knoedler's, which was beginning to jockey for position as the leading international art dealer. So when the paintings were sent for auction at Christie's on May 4, the stage was set for a confrontation. Duveen sent detailed instructions to his brothers Eddie and Ernest, representing the firm. They knew how he felt about the Van Dyck. They were not to lose that under any circumstances. As for the Cuyp, Duveen set a price limit, which they were at liberty to disregard if Knoedler's was in the race. In that case they had to buy it no matter what. However, if another dealer wanted it, they could let it go. As for the Bellini, Duveen wanted them to turn in an order at the last minute in the hope that it might be knocked down in their name. They should show a marked lack of interest in that work and be sure they hesitated appropriately.

The great day came and, as predicted, it was a fight to the finish between Duveens and Knoedler's. The Van Dyck had almost sold for the bargain price of $75,000. "Just as it seemed the hammer would fall Messrs. Knoedler challenged and the bids went up until the picture was knocked down to Messrs. Duveen for 28,000 guineas, the contest between the rival sides having lasted only ninety seconds." Duveens also paid through the nose for the Cuyp, which cost them $90,000, said to be the highest price ever paid for a Cuyp in the English market. They did pick up the Bellini *Adoration of the Shepherds* for a relatively modest price; the price of the Cima was £9,200.

It was a glorious, a fantastic success, Ernest and Eddie cabled a day later. This showed that Duveen Brothers had the international art market in the palms of their hands. Everyone was being congratulated. However, Duveen should remember that they turned down these four pictures for £50,000 and ended up spending a good deal more for them at auction: £61,000. This was not good news. Sellers were bound to take note of the message, that there was more money to be made at auction than in a private sale. So

Duveen should not be too pleased with himself, Ernest and Eddie continued. No doubt the cautionary words did not have much effect on his
mood. At least in one arena, he had wrestled with an adversary and won.

DUVEEN, HIS WIFE, AND DAUGHTER sailed to Europe on the *Mauretania* in June. There was another big sale brewing, this time two paintings
by Sir Joshua Reynolds, *Lady Crosbie* (afterwards Countess of Glandore)
and *The Young Fortune Teller,* portraits of the two children of the Duke of
Marlborough. These belonged to Sir Charles Tennant, and although he
feigned ignorance about their eventual owners, in fact Duveen knew perfectly well that both were going to the Huntingtons, who were continuing
to buy on a princely scale. So was Duveen. Gimpel wrote, "A month ago he
bought a Dürer. At the same time he showed me a Fra Angelico and a
Rembrandt, *Portrait of a Man in a Red Toque.* A few days ago he sold Lord
Carnarvon's Lawrence *Woman and Child* for an enormous price, and
Turner's *The Queen of the Adriatic* for $300,000." Wherever he went,
Duveen was the talk of the art world, which must have gone some distance
to console him for Levy's brusque admonition to keep his mouth shut.

That summer of 1923, having made numerous gifts to France, the Petit
Palais, the Louvre, and various societies, Duveen was awarded the rosette
of the Légion d'Honneur. Gimpel wrote, "He hopes one day to receive a
peerage in England."

DEMOTTE, TOO, WAS IN EUROPE. Samuel Frankel, of *American Art
News,* had dinner with him that August in his Paris apartment. Demotte
was determined to press his suit, Frankel said. He would not accept a
penny less than half a million dollars and planned to divide the prize
between the Louvre and the Metropolitan Museum of Art. He was to sail
for New York on September 23. He had just taken another five-year lease
on his Fifty-seventh Street quarters and was even toying with the idea of
publishing his own newspaper.

That was August. Early in September Demotte accepted the invitation
of an old friend, one of fifteen years' standing, for a weekend in the country. It was the beginning of the hunting season, and Otto Wegener, a
Parisian antique dealer, had a château, the Parc du Petit-Jean, in Chau-
mont-sur-Tharonne, not far from Blois. On Monday, September 3, the
house party gathered in the extensive grounds of the château for the first

day's shoot. After a morning spent looking for targets they went in to lunch. The official report reads, "After lunch, as several hunters and beaters remained in the room, Wegener left, carrying in his arms the gun he had deposited in the dining room during lunch. When one of his assistants asked him whether his gun was recharged, Wegener replied in the affirmative, and in order to convince those present, lifted the gun in the air and pulled the trigger. The gun fired and then recoiled, flying out of Wegener's hands. It fell to the ground and the impact set off a second shot. Demotte was hit in the chest and died a few minutes later."

If the court findings are to be relied upon, Wegener and Demotte were not alone when the gun went off, and there could be no question of a murder being made to look like a hunting accident. Still, the manner of Demotte's death is one more bizarre aspect of the extraordinary chain of events set off by the forged, or genuine, champlevé enamel figurine. Duveen could barely contain his glee at the news that he no longer had to prove anything. This made Louis Levy even angrier. Duveen must remember that there were a widow and a son and the case could still be revived. In fact, the case against Vigouroux went forward and he was found guilty by the Seine Assizes. (He was fined a token twenty-five francs and spent a month in jail, a judgment that was later reversed.) Levy continued that Duveen must do absolutely nothing, say absolutely nothing and not even think it, whatever the provocation, or Levy would not be responsible for the consequences. Duveen wisely took his advice. Once again, the maddest kind of luck had released him from a very tricky situation.

It was convenient not to have Demotte around for other reasons as well. Now that he had been "eliminated," as Duveen so delicately put it in December of that year, there was one less competitor in the Brauer sale. And his grudge against Demotte continued for several years. When Helen Frick, Frick's daughter, bought a sculpture said to have come from the forger Alceo Dossena and sold through Demotte, Duveen happily sat down and wrote her a reproving letter about buying fakes without seeking his advice. Inside knowledge could be very useful when it was a matter of bringing a client to heel. Still, events sometimes had a way of backfiring, even when the client was demonstrably loyal.

It is said that shortly after Demotte's death, Duveen was lunching with Mrs. E. T. Stotesbury at the Ritz in Paris.

"Am I a friend of yours?" she asked. He replied that of course she was.

"Oh dear," she said. "All your friends appear to get shot."

Chapter Twelve

LA BELLE FERRONIÈRE

THE TROUBLE STARTED AT 1 A.M. on June 17, 1920. Duveen, in London, was awakened by a telephone call from a reporter with the *New York World*. It was a routine inquiry: Andrée Hahn, a lady in Kansas, claimed to have a Leonardo da Vinci for sale, *La Belle Ferronière*. The name means, literally, "the pretty wife of an ironworker." In this case it refers to the chain with a single jewel which the sitter is wearing around her forehead. Duveen, half asleep, reacted almost automatically. It could not possibly be a Leonardo, he said. Why not? the reporter wanted to know. How could Duveen know without having seen it? Because, said Duveen, the original painting, c. 1499, was in the Louvre. With that offhand remark he unleashed a ten-year saga that would culminate in the most celebrated art trial of the twentieth century.

La Belle Ferronière shows a young woman in a red dress in three-quarter-face. The jewel in her headband is centered on her forehead, and the necklace wrapped around her throat contrasts prettily with the square neckline of her dress and its full, ornamented sleeves. Her hair is parted in the center and smoothly drawn over her ears. She is looking toward the viewer with a calm, questioning gaze that has baffled and fascinated the experts for decades. It is undoubtedly a beautiful and historic work. But is it quite good enough to be a Leonardo? Perhaps it is an early work. It may only be *close* to Leonardo, as Kenneth Clark thought; he and Bernard Berenson hypothesized that it might have been painted by one of Leonardo's best pupils, Boltraffio. On the other hand, its provenance could be traced back to the art collections of Francis I, and there were technical aspects, involving the techniques used and the particular kind of craque-

Above: La Belle Ferronière: The version owned by Andrée Hahn,
which Duveen claimed was not by Leonardo da Vinci.
His verdict got him into a great deal of trouble.
Below: La Belle Ferronière: the Leonardo da Vinci owned by the Louvre

lure of the portrait, that pointed to Leonardo. Opinions had shifted up and down during the intervening centuries, but when Duveen made his confident pronouncement, *La Belle Ferronière* was hanging in the Louvre as a Leonardo.

The *Belle Ferronière* owned by Andrée Hahn, while outwardly identical in outline, shows certain differences, notably in the features. Close examination reveals that the eyes are slightly larger and have a more bulbous look. The bridge of the nose is blunter. The cheeks are fatter, giving the girl a moon-faced look. In contrast to the Louvre version, there is much less of the exquisitely delicate molding which gives Leonardo's facial paintings their characteristic look; the contours seem almost flattened by comparison. The difference is quite striking in the modeling of the mouth. In the Louvre version the lips are hardly suggested, but in the Hahn version they are fuller, almost pouting. But the clearest difference is in the expressions, which bear only a superficial resemblance to each other. This other *Belle Ferronière* is ever-so-subtly pleased with herself. She looks placid, somehow coquettish, as if the grave and guileless girl in the Louvre painting, who is barely in her teens, has been transformed into a plumper and all-too-knowing twenty-year-old flirt.

Although the issue was, from the first, a contest between the "real" Leonardo and the copy, and although advocates for the Hahn painting liked to give the impression that there were only two versions extant, the fact is that *La Belle Ferronière* has, like Leonardo's *Mona Lisa,* been copied endlessly down through the centuries. The Louvre version could be an old copy. The Hahn version could be an old painting, but still a copy made, say, two or three hundred years ago. There were endless possible permutations, but very few were touched on, because they did not suit either argument. Nor did each side spend much time considering who might have painted the Louvre version if not Leonardo.

On that night of June 17 the irony was that the painting's owner had already asked Duveen Brothers whether they would like to buy her painting. She received a routine reply from one of Duveen's functionaries. Duveen never saw the letter, and how he would have reacted is impossible to say. But, as has been seen, he was far too casual about these kinds of statements and far too ready to use his powerful position to disparage the wares of other dealers. Andrée Hahn would have been right to suspect his motives, because one never knew. He could have deliberately killed the sale, waited a decent interval, bought the painting himself for a pittance through an intermediary, and subsequently restored it to full Leonardo status.

Andrée Hahn and her husband, Harry, had a particular reason to be annoyed. They claimed that a sale had been ruined. According to them, a wealthy donor had guaranteed their asking price of $225,000 and was about to present the painting to the Kansas City Art Institute. Because of Duveen the deal had fallen through. But now no one else would buy it, either. The only way to restore the credibility of the painting was to confront the problem head-on.

With Duveen it is sometimes difficult to decide when he was being recklessly overconfident and when he was sure of his ground. In this case the latter is probably true. As an experienced dealer, he knew that if the Hahn painting really rivaled the one in the Louvre, it would be for sale for two million or three million dollars, not the relatively modest sum of $225,000. To be accepted, the painting would have to be introduced in careful stages. There would first need to be articles in respected art journals, to the effect that a new Leonardo had been discovered. There would need to be a chorus of expert voices, all staking their reputations on that finding. The Hahns only had one expert, Georges Sortais, one of the art experts accredited by the French courts for his opinions in public auctions and legal appraisals. Besides, Sortais had been paid for his certificate of authenticity when the picture was first offered for sale, and to insiders, such opinions were worthless. Anyone could claim to have a Leonardo, and people regularly did; they were always wrong. It was storm in a teacup as far as Duveen was concerned. And, to do him justice, in contrast to the Demotte case, where opinion was against him, the art world was sympathetic, even indignant. Every dealer had been in the same position at one time or another. If a man could not express an honest opinion, what was the world coming to?

Duveen was quite jolly the day Helen Rice, a pretty and fashionably dressed young woman, appeared at 720 Fifth Avenue in the role of process server. It was November 1921, and Sir Joseph had just returned from London on the SS *Olympic.* The lady had called four times before at the galleries but would not relinquish her papers until she could hand them to Sir Joseph in person. "No attempt was made by the art dealer to avoid service, and he thanked her most cordially when she thrust the documents in his hands." The suit by Andrée Hahn claimed that Duveen had falsely and maliciously slandered her painting. It further claimed that "fingerprints imprinted on the surface will prove its authenticity to Leonardo." Andrée Hahn sought damages of $500,000. It seemed to be the magic number.

The Rape of La Belle, a diatribe against Joseph Duveen by Harry Hahn, was published in 1946, seven years after Duveen's death. In the book Hahn

used a variety of arguments to further his belief that his family's *Belle* was
the real Leonardo and the Louvre's was a copy. Hahn said it had taken him
years of research in the National Archives of France looking for documents
which would establish a history of the two paintings. By common agreement, an inventory of the king's paintings by Bernard Lepicie in 1752 is the
first to shed light on confusing earlier descriptions about which titles per-
tain to which paintings in the royal collections. The Louvre portrait, on a
wooden panel, has the same dimensions as one of the portraits described
by Lepicie. The second is three and a half inches longer, also on wood, and
described as having hands holding a wispy lace handkerchief. That version,
Hahn writes, was at some point transferred from wood to canvas by
G. Hacquin, the king's restorer, in 1777. Hahn writes that entries by Lepicie describe the Louvre painting as "in the manner of Leonardo da
Vinci," while the version with hands is called a Leonardo. Since the Hahn
version shows signs of having been cut off at the bottom, and has been
annotated on the reverse with a signature by Hacquin, Hahn argues that
the Hahn version is the real Leonardo and the Louvre version is the copy.

However, the Louvre version remained incontestably in the royal collection, so its provenance is assured, at least as far back as Francis I. The
Hahn version's history is less easily ascertained. According to Hahn again,
the painting that once had hands was acquired by General Louis Tourton,
head of a large Parisian banking firm, Tourton and Thellussion, during the
final days of the French Revolution in 1796. It remained in the general's
collection until 1847, when it was one of six paintings to be sold; but Hahn
does not take the story of its wanderings any further than that. He seems to
feel he has proved his case. But S. Lawrence Miller, who eventually became
their lawyer, was less confident. The *New York Times* wrote, "He must
prove that the painting Lepicie saw and catalogued nearly 200 years ago
was the original, and that the one which Mrs. Hahn now presents is the
same one." His first point, as Miller was well aware, might be impossible to
prove. As for the second, the Hahn argument hinges on the Hacquin testimonial on the reverse. But, as the art trade knows well, testimonials on the
backs of paintings may be just as suspect as anything else in the shady
world of fakes and forgeries. The art trade likes paintings that have signa-
tures, or failing that, unanimity from specialists in the field. What it likes
best of all are paintings that have incontestably remained in the same
hands. And, in this case, all the evidence was against the work. The Hahns
must have known Duveen would use all his influence to buy a chorus of
damning criticism from the experts and, in the days before advanced X-ray

Andrée Hahn at the time of her lawsuit against Duveen in 1929

and infrared techniques, it really did come down to the aesthetics of the matter. Making a case for this *Belle Ferronière* seemed almost quixotic.

Miller's version of the painting's provenance was that the painting had been acquired by a general, although his name was not Tourton but Pourtonne, and that the painting was not sold in 1847 but remained in the Pourtonne family until it was given to Andrée Hahn in 1919. It was a wedding present from her godmother, a descendant of the Pourtonne family.

Andrée Hahn confused the issue further by giving a variety of explanations. She, a French war bride, had met and married Captain Harry J. Hahn, an aviator with General Pershing's staff in France and who won the Légion d'Honneur and the War Cross. Smuggling the painting out of France was the first challenge. "The painting was packed in a basket of washing and carried by a young Frenchwoman, Mlle. Massot, through the French lines and into Belgium; to Brussels and Antwerp and on the steamer *Finland* of the Red Star Line to New York." Why that should have been necessary in 1919, a year after the war ended, was not explained.

She sometimes said she was a niece of the former owner, the Marquis de

Chambure of Brittany, and, almost in the same breath, that she was the daughter of the Marquis de Lardoux, a wealthy Breton nobleman. A few days later she told the *Kansas City* (Missouri) *Star* that the painting had originally been given by General Tournon to his adopted daughter, Madame Antoine Vincent. Andrée Hahn asserted that from her it went to the Comtesse de Pontbriand, her aunt. She herself had been given the painting jointly with her closest friend and relative, Mlle Louise de Montaut. Maurice de Montaut, heir to the Chambure family, subsequently declared that he knew nothing about an Andrée Hahn and that she was in no way connected with his family.

As might be expected, the differences between the versions were too interesting to ignore. Duveen started some quiet investigations and discovered that Andrée Hahn's maiden name had indeed been Lardoux, but the family was not wealthy or aristocratic. She was born in Argentan in Normandy, the daughter of a small jeweler. Her father remarried when she was small and she went to live with an aunt, Josephine Massot, who had a novelty shop in Dinard. Andrée Lardoux grew up there and was making or selling hats in Dinard when she met and married Harry Hahn in July 1919. When the couple decided to settle in France, Andrée Hahn's aunt remodeled her premises to allow for the installation of a bar, called the Celtic Bar, and then a cabaret called the Rallye Bar. This was being run by the Hahns.

According to the detectives' report, the aunt, Josephine Massot, had a good friend, Louise de Montaut, who was a nurse in her fifties. She had inherited the painting from her mother, née Vincent. She in turn got the painting from her parents. The painting was traced as far back as a banker who lived in Paris during the First Empire (1804–14). Presumably he could have been General Tournon, but no name was given. Louise de Montaut found herself in financial difficulties and approached a number of Paris art dealers, but was told the painting was worthless. She said she gave it away because she could not bear to hear anything more about it; its fate, the report states, was the cause of many painful family arguments. There was no relationship between the Montaut, Lardoux, and Chambure families, but the Marquis de Chambure had been something of a surrogate uncle to Louise de Montaut because he had been a witness at her parents' marriage. So when she tried to sell it, he suggested it be hung in his house to give it a spurious provenance, presumably, and increase its chances. It was there, in 1917, that Sortais looked at it and certified it as a Leonardo. Shortly after their marriage the Hahns went to the U.S., taking with them their certificate and their *Belle Ferronière*.

The Hahns first engaged Hyacinthe Ringrose, a well-known trial lawyer formerly of New York, now based in Paris, who appeared to like the argument that Leonardo da Vinci habitually used his fingertips to push around the wet paint on his canvases. Fingerprints were clearly visible on the Hahn and therefore it followed that . . . Quite how the famous attorney planned to demonstrate that these prints belonged to Leonardo in the centuries before fingerprints were registered to their owners is not clear. As Duveen commented, "I have handled the picture in question and genuine Da Vincis a number of times and I am afraid if Mme. Hahn is after fingerprints she may come into court with some of mine and contend they are Leonardo's. If that contention should arise I would be forced to believe in the transmigration of souls." Wilhelm von Bode in Berlin dismissed the argument, saying it was impossible to distinguish an original painting from a copy by fingerprints. Those found on Old Masters in the wet paint were invariably those of a carpenter who framed the picture, a varnisher, or even a restorer. This argument surfaced occasionally in the long-drawn-out wrangling that followed and was finally buried by one expert who insisted that no Leonardo prints were known to exist.

Duveen soon mustered his first battery of experts to challenge the Hahn attribution to Leonardo point for point. Stanchfield and Levy, representing Duveen as usual, had decided to call together a distinguished group. Since Andrée Hahn was willing to have her painting go back to Paris, the witnesses would examine both paintings at the Louvre, side by side.

One of the main witnesses was Sir Charles Holmes, director of London's National Gallery, who had pronounced the Hahn a copy based on photographs and whose opinion was reinforced, he said in the autumn of 1923, now that he had seen the original. Holmes resisted all attempts by Ringrose to question his expertise or shake his original assessment of the Hahn version. He was the first to introduce any kind of technical discussion. He said, "In the Louvre picture the pigments used all the way through are comparatively thin, and each pigment is ground up and worked in a way peculiar to itself. In the Hahn picture, as you will see . . . the pigments have all the same sort of consistency and quality . . . It is a sort of half-way house to our present practice of using oil paint." The result is that "the pigments in the Hahn picture are very much more uniform in substance and consistency than the pigments used in the Louvre picture. It represents a later stage of oil painting." That to him was quite enough to settle the matter of the date of the painting. It could not be as early as a

Leonardo; he thought it was probably the beginning of the nineteenth century and not earlier than the beginning of the eighteenth. He also dismissed the painting on stylistic grounds. There really was no comparison, he said. Holmes wrote, "When I was cross-examined for some three hours by Mr. Ringrose, the clever American counsel for the plaintiff, a picturesque Paris journalist described me as 'pâle, mordillant sa moustache.' There was reason for being a little nervous. I had left my spectacles behind in London, and should have been floored if Mr. Ringrose had handed me any document to read."

One by one the experts lined up with the same verdict. As luck would

Berenson at i Tatti in 1909, posed in front of his famous
Madonna and Child, which he bought as a Baldovinetti
and later attributed to Domenico Veneziano

have it, on September 4, the very day Georges Demotte was killed in a hunting accident, Berenson was in Paris giving testimony on *La Belle Ferronière*. He had done so with great reluctance. He had often published doubts about the Louvre Leonardo, and at one time had attributed the painting to Boltraffio. This was well known in the trade and was bound to be used against him even if he claimed the right to change his mind based on mature reflection, etc., etc. More to the point, he had managed to keep secret the fact that he had been under contract as Duveen's expert for years, maintaining the fiction that he was an independent scholar, even that he had no connection with the market, but it was clear he could do so no longer. Someone was bound to suggest that his change of opinion had been bought.

As usual when he was on the defensive, Berenson was at his most imperious and sarcastic. The Louvre version was the only genuine painting; the Hahn version did not even come close. The girl was "saggy and bulgy looking, like a child's balloon, instead of having the tightness and firmness shown in Da Vinci's works." In addition, "the weak mouth and dull eyes, the dark opaque shadows and the smoothness and oiliness of the texture . . . made the picture look like an oilcloth." Nicky Mariano, who arrived late, asked Mary Berenson "How is it going?" and Mary whispered back, "Berenson has already made a fool of himself," but this was hardly the case. Gimpel wrote:

> I have seen Joe, who told me the inquiry has begun at the American consul's, and that Berenson was cross-questioned for three hours; apparently he was hard put to contain his fury; but how clever he is, the old boy!
>
> The lawyer asked him: "You've given a good deal of study to the picture in the Louvre?"
>
> "All my life; I've seen it a thousand times."
>
> "And is it on wood or canvas?"
>
> Berenson reflected a moment and answered: "I don't know."
>
> "What, you claim to have studied it so much, and you can't answer a simple question?"
>
> Berenson retorted: "It's as if you asked me on what kind of paper Shakespeare wrote his immortal sonnets."

A week later Duveen was in a mood of euphoria, not just because of the way the testimony was going but also, no doubt, because Demotte was no longer on the scene. He had dinner with Gimpel and was "as happy as a child," Gimpel wrote, "thinking that on the day of his death he'll be remembered as the man of *La Belle Ferronière*. How can anyone be so naive!"

THE EXPERTS WERE GETTING UP at six a.m. to arrive at the doors of the Louvre by eight o'clock, and the press was furious at being excluded. A crowd had already assembled, and when the rumor got out that some American journalists had slipped inside, "the pack had to be appeased," Gimpel noted in his diary for September 16. Apparently, the word was that Sir Charles Holmes had burst out laughing when he set eyes on the Hahn version. Gimpel thought it was perfectly amazing that Duveen had to call in the most famous experts in the world to prove that "a horrible copy of a famous picture was only a copy," and thought, too, that the "only interesting aspects of this huge hoax" is that the experts could finally agree, to a man, that the Louvre Leonardo *was* a Leonardo. Without doubt they were an impressive group. Besides Holmes, Roger Fry, and Berenson, there were Professors Adolfo Venturi of Rome and Schmidt Degener of Amsterdam; Sir Martin Conway, the British art critic; Captain Robert Langton Douglas, connoisseur and dealer; Marcel Nicolla of Paris; and Professor Arthur Laurie of Edinburgh University, who was Duveen's chief technical advisor. Based on the first round, the Hahn forces were in retreat, and the whole thing looked, as Fry said, perfectly absurd.

NOTHING MUCH HAPPENED for the next few years. Duveen must have thought the Hahns would drop their case and perhaps tried to use some gentle persuasion. They could and should have settled out of court but proved to be surprisingly recalcitrant. They genuinely believed that the painting catalogued by Lepicie was the one they owned. They must have felt they had cast some doubt on the authenticity of the Louvre version. In any case the experts had been unable to discredit their painting on technical grounds. There really was a multimillion-dollar pot at the end of the rainbow if they could prove their claim. Ringrose was dropped at some point and S. Lawrence Miller engaged. He accepted a 10 percent interest in the picture in lieu of a fee. Miller, young, tall, and highly aggressive, believed he had a case, and it went on the docket of the New York State Supreme Court in February 1929. By then everyone knew that something was being contested by somebody and Duveen was in the news again. The London *Times* wrote that the case seemed "destined to create almost as great a commotion in art circles as the theft from the Louvre of *La Gioconda* in 1912." As another paper had it, it was a "highbrow and lowbrow circus, the smartest show in town." What struck people as particularly absurd was that the twelve men of the jury, no matter how good and true, should be asked to decide a complicated technical matter about which they knew absolutely nothing. Their list of occupations bore out the point. Two were clerks, one was an accountant, two were in real estate, one was a shirt manufacturer, one was in ladies' wear, one was an upholsterer, one was an agent, and one had no occupation at all. Only two were artists.

The case hinged on slander of goods, a basic point of common law to protect property from being depreciated as a result of statements made against it. Miller maintained that Sir Joseph had "a stranglehold on the old-picture business" and that he had recklessly pronounced the painting to be a copy "in order to kill the sale because he was not the salesman." Duveen was the first and star witness the day the trial opened, Wednesday, February 6, 1929. The late Sir Ellis Waterhouse later wrote that Duveen "fancied himself as a witness," and this was perfectly true, even something of an understatement. His chutzpah is reminiscent of that displayed by Frank Lloyd Wright in a similar situation. Asked to say who was the greatest architect in the world, he said he was. Twitted about that later, he replied, "Well, I was under oath, wasn't I?" That same air of innocent braggadocio was displayed by Duveen. Almost Miller's first question was whether he could recall ever having made any mistakes. He thought for a minute and said he never had. Well, he might have when he was a youth, but these concerned authorship of paintings. If it was a question of whether the work was an original or a copy, he was never wrong.

It is always difficult to try to shake a witness willing to show himself as a shameless self-promoter, but Miller tried. A long discussion followed about what an expert sees in a painting, as Sir Joseph attempted to distinguish between a copy and a replica, occasionally interrupting further questions with "Oh no, no, no, I didn't say that." Miller scored several points by getting Duveen to admit that although he had said the genuine Leonardo was in the Louvre, in fact he did not think so. Like Berenson and Clark, he thought it was "close" to Leonardo, and perhaps Boltraffio, but not Leonardo. This made Miller's point, that he had rejected the Hahn version without having seen it, a telling one. Miller also focused his attack on the nebulous argument that Duveen had in common with his experts, i.e., that he trusted his aesthetic judgment and that others had to take his word for it because he was the authority. That would not do for Miller. He wanted a knowledge of pigments and techniques, and that was one

Joseph Duveen, waiting to appear in a New York court
during the $500,000 action for libel brought
against him by Andrée Hahn in 1929

Duveen admitted he did not have. This was an honest statement; technical matters acutely bored him.

Miller interrupted the witness so often that Duveen's lawyers were continually objecting. Finally, Justice William Harman Black told Duveen, "The questions are quite simple," to which Duveen responded, "Not quite so simple, Your Honor. Permit me to go on." After completing a discourse on the distinctiveness of an artist's work, as clearly identifiable as a signature, Miller objected for the umpteenth time to Duveen's long-winded explanations. "Please stop letting him make speeches," he asked Judge Black. Then he suddenly switched tactics and tried to suggest that Duveen had sold Morgan some fake porcelains. Lawyers Louis Levy and George W. Whiteside jumped to their feet. "This attack on the witness is thoroughly improper!" Whiteside roared. His lawyers tried to prevent Duveen from responding, telling him the question was irrelevant, but Duveen was infuriated. "This is a perfectly disgraceful insinuation," he said. "We have

The courtroom scene during the *Belle Ferronière* trial

never taken back any work of art from Mr. Morgan or any person in this country because it has not been genuine." Miller, satisfied that he had properly nettled his opponent, dropped the matter.

The day's testimony on Friday, February 8, was spent in another lengthy lecture to the jury telling them exactly what the differences were between the Louvre painting, a copy of which Duveen held in his hand as a black-and-white photograph, and the Hahn painting, which was on an easel. The comparisons were hard to follow and the jury sensibly suggested that both paintings be on display as black-and-white photographs of equal size so that a more equitable comparison could be made. Meanwhile, Miller, who was attacking Sir Joseph's connoisseurship at every turn, demanded that he deal with specifics, beginning with the face in the Hahn version.

> "You said," Mr. Miller read, " 'her eyes are leaden and lifeless'; may I ask you if both eyes in this painting, in your judgment, are equally leaden and lifeless?"
> "The left eye has a little life," said Sir Joseph.
> "How about the right eye?"
> "It's dead," he said sadly. "Dead," he said again. He shook his head morosely over the painting: "Very dead."

On his fourth day of testimony, February 9, even the master showman confessed he was getting a little tired. He said to his counsel, "Please, can't we stop here? You know I haven't been able to sleep for two nights and I can hardly see because I'm fatigued." Because the Louvre version had not been allowed to leave Paris, Duveen had been permitted to make compar-

isons with the two black-and-white photographs even though the Hahn
painting was on an easel in the courtroom. Then the Hahn photograph
disappeared. After a thorough search, Sir Joseph was found to be sitting on
it. Despite his command of courtroom tactics, he had to know that Miller
was scoring a great many points at his expense. Still, there were moments
when the shoe was on the other foot. When Miller attempted to introduce
a book by Francesco Malaguzzi Valeri and asked if Sir Joseph had ever
heard of the co-author, "Privata Vita," Duveen started laughing so hard
that his lawyer had to reply. Levy explained that "Privata Vita" was Italian
for "Private Life."

If Duveen had wanted his name linked with Leonardo's *La Belle Ferronière,* he was getting it. Newspapers published photographs of both
paintings and challenged their readers to guess which was which. Cables
flew between New York, London, and Paris. Paris had been in contact with
Seymour Ricci, who could recall seeing only one old copy of *La Belle Ferronière*—all the others were nineteenth-century—and it had been catalogued in the Louis XIV collection in 1709. He believed this was the Hahn
picture. Duveen's Fifth Avenue offices were swamped with letters, cables,
and telegrams from critics and patrons of the arts in sympathy with his
cause. He had become a champion of free speech, even a kind of martyr,
mounting the witness stand day after day to defend common sense against
lawyers trying to tear him down with trick questions. And indeed Miller
was preparing one. As Duveen took his place on the witness stand for the
sixth time, Miller produced two photographs of apparently identical
*Annunciation*s. Duveen had already said the one in the Louvre was by
Leonardo and the other, in the Uffizi Gallery in Florence, was by Leonardo
and his pupils. Which, Miller wanted to know, was which? Duveen studied
them for a long time. "I'm a bit mixed," he said. Then he made his choice.
He was right.

That was the day that Conrad Hug, a Kansas City picture framer and
sometime dealer who had put the Hahn picture up for sale, took the stand.
The *New York Times* reported, "Mr. Hug is understood to have mortgaged
his home and his business to push this damage suit against Sir Joseph. As
the tall, ruddy-colored British baronet rejoined his counsel Mr. Hug was
almost carried into the room—a small man with hollow jaws and light-
colored eyes that peered through his glasses as he sat panting in the witness
stand." In fact, Hug was ill with cancer and did not have much longer to
live. Hug's version of events was that Jesse C. Nichols, president of the
Kansas City Art Institute, had been ready to buy if the painting could be

proved to be a Leonardo and that it was Duveen's pronouncement in the *New York World* that stopped the sale. Since then there had been no takers.

As the trial dragged on into its third week, Robert Langton Douglas turned out to be a compelling witness. During his ten-hour testimony, he was fully equal to anything the plaintiff's lawyers could insinuate, and they tried hard. Douglas said he deplored the procedure of the American courts, so unlike British courts, which allowed one to talk as long as one had something to say. "Mr. Miller walked up and down in front of him, waving his forefinger and shouting, 'You keep quiet until I ask you a question and then give me a "yes" or "no" answer.' Justice Black banged the desk with his gavel and cried out: 'Wait. Wait!' Whiteside, Levy, and the assistant counsels for Sir Joseph were crying in chorus: 'We object!' And through the uproar, which arose in this way every few minutes, came the persistent murmur of Mr. Douglas always finishing his answer."

Miller did his best to discredit previous testimony that had been offered by Duveen's witnesses. Hadn't the technical points made by Professor Laurie supported the plaintiff's view that this was an ancient work? he asked Douglas. Didn't Laurie say that the green in the Hahn painting had been used before 1550 and not afterward? "I don't know that he said anything of the sort," Douglas replied, "and I wouldn't believe it if he did."

Miller made no particular mention during the trial of the Hacquin affidavit on the back of the Hahn painting, to the effect that it had been transferred from panel to canvas, but that particular bit of evidence was repeatedly addressed indirectly. Douglas was one of a number of witnesses to say he did not believe the painting had ever been transferred because the normal aging of the paint on a panel followed the line or grain of the wood. This painting showed no such telltale signs. Instead, the pattern of cracks was perfectly consistent with that of paint on canvas.

Douglas's assertion was supported by other witnesses. William Suhr, a highly respected restorer and connoisseur, declared, judging from the pattern of cracks he had seen, that the painting could not possibly have been made in Leonardo's lifetime. Another highly respected expert, Stephen S. Pichetto, for many years restorer of paintings for the Metropolitan Museum, took the stand and was willing to "stake his reputation" that the Hahn painting had never been on a panel. He also doubted the Hahn assertion that the painting had ever been trimmed at the bottom. He said, "Based on my experience in restoring tens of thousands of pictures, I would say that gray strip was put there when the painting was done." Asked why the strip was there, he replied, "To me, there are so many things unexplainable and senseless in this picture." He looked at the painting and began to laugh. Miller, plainly uncomfortable, removed it.

ONE OF THE IMPORTANT WITNESSES in the case, Jesse C. Nichols, president of the Kansas City Art Institute, was not at the trial. Nichols was ill and an affidavit was read in court that raised questions in Judge Black's mind. So a delegation of lawyers representing both sides of the case was dispatched to Kansas.

The lawyers took testimony from Mrs. George E. Powell, who was art editor and music critic of the *Kansas City Star* in 1920. She said that Andrée Hahn came to see her, saying she had a Leonardo. She was skeptical, because she could not imagine how such a painting could have ended up in Kansas City. "I tried to make her understand that Kansas City business-men would not buy it on a French expert's opinion, and she grew very angry."

The delegation also interviewed Nichols, who had, according to Andrée Hahn and Conrad Hug, been about to buy the painting until he read that article in the *New York World*. Nichols readily explained that the grand-sounding Kansas City Art Institute was actually an art school that he was running on the top floor of the local YMCA. It owned a dozen paint-ings worth a total of about $15,000, and the usual price paid for a work was $1,000 to $1,500. Nichols denied that he had offered to buy the painting when approached by Hug. He denied that he later told Hug that the pur-chase depended upon whether the painting was authentic. He denied that Duveen's words had the slightest influence on him; in fact, he said he had never read the article. He denied having said he would reconsider if Duveen would retract his statement. What he did tell Hug was that if a subscription drive raised most of the money to buy the work, he would contribute $5,000.

The *New York Times* wrote, "Every question which Mr. Nichols answered in direct testimony tended to relieve Sir Joseph of the onus of having prevented the sale of Mme Andrée Hahn's painting to the institute by his comment on its authenticity." The Duveen lawyers were jubilant. Here, it seemed, was proof positive that the Hahn claim was spurious. Andrée Hahn listened, the same paper noted, "with a sad expression."

Duveen had undoubtedly scored, but there remained the question of the authorship of the two *Belle*s. That, his lawyers argued, would never be settled by a legal opinion. Even technical analyses, e.g. the dating of pig-ments, could prove whether or not a work was old but could not prove who had painted it. For that, one would have to do what the art market always did, which was to accept the opinions of a preponderance of experts. It was a safe argument, given the unanimity of their experts' opinions; but in this case Duveen, with his disdain for technical evidence, had misjudged the mood of the jury. So did his legal team. Miller had adroitly cast doubt on the opinions of experts who had changed their minds—as many of them had, including Berenson—and voiced his suspicions about their impartiality, which, given the state of the market at the time, he was quite right to do. Amid the welter of conflicting views the jury members were grasping for straws, some kind of concrete measurement. Miller had ordered X-ray photographs of the Hahn *Belle*—when Levy queried Duveen on the matter, he replied that he "did not believe in it"—and these were produced. They were, however, being discussed by a medical technician who was plainly at sea on the subject of paintings. Whiteside moved to strike his entire evidence as irrelevant, and Justice Black agreed.

That, however, left the "shadowgraph" material in limbo. The defense team went to work and produced, overnight, one of the few radiographers who did understand the significance of X-rays as they related to paintings: Dr. Allan Burroughs of the Fogg Museum at Harvard University. When Burroughs happened to mention that he also had shadowgraphs of the Louvre *Belle Ferronière*, the jury wanted to see them. Whiteside, knowing his client's views, temporized. Permission to use the shadowgraphs in evidence would have to be given by the Louvre, he said. The jury insisted. Whiteside made a transatlantic telephone call and permission was duly granted. At long last both paintings could be compared with something like objectivity.

The shadowgraphs "revealed a difference for which no one in the courtroom needed a connoisseur's eye." The issue involved the jewelry—the headband and the necklace—on the two paintings. In the Louvre version the X-rays showed that the face and neck had been fully painted and the jewelry added later. By contrast, the Hahn version seemed almost painted by numbers. The skin was colored around the spaces left blank for the jewelry. The obvious conclusion seemed to be that whoever had painted the Louvre version had added the jewelry as an afterthought. Since whoever had painted the Hahn version had treated the jewelry as an integral part of the design, the logical argument seemed to be that this must be a copy. It was a highly relevant discovery, but Duveen could not be bothered to listen, and even the lawyers admitted that it had taken a while for the importance of Burroughs's testimony to sink in.

Leonardo never worked on canvas. The Hahn explanation, that their painting had been transferred from panel to canvas, was seriously doubted by a number of experts whose opinions ought to have carried weight. There was the evidence of the small-time operator of an art school for whom the idea of buying a $225,000 painting was preposterous, no matter what the plaintiff and her agent had claimed. There was the lack of an adequate provenance. There was the fact that the Louvre version was known to have come from the royal collection. There was the further matter of the X-ray evidence. All this ought to have cast serious doubt on the Hahn claim. But by attempting to dazzle the average layman with technicalities based solely on connoisseurship, Duveen and his defense team had alienated their listeners. The jury stated that this testimony "had given them little but an exotic vocabulary and a distrust for connoisseurs." On the other hand, they believed that evidence asserting the venerable age of the Hahn painting through pigment analysis must mean that it was a Leonardo.

They deliberated but could not reach an agreement. After ten hours they sent a note to the judge asking whether they could return a verdict awarding a certain amount of money to the plaintiff and stating that there was a reasonable doubt about the authenticity of the Hahn painting. It was the only fair conclusion, but the judge said they could not. So, after fourteen hours they returned a verdict of nine to three in favor of Andrée Hahn. They were deadlocked. The judge took the case back to decide the law himself. Suits for slander of property were so rare, he explained, that the application of the law invoked was uncertain and should be clarified before another expensive jury trial was begun. Sir Joseph declined to comment. Andrée Hahn expressed her determination to sue him for another nine years if necessary. Duveen moved to have the suit dismissed but lost his plea. Justice Black directed that the case be restored to the calendar and set for a retrial. It was a bitter defeat. Shortly afterwards Duveen settled out of court for $60,000, still maintaining his view that the Hahn painting was not a Leonardo.

In his instructions to the jury Justice Black had said they had been privileged to take part in an exceptionally interesting case. Outside the courtroom the general verdict was, as the *Evening Post* wrote, "How can anyone outside of a comic opera expect the authenticity of an old painting to be settled by a lawsuit? . . . A verdict of damages against Sir Joseph Duveen might have meant the silencing of all expert comments in our country. This would have been a very real calamity." The huge publicity given to the case was useful, however, not only in demonstrating the complexities of attributing Old Master paintings but, one guesses, in showing Duveen himself just what kinds of consequences would follow a remark carelessly and arrogantly made by the world's biggest art dealer.

What is interesting is that diatribes from the Hahn side have continued to be directed at Duveen, decades after his death. *The Rape of La Belle,* Harry Hahn's selective account of the trial, charging that Duveen systematically set out to destroy the work, was written in 1933 but remained unpublished during Duveen's lifetime—it was probably libelous. Its eventual publisher, Frank Glenn, a well-known dealer in Western Americana, agreed in 1946 to help Hahn sell the painting; whether he, like Miller, would receive a percentage of the sale of the work is not known. Still the painting did not sell. In a British half-hour film documentary in 1993, more than sixty years after the trial, the new owner of the painting, Leon Loucks, claimed it had not sold because of "greed, money, and corruption. Duveen, the godfather of the art world, is the one who caused this painting to lay in obscurity, because he wanted to steal it. Not buy it; steal it!" In 1978 Kenneth Clark said he did not know what had become of the Hahn *Belle Ferronière.* "It was an obvious replica and only the most corrupt kind of pressure could have led to its being put forward as an original." The only reasonable conclusion seems to be that neither version is a Leonardo, although X-rays taken by the Louvre during the five hundredth anniversary of Leonardo's birth in 1952 show that its preparatory sketches under the paint are similar to those of the *Mona Lisa.* Whether modern X-ray, infrared, ultraviolet, or pigment dating techniques have shown anything more conclusive about either painting is not known.

Meanwhile the painting, to this writing, remains unsold.

Chapter Thirteen

THE DISAPPEARING BABY

WHEN SIR JOSEPH DUVEEN said under oath in 1929 that he could not recall ever having made a mistake about a painting, he was, of course, quite wrong. He frequently and regularly made mistakes about paintings, some of them extraordinarily expensive ones. He might have claimed to have an infallible eye, but his eye was no more infallible than those of countless other connoisseurs, dealers, collectors, and curators who, to their eternal chagrin, wept tears of admiration over the clumsiest and most obvious kinds of fakes that, for a time at least, were hung on museum walls. To fake is human and to err—if not desirable—certainly such an everyday occurrence that it hardly bears mentioning.

More to the point, did he knowingly sell a fake? The evidence is that he did not. Duveen the master salesman, who would tout anything within his grasp, was one aspect of his compulsively striving, mesmeric, and wholly amoral personality. Without someone around to apply the mental brakes, as has been seen, Duveen would get himself into trouble almost as soon as he got out of bed. This was particularly true of objects about which he knew little, such as medieval sculpture, medieval champlevé, and Italian Renaissance paintings and sculpture. But to have blanks in his fields of expertise was an admission he would never have made, since it contradicted his private image of himself. And there were many areas in which he could rightly claim a specialist's knowledge. He knew his porcelain and Sèvres. He knew Dutch and Flemish painting, tapestries, and eighteenth-century French furniture. His strongest point was eighteenth-century English portraiture, and there he could not be beaten. When Gulbenkian expressed an interest in three Gainsboroughs from a collection that was for sale, Duveen told Ernest that he had already warned that suspicious collector against two of them on the grounds that they were overcleaned, removing the delicate highlights that made the painter's work so valuable. He also told Gulbenkian that the furniture he admired had been almost totally regilded and that Duveen Brothers would not touch it. What Duveen said was one thing, but the assumption that he never knew the difference is not borne out by the facts.

All his life, whether by accident or design, a realization that he sometimes needed to be saved from himself caused Duveen to surround himself with cautious personalities. There was Elsie, who never said a word if she could help it. There was Uncle Henry, that cunning and genial old scout who, time and time again, saved Joe from pontificating in ways he would later regret. There was Louis Levy, whose mission in life was to stop Joe from talking to the papers. There were his brothers Eddie and Ernest in London; his loyal second-in-command in Paris, Edward Fowles; and his sensitive and perceptive nephew Armand. What is always misunderstood about Duveen is that, although he spent chunks of his year abroad, for the most part he was in New York to do the selling. That left the buying up to Eddie, Ernest, Edward, and Armand. As the interoffice correspondence shows, they proposed and Jove disposed, but they would never propose anything if they had the slightest doubts about it. Eddie, Ernest, and Armand had the keenest eyes, but Edward was no slouch. One of Fowles's proudest moments came in 1937. Henricus Antonius van Meegeren was an exceptionally clever forger who faked paintings by Jan Vermeer. Since this seventeenth-century Dutch artist painted at most forty works, that made them most desirable; on the other hand, it took the eye of an artist to create new Vermeers in the convincing style of the old ones. Van Meegeren was up to the task. He spent years studying his pigments and surfaces and then composing works that convincingly mirrored Vermeer's special themes, ordinary people in the intimacy of their seventeenth-century lives. He then infiltrated his forgeries onto the market in clever ways. As Van Meegeren grew more and more successful, he grew bolder; one might say more of Van Meegeren himself began to creep into his "Vermeers." His so-called masterpiece, *Christ at Emmaus,* was painted on a genuine seventeenth-century canvas which still had its original stretcher—a rare find—and was called a Vermeer by a famous Dutch art historian, Dr. Abraham Bredius. It was then bought for the Boymans Museum. That the painting is second-rate Van Meegeren rather than top-quality Vermeer is very clear to modern eyes, but escaped the world's foremost authorities in 1937. Edward Fowles and Armand Lowengard went to see it and other

"Vermeers" and pronounced the work "a rotten fake." This has been the belated verdict of posterity.

Besides being astute, these were serious-minded men who were perfectly aware of the dangers lurking all around the Old Master market. Prices were soaring—that was the good news—but that also meant that, with more and more at stake, the forgers were becoming, like Van Meegeren, cleverer and cleverer. Their solution continued to be the path Duveen had set for himself years before, i.e., to buy at the top of the market. This was partly because Duveen loved the intoxicating effect of being the world's biggest art dealer spending the most money, but also because paying so much was, as has been noted, a kind of guarantee that one bought the best. It might not be a bargain but, on the other hand, the "bargain" might not be worth having. Consistent comments, in cable after cable from London and Paris, that a painting or sculpture or collection was not big enough for Duveen showed a lifelong aversion to taking unnecessary risks. In that they were remarkably successful. All those wonderful purchases from the Rodolphe and Maurice Kann collections, the Hainauer, Morgan, Chabrières-Arlès, and so many others, formed the gilt-edged stock in trade of Duveen Brothers' daily transactions. The genuine Bouchers, Fragonards, Van Dycks, Canalettos, Cuyps, Goyas, Hals, Holbeins, Nattiers, Raphaels, Titians, Watteaus, Rembrandts, and van der Weydens that were bought and sold are typical of the hundreds, if not thousands, of objects of all kinds—including furniture, tapestries, carpets, and the like—that have turned out to be "right."

When not much was needed to turn a painting into sparkling shape Duveen, to his credit, did little. In the days when varnish always yellowed—twenty-five years might be the absolute limit—this was, as a matter of course, removed and replaced. Very little touch-up might be needed. The canvas would be minutely examined to see whether it should be relined and new stretchers would be applied. According to Mark Leonard, conservator at the Getty Research Institute, the characteristic look of Duveen canvases is visible in these relinings which, though skillful, tended to flatten the surface too much. Duveen loved big expensive gold frames with lots of elaborate detail—another trademark. Naturally the works for sale always came with fresh varnish, which may be one reason Duveen was open to the charge that his canvases had a suspicious smell.

Eighteenth-century British portraits of titled lords and ladies, the vast majority with safe provenances and in good condition, are another huge category that has never been questioned. Sculpture was a different matter, but as has been noted, such works of art are notoriously difficult to authenticate. Giovanni Bastianini and Alceo Dossena are examples of two fiendishly clever nineteenth-century Italian sculptors, whose busts and bas reliefs "in the manner of" Simone Martini, Donatello, Mino da Fiesole, Desiderio da Settignano, and others were sold as the real thing and scattered in collections all over the United States. There were always problematic paintings but most of them came from the most difficult area of all, i.e., the Italian Renaissance. If one believes Kenneth Clark, Duveen was almost comically gullible in that department. He had to believe Berenson and, time and again, Berenson let him down.

One of the sticking points in any discussion of the Duveen-Berenson relationship is the problem of knowing why Berenson was reacting in a particular way at a particular moment. With Duveen, it was easy. He wanted first-rate pictures. He was willing to pay Berenson handsomely. He wanted his exclusive contract with B.B. honored and was ready to suspect that B.B. was doing business on the side even when he was not. He never particularly wanted to send B.B. money owed but, in fairness to Duveen, sales were invariably on paper only, the money being deferred for months or years. That was a point the Berensons frequently failed to understand or take into account. Whenever he could put business aside, Duveen wanted to be friendly, even cozy. Mary Berenson wanted to be cozy right back, but she had to deal with B.B.

With Berenson, the problem of how he was reacting at any particular moment and why, becomes problematic, because all the nuances: the mood swings, the frowns, the sarcasm that does not make its way onto the page, and the rumors and in-fighting with which the world of art in Florence was rife, will forever be unquantifiable. One could make a fairly good guess that moments when B.B. needed money—and given his grandiose ambitions for i Tatti, he always needed money—could probably be shown to coincide with moments when a particular painting's drawbacks were swept under the rug. There is a further factor, one that Duveen recognized early in their relationship. Berenson, after all, was scouting for paintings just as assiduously as Duveen was, and in a way had a harder time of it, given the well-known venality and deceptive business practices of Italian dealers. The result was that paintings coming through Berenson turned out to be not as billed more often than Duveen would have liked, and he would periodically decree that Berenson could no longer propose works for sale. Berenson, of course, found the whole idea immensely frustrating and would complain to Fowles about Joe's unfounded "suspiciousness." This issue was never satisfactorily settled. In a cable sent to Armand in 1936, almost at the end of the Duveen-Berenson relationship, Duveen instructed

Armand not to take anything from Berenson that he had not independently decided was worth buying: "have to be very hypercritical," Duveen wrote, "otherwise are going to be landed again with dead stock."

By the 1920s Duveen was selling his Italian Renaissance works solely on the probity of Berenson's judgments. As he knew very well, the difference between a painting by Bellini and one that had been judged "Bellini and Assistants" was enormous—worth hundreds of thousands of dollars. Berenson also knew this, and since he picked up anything from 10 to 25 percent of the profits, the incentive to attribute as optimistically as possible goes without saying. Everyone, i.e., all the connoisseurs, did it as a matter of course. Berenson had somehow managed to present himself as a man apart, a genuinely disinterested scholar. The fact is that he had been genuinely disinterested in the early days. His famous "lists" have never been equaled for the sheer versatility and range of his knowledge, and the almost uncanny way he either identified or ignored old claims for optimistic attributions that were clearly wrong or, on the other hand, discovered neglected masterpieces. To make his lists, Berenson had personally visited and inspected every painting.

By the height of his fame, in the 1920s, this was no longer true. He was now invariably judging based on photographs, and those, based on inferior technology, were barely acceptable as evidence for the work, as he himself knew and complained about often enough. Such testimonials in black-and-white gave no concept of the painting's overall effect but also no hint of surface condition. He had, of course, a remarkable, almost photographic memory, allowing him to conjure up details of paintings he had seen decades before. But he had a kind of disdain for the technical aspects that seems to have been common for his generation; certainly, as has been seen in the *Belle Ferronière* controversy, it was one Duveen shared. Fowles tells an interesting story of visiting Christie's one day with Duveen and stopping to look at a painting, *Madonna and Child with St. Catherine,* that the label said was by Leonardo. Obviously it was not a Leonardo, but it looked rather good. What did Duveen think? "Nothing! It's rubbish!" Duveen said, brushing past. On Fowles's return to Paris he was asked by a small dealer, Charles Wakefield Mori, whether he had seen anything that was not good enough for Duveen's but that he might like. Fowles recommended the "Leonardo" and Mori bought it. He had the picture cleaned and reframed and showed it to Berenson. Berenson said it was a fine work of Bernardino Luini. Fowles wrote, "Mori sold it to Joe, who apparently liked it since B.B. had given it a name." The painting was spruced up and sold once again, this time for $180,000 to a Cincinnati patron of the arts. (It now hangs in the Cincinnati Art Museum as a Luini.)

That was Duveen, but that was also Berenson. Only a consistent and stubborn lack of interest in what might have happened to the work, coupled with an equal lack of concern about what was likely to happen to it once Duveen's restorers got hold of it, can account for this blind spot in Berenson's philosophy that led to so many mistakes. Or perhaps the matter is even subtler than that. Given Berenson's prickly conscience and his perfectionistic expectations for himself, traits so evident in his later diaries, perhaps the only way he could live with himself, in the thick of a very murky and conniving world, was to judge from evidence that, after all, told him so little. He could always blame the evidence.

There was the further problem of supply. When B.B. first started buying Italian Renaissance paintings for Isabella Stewart Gardner in the 1890s, he was clearly indulging in a specialist's taste, and prices were modest. As they mounted by leaps and bounds in the years before and after World War I, more and greater paintings came onto the market. These disappeared into private collections, the vast majority of which were destined to end up in American museums. The supply was dwindling, but Duveen still needed to sell and Berenson, more than ever, was thinking about his legacy. Duveen was always pushing for the best possible attribution; Berenson, hating him for putting him once again into emotional torment, would capitulate. It could never be an easy relationship.

ONE DAY G. F. IONI, the Italian sometime dealer and expert faker of Italian Renaissance paintings, came to tell the Berensons that he had discovered an unknown masterpiece in a tiny church some distance away. They traveled into the countryside and found the church dusty and neglected. Ioni pointed out the old painting hanging over the altar. "There it is," he said. Berenson and Mary, who was his best student and almost as expert at this point, peered at the painting in the penumbra. Mary said, "Oh, Ioni, you old monster; now you have to pay for the cab."

It makes a good story, but the implication, that the Berensons were up to Ioni's tricks, was not necessarily the case, at least in the early days. Ioni's assertion that Berenson could not tell a fake from the real thing would be closer to the truth. Even Berenson, who admitted nothing, conceded at one point that he could spot a fake sculpture more easily than he could a painting, in part because fakers were so diabolically clever. Like other connoisseurs of his generation, he was blinded to the astute pandering of Ioni and others like him, who so exactly matched their Madonnas to the expectations of the age. Although Ioni might not take as many pains as Van Meegeren did to match his techniques to those of the quattrocento, his favorite period, his method of taking elements from various known paintings so as to give them plausible variants was the one chosen by the best fakers. Some of the resulting works were achievements in their own right. One unknown imitator of Botticelli fused elements from several of that master's paintings to create a "new," highly plausible "early" Botticelli, titled *The Madonna of the Veil.* This depicts a young woman—hardly more than a girl—wearing a blue cloak and rose-colored dress, holding a naked baby who is pulling at the transparent, veil-like fabric loosely draped around her hair. The work has the delicacy of touch and otherworldliness of Botticelli himself and was bought in 1930 by Lord Lee for the Courtauld Institute of Art, London University. Even without an attribution, Lee paid $25,000 for it, impressed no doubt as much by its grave and poetic manner as everyone else. If one looks very closely at the Madonna, however, one can see that she is a bit too much like the ideal of beauty promoted by Hollywood, 1920s version. The young Kenneth Clark pointed it out, and once the tests were done the verdict was in: no Botticelli. It is still a remarkable work. What's in a name? The telltale signs of a contemporary imagination at work remind one of Salvador Dalí's famous maxim: "Don't bother about being modern. Unfortunately it is the one thing that, whatever you do, you cannot avoid."

Another industrious group of fakers caused Berenson one of his biggest embarrassments. He kept coming across a large and homogeneous group of Florentine painters from the fifteenth century. When faced with this kind of puzzle, he often created a name for the unknown author that went something like this: "Master of the San Miniato Altarpiece," or whatever it was. In this case he decided that the paintings had to be the work of Pier Francesco Fiorentino, the minor master whom the art expert Georges Sortais could not identify when questioned at the *Belle Ferronière* trial. Pier Francesco's autograph works are in San Gimignano and Montefortino, and Berenson thought he saw the master's hand in this new group even though there were decided differences, according to the art historian Federico Zeri. This new group "are lacking in genuine individuality and are characterized by a firm, even rude technique, with sharp, definite outlines, flat, bright areas of color, and often embellished with tooled gold in the haloes and rose hedges as backgrounds." A *Madonna and Child with Infant St. John the Baptist* was sold as a Pier Francesco Fiorentino with a Berenson certificate in 1917–19 and ended up at the Metropolitan Museum. It has since been identified as one of a group of fakes by this most industrious school of fakers, all operating out of a single Florentine workshop, who borrowed shamelessly from a host of their betters, particularly Filippo Lippi and Pesellino, a kind of object lesson in just how early the art of faking began in Italy. (The painting is now attributed to "the Lippi-Pesellino imitators.")

Carl Hamilton, who seemed to be strangely unlucky in the paintings that were recommended to him by Duveen and Berenson, briefly owned another fake, this one a *Madonna and Child* by Verrocchio. (It later went to Clarence Mackay.) Berenson called it Verrocchio's "most impressive work in existence. In its presence I feel almost as if I were looking at the Colossi of Egypt." The painting was exhibited at a loan exhibition of Duveen's works at the firm's New York galleries in 1924. Shortly thereafter, the New York critic Richard Offner published the painting beside an almost identical *Virgin and Child* in the Kaiser Friedrich Museum in Berlin. It was perfectly clear that the latter was the original and the Hamilton version a later copy.

If Berenson was taken in by Ioni, he was equally deceived by a clever and unscrupulous dealer, "Baron" Michele Lazzaroni of Paris and Rome, who specialized in radical restorations that, like Ioni's best work, conformed to contemporary expectations. The only problem was that Lazzaroni was so industrious and his amendations so predictable that all his paintings had a way of looking exactly the same, as the Italian art historian Luisa Vertova noted in a 1971 article in the *Burlington Magazine*. This ought to have sounded a warning bell in Berenson's visual imagination far sooner than it did. As it was, there were the prettified *Madonna and Child with Saints* by Bonfigli that was sold to Mrs. Otto Kahn; a Crivelli *Madonna and Child Enthroned,* now judged to be a ruined work painted to resemble Crivelli; a *Madonna and Child with Angels* by Sebastiano Mainardi with the characteristic Lazzaroni look; and two Bellini *Madonna and Child* paintings defaced by similarly vapid expressions. These purchases, for the most part, were made from 1911 to 1915, and the wonder is that even as late as 1927 Lazzaroni was being let loose on extremely valuable paintings. One of them was Domenico Ghirlandaio's *Francesco Sassetti and His Son Teodoro,* which came from the Robert H. Benson Collection, went to Jules Bache, and is now at the Metropolitan. The father's face has been repainted, what were figures in the background have been lost, and other heavy-handed improvements were added in the cause of prettying up a great work of art.

BAD PAINTINGS WERE BOUND TO BECOME a part of Duveen's stock in trade for the reasons mentioned, which is not to say that he liked the idea, and in fact Duveen Brothers did its best to minimize the damage. That was the case with a so-called Leonardo *Portrait of a Young Lady,* sold to S. H. Kress, which ended up at the National Gallery of Art in Washington, D.C. When, some years later, Kress's restorer, Mario Modestini, denounced the painting, saying that it was by a pupil or assistant, Fowles offered Kress something else by way of compensation. It turned out to be the *Portrait of the Marchesa Brigida Spinola Doria* by Peter Paul Rubens, along with a small painting attributed to Verrocchio. These were acquired at bargain prices, which struck Modestini as a very nice deal indeed. The National Gallery also got to keep its Leonardo, now labeled "studio of."

In terms of deceptive practices, what was of equal concern was the deplorable and wholesale repainting of pictures, particularly Italian Old Masters. Dealers were selling to millionaires who were as "ignorant as swans" but wanted value for money. That meant paintings that looked like something. If time and its inevitable wear and tear had dirtied the varnish and faded the colors; if figures were smeared and flaked and cracks had appeared, off they came. Nice new shiny paint was added with no particular relevance to whatever lay beneath. Canvases were turned from ovals to rectangles, something even Holder, that model of rectitude, found acceptable. Faces were retouched or repainted and double chins removed. Canvases were chopped at the top or bottom and folded at the edges, as happened with Diego Velázquez's famous portrait *The Infanta Maria Theresa,* now at the Metropolitan. Backgrounds were painted in or out. Figures appeared and disappeared. Even more insidious was the widespread practice of turning a modest anonymous Renaissance work into something that looked like Bellini, Crivelli, Fra Angelico, or any of those other major figures with nice price tags attached. John Walsh, former director of the Getty, said of such calculated deceptions, "It was don't ask, don't tell and no penalties were paid."

Clark said that when he was director of the National Gallery he was hounded by dealers who all had paintings to sell. "One day I was summoned by an art dealer who normally dealt in paintings of daffodils and Swiss alpine scenes who produced a rather battered Madonna and Child, a 1480 Florentine work, and asked what he should do with it. The man who had given it to him to sell wanted 750 pounds for it. I advised him to try it at auction. It went to Sotheby's and fetched 12,000 pounds. The next time I saw it, it was in the National Gallery in Washington with a certificate from Berenson as a work by Domenico Ghirlandaio. A rubbishy wreck of a picture in three days becomes a shining new one, and is very convincing." When asked about that painting, the late John Walker, then director of the National Gallery, a protégé of Berenson's, said, "B.B. was very enthusiastic about it. It was called a Verrocchio at one time. I never really questioned its attribution, partly because of B.B. It's rather unfortunate. It would be much better labeled as 'Florentine school,' as was my preference." The painting is still attributed to Ghirlandaio.

Marco Grassi, a respected master of the art of restoration, observed, "What difference does condition make? A great deal. There comes a point

An undated photograph of Bernard Berenson and John Walker
in the garden at i Tatti, probably in the 1930s

after which the message of the picture is no longer readable. It can be restored, but it is essential to know whether the picture has passed the point of no return. Unless you know that you don't know anything."

An example of such a restoration is provided by *Head of the Madonna,* a painting purporting to be by Fra Filippo Lippi which was sold to Kress and entered the National Gallery collections. The original painting shows a Madonna in three-quarter-face beneath an archway with what looks to be mountains in the background. At the lower-right foreground, a curly-headed baby with one pudgy hand raised is looking up at its mother. Only part of the baby—its head and a hand—is visible, suggesting that the picture has been chopped off. One might call this a face only a mother could love. Nevertheless the baby, battered, scratched, and abraded though it is, is definitely there. As the restorer went to work, photographs were taken at successive intervals. All kinds of scratches and abrasions were removed. Details of the Madonna's headdress were filled in, along with her hairline. Subtle changes in the eyes, nose, and mouth had a curious effect on her expression. A rather distinctive, enigmatic-looking fifteenth-century face seemed to metamorphose into an intellectual, even bluestocking, twentieth-century one. Superfluous details were added, such as a white line following the curves of her forehead and cheek, around her chin and down her neck; and a shiny new halo, prettily speckled, was appended. But the biggest surprise was the disappearing baby. Not a trace of him was left, and where he lifted his tiny hand there was nothing but dress fabric.

Perhaps the most famous example of a ruined work, one twice radically repainted, is the *Madonna of Humility* by Tommaso di Giovanni, called Masaccio, a fifteenth-century Florentine generally considered, with Giotto, as a founder of the Renaissance school of painting. Although he was only twenty-seven when he died, Masaccio's depiction of real people in ordinary situations, painted with great economy and a kind of natural dignity, is akin to Giotto's. Just like the humanist and intellectual art then being developed by Donatello, in sculpture, and Brunelleschi, in architecture, it speaks of a new age, a way of seeing that would revolutionize Italian art. So when it was announced in 1929 that a new Masaccio had been discovered, articles were published in such distinguished magazines as *Dedalo, Art in America,* and the *Burlington Magazine.* Royal Cortissoz called it a "truly heavenly" picture, and his opinion was echoed by other critics who saw in it the handiwork of the master. To Berenson, here was a painting without equal "since the builders of the Pyramids and the sculptors of the Chefrens, and Mycerinus, . . . Ranefers, and their contemporaries."

The painting shows a Madonna, her head covered with a cloth, in

The ruinously restored *Madonna of Humility*
by Masaccio

loose, flowing robes. Two angels hovering behind her are holding a large drapery as a background, and a dove flies over her head in a sunburst of gold. She is holding a naked baby who has an arm around her neck. Again, the baby is amazingly plain, rather like a wrinkled newborn who resembles his grandfather, and the Madonna's expression looks less monumental than blank. What no one saw fit to mention was that the version they were admiring was almost completely the work of another artist. She was Duveen's French restorer Madame Helfer, and the rumor was that she had used her own niece as a model for the Madonna.

There were other rumors almost as soon as the Masaccio had been launched. One story had it that the painting was a much-repainted Madonna and Child that had ended up in a Viennese restorer's studio. When the accretion of years was removed, there remained a ghost of a picture that three specialists repainted in the manner of Masaccio. The New York office had its own version; it had somehow learned that the same painting had been seen in the studio of a clever restorer named Hahn. Duveen just knew it was all a sinister plot concocted by Roberto Longhi, the expert for Alessandro Contini-Bonacossi, a self-styled count, dealer in Rome and no friend of Duveen Brothers. Then, in April 1930, Duveen learned that Dr. August Mayer in Berlin, whom he frequently consulted, was about to publish an article stating that three paintings Duveen was handling were fakes. One of them was the Masaccio. Duveen went into high gear. He had had the paintings examined by the best experts. He could not believe someone of Mayer's standing could be influenced by idle gossip. If something did not look "right" about the painting, it was the fault of the reproductions. Dr. Mayer dropped the idea and the furor died down. Thank heavens, Duveen wrote, that at least he had not sold the painting yet.

Paintings that gave him trouble were, not surprisingly, paintings that Duveen came to dislike intensely. They were one more albatross around his neck, particularly when they had been foisted on him by Berenson and his staff and had the cold, unpromising look of this particular concoction by Madame Helfer—and he must have known just how much of a concoction it was. Behrman's famous story is that the day came when Duveen sent Bertram Boggis out to get an axe so that he could chop it up. Boggis's famous reply was, "Don't chop it up, Joe. B.B. likes it." Reprimanded, Duveen turned the painting over to the care of a second restorer, William Suhr in New York. Essentially, Duveen was giving the painting to a new artist to let him paint yet another version of what he thought the work ought to look like. This one sold, to Andrew Mellon, and the *Madonna of Humility* went to the National Gallery of Art in Washington. When, in 1981 the paint was removed once more, only the general outline of the figures was left, along with a few faint brushstrokes. What is left is still considered to be by Masaccio.

FOR SHEER COMIC ENTANGLEMENT, however, nothing beats the story of *A Portrait of a Lady* by Albrecht Dürer. This painting of a plump little bourgeois with an unfortunate chin and the silhouette of a pouter pigeon seems made to order for a Feydeau farce in which complication is

A Portrait of a Lady, now considered to be
in the "style of" Albrecht Dürer, which
Duveen tried valiantly to prove
was the genuine article

piled on complication until the whole tragicomedy collapses in an exhausted heap. And it all started, as such plots do, in the most innocent possible way. Early in January 1929, Paris sent New York a message to say that Lowengard had discovered a Dürer portrait belonging to a German prince, of a lady with fair hair and a green dress, aged about forty. It was not yet for sale, but they were "working" the picture through a Berlin dealer named Cassirer. The great Max J. Friedländer, leading expert on Flemish painting, who had just succeeded Bode as director of the Kaiser Friedrich, was not yet completely convinced that the painting was by Dürer, but Lowengard was sure it was "right" and had begun negotiations with Cassirer. Fearing competition, and also knowing Duveen's weakness, he did not want Duveen to say a word about it as yet. Friedländer had had one of the restorers in his museum remove the nineteenth-century over-paint and had "passed" the picture. It had the initials "J.D." spelled out in pearls in an ornament in the sitter's bodice, along with the date 1506. Further initials had been scratched into a kind of medallion in the black background. Lowengard bought it for the serious price of £46,200. The name of the owner was Wilhelm Herzog von Urach, Graf von Württemberg, head of the Catholic line of the Württemberg family, one of the oldest noble families in Germany, dating back to the twelfth century.

When Paris took possession of the painting at the end of January, Duveen's immediate concern, as always, was how to present it to best advantage. Since he wanted to sell it to Jules Bache when the latter returned to New York, it had to be "wonderfully, beautifully" framed. Could they get the painting to him no later than April 15? It meant a rush job at the restorer's, but the painting was duly shipped to New York and sold to Bache almost at once. Then a new query came in. New York needed a provenance for a catalogue of the Bache collection that was being prepared. Who was this Duke of Urach? They could not trace him. Which King of Württemberg, they asked, was he the son of? They also wanted the picture published, the normal route of authentication following a sale. August Mayer agreed to write a favorable article for the June 1929 issue of *Pantheon*.

Six months or so later, rumors began to circulate on Bond Street that the Dürer was a fake. Ernest wrote that obviously the whole thing was being said out of spite by people who were jealous of Joe's discovery, but he thought his brother should be warned. The doubts this news raised in Duveen's mind translated themselves into instant action. Armand was asked what guarantees had been given to him by Cassirer at the time of the sale. The news from Cassirer was not reassuring. The affidavit stated only that the attribution to Dürer had been made by Friedländer. In other words, there was no chance of a refund from Cassirer. On the other hand, the great Dr. Friedländer, the world authority on Dürer, had actually seen the painting, and so it must be "right."

Lowengard was on the defensive. He could not understand why Duveen should now be insisting on proofs. His backbone needed some stiffening. Lowengard's criticism seems unfair since his uncle was, at that moment, settling a nine-year lawsuit that had come about precisely because he would *not* change his mind. A new mistake would be disastrous, as Lowengard was well aware.

Duveen's doubts had been reinforced by a letter from August Mayer, who had heard that the Dürer had been bought by the Duke of Urach shortly before it was sold. This was not as farfetched as it might seem, since the young man was broke and eking out a living in a garret on the Left Bank by painting street scenes. The conclusion that some dealer, perhaps Cassirer, had put him up to it so as to trade on his family name, made Duveen most uncomfortable. What also made Mayer, who had put his own reputation on the line, uncomfortable was the discovery that the painting seemed to be almost exactly like an early Italian engraving that preceded it; an ominous discovery indeed.

Duveen then turned his attentions to the Duke of Urach. Fowles and Lowengard were dispatched to confront him, and the news that spring of 1930 was not reassuring. Armand and Edward said that the Dürer, as Duveen feared, had never belonged to his family. The duke had merely passed it around as a favor to a friend, who did not want his or her name used. The duke felt he was in a very awkward position. Fowles and Lowengard immediately threatened to sue him for fraud. They wanted a name, or else. That very day Wilhelm von Urach, Count of Württemberg, sat down and wrote a letter saying that he had owned the painting after all. Well, he did not quite say that. The painting came either from his own private collection or that of a relative. It was obliquely worded, but Duveen decided it would have to do.

There the matter rested until December 1930, when Dr. Mayer, who had raised the gentlest of questions in his original article of the year before, again decided his reputation was at stake and that he had to clear his conscience. He cleared it by writing another article for the same magazine in which he complained in more forceful terms about what he considered to be a bungled restoration, and brought up the subject of the earlier engraving. This was the worst news, since everyone knew that a painter of Dürer's stature would never copy someone else's work. It could only mean that the painting was not by Dürer.

By then Jules Bache was getting worried and wanted to know what Dr. Mayer's new article meant. How could a painting that was "only slightly damaged" in the first article have metamorphosed into one that was "not well preserved and poorly restored" in the second? Dr. Mayer responded with some soothing words and no mention of the questions raised by the engraving. That should have settled matters, but Duveen was still persecuting the Paris office with further demands for absolute certainty about the Dürer. He asked for X-ray photographs, the newfangled method of inferring intent, the possibilities of which had been demonstrated to him in the *Belle Ferronière* trial. He had turned away from Mayer and was looking for a new expert, and thought he had found him in Hans Tietze, an art historian who had also doubted the painting, but now was changing his mind. Or so he said after having seen it in Bache's apartment in February of 1932. Meantime, Duveen had made up his mind that the botched restoration had to go. The painting was sent back to Paris.

It seems clear in retrospect that whatever was wrong with the Dürer was unlikely to be repaired by restorations, however skillful. And in fact the man on whom Duveen had pinned so many hopes refused to be persuaded by whatever had been amended, or removed, saying he would reserve judgment. It was now November of 1932, and Duveen turned back to his first choice, Friedländer. The only way to put this infuriating controversy to rest was to get Friedländer to publish the painting himself. Then he ran into yet another hurdle.

By then Adolf Hitler had come to power, and almost his first priority was the removal of Jews from influential positions. Friedländer was being attacked by people who wanted him out. The argument being used was that he gave bogus certificates to his friends. Duveen must see, Friedländer pointed out, that publishing something in favor of the Dürer might add fuel to this argument. He sounded very scared.

Duveen did nothing more for several months, but then another blow fell. Tietze wrote an article for *Art Bulletin,* published by the College Art Association of America, in which he questioned the authenticity of both Bache's Dürer and another portrait by Dürer that Andrew Mellon had just bought, although not from Duveen. This time Duveen would not be put off. Friedländer just had to make his opinion public. Friedländer agreed, but again reminded Duveen of the awkwardness of his situation that spring of 1934. Duveen kept waiting, but by autumn he could wait no longer. He told Paris that Friedländer's opinion absolutely had to be published. Unless an article was in hand within two months, Duveen would have to take the picture back.

What Duveen had avoided telling Paris until the eleventh hour was that the painting had never been paid for. Since the effects of the Depression were still being felt, the gravity of the situation hardly needed to be underlined. By then, Friedländer was on the point of leaving the Kaiser Friedrich and settling in Holland. (He survived the war.) He would see what he could do.

After the infuriating six-year effort to prove the painting's authenticity, the dénouement was anticlimactic. Friedländer published his article in the March 1935 issue of *Art in America.* Bache presumably paid for the painting eventually. The painting went to the Metropolitan Museum of Art. According to present curatorial opinion, it is a copy after Dürer. In other words, a fake.*

---

*Mellon's portrait is now attributed to Hans Schaufelein, a painter and designer of woodcuts much influenced by Dürer.

Chapter Fourteen

"KEEP ALIVE"

BY 1920, JOSEPH DUVEEN'S YEAR was as sedate and predictable as any wealthy Edwardian's at the turn of the century, except that he had followed pleasure and Duveen's itinerary was dictated by money. At the end of May he left New York for London, where he always stayed at Claridge's. In June and July he was in and out of 4 Grafton Street. Then he was off to the Ritz in Paris for more consultations and plans for the big autumn sales. He, Elsie, and Dolly then traveled to the Grand Hotel Vittel, a health resort in the Vosges mountains, for three weeks of what must have been excruciating boredom for Dolly, but not for her father, since the cure was in name only and urgent business followed him there. Then it was back to London, sailing for New York in September. Dolly went back to college and he went into another concentrated round of client cultivation, followed by split-second decisions and cables twenty-four hours a day.

Raymond Duveen, Eddie's son, said his father, who ran the London business, was terrified of Uncle Joe. "Most of them were. With the result that my sister and I always knew when Uncle Joe was coming over because the household was in a frantic state and my father was impossible. Absolutely on edge. No doubt he expected to be criticized and reproached for everything he hadn't done already. My father had contacts with all the aristocrats who had pictures on their walls and who were all terribly hungry, so he would buy the pictures at a fraction of the cost. Then the recriminations would start from Joe: 'You've paid too much for this,' and my father would retort, 'You wanted it in a hurry.' There'd be terrible sorts of factions and things."

A photograph of the unfurnished interior of 4 Grafton Street, London,
for many years Duveen Brothers' London headquarters

Eddie, who was on a salary, was the only sibling who was not willing to
be bought out, Raymond said, a reference to Ernest, who left the London
office to found an insurance company, Duveen and Walker, and also to
Benjamin, who left the New York office. "He really enjoyed the art world,"
his son recalled. But the persistent belief that the Duveen brothers and sisters who had been forced out of the family business remained hostile and
resentful has been somewhat overstated, according to family members.
Most of the brothers did pretty well financially (with the exception of
Charles, who had no head for money) and branched out into successful
businesses on their own. The sisters were comfortably off, and since so
much distance separated them, the Duveen family members took a desul-
tory interest in their famous relative and only vaguely disliked him. That
may be because Duveen resisted the idea that their sons and daughters
should join the business. When Eddie proposed Raymond as a new member of the firm, he was repulsed. Duveen said he did not want any Duveen
to follow him, a rebuff that might have come about because he had been

Grafton Street, just off Piccadilly, in the 1920s

asked once too often. After the huge and costly battle he had waged to gain control, one can hardly blame him for his instinctive emotional defenses.

The only Duveen who might have succeeded him was Dolly, and it was becoming clear that she was the heir apparent. She had the same lively and impudent personality. She was flamboyant. She had an authoritative manner. She was extremely well organized and she liked the idea. People who knew the late Dolly Burns believed that she never had the slightest interest in art, but this was certainly not true when she was at Smith College. She wrote an article about Botticelli when she was twenty that Duveen proudly sent to the Berensons. They were full of advice. Dolly had a pronounced gift, they said. She should study Berenson's new method, an advance over the Morellian. In fact they thought she should take over the business. Duveen assured them that Dolly was reading B.B.'s books over and over and "getting very keen." With his natural instincts as a teacher, it would have been surprising if Duveen had not seen an ideal pupil in his bright, lively daughter. He took her to galleries and openings. He introduced her around. He was immensely proud of her. She was Daddy's girl.

Dorothy was growing tall and large bosomed, with long, slim legs and a piquant, heart-shaped face, handsome rather than conventionally beauti-

Right: An early drawing of Dorothy Duveen

Below: Dolly, now the Hon. Mrs. William F. C. Garthwaite, attends an exhibition of the drawings of Percy Crosby, an American cartoonist, at a gallery in Old Bond Street with her father. It was 1935 and, Duveen said, she was "very keen."

Duveen, Elsie (at left), and Dolly, on one of their innumerable transatlantic voyages. Duveen once reckoned that he had crossed the Atlantic a hundred times.

ful. She was photographed on her father's arm at art exhibitions or on their interminable trips back and forth across the Atlantic. Her mother was becoming heavier as she grew older. She favored wide-brimmed, Vita Sackville-West–type hats and expensive jewelry and furs. Sir Joseph wore impeccable double-breasted suits with a faint banker's stripe and natty hats. His mustache turned gray before the rest of his hair did, and even by the unrevealing standards of the age, an expression of jaunty determination shines through the news-agency pictures.

There are endless portrait photographs of Duveen at a certain age, presumably during the 1920s and '30s. As his father had done—there is a fine portrait of him by Emil Fuchs—Duveen also sat for his portrait in oils numerous times, although only one of them, by Adolfo Müller-Ury, caught the likeness of a man whom one sees as constantly in motion, and expressing a thousand fleeting changes of mood. Elsie was also required to sit endlessly for portraits. These, particularly rapid sketches executed in the 1920s, are more successful, although too flattering to be very revealing. As for Dolly, there is a famous portrait of her by Augustus John wearing an outrageous hat. The painting perfectly captures the relationship between her

Dolly in the sitting room of her Mayfair house
beneath a painting of herself by Augustus John

widely spaced eyes, long, straight nose, and determinedly pointed chin. She
was extremely proud of it and hung it over her living-room mantelpiece.

In New York the Duveens lived in an immense corner suite on the second floor of the Plaza Hotel; like Eloise, Joe luxuriated in hotel life. But in
1925 he decided the time had come to find a place where he could entertain
in proper style. He settled first on the Willard Straight house, a mansion on
Fifth Avenue, and thought he had bought it, but at the eleventh hour the
owner changed her mind. (It later went to the chairman of U.S. Steel,
Judge Elbert H. Gary, and his wife.) But then he found a large house on
the corner of Ninety-first Street and Madison Avenue that was only nine
years old. It had been built for Charles M. MacNeill, president of the Utah

Copper Company, by the architect Frederick Junius Sterner, and "is considered one of the finest houses in the city," the *New York Times* reported. The central hallway was a full five storeys high and accommodated a suitably grand staircase. There were two elevators, and Duveen added to its stature by redesigning the house with an art gallery from drawings made by the man who would become his favorite architect, John Russell Pope. Since he wanted lots of overnight guests, a whole floor was being remodeled to receive them. There were numerous reception rooms. One of them, in eighteenth-century French, had a handsome fireplace, overmantel, and full-length mirror reminiscent of the front parlor in Home House, London. It contained a set of two settees and six armchairs, the backs of which were inset with painted glass panels, as well as the Chinese vases and bowls, famille rose eggshell plates, Sèvres and Dresden porcelains, and French terra-cotta figurines that Elsie loved. Another room was more family focused, with capacious armchairs in the English country-house manner and other pieces of uncertain pedigree that would win no prizes at auction. Photographs taken when the house was opened for charity in 1933 show a formidable art collection. There were a Van Dyck over one of the mantelpieces and two fine full-length Gainsboroughs flanking another handsome fireplace. But the feature that made the house most extraordinary was the size of the property. There was room for an elaborate Italian garden, in crowded Manhattan perhaps the biggest luxury of all.

One of Duveen's favorite artists was Sir John Lavery, best known for his society portraits. When the Modern Foreign and Sargent galleries that Duveen gave to the Tate were opened by George V and Queen Mary in 1926, Sir John was engaged to record the scene. The king and queen are seated on a dais in the distance, surrounded by paintings. The proud donor is, presumably, standing at far left facing the viewer, and a young woman who could be Dolly is sitting beside him with an open book on her lap. But Sir John's most important commission by far was that given him by Duveen after he and his family moved to 15 East Ninety-first Street. The most handsome room of all was the Grand Salon, its huge vertical windows looking out over the Ninety-first Street side, with a vast cavernous double-doored entry memorialized by pillars on the other. There Duveen sat in a capacious wing chair, a little left of center, surrounded by his adopted ancestors, his chandeliers, his busts, and his flowers. At far left sat Elsie, looking toward the windows with two terriers at her side. Dolly, in something white and flowing, stood behind her mother's chair. Curiously, no one was looking at anyone else except for the dogs, and the physical distance between Elsie and Joe was wide. "I lunched with the Duveens at the

Ritz," Mary Berenson wrote from Paris in 1922. It was "most uncomfortable, as he and she are on each other's nerves and show it every second. He bought her some gorgeous pearls afterwards, which she didn't want, as she found them too white." When Dolly returned from Smith without graduating, the explanation given was that her father needed a hostess. Since Elsie could only have been in her mid-forties at the time, this raises some interesting questions about her interest, or lack of it, in her husband's life. It also suggests that Elsie willingly accepted a secondary role so that Dolly could be groomed in the complicated business of becoming her father's successor. Eventually Elsie took a companion, and the two ladies were inseparable for twenty-five years. Her companion inherited substantially from Elsie's estate.

Duveen was always importing paintings and objects for himself, although how long he kept them is a moot point. No doubt he used his own sumptuous quarters as display rooms as indiscriminately as he used Carl Hamilton's and many others'. And he entertained all the time. Jean Fowles, who was first married to Robert Langton Douglas—she married Edward Fowles after Douglas died—went to many of the Duveens' dinner parties. She recalled meeting all kinds of people there, from Carl Van Vechten, the novelist, critic, and photographer, to the owners of Macy's department store and their wives, to Sir John Lavery and his wife, Hazel, H. L. Mencken, and Ramsay MacDonald, the first Labour prime minister of Great Britain. Dolly Burns, who would become a famous hostess herself, benefited from this early training in random conviviality. Jean Langton Douglas liked Elsie, whom she found exquisitely stylish—she bought all her clothes from the French couturiers—with delicate pink-and-white skin and soft, natural-looking hair. She was quiet and not unkind, she thought, and full of common sense. Jean had just arrived in New York as a young wife, and Lady Duveen told her where to shop, where to buy wine (it was Prohibition), the best doctor, the best dentist, and so on. Her hostess would talk about literature and the theatre but seldom about art.

Jean Langton Douglas had heard about Joe Duveen and was prepared for a lively intelligence but not for the effect of his eyes, which were a brilliant, almost hypnotic blue, and his boisterous humor. When she remarked on a huge aquarium in the entrance hall that seemed to go up to the ceiling, Sir Joseph said he was getting bored with the fish because they never did anything. He was proposing to put a huge cage of monkeys there, along with a miniature African forest. His wife did not like that idea, he said. She was sure the monkeys would smell, but he had an answer to that:

The Duveens at home in their great New York salon, painted by Duveen's favorite artist, Sir John Lavery. The two dogs may be props.

He intended to spray them constantly with Guerlain perfume. When he saw the look on Jean Langton Douglas's face, he burst out laughing.

Although he had no hobbies and no other life apart from art, he loved to walk. Whenever he was in London, he went for his daily constitutional, and Edward Fowles would be summoned from Paris to accompany him through Hyde Park. In Paris, his daily tour took him from the Place Vendôme through the Tuileries, past the Rond-Point, toward the Champs-Élysées, usually in the late afternoon or early evening. He tried to time himself so that he could catch sight of the sun setting through the Arc de Triomphe.

He was a hard taskmaster, but fair, and liked by his Ninety-first Street staff. The maid who dusted the precious porcelains and served tea every afternoon at four would place a rose on his desk every day. She paid for it herself, and when she died, she provided for that service to continue in her will. It was only then that Duveen found out what she had done. His memory for detail was terrifying. He could, for example, remember the precise instructions about the alterations to be done to Mrs. George Widener's corsets, which were shipped to Paris at his expense. It was more than any human being could be expected to cope with, and he began to have periodic spells of exhaustion. In May 1924 he confided to Judge Gary and his wife that he had been unable to move and was sent to bed. The Garys sent soup, cakes, and new-laid eggs and improving books about eating the right food. Speaking confidentially, Duveen could not be sure that he was ever going to be able to handle the same amount of work again. (He was then aged fifty-five.) But within a month he was up and about, working harder than ever. At the end of 1924 he could say that the year's purchases had been the most perfect of all.

ALISTAIR COOKE CALLED HIM a ruthless catalyst and noted that his most pronounced successes were "not with the hereditary rich but with men who lusted to belong to it." To Peter Quennell he was an arch diplomatist. Raymond Mortimer thought his career belonged in the realm of "succulent, invigorating satire"; he was a rogue out of Ben Jonson, "up to every artful dodge." Harold Nicolson thought he had a Napoleonic grasp of detail along with a disarming ease of manner. To Orville Prescott he was a one-man phenomenon, and to Lloyd Morris, the "most spectacular dealer of all time."

However you looked at it, these were great days for Joseph Duveen; he knew it and luxuriated in that fact. KEEP ALIVE FIND ME GREAT THINGS I CAN SELL THEM, was perhaps his most memorable telegram in those halcyon days of the 1920s. He was becoming a legend in his own time. He once said, "I don't have any more of a gift for selling than anyone else but it's that I truly believe in the work I want to sell. It is my inner confidence that makes me eloquent." He might have alluded to that sense of impishness which was never far below the surface. One day he was examining a certain painting in a Parisian antique dealer's gallery when a woman came up to him and said, "Do you know the reputation of Lord Duveen of London? He told us last week that this Virgin of Leonardo was an admirable copy of the period." Duveen replied, "Are you sure you haven't been dealing with an admirable copy of Lord Duveen?"

In pursuit of ever more influential clients in ever more exalted circles, Duveen made a careful point of cultivating the right people, whether they were politicians like Ramsay MacDonald or aristocrats with particular diplomatic, financial, and court connections. To these gentlemen, like Lord Esher, private secretary to Edward, Prince of Wales; Lord Farquhar, banker to King George V; and Lord Lee of Fareham, an amateur collector and later chairman of the board of trustees of the National Gallery, Duveen was endlessly obliging, although frequently out of pocket as a result. The well-placed Sir Philip Sassoon was assiduously courted and so was his sister Sybil, Lady Cholmondeley. In 1924 she wanted to sell a painting of a young girl with a squirrel which might or might not be by Holbein. No one knew, and in any case it was so defaced with a thick dirty varnish that no one could tell. It might be valuable. Agnew's thought the best she could hope for was three thousand pounds; so when Duveen offered ten thousand, she told the London office that they could come and take it away and to send the check to her husband. Then Duveen, who was cleaning off the old varnish, made the mistake of telling her that something exciting was emerging and it was probably indeed a Holbein. All of a sudden there were complicating reasons why the painting needed to be returned and the check held in abeyance. Lady Cholmondeley was now sure the price ought to be thirty thousand or forty thousand—if she ever decided to sell. There was nothing Duveen could do about it, and the check was returned.

Something of the sort happened with George V. Joel Duveen had been in and out of Buckingham Palace, and Uncle Henry, that champion stamp collector, had become very friendly with the king, who shared the same passion. It was only natural that Sir Joseph Duveen should be invited to admire the beauties of the royal collection and pass a practiced eye over whatever objects the monarch should want to know about. On one of those tours they paused before a particularly horrid object, a bronze river god that the king, with a wave of the hand, pronounced a Leonardo. Duveen, secure in the knowledge that nothing could be sold, dutifully admired it and expressed the polite wish that he might own it one day. Nothing simpler, said the king: It happened to belong to him. Duveen was obliged to part with ten thousand pounds, and since the statue went to the Norton Simon Museum—Simon was the last owner of Duveens—the conclusion is that it never sold during Duveen's lifetime. It was, of course, not a Leonardo.

These were galling but minor setbacks, the price to be paid for ever more influential contacts that would one day translate into sales. After Duveen died, Berenson wrote that he "stood at the centre of a vast web of corruption that reached from the lowliest employee of the British Museum to Buckingham Palace itself." This comment was, like much that Berenson said of Duveen in his old age, colored by longstanding grudges and resentments, most of them having to do with the money he could have had if only Duveen had been less grasping. Still, to suggest that Duveen was buying the loyalty of minions in the palace and the museum was probably true. Nevertheless, as the story about King George shows, Duveen was far from gaining the upper hand. What he wanted was not a sale, which would always involve a lesser object forced upon him, but the association itself, the social validation at the highest circles and, most of all, insider knowledge. He was equally interested in the rapidly dwindling band of European royals for the same reason. They, with valuable objects to sell and increasingly uncertain futures, were very interested in him. Fowles wrote from Paris that the King of Portugal had put his head around the door recently and wanted to know when Duveen would be back. He wanted to speak to him personally. That was just the kind of anxious hovering that made Duveen feel very secure.

As it happened, one of the great coups of his career did not come through his influential connections, courtly or otherwise, but through Agnew's. The seventh Earl Spencer happened to mention to Colin Agnew in May 1923 that he had some paintings to sell. This was staggering news, analogous to the notion that the National Gallery in London had some masterpieces it intended to offer to the highest bidder. The Earls Spencer had inhabited their lush corner of Northamptonshire since the reign of Henry VII, almost five hundred years. There they established their country seat, Althorp, one of the most beautiful Palladian and neoclassical houses in England, filled with books and paintings. At one time they owned the greatest private library in the world, forty thousand volumes of rare books. They were farmers but also collectors and connoisseurs, commissioning great eighteenth-century portraitists like Reynolds, Lawrence, Copley, and Gainsborough. These they displayed in a huge portrait gallery almost 140 feet long. They owned paintings by Holbein, Van Dyck, Sir Peter Lely, Rembrandt, Frans Hals, Titian, Teniers, Watteau, Tintoretto, and so many others.

In London they lived in palatial grandeur in Spencer House, built in the eighteenth century and containing some of the most imaginative interiors. The Palm Room still exists; it is an alcove with a domed ceiling and a recurring theme of carved pillars and arching palm fronds. In 1768, when it was just completed, Arthur Young wrote, "I do not apprehend there is a house in Europe better worth the view of the curious in architecture, and the fitting up and furnishing of great houses, than Lord Spencer's in St. James's Place." Besides being farmers and collectors, the Spencers served so often in Parliament down through the generations that by 1900 they were "political aristocracy," to be grouped with the Derbys, Salisburys, Shaftesburys, Roseberys, and Hartingtons in terms of their influence.

However, by the time the estate was inherited by the seventh earl in 1922, they, like so many others, were struggling under the burden of huge fixed costs, dwindling incomes, and increasing taxation. Lord Spencer, who was the grandfather of the future Diana, Princess of Wales, was just thirty. The year before, in 1921, his father had closed Althorp because he could not afford to run it. The heir tried to live in Spencer House but found even this ruinously expensive and lived there for only two years. There were huge debts and death duties to pay. By nature a scholar, more at home in a library or art gallery than running a huge estate, the seventh earl found himself in the position of looking for a ready source of cash. Americans liked pictures; pictures they should have.

Duveen had already handled one Spencer portrait, sold to Henry E. Huntington in 1911, but it did not come from Althorp. The Spencers were related by marriage to the Dukes of Marlborough, and one of them, the fourth duke, had paid Romney to paint portraits of his daughter Caroline, the oldest of eight, and her sister Elizabeth. The double portrait shows the two girls in the pursuits considered appropriate for their breeding and social position: Lady Caroline sits at her drawing and Lady Elizabeth is playing something on the harp. Curiously, the same year of the fateful decision by Diana's grandfather, Duveen was also to buy another Spencer family portrait that went to Huntington. This one came from Christopher Tennant, the second Lord Glenconner, and depicted two more children of the fourth Duke of Marlborough, Lady Charlotte and Lord Henry. They are wearing party costumes; she is a fortuneteller and he is her wealthy dupe. The painting was by Reynolds, who enjoyed the conceit of having children—she was five and he was four—playing the parts of grown-ups. (As was almost the rule for that generation of aristocratic children, they were subjected to callousness and neglect by their parents and were doomed to die young, Lord Henry at age twenty-five and his sister when she was just thirty-two.) The theatrical and mannered poses of both paintings pleased the Huntingtons well enough, but were no match for the glories they were about to acquire.

The first paintings mentioned by the seventh earl were two full-length portraits of one of his ancestors, Georgiana (Spencer) Cavendish, Duchess of Devonshire. This fascinating creature was never particularly pretty; she had somewhat bulbous eyes and a distinctly upturned nose. But what she lacked in statuesque beauty was more than compensated for in a naturally vivacious, unaffected personality and a gift for attracting interesting people. She was married off to the fifth Duke of Devonshire when she was just sixteen and plunged into a demanding world requiring political and diplo-

matic skills that she was far too young to have learned. While growing
steadily estranged from her dull, conventional husband, she gambled, ran
up huge debts, and had a string of miscarriages. She finally found her voice
in novels (one of them was *The Sylph*, a roman à clef that satirized the
morals of her social circle). She published a poem. Then she became a
political hostess. Without ever being beautiful she became a glamorous
trend-setter. There were the "Devonshire hat," the "Devonshire minuet,"
and even a special Devonshire shade of brown.

Lord Spencer wanted to sell Gainsborough's portrait of her which is, by
Gainsborough standards, distinctly uninspired. She leans backwards grace-
fully enough, but her regard is empty, even vacuous, and in fact the artist is
said to have thrown down his brush exclaiming, "Your Grace is too hard
for me." The real prize was the portrait by Reynolds. The artist has decided
to depict her walking in a garden. She is just about to descend a flight of
stone steps, and the forward movement implied in her stance was his first
good idea. His second was to draw on her handsome wardrobe—her
mother called her the most "showy" girl she ever met—depicting her in a
flowing white dress trimmed at the waist, shoulder, and sleeves with heavy
gold lace. Since the duchess was famous for her high-dressed hair style, on
which she liked to perch longer and longer ostrich plumes, this was the
way she must be depicted, although the painter has prudently trimmed the
length of her feathers. The lights and shadows on her pretty pink cheeks
and delicate bosom, the hand placed against the balustrade, in short the
image of an elegant young woman passing through her magical landscape,
was Reynolds at his very grandest, one of the most wonderful paintings
Duveen had ever seen. As soon as he received the news, there was no question that Duveen was willing to pay Agnew's its 5 percent commission and
take both pictures. But, he told Ernest, since the paintings were rather
expensive—the price quoted was £75,000 each—he wanted to know
whether the duke would throw in a couple of smaller portraits by Reynolds
as well.

From then on negotiations became extremely complicated. Agnew's
had to be paid no matter what. Duveen also wanted Arthur Ruck, the
small dealer who had pulled off several such negotiations for him and was
a fine judge of pictures, brought in as a second intermediary for another 5
percent. He wanted Holder to look at the pictures. Eddie had to be consulted, and the business of how to bid, and for what, pondered with exquisite care. Should they take an option or not? Meanwhile the seventh earl,
who was away guarding Windsor Castle as a captain in the Coldstream
Guards, was hard to pin down. He finally told Ruck that something had to

be done. He had been told that selling two pictures would clear up his debts, but this had turned out to be "bunkum." He had to make money fast or start selling off his land. The question of which paintings, and for how much, dragged on through the winter and early spring. Duveen was sure that Knoedler's was about to get into the act, and his tactical arabesques grew ever more convoluted. He kept pressing Eddie and Ernest to secure the pictures somehow, if only to foil Knoedler's. He told them what to say to Agnew's and what not to say to Ruck. By the end of January the negotiating had shifted to Gerald Agnew, who was not very forthcoming; he "likes to be secretive," Edward and Ernest complained, as if this were a new idea.

Meanwhile Duveen had his own reasons for moving slowly. The only clients for full-length portraits in the grand manner were the Huntingtons, but a big sale of Chelsea porcelain was hanging fire and H.E.H. had suddenly put up some stiff sales resistance over another purchase that was almost as important, Romney's portrait of Emma Hart, later Lady Hamilton, wearing a straw hat. This enchanting portrait was of the young Emma—she was about nineteen—looking out from underneath an enormous brim trimmed with a huge black ribbon. She had been introduced to the artist by her lover, the Honorable Charles Francis Greville, and Romney painted her obsessively. This particular painting is perhaps his most famous, both for the appealing nature of the pose and also for its suggestion of a tempestuous and uninhibited personality in hiding underneath a perfectly proper exterior. Duveen had acquired the painting from Almina, Countess of Carnarvon, and meant it for Huntington; but the latter was balking at the price of $175,000. Huntington had to concede it was a beautiful picture, but $125,000 was his maximum. If Duveen could not relent, he feared he and Emma would have to part.

While all this haggling was going on—Duveen must have dropped his price, because the picture went to the Huntington museum that year—Duveen would have felt he could hardly start extolling the merits of another expensive round of purchases. No sooner was the Emma Hamilton argument settled than, in the fall of 1924, Arabella Huntington died. Knowing how devastated her husband would be, Duveen must have decided this was hardly the moment to start talking about new business. So the matter remained.

The Spencer sale was finally brought to a conclusion at the end of 1924. Duveen Brothers bought the two portraits of Georgiana, Duchess of Devonshire. They bought a smaller portrait of another member of the family, Frances Molesworth, the future Marchioness Camden. They bought a marvelous Frans Hals portrait of a seated man and a lesser work, *Daedalus and Icarus,* by Anthony Van Dyck. They also bought *Lavinia (Bingham), Countess Spencer, and John Charles Spencer, Viscount Althorp, later Earl Spencer,* a charming portrait by Reynolds of the lady and her son, who was a year or two old when the portrait was painted. He has just fallen and bumped his head and she has kneeled to put her arms around him fondly, although in effect she is not looking at him but at something just beyond the picture frame. This puzzling discrepancy may be related to that convention of the operatic stage which requires lovers to sing a duet past each other's ears, and exacts the same suspension of disbelief from the viewer. But, again, the lady was not very domestically inclined. For the sake of the picture she has succumbed to the newfangled idea that mothers should comfort their infants personally, rather than leaving it up to the maid.

It appears that there were several portraits of Lavinia, Countess Spencer. One of them was a three-quarter-length study of the lady sans infant; Huntington had been given a personal tour of the Spencer portrait gallery some time before the sale was concluded, and this was the one he wanted. But since this particular version was not for sale, he reluctantly took the Lavinia that was offered. He also bought the portrait of Frances Molesworth and, most important, the great *Georgiana, Duchess of Devonshire* by Reynolds. The lesser Gainsborough version was accepted by Mellon. The sale of six incomparable paintings from Althorp was widely reported on both sides of the Atlantic, which would have pleased Duveen, although the reported price of $1.5 million, or £300,000, was termed a gross exaggeration by the earl. He hastened to say he would not see a penny of the money, as it was all going to death duties. Since some wonderful paintings were still at Althorp, the alarm caused by this newest exodus was muted.

Another British treasure left the country at the same time, also bound for San Marino, apparently unnoticed, although it was of equal importance: *View on the Stour Near Dedham,* by John Constable, from the estate of Thomas Horrocks Miller of Poulton-le-Fylde, Lancashire. This tranquil depiction of an area of Suffolk near Constable's birthplace was one he painted continually. The river undulates with black lights in the lower left foreground, turning and twisting its way toward the distant horizon, where it shimmers with fractured reflections from a sky full of hurrying clouds. The contrast between the etched stillness of the scene, which includes some bargemen in petrified attitudes, and the lovely tumble of drifting clouds and their sparkling patterns of light and shade, mark this as one of Constable's most successful works, all penumbral depths and bleached grass. Duveen observed that with Turner's *The Grand Canal: Scene—A Street in Venice,* which Huntington acquired in 1922, and Gainsborough's *Cottage Door,* he would have "the three greatest landscapes possessed by any private collection in the world." That was, of course, not true, but true enough. The Huntington acquired one more Constable, his view of Salisbury Cathedral seen from the Bishop's Grounds, but that was well after H.E.H. and Duveen had both died. At the time of these earlier sales that curious art lover Henry Edwards Huntington, who had become an aesthete despite himself and had lavished millions on his paintings, statuary, furniture, tapestries, rugs, objets, and porcelains, all of them from Duveen Brothers, did not have long to live. He died in 1927, quite soon after taking possession of *Pinkie,* his last great purchase, and an era in the saga of Duveen Brothers died with him.

In those last years Huntington bought one more portrait of a member of the Spencer family from Duveen. Behrman's version is that the portrait of Lavinia as a mother was not really what he had in mind. He wanted a younger Lavinia, unencumbered by offspring, but the seventh earl was never going to part with that one. So Duveen cast about for an acceptable substitute and came up with a replica which, it was said, had also been painted by Reynolds, this one for the dowager duchess, mother of the second earl. Huntington bought it for $250,000, and all was well until he died. His trustees, faced with the monumental task of turning a private house into a museum, invited Charles Henry Collins Baker, surveyor of the king's pictures and keeper and secretary of the National Gallery in London, to publish a catalogue of the British paintings for the new museum. Then the trouble started, because Collins Baker began to question some of the paintings, and three of them came from Duveen Brothers. One was by Raeburn, a portrait of Master Blair; the second was supposedly a portrait of Mrs. Bedford and her son by Hoppner; and the third was the portrait of Lavinia that Huntington had admired enough to buy for a large sum of money. Collins Baker said that the first was inferior, the second was not by Hoppner, and the third was not by Reynolds.

This was a serious vote of no confidence. Duveen naturally tried to get Collins Baker to change his mind, particularly over the Reynolds, which, one assumes, had been the most expensive. Collins Baker insisted in a letter to Duveen that the painting was a studio version and regiments of archangels armed with affidavits could not change his mind. The Huntington trustees duly filed a claim against Duveen Brothers in 1931. Duveen, who had happy memories of the role recently played by Sir Charles Holmes in the *Belle Ferronière* case, decided he was the only man "big enough" to overrule Collins Baker, and Holmes was subsequently invited to arbitrate the matter. Sir Charles found no merit in Collins Baker's first claim, that the Raeburn was inferior; it was fully equal to an earlier Raeburn portrait of Master Blair. He agreed with Collins Baker, however, that the Hoppner portrait of Mrs. Bedford and her son was, in fact, not a Hoppner, but by the lesser-known Sir Martin Archer Shee. As for the Reynolds, Collins Baker's belief that the master's brush had never touched the canvas was a view that Sir Charles did not share. He believed he saw evidence of the master's hand, although there certainly were lesser artists at work. Given the numbers of paintings Duveen sold to Huntington, that only three had been questioned was a sort of victory. Just the same, Duveen Brothers had to make financial restitution, and the new museum used the money to buy some more pictures. (Incidentally, the museum itself does not believe it has a Reynolds in its Lavinia: The painting is now classified as "after Joshua Reynolds," whatever that means.)

One of the great paintings the Huntington did not get to keep, through no fault of its own, was Rembrandt's *Aristotle Contemplating the Bust of Homer*, which Arabella Huntington first saw in 1907 in the Duveen galleries on the Place Vendôme. After she died the painting was one of the treasures inherited by her son, Archer, along with her jewels and a trust fund of $2 million. Archer gave two Rembrandts to the Huntington, one of Flora and another of Rembrandt's servant Hendrickje Stoffels, as well as a portrait by Frans Hals; but he specifically declined to part with this particular painting because, he explained, he wanted it for his own home. As it happened, he sold it to Duveen instead.

The painting was commissioned by Don Antonio Ruffo, a wealthy Sicilian nobleman and Rembrandt's only foreign patron, who asked for a portrait of a philosopher, but did not seem to mind which one. The artist ingeniously hit upon the idea of representing three great men from antiquity. Aristotle, the fourth-century B.C. Greek philosopher, stands beside a table, his left hand on his hip and his right resting on the head of a bust of the blind Homer. He is wearing the robes of a Renaissance humanist, a dark sleeveless tunic over a heavy shirt the loose, cascading sleeves of which are trimmed with metallic braid. Over it is a handsome chain bearing a medallion of Alexander the Great, who was once Aristotle's pupil. No artist ever painted faces more expressively than Rembrandt, and this particular painting is perhaps unrivaled for the mood of melancholic, almost painful contemplation that is displayed here, almost as if, as Wordsworth said, the exercise brought thoughts "that do often lie too deep for tears." The dignity of the subject, the depth of feeling, and the complexity of means

Aristotle Contemplating the Bust of Homer by Rembrandt, one of
the most famous paintings that ever came through Duveen's hands

within a very limited range make this one of Rembrandt's incomparable
works. If Duveen had only bought and sold this painting once, his position
in art history would have been secure. As it was, he bought and sold it three
times.

The second transaction involved Alfred W. Erickson, co-founder of the
McCann-Erickson advertising agency in New York. Erickson had assembled a small but highly select group of masterpieces by such painters as Van
Dyck, Hals, Holbein, Nattier, Fragonard, Romney, Raeburn, Gainsborough, and Crivelli. He already owned two smaller Rembrandts, but this
was the prize and he paid Duveen $750,000 for it. It was the kind of sale
that gives a dealer like Duveen particular satisfaction. But then the crash of
1929 came, and one Saturday morning Erickson called on Duveen. Hardly
had he gone through the doors at 720 Fifth Avenue when Sir Joseph began
to speak and instructed his bookkeeper to make out a check for $500,000.
He gave it to Erickson with the words, "At a time like this, you've not come
to Joe to buy pictures. You know that I am always ready to take back from

a client any work of art at my sales price. I'll send for the picture tomorrow." Paul Sachs, who knew the Ericksons well and was a frequent visitor at their house, 110 East Thirty-fifth Street, said Mrs. Erickson's comment was, "You can imagine how my husband felt when at night he traced the empty space where the large Rembrandt should have hung."

Some years later, in 1936, things were looking up for Erickson and he resumed his Saturday-morning rounds. This time Sir Joseph said, "Your *Aristotle* has been in hiding. I knew you would come back for it." This is a nice story, but not quite true. Sir Joseph had tried it out on Mellon, even going so far as to let him hang it on his walls, and it should have gone to the National Gallery. But Mellon was not charmed, and it was Duveen's good luck that it was still there for Erickson when he wanted it. The collector bought it back for $590,000, which was not a bad price when one considers what happened eventually. After Mrs. Erickson died in 1961, the painting was put up for auction at Parke-Bernet and was bought by the Metropolitan for $2.3 million.

So many Rembrandts went through Duveen's hands that he almost seemed to be specializing in them. In addition to the Rembrandts from the Kann Collection that went to Altman, there were *Pilate Washing His Hands,* which Altman bought for $280,000 in 1910; *The Auctioneer,* which he bought for slightly less, $262,000, in 1909; and *Old Woman in an Armchair,* another Altman purchase: twelve Rembrandts in all bought by that one collector. There were a supposed Rembrandt self-portrait, which Duveen bought for a mere £5,000; *Jewish Philosopher,* which Duveen bought in 1925 amid similar doubts, for only £15,000 (it finally went to the Norton Simon); yet another portrait of Hendrickje Stoffels, which went first to Lord Melchett and then to Norton Simon; a *Minerva;* and the *Portrait of an Old Lady,* or the "Montgermont Rembrandt," which caused a sensation when it was sold in Paris in 1920 and Monet came to see it. (It is now at the National Gallery of Art.) There was also the "Wachtmeister Rembrandt," *A Young Man Seated at a Table,* which Duveen bought for $169,000 and sold to Mellon at a tidy profit for $410,000.

Chapter Fifteen

"I CANNOT WAIT"

T HEN THERE WAS THE CURIOUS MATTER of the paintings themselves. Once they had been handled by the company, they were always called Duveens. This is not so strange nowadays, when one considers the number of handbags, shirts, sweaters, hats, scarves, and the like bearing the imprint of the company making them, for which the customer becomes, as it were, a walking advertisement. But at the time, the concept of branding a work, particularly one bearing a rather more famous name, i.e., Raphael, Rembrandt, Leonardo . . . would seem to reveal a certain hubris. Even the boldest of dealers would not go that far, and still do not, although it should be noted that umbrellas with sunflower designs on them sold by your average museum bear that institution's name at least as prominently as that of the hapless artist who created the painting in question.

But no; if Duveen had been lucky enough to get his 20 percent (or more) on these rare and costly items, they were forever linked with his immortal name, as one can see from the title page of two catalogues, *Duveen Pictures in Public Collections in America* and its companion volume on sculpture, that were published shortly after his death. The outrageous nature of the assertion did a great deal to antagonize Duveen's art-dealer contemporaries, not that they needed an excuse. It was typical of everything that Duveen had always symbolized in a world that prided itself on genteel manners, at least on the surface. To our eyes it looks rather like the forward-thinking of a salesman far in advance of his age. Still, one suspects that more was involved, having to do with the way Duveen began to see himself. In a classic essay about the qualities that go to make a collector,

Kenneth Clark enumerated attitudes of mind that apply equally well to Joseph Duveen. To begin with, there is the artistic sense; there is no doubt that Duveen had it. Professionally, he bought and sold great paintings. Privately, he admired and bought contemporary works with an intuitive and unerring eye: Stanley Spencer, for instance, decades before anyone knew his worth; Augustus John; and the young Georgia O'Keeffe, whose flower paintings he bought in quantity. He was that rare being, someone who can enter the artist's world and perceive at least some aspect of his or her struggling vision, sense it and respond to it. There is no evidence that he ever tried to draw or paint, but his was the lucky accident of birth that allows a man full scope to do precisely what he likes best.

Then there was, Clark continued, the desire to possess, reaching its ultimate in the person of Calouste Gulbenkian, who thought of his works of art as his harem, to be sequestered and jealously guarded. In fact Gulbenkian even said at one time that he wished his collections to be burned upon his death, although, fortunately for posterity, this did not happen. Then there is the image of the dying Mazarin stumbling through his picture gallery, full of Correggios, Titians, and Carraccis, saying, "Adieu, chers tableaux, que j'ai tant aimés." One cannot imagine Duveen ever doing this. His was a much more buoyant spirit; because he had experienced the exhilaration that comes with ownership of a world-famous Raphael, however briefly, no matter what happened to it, it was his forever.

Coming to the next attribute, what Clark called the sporting instinct, or the thrill of the chase, to Duveen that was as natural as breathing. One thinks of him as the ultimate in bald-faced salesmanship, yet, as Clark wrote, "Dr. [Albert C.] Barnes and Sir William Burrell, two of the greatest collectors whom I have known, would tell with relish hair-raising stories of how they had watched at the bedsides of dying widows or paid monthly calls on poor clergymen, in order to get their teeth into some delicate morsel . . ." There is no evidence that Duveen ever sat at anyone's bedside with a contract in hand and pen raised, although he did almost everything else. Conquest, power, self-assertion, the sense that an object is infinitely more desirable because someone else wants it—all these qualities were certainly aspects of Duveen's personality. So was snobbism and the desire to advance one's social status. His collectors luxuriated in the solemnity of wealth and so did he. One has only to look at the house on Madison Avenue and Ninety-first Street.

One comes to the final attribute of the great collector, particularly American. Almost from the start Duveen was surrounded by men and women who were buying for themselves, but with a generosity that is still extraordinary, even in our own age: in order to give them all away. One thinks of Isabella Stewart Gardner's museum, Fenway Court; of Henry Walters and the Walters Art Museum; of John G. Johnson, whose collection went to Philadelphia; of Morgan, Altman, Frick, the Wideners, the Huntingtons, and so many others. That urge to give back something precious, something immortal, that had been salvaged from the struggle and even wreckage of their private lives is the most puzzling yet admirable aspect of these great American collectors and philanthropists. Duveen's farsightedness in the selection of these objects cannot be overstated. He instructed and cajoled, and as a result American museums are filled with Old Masters rather than the tenth-rate salon paintings of the *dernier siècle* that they might otherwise have contained. So of course there should be a book about the objects that, thanks to him, went to museums, and of course they should be called Duveens. Otherwise someone might not appreciate the connection.

In the last decades of Duveen's life one sees him blurring the line that separated agent from client in the most natural possible way. Their goals had become his own. If, because of his actions, untold treasures had left Britain, then the least he could do was to give something back, and his final years are full of generous gestures, always more galleries to house works of art in great British institutions. He must have believed, with the Italian poet and dramatist Gabriele d'Annunzio, "Io ho quel che ho donato," or, "I have what I have given away." The push and pull of holding fast and letting go had always been part of his character, but now altruism had become the dominant motive. To have given away all those wonderful objects was the legacy his clients had assembled. He would have been inhuman not to consider it also his own.

LAWRENCE'S *PINKIE* HAD BEEN OFFERED to Andrew Mellon, but at that point he held the high cabinet position of secretary of the treasury and was reluctant to be seen publicly spending so much money on a single painting. As before, Duveen personally escorted the painting to San Marino in January 1927. Early in the journey he cabled Huntington: PINKIE ONLY FAIRLY WELL LAST NIGHT CRYING FOR GRANDPA BUT AM TAKING GREATEST CARE OF HER UNTIL SHE RETURNS HOME. That should have settled matters, but then it turned out that another possessive parent was back in the picture. Mellon decided that Pinkie looked exactly like his own daughter, "and of all the pictures he owns he coveted this the most." Duveen was placed in the horrid position of asking H.E.H. to part with a painting he had previously persuaded him to buy, but by then he had done his work too well. His exquisitely diplomatic overture was met with an equally diplomatic refusal, and the painting stayed in San Marino. In short order Duveen had to come up with something Mellon would like almost as well.

He hit upon the idea of *Mrs. Davenport,* a head-and-shoulders portrait of another society beauty that George Romney painted between 1782 and 1784. A good decade in age separates this lady from the preadolescent Pinkie, and there is no doubt which is the superior painting; but Mrs. Davenport, with her straw bonnet decorated with a brown bow, her capelike pink satin coat trimmed with fur, her calm gaze, and her delicious English complexion, has a certain charm. As soon as he knew that she was up for auction at Christie's, Duveen sprang into action. She was just right as a consolation prize. Knowing his methods one gathers he already had the nod from Mellon who was, despite his outward demeanor, as vulnerable to a pretty face as the next man. Another Romney, technically unfinished, *Lady Hamilton in a White Turban,* was for sale in the same auction. Both paintings had recently been in the news. They were owned by Sir William Bromley-Davenport, who had hung them in his country house and then decided to transfer them to his London flat. He soon thought better of the idea, put two less valuable portraits in their places, and removed the originals to a strong room. This, as it turned out, was prescient. The word had leaked out that there were two valuable paintings hanging on his walls. Burglars broke in and carefully removed the two substitutes. "Evidently they had received orders to take the two portraits hanging in certain positions, for they took nothing else." This sobering experience may have made their owner decide that the time had come to find new homes for his paintings.

Duveen, who was taking his usual cure in Vittel that summer of 1926, cautioned Eddie not to let Knoedler's have either painting. He wanted Christie's auctioneer, Sir Alec Martin, to buy *Mrs. Davenport* on their behalf.

No doubt Duveen fully expected the ruse to work, but then something went wrong. Sulley began the bidding for *Mrs. Davenport* at £5,000, but he soon dropped out, and the bidding was taken up by Charles Carstairs, acting for Knoedler's. The price soared upward and finally stopped at 58,000 guineas, or almost £61,000. That must have given Sir Joseph an awful shock, but it could not be helped, the word came from London. Martin said that Knoedler's had asked him to buy the painting for them. He was bound to say he was committed elsewhere, and Knoedler's must have concluded that could only mean Duveen Brothers. Lowengard, in Paris, also came to the same conclusion. As he pointed out, Duveen had publicly stated his determination to control the market for great English pictures, and so he must expect Knoedler's to make him pay dearly.

Duveen did not seem to mind being reproached. Still on holiday in Vittel, he wanted to know how many papers were carrying the story. What were they saying? At $300,000 it was the biggest price ever paid for a Romney so far. That seemed to satisfy him. Berenson was merely disgusted. If Duveen was determined to compete directly with Knoedler's, it was hopeless for him to try and tell him anything, he wrote to Fowles.

TRY AS HE MIGHT, Duveen could not always set new sales records; sometimes he had to be content with the merely satisfactory. A case in

Portrait of Arthur Atherley as an Etonian by Sir Thomas Lawrence

point is a painting by Lawrence called *Arthur Atherley as an Etonian.* This fierce-looking youngster, who has just left Eton, is standing in front of a wide landscape that includes Eton College in the distance. As with *Pinkie,* Lawrence has deliberately lowered the horizon to give the young Atherley a commanding aspect, and the storm clouds billowing behind him add to the theatricality of the setting. Atherley has all the accoutrements that go with the role of a young gentleman, including fur collar, top hat, and gloves. But, despite his provocative stance there is something endearing about his expression of mingled vulnerability and defiance that gives the portrait its charm. It was, in fact, immediately engraved and became well known. The picture was offered to Duveen's by a small London dealer. Walter Dowdeswell thought it very fine; so did Eddie and Armand. The only drawback, they agreed, were those dreary storm clouds. If only the painting had a more cheerful background it would be priceless. As it was, they thought they ought to be able to get it cheaply and bought it for something under £10,000.

Duveen had very little time or money invested in the affair, but the instinct to sell was so ingrained that when the film star Marion Davies, William Randolph Hearst's mistress, saw the painting in London and liked it, he gently told her it was not for sale. Anna Thomson Dodge was offering $600,000 for it. He would not answer for the latter's state of mind if the painting went to someone else. Davies reflected that Mr. Hearst would be so disappointed that he would probably never buy from Duveen again, but that was all right. What was a poor dealer to do? Davies had won. He rang back and offered her the painting for a mere $150,000. She countered with $140,000 and the deal was made. When she heard the news Anna Thomson Dodge ran down the stairs, fell, and broke her leg. Or so Duveen said. Davies went away feeling very proud of having beaten down the world's biggest art dealer. Duveen, putting up a brave front, sighed and retired with a profit of $90,000.

New clients with plenty of money were filling in the ranks left by the Huntingtons. Mrs. Dodge in Detroit was a promising newcomer. So was the young Mrs. Marjorie Merriweather Post and the future governor of New York, John D. Rockefeller Jr., if only he could be weaned from his regrettable interest in primitive African sculpture and the moderns.

John R. Thompson, owner of a chain of restaurants in Chicago, was another blank slate, offering all kinds of opportunities for re-education in the finer things of life. Duveen started him off slowly with a Frans Hals, *The Laughing Mandolin Player,* from the Paris collection of Arthur Veil-Picard. No one was better at portraying a bibulous, Falstaffian, rib-tickling laugh than Hals, and Thompson parted with $250,000 for his prize. The tenor John McCormack, who bought *Portrait of a Man,* another Frans Hals, became another good customer and friend. As one great sale followed another, in Britain in particular, there was always some newspaper comment about disappearing treasures.

Before the First World War, Duveen's fame had been limited to the art world, but in the postwar boom he became known to the public as "a magnificent, dramatic and astute plunger." He was so successful that other governments, not just the British, were finding it necessary to defend themselves against the charge that they were letting him abscond with national treasures. Shortly after yet another Titian, this one a *Portrait of a Venetian Nobleman,* left a Venetian collection bound for the U.S. at the price of £45,000, an official in Rome dismissed the sale, because, he said, the painting was not by Titian. He attributed it to Moroni.

"A magnificent and dramatic plunger": Duveen in the 1930s

"Not a real Titian?" Duveen exclaimed when he was asked about its purchase. "Do you think I'd give forty shillings, let alone over 30,000 good pounds, for a fake?" One could of course counter that he might be mistaken, as he was in this case. (The painting is now given to the very minor Lambert Sustris.) But obviously, no one was going to argue with the world's greatest authority on Old Masters.

Paintings by Bellini—that family of fifteenth-century Venetians that included Jacopo and his sons Gentile and Giovanni—were speculative undertakings, not only because so many were made by their own workshops but because their styles were widely admired and imitated, even during their lifetimes. For authentication Duveen was dependent, as usual, on Berenson, and Berenson "passed" so many Bellinis that Duveen sold them in quantity. He naturally liked to boast, as Sir Ellis Waterhouse recalled, "I can assure you that the stock of Giovanni Bellinis is absolutely inexhaustible." Many of the Bellinis Duveen bought and sold during the 1920s have subsequently been demoted to "workshop of," or minor masters, but at the time they looked like bargains. As usual, Lowengard was the one who approached the field with caution. Do not forget that Berenson is getting old and becoming far too liberal with his labels, he remarked to Duveen in the mid-1920s, when B.B. would have been about sixty. Duveen forgot.

A case in point is the *Madonna and Child* that came up for sale at Sotheby's in December 1927. It was being sold as a Cima da Conegliano, and B.B. had formerly given it to Marco Basaiti. B.B. now decided it was by Giovanni Bellini, the most famous name, which bumped the price up tenfold. The Virgin in a mauve-colored robe holds a naked child in her lap, with a symbolic landscape and a bright blue sky in the background. The jewel-like colors, the pretty conceit of the baby with a swallow perched on its hand, the gently inclined head of its mother and the distinguished provenance of the painting itself (it had come through William Beckford and the Dukes of Hamilton) made it a winner. Naturally no one at Duveens dared breathe a word about its really being a Bellini; they could barely think it. They themselves could not be seen buying it. There was a further complication; Gulbenkian had asked about it, and knowing how keenly he would be watching the price paid, they would be lucky to get a 5 percent markup if he bought it. Somebody had to keep Gulby at bay without arousing his suspicions, a difficult task. A front man had to be found and appointed. A small-time dealer with no known Duveen connections was delegated to bid. Since the man had no account with Sotheby's, he had to be provided with a large wad of cash. Duveen fretted about the idea that anyone from the firm should even be in the room.

The precautions seemed unnecessarily elaborate, but the result was a resounding success. Duveens had been prepared to pay as much as £15,000 but picked up the painting for a mere £4,400. No sooner had their agent left with the prize than he was contacted by numerous other dealers, among them Colnaghi's and Knoedler's. Gulbenkian no doubt found the whole exercise highly suspect but had no proof of anything. The painting was removed from its frame and protective glass and pronounced "an absolute peach." It was one of the most successful auction-room bids ever, repaying all of Duveen's anxious hovering. Duveen cabled, WHAT MARVELOUS HEADWAY WE ARE MAKING—PICTURE WILL REALIZE FORTUNE. He was right. The painting was bought by Jules Bache for $200,000, ten times the price they had paid. It is now labeled "workshop of."

In his constant pursuit of high-sounding collections with cachet, names that were as valuable as the objects to which they were attached, nothing was more useful to Duveen than a royal provenance. After World War I, when some aspects of the collection formerly belonging to the crown of the Austro-Hungarian monarchy were rumored to be for sale, Duveen was on it like a flash. He himself planned to take the Orient Express to Vienna, accompanied by Walter Dowdeswell; but in his zeal to get first pick of the best Sèvres, the Gobelin tapestries, the Regency silver, rare Spanish rugs, and the like, he had underestimated the obstacles. These followed in short order. First, the Austrian government possibly did not want to sell but merely to acquire a loan with the Hapsburg objects as collateral, which did not suit him at all. Next, there was the whole issue of which entity actually owned the objects and whether, having paid for them, Duveen might have to give them back. Then there was the problem of political instability and wild currency fluctuations. All these obstacles were as nothing to Duveen's temperament, and he pressed on manfully in pursuit of objects with ermine attached. However, after four years disenchantment set in. The prices being asked were in the millions of pounds for unsalable Rembrandts, disappointing Van Dycks, and paintings said to be by Velázquez that were probably not as billed. He would also have been amused by the news that his competitor Jacques Seligmann went to Vienna to see the tapestries and practically had a temper tantrum. He would not have them as a gift.

The end of World War I presented similar opportunities and pitfalls in Germany. After Kaiser Wilhelm II escaped to Holland, he was interned there in the castle of Doorn. Since he owned twenty castles of his own, all of them bursting with works of art and enviable furnishings, these would certainly be for sale at some point. Some of them were already finding their

way into the international antiques market. Duveen was particularly interested in the Kaiser's French eighteenth-century holdings, but it was said
that despite his present predicament, the Kaiser would never sell. This view
was somewhat modified in 1927, a year or so later, after Fowles had
reviewed the situation at first hand in Berlin. It was true that the Kaiser was
rich, but he owed the German government a huge sum in reparations, and
since forty-eight members of his family were dependent upon him, money
had to come from somewhere. The thought of art bored him and he was
perfectly willing to sell whatever the government said he still owned, which
was not much. Duveen Brothers knew they would have to pay top prices
for whatever they bought. That did not matter so much because of the
cachet. But the Kaiser would be no fun to deal with, Fowles wrote; he was
"still the most autocratic, capricious man in Europe." There was the slight
problem of their being English as well. The Kaiser refused to sell to an En-
glishman or Frenchman, so Fowles airily commented that of course they
were dealing through someone else, in this case a Spanish nobleman. None
of this particularly mattered to Duveen, who was in his usual ebullient
mood in the winter of 1927. Business prospects had never looked better. By
early January of 1928 they were negotiating for five pictures, and Fowles
was sending long, careful letters with detailed descriptions of the pros and
cons, the prices they might have to pay, the desirability of the subject matter, the question of provenance and all the complex considerations that
went into any decision about a sale. Since the Kaiser was such a potentially
rich source, they might even want to pay a bit more than he asked, Fowles
wrote, to show what good sports they were.

The painting they most wanted was Watteau's *La Danse,* which, according to old records, had been bought by the German ambassador in Paris
after Watteau's death. Since Emperor Frederick the Great only liked big
pictures, the painting had been enlarged, but so skillfully that it had never
been detected. Even so, Fowles had never seen a more idyllic scene. The
lovely dancing girl standing in the center was a larger figure than was usually found in a Watteau, almost two feet tall and dressed in red and green.
The children watching on the side wore harmonizing shades of blue, yellow, and mauve. In short, it was a very great picture and one they should
not miss. Unfortunately, *La Danse* was not yet for sale, and the problem
was that if an offer was made, the state had reserved the right to buy it at
the same price. Still, they should keep trying.

While this affair was pending, Duveen Brothers went after some other
eighteenth-century French pictures they liked almost as much. Lancret, a
follower of Watteau's, had painted *La Camargo Dancing,* a depiction of the

famous ballerina performing a stately minuet with a partner in one of Watteau's magical woodland dells, observed by a circle of charmingly dressed courtiers. Lowengard said this was one of Lancret's most celebrated works and there was nothing finer in Paris. They also bought Watteau's *The French Comedians,* a group of actors recognizable as famous figures of the theatre in Watteau's time. The painting lacks the brio of Watteau's other painting of a troupe of Italian comedians, but Lowengard thought it had historical importance and, as they thought he would, Jules Bache snapped it up right away. They took two lesser Watteaus, *Fête Champêtre* and *Embarquement pour Cythère.* They also bought a large, imposing portrait of Louis XIII by Rubens, after agonizing over whether it really was by that master. The king was in full uniform, which they considered a drawback, but there was plenty of color—blue cloak, red curtain, even some red feathers—which brightened it up a bit. As for the anxiously watched *La Danse,* the Kaiser finally said he would be willing to sell. However, he was required to get the German government's permission, and he would be dammed if he would ask them.

Since his staff had given him stern instructions not to crow about this latest coup for fear of antagonizing the Kaiser, Duveen obediently kept quiet. But the London *Sunday Times* found out about it anyway and claimed Sir Joseph had spent £500,000 on the purchase, a gross overstatement. The Germans were up in arms about the sale, and Bode, who had known all about it and had advised Duveens, said he was shocked, shocked. Duveen also confirmed he had bought a fragmentary work from the Kaiser that belonged to a Pesellino altarpiece that was at the National Gallery in London. He had donated it to the gallery. After this publicity, which for once Duveen did not relish, the supply of pictures from the Kaiser dried up, and Duveen never did get *La Danse.*

To buy or not to buy tormented them all. Given the necessity of making instant decisions, it was easy to be wrong, and an expensive mistake was just too painful to contemplate. A case in point was the Fra Angelico *Madonna and Child with Side Pieces,* owned by Sir John Ramsden, which had come up for sale at Partridge's in Bond Street early in December 1929. Ernest went to see it and became very excited about it when he learned that a few years earlier, Langton Douglas, an expert in the field, thought it must be by the great master and offered £16,000 for it. To have Langton Douglas prepared to pay that kind of money must mean the painting was genuine, and Duveen sprang into action. It sounded wonderful, and he was terrified the painting would slip away. Armand, his best eye on the Italian Renaissance while they waited for B.B.'s reaction, must take the first train to London. If the Channel services were not running because of bad weather, Duveen said grandly, he must figure out some other way to get there, as if swimming were not out of the question. Meanwhile, the London office must arrange to have a photograph delivered to Paris by hand—they were not to depend on the Christmas mail—and also keep a copy in the office in case Armand arrived in London before the photograph arrived in Paris. They must leave nothing to chance. Duveen cabled, MUCH THRILLED AND SCARED ANY RISK LOSING IT AS MUCH AT STAKE STOP.

From then on cables flew across the Atlantic by the hour. A day later, on December 9, Ernest went back and studied the painting, then compared it to other Fra Angelicos in the *Klassiker der Kunst.* He was no longer completely sure that it was by the master. The boats were running again. Duveen should not worry as Partridge, their friendly business partner, was reserving the picture entirely for them. Meanwhile, another photograph was being delivered by hand to B.B., who was about to arrive in Montpellier in southern France. None of this was good enough for Duveen, who made an urgent phone call. He wanted an answer within the hour. When was Armand scheduled to arrive? A few hours later on the 9th, the messenger with the photograph bound for Paris telephoned from Dover to say he was stuck; the boats had stopped running again. Meanwhile, Ernest was more sure than ever that the painting was not a Fra Angelico, much as he liked it. By December 10, the flurry was over. Armand had arrived and was equally sure the painting was not a Fra Angelico. Berenson had arrived in Montpellier and agreed with them both. He thought it was a "very typical" work of Andrea di Giusto. The chase was dropped after four days, almost as abruptly as it had begun.

IN THE FAST-CHANGING WORLD in which they lived paintings worth £100,000 might, two or three years later, be worth £10,000, or the reverse. Everything depended on market conditions and how many rich collectors were bidding for that kind of painting at any given moment. Such was the case with *Portrait of the Marchesa Balbi* by Sir Anthony Van Dyck. The subject is in black, wearing a somber, gold-embroidered mantel and a ruffed collar, and there is none of the color that Duveen looked for in a major work. Its most striking aspects are the face and hands, which glimmer against the surrounding darkness; in short, the work's effectiveness lies in the contrast between the pale, alive face and graceful hands, one holding a folded fan and the other cupped in what could be a formal dance position, and the somberness of the setting. Despite the subject's obvious status and wealth, she seems acutely alone, almost melancholic. When the painting, which came from Sir George Holford, was suggested to Duveen by Colin Agnew as a joint purchase in the summer of 1924, the price was £50,000. That was a joke, Duveen said. The problem was that Agnew's were far too timid in negotiation and did not dare to approach wealthy owners unless they could make grand offers. Duveen thought the work was worth £35,000 at the most. But the point was not to make any offer, which only encouraged the owner to shop around for a better deal. The dealer must insist that the owner name his price. Until Holford did there was no point in touching the Van Dyck. But then, curiously, a year later, in July 1925, Duveen wanted the painting. What is more, he paid a staggering price for it, twice what he said it was worth: £70,000. He knew, of course, just what he was doing. When the Van Dyck reached New York in December 1925, he wrote that it was an absolute miracle; the greatest painting he had ever owned. That was a typical overstatement, but he was extremely happy about something, and the reason followed shortly. He was taking the painting to Washington along with two Titians, a Raphael, a Metsu, and the Reynolds of Lady Caroline Howard. He expected to sell them all.

Sir George Holford's sister Evelyn had married Robert H. Benson, senior partner of a London firm of merchant bankers and a passionate collector of Italian Renaissance art. Over a period of forty years the couple amassed 114 paintings from the fourteenth to sixteenth centuries, with particular emphasis on the Venetians. The Bensons were on friendly terms with the Duveens, and the story is that one evening over dinner, Duveen leaned across the table and offered Benson a blank check. Whatever the truth of the matter, the Benson Collection changed hands in July 1927 for the staggering price of $2.5 million. It was clear that Duveen intended to dominate the market for Italian Old Masters just as he had for the British ones. Berenson, who could see the writing on the wall, chose that moment to negotiate for a new and more favorable contract. Although the Benson Collection had been authenticated by Tancred Borenius, a Finnish art historian who settled in London and was a picture expert at Sotheby's, his name had none of Berenson's authority, and B.B. would be needed if all these Italians were to find new homes. It was either a big name or no kind of sale, and Duveen had paid too much to contemplate the latter. So Berenson got his improved contract, plus £50,000 for his expertise on the Benson Collection alone.

Some Duccios went to Clarence Mackay and John D. Rockefeller Jr.

for handsome prices. The Frick Collection paid $500,000 for two paint-
ings, Berna's *The Way to Calvary* and Duccio's *The Temptation of Christ*.
Bache bought pictures by Domenico Ghirlandaio, Luca Signorelli,
Cosimo Tura, and Bellini, paintings that eventually went to the Metropolitan. Kress bought fourteen Bensons. Other paintings eventually ended up
in the Fogg, Cincinnati, Wadsworth Atheneum, Los Angeles County, and
Getty Museums and even the Ringling Museum. Just the same, how to dis-
pose of all those Italian Renaissance paintings defeated even Duveen.

ONE OF THE VERY FEW CLIENTS with whom Duveen was on chatty
terms was Judge Gary, who, with Mellon, had founded the U.S. Steel Corporation and had been buying paintings, sculptures, Sèvres porcelain, and
the like from Duveen Brothers since about 1912. To say that Duveen's
friends were financial titans would be a truism; all his New York clients
were self-made millionaires, but there was something about this short,
cocky "czar of the steel trust" with his pretensions to aristocratic status that
appealed to the vaudevillian in Duveen. Bit by bit Duveen managed to
wean the Garys from their fondness for the Barbizon school and such
painters as Anton Mauve and Charles-François Daubigny. He must have
cringed when he saw the painting *The Dying Soldier* by J. Berne Bellecour
on their wall; but he rallied, managed to persuade them to put it on the
market, personally found a buyer, and shipped it off to San Francisco.
Before long they were appreciating the virtues of such marbles as *Venus
Chastising Cupid with a Bunch of Roses* by Etienne Maurice Falconet, which
was once in the Morgan Collection, an antique Beauvais tapestry sofa and
chairs, some marvelous silk carpets, choice tables and bric à brac, Dresden
porcelain, a terra-cotta Houdon bust of the sculptor's infant daughter and,
most important, Gainsborough's *The Harvest Waggon*. Duveen bought the
painting, which was owned by Sir Lionel Phillips, at Christie's in 1913 for
the comparatively modest price of $100,000 and sold it to the Garys for
$160,000.

The Garys were especially fond of china. They bought a set of apple-
green Old Sèvres that had belonged to Lord d'Abernon, a gold dinner service for eighteen, and, among much else, a set of Sèvres that had belonged
to Queen Marie of Roumania—a million dollars' worth of china alone. So
when, in 1926, Queen Marie came to New York, she was invited to dine
with the Garys, and of course the Duveens were included. Next morning
Duveen sent a handwritten note to thank Mrs. Gary, who was easily overwhelmed in such situations, and tell her what a great success she had been

as a hostess. Reassuring wealthy clients was the kind of thing he was terribly good at, and the note, hand-delivered, was probably on her doorstep by nine a.m. He also thoughtfully cabled Henry Huntington to say that since the queen was to be in Los Angeles a month later, perhaps that multimillionaire might like to entertain her, too. Linking up the world—nobody did it better than Duveen. Eventually, with the Garys, Duveen slipped into a kind of relationship he also did well, of infiltrating their private life so unobtrusively that they became dependent on him for all those little services that help smooth life's path for multimillionaires.

A few months before Gary died, he and his wife moved from their palatial residence at 856 Fifth Avenue to an even grander dwelling at 1130 Fifth Avenue, at Ninety-fourth Street. Bert Boggis was instructed to personally assist Mrs. Gary so that the fine French eighteenth-century furniture, the Hals, the Rembrandt, the Gainsborough, the palatial carpets, the Sèvres and peach-bloom bottles might be suitably placed in their new quarters. Duveen was in mid-Atlantic on the SS *Mauretania* en route to Paris when Boggis cabled in July 1927 to say he was taking great care of Mrs. Gary as they settled into their new home. The judge had not been well for several weeks, something he did not wish to have known, but was now completely well. Boggis spoke too soon. By the middle of August Judge Gary was dead, aged eighty. Duveen Brothers sent a beautiful wreath of orchids. His widow, who along with their daughters retained a life interest in the estate, said that all the furniture and works of art in the new town house would have to be sold. But she refused to do anything until Sir Joseph, whose advice was crucial, she said, returned from Europe in October. The moment came for an evaluation of all the antique furniture, statuary, rugs, and paintings. Duveen's figure was $1.25 million and he offered to buy the collection outright. It was a fair offer, and no doubt the lady, who at that stage lived only to please him, would have accepted. But the executors of the estate, the New York Trust Company, thought otherwise and arranged for an auction by the American Art Association in the spring of 1928.

The question at that point became, What did Duveen want? Naturally, *The Harvest Waggon*. He also wanted his Houdon bust back. He loved the sofa and chairs with their Beauvais tapestries and had to have those as well. Anyway, Gulbenkian wanted first refusal on this item. Gulby also said he would pay up to $55,000 for a remarkable Louis XV boudoir table in acajou and kingwood marquetry. Paris was rather interested in some green hawthorn vases, but Duveen said the color was too pale and one of them was broken. He had similar objections to the black hawthorn vase they asked about. He thought that the Gainsborough, the Houdon, and the

Louis XV table were going to make headlines and began to plan his publicity campaign. The first day of the sale would be on the evening of Friday,
April 20, and he thought there ought to be some news by nine-thirty or
ten. He wanted a staff person to wait at 4 Grafton Street in London for a
telegram that, given the time difference, would probably arrive at about
three a.m. on Saturday. Then the morning papers were to be told immediately so that the news could be on the front page all over London. That was
the idea, but it transpired that the final deadline for the morning dailies
was two a.m. The best London could arrange was coverage in the Saturday-
afternoon papers. The Sunday papers would have much more space, and
A. C. R. Carter of the *Daily Telegraph* had already promised to come
through with a big article.

As expected, the Gary sale was the event of the season. The American
Art Association had originally planned to hold the auction in its own
rooms, but the demand for tickets was so great that it was moved to the
ballroom of the Plaza Hotel. That room held sixteen hundred seats, and
thirty-six hundred people applied for admission. Seats were not reserved,
so youngsters from the YMCA were dressed up in borrowed finery and sent
ahead to secure the best places; they were tipped as much as fifty dollars.
Among the socialites in black tie and full evening dress were Mrs. W. K.
Vanderbilt Jr., Mrs. Cyrus McCormick, J. E. Widener, C. S. Phipps, Mr.
and Mrs. Percy Straus, E. F. Albee, Samuel Untermyer, and Otto Bannard.
Every big international dealer was represented, and when the auctioneer,
H. H. Parke, made his entry, it took him twenty minutes to make his way
through the crush to the stage. Gary's remaining Barbizons were soon dispensed with, but then the serious bidding began. Duveen bought *Mrs.
John Allnutt* by Thomas Lawrence for $45,000, one of a series of record
prices: $44,000 for a Raeburn, a Fragonard self-portrait for $52,000, and
even a Corot for $32,000. As the *New York Times* commented, "So much
speculation had been aroused among collectors and dealers . . . that the
mounting bids took on something of the aspect of the gradual unfolding of
a plot on . . . opening night . . . Each painting, as it came up for sale was
shown on the stage at the west end of the ballroom and many were greeted
with applause . . ."

Knoedler's opened the bidding for *The Harvest Waggon* with $200,000,
and the price mounted by rapid jumps of $5,000 and $10,000 to
$300,000. At that point Sir Joseph grandly entered the competition. Gov-
ernor Alvan T. Fuller went him one better with $335,000. An anonymous
French bidder offered $340,000. "Not more than perhaps three minutes
after the first bid the hammer fell on Sir Joseph's offer of $360,000."

The Harvest Waggon (sometimes called The Market Cart) is one of a series Gainsborough painted in which a group in the left foreground is seen either coming or going, with trees massed against the horizon and a tranquil sky. The figures are, as in The Mall in St. James's Park, subordinated to a harmonious design of man, animals, and landscape. The companions pause to drink, comfort their babies, and welcome a newcomer aboard. Dogs follow along, and small pools pick up the glittering light. This particular version is unique because Gainsborough's daughters, Mary and Margaret, figure in the composition, and the team of horses depicted belonged to the artist's favorite mover. Gainsborough also did something he seldom did, which was to sign the work: The initials "T.G." appear on a rock in the foreground. So it has particular associations with the artist; but still, the idea that in fifteen years the painting had more than doubled in value stupefied the art world. "People were dazed," Art News commented.

The chief attraction on the second day was Sabine, the small marble bust of Houdon's baby daughter. Duveen had always loved Houdon, the most celebrated French sculptor of the eighteenth century, whose busts of children are particularly prized. A Houdon could once be picked up for $25,000, and at one point Duveen owned fifteen of them. Being Duveen, he began looking for a way to increase their value. The only way to get more was to be willing to pay more. He caused a sensation during the Yerkes sale of 1910 by bidding $51,000 for Houdon's life-size bronze Diana, one of three copies, the others being in the Louvre and the museum at Tours. From then on the pattern was set, and Sabine, which Duveen had bought for $96,000 from the Jacques Doucet collection in 1912, was going to fetch a great deal of money. Exactly how much, even he was not quite sure.

Gulbenkian got his set of Beauvais tapestry furniture for $60,000 plus commission. The Louis XV table that he had been willing to pay $55,000 for fetched $71,000. That, and a number of other select items, including two sixteenth-century gold-and-silver-woven silk Polonaise rugs and two other sixteenth-century carpets from the Ispahan palace, went to John D. Rockefeller Jr., for whom Duveen was bidding at no cost, no doubt to encourage him. A private buyer named John Grosberg had bought Hals's A Young Cavalier, paying $85,000. Whether or not he was buying for Duveen is not quite clear, but in any case Duveen decided he had to have this salable item, so he took this as well and sent it to Paris to be cleaned.

The single disappointment was the Houdon bust. Wesley Towner wrote in The Elegant Auctioneers: "Now, with the particularly exquisite Sabine on the block, Sir Joseph, in the front row, was obviously prepared to vanquish all niggling contestants." But to the auctioneer's surprise, five bidders kept raising the price. It should have stopped at $175,000, which would have been about right. "But well to the rear . . . a self-composed young woman continued nodding. Up and up the melody of numbers floated, until—at $245,000—Duveen hesitated and grimly shook his head. Parke leaned over to him. 'Are you all through, Sir Joseph?' he asked, as if incredulous at such a show of penny-pinching.

"Sir Joseph remained grim and immobile. Parke knocked down *Sabine* to the lady in the rear. Then, pointing his gavel at Duveen, he said graciously, but with just a trace of covert irony, 'Sir Joseph, this is the first time I have ever known you to be outbid on an item of this rare caliber.' "

This was perfectly true. As Duveen relayed to London: AFTER EXCITING DUEL KNOEDLER BOUGHT HOUDON TWO HUNDRED FORTY-FIVE FOR MRS. HARKNESS AGAINST ME STOP. FIRST TIME IN HISTORY HAVE BEEN BEATEN STOP. He was genuinely annoyed. To allow Knoedler's to get the better of him was not only bad form, but set a very bad precedent. Just the same, London thought it was a good thing, because it showed that he had real competition and that the sales were not window dressing, as some people claimed. This was a poor consolation, but the publicity in New York, London, and Paris had been tremendous, and that was almost as good as a Houdon. Besides, he had his Gainsborough, even if temporarily. He sold it to Frank P. Wood of Toronto for $450,000. It is now at the Toronto Art Gallery, where it was once again in the news in 1959 when some thieves, attempting to cut it out of its frame, damaged it badly. As for the widow of the judge, she took a modest suite of rooms in the Savoy Plaza and continued to seek Sir Joseph's advice about what to do with her possessions.

Chapter Sixteen

IN THE ELEVATOR

THERE IS A WONDERFUL STORY about the way Joseph Duveen is said to have wangled an introduction to one of the last great collectors in his career, Andrew Mellon, the future benefactor of the National Gallery in Washington, D.C.

According to this version the legendary meeting was one Duveen had been trying to orchestrate for years. Finding that he and Mellon were passengers on the same transatlantic liner, he dispensed his usual liberal tip to the deck steward with instructions to place his chair beside Andrew Mellon's. Day after day he waited expectantly, but Mellon, sensing trouble, merely paced the deck and retired to the safety of his cabin.

When in London Duveen always took the same spacious fourth-floor suite at Claridge's, which was handsomely arrayed with the latest Old Masters for sale in the London galleries. One day in 1921 he happened to learn that Mellon was staying on the third floor. He made the discreet acquaintance of Mellon's personal valet and asked to be apprised of the great man's comings and goings. Then he had himself moved to a different suite on the second floor just below Mellon's and, like the great actor he was, waited for his cue. It came one afternoon. Mellon's valet telephoned to say that his master was about to go out for a walk. Duveen rushed out of his apartment and was just in time to catch the elevator as it reached the second floor. Then the door opened.

The cartoonist Edward Sorel captured the moment when the consummate salesman, a huge pussycat in top hat and striped pants and carrying an umbrella, entered the elevator to the consternation of a very aged and tiny bird. Doffing his hat, Duveen practically purred with pleasure. "Mr.

The cartoonist Edward Sorel celebrates the moment when, it is said,
Duveen first met a most reluctant prey, Andrew Mellon.

Mellon, I presume? What a delightful surprise!" As it happened, Duveen
was about to take his daily constitutional. Was Mr. Mellon going far? Perhaps he would like to take a tour around London's National Gallery? It
would be no trouble. It would be his pleasure. That cunningly arranged
coincidence, it is said, was the beginning of a beautiful friendship.

For the likely story one has to go to the more reliable and perhaps
equally intriguing account furnished by Edward Fowles. He dates their
first meeting as eight years earlier, in 1913. Just after the Merchant Marine
building was opened on Fifth Avenue, three visitors appeared: Judge Gary,
Frick, and a younger man, Andrew Mellon, whom Frick predicted would
one day be "the greatest collector of us all." Shortly after that, Mellon visited Duveens in Paris at the Place Vendôme and Fowles showed him a
model of the museum in which the Edward Tuck Collection was to be
housed in Concord, New Hampshire. Mellon showed no great interest in
the paintings and marbles but was fascinated by the scale model. He stood
there examining it intently. "In my mind, I can see him standing there to
this day: saying nothing; just looking . . ."

Andrew Mellon, looking forlorn, on the empty deck of a ship

Mellon, the son of a Pittsburgh banker, was a quiet, unassuming man with a genius for backing entrepreneurial ventures in oil and metals, taking repayment in the new company's stock. Among the businesses he helped establish were such corporate giants as Gulf Oil, Alcoa, Carborundum, American Locomotive, and Standard Steel Car, not to mention the Mellon Bank, which he nursed from a modest local business to one of the country's largest. Incidentally, he became vastly rich, a secretary of the treasury under three presidents, and a collector of art.

Mellon, with his high forehead, wide cheekbones and square jaw, would grow up to look uncannily like his father, Judge Mellon, the look of a natural aristocrat. Like his father he was reserved and taciturn; he stooped slightly and, when he was not consumed by business matters, began to study art with a similar passion and concentration. He was buying art from Knoedler's as early as 1899, making all the common mistakes of choosing minor artists and sentimental scenes, although an occasional fine Corot or superb Cuyp began to slip through. In this case, Charles Carstairs of Knoedler's was the chief influence on Mellon's artistic education, coaxing and cajoling him into an appreciation for Turner, Romney, Gainsborough, and Vermeer.

John Walker, who would become a future director of the National Gallery, recalled an early meeting in Pittsburgh in which Mellon showed him his picture collection. The "frail, fastidiously dressed" old man was completely tongue-tied, he said, and unable to say why he liked a work. He even forgot the names of some of the artists. "But from the way he looked at his paintings, from the sheer intensity of his scrutiny, I knew that he had a deep feeling for what he collected . . . He seems to have wanted paintings which would offer him an escape into an ideal world . . ."

The thread of an aesthetic awakening seems to have been the one self-indulgence in Mellon's austere regime of thrift, hard work, and self-denial. Since he lacked the slightest understanding of his own emotional needs or anyone else's, there were bound to be repercussions in his private life. He made an advantageous marriage to a well-born Englishwoman, but she was appalled at the grimy, dust-filled air of Pittsburgh's blast furnaces and steel mills and felt shut out of her husband's life. She left, taking their children, Ailsa and Paul, and asked for a divorce. Her husband hired private detectives, had hidden microphones installed in her house, and tried by numerous tactics to gain custody of the children. Such an aspect of his character was known only to intimates. To others he seemed inoffensive and bland to the point of invisibility.

By the time Mellon was ready to twitch an eyebrow in Duveen's direction, he had been buying art for almost twenty years and had formed firm personal friendships at Knoedler's. He was modest, he was retiring, he was immensely successful and the kind of person who will stay loyal. He was also capable of devious ways of getting even, as his divorce tactics showed. So it is perhaps curiously appropriate that the one man Duveen tracked down with equal deviousness was Andrew Mellon. He bribed the butler. He bribed servants, even Mellon's personal valet and one of his secretaries. If he did not arrange for encounters in elevators and on the decks of ships, he was perfectly capable of doing so. Mellon's splendid evasiveness was matched only by Duveen's determination to capture him as a client, for two reasons. In the first place, he belonged to Knoedler's, and Duveen was bound to take that as a personal challenge. In addition, one has to believe that Duveen had an instinct about such things. Years before Mellon let it be known that he was going to found a great national gallery, Duveen had sniffed the air and decided that, sooner or later, Mellon would do it. He might have known it before Mellon did. One believes that these naturally opposed temperaments were meant for each other. Mellon's acute and penetrating silences might have unnerved some people, but not Duveen. He would have burbled on happily, hardly needing an answer. What would have driven Duveen mad was Mellon's inability to say whether or not he wanted a painting. The usual procedure was that a painting Mellon might get to like would be hung somewhere in the house. Then Duveen Brothers waited. And waited for their mute prey to indicate by the flutter of an eyelash whether he wanted it. They might wait for a year. Somebody around him had to read the signs and portents and signal the possible outcomes. Duveen almost had to pay informants in self-defense.

Just the same, it is a bit unnerving to see how many confidential reports there are in the Mellon correspondence files that were kept in the Duveen Archive. From about 1918 onward, when Mellon bought his first painting from Duveen, a Frans Hals, *Portrait of an Elderly Lady*, Duveen kept a dossier on Mellon's movements, his visitors, his art collection, his dinner parties, and whatever thoughts were heard to escape from his lips. Bert Boggis, who had graduated to Duveen's confidential assistant and probably took more secrets about Duveen Brothers to his grave than anybody else, was delegated to stalk Mr. Mellon. He was heard to boast, when Mellon was secretary of the treasury, that "the contents of his wastebasket reached the train to New York in the time it took the Secretary to walk home from the office."

If Mellon could have brought himself to buy *Pinkie* when the time was right, he might have been acquiring Duveen's choicest specimens far sooner than he did. As it was, the trickle of Duveen paintings that eventually became a flood started late in 1920. Duveen won at auction in Paris the famous "Montgermont Rembrandt," so called because it had been owned by Louis Leboeuf de Montgermont, among others. This stark portrait of an old lady holding a Bible would be likely to appeal to Mellon's austere tastes, and its authenticity was unquestioned, along with its fame as one of the artist's most uncompromising studies of character. Duveen tried his best to follow this victory with two Tintoretto portraits of Venetian senators, from the collection of the Dukes of Abercorn. He wanted $350,000 for the pair. He also sent a seventeenth-century Dutch scene by Gerard ter Borch of a suitor in black entering a room in which a lady, dressed in velvet and satin, awaits him with a look of shy interest. Behind her a young girl is playing an early version of a guitar and a small brown-and-white dog looks up expectantly. It is the moment when no one quite knows what to say. The musician, the father in the background, and the fussily dressed suitor, with his big square buckled shoes, his puffed sleeves, his oversize hat, and his attitude of almost excruciating deference, are positioned to suggest a world of feeling. That this is a charged encounter is further suggested by the contrast between the dim light in the room and the spotlight that seems to shine on the woman's high, pale forehead, her clasped hands, and the brilliant sheen of her skirt.

The Suitor's Visit is a magical painting and must have charmed the collector. But Duveen had asked $220,000. True, he had already given Mellon a 10 percent discount. But Mellon still thought he was paying too much. His genuine inability to decide—and his vagueness about titles and artists once he had decided—were coupled with a conviction that one could bring down the price by delaying because (as he would have reasoned) dealers always asked too much. He held the trump cards in this waiting game. The paintings over which he dawdled might well have been financed with a loan from one of his banks on which Duveen was paying interest. So Duveen might be in the comically disadvantageous position of borrowing money from Mellon in order to find out whether Mellon wanted a painting. No more nail-biting, stomach-churning dilemma could be imagined. Two years later Mellon sent a check for $175,000 for *The Suitor's Visit* and the Tintorettos were packed up and sent back to New York.

Naturally, Duveen tiptoed around Mellon. When the latter was named secretary of the treasury in March 1921, Duveen "permitted himself the pleasure" of writing to congratulate him. He also mentioned a very pretty house in Washington that his friends, the Belmonts, were willing to sell or rent; whether Mellon explored the idea is not known. By October 1922 Duveen was angling for a contract to decorate the Mellon apartment but had been beaten out by French and Company, according to one of Duveen's own moving men. This was a huge disappointment. Perhaps their bid was too high or their representative had not made the right impression. Cabling from London, Duveen wanted to know whether work had begun and when Mellon would return to Washington. He kept trying. Learning that Mellon might want to have his portrait painted, Duveen recommended Oswald Birley, a British society painter who had had numerous commissions, including portraits of both Huntingtons—his of Arabella became widely admired. Decorating someone's apartment, making suggestions about where he should live and which was the best choice for a certain project: all these were second-nature to Duveen as he lay siege to a client he was determined to have. Mellon was much too cagey and stubborn to make a satisfying target. He would think about it. In the case of Birley, he thought for ten years, but in the end he engaged the painter, who produced a remarkably fine likeness, one in which pain and loneliness struggle for dominance in an otherwise closed-off face.

At this stage in their relationship every purchase Mellon made from Duveen Brothers included a carefully worded agreement that he could return the painting within a certain period if, for any reason, he did not like it or it did not look well in one of his houses. This might have been the prudent result of many horrid early mistakes. A man whose eyes have been educated can no longer look at a salon painting without a shudder, and Mellon must have sold a great many bad early choices at a loss. Just when the idea of founding a national gallery became lodged in his mind is not exactly clear. But it may be significant that the clause about the return of pictures was dropped in the autumn of 1926, possibly signaling that Mellon's plans for his collection had undergone a sea change. That was a great year for Mellon sales from Duveen's point of view. On April 15, 1926, he cabled Paris that he was seeing Mellon that day and would be hanging Van der Weyden's ravishing *Portrait of a Lady* and the "Wachtmeister Rembrandt," *A Young Man Seated at a Table,* in the house the following week. He also hoped to sell a Velázquez, a Rubens portrait, and the Giovanelli Titian, a portrait that eventually went to Bache. Since Duveen was at the pinnacle of his fame as an international art dealer, it would have been curious if Mellon had not begun to thaw, and he did. When his daughter Ailsa married David K. E. Bruce in Washington in 1926, the Duveens were invited, among a guest list that included President and Mrs. Calvin Coolidge, Vice President and Mrs. Charles Dawes, Supreme Court justices, cabinet members, the secretaries of war and the navy, eleven senators, thirteen ambassadors, and other similarly prominent members of the Washington establishment. On hearing of Ailsa's engagement, Duveen drafted a letter saying that he had been fond of her ever since he realized she and his wife had the same name, but thought better of it.

In September of that year Mellon uncharacteristically confessed he would rather have Duveen's opinion than that of any museum official. By then they were in London and spending every day together. Four days later Duveen sent an ecstatic report to New York. They had had "marvellous interviews." Mellon was taking the Rembrandt and the Van der Weyden. If Duveen did not sell the Davenport Romney to Huntington, Mellon wanted the second refusal. (He took it.) He wanted the ex-Michelham Gainsborough, *Miss Catherine Tatton.* He also asked about their Giorgione, not identified, and a Vermeer Duveen had just bought. All of these possible sales thrilled Duveen. But he was equally enthusiastic about the future as well, another hint that he expected Mellon's pace to quicken. A year later he had even better news. Mellon was "in a wonderful humor and very interested," he cabled. There was enormous business to come; "more than you realize."

As with any relationship, there were bumps along the road. The Vermeer to which Duveen referred was *Laughing Girl,* a painting of a young woman in three-quarter-face, her head turned toward her left shoulder, her brown eyes rolling with amusement. Fowles and Lowengard had responded soon after Bode had declared it to be an early Vermeer. It was a rare discovery, and they were naturally excited. But once they saw it they were full of doubts. They did not like the girl's fixed smile, her staring eyes, or the stiff handling, and were not impressed by the color scheme, either. They should have trusted these impressions. Somehow they convinced themselves that the painting was genuine; Duveen did the rest. Mellon, who needed a Vermeer, bought it; it is now considered to be by an imitator, i.e., a fake, and has not been exhibited for years. The same fate awaited *The Lace Maker,* another weak painting supposedly by Vermeer which Bode authenticated. One of Vermeer's masterpieces, *Girl with a Red Hat,* was bought by Mellon and is one of three by that artist now at the National Gallery, but it did not come from Duveen.

Since questions about the two Duveen Vermeers were safely in the future, these sales would not have ruffled the atmosphere of trust that was developing between Mellon and Duveen. But something Berenson did was unsettling and centered around one of the paintings for sale at Christie's from the Darnley collection. There were a so-called Giorgione, *The Head of Pompey Brought to Caesar,* which Berenson called a decorative item, and a painting, *The Lords John and Bernard Stuart,* a copy by Gainsborough after a work by Van Dyck. This painting absorbed a great deal of Duveen's attention. After all, it was a famous painter, but Gainsborough had put as little of himself into it as possible and as much of Van Dyck's style as he could. Walter Dowdeswell asked, Would anyone want a Gainsborough that wasn't? Ernest Duveen was similarly unimpressed; the predominant colors were brown and yellow and the whole canvas uninteresting. Duveen, who hated the idea of passing up a Gainsborough, even a dull one, cabled, IS THERE ABSOLUTELY NO GAINSBORO BLUE STOP SURELY SOME BLUE SOMEWHERE STOP. There was not. There was also a painting by Titian, *Venus and Adonis,* showing Adonis leaving on his fatal hunt while a nude Venus, her back turned and eyes raised, tries to prevent him. The famous scene had been painted many times, and they agreed with "Doris," pseudonym for B.B., that it was only a studio copy. The one authentic version was in the Widener collection in Philadelphia. In other words, they would not recommend it for Mellon, which turned out to be lucky, because Widener's collection ended up at the National Gallery. The Darnley version was bought by Knoedler's and Colnaghi's jointly and went to Jules Bache two years later. But before it was sold, Otto Gutekunst of Colnaghi's, whom Berenson had known for almost thirty years, tried to sell it to Mellon. He sent it to be hung in the house with a testimonial letter from Berenson saying the work was a Titian. Mellon naturally asked Duveen what this was all about.

Duveen saw Berenson's letter as a rank betrayal. How could B.B. tell Duveens that *Venus and Adonis* was not a Titian and then tell another dealer that it was, adding incalculable numbers of zeroes to the painting's value? He was extremely upset about it. Edward Fowles was delegated to make a visit to i Tatti and read Berenson the riot act. The least Berenson could do, Fowles subsequently said, was to let them know about his change of opinion. They were trying to introduce Mellon to the idea of buying Italian pictures and it was hard going. Now here was their Italian expert, changing his mind capriciously. Even someone who did not share Mellon's towering suspiciousness of dealers was bound to think that B.B. blew with every wind. As a result Mellon had sent back the Giovanelli Titian and the Giorgione and would be unlikely to keep the Darnley picture, either. Berenson made some feeble excuses. The fact that they were right about the Darnley "Titian" and Berenson was wrong probably did not help, at least then.

The more promising their Mellon prospects became, the more the Duveen espionage network moved into high gear. Ailsa Mellon Bruce was heard to remark just before her wedding that she was expecting a wedding gift from the Duveens, but since one had not been forthcoming she supposed she would have to make do with the one they sent at Christmas. (Their gold box arrived just before the ceremony.) Mellon had been away from Washington. While he was there, he frequently saw Mr. and Mrs. Robert Woods Bliss, who owned an estate in Georgetown, Dumbarton Oaks, and usually asked their advice about pictures. He had shown them some, and Mrs. Bliss had advised him to keep the Rembrandt; she did not like the Raphael. There had been no visitors recently except the Blisses. Messmore, of Knoedler's had not been there. Two months later Duveen's informants sent a cable to Paris saying that Mellon was sailing on the *Majestic* but was not going to Paris. Two cars would meet him at Cherbourg and he was motoring directly to Rome. Wherever Duveen went, reports followed. In August of 1926 he was at the Lido in Venice, and Armand cabled him there. An informant Lowengard referred to as their "friend" said that Mellon—his code name was "Timothy"—would probably not arrive in Paris before early September and was going to London afterwards. The friend thought the Mellon eye was ripe for Botticellis and the great masters, not to mention the Giorgione and the Vermeer. The trail was picked up in London in September. Mellon was due to arrive on a Friday night, staying at the Berkeley. Since he was sure to have an appointment with Carstairs of Knoedler's, Duveen Brothers must get to him first on Sunday morning at nine o'clock sharp—Mellon was an early riser. Duveen wanted a full report awaiting him when he arrived at Claridge's on Sunday evening.

Mellon was back in Washington in mid-September and his valet, Flore, took up the commentary. Mellon, he told Boggis, had been delighted with the hamper of fruit that Duveen sent to his cabin for his return voyage; he had eaten some every day. When he asked who had sent it, and Flore told him, he laughed. By November 1926 the Darnley "Titian" was hanging in the library in place of the portrait of Ailsa, and Messmore of Knoedler's had lunched with Mellon: The main topic of conversation was the coming Michelham sale in London and what kinds of prices Messmore thought various paintings would bring. And so it went. Anticipating Mellon's moves evidently paid off because, as the famously apocryphal meeting in the elevator demonstrated, everything depended on catching Mellon by surprise.

Then the first inkling that something might be brewing was picked up by the papers in the winteer of 1927. The rumor that a site had been selected on the Mall for the proposed National Gallery of Art was coupled with the further rumor that a public-minded citizen was offering to erect the building at his own expense, at a cost of $10 million. There was speculation that this person was, in fact, the secretary of the treasury. Ostensibly Mellon would provide a building for the nation's own rather haphazard collection of art that had been accumulating over the centuries. In fact he was planning to include his own collection to provide a nucleus for what would follow and become an inspiration to other collectors, as indeed it did. It should have been the Andrew Mellon Museum, but that was not in his character. Doing good by stealth, he left bombast and self-congratulation to others.

DUVEEN HAD ALWAYS been as adroit in the politics of art as in every other area of life. One of his new friends of those days, Ramsay MacDonald, was leader of the Labour Party and twice prime minister of England. Duveen and MacDonald struck up a friendship, and as Duveen escorted

MacDonald around the public galleries, as a born proselytizer he would have been pleading the cause of art from every direction, not only his own. He was becoming an establishment figure himself, a trustee of the Wallace Collection (later, of the National Portrait Gallery and the Tate), a member of the Council of the British School at Rome, an honorary member of the Council of the National Art Collections Fund, a director of the American Institute for Persian Art and Archaeology, and many others. Another pivotal figure in his political maneuverings was Lord D'Abernon, a banker, collector, and former ambassador to Germany who became chairman of the Tate Trustees in 1923. D'Abernon was often short of money, and for years Duveen had been obligingly buying and selling, undertaking those exhaustive courtesies which must have consumed endless man hours in the London office. Nothing was too much for D'Abernon, and D'Abernon obliged. He sent the king a helpful list of all of Duveen's accomplishments in 1926, and Duveen's name subsequently appeared on the 1927 honors list. He had been made a baronet, the final step before being named a peer of the realm in 1933. Asked how he wished to style himself, he said he wanted to be called Lord Duveen of Millbank.

By then he knew his legacy would not include his daughter's choice of career. After her early interest in Botticelli and the Italian Renaissance, Dolly had turned to politics and economics and in time would disclaim any knowledge of art, although she was always very proud of her father's accomplishments. In 1931 she would make a proper marriage to William C. Garthwaite, son and heir of a titled shipping magnate, and embark on her lifelong career of political hostess.

As for Duveen, almost as soon as his long-delayed Modern Foreign and Sargent galleries opened at the Tate in 1926 he was asking himself what else he could do. He offered to pay for a mural to brighten up the dingy and claustrophobic room that passed for a restaurant at the Tate. He had in mind Rex Whistler, then a young student at the Slade, who was an admirer of the architecture of Inigo Jones and the most imaginative and accomplished muralist in Britain of the prewar years. (He died during World War II.) Whistler was just twenty-one when Duveen spotted his talent and encouraged the Tate to let him loose on the Refreshment Room. Whistler hit upon the story idea "In Pursuit of Rare Meats," or the adventures of a hunting party. The group, fancifully dressed in nineteenth-century costume, set out in one corner of the room on a journey that takes them through various countries and time periods, searching for truffles in the forest, spearing fish and meeting mythical beasts such as a unicorn. They hurdle the Great Wall of China and have various other hair-raising adven-

tures before coming to a halt in a landscape worthy of Claude. The exquisite detail, the playful imagination, the fairy-tale-like progression, and the
wit and originality of the conception were quite unlike anything Londoners had seen before. Whistler was launched on his career, and the Tate
restaurant became instantly famous. The mural is still there.

The great flood of 1928 offered Duveen a new opportunity. There was
an unusually heavy snowfall that winter, and a sudden thaw early in the
new year sent a wall of water surging down the Thames. The Embankment
wall collapsed and the flood roared into the lower galleries. Nine of them,
hung with paintings and drawings, were completely flooded. The museum
was built on the site of a former prison, and some of the old vaults had not
been completely filled in. Water found its way into the main building
through these empty chambers, and under the main floor. Many paintings
were ruined, others were badly damaged; drawings were covered with mud,
floors and walls destroyed; the lighting went, and so did the heat. Fortunately, the Whistler murals, painted in a mixture of wax and oil, were none
the worse.

Saving what could be saved was the first priority, but a quick decision
about rebuilding was equally vital. As a temporary measure, storage was
moved to the main floor, and Duveen came in with an offer to rebuild
three-fifths of the basement area. He would also build a great new gallery
to house foreign sculpture, a favorite project that he had already proposed.
It was another munificent gift, but exactly how it was to be done was the
subject of endless wrangling. There was an architect-manqué somewhere
in his character, and thanks to his annoyingly acute memory for details,
nothing could get past him until it had been exhaustively analyzed and
usually rejected. Just when it seemed everything had been decided, Duveen
came up with a new idea. None of it would do. He wanted the plans completely redone by his favorite architect, John Russell Pope, the one who had
designed the art gallery for his New York house.

Duveen had probably known Pope for years, perhaps ever since the
architect married Sadie Jones, stepdaughter of the collector Henry Walters,
in 1912. Pope's serene, monumental neoclassical style was in great demand.
He had been engaged by the U.S. government to design some massive government offices for a downtown Washington site called the Federal Trian-
gle, and in 1926 the official overseeing the construction of that project was
Andrew Mellon. There was yet another connection, through the Frick;
that institution had engaged Pope to build a wing for its reference library.
The Metropolitan Museum of Art also hired Pope at about the same time,
in 1929, to design a wing for its own building. (Never built.) The idea of

Dolly and William Garthwaite, her first husband, at a nightclub

Duveen's favorite architect,
John Russell Pope

Pope was in the air, perhaps because his designs had the power and time-lessness that important men thought ought to be symbolized by the buildings of a great nation. As Kenneth Clark remarked, "If I had to say which was telling the truth about society, a speech by a Minister of Housing or the actual buildings put up in his time, I should believe the buildings." Duveen just knew Pope was the right man, and although the Tate officials were infuriated, there was not much they could do about it. Pope and Duveen had studied the new barrel-vaulted sculpture gallery being built at the Metropolitan during the anxious period of deciding just what they wanted. Duveen was determined to have a gallery "which would in itself rank as a work of art comparable to any modern building of its kind." Then Pope went to work.

IN THOSE HEADY DAYS of the 1920s Duveen seemed to be everywhere at once, buying, selling, cajoling, spying, designing for the Tate, and making forays into the National Gallery (he erected an annex there for the effective display of Italian Primitives), the National Portrait Gallery (which, it seemed, also needed a new building), the British Museum, the University of London, and, it seemed, everywhere else. But he had been given a warning in 1924 that his energies had a limit. His way of paying for too much stress was acute indigestion, despite his careful eating habits and abstemious ways. He continued to be a heavy smoker, and there had been a series of annoying polyps in his throat. Some time in the late twenties he was given the bad news that he had cancer. In 1930 he underwent an operation, not described; it came at the end of the *Belle Ferronière* trial. There was a setback, and he was convalescing for several months. A report that he underwent a colostomy in 1927 could not be verified, but he did make a will that year, the first of several, and also took out a life-insurance policy of $50,000 in favor of the company. He was building his legacy just as Mellon was making the same decision and, as with the friendship between Altman and Uncle Henry, their common purpose would unite them. Perhaps, as Altman had when Uncle Henry was building the "Merchant Marine" building, Duveen began to think of Mellon's new National Gallery as "ours."

Mellon went on buying fairly carefully from Duveen through the late 1920s and, despite Duveen's panegyrics, seemed to be increasingly sales resistant. Writing in the summer of 1929, Duveen said he had worked hard to secure a new group of important paintings. He wrote, "I recall a phrase my father once used to me, when I returned from an auction sale, and had to confess that I had missed something. He said, 'Pray don't tell me what you have missed, only what you have secured.' This is something I have never forgotten." He then went on to describe a group of paintings he thought Mellon ought to take seriously. What he did not know was that Mellon was angling just then for a huge purchase of some of the most famous paintings in the world, and none of them would come from Duveen.

The idea that the Soviet government might decide to sell off treasures from the Hermitage had been rumored for years. The great museum in St. Petersburg, then called Leningrad, began as a showcase for the art treasures of the tsars and was expanded, after the Bolsheviks seized power in 1917, to include the huge holdings of the imperial family in their numerous palaces and vast, confiscated collections belonging to the Russian nobility. Among them were the greatest compilation of French eighteenth-century art outside France. The Soviet government had an *embarras de richesses* at the same time that it was becoming increasingly desperate for money. The Paris office of Duveen Brothers had been monitoring the Hermitage situation for several years. Replying to a query from Duveen in New York in the spring of 1928, Fowles and Lowengard said that they were well aware of the rumors but convinced that the Soviets were not serious, at least not yet. Harry Abrahams, who had married Armand's sister Annette and was a director of the De Beers diamond syndicate, had already bought diamonds, and sent an emissary to buy some silver; but on leaving the country the Soviet authorities exacted such a heavy export duty that the business was profitless. Paris kept hearing about dealers who had sent men to make inquiries and who all returned with the same story, i.e. that the goods the Russians were offering were mostly rubbish and the remainder of minor interest. It seemed that the price of getting even one moderately good piece of merchandise was a great many items no one wanted. The authorities were refusing to name their prices. It was worthless bait, a ruse; just a game.

Germain Seligman had been one of the dealers invited to inspect the possibilities. He made the arduous train trip to Leningrad only to be shown a vast hall full of such objects as writing sets, boxes, and the like, of minimal interest to him. When he demanded to see something more important, he was shown other rooms full of "reserves," treasures the government might or might not be willing to part with. "One room was an extraordinary sight—a vast hall which gave the impression of being a great cave of ormolu and gilt-bronze, with stalactites and stalagmites of gold and crystal. Hanging from the ceiling, standing on the floor or on tables, was an incredible array of chandeliers and candelabra, small, large, or huge, all glittering . . . with gilded ornament and glass or crystal pendants. Nor were the tables they stood on less resplendent, with ormolu ornaments and tops of marble, onyx, agate, or that vivid green malachite of which Russians are so fond."

The Russians might sell or they might not. The reasons for their evasiveness became perfectly clear in retrospect. The Soviet government was desperate for foreign currency for its first Five-Year Plan, and exports of antiques and jewelry would eventually be measured in the hundreds of tons. However, none of this was evident at first. What was clear was that the Soviets needed help in dumping crude oil at cut rates on the world market, and Calouste Gulbenkian, who was then head of the Iraq Petroleum Company, reportedly facilitated the sale. In exchange the great collector was allowed to make his first transaction, £54,000 for what Duveen would have considered high-class material. This group included twenty-four gold and silver pieces of eighteenth-century French origin; two paintings by Hubert Robert of Versailles; Dirk Bouts's *The Annunciation;* and a Louis XVI writing table. After the usual prolonged haggling Gulby made further purchases, Rubens's *Portrait of Helene Fourment* and fifteen silver objects, all from the Hermitage. He would eventually end up with Houdon's statue of Diana and five more paintings from that great museum: Rembrandt's *Portrait of Titus* and *Pallas Athene,* Watteau's *Le Mezzetin,* Ter Borch's *The Music Lesson,* and Lancret's *Les Baigneuses.*

Then another collector with huge financial resources and the right political connections entered the picture. One morning in 1930 a curator of paintings at the Hermitage was given instructions to take a painting by Jan van Eyck, *The Annunciation,* off the wall and deliver it to a representative of the People's Commissariat for Foreign Affairs. She was then to rehang the display so that the painting's disappearance would not be noticed. The painting just vanished. After a decent interval it ended up in the U.S., sold for half a million dollars. The buyer was the secretary of the treasury, Andrew Mellon.

In *Russian Art and American Money,* Robert C. Williams has described the complex set of circumstances that made the Soviets decide that their art collections, the jewels of which would be snapped up everywhere, ought to go to the people who had useful political positions. For years the U.S. had been one of the biggest suppliers of manufactured goods like cars and tractors, but also raw materials such as cotton and metals, to the Soviet Union. Most of the sales were made on long-term credit from big U.S. companies like Standard Oil and General Motors, but trade from Russia to the U.S.

was so tiny as to be almost invisible. Its trade imbalance was huge and growing worse. Money had to be found from somewhere to carry out the modernization called for in the Five-Year Plan, and the stock market crash of October 1929, coupled with the depression that followed, only exacerbated the problem. Selling crude oil cheaply so as to corner the world market was followed in short order by the similar dumping of commodities such as asbestos, manganese, lumber, and matches.

The reaction was predictable and swift. During the first six months of 1930 State Department officials and businessmen began urging Congress not to buy the Soviet lumber that was flooding the world market. The ostensible grounds for an embargo were that the wood had been cut by inmates of forced-labor camps. Other arguments were used to protect American industries against the avalanche of cheap steel, asbestos, matches, and the like. This did not suit the Russians at all. Andrew Mellon was a great art collector, and they had what he wanted. He had what *they* wanted: the power to influence what happened in American trade. It was all very businesslike.

Van Eyck's *Annunciation* arrived in the U.S. in June 1930, the first in a coveted group of treasures to end up in the Mellon collection and, ultimately, the National Gallery of Art in Washington. The painting describes the moment when the angel appears to Mary, greeting her with the words "Ave Gratia Plena," to which she answers "Ecce Ancilla Domini." The letters are reversed so that the Holy Ghost, who is descending on a ray of light, can read them on his rapid flight. Mary, her head to one side and her hands raised in a gesture of amazement and obedience, is seated in a churchlike setting with a carpet at her feet and a book in her lap. The Angel who has come to make the announcement is crowned and very much flesh and blood, looking a bit like a teenager, with many-hued wings, coronet, and a rich cloak of gold embroidered brocade, trimmed with ribbon. The painting is full of Christian symbolism, but no particular knowledge is required to appreciate the magical realism involved, the delicacy of the conception and the vividness and power of the moment. Nothing Mellon would buy in the following years could surpass this rarest and most beautiful of works from a fifteenth-century Flemish painter. In July 1930 Mellon decided that there should be an embargo of any lumber where it could be demonstrated that slave labor had been used—quite difficult to prove. He ruled against imported Russian matches, but his ruling on February 1931 in the case of manganese dumping was favorable to the Soviets. Williams wrote, "Many businessmen and government officials sought far more extensive limits on Soviet imports in the United States and found Mellon's decisions too little and too late." Meanwhile the paintings continued to roll in: a total of twenty-three masterpieces for more than $8 million. The result is that these paintings ended up in a museum built by a capitalist society that was the mortal enemy of the country selling them. Such are the ironies of fate.

Since Mellon had money and influence and Duveen only had money, the struggle was doomed from the start. Still, he threw himself into the effort with his usual enthusiasm. Williams wrote that in the winter of 1928–29 a syndicate of American dealers had offered $5 million for forty masterpieces, and he assumed that this plan was headed by Duveen. This seems unlikely. Duveen would hardly make the mistake of offering so little for so many, and as might be expected, the Soviet authorities rejected the offer out of hand. Duveen's version of events is that representatives of Duveen Brothers went to Russia in about 1928 but were unable to find out what was for sale or how much. Since even these elementary questions were not being answered, there seemed no point in going any further. Then in the summer of 1930 the Soviets made a new overture to Duveen Brothers which looked particularly promising. By then Duveen knew that Mellon was buying through Knoedler's, and Gulbenkian had mentioned the political implications, although just how specific he was is not clear. About two weeks after that, on August 12, 1930, the international press got wind of the story that a wealthy American collector was buying the art of the tsars. There were varying accounts. The *New York American* claimed that thirty paintings had been sold, whereas the *Daily Telegraph* in London contented itself by naming a few paintings that seemed to have disappeared. Besides the van Eyck, these were *Portrait of a Polish Nobleman* by Rembrandt, *Lute Player* by Watteau, and Frans Hals's *Portrait of a Dutch Admiral.* The name of the collector was not given. Fairly soon afterwards Mellon's recent Russian purchases were removed from his walls and placed in a secret room in the Corcoran Gallery of Art in Washington. Mellon denied that he had been the major purchaser from the Hermitage for the next five years. Being seen to be spending millions on paintings at a moment when millions of Americans were out of work was only slightly more heinous than the idea that the Hermitage was selling off its treasures in the first place. But there was another reason why Mellon did not want the sales to be known. To be dealing with the Russians at a time when he represented the U.S. government's interests was a clear conflict, one that might have forced him out of public life.

No such constraints bothered Duveen, and in fact, in the summer of 1930, he thought he had a chance to capture his share of the loot from the

Hermitage at last. He ordered Boggis to take a telegram to Mellon in Washington and deliver it by hand. The gist of the message was that Lowengard was going to Leningrad to offer a tempting $5 million for nine paintings. Duveen wrote, FEEL CONFIDENT I SHALL SUCCEED UNLESS OF COURSE I AM COMPETING AGAINST YOU . . . He was on his way to London on the SS *Berengaria* and subsequently received the kind of detailed description from Boggis that no doubt made him extremely grateful that he had hired him all those years ago. Boggis reported that he took the morning train from New York to Washington, arriving in the early afternoon. He went straight to Mellon's house but missed him by three minutes, so he followed the secretary to his Treasury office. But before he left he took the opportunity to have a good look around, and his sharp eyes missed nothing. The Rembrandt *Man with the Moustache* was still hanging to the left of the full-length Van Dyck, with their Titian *Woman* on the right. The Rembrandt portrait of the girl from the Hermitage was still in the entrance hall, to the right of the door, and the Frans Hals, also from the Hermitage, was displayed on an easel in the small corridor where their Titian landscape used to be. He went on to describe what was hanging in the drawing room and even one of the bedrooms—he was all over the house. Messmore had not been there, and he thought that given the circumstances, the man from Knoedler's would probably confine his visits to the Treasury.

Once he was alone with Mellon, it became clear to Boggis that the secretary was extremely surprised. He had believed that he had a clear field, but now, it seemed, Duveen was in the running. Mellon wanted to know which paintings Duveen wanted. Boggis was far too cagey for that. He replied that Mr. Mellon could safely assume that whatever he wanted Sir Joseph would also try to get. Just then, Mellon was negotiating for four paintings, but there seemed to be some kind of delay; the Russians were asking for more money. It took no great imaginative leap to see just where Duveen fitted into that scenario. On the other hand, competing with Duveen was the very last thing Mellon wanted. One of them, clearly, would have to withdraw, but why should it be he? Mellon was late for a meeting, and the interview was interrupted several times by reminders from his secretary that a group of prominent bankers was waiting for him. Still he hesitated. He kept reading and rereading the telegram. He finally told Boggis to telephone Duveen and explain that the art dealer was interfering with his business affairs. Boggis left the room, but as soon as the door closed behind him he put his eye to a crack and saw Mellon still standing there with the telegram in his hand.

More telegrams and phone calls followed. For the moment, Duveen had the upper hand and made the most of it. He explained to Mellon that he had made a bulk offer that included two lesser paintings in order to get the three fine ones he wanted. In the normal business world this would have been the best way to do things. Mellon had to agree that it was smart. By the end of the exchange Mellon had decided to leave matters entirely in Duveen's hands. The one point, however, that Duveen, for all his undercover work, had failed to grasp was that if it was a question of selling to Gulbenkian, Mellon, or Duveen, in the Soviet world he would always come in last. In other words, his role in that affair was simply to get Mellon to improve his offer.

Duveen never got his pictures. In fact, he never bought a single canvas from the Hermitage but was limited to lesser objects such as furniture, tapestries, silver, candelabra, and objets d'art. If that represented a demotion to the world's greatest art dealer, as a true son of his father he would never admit it. His story was that he went to Leningrad in the autumn of 1931 and spent a lot of money. He said, "I made considerable purchases in Russia . . . and . . . bought the contents of the palaces . . . great tapestries and objets d'art from the summer palaces of the Tsars," picking and choosing from the almost unlimited holdings of the French eighteenth century. He, of course, never admitted he had any health problems, either, although he had no business undertaking such a long and difficult trip. At the eleventh hour, Lady Duveen put up a stiff fight, and it was only after Edward and Armand successfully argued that it was useless to go otherwise that she stopped arguing. They all agreed that Duveen's personal valet would accompany him. As for the huge business transactions that Mellon had made through Knoedler's, Duveen was amazingly forgiving. Perhaps he knew it would all turn out well in the end. At about that time, the *Frankfurter Zeitung* published an article about the fact that Knoedler's had beaten out "the Napoleon of the art dealers." In retaliation, the newspaper said, Duveen had decided to "buy the entire Hermitage en bloc." Duveen would have loved that idea.

Chapter Seventeen

A PROPER ENGLISH GENTLEMAN

THE NATIONAL GALLERY MELLON admired more than any other was in London, but, admirable as it was, it contained only pictures. That would not suit Duveen at all. A gallery worthy of the name had to show sculpture as well. He persuaded Mellon that John Russell Pope's drawings should include garden courts and halls wide enough to accommodate the most expansive pieces of statuary, something more like the Metropolitan or perhaps the Louvre. Duveen always had a plan, and his concept of the new National Gallery was influenced by the fact that he had just bought another huge collection. This one contained all kinds of sculptures. Since he had them, Mellon was delegated to buy them.

The Dreyfus Collection was, like the Rodolphe and Maurice Kann collections, one of the glories of Paris before World War I. David Finley, first director of Washington's National Gallery, said, "The Dreyfus Collection was undoubtedly the most important collection of Renaissance sculpture in private hands in the world. It was started in Paris by Charles Timbal (a French art critic) who had quite an important collection when the Germans marched into Paris in 1870. He became frightened lest his collection be confiscated by the Germans, or even destroyed. Gustave Dreyfus bought the whole collection from him and from 1870, continued to add to it . . ."

Dreyfus had far more objects than he could possibly cram into his eighteenth-century house, hard against the southern side of the old church of St-Germain-des-Prés in the Quartier Latin. But he was as generous about showing his treasures as the Kanns had been, and his house was one of the major stops for art lovers on an international pilgrimage. When the great collector died in 1914, the objects—paintings, marbles, terra cottas, and wood carvings, as well as medals, plaquettes, and small bronzes—were inherited by his son Carl, a curator at the Louvre, and two married sisters. Carl Dreyfus, "a gentle blond boy," as René Gimpel described him, would willingly have given the whole collection to the Louvre, but his sisters had other ideas. Edward Fowles and Armand Lowengard, who had been keeping an eye on the collection for years, knew the minute it went up for sale in 1929. The price was huge: 150 million francs, or something like $10 million. Gulbenkian was interested, but not at that price, and the Frick Collection was also in the market.

Fowles, who was the chief negotiator for Duveen Brothers, recalled:

I had, I think, months of seeing an Algerian Jew, who was the son-in-law of the family, who had been delegated by the family to do the negotiation because he was a hard bargainer. And I used to go over and see that man day after day, talk it over, talk it over, talk it over . . . and finally he got down to the stage where one day he said to me, "Now listen, you don't come up to my price and I don't come down to yours, but I tell you what we'll do. If you will go up one million francs I will come down one million francs." I said to him, "That means to say you'll split the difference, and I won't give it." That old man was floored. He had to sit down and work it out with a piece of paper. He told Lord Duveen afterwards, "That was a very smart trick that young fellow worked on me."

Nevertheless, the price finally paid, 80 million francs, was still around $5 million, a very big price to pay for the privilege of getting front-page coverage in London and New York. Duveen partly financed the purchase with the help of Wildenstein's and Seligman's and sold the best pieces quite soon thereafter. Some fine Italian sculptures went to John D. Rockefeller Jr. and Andrew Mellon. So did some of the paintings; and a unique collection of Italian commemorative medals was sold to Samuel H. Kress. He bought them in their hundreds and presented them to the National Gallery.

What was particularly newsworthy about this latest coup by Duveen Brothers was its timing. The stock market crash on "Black Friday," October 24, 1929, which wiped out so many fortunes, had not materially affected Duveen, who was given advance warning by Gulbenkian and pulled out of the market just in time. Although he could see clearly enough that his halcyon days were over, at least for the time being, his professional position was that this was a mere blip on the financial landscape. Eddie wrote from London ten days later that he had received Duveen's gloomy cable that morning with regard to the American economy. Everyone in London was similarly depressed, although Eddie had been putting the word around that his brother was "extremely bullish." The response to that was, "We have never seen him depressed," which was probably quite true. It was not good for business to make one's secret fears public knowledge, and besides, as Gerald Reitlinger observed, the art market was not badly affected at first. "The result [of the stock market crash] was to keep pictures out of the market, rather than to bring down prices. In the season ending in July 1930 the London stock market was not entirely overturned by the first series of Wall Street crashes, but the number of pictures auctioned in London at 1,400 guineas and over, a hundred and thirty in 1927, was now down to sixty-three. In the season ending July 1931 it dropped to thirteen. In August there occurred the credit crisis, the suspension of bank-payments and the creation of the National Government . . ." The pound was devalued from $4.86 to $3.23 and did not recover its position until the dollar itself was devalued in 1933 as part of Roosevelt's emergency measures.

Foreign exchange and the cost of money would, whether he liked it or not, have forced itself on Duveen's awareness, and the odds are that he did not much like it. When he was testifying for Mellon on a tax case in 1935, Duveen said that during his worst business year, 1932, he could not remember whether he had made $2 million or lost $2 million and was disdainful when pushed to remember which it was. He probably had an ulterior motive, since the Internal Revenue Service was after him as well for back taxes, and he eventually had to pay up. But there was a kind of grandeur about his lordly refusal to mind. His attitude had always been that he made the sales and paid other people to worry about where the money would come from. After fifty years in the business, he knew it would come from somewhere. When the Depression hit, Berenson wrote that Duveen was "finished," but he was always pessimistic. Duveen was far from finished, but he was badly handicapped, partly because banks were not so free and easy with their overdrafts but also because he had bills outstanding which his clients could no longer meet. As one of them said a few years later, buying the Dreyfus Collection just then had been a very bad idea for Duveen, because it had crippled him financially.

That collector was Jules Bache, one of Duveen's largest headaches for the next few years. Bache, once called "one of the Wall Street princes who rule the world's finance," was assembling an enviable collection, one that rivaled Widener's, according to Gimpel, who would have liked to have him as a steady customer. He wrote, "I don't believe in Bache's large Bellini, any more than his Botticelli; his Dürer of Venice is poor. His Fra Filippo Lippi is doubtful; his Vermeer, a portrait, is by no one special. But the rest are superb: Bellinis, [four] Holbeins, Memlings, Gerard Davids, Titians, Rembrandts, a Bouts, a Petrus Christus, a Roger van der Weyden, Signorelli, Cosimo Tura . . ." Bache, who had an office on Broadway, lived on a princely scale. Besides having a town house at 814 Fifth Avenue, he had an estate in Roslyn, Long Island, another town house in Paris, and a house in Palm Beach, Florida. By 1929 Duveen was taking regular vacations in Bermuda and often stopped in Florida to visit Bache even when he did not want to see anyone else. As he wrote, "It bores me to death to have to visit so many people whom I may know there."

Duveen had a curiously detailed knowledge of Bache's private life, leading to the suspicion that he had paid informants there too. He knew where every painting was hung—the list was revised at regular intervals—and had somehow taken charge of the Fifth Avenue house's interior decor as well. When he learned that Bache planned to completely replace the walls and floor of one of his rooms on the fifth floor rear, Duveen suggested that Bache assemble a "very select" group of early primitives. As before, when Duveen had advised Bache to gather together an early Flemish collection for the den, he wrote, "I now seriously counsel you to allow me to go ahead with the suggestion I have above made." Bache obediently did as he was told and bought ten paintings for the redecorated room, mostly Virgin and Child paintings by Luini, Vivarini, Francesco Fiorentino, Lorenzo Costa, and others. Duveen chose the flooring, put opaque leaded glass in the windows, changed the doors to a fine walnut, and selected the wall colors, furniture, and rugs. Bache was compliant and it all went on the bill.

Bache even allowed himself to be coaxed into Berenson's circle, where he was to study the Italian Renaissance at the feet of the master, with Berenson's condescending permission. "If you can trust my honor as well as my judgment I shall be glad to help you. If you are not big enough for that, apply elsewhere." The Berensons shared a disdain for Bache and seemed particularly uncomfortable about the role they felt themselves to be playing as shills for Duveen's merchandise. Commenting about a plan to sell some Bellinis to Bache, Berenson wrote to Fowles, "It will be easy to say nothing about it, but it will then become extremely awkward to pop out all this chain of sausages exactly when it suits Sir Joseph to dangle them before Doggie." The same cynical tone is evident in a letter from Mary Berenson to Duveen on the theme of Bache's education. Bache had been the only buyer for Italian Renaissance recently, she wrote in 1929, and for that Berenson, who had helped Duveen unload some real dogs on Bache

(Berenson's term for that was "cold pig"), deserved the credit. Naturally Bache, like everyone else, was paying on the installment plan. When he was wiped out by the stock market crash of 1929, he owed Duveen $4 million. Even Duveen was bound to find a debt on that scale impressive.

Almost as soon as the news was out, Duveen started dunning Bache for payment not, perhaps, because he particularly needed it just then, but on general principles. Bache had agreed to make twice-yearly payments of $250,000. When January 1930 came and went with no payment, Bache was reminded of the agreement that he could only defer one payment a year. Another was due in July, and soon that one was also in arrears. By October 1930 it was clear that Bache could not pay anything that year. Bache hoped that Duveen had other clients who were less financially embarrassed. At that point Duveen agreed to wait, at least until the beginning of 1931.

And in fact, despite the huge Dreyfus sale and the indebtedness of Bache and other clients, he was in a better financial position than most dealers. Hearing of an enchanting *Nativity* by the Flemish painter Petrus Christus that was in Spain, Duveen was able to buy it mostly because the dealer who had it, Zatzenstein, was desperate to sell it. It went for a bargain price because in April 1930 Duveen could afford to pay £30,000 in cash. Mary and Joseph are seen in a garden setting underneath an elegant arch, worshipping the baby Jesus, who lies in a golden aura. There are also four tiny angels like flower fairies clustered around the baby. The playfulness of the concept, the homely touch provided by Joseph's sandals, kicked off and lying in the right foreground, and the exquisite meadowland beyond, make this one of the most artless scenes of the Nativity ever painted. Mellon snapped it up for the National Gallery.

The painting is significant for another reason. So often before, particularly with a seldom-reproduced work, New York had to trust the judgment of its men in London and Paris because the only way to get a photograph across the Atlantic was by boat. That would mean a five-day delay in making a decision, and sometimes that was four days too late. But things were changing. The era of international air travel was approaching, and there was something else very novel in the works: the transmission of photographs by radio. This was in such a rudimentary state that it hardly existed, but the tactical advantages were so obvious that Duveens were determined to try it out. The order for the Petrus Christus went by cable from New York on the 23rd of April. Paris said it was sending the photograph on the 1:30 p.m. flight to London the next day, but it did not arrive until the nine o'clock plane. On April 25, the Marconi Company was to have sent the photograph by radio, but atmospheric conditions were unfavorable and the picture did not arrive until the 26th. By then the painting had been bought. Given the primitive nature of the technology, it is a marvel that Duveen thought it was a wonderful new way to beat the competition, but he did. London and Paris were to keep very quiet about it in case other dealers found out about the radio photograph. In the meantime, two visitors from the Prado, the great museum in Madrid, were in New York, and Duveen was making a huge fuss over them, because one never knew what might happen in life. It was the end of April 1930.

The promise of transatlantic decisions based on an actual photograph instead of the cumbersome business of a barrage of cables was one of the few bright spots at the start of the new decade. Like Bache, Clarence Mackay, director of the Guaranty Trust Company, had suffered heavy losses and would begin selling off his collection. As Duveen knew, Bache intended to give his collection to the Metropolitan, and kept offering assurances that he did not want to part with anything till then. He would pay Duveen back as soon as his deeply devalued Chrysler stock went back up to forty dollars a share. In the meantime, there was $4 million worth of unbought works of art in his houses that could, conceivably, be seized by his creditors. Something had to be done to protect them legally, and Duveen's lawyers set up a holding company. As the Depression deepened, so did Duveen's financial worries. He wrote to Bache saying he had been willing to wait for his money the year before, but now he was as badly off as anyone else. If Bache could not scrape up an installment of $500,000, could he manage half of that? Or anything? The Chrysler stock had reached $25.75 that day. Could he not sell *something*?

The situation would not change much for the next few years. The one collector who was swimming in money, Andrew Mellon, was pouring it all into paintings from the Hermitage. All kinds of other clients owed sums, large and small; Lord D'Abernon's bill of almost £16,000, for example, was still outstanding in 1935. For his part, Duveen continued to use credit wherever he could. He had often taken shares on a large purchase with Wildenstein's and Agnew's; now he did it more and more often and was even cooperating with Messmore of Knoedler's by 1933. He renegotiated his contract with Berenson—who had also suffered heavy stock market losses—and obliged him to accept a smaller fee. He tried to curb his expenses—which, given the expensive habits of a lifetime, was more difficult. And he always owed his attorneys money; unpaid bills languished for years. Duveen considered himself virtuously reconciled to hardship and lectured Edward and Armand on their profligate ways. He wrote, "You will all have to realize that pictures . . . must be revalued today upon totally different basis. You may reply things will change immediately business improving. My reply is not in my lifetime will pictures and works of art ever fetch prices they have. Sooner you realize we live in new era, the better."

The market was plunging just as getting pictures out of Europe was becoming more difficult. The Petrus Christus had been routed from Madrid by sea to Hamburg and Berlin and thence to Paris before being sent to New York, the roundabout route being used simply to avoid the 10 percent export fee which would have been levied had the painting taken a direct route to New York. That was bad enough, but since Mussolini had assumed power in 1928, things in Italy had gone from bad to worse. A case in point was the *Portrait of a Man* by Antonello da Messina, which Duveen was offered that year by Prince Giovanelli for £70,000. Sometimes called *Portrait of a Youth,* the painting was immediately referred to B.B. He first said it was not by Antonello, the fifteenth-century Sicilian painter who had been a major influence on the development of the Venetian school. But he changed his mind about the work a few days later. He then thought it might just be by Antonello, although other authorities, notably Lionello Venturi, did not. He wrote, "It is perhaps the weakest of his portraits and I beg you to do all you can to prevent Joe fr. biting too hard at it." Lowengard was of much the same opinion. He wrote that the painting was of fine quality but not all that attractive. He did not think his uncle would particularly like it.

A month later a certain Count Labia, acting as Giovanelli's agent, was in the picture trying to get Duveen Brothers to take his bait. The price had dropped to £40,000, but that was still too high. By the time export charges of 40 percent of the sales price were added on—along with commissions, pourboires, freight charges, and all the rest—they were looking at another £12,000 to £15,000. Labia kept dangling lower and lower prices and Paris kept refusing. Paris thought the Antonello was worth £25,000 at most, everything included. By then Duveen had received a photograph and wanted the picture for Bache. Duveen kept insisting that Labia quote the price of the painting exported from Italy and Labia was refusing. Everyone knew what a snake pit that would be. The Fascist government, which was as interested in hard cash as Russia, saw the export of Old Masters as a lucrative source, and a pervasive culture of corruption and bribery in all circles of government did the rest. Then Labia somehow deduced that Bache was the customer Duveen had in mind and was threatening to sell to him directly for £60,000. The impasse dragged on until the stock market crash. Early in 1930 Bache was removed as a likely customer and Labia was ready to talk business. He got a commission of £2,500 for himself and Giovanelli sold his painting for £22,000.

That still left the problem of how to get the painting out of Italy. While Berenson sent letters saying "I told you so," Duveen appealed to Bache, who had some useful contacts, and they both began to do some serious string pulling. Finally, in March 1930, the bill was presented. The Italian authorities wanted 500,000 lire for the Fine Arts Department, 150,000 for a Fascist school, and 150,000 in bribes to various officials. Along with 800,000 lire in export taxes, that meant a total bill of £7,000 which Duveen refused to pay. Writing to Paris in March 1930, he said the selling season was over anyway. He knew that Bache could not give him cash. He might as well leave the painting in Italy, "particularly in view of their excessive demands, thus teaching them that we are not so keen as to pay any price." The painting went into a bank vault, the fate that was to await several others. Meanwhile Duveen, who was at home recuperating from his operation, had a much bigger prospect in mind.

For some years past he had been trying to buy another Giovanelli painting by that rarest of artists, Giorgione, whom Vasari ranked with Leonardo as one of the founders of modern art. Giorgione specialized in small oil paintings, and his clients were usually private collectors rather than the churches which had traditionally been the patrons of the arts in Italy. His paintings were frequently enigmatic, in a style that predates the Symbolist movement by several centuries. In *The Tempest,* the small painting that particularly interested Duveen, a classical landscape is being hit by a thunderstorm. A soldier stands in the left foreground, and on the right a naked woman, who may be a goddess or perhaps only a Gypsy, is nursing a baby. The mood is not so much somber as full of hidden significance, rather as if Giorgione were half dreaming when he painted it. Everything stands out with exemplary clarity and vividness, yet the total effect is haunting, like a memory in which something just outside consciousness is struggling for expression. Byron, who was enchanted by the work, wrote a poem about it, which, referring to the woman, ends with the lines: "The face recalls some face, as 'twere with pain, / You once have seen, but ne'er will see again."

For centuries *The Tempest* had been housed in the Giovanelli Palace, a fifteenth-century Gothic building near the church of Santa Felice in Venice. Armand had seen it there and considered it the equal of that artist's *Concert Champêtre,* an equally disturbing painting in the Louvre. People had, of course, tried to buy it for years, Wilhelm von Bode and Isabella Stewart Gardner among them. To be offered *The Tempest* was a bit like being told that Hadrian's Column was for sale, and when Berenson heard about it he was caustic. The dealer who was offering the painting was a member of a rogues' syndicate, he wrote, "consisting of nearly every bad element in Italy." The man was playing on Duveen's gullibility. Duveen did not have a hope of getting *The Tempest,* and besides, he was already so overstocked that the idea of another huge purchase eating interest was almost mad. Duveen, of course, was not gullible at all and must have had Mellon in mind to even think of buying the Giorgione. But he was cautious for a different reason. "Remember," Lowengard wrote from Paris, "Italian dealers are all spies." If they went to Venice at that stage, the dealers would all conspire to make sure Duveen Brothers did not get the business. The best idea was to work directly with Prince Giovanelli, but the owner seemed to have an extraordinary idea of the painting's value and was asking for £500,000. Duveen offered £100,000. Nothing much happened for the next several years.

Finally, in January 1930, a sale looked possible at last, and the only problem, provided the Italians would even allow a great painting like that to leave the country, were the huge export costs. Duveen was unwilling to invest a vast sum in another painting which Mussolini's bureaucrats would also hold up for ransom. Much as they wanted his money, the Giovanelli family were equally unwilling to confront the fearsome export authorities. So the matter stood until 1932, when they sold the painting to the Gallerie dell'Accademia in Venice for the reported, and very modest, price of £75,000. As for the Antonello, this painting, along with a Filippo Lippi *Madonna and Child* and a Botticelli *Virgin and Child* tondo, both from the Corsini collection, remained in Italy until 1936. By then Mussolini had invaded Ethiopia and was desperate for hard cash. The Italians presented Duveen with a bill for £8,000 for all three and he paid up. The Chrysler stock had recovered at last, and he could sell the Antonello to Bache with some hope of actually getting paid.

IN JANUARY 1929 Duveen wrote to Bache to tell his "dear friend" that "my people," as he grandly called Fowles and Lowengard, were negotiating for the Dürer and confident of getting it. He was delighted to see, in the *Illustrated London News* for the week of January 12, a drawing of Queen Mary admiring one of Bache's paintings, Rembrandt's *Christ with a Pilgrim's Staff,* which the collector had lent for an exhibition of Dutch art. Duveen would eventually unearth the original watercolor sketch and send it to Bache as a souvenir. Friends told him that Bache's pictures were making "a tremendous sensation," and he thought Bache would be glad to know this. "I assure you that I feel a considerable amount of pride in having assisted you to acquire them." Duveen was always boasting dreadfully about his Buckingham Palace contacts, usually by means of helpful hints or, if these failed, blatant name dropping. The king's health was improving, he wrote, and it was "on the *tapis*" that he would spend some time recuperating by the seashore before going to Bermuda on his yacht. Duveen planned to go there once the king arrived even if it meant taking a steamer from Nassau. The assumption was, of course, that he would be warmly received whenever he cared to appear. For a man "in trade," from a family of self-made men, and with the wrong kind of political sympathies, Duveen was a marvel, almost a Buckingham Palace pet. It did not hurt, either, to have been taken up by Ramsay MacDonald, who had just been returned as prime minister in the summer of 1929. He, Elsie, and Dolly had such a lovely time at Chequers the weekend before. There was no one else there except them, the prime minister, and his family. Duveen's frequent references had a double purpose, not just to flaunt his own status but to underline the cachet that pertained to associating with him. Meantime he continued his dauntless assault upon the social pecking order. He, the prime minister, and his family were sailing to New York together on the *Olympic* in the autumn of 1929. He, the curiously titled Count John McCormack, and family were all sailing to Europe together in 1930. He, Elsie, and Dolly had been invited to Windsor for . . . fill in the blanks. He had made headway with the Prince of Wales's circle and they were invited to a party to meet Mrs. Simpson. He must have become impossible after the announcement in the *Times* for February 8, 1933, that "the King has been pleased to confer the dignity of a Baron of the United Kingdom on Sir Joseph Duveen by the name, style and title of Baron Duveen of Millbank in the City of Westminster."

The new baron was formally inducted as peer in the House of Lords a few months later. In a ceremony as quaint as it was irrelevant Duveen, wearing an ermine-trimmed red robe and cocked hat, was escorted into the House of Lords with his sponsors, Barons Conway and Melchett. The newcomer took the oath of allegiance and subsequently subscribed to the roll. Bowing profusely in all directions, he and his sponsors were then escorted from the chamber. Duveen, sans regalia, reappeared shortly thereafter with no ceremony at all and took his seat. A man who is achieving such rarefied heights needs an adequate setting. The newspaper report that Duveen had never owned property in Britain was incorrect, but for years he had been happy to live in hotels. It was clear, however, that if Dolly was to marry well, she must have a London season. So Duveen leased a town house off Park Lane early in 1931 and also bought his first country house, a mansion with fifty acres of parkland in Hawkhurst, Kent. He was a proper English gentleman at last.

JOHN RUSSELL POPE'S DESIGN for the new sculpture galleries at the Tate took the eye from the main entrance straight down two rectangular sculpture galleries which effectively bisected the building. The first was almost 100 feet long. This ended in a central octagon, to be continued by a second gallery almost 120 feet long; all told, a vista of some 300 feet. This was the central design to which all the museum's other galleries were subordinated. As might be expected Pope's designs, using marble for walls and floors, Ionic columns, coffered rosettes, and other classical themes, placed an almost overwhelming emphasis on the idea of a museum as a temple of art. Whether the scale was too intimidating even for the largest modern sculpture was an immediate subject of debate, one that continues to this day.

Duveen was prepared to spend the munificent sum of £50,000 on these additions, the first public galleries in Britain to be designed specifically for sculpture. Pope had a kind of genius for working with marble. He knew how to handle the natural variations in the stone so that there was an imperceptible transition from dark to light. The final impression was of a greenish gray, an elegant contrast to objects made of stone or marble but not a particularly striking one. The overwhelmingly classical allusions were another issue. Would they be inappropriate for the increasingly abstract designs of a Jacob Epstein or the young Henry Moore? Duveen, as usual, dealt with such objections by grandly ignoring them. He fought with the Tate's bureaucracy, the contractors, and finally the director, James Manson, a former banker turned painter. Duveen was probably impossible to deal with but, in fairness to him, so was Manson, who, Kenneth Clark wrote, "was so confident of his charm that he appeared at Board meetings drunk." When the galleries were finally opened by George VI in the summer of 1937, Duveen refused to communicate with Manson and the arrangements had to be made by his deputy. It was quite a grand affair. The Victoria and Albert Museum sent its Rodins and a tapestry, among other items. The Treasury coughed up for a visitor's book bound in dark blue morocco and lent the state inkstand. Duveen contributed more money for some proper pedestals. The king remarked that the Tate now had "the greatest sculpture gallery in the world." It was a thought worthy of Duveen. Years later Pope's design has proved so recalcitrant that, despite the changes in tastes, nobody has been able to think of a way to get rid of it. That would have struck Duveen as most gratifying of all.

Duveen wanted Pope for his next big challenge, the galleries for the Elgin Marbles at the British Museum. These relics of the Parthenon, or the temple of Athena Parthenos, the deity protecting the city of Athens, have a curious history. They were brought from Athens to England early in the nineteenth century by Thomas Bruce, seventh Earl of Elgin, who was Britain's ambassador to the Ottoman Empire and passionately interested in improving the study of Greek architecture in Britain. At his own expense he undertook an expedition to Athens to make accurate plaster casts and architectural drawings of whatever fragments of the Parthenon, and two other buildings on the Acropolis, remained after centuries of neglect and disuse. In the inevitable way of things, he ended up buying all kinds of bits and pieces. His most valuable finds were parts of a giant frieze, a stone bas relief running all the way around the ceiling of the temple. The subject was a huge procession. Preparations for the stately promenade began at the west end. Horsemen with chariots, male figures leading animals for sacrifice, women carrying trays and pitchers, musicians, elders, stewards, and others then made their way along both sides of the building to meet at the eastern end. One of the surprising discoveries of eighteenth-century archeological research is that the figures, which have survived as plain unadorned stone, were actually brightly colored, against a blue background. Such news was greeted by artists and connoisseurs with disappointment and disbelief. To think such ancient adornments were garishly painted was so much against the natural order of things that, William St. Clair wrote in *Lord Elgin and the Marbles,* people refused to believe it. They continued to regard such artifacts the way they had always seen them, i.e., with vacant eyes and a nice white finish.

One way or another Elgin acquired fifty-six panels from the frieze, along with seventeen figures, some pediments, and parts of the metopes, a second series of bas reliefs running around the Parthenon's exterior. Some time after that Lord Elgin went bankrupt and, in 1816, sold his souvenirs to the nation.

At first, the main interest of these fragments from an ancient civilization was to serve as models for artists in their study of classical methods and themes. As archeological investigations continued, the Elgin Marbles came to be valued for their historical context and were exhibited with diagrams, plaster casts, models of the building, and so on. Still later, that view changed again as the sheer beauty and complexity of the sculptures themselves took hold of the popular imagination. The poet Keats felt "a most dizzy pain" on viewing them for the first time and recorded his other impressions in "On Seeing the Elgin Marbles." It was clear that these exquisite remnants deserved a respectful setting. Duveen offered to provide one.

Late in 1929, in his usual thorough way Duveen went to Berlin to study the installation of the Greek and Near Eastern antiquities in the Pergamon Museum. He had already set Pope to work and in the summer of 1930 Pope produced rooms on such a massive scale that the museum's director, Sir George Hill, is supposed to have said, "It will make the rest of the British Museum a dog house." Pope's plan was an I-shaped hall in which the Parthenon frieze would be set into the walls while two pediments would stand at each end in rooms reached by a flight of steps. There would be Doric columns, green-gray marble, classical allusions—it was all very typically Pope.

Given the enormous size of the British Museum, Sir George was rather overstating the case, but it is true that, as envisioned by its designer and chief benefactor, the project begins to sound like an airport hangar. No one challenged Duveen's theory that the Marbles ought to have a classical setting, the best money could buy. There was, however, the nasty suspicion that the scale of the design had more to do with glorifying the name of Duveen than with acting as a discreet backdrop for the marbles themselves. This hall was so conspicuous it threatened to overwhelm even them. Three professors of ancient art were called in to pass judgment, and in the typical way of committees they proceeded to tear the idea apart by means of endless tiny objections. The sculptures had not been properly assembled. The plinths on which the metopes would stand were the wrong design. They did not like the use of a single pedestal base for the pedimental sculpture. The friezes should not be set into the walls. The nitpicking actually went on for five years, but in the end, the scale of the design was reduced by half, various other objections were met, and work actually began. In about 1936 the Elgin Marbles went into storage. Meanwhile, Duveen decided that they looked dirty and he ought to do something about that.

As all this was going on, he had his hands full with another splendid project, an entire new wing for the National Portrait Gallery, called the Duveen Hall. Opening new buildings in the Depression years, courtesy of Lord Duveen, was becoming almost routine. This latest inauguration, in 1933, was attended by the Archbishop of Canterbury and Prime Minister MacDonald. The king said some kind words about this latest benefaction, and Sir John Lavery, sitting in a corner, sketched the ceremony for posterity.

IN VIEW OF THE INCREASINGLY FRAGILE STATE of his health, the amount of work Duveen was able to accomplish in the 1930s is astonishing. He seemed to be looking for things to do, and where the state of British art was concerned, he did not have far to look. Everyone knew that, as the Depression took hold, young artists trying to make a living were in the worst possible state. The precipitous decline in patronage of the past fifty years was a gap that had not been filled by the emerging middle class. Bright young things decorated with such understatement that there was hardly anything left to look at. Meanwhile, Graham Sutherland and his wife, like so many others, were living in near poverty in one room with a single gas ring and meals of lentils and salad.

As the Depression deepened, Kenneth Clark's solution was to commission artists. Wilson Steer, whom he considered Britain's best living painter, was hired to paint Clark's wife's, Jane's, portrait, and so was Duncan Grant. Clark also set up a small trust fund, a modest ten pounds a month per artist which, small as it was, kept people from sleeping under bridges. Clark was acutely aware of the problem once he became director of the National Gallery in 1934. By then Duveen was already well aware of it. His book *Thirty Years of British Art,* which was fortuitously published in 1930, assembled an extremely handsome group of landscapes, portraits, still lifes, seascapes, mural decorations, drawings, and watercolors in color and black-and-white to demonstrate the quality and variety of the British scene. Besides such well-known artists as Steer, Ambrose McEvoy, Augustus John, Sir John Lavery, C. J. Holmes, Sir William Orpen, Walter Sickert, and Muirhead Bone, there were such relative newcomers as Vanessa Bell, Eric Gill, Gwen John, E. McKnight Kauffer, Dame Laura Knight, Henry Lamb, Paul Nash, William Nicholson, Eric Ravilious, Stanley Spencer, Rex Whistler, and Gerald Brockhurst. (Duveen had to stretch a point occasionally; the French sculptor Henri Gaudier-Brzeska, who had lived in London before dying in World War I, became for his purposes "British.") His eye told him how good the work was, and as a practical businessman, he knew how small the financial rewards were. He estimated that there were between ten thousand and twenty thousand practicing artists in Britain. They should be given a chance to shine. He would organize a series of exhibitions.

Once the word was out that the first exhibition would be held in the City Art Gallery in Leeds, in 1927, his fledgling committee was overwhelmed with applications from artists. One of them sent "two solid flagstones which he had decorated in his patriotic and not too finished style," Duveen wrote. He turned out to be a pavement artist. Duveen persuaded Augustus John to open the exhibition and then sat back to await events. The results were so promising that more exhibitions followed, in Leeds, Manchester, Bradford, Belfast, Plymouth, Liverpool, and Glasgow; even one on the SS *Berengaria*. The next step was to take British art overseas, and traveling shows were sent to Paris, Brussels, Buenos Aires, Stockholm, Tokyo, and Rome. It was tedious work that did not produce a penny, but to a man who has refined the art of ordering corsets for his clients' wives, it no doubt seemed like child's play.

Exhibitions: how to organize and exploit them, had always been an essential part of the Duveen strategy. As a buyer he knew that owners routinely lent to exhibitions works they were about to sell, making his attendance obligatory. As a seller, he knew that a Duveen Titian now belonging to Altman or Bache gained that much extra authority if it was exhibited, particularly by a museum. A request for a loan became a kind of command, and some of his most flowery appeals to collectors were bent to the task of persuading them to send their precious works several thousand miles away.

A case in point was the exhibition of Italian art in Burlington House, the premises of the Royal Academy, in 1930. The custom was to have an annual exhibition of works from a different European country every winter. The Spanish and Dutch shows had been particularly successful, and a proposal for an Italian show grew out of a friendship between Mussolini and Lady Chamberlain, the energetic and determined wife of the British foreign minister, Sir Austin Chamberlain. Young Kenneth Clark, then aged twenty-six, was called in to join the committee. He described the exhibition as infamous, because it was "basically a piece of Fascist propaganda." He also thought it "a wicked risk to send so many of the world's greatest pictures in a single ship to a single exhibition. None of this occurred to me at the time . . ." The Italian in charge was Ettore Modigliani, director of the Brera museum in Milan and *soprintendente delle belle arti* of Lombardy. Clark called him "a ridiculous figure by any standards [who] must have risen to his high office by sheer volubility. He never stopped talking for a second, and hard-pressed officials must have given him anything he asked for in order to get rid of him." Clark's reference to some of the world's greatest works of art arriving on a single ship was to the point. Of the six hundred paintings that went on view, well over half came from Italy, and these were all shipped to London from Genoa on the *Leonardo da Vinci* in December 1929. They arrived nine days later, having been badly battered by huge storms off the coast of Brittany. Among the precious cargo were Botticelli's *Birth of Venus,* Piero della Francesca's *Duke and Duchess of Urbino,* Donatello's *David,* Giorgione's *Tempest* (then still owned by Prince Giovanelli), Titian's *La Bella,* Masaccio's *Crucifixion,* Carpaccio's *Courtesans,* and others of similar renown. Clark described the moment when the committee, accompanied by Modigliani, went down to the docks to retrieve the shipment. "The strong-room of the ship was locked, and he had the only key. As he approached the door a look of agony came over his face and his hands beat the air. 'La chiave, dove?' (Where is the key?) Only those who have had long experience of Italian sacristans will enjoy this story. The key was found in his hotel bedroom."

The Italian works from public collections were by far the most important, but there were others from private holdings and there were also sculpture, manuscripts, and drawings. Something like a quarter of the pictures were on loan from British holdings, and others came from France, Germany, Austria, and elsewhere. A further group of thirty was to be sent from the United States. One can imagine Duveen happily torn between the prospect of having so many sumptuous possibilities for sales under one roof and the prospect of his own Duveens displayed beside Botticelli's *Venus* and Donatello's *David.* He could not wait to round them all up. Berenson, by contrast, was horrified, incidentally revealing how much he knew about the artificial respiration that had been given to Italian Renaissance paintings he had attributed through the years. He told Fowles that if the paintings owned by American collectors were exhibited in Burlington House, people would be bound to see that they looked too much alike. That, of course, was Joe's fault, because he always wanted them right away and would not give Madame Helfer, their chief Paris restorer, the time she needed to make those delicate amendations and corrections that made all the difference. She worked in a continual rush, and so a certain similarity was bound to creep in. Some bright-eyed critic would be sure to notice. Berenson warned of SERIOUS DISASTER—the capital letters were his. Fowles must do all he could to stop Joe from sending pictures to London.

Fowles knew he might as well try to stop Niagara Falls during the spring thaw. In any event, Berenson had overestimated the ability of any critic to seek out and compare a tiny minority of American paintings from among the several hundred on view. He could not have known that W. G. Constable, A. E. Popham, and Kenneth Clark, who assembled the catalogue, would take the attributions of paintings from British, American, and European private collections at face value. Clark characterized his entries as "puerile," explaining that he simply did not know enough, which was true. Too many pictures were not as billed, which must have bothered some people but not the general public. The night the private view was held, the traffic jam went from Burlington House in Piccadilly as far as Harrods in Knightsbridge, and bus drivers in suburban Cricklewood complained they were an hour behind schedule. The exhibition was visited by over half a million people, almost twice as many as had seen the Dutch exhibition the year before. There were lengthy articles about the lectures, the poetry, the sculpture, the American and European loans, and so on; the coverage went on for weeks. As for the American loans, these were uncritically admired. John G. Johnson of Philadelphia lent a set of four predella panels by Botticelli representing the legend of St. Mary Magdalen, and F. Maitland Griggs of New York lent Sassetta's *Journey of the Magi,* though neither work had come from Duveen. Joseph E. Widener lent Mantegna's *Judith Before the Tent of Holofernes,* and Henry Goldman of New York a *Virgin and Child* attributed to Giotto, both acquired through Duveen. There were Pollaiuolos and Tintorettos that were equally admired. It was a triumph.

Duveen, who was in New York, was advised by the London office not to approach the owners of the British paintings which had been included in the show as yet, because all the dealers were writing and they had been inundated with letters. The best idea was to wait. Duveen, who had his eye on Raphael's *St. John the Baptist Preaching,* lent by the Marquis of Lansdowne, did not believe in letters and wanted someone to approach Lansdowne at once. (They did not buy the Raphael.) Ernest and Eddie preferred a Titian that Lansdowne also owned; they did not buy that one, either. Duveen had a copy of the catalogue, and his brothers, after examining the paintings with care, sent detailed notes. The Earl of Crawford's Duccio *Crucifixion* was not a Duccio. Lycett Green's Nardo di Cione *Pietà* was small and unimportant; ditto Giunta Pisano's *Crucifixion,* lent by Henry Harris. Giotto's *Christ and the Magdalen,* owned by Lord Lee of Fareham, had nothing to do with Giotto or his school. And so it went. They liked a Moroni and several Titians and were particularly attracted to a highly unusual painting, *The Adoration of the Shepherds,* owned by Viscount Allendale. They were seeing this wonderful painting, of a couple of simply dressed young men kneeling before an infant, for the first time. It might be by Giorgione or it might by Titian, but it did not matter, because it was a very great painting. They wanted Duveen to see it as soon as he returned to England.

HAVING TO GIVE UP SMOKING for health reasons after a lifetime was a deprivation that Duveen accepted with good grace. He had "a remarkably lifelike ivory cigarette made plus a light which he kept perpetually in his mouth or in his hand so that he always seemed to be smoking," Behrman wrote. In his usual generous way, what he could no longer allow himself was to be shared. When Louis Levy sent him a box of fine Coronas, Duveen passed them around at a dinner party and enjoyed the enjoyment of his guests. Levy did not know he could no longer smoke and, indeed, most people did not know how many pleasures Duveen had been denied. Although he would eventually need a nurse constantly in attendance and daily medical attention, he kept up the pretense of being only slightly indisposed. Behrman wrote, "Something of a gourmet, he would account for the fact that at this period he hardly ate anything by saying his doctor had put him on 'a bit of a diet.' " Keeping up the façade was a lifelong trait, but so was his refusal to feel sorry for himself. Behind the bluster and bravura was a quiet stoicism. Only those who knew him well had any idea he was constantly in and out of hospital. In early February 1934, for instance, at the end of a long letter to Bache he wrote that he was dictating it from his bed, where he had been laid up for nearly a week with a temperature of 102, feeling miserable. Ten days later he was relieved to discover that instead of the "old trouble," not described, he had simply picked up some sort of bug during his visit to the Chicago Exposition the previous December. He recovered rapidly from this setback but was ill again in November and underwent an operation in Mount Sinai Hospital in New York City. The operation was described as "minor," as was another operation about six months later, again at Mount Sinai, where he was "resting comfortably" early in July. His attending physician, Dr. A. A. Berg, reported he had had "a satisfactory day and was doing as well as could be expected." With Duveen, illness was an inconvenience, to be ignored the way he had surmounted so many obstacles in the course of a long and brilliant career. He did not have time to get ill. A cable to Paris early in January 1935 is full of enthusiasm for improving market conditions. He wrote that although the market was still poor for the second-rate, he believed that great things in art would fetch as much as ever within the year.

His ability to discover the silver lining whatever the cloud is intrinsic to his nature, as the following example shows. Some time after Hitler assumed power in 1933, Duveen chanced to be traveling through Germany by train. He was taken ill and had to spend the night in a small hotel in the provinces. The future director of the National Gallery of Art, David Finley, said, "The next morning he visited the local art gallery and spoke to the director, who said that he was going to Berlin to replace Dr. Friedländer at the Kaiser Friedrich and that he might be able to exchange some pictures for German ones." Finley was referring to the fact that the Nazis had labeled as "degenerate" art not only all the French impressionists and such contemporary giants as Picasso and Matisse but German expressionists as well, along with any artist judged to be part of the "Judeo-Bolshevist" school. Since their museums were so contaminated, the Nazis were going on a thorough housecleaning. Extraordinary works—by Picasso, van Gogh, Matisse, and the like, all from German museums—went up for auction in a famous sale in Lucerne in 1939, one that scandalized the art world. What the Nazi-affiliated Combat League for German Culture wanted to exhibit were works by such minor nineteenth-century Swiss and German genre painters as Carl Spitzweg, Wilhelm von Kaulbach, and Arnold Böcklin, along with Caspar David Friedrich, Hans von Marées, and Anselm Feuerbach, as well as examples of German Gothic art. They did not seem particularly interested in the Italian Renaissance.

At the news that some kind of exchange might be possible, Duveen was all attention and invited the new director to lunch. Finley continued, "Lord Duveen told him he had a Holbein which he would exchange for some pictures." One of the paintings the Kaiser Friedrich was willing to exchange was Duccio's *Nativity with the Prophets Isaiah and Ezekiel,* a fourteenth-century triptych on wood. Mellon was delighted to buy it and it is now at the National Gallery. That was one of many paintings that Duveen's activities succeeded in obtaining for British and American collections, often through Swiss or Dutch intermediaries. Ian Locke, a British specialist in the field of Nazi stolen art, said that Duveen only dealt with the best items that came from German museums and eventually sold numbers of such paintings to Samuel Kress. "He bought directly at a time when some of the London dealers were complaining about having to go to Munich and Berlin to buy, and they also thought that the works were mostly second-rate." Duveen did not complain; he knew better. The first big round of sales came in 1933–34 and mostly involved works that had been taken from museum collections. The second round of sales, in 1936, "were paintings owned by so-called enemies of the state; all sorts of categories from ship owners to bankers, forced sales and confiscations of a lot of their property. Or people put on trial for treason would lose their possessions, another easy way for the Germans to pick up art treasures."

By early 1934 the Paris telegrams were beginning to make references to the willingness of the Kaiser Friedrich Museum to part with some Italian-school pictures in exchange for a work by Stefan Lochner of Cologne, a fifteenth-century exponent of the International Gothic style. There are many cryptic references to "the Berlin business," which for obvious reasons had to be kept entirely secret. By April 1937 Berlin pictures, including a wonderful Filippo Lippi, were being shipped on the *Bremen* and Duveen was trying to get a first-rate Vermeer from Vienna. Duveen was perfectly willing to wash and brush up as many mediocre German works as the Nazis thought they wanted if he could get his hands on something really useful. Pretty soon, he did. Perhaps the most important purchase from Germany in those years was Raphael's portrait of a fifteenth-century Florentine banker named Bindo Altoviti. The painting had been owned by Crown Prince Ludwig of Bavaria and had entered the collection of the Alte Pinakothek in Munich. How or why that museum was ever persuaded to part with such a masterpiece is a mystery. It apparently accepted with pleasure some worthless German paintings from Duveen's vast stock, and *Bindo Altoviti* went to Kress. It is now at the National Gallery in Washington.

Such quiet triumphs were tempered by major disappointments. Among the many victims of the Nazis were members of the great Rothschild family of bankers, industrialists, and collectors. One by one their palaces and their remarkable contents were confiscated, that of Alphonse in Vienna being one more example. As soon as Duveen learned that this particular collection was being put up for auction, he sent Fowles and Lowengard to meet with a firm of Swiss bankers in an effort to negotiate a price. It is believed he even tried to get Hitler to mediate. It is certain that Duveen intended to turn the collection over to the Rothschilds, but the auction never took place. Hitler had decided to make Alphonse Rothschild's Old Masters, Sèvres, and Louis XV furniture the nucleus of a new German art gallery at Linz. He would "give the Reich its Louvre," Niall Ferguson wrote in *The House of Rothschild.* "It was the beginning of one of the greatest art thefts in history."

Then there was the Spanish affair. The slight hint that there might be some art for sale came to Duveen in 1931 after the Republican Party in Spain won a great victory in the municipal elections and King Alfonso XIII abdicated. Paris, as usual, was watching the political developments closely, and sent word to Duveen in New York that the king had thoughtfully removed trainloads of possessions out of the country before he stepped down. Since the king had also transferred several million pounds to foreign banks, Armand and Edward did not think he would need to sell anything just yet. But they expected a great many Spanish aristocrats would take up residence abroad and that those with villas in other countries would be allowed to export their treasures, which would include artworks. Then there was the distinct possibility that the Catholic Church would lose its favored position, along with much of its property, which did indeed take place a couple of years later. They wrote, "In this case there will be enormous quantity of works of art in the market much more serious than Russia." They had heard that Wildenstein was already investigating the business aspects, ditto Arnold Seligmann, Bacri, Knoedler's, and Colnaghi's. That was all Duveen needed to know. They were not to hang around in Paris, where they would learn nothing, but to take the first train to Madrid and talk to Salazar, a trustee of the Prado whom Duveen had entertained in New York the year before. Meanwhile, they should stay on the alert for every rumor.

That, for the moment, was that. The next time the subject came up it was 1936. A military rebellion led by General Francisco Franco, a nationalist and conservative in his mid-forties, had precipitated the great Spanish Civil War. There was fighting in the streets between Franco's Nationalist Party, which included the monarchists, Carlists, clericalists, landowners, and industrialists, and the Popular Front (Socialists, Communists, and syndicalists). Naturally this led Duveen to think about pictures. Returning to New York from Marienbad on the Cunard White Star liner *Queen Mary* in October, he said he hoped "the art treasures in Spain were being hidden to protect them from vandals." He seemed particularly interested in the fate of Old Masters in the Prado. Three months later, in January 1937, he became even more interested. Edward and Armand cabled from London that a Parisian diamond merchant had approached them asking whether they were willing to spend a couple of million pounds buying fine pictures from the Spanish government (presumably the one represented by the Popular Front, which was still in power). They replied they would love to buy from the Prado. Naturally, they wanted to know exactly what was going on, because at least three other intermediaries had approached them, all claiming a direct line to the Prado's treasures. In the meantime, Duveen should send a wish list of what he wanted.

Duveen responded a day later with details of about twenty pictures he would be delighted to buy. Eleven of them were by Velázquez, most of them portraits of King Philip II, Don Carlos, his son; the Duke of Olivares; the dwarf; the court jester; and so on. Others were by Fra Angelico, Mantegna, Raphael, Titian, Dürer, and Memling. Edward and Armand made immediate plans to go to Madrid. But before they left they thought they had better get some legal advice. It had occurred to them that the British government had taken a position of strict neutrality and had passed a law prohibiting assistance to either side. Since buying pictures could be construed as assistance, it might be as well to get advice from their British law firm before committing themselves to another big chase.

The advice was not long in coming. Their chief advisor at F. M. Guedella and Company in London replied that the whole suggestion was perfectly preposterous. They must be mad. The cable continued: WHAT-EVER GOVERNMENT SUCCEEDS, PRESENT ONE IN SPAIN WOULD CLAIM RETURN OF PICTURES AS SALE ILLEGAL. NATIONAL PARTY HAVE STATED ALREADY THAT THEY WILL CLAIM RETURN OF GOLD TAKEN FROM BANK OF MADRID; FURTHERMORE GUEDELLA SAYS THAT BRITISH GOVERNMENT WOULD NOT UPHOLD YOUR ACTION AND EVENTUALLY YOU WOULD BE OSTRACIZED BY EVERYONE AND MIGHT EVEN LOSE YOUR PEERAGE AS YOU HAVE NO RIGHT TO TAKE ANY PERSONAL ATTITUDE . . . That, it seemed, was that.*

IN THE SPRING OF 1935 Duveen was, if possible, busier than ever. Before he got to London Guedella sent him an advance report on *Art Treasures and Intrigue,* the first of three books about the art world that James Henry Duveen, otherwise known as Jacques or Jack, would write that, one way or another, dealt with the history of Duveen Brothers. What must have rankled was the flowery introduction that characterized the author as "a member of that notable family whose exploits are known all the world over, and his very name stands in all civilized countries as representing vast knowledge, keen enterprise and amazing skill." It was very flattering to the author and may even have been true, but to Guedella it looked like a shameless attempt to trade on Duveen's fame. Besides, in the spring of 1935, Jack was bankrupt. In an attempt to explain his downfall he had given an examining magistrate a confused tale of disappearing stock, mysterious fires, and ruthless moneylenders two years before. In the autumn of 1933, when he declared bankruptcy, he had a bank overdraft of £19,000, other debts, and about £1,000 in assets. Jack's insistent references to his wife, Esther, as the great love of his life also had an ironic ring, since the marriage had broken up. His wife gave him an allowance of ten pounds a month, and Duveen was contributing another twenty, so he was in no particular danger of starving. The solicitor was vastly irritated and wanted Duveen to disavow Jack as a relative, an idea Duveen immediately dismissed. His new tolerance seemed of a piece with the comment made by Berenson after a

---

*The paintings at the Prado were never sold. Duveen helped raise the money for an international committee to save Spain's treasures and was able to hammer out an agreement that the paintings and other works of art be sent to Geneva for safekeeping. (Duveen obituary, *New York Times,* May 26, 1939)

distant relative fell asleep at the dinner table and started snoring. "Oh, leave him alone," Berenson said. "We all make some sort of noise."

Duveen had always been particularly successful with women collectors. He had taken great pains with Arabella Huntington and had been slowly rewarded; his relationship with her remained satisfactory, even fond, until her death. Similarly, with the immensely wealthy American heiress Marjorie Merriweather Post, Duveen took it upon himself to educate her tastes and sent her a handwritten guide to the Louvre beginning with the thirteenth-century Florentine school, essentially a cram course in art appreciation. Mrs. Post never did get to like Italian primitives, but she showed an instinctive preference for eighteenth-century French, which suited Duveen almost as well. He helped her acquire a valuable collection of Sèvres and guided her toward the tapestries and superb pieces of French furniture that now decorate her home of Hillwood; she also bought Nattier, Largillière, Rubens, and Gainsborough. She called Duveen "one of the most important men in my life."

One of Duveen's clients, Marjorie Merriweather Post,
dressed as Marie Antoinette

Anna Thomson Dodge, painted as
Madame de Pompadour, by Gerald Festus Kelly

But perhaps the most prominent woman collector of those years, from
a business point of view, was Anna Thomson Dodge, widow of the auto-
mobile magnate, with millions to spend and no one to instruct her. Naturally, Duveen would. He knew exactly how to instill in her the idea of
living on a scale commensurate with her status, how to make her appreci-

ate the finest and rarest, and how to inspire in her a proper respect for his gentle despotism. One can imagine him saying, as he did with Bache, "Now, dear lady, I must insist on advising you to take my advice." She did, allowing him a free hand decorating her mansion, Rose Terrace, in Grosse Pointe, Michigan, and her summer palace in Palm Beach; and the Detroit Institute of Arts is the richer for her many bequests. Duveen subsequently organized a multivolume catalogue of her works and (one suspects, as a reward) introduced her to the highly accomplished portraitist Sir Gerald Kelly. He painted her, naturally, as Madame de Pompadour.

Prices were going up again, and Duveen's optimism index was rising with them. One of the coups of 1935 would be his purchase of *Mrs. Pemberton,* a Holbein miniature that his father had sold to J. Pierpont Morgan thirty-one years before. The portrait reappeared in a sale of the $2.5 million collection of Morgan miniatures at Christie's in London in June. Morgan had paid $14,264 for it; Duveen bought it for almost $31,000. Duveen never minded paying more for something. That was part of his mantra, and from that perspective one can guess what an awful admission it was when prices started going down. But it was back to heady profits, and he was ready for them as his galleries in London and Paris shipped over Romneys, Gainsboroughs, Van Dycks, a Velázquez, and two Hoppners in September of 1935.

But the best sign that things were returning to normal was the fact that Knoedler's had become the enemy again. This was the case during a sale at Christie's of the Henry Oppenheimer drawings in the summer of 1936. Duveen made a dramatic appearance at the final session. He wanted a small silverpoint head-and-shoulders study, *Portrait of an Ecclesiastic,* by the fifteenth-century illuminator and illustrator Jean Fouquet. Knoedler's opened the bidding with an offer of 5,000 guineas. Duveen immediately raised that to 5,005. Knoedler's retaliated with 6,000 guineas. The antagonists, circling each other warily, went up by small increments until the price reached 9,800 guineas. Suddenly a contender, appearing from nowhere, entered the struggle with a bid for 10,000 guineas. Knoedler's threw in the towel and Duveen emerged victorious at 10,002 guineas.

Duveen had also started selling to museums, a market that had recently showed surprising strength. One of the Titians he owned, *Venus and the Lute Player,* came from Holkham Hall, Norfolk, the seat of the Earl of Leicester. It had been acquired by Sir Thomas Coke, an ardent collector who built the great house, and bought most of the items in his collection during a grand tour of the Continent. It was a distress sale; the earl was inconsolable, but Duveen Brothers was ecstatic and the price, in 1930, was a

rock-bottom $200,000. When it arrived in London, Eddie cabled: SIMPLY
MARVELLOUS AND STUPENDOUS CONSIDER ONE OF THE GREATEST WORKS
OF ART YOU HAVE EVER HAD. Its purchase for the Metropolitan Museum of
Art five years later at twice that price was hugely satisfying. The *New York
Times* gave it a full column, and as usual, A. C. R. Carter of the *Daily Tele-
graph* did the honors in London. Eddie, however, had leaked to Carter that
the painting had been in their stock for five years because it was too big to
sell. He had also breathed some suggestion about the price. Duveen was
furious. NONE OF YOU MUST INTERVIEW PRESS WITHOUT ASKING OUR
INSTRUCTIONS, he wired sternly. YOU ARE NOT TO BE TRUSTED.

The treatment by the London papers could only be helpful, Eddie
replied soothingly, because it was a long time since Duveen had had any
publicity at all. This was not quite true. The summer before, Duveen had
landed himself squarely in one of the biggest controversies ever to involve a
senior member of the United States government.

The occasion had to do with the complicated financial and political
fortunes of the former secretary of the treasury, Andrew Mellon. In 1935
the great old man was eighty years old and had been spending his senior
years making detailed plans for the financial well-being of those who
would follow him. The intricacies of this legacy are not relevant to this
account. It is enough to know that a Democratic administration, headed
by Franklin D. Roosevelt, was looking askance at any wealthy Republican
who seemed to have figured out a way to avoid paying taxes. Mellon provided a handy target, not just because he was so rich but because he had, a
few years earlier, established the A. W. Mellon Educational and Charitable
Trust. The whole point of the trust was to take charge of the Mellon collection of paintings, worth something like $40 million. This munificent
gift was destined for the National Gallery of Art, or so he said. The government did not believe in mighty fortunes being donated to galleries that
might or might not materialize. The prosecutors were sure there was a
catch in it somewhere. Their argument went that Mellon had not actually
given up control of his paintings, and therefore should not be allowed to
make tax deductions of their value. There would be heavy gift taxes to pay.
Mellon had also underpaid his taxes for 1931. They were after him.

The trial, which dragged on for weeks in Pittsburgh and Washington,
was a long and involved wrangling, much of it over aspects of the tax code.
Only a money man would find it interesting, and Mellon, alert and
informed, naturally did, showing himself in command of the facts and
cool under pressure. Since Mr. Mellon's dream, to give the nation a building, a trust fund, and an art collection as well, had never been public

knowledge before, it made for huge press coverage. His lawyer's defense was also widely quoted: "God did not place in the hearts and minds of men such diverse and opposite traits as these. It is impossible to conceive of a man planning such benefactions and at the same time plotting and scheming to defraud the government," which turned the government's argument neatly on its head.

One of the points it seemed essential for the defense to make was that Mellon had thought of his National Gallery years before and that this was not just the whim of the moment, designed to hide some crafty tax dodge. Mellon naturally thought of Duveen. Duveen immediately responded. Of course he would help.

In a duel of wits, even one stage-managed by the best lawyers the U.S. government could summon, it took a lot to ruffle Duveen. Robert H. Jackson, the prosecutor, said in his reminiscences that Duveen was "about the most fantastic witness I ever saw on the witness stand." He was quick. He was evasive. He quibbled. He danced. He twirled. He was always three or four moves ahead of whatever stratagem the prosecution had devised for trapping him. Jackson was amused, annoyed, and admiring. He quickly lost a round when the Board of Tax Appeals refused to admit as evidence the fact that Duveen Brothers had paid a heavy fine in the old customs case of 1910. Then Jackson tried to show, with no success, that Duveen himself

At left, Duveen, as usual, enlivens the proceedings when he testifies at Andrew Mellon's tax trial, to the great gratitude of the former secretary of the treasury. With Duveen are (left to right) Mellon; Mellon's attorney, Frank J. Hogan; and William R. Valentiner, director of the Detroit Institute of Arts.

was a tax dodger. That was the occasion for the lordly remark that he could not remember whether he had made $2 million or lost it. The whole issue of how the paintings arrived at their value took up an endless amount of questioning and cross-examination. When the subject of the Niccolini-Small Cowper Madonna came up, that Duveen bought from Lady Desborough in 1929, Duveen agreed to disclose the trade secret that he had paid as much as $750,000 for it. Since Mr. Mellon thought the price was very high, Duveen said, he had only taken a profit of $75,000. Duveen said he thought it a very low price. "But Mr. Mellon thought it was a very high price. One day after lunch I gave way." *News-Week* added, "Duveen beamed at Mellon. The banker stopped chewing gum long enough to wink at Duveen."

Whether the paintings in Mellon's collection had some kind of absolute value apart from the market became part of the discussion. Duveen, who was perfectly capable of arguing either way, chose to uphold the idea that paintings never deviated in value. Jackson: "They are not a fluctuating commodity?" Duveen: "No. They are not a commodity. You cannot buy a picture like you buy a load of copper or a tin mine."

But his main usefulness was the testimony he provided that the idea of a National Gallery had been in Mellon's mind for a number of years. Duveen said he was the one who had thought of John Russell Pope. (Whether or not this was true, Mellon did not seem to mind.) He had even recommended the site. The journalist and author Marquis Childs recalled, "This was a beautiful clash between Jackson, the homespun American, and Duveen, this arrogant Britisher. I remember a marvelous exchange between them when Jackson was pressing him to say where [the site] would be and Duveen, with some impatience, said, 'Well, I really can't quite remember, you know. He showed me a little sketch on the back of an envelope. I think it was by the pond, by the little obelisk.'

"Jackson said, 'A pond with an obelisk? What do you mean?'

" 'A little obelisk, a what-do-you-call-it.'

"Then Jackson realized he was talking about the Washington Monument."

Duveen did his star turn in Washington in May 1935 and sailed for London the next day. David Finley sent a grateful letter to his office there. "You kept your self-possession and good temper under very trying circumstances, which seemed to have the effect of disconcerting the attorney conducting the cross examination . . ." His tone was gratifyingly cordial. Just how warmly Mellon felt is not recorded, but the wink during the tax trial spoke volumes. A year later, in the summer of 1936, Duveen, again in London, sent a jubilant telegram back to New York. He had spent three hours with Mellon and there was a huge deal in the works. Not only did the collector want their Italian Renaissance paintings but much more besides. Duveen had finally triumphed.

Chapter Eighteen

RAIN ON THE LAWN

THE YOUNG RICHARD KINGZETT, a future director of the grand old firm on Old Bond Street, went to stay with his uncle Colin Agnew in London in the summer of 1938. Agnew had a flat near Grosvenor Square, where he was looked after by his Swiss housekeeper, Mrs. Stansel. Kingzett wrote, "My father always maintained that she had accompanied Colin to the trenches in the First World War. This seemed unlikely, but had she done so I am quite sure that she would have continued to serve the same delicious food in his mess tin throughout the Battle of Mons as she had always done at his dinner parties in South Audley Street."

Kingzett, then just seventeen, was in London to attend the Rugby–Marlborough match at Lord's, and was invited to a dinner party that night being given for Lord Duveen. The name meant almost nothing to him, and he is not sure who all the other guests were, but remembers Horace Buttery, the picture restorer; Sir Osbert Sitwell, the writer; Raymond Mortimer, the literary editor of the *Sunday Times;* and Edward Sackville-West, the musicologist and inspiration for one of Nancy Mitford's characters in *The Pursuit of Love.*

As was his custom, Duveen arrived last, even later than usual. He was warm and effusive with everyone, although Kingzett noticed he asked questions but never waited for the answers. When he arrived at Kingzett himself, he flatteringly said that he had heard a great deal about him. Kingzett remarked wryly, "I was still at an age when I believed that grown-ups meant what they said." Once he found out that the young man was in London for the cricket match, Duveen announced that he was passionately interested in cricket. This came as a great surprise to everyone, particularly when Duveen insisted on developing this theme all through dinner. Here were all these people who had come to hear him talk learnedly about art, the state of the market, the future of the National Gallery in Washington, the new sculpture galleries at the Tate, the rooms at the British Museum, even perhaps the future of British painting. All Duveen would talk about were the merits of Trumper and Spooner as opposed to Larwood and Verity, and that great old cricketer, a personal friend of his, Jack Hobbs. Did Kingzett not agree that Hobbs was the finest batsman who ever lived? All this was said with the greatest élan, vitality, and self-assurance. Kingzett said, "He was exactly like the man who came to dinner. The party simply revolved around him and, quite honestly, you didn't notice anyone else." Duveen struck him as being a great actor, with an instinctive stage presence. "He was also extremely funny, a point which most people who have written about him seem to have missed."

In this case Kingzett believed Duveen was avoiding talking about art altogether out of sheer mischievousness. "Any attempt to divert his conversation to more cultural matters was stonewalled. In cricketing parlance he 'played it back to the bowler.' I remember one particularly effective stroke: Sackville-West, clearly no aficionado of our national game, tried to introduce music as a topic." The subject was a recent performance of *Don Giovanni* at Covent Garden. " 'Ah,' said Duveen, 'the Don. Now in my view Don Bradman is the greatest batsman playing today . . .' "

The only other person to whom Duveen gave his attention was the housekeeper. Learning that she was suffering from rheumatism, "at once the famous Duveen empathy came into play," Kingzett wrote. He had the same problem, Duveen said, and the two launched into a long conversation about symptoms and remedies. Duveen was delighted to learn that Mrs. Stansel was giving them his favorite dessert, chocolate mousse, but Kingzett noticed that he ate very little of it. Duveen left early, explaining that he was leaving for New York the next day. Colin Agnew explained that Duveen was undergoing an exhausting form of cancer treatment. "As he always wanted to dominate any party at which he appeared, when tiredness set in he would simply . . . go home." At Christmas that year Kingzett paid another visit to the flat and learned that Mrs. Stansel's Christmas present from Duveen was an electric blanket for her rheumatism. This exotic device, almost unknown in those days, thrilled and terrified her. She would not dream of using it in case it set the sheets on fire. Instead, she had laid it out on a table, "where she displayed it with all the unction of the *parroco* of a small village showing his church's one treasure to a visiting tourist." Kingzett was also given a present from Duveen, a book about cricket. It was inscribed to him with his name misspelled, which did not bother him in the least. He wrote, "I doubt that any present has ever given me more pleasure."

JUST HOW PHYSICALLY TAXING those last years were is not known, but Kingzett's description of Duveen as the dominant presence at a dinner party a matter of months before he died is highly illuminating. In those prewar years, several large, divergent events were coming together in ways that would have tested his energies to the utmost even if Duveen, with his clear mind and ability to plan far ahead, could have foreseen them. In the first place, he would certainly have been alarmed at the Nazi persecution of the Jews and the future of world Jewry, not to mention his own relatives if they were stranded in Europe. This fear would have been well founded, since his sister, the outspoken Florrie, René Gimpel's wife, was only just rescued in time, her children fought with the French Resistance, and her husband died in Neungamme concentration camp. There is no doubt that Duveen must have had to deal with anti-Semitism as a matter of course. René Gimpel told the story of a Van Dyck painting of two young men that Duveen had hung in Frick's house in 1918 in the hope that the collector would buy it. Frick's wife did not want it; "she couldn't bear to have those Jewish noses constantly before her eyes." The noses, Gimpel recorded, belonged to the brothers Stuart, nephews of Charles I, King of England. There is no evidence that Duveen tried to pretend, as had the young Berenson, that he was not a Jew. But like Disraeli, he occupied a highly unusual position. His father had transcended his origins and social handicaps and been accepted in the highest circles, and so would he. If he was ever snubbed and rebuffed, he had long since developed useful defenses, and his elevation to the peerage was enough to silence most people. He was married in a synagogue and would be buried in Willesden Jewish Cemetery, but there is no evidence that he observed Jewish holidays or dietary laws, and neither did his daughter. As for Elsie, one wonders what she felt. In the spring of 1934, shortly after Hitler's rise to power, Eddie in London sent her a telegram in code: THERE IS A RUMOR YOU CONTEMPLATING TRAVEL GERMAN STEAMER. YOU CANNOT DO THIS. ERNEST SAYS HE TIRED TELLING YOU.

Duveen must have realized that another world war would mean the end of his international eminence as an art dealer. He had to decide, and soon, how Duveen Brothers would continue, and if so, where. The question was equally pressing for another reason. Like his father, he was tiring. The career he had chosen depended on a young man's energies; who would succeed him? How long would he himself live? What kind of life could he anticipate? Where did he want to spend his final years? These were the issues crowding in on him as he struggled with the immediate aftermath of the Depression and the formidable challenges presented by the legacy he had chosen for himself. There was another problem absorbing his depleted energies. Dolly, whom he had thought safely and suitably married off, was not happy with William Garthwaite. The cause of her unhappiness is not known, but her husband may have met someone else, or perhaps she had. Sir John Foster, a leading barrister who first met Duveen when he was a fellow at All Souls College, Oxford University, may have caused the breakup. He was thought of as something of a womanizer and told an interviewer he had divorced his wife for Dolly. The rumor is that after they got engaged, Foster sent a telegram to her father breaking the engagement. Whether or not this is true, Foster remained an important presence in her life for several years, to be replaced by Bryan Hartopp Burns. Burns was an orthopedic surgeon with a distinguished reputation who was described as "tall, elegant, and charming" by one of Dolly's relatives by marriage, Anneta Duveen. When it seemed clear in 1937 that Dolly's future happiness was in the balance, Duveen bought her out of her childless marriage to Garthwaite and no doubt underwrote the agreement that, a year later, gave Burns a prenuptial settlement of £20,000 in trust. Dolly, who settled into a charmed lifestyle with a house in Ascot, another in Chesterfield Hill, London, and a winter home in Jamaica, was well cared for by her father. Before he died, Duveen set up for Elsie and Dolly tax-free trusts on the Isle of Man of a million pounds each.

The author Brian Masters recalls his first meeting with Dolly, at the home of Lady Selina Hastings: "looking like some great black object; luminous black hair and ruby red lips, a prewar style, and of indeterminate age. Far too many rings, jewelry, and lipstick. She was absolutely charming to me. I was telling her how I grew up, came from nowhere, and spoke with a Cockney accent. She grabbed me. I became a kind of trophy. She had enormous regard for self-made men. She claimed many times to be a Communist. A supporter of the Labour Party. Had she been born poor, she would never have gone anywhere, and she secretly knew it. She absolutely adored her father. As a professional hostess you don't talk about personal matters, but she called him 'Daddy,' a term of endearment. She gave me a biography of her father which she kept hidden away. Even between two covers, he belonged to her and her alone."

She was a mixture of opposites. "She had a ruthless streak and was

Dolly Duveen Garthwaite gets married to Bryan Hartopp Burns in 1938.

amazingly contradictory. She was generous and yet mean about things like postage stamps. I've seen her berate servants for spending a dollar too much on a lobster. Screaming and humiliating them."

She gave dinners constantly, "five nights a week and never less than fourteen, black tie and women in long dresses. A splendid mixture of politicians, writers, shoe designers. She threw people together and expected intelligent, rewarding conversation. She fancied herself as an intellectual. It was current politics. There was never that acerbic cruel tone. She liked wit in the eighteenth-century sense of knowledge and wisdom. She couldn't abide the idea that someone was being humiliated—except by her! She was a good judge of talent and worth, but she couldn't spot a con man and was taken advantage of. A girl named Marilyn took a ring off Dolly's dying finger. I think Bobbie [her husband] saw through that but had long since given up trying to advise or influence her. When she got angry with her husband she'd attack him and say, 'Why on earth did I marry you?' 'Daddy would have got me someone' was the tone. Bobbie would wink as if to say, this is the way she is. She's not as bad as all that."

Robert Skidelsky, an eminent academic and the biographer of John Maynard Keynes, was another frequent visitor. He said, "I'm quite interested in finding out about people, but I don't think it was very easy to get to know Dolly. I used to ask her questions but she wouldn't really respond. The trouble was, it was very hard to get her alone. She always went to Cannes for the season, and we had a house just outside, in a little village in Provence. So I usually got asked to Cannes for her dinner parties and once she came to our house and it was wonderful, in a way. This great Rolls-Royce drove up the village road full of bumps and lots of peasants running about, and out stepped Dolly with a huge hat and the usual diaphanous clothes in purple. And then the entourage followed and they all trooped in and she is saying, 'How very charming. I've never been to a French village before.' Her circuit was not that. It was the same in Jamaica. Always lots of people around, and when there weren't lots around, the chances of having a conversation with her were almost nonexistent. The obvious thing one concludes is that she had a hole in the middle of her life which she needed to fill." Unlike her father, she hated fast cars and was always slowing her chauffeur down to a crawl. "Curious, isn't it?" Lord Skidelsky said. "There was a fear there. No one whose life is lived in such a public way, even though she wasn't a public figure, has a rich inner life. It seems to me she was alive when she was with lots of people and dead when she wasn't."

Perhaps getting Dolly settled had something to do with it, but Duveen had made up his mind that he wanted to move to England, whatever the

The house in Kensington Palace Gardens, or "Millionaire's Row," that John Russell Pope designed for Duveen in 1937 but that was never built

future held. He had engaged the services of his favorite architect, John
Russell Pope, to design a mansion for himself and Elsie on the western edge
of Hyde Park near Kensington Palace and its gardens. Drawings of the
front and rear elevations have survived, and these show a very simple,
almost severe classical façade using pillars, pediments, and decorative
schemes based on Greek revival motifs. The rear, facing the garden, showed
a gentler aspect, with French windows opening onto terraces and bal-
conies. The house, with its wide terraces, would have sloped down to lawns
and herbaceous borders and a view of the park beyond, just like The Elms
on the edge of Hampstead Heath. There would be visits to museums and
walks in the park, and perhaps, in the late afternoon, he could have rested
on his spacious terrace and watched the sun setting or rain crossing the
lawn. As Lord Skidelsky observed of Dolly Burns, Duveen was not the
kind of person who looks backwards. He was, as was she, "one of those
people who is always interested in what is to come, and that's quite
unusual."

MELLON'S TIRING TAX TRIAL ended in June 1936. (He won his case
but never knew it; the verdict came down after he died.) Almost immediately, Mellon decided he deserved a vacation. Finley, his wife, and his
mother were already in London, and Mellon joined them there. They
made the usual visit to 4 Grafton Street and were met by the great man
himself. As Finley remembered it, Duveen told Mellon, "I am going to
retire from business and you are getting ready to give your collection for a
national gallery. This is a combination of circumstances which could never
happen again. I have quite a number of pictures of the first quality which
are needed to build up your collection." Mellon agreed to a meeting in
New York to see the paintings and sculpture in the storage vaults at 720
Fifth Avenue. But after he returned to Pittsburgh in September, Mellon
came down with a cold and sent Finley in his stead. Finley took the train
for New York at ten o'clock that night, arriving at Duveens at ten the next
morning, and spent three days going over his entire stock. He selected
thirty paintings and twenty-one pieces of sculpture, all from the Dreyfus
Collection, and all destined for storage in the drab basement of the Corcoran Art Gallery in Washington. But then it turned out that Mellon, who
had a large apartment at 1785 Massachusetts Avenue in Washington,
should not be subjected to the relatively short trip across town to ponder
over all those new Duveens. David Finley said it was his idea that Duveen
should rent an apartment directly underneath Mellon's own on the second

floor. Whether he actually thought of it, or Duveen did, really does not matter because Duveen would have usurped it fairly soon. It was of a piece with his large vision of life, which was to show unimaginative millionaires how they ought to live. One can imagine just how splendid that demonstration turned out to be, with its carpets, its tapestries and paneling, its Louis XV and Louis XVI furniture, its silks, brocades, ribbons, tassels, lamps, porcelain, Sèvres, and the rest, all of them produced like magic from the Fifth Avenue vaults. Duveen installed a caretaker, guards around the clock, and gave Mellon a key.

The caretaker, of course, kept Duveen informed almost on a minute-to-minute basis. Mr. Mellon had taken to dropping in, sometimes in his dressing gown and slippers, to examine the treasures. Pretty soon he was

All the things that didn't sell:
the storage vaults at 720 Fifth Avenue

coming and going on a regular basis, and perhaps the apartment began to look even better than his own, because he started giving dinner parties there. Finley said, "One day, as Duveen was leaving after a visit to Mr. Mellon, he turned at the door of the apartment and looking at the Van Dyck of the Marchesa Balbi, said, 'Look at that picture, Mr. Mellon, with the light falling on it. Have you ever seen anything so marvelous!' Mr. Mellon replied drily, 'Lord Duveen, my pictures never look so marvelous as when you are here!'" Nevertheless, the idea was growing on him. Behrman wrote, "Gradually, Mellon must have begun to feel that the paintings he showed off to his friends as Duveens were his own. There came a moment when he felt he couldn't go on living a double life. He sent for Duveen and bought the contents of his apartment lock, stock, and barrel!"

Making allowances for Behrman's theatrical flourishes—perhaps Mellon did not actually buy the teaspoons—this sale was an incredible triumph, the biggest of Duveen's career. Mellon bought twenty-six of the thirty paintings and eighteen of the twenty-one sculptures, for a total of $21 million. This far surpassed the measly $8 million that Mellon had paid for the twenty-three Hermitage paintings acquired through Knoedler's. In fact it was so much money that even Mellon could not find that much ready cash and had to pay Duveen in securities, not that Duveen minded, of course. All the gems of the Dreyfus collection went to Mellon: Desiderio da Settignano's charming bust of a little boy; Verrocchio's *Giuliano de' Medici;* the two exquisite marble reliefs of *Faith* and *Charity* by Mino da Fiesole; the unique painted and gilded terra-cotta *Madonna and Child* labeled as fifteenth-century Florentine but now thought to be by Donatello; and so many others. Since Mellon had always resisted buying Italian Renaissance works, Duveen's salesmanship was bent to persuading him that his collection needed drastic help in this department, and the paintings were also chosen with an eye to correcting this deficiency, with works by Botticelli, Cimabue, Giotto, Lippi, Matteo di Giovanni, and Antonello, along with the ill-fated Masaccio *Madonna of Humility,* which somehow slipped through.

Mellon's holdings were also weak in one of Duveen's favorite artists, Gainsborough. Apart from the less successful portrait of Georgiana, Duchess of Devonshire, the pleasing but unremarkable portrait of Miss Catherine Tatton, and the portrait of Master John Heathcote that Duveen had sold even though he did not like it, there really were no Gainsborough holdings to rival those at the Huntington. Duveen was determined to remedy this. One of his late great coups for Mellon was a full-length portrait of Mrs. Richard Brinsley Sheridan, the wife of the celebrated English wit, playwright, and Member of Parliament, from the collection of Baron Nathaniel de Rothschild. It cost Mellon $450,000 and its worth is almost beyond price nowadays, not just for its exquisite execution but for its subject. The lady, the former Elizabeth Linley, is as romantic a heroine as ever stepped out of a Gothic novel. She was from a celebrated family of musicians with ties to Mozart, and she herself acquired a national reputation as a singer when she was still an adolescent. When her father tried to marry her off to an aging rake, Sheridan fought two duels for her and was seriously wounded in one of them. Linley gave up her singing career when she married, and became a Whig hostess; she died, still quite young, of tuberculosis. The music-loving Gainsborough painted everyone in the family, and Elizabeth several times, but this portrait is his masterpiece.

Mellon went on buying and Duveen went on selling, but even so Finley and his chief curator, the young John Walker, were presented with a problem. Walker wrote, "Mr. Mellon had donated only 125 paintings and twenty-three pieces of sculpture. We were about to open a vast building, designed to provide well over a hundred galleries, with 148 'items,' to use Mr. Kress's term. That was all we had. No one else had given anything. The Mellon works of art would seem as scattered as sheep on a Scotch moor."

There were, of course, the Widener holdings. That glorious collection with its objets d'art, its great paintings, its sculpture, furniture, carpets, tapestries, and the rest, ought to have gone to the Philadelphia Museum of Art. But as Agnes Mongan, who became director of the Fogg Museum at Harvard, remembered, "The Wideners were not pleased with the way the Philadelphia Museum was being run." They were also amenable to the argument being made by David Finley that Washington would become more of a center for the arts than Philadelphia would ever be. Duveen naturally threw himself into the business of persuading the Wideners. The Wideners must be made to see reason; they soon did. Now the problem was that the gift would come with strings attached. If the National Gallery wanted the works of art, it would have to take everything else in Lynnewood Hall, including the tapestries, armor, porcelains, and so on, and the decorative arts had been specifically excluded by the terms of Mellon's gift. When the trustees began to waffle, Duveen cut through the dilemma with a bold solution. He would buy the whole thing. He thought the cost might be $25 million. He would then sell the National Gallery whatever it wanted for that price, and in the end he would have all those choice tapestries, porcelains, and the like. He would make a tidy profit from those. It was boldly simple, even breathtaking. But the logic of it escaped the trustees, as perhaps Duveen thought it might. Why should they pay $25 million for

Samuel H. Kress, painted by Leopold Seyffert

something they were being offered for nothing? They swallowed their objections, and the Wideners' wonderful tapestries, pieces of armor, chalices, select groups of French furniture, Chinese porcelains, and the rest are now at the National Gallery.

SAMUEL H. KRESS, founder of the chain of five-and-dime stores, and his brother, Rush, were two other major benefactors of the National Gallery. By the time Sam Kress swam into Duveen's consciousness at the end of World War I, he had consolidated his single modest store, selling cheap items most people wanted, into a vast coast-to-coast conglomerate of about two hundred and fifty stores, employing twenty thousand people. He lived in New York; he was clever, single-minded, and hard-working, and, thanks to frequent holidays in Europe, which he supposedly took for his health, he had acquired an admiration for Italy and all things Italian. This translated itself into an interest in amassing a collection of Italian Renaissance works. At that point Sam and Rush Kress should have been taken over by Duveen and Berenson, but there was a slight hitch. Sam Kress had already been pounced upon by Count Alessandro Contini-Bonacossi, the collector-dealer, about whom reminiscences are ambivalent. It is true that he knew fine painting and had some wonderful things himself, but opinions are divided on whether he always advised Kress wisely or sometimes threw in a lot of rubbish with the certain knowledge that Kress did not know the difference. Given the cavalier attitude toward condition and provenance that pertained in the wild and woolly art market of the 1920s, the probability is the latter. But in any event, Contini acted the part: "In his good looks, his tall slender figure, his spacious forehead and air of breeding and authority, he might have had the successes of a Casanova," John Walker wrote. Contini had prospered, mostly because he was persona grata in the highest Fascist circles and so, one assumes, the laws were bent for his benefit. This made him, according to the distinguished restorer Marco Grassi, "the only major buyer in Italy."

Kenneth Clark said, "For many years B.B. would have nothing to do with him; he thought he was a crook. Then he began to sell all these things to Kress—a meal ticket—and Berenson took him on. He began to authenticate all of Contini's pictures, and they are not all authentic. There is a dish in Italy made of mozzarella, the soft white cheese, called 'in carrozza.' Contini had a wife, a horrible soft white fat woman who drove around in an open carriage and was always known by that name. They owned a villa, Il Nonno, in Florence, an enormous hideous house near the station, full of marvelous Spanish pictures and some very good things. You couldn't laugh off Contini."

Sam Kress, who is always described as austere, abstemious, and ferociously penny-pinching, referred to Contini deferentially as "the Count" and bought and bought. The idea in the back of his mind was that he would found his own museum, but in the meantime he wanted to enjoy his treasures and had distributed them widely in the rooms of his two-story penthouse at 1020 Fifth Avenue, furnished in what Walker called New York Renaissance. Walker wrote, "Heavy tables and elaborately carved *cassoni* supported a plethora of majolica, plaques and small bronzes, and the Savonarola stools and Medici chairs on which we uncomfortably sat were

upholstered in stamped leather . . . Italian paintings, lighted with reflec-
tors, were hung from dado to ceiling in every room . . ."

Even Duveen, who always took the long view, was not able to make
much of a dent in Kress's well-fortified defenses until the Depression years,
when the shrinking market made him look again at the very few collectors
who were still buying. The correspondence shows that he had tracked
Kress for years, thanks to the indomitable Boggis, following him from his
visits to the Kellogg sanatorium in Battle Creek, Michigan, to California
and back, always accompanied by a Contini expert, presumably to make
sure that he did not fall in love with the wrong things, or anything. They
had known each other casually for a decade when Kress, to Duveen's surprise, must have read in the papers that the latter was hospitalized and
called to see how he was progressing. This struck Joe, who was always surprised and touched by any non-business-relationship interest in him personally, as very kind. He subsequently wrote to thank him. One thing led
to another, and in the summer of 1932 Joe went on the hunt. He was going
to find Kress somehow. He was in Europe in the summer of 1932 and
cabled New York for information on Sam Kress's European itinerary. He
then wrote to Kress to make a forceful case for some "very fine pictures of
great importance." If Mr. Kress would indicate his itinerary, Duveen could
meet him in London, or Paris, where he would be staying until the beginning of September. Kress replied cordially enough from his spa in Bad Kis-
sengen, but vaguely; their dates would not coincide in Paris, and he had no
plans to go to London. Duveen was willing to meet Kress at his next stop,
another spa in Bad Gastein, Austria. Kress again adroitly eluded him. In
fact, Kress did not reach Paris until November, when the office at Place
Vendôme reported that he was impossible to approach, being surrounded
by Contini and his family, acting as bodyguards.

Duveen persevered and, once back in New York, succeeded in showing
Kress a batch of paintings (he knew how much the collector liked buying
in bulk) that included the Mackay Sassettas that eventually went to London's National Gallery and a small, perfect Duccio. This was *The Calling of
the Apostles Peter and Andrew,* a fourteenth-century painting of tempera on
panel that had been part of the Benson Collection. Christ, on a rocky
shore, is calling to the Apostles, on an amusingly carved boat, who are just
about to make a nice haul of fish. They are obviously torn between the fish
and the commanding figure on the rocks, standing barefoot, wearing a red
gown and gold-edged cloak of royal blue. The scene is simplicity itself, and
the lovely clarity of the composition is embellished by its gold background
and tapestry-like, stylized sea, teeming with fish. It was a rare find and a

real prize to dangle at Kress. It must have occurred to the collector when he saw it in January 1933 that this was an exceptional work, and it did. Duveen, however, wanted $250,000 for it, and Kress steadfastly refused to pay. It took another year and a half of solid salesmanship on Duveen's part to bring Kress round. The sale was made along with two other, lesser works, both fifteenth-century Sienese paintings, *Madonna and Child with St. Jerome and St. Mary Magdalen* by Neroccio dei Landi and *The Annunciation* by Giovanni di Paolo. The price for all three was slashed from $460,000 to $360,000, and Kress got his Duccio for something like $195,600. Duveen ended up selling at a loss. It was rather adding insult to injury when brother Rush—Sam having taken off for Europe—threw up one excuse after another to avoid paying the first installment. The matter was finally cleared up by Sam in Europe, with profuse apologies.

Whether this embarrassing incident placed Samuel Kress under some kind of obligation to treat Duveen in a less high-handed way, or whether he concluded that Duveen's prices were not so bad, after all, cannot be known, but the likelihood is the latter. Duveen had reeled him in, and could gradually improve substantially on his own profit margin as the years went by. The first really big sale to Kress came just two years later: eleven paintings and a marble bust, *Isotta da Rimini* by Desiderio da Settignano, for $1.5 million. By then Kress, who must have been rapidly running out of space in his New York duplex, was thinking in grander terms and would end up leaving his whole collection to the National Gallery in Washington. That led its director to ponder the sticky problem of what to do with the mediocre works acquired through Contini, but that is another story. From Duveen's point of view Kress, who had always bought in bulk, was buying wholesale—he would eventually amass 3,210 works of art—and the Contini stranglehold had been broken. In the spring of 1937 Kress bought an even larger batch of twenty-four Italian Renaissance works for $2.3 million, and in the summer of 1938, a further purchase of eight more paintings for $1.25 million. Duveen's decision to take a loss had been handsomely rewarded, but then, he knew his man. Among the paintings in this group was the Allendale Giorgione.

THAT FIRST BIG SALE TO KRESS in the spring of 1936 had impressed on Duveen the importance of cultivating in him a proper appreciation for Berenson's position in the Italian culture he so fervently admired. It seemed only right and proper that Kress should pay a call on B.B. and sit at his feet as Bache had done. As with the New York banker, Berenson took his role with a very bad grace, saying the fact that Kress might become "the greatest buyer of Italian art does not personally interest me unless my financial relations with the firm are greatly altered to my advantage."

That comment referred to the dwindling rewards of expertising exclusively for Duveen at a time when B.B., now in his early seventies, was becoming increasingly anxious about the future of i Tatti. He was particularly upset about a longstanding debt of $150,000 that the firm had still not paid him. That autumn of 1936 a contract was hammered out in which Duveen agreed to pay off the debt in two installments and to increase Berenson's yearly retainer from $20,000 to $40,000. In prewar dollars that has to be considered munificent, but Berenson was still annoyed and resentful, because he was obliged to agree that he could no longer expect a percentage of the profits. The new two-year arrangement began on January 1, 1937, and ran until December 31, 1938. Either party could terminate at the end of 1937 if certain stipulations were met. So there was a way out. Both of them apparently wanted one, for different reasons.

The sharp-eyed Mary Berenson had not missed the change in Duveen. Although "bragging and blustering as if he were in perfect health," she realized he was "very, very ill." She did not think he could live much longer. Her opinions always carried great weight with B.B., and what she saw, or thought she saw, would have been a spur to get him thinking about new sources of revenue. As for Duveen, he was thinking too, but along entirely different lines. Whether or not Berenson knew it then, Duveen was planning to retire, as he had told Mellon just that summer. The firm's charter was set to expire in May 1938, when it made sense to liquidate. But exactly how that would be done and what the future of the firm would be were still in doubt and took a year to hammer out. Talks began in the summer of 1937 and caused a huge upheaval in his life, with the predictable consequences to his health. Just at that pivotal moment, one of the most famous paintings in the world came up for sale.

The Allendale *Adoration,* or *Nativity,* as it is usually called, has always been considered a work of Giorgione's although to this day there is talk about whether it could be an early Titian, or perhaps could have been painted by Giorgione with some amendations by Titian. No one disagrees about the astonishing beauty of the painting, with its idyllic grouping of shepherds and the holy family against an ideal landscape, suffused in a golden light. In terms of appreciation, the game of who painted it is irrelevant. But from a commercial point of view, the Allendale *Nativity* was being sold for a Giorgione price and therefore had to be a Giorgione.

In 1924, years before it came up for sale, Berenson told Duveen that the painting had baffled him for thirty-five years. He thought it might be by Giulio Campagnola. He thought a lot of things, including that it was an early Titian. Fowles had the idea that this opinion might have been influenced by a very old snub. He said, "I remember when Berenson wrote to me about going to see that picture. That picture belonged to Lord Allendale, an old and very sniffy, weird sort of family. It was hanging in their dining room for years as a Giorgione. It had always been a Giorgione. And Berenson said, 'If you go and see the picture don't mention my name.' I thought to myself afterwards, there's something behind this. I'm perfectly certain that Berenson must, in his grandiose manner, have turned around and said, 'Lord Allendale, you know this is a very nice picture but, of course, it isn't a Giorgione, it's only an early Titian.' Lord Allendale would have said, 'Call the butler,' and then, 'Do you mind showing this gentleman out.' " Since Fowles had encountered other examples of what he judged to be Berenson's refusal to pronounce favorably on a work for petu-

The Adoration of the Shepherds (the Allendale *Nativity*) by Giorgione

lant reasons, this made sense to him. In addition, the painting came up for sale in the early summer of 1937, just before either party could terminate the agreement—in December of that year. Berenson would not call it a Giorgione. Duveen insisted that it was.

In retrospect, a great many things could have happened. Since the word was out that Duveen was ill, perhaps dying, Berenson might have been approached by Wildenstein and offered a nice price to get out of his exclusive contract. Or perhaps it was Contini; in any case there would have been no shortage of alternative arrangements, given his reputation. In *Artful Partners,* Colin Simpson states that Louis Levy, Duveen's lawyer, had a secret plan to take over the firm, merge it with Parke Bernet, and hire Berenson as artistic advisor. This sounds plausible, but a search of the Duveen Archives has yielded no clues. What is known is that Levy was not part of the partnership that assumed control of Duveen Brothers in 1938. His career ended ignominiously in 1940 when he was disbarred as a lawyer. He was convicted of obtaining a $250,000 loan for a business associate of a judge in the Federal Circuit Court of Appeals at a time when one of his clients had a suit before that court. Neither is there any correspondence supporting the assertion that Berenson formed a four-man syndicate to buy the Allendale *Nativity* himself and that the plot was discovered by Duveen, who managed to outbid his rivals. Again the idea is possible, but nothing in the archive supports it. What is clear is that in June 1937, Duveen paid the huge price of $315,000 for the painting, plus a further $5,000 commission to the dealer Charles Ruck.

What is also clear is that it was very much to Duveen's advantage to keep Berenson in his self-imposed corner. The extensive discussions in Europe that summer, which Levy attended along with, presumably, all the pivotal members of the firm, had settled the future of Duveen Brothers. If Duveen could get out of his contract with Berenson by the December deadline, he would save himself $40,000, a very useful sum under the circumstances. Whether Berenson baptized or not, Duveen had the upper hand, because he knew he could sell the painting as a Giorgione. He had bought it with Mellon in mind. But by the time the formalities were concluded, it was July; Mellon died a month later, on August 27, 1937. Duveen transferred his hopes to Samuel and Rush Kress and was gratified to have them confirmed when they bought the painting a year later for the handsome price of $400,000. By then Duveen Brothers Inc. had been dissolved and a new company, the Imperial Art Corporation, had acquired the company's assets. By the end of 1938 Lowengard, Fowles, and Boggis were the new owners, and Duveen reluctantly relegated himself to the status of an employee. His former right-hand man in New York, John H. Allen, had become his boss. It was the only thing to do, but it was horribly painful. Not surprisingly, Duveen became ill almost at once. Writing to W. G. Constable of the Boston Museum of Fine Arts, Duveen thanked him for his kind inquiry. "I am glad to say that the trip [to London] was very smooth and pleasant and helped me to recover from that wretched attack of pleurisy. I still felt, on arrival, the effects of it . . ."

THE ALLENDALE *NATIVITY* was almost the last great painting Duveen would ever sell, and that it was the subject of such contention between him and his expert advisor is one of those questions that will never be completely explained. It is clear enough that it was a pretext, and a very poor one from Berenson's point of view, as Kenneth Clark observed, since it *is* a Giorgione, as posterity has confirmed. The irony of the whole story is that Duveen did not think it was a Giorgione, either, at least when he saw it at Allendale's in the autumn of 1931. He did not like it much—hard to believe—and did not think it would sell in America and believed it to be a Titian. But that was during the Depression. In 1937, with business improving and two possible collectors in mind, he changed his opinion pretty smartly. Writing to the German art historian Georg Gronau just after he bought it, Duveen said, "You will no doubt be interested to know that I personally saw the picture in a proper light only a few days ago. For many reasons I eliminate the possibility of its being a Titian and am absolutely convinced that it is by Giorgione himself . . ." As for Berenson, he chose to consider himself insulted that Duveen would reject his own gilt-edged opinion in favor of such pathetically minor authorities as Duncan Phillips, the distinguished Washington art collector. (He had a point there.) It was such an insult that he would never work for the firm again.

In the cynical world they both inhabited, "no" meant maybe. It was a kind of chess game, the aim always being to press one's tactical advantage at the expense of one's opponent. It is a safe guess that what rankled most for Berenson was being denied his usual share of the profits. His comment that he did not care how good a customer Kress was going to be—unless there was something in it for him—supports this. He surely wanted a percentage in exchange for his valuable attribution to Giorgione. In fact, he had used this tactic often enough when Duveen was pressing for a "bigger" attribution, and Duveen had always improved on the terms. But this time Berenson had miscalculated. He wrote years later, "If Duveen abetted by his lawyer had played fair by me I should have at least double the capital I now

Lord Duveen in all his finery, posing for
a Coronation portrait in 1937

have. I should be able to endow 'i Tatti' . . ." The dream—it was all that
mattered.

ONE OF DUVEEN'S LAST CEREMONIAL APPEARANCES was the
coronation of George VI and Queen Elizabeth at Westminster Abbey on
May 12, 1937. He wore a proud and hopeful smile as he was photographed

in his red ermine-trimmed cape, his gold-buttoned waistcoat with his sword, his decorations, his rhinestone-buckled shoes, and his ermine-trimmed peer's cap. There was still a shadow of youthful eagerness to please in that beaming look, although the same could not be said of his unsmiling wife, who posed for her own photograph by Dorothy Wilding, the society portraitist who attended almost everyone on such occasions. The photographer has done her best, but Elsie, with her developing chins and disappearing waistline, her dowdy cape-sleeved dress and obligatory train, has the look of a woman who knows she will not enjoy herself. This would have been a pity, because the coronation really was a great occasion, full of pageantry and symbolism, with peers and peeresses in rows looking like so many red and white carnations, as Kenneth and Jane Clark observed. The diarist Sir Henry ("Chips") Channon, who was also there, wrote, "I tried to remember the great moments of the ceremony: I think the shaft of sunlight, catching the King's golden tunic as he sat for the crowning; the kneeling Bishops drawn up like a flight of geese in deploy position; and then the loveliest moment of all, the swirl when the Peeresses put on their coronets: a thousand white gloved arms, sparkling with jewels, lifting their tiny coronets." To have become an integral part of all that was to have attained all that British society had to offer, and would have gone some distance to repair what was to follow. Duveen's term as a trustee of the National Gallery, London, was ending, and he insisted on believing he would be re-elected. Several trustees, including Evan Charteris, Lord d'Abernon, and Sir Philip Sassoon, supported him; Kenneth Clark, as director of the gallery, did not, and neither did his chairman, Samuel Courtauld.

Clark was still smarting over the business of the Sassettas. He was convinced that whenever Duveen proclaimed the worthlessness of a painting, it was because he wanted to buy it himself. This had happened with a particular Italian Renaissance work which Clark had hoped to buy for the gallery at a pittance: £3,500. Duveen talked the trustees out of it and then quietly acquired the work. Clark was determined that Duveen should not be reappointed and bent his efforts to make sure that did not happen in late December 1937 and early January 1938. Then he learned that Duveen was ill with cancer and felt remorseful. He wrote, "In Mr. Andrew Mellon's immortal phrase, 'No good deed goes unpunished.' " Clark was convinced the rejection added to Duveen's misery, but this is far from certain. Duveen had been told a year and a half earlier that there was "not the smallest chance" of his being re-elected. The word came from Charteris, one of his supporters, who said that Duveen simply had not attended enough meetings (as was possible, given his habitual six-month stay in New York). So Duveen was forewarned; and the realist in him would have wondered how useful the reappointment would be anyway, since he would soon have no more pictures to sell. Still, he had been generous with the National Gallery, as with every other large British public institution, and to think they would dispense with him so cavalierly must have hurt.

That, however, was as nothing compared to the final confrontation of his declining years. Duveen would not be Duveen without some kind of legal fight looming; as John Allen, who became president of Duveen Brothers, observed, he was "a man of battle and naturally made many enemies." As late as 1935 Duveen had relished the fight and gone into the Mellon tax case with all of his old insouciance. But as the days and months ticked away, his strength was slowly ebbing, and Carl Hamilton, that once bright young star in whom he had placed so many fond hopes, was the one probing for the weak spot, and finding it. With his usual dry assessment, Gimpel called the Hamilton debacle an "odd case," and he was right. Some vital fact is missing that would explain the incomprehensible way Duveen fell for this blatant self-promoter and allowed himself to be exploited. At one point Hamilton supposedly owed him £400,000. As it is, one is left wondering how this titan of the art market could have willingly turned over dozens of paintings he must have known Hamilton could not buy, and then allowed Hamilton to continue postponing the day of reckoning with ever-more-complicated agreements about how the hypothetical profits were to be divided. In 1922 Duveen finally took most of the paintings back, having wasted several years waiting for something to happen and paying dearly for the privilege in the form of bank loans.

Even then, relationships continued to be cordial. As a letter from Hamilton in the summer of 1927 reveals, the collector was conceding that he had been in some financial difficulty for the past seven years but, he wrote, he had just paid off the last of his debts and was trying to sell a *Madonna and Child* by Filippo Lippi. This was one of the few works he had actually bought from Duveen, and at modest prices. He was just about to sell the painting to a Detroit collector and wanted an appraisal from Duveen to the effect that it was worth $350,000. Duveen gave him the letter, but the painting still did not sell, and Hamilton's financial woes continued. Duveen was not the only dealer whose patience was tried by what Alice de Lamar called Hamilton's "folie de grandeur." Sulley soon took back his wonderful Bellini and sold it to Widener. Hamilton's blatant attempts to display his unbought wares at exhibitions were becoming suspect. When he sought to lend numbers of his paintings to an exhibition of

Old Masters being held in San Francisco, the organizer, an old friend of Duveen's, cabled him in confidence asking about the rumor that Hamilton did not own them. She liked the collector but could not afford the adverse publicity should it be known that her exhibition was being used as a de facto promotional tool. If Mary and B.B. knew what Hamilton was up to in 1920, it would not be long before everyone else did, and in fact Hamilton had shopped his wares around for years. As everywhere else, tired merchandise in the art world is sold at giveaway prices. So when Hamilton decided to sell his Piero della Francesca *Crucifixion* and his Lippi *Mother and Child* at the Anderson Galleries in the summer of 1929, he was luckier than he had any right to be. The *Crucifixion,* which he bought for $65,000, went for $375,000—in fact, Duveen bought it himself. The Lippi *Madonna and Child,* sold to Hamilton for $50,000, went for $125,000. (Leon Schinasi, a cigarette manufacturer, bought it after two minutes' bidding.)

Hamilton picked up a profit of $385,000 on these two paintings and another profit of $115,000 on the two others he bought from Duveen, for a total of $500,000. Anyone else would have been well satisfied, but not Carl Hamilton. The auctioneers announced before the sale that the *Crucifixion* was valued at $800,000 and the *Madonna and Child* at more than $650,000. Their expectations were highly unrealistic. Lawrence's *Pinkie,* which had sold in London three years before, had reached the world's record price for a painting at $377,000. The Piero had sold for just $2,000 less; so the idea that it ought to sell for more than double, given the scale of relative desirability, was so absurd as to be farcical. Hamilton, however, took the estimates literally. Word came through Stephen Pichetto, the restorer who was Hamilton's new friend, that Hamilton was deeply disappointed because the profit had not covered all his debts; he still owed the Harrimans $150,000. He had been given notice to move out of his apartment. He was looking for someone to blame.

Hamilton's mistake was clear enough in retrospect. When he looked at Duveen's astonishing success and started to think about how much money he, too, could make (and how clever he had been to get all those paintings for nothing down), he overlooked a big lesson. As Fowles said, the Duveen maxim was to sell first and buy later. Even when Duveen paid $375,000 for the Piero, he knew what he was doing, because he had a buyer in John D. Rockefeller and his wife. In following Duveen into the realms of high-stakes art dealing, Hamilton had not hedged his bets. He had "bought" first and found out just how hard it is to sell later.

As for Duveen, all the mistakes he had made in Hamilton's case are tiresomely obvious and need no reiterating here. It is enough to point out that he made one very large mistake, given Hamilton's paranoid suspicions, in buying the *Crucifixion,* even at a record price. A comment in the *New York World* underlines this: "There were those who said Sir Joseph had retained a major interest in the picture all along, and was just taking it now because he was determined not to let it go for under half a million." Those kinds of thoughts were tailor-made to arouse in Hamilton, whom Alice de Lamar only saw in his manic phase, the deepest and most profound suspicions. Word came through Pichetto that Hamilton had made inquiries to Messmore of Knoedler's and had learned all about the clever ways Duveen had of queering a sale. Hamilton just knew this had happened to him. Because of it, he had been cheated out of $2 million. Why had he ever trusted Duveen?

That was the summer of 1929. Then nothing happened. The statute of limitations on grievances was just about to run out when Hamilton decided to take action. Presumably he had reached another crisis, when bills outstanding could no longer be ignored. Or perhaps Duveen had made some allusion to the past that Hamilton chose to find offensive. Or perhaps Hamilton heard that Duveen was seriously ill and decided this was the moment to get back all the money Duveen owed him. At any rate, he filed suit in July 1935, six years later; the suit became public knowledge a year after that. Just what he claimed had happened makes sense only if one accepts the reasoning of a tortured and spiderish mind. According to Hamilton, he had spoken at length to Duveen about getting his wealthy clients to come to the Anderson Galleries and make handsome bids. Duveen assured him that he certainly would tell his clients just how valuable the paintings were and make sure everybody came. Because of these assurances, Hamilton said, he had made no effort himself to round up the usual prospects.

But then, to his horror, he found out that Duveen had taken his clients around before the sale and told them the paintings had recently been repainted and were therefore worthless. (This was a particularly low blow because, of course, Hamilton routinely did this himself.) The suit alleged that Duveen did this to make sure he had no rivals when the sale took place and he had therefore picked up the *Crucifixion* for nothing. Hamilton had other suspicions about the sale to Schinasi, supposedly at another throwaway price. He included six other paintings in the suit, though why he did so is not clear. He had further suspicions about a 1933 catalogue of Italian paintings edited by Lionello Venturi that Duveen supposedly influenced in some sinister way. He had been betrayed by Duveen. He wanted justice, to the tune of $2 million.

It must have looked like some grotesque joke to Duveen, who by now was used to swatting away disgruntled clients. There was one small problem: an eyewitness. The lady, Hannah Counihan, had been working for the Anderson Galleries as a receptionist when the sale took place and said she heard Lord Duveen loudly declaiming the worthlessness of Hamilton's paintings to anyone who would listen. The horrid truth is that, given Duveen's lifelong inability to keep his own counsel, the allegation sounds perfectly plausible. Louis Levy must have thrown up his hands in despair at such terminally brash behavior. What Fowles and Lowengard thought can only be guessed at. There was no one around to stop Duveen from making a fool of himself except Boggis, and he was too much under Duveen's thumb to tell him anything. The fact was, Duveen's claims were perfectly true, not that it helped. Both paintings had been extensively reworked, probably by Pichetto, and the Lippi has been called an "Ioni fake." That was beside the point. As Hamilton saw it, Duveen had made public statements that affected the value of his possessions, and he therefore wanted to punish him where it hurt most.

Obviously the case succeeded or failed on the testimony of Hannah Counihan. That lady had been in an accident some time before—she had been hit by a car—and was in fragile health. Since the case would not come to trial until 1938, she had to be interviewed at once, and a deposition was taken in June 1936. She said that the two Hamilton paintings had been hung in a small gallery and that Duveen came to see them a few days before the sale. He was one of a crowd of people. "We went into the exhibition room and when we got to the door he got very loud and threw his hands up and said, 'Ruined, ruined, retouched, no good, not worth anything' and of course I was naturally crushed." She could not name any of the people in the room when that remark was made, but this was not good enough for Hamilton. He was sure Duveen had transmitted his negative opinions to every one of his clients, including Bache, Mellon, Rockefeller, Widener, Helen Frick, Hearst, Mrs. Henry F. Du Pont and so on. He intended to compel them all to testify.

Duveen was examined by Hamilton's lawyers in four lengthy sessions during the spring of 1936, with Louis Levy acting as a particularly pugnacious defending counsel. Hamilton's lawyer kept asking the same questions and Levy kept objecting: "on the ground that it has been asked at least three times and answered categorically. There must be some end to this thing. There are pages of it. Don't answer that question." Levy was equally abrupt with his client, whom he would have liked to follow the discipline of simply replying "yes" or "no." The inference was that Duveen had done enough damage already, as the following exchange shows.

> MR. LEVY: He has answered the question.
> THE WITNESS: I have answered the question. Now allow me, pictures—
> MR. LEVY: There is no question before you. This is not a class being instructed. You are just to answer questions.
> THE WITNESS: All right.

Levy was right to be on guard, but even a tired Duveen who had a nurse in constant attendance was better than almost anyone else. Duveen defended himself successfully against the assertion that he had ever said anything negative about the two paintings; he had made only glowing comments to Jules Bache (who was interested in buying the *Crucifixion* up to $200,000) and to the Rockefellers, who eventually bought it at the price he paid. Duveen even had some kind words for Pichetto's amendations. He denied having discussed the sale with any other collector. There was nothing here to give any hope to Hamilton's lawyers.

Duveen managed to get in a couple of jabs of his own. Clearly, he felt he was the one who had a grievance. Hamilton had deceived him and everyone else. Hamilton said he had millions, "and never paid me the interest [on the installment purchase], even kept my pictures and said I gave them to him. I could not get them back from him," Duveen said. Sulley told him that Hamilton had also represented himself to him as being very rich and "bought" his Bellini for a hundred thousand pounds, which Sulley later discovered he had no intention of paying. Duveen heard from reliable sources that Hamilton had taken out first, second, and third liens from friends and acquaintances on the same pictures. He did not quite say the man was a con artist. A note of real exasperation creeps into his answers. "Could anybody have helped him more by giving him the letters I gave him at all times at his beck and call; telegrams, whenever he had a prospective client he would send him a wire, and I would send him a wire, and never refused to answer it. Can any man do more than that?" The idea that a man who had made half a million dollars would have the gall to find himself abused was more than he could stomach.

The trial was set to begin in mid-March of 1938 in the New York State Supreme Court. Hamilton had made an ambitious claim about all the wealthy collectors he would summon, including Bache, who had already shown his support for Duveen, and there was a reference to the late Andrew Mellon, who had given Duveen a supporting letter two years before. On March 18, 1938, the day the *New York Times* article appeared announcing the opening of the trial, Mrs. John D. Rockefeller was examined by Hamilton's attorneys. She turned out to be an even more obtuse and defensive witness than Duveen had been, absolutely refusing to give the Hamilton side any comfort. Whether that was the reason for the sudden postponement is not known, but there were several other postponements in the month that followed. It was clear to the presiding judge that a protracted struggle was likely and that neither side had a clear advantage. He urged both to seek a settlement. Hamilton was then said to be recovering from an operation, but in court. Duveen was absent with the attack of pleurisy that ruined a good part of his summer. Six months later, in the autumn of 1938, Duveen settled out of court for an undisclosed sum. He did so against the advice of his lawyers, who were certain he could have won. When the announcement came that Hamilton was dropping his suit Duveen was in London. He was told to say nothing and to refer all questions to his lawyers. For once, there was no need to underline the point. He said at one stage during his deposition, "I am afraid I cannot go any further. I am tired." Edward Fowles's wife, Jean, who did not trust Hamilton any more than her husband had, remarked, "Carl Hamilton got more out of Joe than Joe ever did him. But Joe always had a great weakness for a crook."

DUVEEN WAS HAVING HIS PORTRAIT PAINTED again by his favorite artist, Adolfo Müller-Ury, who had painted him in 1923 and 1929 and executed that particularly sympathetic study, uncharacteristic and revealing. Müller-Ury had moved to San Marino, and his biographer, Stephen Conrad, believes Duveen bought land next to the artist's studio and built a bungalow there, although he may never have used it. Müller-Ury kept Duveen in touch with developments at the Huntington and was frequently recommended by Duveen as an accomplished portraitist for socially prominent collectors and their wives. Duveen sold his house at the corner of Madison and Ninety-first in April 1938 for $1 million and then turned all his efforts to building the mansion Pope had designed for the site in Kensington Palace Gardens. According to Müller-Ury, whose last portrait of Duveen was not finished during the latter's lifetime, Duveen told him that a room was being planned for his express use, presumably whenever he visited London. Plans to build were continuing even though the architect had died, unexpectedly, a day before Mellon, on August 26, 1937. Pope had been suffering from jaundice, and then cancer of the pancreas was diagnosed. He was operated on, seemed to recover, suffered a second relapse, and died during a subsequent operation. Fortunately, his daughter said, he had completed his plans for the National Gallery in Washington the year before his death. He had also completed drawings for the Elgin Marble galleries in the British Museum and the house in Kensington Palace Gardens. When Duveen wrote his will that summer of 1938, he confidently expected that all the furniture from the New York house that was then in storage would be moving into their new London home. Work had apparently started, but just how far it had progressed is not known.

While devoutly hoping for peace, Duveen was, in his usual practical way, planning for war. Unlike in 1914, they would not be caught unawares. Anyone could see that the Germans were mobilizing. The Nazis had marched into Austria in March of 1938 and assumed control without a shot being fired. In the summer, Hitler was making threatening moves in the direction of Czechoslovakia. Prime Minister Neville Chamberlain went to Munich in late September and returned with his famous agreement in which the Czech Sudetenland was sacrificed for "Peace in our time." There were public cheers and private doubts. Meantime, Londoners began preparing for possible bombing raids, digging trenches and fitting gas masks. Appeasement, most people realized, would only buy time. Paintings were leaving Paris for the United States every week, and in Grafton Street, there was only a single work on display in the ground-floor galleries. The rest were hidden in basement vaults. As had happened during World War I, Duveen Brothers was happy to provide useful cover for counterespionage. Colonel Claude Dansey, who became deputy chief of the British Secret Intelligence Service, operated from Duveen Brothers on Grafton Street, as well as a travel agency in Highgate and other supposedly innocent establishments. In those war years, the export department of Duveen Brothers had few goods to send out of the country but plenty of useful anti-Nazi intelligence.

WHATEVER THE FUTURE HELD, Duveen had a few great pleasures left. One was building the new house in Kensington Palace Gardens; another was the opening of the new Elgin Marbles wing at the British Museum. This was set for May 1939 and the king had agreed to officiate. He was discussing the Elgin Marbles with a friend one afternoon in the autumn of

1938. It had been an arduous search to find exactly the right color of marble to serve as a background, he said; there had to be enough of a contrast, but on the other hand it must be perfectly plain and unobtrusive. The friend wrote, " 'At last,' he claimed, 'they will be seen for what they are.' To him these sculptures stood supreme above all other human work, and he dwelt on them with the reverence of love and youth. He believed that cleansed, they would come as a revelation to the world. 'Wait until you see them with the London grime removed and in their first purity. They will be luminous . . .' "

The comment is enlightening because it makes clear exactly how Duveen wanted the Elgin Marbles to look when their latest cleaning, done as a matter of course before they were put on display in the new quarters, was completed. Dr. Dyfri Williams, keeper of the Department of Greek and Roman Antiquities at the British Museum, has found no indication that Duveen paid for the cleaning himself, at least officially. But Duveen's intense interest in how they should look betrays a close involvement at the very least. As far as he was concerned, the brownish stain on the surface was just the accumulated dirt of decades. He would no more exhibit a painting with a horrible old varnish still on it than attend a royal levée in tennis shorts. Why then, he would have reasoned, should something as exquisite as the Elgin Marbles be exhibited covered with the grime of neglect and mistreatment? He wanted to see the marbles glowing "in their first purity." The artless remark reveals that he had no idea that the marbles were originally painted. He thought he was restoring a beauty that had been lost.

That was exactly the problem. He was determined they should be cleaned his way and would not give up. Lord Crawford, one of the trustees, noted in his diary that at one of the meetings, "Duveen lectured and harangued us." He continued, "I suppose he has destroyed more old masters by overcleaning than anybody else in the world, and now he told us that all old marbles should be thoroughly cleaned—so thoroughly that he would dip them into acid."

William St. Clair, author of *Lord Elgin and the Marbles,* an authority on their history and treatment, said that whatever the man in the street may have thought, it was known in Duveen's time by the specialists, the curators and archeologists, that one did not tamper with the surfaces of these ancient artifacts. This being so, the experts at the British Museum must take the blame for allowing Duveen to exert such an influence on the cleaning, particularly since, if one believes Crawford, they knew how radical it was likely to be. Daniel, a mason employed by Duveen, and his men were given free and easy access, and they went at it with a will. They scraped and scrubbed and polished. They used steel wool, carborundum, hammers and copper chisels. They were supposedly being monitored, but nothing happened. One museum official who did become alarmed passed the word along that this was to stop. The men went on working even after they had removed the stains and arrived at a pleasing patina of yellowish gold. Duveen, on a visit, said that was not white enough. He wanted the marble whiter than white.

Nowadays such methods are rightly condemned as barbaric. Opinion has shifted so far in the opposite direction that, in 2003, when a respected Italian restorer proposed cleaning Michelangelo's *David* with nothing more abrasive than swabs and a badger-hair brush, even these gentle methods raised an outcry. But, in 1938, the kinds of tools used to clean the Elgin Marbles were routinely employed. In any event, Duveen had had decades of experience sprucing up grimy sculptures, or so the reasoning would have gone. He must know what he's doing.

The more pleased Duveen became as the workmen banged and scraped away, the more worried officials at the British Museum became. Someone finally felt constrained to say something, and the search was on for a way to blame the staff and exonerate the trustees. Meantime, Duveen was warned that a storm was brewing. Ernest sent New York a telegram in November 1938 to say that John Forsdyke, the director, had discovered the unauthorized use of metal tools, which had badly scarred the marbles and obliterated some priceless details. As William St. Clair wrote, Forsdyke was as horrified by the well-skinned whiteness as everyone else but was loath to put the blame where it belonged, if only because of the vast cost of the new construction—or so one assumes. Forsdyke told Lord Macmillan, British Museum trustee who was chairman of a secret board of inquiry, "I must ask your advice upon one more point, as to how I am to try to keep Duveen out of any further statement that I may have to make. My instinct is not to keep him out but to let him appear for what he really is, the villain of the piece. But I know that I must be careful . . ." Although one cannot be sure Duveen was entirely to blame, the cables flying between New York and London at the time make that conclusion likely. After an article appeared in the *Daily Mail* on March 25, 1939, London summarized the points raised in a cable to New York, along with the comment, WE FEEL THESE REPORTS CERTAINLY CLEARED ATMOSPHERE IN YOUR FAVOUR AS YOUR NAME DOESN'T APPEAR IN CONNECTION WITH CLEANING.

Duveen was planning to set sail on the *Queen Mary* in April 1939 to attend the official opening of the Elgin Marble galleries on 1 May. Just before the Tate sculpture galleries had been opened, he and Elsie had been given a preview behind closed doors. An official, peering behind a curtain, saw them sitting on chairs in the center of the vast and serene space, marveling at its beauty. They were holding hands. Duveen would not have been human if he had not been anticipating, with almost childlike delight, all the pomp and ceremony that a royal opening would bring with it, not to mention all that delicious publicity.

Then the telegrams began to arrive. Forsdyke was firing his staff and did not know when the marbles, all seventy-five tons of stone, would be moved into position. The king would not be opening the galleries after all. In fact there would be no formal opening.

Of all the disappointments, this must have been the keenest. Fortunately Duveen did not live long enough to witness yet another snub that summer of 1939, this time coming from the other side of the Atlantic. It concerned the construction of the Founders Room in the National Gallery. Among John Russell Pope's additions to Duveen's New York town house was a magnificent oak room, decorated with handsome and very expensive paneling over which the architect and the patron had taken enormous pains. Two months after Duveen's death, in August 1939, Lady Duveen was ready to offer the paneling, which had been removed when the house was sold—presumably to install it in the new London house—to the National Gallery. It was a nice touch, the idea that the architect's design and Duveen's furbishings should carry over to the grand new building, a fitting memorial to the importance of both. David Finley, the gallery's new director, thought it was a wonderful idea but added that the trustees would have to make the decision. They did. The paneling was the wrong size, or some such. They turned the offer down.

Duveen arrived in London at the end of April and moved into his favorite suite in Claridge's. The news was very bad. The *Daily Mail* article in March repeated what other commentators were saying, that irreparable damage had been done to the marbles. This view was summarized by Robert Bryan, an art historian writing in the *Sunday Times* on May 14, 1939: "Anyone who knows the patina of Pentelic marble, who has run his hands over the knife-like edges of the Parthenon or the objects in the Acropolis Museum and felt those innumerable tiny asperities and translucencies which make that stone the most vivid material that ever rewarded a carver's skill, can see at once that the marbles in Lord Duveen's new gallery have lost this patina. The lustre and the gentleness have vanished. The lumps of stone remain, robbed of life, dead as casts." On May 22, 1939, the eminent sculptor Sir Jacob Epstein added his voice to the indignant chorus decrying the damage. It was not just the loss of lovely color, he wrote in *The Times,* but the ignorant and disfiguring scraping that had ruined these priceless objects. Naturally enough, the museum began to close ranks. The gallery was never opened to the public. The less people who came to see and criticize, the better. There were mutterings in the House of Commons.

Duveen was ill with a second bout of pleurisy. He had a temperature, was coughing and having great difficulty breathing. He was, as A. C. R. Carter wrote, "very worried over the Elgin Marbles controversy during the past two months. I hear that he took very much to heart the suggestion that the cleaning which the Marbles have lately undergone was in some way his responsibility." Of course it was not, the loyal Carter wrote, the official Duveen position. It was kind of Carter to defend him, but Duveen would have known how untrue this was. The gift that had cost him £80,000 ($68 million in today's dollars) was being thrown in his face. He found himself too ill to visit the newly completed rooms. The Duveen Gallery was hardly finished before war was imminent and the marbles were put in storage. The Duveen bequest was badly damaged by bombs; it is now restored.

In mid-spring, dawn in London arrives before five a.m., and Duveen had always been an early riser. On Thursday, May 25, 1939, he was probably awake long before they brought him his morning tea and the usual newspapers, which would have included the *Times,* the *Daily Telegraph,* and the *Financial Times.* The day before had been Empire Day. The king and queen were traveling across Canada, and the king made his yearly radio address from Winnipeg. Lord Roseberry's Blue Peter had won the Derby. Some doctor had locked a naked woman up in a chicken coop and kept her there. The Financial Bill was to get a second reading in the House of Commons. Joseph P. Kennedy, U.S. ambassador to Britain and father of the future president, had toured Scotland Yard and visited the Black Museum. Queen Mary had been in a car accident and sustained an injury to her left eye. Evacuation plans for children, should war come, were discussed in the House of Commons. Jacob Epstein had another indignant letter in the *Times* in which he took issue with somebody's assertion that blunt copper tools would not have scratched the marbles because marble was harder than copper. Again, there was no mention of Duveen's role, but Duveen knew there would be questions in the House of Commons the next day. The issue of how badly the marbles had been damaged was bound to be asked. This would have been a subject Duveen did not relish. He was drinking his morning tea at eight o'clock when he suffered a cerebral hemorrhage. This, along with "pleurisy with effusion and arteriosclerosis," was listed on the death certificate. Elsie, Dolly, and Bryan were at his bedside.

There were articles in national and international papers and numerous tributes from friends and colleagues. One of the best, however, had come four years before. After one of Duveen's hospital stays, B.B. told Fowles to give Duveen his love and say that his continued health and happiness were of real concern to his friend. "In any case I regard him as one of the most vital, life-enhancing energies I have ever approached . . ." Given the equivocal nature of their relationship, it was a real compliment. Even those who did not like him much knew that some vital force had swept out of their lives. No one remarked on the peculiar aptness of his departure. It is hard not to think he timed his exit as perfectly as he had done his entrance into that great arena in which he played such a pivotal role. For the world, a war was about to begin, but after so many campaigns fought and won, for Duveen, the long chase was over.

One afternoon in late September 1938, Duveen was walking on the grounds of his temporary home, Sheffield Park, with a friend. This splendid country house in Uckfield, Sussex, which Duveen was renting, had replaced his estate in Hawkhurst, Kent, which he had sold a few years after buying it, possibly because it was too far from London. Or perhaps he needed the money for the Kensington Palace Gardens project. In any event he saw no cause to economize upon his habitual style of living. Sheffield Park, with its eighteenth-century façade remodeled in the fashionable Gothic style by James Wyatt, its crenellated lodge, and its model home farm, was if anything even grander than the mansion he had left behind.

But its real prize was its gardens, a hundred acres of rolling meadow and woodland that already included a strategically placed manmade lake, called the "Great Water." When John Baker Holroyd, first Earl of Sheffield, inherited the estate, he wisely put himself into the hands of the great landscape architects Capability Brown and Humphry Repton. One lake made a handsome effect. The owner was advised to add three more, ascending the gentle northwest slopes of the valley the house overlooked. Paths were cleared through the Sheffield Woods. Tasteful clumps and groves of trees were scattered about in the typical Capability Brown fashion. Picturesque vistas appeared, along with statues, strategically placed benches, stone bridges, and waterfalls. Great masses of plantings: rhododendron, azaleas, silver deodars, golden retinospora, golden-leaved weigela, ferns, roses, and all manner of hydrangea, gentians, lilies, daffodils and spring flowering bulbs were employed in their hundreds and thousands. What was a muddle had, with so many years of exquisite dedication, been transformed into a paradise of color, light, and floating movement. For the moment at least, it all belonged to Duveen. (The gardens are now owned by the National Trust.)

Their walk was a leisurely one and they paused frequently to admire what Virginia Woolf, in "Reflections at Sheffield Place," called the "shake and break" of reflected leaves and branches on the surface of the lake in their autumn bronzes and golds. The friend wrote, "The feelings stirred in him were too strong for silence and he talked of much beauty seen and of dreams still to be realized. 'I have had a wonderful life,' he said." Indeed he had.

Notes

Abbreviations

ART   *Art Treasures and Intrigue,* James Henry Duveen, 1935

BBB   *Being Bernard Berenson,* Meryle Secrest, 1979

BEH   *Duveen,* S. N. Behrman, 1972

DA   Duveen Brothers Records, 1876–1981, Getty Research Institute for the History of Art and the Humanities; Special Collections and Visual Resources

ECON   *The Economics of Taste,* Gerald Reitlinger, 1961

FOW   *Memories of Duveen Brothers,* Edward Fowles, 1976

GIM   *Diary of an Art Dealer,* René Gimpel, 1966

RISE   *The Rise of the House of Duveen,* James Henry Duveen, 1957

Chapter One / THE CHASE

3 "She hunted high and low . . .": *The English as Collectors,* Frank Herrmann, p. 334.

5 "The tradition is . . .": ART, p. 16.

6 a Dutch chronicler: Thijs Rinsema, in the *Meppeler Courant,* May 3, 2000.
   a future in manufacturing: *Let Me Tell You,* A. C. R. Carter, p. 20.

8 This picturesque version: John B. Stanchfield, letter, *New York Times,* January 23, 1919.

9 ". . . show me the stock.": RISE, p. 16.

10 "with a fine collection . . .": RISE, p. 22.
   the best-paid employee: RISE, p. 23.
   he set himself up in partnership: RISE, p. 27.

11 "Look here, Barney . . .": RISE, p. 29.
   "From then onwards . . .": RISE, p. 29.

12 "It was the first time . . .": RISE, p. 30.

12 "Stop! I won't sell . . .": RISE, p. 31.
   "loved his stock better . . .": RISE, p. 31.

13 "It was a very clear day . . .": RISE, p. 34.
   RETURN IMMEDIATELY . . .: RISE, p. 40.
   "Joel Duveen . . . chartered . . .": RISE, p. 41

14 A hawthorn vase: RISE, p. 41.
   "the reflection of the azure sky . . .": RISE, p. 42.
   "There in front of him": RISE, p. 42.
   two thousand gulden: RISE, p. 43.

15 a derisory sum: RISE, p. 173.

16 ". . . painted old shays . . .": RISE, p. 174.
   "my usual fever . . .": RISE, p. 174.

17 ". . . nevertheless stunned . . .": RISE, p. 177.
   "In less than two hours . . .": RISE, p. 178.

18 ". . . not a watch . . .": *Let Me Tell You,* A. C. R. Carter, p. 19.
   They were married: On the wedding certificate, Joel Joseph Duveen was described as
   a hide, skin, bone, and wool merchant, and Rosetta's father was described as a pawn-
   broker.

Chapter Two / BOND STREET

19 ". . . a clever mechanical movement . . .": RISE, p. 46.

23 She was too delicate: RISE, p. 84.
   To go to Oxford: undated memoir.
   their doting father: RISE, p. 80.
   his father's tapestries: *Thirty Years of British Art,* Sir Joseph Duveen, p. 1.

25 prepared to leave: RISE, p. 66.
   "knew how to get . . .": RISE, p. 67.
   "our beautiful stock . . .": RISE, p. 67.
   ". . . on the cheap . . .": RISE, p. 67.

27 a matter of months: RISE, p. 71.
   almost three hundred cases: Edward Fowles, oral history, *Archives of American Art,*
   p. 2.

28 "his Oriental porcelain . . .": RISE, p. 73.
   ". . . finest and rarest . . .": RISE, p. 73.
   "crazy" prices: RISE, p. 74.

29 ". . . sarcastically sorry . . .": RISE, p. 74.
   "Of course I denied . . .": RISE, p. 75.
   ". . . a very bad storm . . .": RISE, p. 75.
   ". . . the finest advertisement . . .": RISE, p. 77.

30 "He . . . greatly admired . . .": RISE, p. 88.
   ". . . a rush at the woodwork . . .": RISE, p. 89.

31 ". . . exquisite taste": RISE, p. 90.
   "the Duveen Lighthouse": FOW, p. 3.
   ". . . so much wealth!": RISE, p. 90.

"... bring all the money ...": RISE, p. 101.

32 Both men were in Holland: FOW, p. 3.
"I shall never forget ...": RISE, p. 97.

35 "and you are not going to make me ...": RISE, p. 103.
a profit of £500,000: RISE, p. 191.
"owned a housing estate ...": FOW, p. 6.

36 Duveen tore it down: FOW, p. 6.
"... probably a Rothschild ...": Edward Fowles, oral history, *Archives of American Art.*

40 laughing so hard: FOW, pp. 6–7.

Chapter Three / LADY LOUISA MANNERS

41 "... what is on the market": FOW, p. 44.
how to build packing cases: *Let Me Tell You,* A. C. R. Carter, p. 19.
in an account he wrote: undated, Huntington papers, DA.

42 "... you will never get them ...": undated account, Huntington papers, DA.

43 owned four-fifths of the land: *The Decline and Fall of the British Aristocracy,* David Cannadine, p. 9.
"... private art collections ...": *The Decline and Fall of the British Aristocracy,* David Cannadine, p. 10.
a noble inheritance: ECON, p. 175.
a calamitous low: *The Decline and Fall of the British Aristocracy,* David Cannadine, p. 91.

44 record-breaking sum: *The Decline and Fall of the British Aristocracy,* David Cannadine, p. 113.
"... beyond all precedent ...": ECON, p. 179.

45 "... afraid even to patrol": *Mr. Clemens and Mark Twain,* Justin Kaplan, p. 19.
"Chelsea porcelains ...": *Morgan,* Jean Strouse, p. 430.
bought by Mrs. Gardner: *Morgan,* Jean Strouse, p. 413.
the price Morgan paid: *Morgan,* Jean Strouse, pp. 413–4.

46 "... channel crossings": FOW, p. 44.

47 determined to go on traveling: RISE, p. 125.
"I am saved!": RISE, p. 126.
"... after two sleepless nights ...": RISE, p. 127.

48 summarily dismissed: FOW, p. 8.
"and thus ended ...": FOW, p. 5.
"... in a good enough humor ...": FOW, p. 8.
a box on the ears: FOW, pp. 5–6.

49 "Uncle Henry smiled ...": *Morgan,* Jean Strouse, p. 382.
"This lucky speculation ...": FOW, p. 12.

51 along with their provenances: Edith Standen, oral history, National Gallery of Art Archives.

52 "We must look and look ...": BBB, p. 111.
Information about the Corcoran copy of Antonio Canova's Hope Venus is drawn

from the essay written by Douglas Lewis in connection with the fiftieth anniversary of the installation of the Clark Collection at the Corcoran Gallery of Art in Washington, D.C., April 26–July 16, 1978.

52 the look of Buckingham Palace: FOW, p. 19.
53 claimed a half-share: FOW, p. 21.
    busier than ever: FOW, pp. 19–23.
54 "The artist worked . . .": *The Taste of Angels,* Francis Henry Taylor, p. ix.
    the "archimandrite": ECON, p. 198.
    "You don't understand . . .": BBB, p. 141.
55 ". . . not of any great value": BBB, p. 139.
56 ". . . its triumphant climax": *Let Me Tell You,* A. C. R. Carter, p. 18.
57 the auction record: ECON, p. 190.
    ". . . a new buyer for the vase": *Let Me Tell You,* A.C.R. Carter, p. 27.

Chapter Four / THE RAJAH'S PEARL

59 "She just said yes and no": Sir John Foster interview by Roger Jenkins.
60 "Yes, it is nice . . .": *Another Part of the Wood,* Kenneth Clark, p. 246.
    how emotionally insecure: FOW, p. 45.
    "swallowed hard": FOW, p. 13.
    ". . . the handsome Duveen couple . . .": FOW, p. 13.
    in bed by 11 p.m.: FOW, p. 201.
61 The chauffeur was fined: *New York Times,* July 18, 1915.
    fine Havana cigars: FOW, p. 201.
    a picnic lunch: FOW, p. 192.
    "an extraordinary character . . .": *Manchester Guardian,* May 26, 1939.
62 claim to be completely helpless: BEH, p. 41.
    "We lived on the corner . . .": Dolly Burns interview with Roger Jenkins.
63 remodel the premises: FOW, pp. 24–5.
64 the dilapidations were removed: FOW, p. 36.
65 "couches, armchairs, screens . . .": *The Flaneur,* Edmund White, pp. 116–7.
    ablaze with light: FOW, p. 43.
    "That was the way . . .": *Civilisation,* Kenneth Clark, p. 332.
    ". . . works of great splendour": *Civilisation,* Kenneth Clark, p. 332.
66 "far the greatest painter . . .": *Civilisation,* Kenneth Clark, p. 284.
    "If I owned . . .": *Evening Standard,* May 25, 1939.
67 "meshugge": *The Joys of Yiddish,* Leo Rosten, p. 237.
    " 'Out of the house!' . . .": Sir John Foster interview with Roger Jenkins.
68 He was still head: ART, pp. 155–156.
71 The spectacular $4.2 million sale: Gimpel and Wildenstein held a quarter interest plus further commissions on sales.
72 ". . . this great coup": RISE, p. 213.
    act as guarantor for loans: established during testimony for the lawsuit of *Duveen v. Duveen,* April 18, 1910.
    ". . . still the master-brain": RISE, p. 215.
    ". . . pictures included!": RISE, p. 233.

"... our savings bank": account written by Duveen, Huntington papers, DA.

"French commentators agreed ...": *Let Me Tell You,* A. C. R. Carter, p. 31.

73 "... without hesitation": RISE, p. 289.

a new agreement was hammered out: testimony during the lawsuit *Duveen v. Duveen,* April 18, 1910, p. 40, Clark Institute.

74 not expected to show their noses: FOW, p. 39.

"was deeply grieved ...": FOW, p. 39.

75 "... keen eye": RISE, p. 253.

"became increasingly perturbed ...": RISE, p. 253.

76 a gullible American: RISE, p. 251.

never ran out of money: Behrman, manuscript, II-16, National Gallery of Art Archives.

paralyzed with indecision: RISE, p. 254.

77 She accepted: on June 28, 1906. On June 29, the *New York Times* reported that the final price was £250,000, or $1,250,000.

traveling through Europe: RISE, p. 255.

78 no desire to compete: *Duveen v. Duveen,* April 18, 1910, p. 3, Clark Institute.

79 "I think my father ...": *Duveen v. Duveen,* April 18, 1910, p. 61, Clark Institute.

changing his name: On July 9, 1908.

80 Rodolphe Kann guest book: DA.

His father was knighted: on June 26, 1908.

"It was depressing ...": FOW, p. 44.

became so agitated: RISE, p. 292.

bribed him handsomely: RISE, p. 292.

"... deeply attached to his father": FOW, p. 45.

Chapter Five / THE SOUND OF A SELL

82 As Daniel Wildenstein relates: in *Marchands d'Art,* pp. 12–13.

83 "If I had never known ...": *Marchands d'Art,* Daniel Wildenstein, p. 71.

84 "I wish you would not ...": *Duveen v. Duveen,* April 18, 1910, p. 74, Clark Institute.

85 at the lowest possible price: letter, July 27, 1909, DA.

86 a profit of 75 percent: July 27, 1909, DA.

The Boucher panels: bought in 1916.

87 "... Do you fancy ...": December 13, 1897, quoted in *The Letters of Bernard Berenson and Isabella Stewart Gardner,* p. 110.

90 "Bernhard went to Duveens ...": *Mary Berenson: A Self-Portrait from Her Diaries and Letters,* p. 147.

"motor-trips, house-furnishings ...": *Mary Berenson: A Self-Portrait from Her Diaries and Letters,* p. 186.

"the grandest surviving ...": *The Letters of Bernard Berenson and Isabella Stewart Gardner,* p. 403.

91 "the most vigorous ...": *The Letters of Bernard Berenson and Isabella Stewart Gardner,* p. 404.

positively hideous: *Bernard Berenson: The Making of a Legend,* Ernest Samuels, p. 52.

for £1,500: RISE, p. 110.

the collection was on loan: FOW, p. 11.

92　"I had heard of . . ." RISE, p. 259.

93　Duveen Brothers paid $3 million: *New York Times,* February 9, 1915.
　　"A man always has two reasons . . .": *Morgan,* Jean Strouse, p. xiii.
　　It was in his library: *Morgan,* Jean Strouse, p. 486.

95　embarrassing personal search: RISE, p. 96.

96　perfectly aboveboard: *Morgan,* Jean Strouse, p. 609.
　　"worked diligently . . . and sent . . .": RISE, p. 265–266.

97　". . . show his face . . .": FOW, p. 59.
　　a false exhaust pipe: FOW, p. 51.

98　entered the country duty-free: *New York Times,* May 24, 1911.
　　The civil suit was settled: *New York Times,* April 11, 1911.

Chapter Six / LIVING WITH CACHET

99　advanced the $75,000 bail: Behrman manuscript, II-18, National Gallery of Art Archives.
　　Let Uncle Henry off: *New York Times,* May 25, 1911.

100　can it really be their fault?: *New York Times,* May 25, 1911.

102　"It was all stage-managed . . .": interview with author.
　　". . . done the circuit several times": *Another Part of the Wood,* Kenneth Clark, p. 245.
　　". . . a sort of bribe . . .": *Another Part of the Wood,* Kenneth Clark, p. 244.

103　missed the prize: Paul Sachs oral history, Columbia University, pp. 70–71.
　　New York auction: on April 5, 1910.
　　"Olympian gentlemen . . .": *The Elegant Auctioneers,* Wesley Towner, p. 234.

104　Uncle Henry, representing Duveen: *The Elegant Auctioneers,* Wesley Towner, p. 237.
　　"Not a feather stirred . . .": *The Elegant Auctioneers,* Wesley Towner, pp. 237–238.
　　"Duveen, simulating despair . . .": *The Elegant Auctioneers,* Wesley Towner, pp. 239–240.

105　"I found myself confronted . . .": *Bernard Berenson: The Making of a Legend,* Ernest Samuels, p. 216.
　　price . . . set new records: ECON, p. 202.
　　"the most lavish . . .": ECON, p. 201.

106　Duveen bought that artist's portrait: *New York Times,* February 7, 1914.
　　". . . the bigness of it all": Edward Fowles oral history, Archives of American Art, p. 18.

108　Duveen commandeered: FOW, p. 47.
　　even Duveen was satisfied: FOW, p. 47. The Petit Trianon Duveen built is still there, along with the red and white marble courtyard, but the annex that fronted onto the rue St.-Honoré has vanished.
　　"the Great Ottokahn": *Families of Fortune,* Alexis Gregory, p. 94.
　　This painting by Patinir looks like *St. Jerome in a Rocky Landscape,* which Duveen bought from Rodolphe Kann and must have lent to the Kahns. It was bought by Mrs. Henry Oppenheimer of London in 1916 and is now at the National Gallery in London. The photograph is reproduced in *Families of Fortune,* Alexis Gregory, p. 134.
　　"a perfect fairy-tale . . .": Berenson to Louis Duveen, May 1, 1913, DA.
　　repaint had to come off: May 7, 1939, DA.

110 only £5,000 a year to spend: *New York Times,* February 8, 1914.

"That the Desborough collection . . .": *New York Times,* February 7, 1914.

111 "how few illustrated books . . .": interview with author.

114 "Do I not *desire* . . .": April 22, 1913, DA.

finished by an assistant: FOW, p. 69.

116 "one of the most perfect . . .": *Rembrandt and the Italian Renaissance,* Kenneth Clark, p. 124.

"an attribution to either . . .": *The Paintings of Titian,* vol. 2, Harold E. Wethey, p. 186.

"Visitors to the Metropolitan . . .": *The Benjamin Altman Bequest,* Francis Haskell, Metropolitan Museum *Journal,* vol. 3, 1970.

117 in one of his letters: FOW, p. 77.

"I don't think . . .": RISE, p. 283.

"MANY THANKS . . .": June 12, 1913, *The Benjamin Altman Bequest,* Francis Haskell, Metropolitan Museum *Journal,* vol. 3, 1970.

118 According to a history: *Agnew's, 1817–1967,* pp. 37–38.

"Contemporary British artists . . .": Malcolm Warner in *Great British Paintings from American Collections,* p. 8.

119 H.E.H. once related: *Merchants of Art,* Germain Seligman, p. 138.

120 spent over $21 million: *British Paintings at the Huntington,* Robyn Asleson and Shelley M. Bennett, p. 2.

she bought several other paintings: RISE, p. 236.

122 "Sometimes she would . . .": FOW, p. 68.

"The few [objects] . . .": letter, July 31, 1907, DA.

buying three Gainsboroughs: FOW, p. 70.

123 arrangements for their wedding: Behrman manuscript, IV-3.

" 'Wait a minute . . .' ": FOW, p. 71.

Chapter Seven / SPY MANIA

124 a thousand reasons: letter, November 10, 1922, DA.

just a small collector: letter, January 9, 1923, DA.

126 doing the bidding himself: *Selected Paintings at the Norton Simon Museum,* Frank Herrmann, p. 13.

sit back, rub his cheek: *Aux Ecoutes,* Paris, May 26, 1939.

127 it would clean up beautifully: letter, London to New York, April 9, 1926, DA.

what Gulbenkian wanted: April 29, 1926, DA.

129 Bache turned it down: correspondence, New York to Paris, January 8, date smudged, probably 1930, DA.

not worth their time: October 7, 1922, DA.

rather "podgy" face: September 10, 1936, DA.

disqualified the male sitter: November 27, 1936, DA.

the picture was very fine: May 5, 1927, DA.

130 indelicately handled: June 19, 1923, DA.

found the painting too dark: June 16, 1936, DA.

130 probably by Reynolds: September 16, 1929, DA.

"no feeling or power": February 26, 1930, DA.

". . . is by Holbein": October 2, 1918, DA.

131 "mending without repainting": *Self and Partners,* C. J. Holmes, p. 329.

The painting was bought: In the summer of 1928. It is now at the Detroit Institute of Arts.

132 "the finest modern portrait . . .": *Great British Paintings from American Collections,* p. 93.

133 He had seen her: on October 7, 1922, DA.

134 he was not a buyer: February 9, 1928, DA.

determined to have her: June 18, 1930, DA.

". . . you don't know Joe": RISE, p. 214.

135 "stabbing the air . . .": *New York Times,* February 20, 1929.

a perfect genius: letter, June 12, 1916, DA.

"devotion to the superficial . . ." Stephen Holden, *New York Times,* May 22, 2002.

136 "The mere pressure . . .": *Self and Partners,* C. J. Holmes, p. 226.

". . . a couple of drinks": *Another Part of the Wood,* Kenneth Clark.

". . . cherubs are homosexual": BEH, p. 10.

137 "So she went on buying . . .": Sir John Foster, interview with Roger Jenkins.

"They are right . . .": GIM, p. 142.

"He travelled like royalty . . .": *Brat Farrar,* Josephine Tey, p. 106.

he played the fool: *Another Part of the Wood,* Kenneth Clark, p. 227.

"More like gin": *Another Part of the Wood,* Kenneth Clark, p. 144.

138 "He got up . . .": *Mary Berenson, A Self-Portrait from her Diaries and Letters,* pp. 248–249.

139 Regular payments: Behrman manuscript, V-13.

Such largesse: BEH, p. 244.

140 "There is no ground . . .": London *Times,* July 9, 1914.

"Daddy was sure . . .": Dolly Burns, interview with Roger Jenkins.

a further $65,000: FOW, p. 82.

141 "I was just leaving . . .": FOW, p. 84.

left by the last train: FOW, p. 85.

142 "Mother and I and a maid . . .": Dolly Burns, interview with Roger Jenkins.

lined up row on row: *Life in the French Country House,* Mark Girouard, p. 116.

143 "It took three days . . .": *Henry Edwards Huntington,* James Thorpe, pp. 338–339.

exceedingly grateful to Duveen: FOW, p. 87.

The announcement was made: *New York Times,* July 22, 1914.

144 "After the czar mobilized . . .": *The House of Morgan,* Ron Chernow, pp. 183–184.

"A dual myth . . .": *The House of Morgan,* Ron Chernow, p. 192.

arrested on suspicion: *Bernard Berenson: The Making of a Legend,* Ernest Samuels, p. 195.

145 Could muster only ten men: a United States Secret Service Treasury Department report on counterespionage 1915–1918, written by an anonymous agent in 1938.

146 He did not appear to welcome: U.S. Secret Service Treasury Department report, p. 27.

Chapter Eight / THE FAY CASE

147 if it stepped off the wall: interview with author.
said he never would: GIM, p. 118.

150 willing to sell it to him at cost: GIM, pp. 43–44. The *New York Times* announced the
sale on February 21, 1915.

151 sent the paneling back: FOW, p. 93.

153 Frick had been taught a lesson: Behrman manuscript, I-41-2, National Gallery of Art
Archives.
acquired from Thomas Agnew: *New York Times,* February 16, 1916.
A Pair of Spectacles: Behrman manuscript, I-39, National Gallery of Art Archives.

154 $500 million worth of war contracts: *New York Times,* July 5, 1915.
"My dear Mr. Lamont . . .": *The House of Morgan,* Ron Chernow, p. 192.
a huge explosion: *New York Times,* July 4, 1915.

155 The fight had only lasted: *New York Times,* July 4, 1915.

156 He wanted to go downstairs: *New York Times,* July 7, 1915.
threw himself to his death: *New York Times,* July 7, 1915.
"The attempted assassination . . .": *New York Times,* July 4, 1915.
Both boats were searched: *New York Times,* July 8, 1915.
bombs in their cargo: *New York Times,* July 8, 1915.
safely on their way: *New York Times,* July 7, 1915.

157 another assassination attempt: *New York Times,* October 26, 1915.
There was a queue: *Artful Partners,* Colin Simpson, p. 160.
The hapless ship: United States Secret Service Treasury Department report on coun-
terespionage 1915–1918, written by an anonymous agent in 1938.

158 "It looks like twenty . . .": *New York Times,* October 26, 1915.
any nefarious intent: *New York Times,* October 27, 1915.
actually a British or French agent: *New York Times,* November 10, 1915.

159 a well-planned escape: *New York Times,* August 20, 1916.
"In less than no time . . .": FOW, p. 104.

160 rejected her arguments: *New York Times,* May 6, 1916.
His complaint made the front page: *New York Times,* May 7, 1915.

161 The *Lusitania* was carrying: *The International Law of Art,* Barnett Hollander, pp.
232–233.

164 checking up on the story: BEH, p. 156.
A sketch, signed by Humphry: *The International Law of Art,* Barnett Hollander,
p. 195.

165 a dreadfully bad painter: GIM, p. 116.
Duveens paid $1.5 million: *New York Times,* May 2, 1916; FOW, pp. 91–92.

166 "These people have . . .": *Thirty Years of British Art,* Sir Joseph Duveen, p. 31.
refused to buy a Cézanne: *The Tate, a History,* Frances Spaulding, p. 46.

167 presented Gauguin's *Faa Iheihe: The Tate, a History,* Frances Spaulding, p. 45.
Green marble doorways: *The Tate, a History,* Frances Spaulding, pp. 49–50.
three more paintings: *The Tate, a History,* Frances Spaulding, p. 48.

167 in 1920 its net profits: *New York Times,* February 1, 1929.
168 "all lazy and not workers": FOW, p. 90.
　　　Ernest was very astute: FOW, p. 91.
　　　discharged two years later: on file in the Public Records Office.
　　　Jack sold it in Amsterdam: RISE, pp. 121–123.
　　　After starting in business: *Duveen v. Duveen,* April 18, 1910, pp 7–8, Clark Institute.
　　　"the vast majority . . .": FOW, p. 106.
　　　He fell, unconscious: *New York Times,* August 9, 1916.
　　　Sided against him: letter to Lockett Agnew, July 10, 1917, DA.
169 "I have told him . . .": letter to Joseph Duveen, July 18, 1917, DA.
　　　region of the lower back: FOW, p. 111.
　　　"He did this . . .": FOW, p. 111.
　　　Henry had a stroke: *Artful Partners,* Colin Simpson, p. 159.
　　　Henry's death: January 15, 1919.
171 to congratulate him: letter, August 24, 1919, DA.

Chapter Nine / THE CHASE CONTINUES

173 "Ernest, the youngest . . .": *Mary Berenson, a Self-Portrait from Her Diaries and Letters,* p. 186.
174 "crazy" about them: letter, April 12, 1921, DA.
175 "If Wildenstein hears . . .": April 22, 1921, DA.
　　　"We talked politely . . .": *Mary Berenson, a Self-Portrait from Her Diaries and Letters,* p. 186.
176 "Privately, however . . .": March 29, 1927, DA.
　　　take up thirty pages: FOW, p. 116.
177 for more than $350,000: ECON, p. 195.
178 "Why should I trouble . . .": *British Paintings in the Huntington,* Robyn Asleson and Shelley M. Bennett, p. 408.
179 six of the two dozen gardeners: *America's National Gallery of Art,* Philip Kopper, pp. 197–198.
　　　Widener paid considerably more: *The Elegant Auctioneers,* Wesley Towner, p. 319.
　　　a unique yellow square vase: letter, January 24, 1916, DA.
180 hinting there were more: letter to Joseph Duveen, January 13, 1911, DA.
　　　a humble-pie letter: dated April 1, 1919, DA.
　　　In the meantime: letter, April 4, 1919, DA.
181 he was about to sail: April 19, 1919, DA.
　　　"great amateur": letter, January 19, 1918.
　　　". . . a great weakness for a crook": to author, January 6, 1977.
182 "he invented the name . . .": to author.
183 intended to become a missionary: *Berenson and the Connoisseurship of Italian Painting,* David Alan Brown, p. 22.
　　　a worthless religious scene: FOW, p. 127.
184 The meeting went smoothly: FOW, p. 102.
　　　but he never did: *Hamilton v. Duveen,* 1936–1938, DA.

"something exhilarating . . ." *Bernard Berenson: The Making of a Legend,* Ernest Samuels, p. 264.

distinct preference for handsome young men: *Bernard Berenson: The Making of a Legend,* Ernest Samuels, p. 264.

185 ". . . the eternal manic phase": letter to David Alan Brown, undated, c. 1979.

"refused categorically . . .": *Forty Years with Berenson,* Nicky Mariano, p. 51.

186 B.B. meekly dictated: FOW, pp. 152–153.

Lucrezia was "dreadful": Sir Joseph Duveen, letter, January 10, 1923, DA.

Never traveled without a ruler: FOW, p. 150.

The Monet disappeared: It is now at the Boston Museum of Fine Arts (FOW, pp. 144–145). The Lehman Collection, further embellished by Philip Lehman's son Robert, is now at the Metropolitan Museum of Art.

187 "the Atlantic cable . . .": *The Big Spenders,* Lucius Beebe, p. 124.

he bought "fabulously": interview with author, 1976.

" 'Of course he hasn't . . .' ": *Another Part of the Wood,* Kenneth Clark, p. 227.

189 is perfectly possible: *New York Times,* January 19, 1927.

No clue in the newspaper: *New York Times,* November 12, 1921.

190 He acquired *Portrait of a Man: New York Times,* November 12, 1921.

Chapter Ten / THE BLUE BOY

191 "Who's the boy . . .": BEH, pp. 146–147.

192 "You know that Gainsborough . . .": *The Letters of Bernard Berenson and Isabella Stewart Gardner,* p. 51.

his father had tried to buy it: *New York Times,* October 19, 1921.

"It's harder to sell . . .": GIM, p. 9

in the Scouts Book: DA.

he had been negotiating: March 26, 1919, DA.

"He didn't realize . . .": Edward Fowles oral history, Archives of American Art.

193 "That was a sound . . .": Edward Fowles oral history, Archives of American Art.

"Duveen had a large desk . . .": Edward Fowles oral history, Archives of American Art.

a letter arrived: on October 7, 1921, DA.

refutes this argument: *Thomas Gainsborough,* William B. Boulton, p. 226.

194 a direct parallel: *British Paintings at the Huntington,* Robyn Asleson and Shelley M. Bennett, p. 108.

195 an intricate blending: *British Paintings at the Huntington,* Robyn Asleson and Shelley M. Bennett, p. 108.

"All those odd scratches . . .": *The Penguin Dictionary of Art and Artists,* Peter and Linda Murray, p. 153.

197 the result was a revelation: Duveen to H. E. Huntington, December 6, 1921, DA.

"In its renewed youth . . .": *New York Times,* January 4, 1922.

not to make it public: on October 21, 1921, DA.

198 "in these hard times . . .": *New York Times,* January 5, 1922.

removing their hats: report to Sir Joseph Duveen, January 3, 1922, DA.

"Au revoir, C.H.": *New York Times,* January 26, 1922.

198 "a worthy setting . . .": *New York Times,* February 21, 1922.

200 there were no takers: in April, 1932.

201 "Red Boy's" value: FOW, p. 150.

The spring of 1783: on March 22.

203 "I become every day . . .": letter, November 16, 1793.

204 most ungentlemanly: FOW, p. 72.

a story in itself: told in *Artful Partners,* Colin Simpson.

205 ". . . a crowd collected": *New York Times,* November 25, 1926.

206 the highest price ever paid: *New York Times,* November 25, 1926.

Duveen Brothers had saved the day: London to New York, November 25, 1926, DA.

Ernest Duveen was surprised: London to New York, November 25, 1926, DA.

"try to upset . . .": letter, March 29, 1927, DA.

CONSIDER YOUR INTERFERENCE . . .: April 7, 1927, DA.

Chapter Eleven / THE DEMOTTE AFFAIR

207 running up and down Piccadilly: *Le Cousin Pons,* June 1923.

208 But the word was out: in January 1923.

sued for slander: *New York Times,* May 17, 1923.

"France, the richest . . .": *Medieval Art in America,* Elizabeth Bradford Smith, Palmer Museum of Art, Pennsylvania State University, p. 138.

209 "a Belgian dealer": FOW, p. 35.

"Romeuf proved . . .": FOW, p. 35.

Romeuf is sometimes described: *Artful Partners,* Colin Simpson, p. 142.

geometric doodles: telegram dated February 3, 1916, DA.

"We cannot make out . . .": letter, March 3, 1916, DA.

210 monumental waste of time: letter, April 21, 1916, DA.

the saddle of her horse: *New York Times,* May 17, 1923.

willing to spend $500,000: *New York Times,* May 17, 1923.

sheer generosity: *Journal d'un collectionneur,* René Gimpel, p. 80.

tightening controls: *Medieval Art in America,* Elizabeth Bradford Smith, Palmer Museum of Art, Pennvylvania State University, p. 136.

211 "no better than a runner": report dated February 14, 1922, DA.

it might be by a Belgian: report, March 9, 1922, DA.

wanted to claim the reward: letter dated May 22, 1923, DA.

212 a model for the Demotte Virgin: letter, May 25, 1923, DA.

Some dead statues: *Le Matin,* May 22, 1923.

B.B. had failed to mention: letter, July 12, 1914, *The Letters of Bernard Berenson and Isabella Stewart Gardner,* pp. 524–525.

In the decades since: *Le Temps,* May 23, 1923.

"dressed the wounds": *Le Matin,* May 23, 1923.

213 This explanation was disputed: *Le Matin,* May 25, 1923.

214 nothing to do with Vigouroux: letter, May 25, 1923, DA.

"some personage of mythology . . .": *New York Times,* June 8, 1923.

215 now in perfect condition: *New York Times,* May 29, 1923.

Then a new witness: *Le Matin,* May 31, 1923.

had been replaced: *Le Matin,* June 3, 1923.

he had sold the statue: *Le Matin,* June 3, 1923.

the American client: *New York Times,* June 22, 1923.

He had to rent studios: *Le Matin,* June 5, 1923.

repeatedly warned the Louvre: *La Presse,* June 3, 1923.

216 "Our patron must . . .": *New York Times,* June 21, 1923.

"M. de Stoecklin . . .": *New York Times,* June 29, 1923.

"I am rather worried . . .": *New York Times,* July 10, 1923.

without regaining consciousness: *New York Times,* July 10, 1923.

217 "I was refused admittance . . .": *New York Times,* July 10, 1923.

"because I don't owe you anything . . .": *New York Times,* July 11, 1923.

". . . truth will be discovered": *New York Times,* July 10, 1923.

belonging to Gilbert Romeuf: *Artful Partners,* Colin Simpson, p. 189.

denied access: A. Pivin to author, July 18, 2002.

218 "I know every . . .": *New York Times,* May 31, 1923.

". . . unscrupulous dealers . . .": *New York Times,* June 2, 1923.

had pocketed money: *New York Times,* June 6, 1923.

had defrauded him: *New York Times,* June 6, 1923.

219 "The growth of museums . . .": *New York Times,* June 6, 1923.

". . . under false pretenses": *New York Times,* June 26, 1923.

220 "You'd better get . . .": Paul Sachs oral history, Columbia University, p. 2318, part IV.

"You are to say . . .": letter, June 6, 1923, DA.

reiterated his confidence: letter, July 17, 1923, DA.

a positive genius: May 25, 1923, DA.

a dreadful picture: GIM, p. 230.

221 ". . . only ninety seconds": *New York Times,* May 5, 1923.

relatively modest price: *New York Times,* May 5, 1923.

spending a good deal more: letter, May 11, 1923, DA.

222 "A month ago . . .": GIM, p. 225.

"He hopes one day . . .": GIM, p. 225.

223 ". . . died a few minutes later": Conclusion of the Tribunal de Grande Instance de Blois, Département du Loir-et-Cher, December 22, 1923.

found guilty . . . later reversed: *New York Times,* November 15, 1924; *New York Evening Post,* May 12, 1925.

not be responsible: letter, September 27, 1923, DA.

the Brauer sale: on December 31, 1923.

a reproving letter: October 12, 1928, DA.

". . . appear to get shot": *Artful Partners,* Colin Simpson, p. 191.

Chapter Twelve / LA BELLE FERRONIÈRE

224 only *close* to Leonardo: Leonardo da Vinci, Kenneth Clark, p. 52.

painted by . . . Boltraffio: *Bernard Berenson, the Making of a Legend,* Ernest Samuels, p. 315.

226 received a routine reply: in November 1919, DA.

227 "No attempt was . . .": *New York Herald,* November 5, 1921.
228 called a Leonardo: *The Rape of La Belle,* Harry Hahn, pp. 168–169.
"He must prove . . .": *New York Times,* February 17, 1929.
229 A French war bride: *New York Herald,* November 5, 1921.
"The painting was packed . . .": *Brooklyn Daily Eagle,* January 15, 1922.
a niece of the former owner: *New York Herald,* November 5, 1921.
230 daughter of the Marquis: *New York Herald Tribune,* November 5, 1921.
the painting had originally been given: *Kansas City Star,* November 8, 1921.
declared that he knew nothing: *New York Herald,* February 5, 1922.
231 hung the painting in his house: *New York Times,* November 5, 1921.
The Hahns went to the U.S.: Detectives' report, an unsigned memorandum, circa August 1929. In *Artful Partners,* p. 243, Colin Simpson writes that "Mrs. Hahn and her sister had been prostitutes, their father a pimp, and their uncle an antique dealer with convictions for receiving stolen property." No assertion that Andrée Hahn's father was a pimp and her uncle a corrupt dealer has been found in the Duveen Archive. A memorandum to Sir Joseph Duveen from, probably, his French lawyer, signature illegible, dated September 23, 1929, states that a detective named Conner investigating her background had found evidence of a certain Andrée Lardoux, a prostitute who kept a brothel in Paris. But since this Andrée Lardoux was born in Rennes in 1875 and Andrée Hahn, née Lardoux, born in Argentan in 1896, they were obviously two different women. There are no supporting notes in *Artful Partners.*
". . . transmigration of souls": *Philadelphia Public Ledger,* July 21, 1922.
impossible to distinguish: *Philadelphia Public Ledger,* July 21, 1922.
no Leonardo prints: *Art Fakes in America,* David L. Goodrich, p. 149.
"In the Louvre picture . . .": deposition, September 15, 1923, pp. 38–39, DA.
"When I was cross-examined . . .": *Self and Partners,* C. J. Holmes, p. 355.
233 published his doubts: *Bernard Berenson, The Making of a Legend,* Ernest Samuels, p. 315.
"Berenson has already . . .": *Bernard Berenson, The Making of a Legend,* Ernest Samuels, p. 316.
". . . his immortal sonnets": GIM, p. 240.
234 ". . . remembered as the man . . .": GIM, p. 240.
"a horrible copy . . .": GIM, p. 239.
". . . this huge hoax": GIM, p. 241.
looked perfectly absurd: *Letters of Roger Fry,* vol. 2, p. 544.
"destined to create . . .": *Bernard Berenson, The Making of a Legend,* Ernest Samuels, p. 315.
235 "highbrow and lowbrow . . .": *Art Fakes in America,* David L. Goodrich, p. 144.
"fancied himself . . .": letter to author, December 27, 1977.
236 an honest statement: *New York Times,* February 6, 1929.
". . . perfectly disgraceful . . .": *New York Times,* February 7, 1929.
237 " 'It's dead' . . .": *New York Times,* February 8, 1929.
238 This was the Hahn: cable, February 9, 1929, DA.
champion of free speech: *New York Times,* February 11, 1929.
"Mr. Hug is understood . . .": *New York Times,* February 12, 1929.
239 ". . . finishing his answer": *New York Times,* February 21, 1929.
"I don't know . . .": *New York Times,* February 21, 1929.

in Leonardo's lifetime: telegram, Dr. Walter Heil, February 19, 1929, DA.

240 began to laugh: *New York Times,* February 27, 1929.

"Every question . . .": *New York Times,* February 24, 1929.

". . . a sad expression": *New York Times,* February 26, 1929.

241 "did not believe in it": to Louis Levy, February 8, 1929, DA.

Justice Black agreed: *New York Times,* February 28, 1929.

"revealed a difference . . .": *New York Times,* March 1, 1929.

it had taken a while: *New York Times,* March 1, 1929.

242 ". . . distrust for connoisseurs": *New York Times,* March 3, 1929.

another nine years: *New York Times,* March 3, 1929.

set for a retrial: *New York Times,* March 3, 1929.

settled out of court: *New York Times,* May 20, 1930.

"How can anyone . . .": *Bernard Berenson, The Making of a Legend,* Ernest Samuels, p. 318.

243 a percentage of the sale: *Artnews,* Summer 1985, pp. 94–95.

". . . Not buy it; steal it!": television film, *The Two Belles,* Illuminations, 1993.

"It was an obvious replica . . .": letter to author, April 10, 1978. In *Artful Partners* (p. 243) Colin Simpson writes that Kenneth Clark wrote privately to Sir Joseph Duveen to tell him that he thought the Hahn Leonardo was genuine. This letter has not been found in the Duveen Archives.

its preparatory sketches: *Bernard Berenson, The Making of a Legend,* Ernest Samuel, p. 318.

remains unsold: as of May 10, 2002.

Chapter Thirteen / THE DISAPPEARING BABY

245 would not touch it: letter, September 12, 1923, DA.

247 unfounded "suspiciousness": letter to Edward Fowles, May 12, 1922, DA.

248 ". . . dead stock": letter, October 9, 1936, DA.

"Mori sold it to Joe . . .": FOW, p. 115.

249 ". . . you have to pay . . .": BBB, p. 214.

250 ". . . lacking in genuine individuality . . .": *Italian Paintings, A Catalogue of the Collection of the Metropolitan Museum of Art, Sienese and Central Italian Schools,* Federico Zeri, p. 106.

251 "most impressive work . . .": March 28, 1944; BBB, p. 261.

looking exactly the same: *Burlington Magazine,* July 1971, p. 427.

252 a very nice deal: Mario Modestini, oral history, National Gallery of Art.

"ignorant as swans": *The Other Side of the Alde,* Kenneth Clark, unpaginated.

"It was don't ask . . .": John Walsh to author, June 27, 2000.

253 ". . . very convincing": to author, April 23, 1976.

"B.B. was very enthusiastic . . .": to author.

still attributed to Ghirlandaio: *National Gallery of Art,* John Walker, *Madonna and Child,* no. 73, p. 104.

". . . There comes a point . . .": interview with author, 1978.

254 "since the builders . . .": BBB, p. 268.

256 three specialists repainted: *3,000 Years of Deception,* Frank Arnau, p. 294.

256 Duveen went into high gear: letter, April 18, 1930, DA.

"Don't chop it up . . .": BBB, p. 268.

257 Lowengard was sure it was "right": letter, January 14, 1929, DA.

the serious price of £46,200: January 17, 1929, DA.

258 one of the oldest noble families: April 22, 1929, DA.

"wonderfully, beautifully": letter, January 25, 1929, DA.

They could not trace him: Letter, April 13, 1929, DA.

people who were jealous: March 14, 1930, DA.

Armand was asked: March 24, 1930, DA.

no chance of a refund: March 31, 1930, DA.

it must be "right": March 25–26, 1930, DA.

He could not understand: March 27, 1930, DA.

in a garret: *New York Herald,* April 1, 1930.

259 an ominous discovery indeed: March 27, 1930, DA.

They wanted a name: April 1, 1930, DA.

it would have to do: April 1, 1930, DA.

not by Dürer: *Pantheon,* December 1930, p. 542.

Bache was getting worried: December 23, 1930, DA.

some soothing words: December 24, 1930, DA.

260 might add fuel: February 25, 1933, DA.

take the picture back: October 13, 1934, DA.

had never been paid for: October 23, 1934, DA.

Chapter Fourteen / "KEEP ALIVE"

261 "Most of them were . . .": interview with author, November 25, 1999.

263 she should take over: letters, July 23, 1923, and August 23, 1923, DA.

"getting very keen": August 14, 1923, DA.

266 It later went to: January 17, 1925, DA.

267 ". . . one of the finest . . .": *New York Times,* January 15, 1925.

his favorite architect: *New York Times,* April 30, 1938.

268 ". . . found them too white": *Mary Berenson, A Self-Portrait from Her Diaries and Letters,* p. 243.

269 She paid for it herself: Jean Langton Douglas, later Jean Fowles, unpublished memoir.

270 soup, cakes, and new-laid eggs: May 22, 1924, DA.

the most perfect of all: letter to d'Arenberg, December 20, 1924, DA.

"not with the hereditary . . .": *New York Herald Tribune,* March 30, 1952.

an arch diplomatist: *Daily Mail,* June 28, 1952.

"succulent, invigorating . . .": *Sunday Times,* June 22, 1952.

a Napoleonic grasp: *Observer,* June 22, 1952.

"most spectacular dealer . . .": *Saturday Review,* March 22, 1952.

KEEP ALIVE . . .: December 14, 1926, DA.

". . . an admirable copy . . .": *Aux Écoutes,* June 3, 1939.

271 The check was returned: based on correspondence in the Duveen Archive, 1924–1929.

272 made Duveen feel very secure: October 3, 1922, DA.

some paintings to sell: May 16, 1923.

"I do not apprehend . . .": *London Interiors,* John Cornforth, p. 44.

"political aristocracy": *Connoisseur,* July 1981.

274 "Your Grace is . . .": *British Paintings at the Huntington,* Robyn Asleson and Shelley M. Bennett, p. 336.

a couple of smaller portraits by Reynolds: letter, May 23, 1923, DA.

275 clear up his debts: letter, January 2, 1924, DA.

He kept pressing: letter, January 20, 1924, DA.

"likes to be secretive": letter, January 25, 1924, DA.

If Duveen could not relent: letter, May 26, 1924, DA.

Arabella died: on September 16, 1924.

276 would not see a penny: *The Times,* January 17, 1925.

277 "the three greatest landscapes . . .": Duveen to H. E. Huntington, May 24, 1922, Huntington archives.

He died in 1927: on May 23.

regiments of archangels: letter, May 7, 1931, DA.

278 lesser artists at work: *British Paintings at the Huntington,* Robyn Asleson and Shelley M. Bennett, p. 14.

"after Joshua Reynolds": *British Paintings at the Huntington,* Robyn Asleson and Shelley M. Bennett, p. 543.

He wanted it for his own home: *Aristotle Contemplating the Bust of Homer,* Theodore Rousseau, Metropolitan Museum of Art *Bulletin,* January 1962, p. 156.

"that do often lie . . .": *Ode: Intimations of Immortality,* William Wordsworth.

279 this was the prize: *The Elegant Auctioneers,* Wesley Towner, p. 603.

280 up for auction at Parke-Bernet: *The Elegant Auctioneers,* Wesley Towner, p. 604; Paul Sachs oral history, Columbia University.

Chapter Fifteen / "I CANNOT WAIT"

282 ". . . some delicate morsel . . .": *Great Private Collections,* Douglas Cooper, p. 15.

284 His exquisitely diplomatic overture: *Henry Edwards Huntington,* James Thorpe, p. 500.

"Evidently they had received . . .": *New York Times,* July 29, 1926.

could only mean Duveen Brothers: letter, July 28, 1926, DA.

285 he must expect Knoedler's: July 29, 1926, DA.

it was hopeless: April 30, 1928, DA.

286 something under £10,000: April 3, 1928, DA.

went away feeling very proud: *The Times We Had,* Marion Davies, p. 165.

287 "a magnificent, dramatic . . .": *New York Herald Tribune,* May 27, 1939.

288 "Not a real Titian?": *New York Herald Tribune,* May 27, 1939.

"absolutely inexhaustible": told to author.

289 "an absolute peach": December 8, 1927, DA.

. . . WILL REALIZE FORTUNE: cable, January 30, 1928, DA.

probably not as billed: April 6, 1922, DA.

He would not have them: May 11, 1923, DA.

290 would never sell: November 1925, DA.

290 would have to pay: November 25, 1927, DA.

"still the most autocratic . . .": November 23, 1927, DA.

a Spanish nobleman: November 23, 1927, DA.

pay a bit more than he asked: January 20, 1928, DA.

291 He had donated it: February 4, 1929, DA.

292 MUCH THRILLED . . .: December 8, 1929, DA.

He wanted an answer: December 9, 1929, DA.

a "very typical" work: December 11, 1929, DA.

293 He expected to sell: December 4, 1925, DA.

got his improved contract: *Bernard Berenson, The Making of a Legend,* Ernest Samuels, p. 359.

294 personally found a buyer: October 17, 1921, DA.

295 cabled Henry Huntington: October 14, 1926, DA.

The Judge had not been well: July 27, 1927, DA.

he offered to buy: February 20, 1928, DA.

He loved the sofa: April 4, 1928, DA.

the black hawthorn vase: April 16, 1928, DA.

296 could be on the front page: April 16, 1928, DA.

". . . the hammer fell . . .": *New York Times,* April 20, 1928.

297 He caused a sensation: *The Elegant Auctioneers,* Wesley Towner, p. 242.

bidding at no cost: May 1, 1928, DA.

"Now, with the particularly exquisite . . .": *The Elegant Auctioneers,* Wesley Towner, p. 446.

298 AFTER EXCITING DUEL . . .: cable, April 21, 1928, DA.

not window dressing: April 27, 1928, DA.

Chapter Sixteen / IN THE ELEVATOR

300 "In my mind . . .": FOW, p. 83.

302 ". . . an ideal world . . .": *Self Portrait with Donors,* John Walker, pp. 105–106.

303 "the contents of his wastebasket . . .": *America's National Gallery of Art,* Philip Kopper, p. 97.

304 beaten out by French and Company: October 3, 1922, DA.

when Mellon would return: October 5, 1922, DA.

305 Duveen drafted a letter: undated, DA.

Mellon uncharacteristically confessed: September 6, 1926, DA.

equally enthusiastic about the future: September 10, 1926, DA.

306 "in a wonderful humor . . .": December 1927, DA.

full of doubts: April 21, 1926, DA.

a Gainsborough that wasn't: March 7, 1925, to Sir Joseph Duveen, DA.

IS THERE ABSOLUTELY . . .: March 28, 1925, DA.

The one authentic version: April 18, 1925, DA.

307 a rank betrayal: December 14, 1926, DA.

some feeble excuses: Fowles to Sir Joseph Duveen, January 18, 1927, DA.

Just before her wedding: May 26, 1926, DA.

Two cars would meet him: July 29, 1926, DA.

308 ripe for Botticellis: August 23, 1926, DA.

a full report: September 2, 1926, DA.

When he asked who had sent it: September 17, 1926, DA.

what kinds of prices: November 18, 1926, DA.

There was speculation: November 9, 1927, DA.

twice Prime Minister: from 1923–4 and 1929–35.

309 opened at the Tate: June 8, 1926.

312 ". . . believe the buildings": *Civilisation,* Kenneth Clark, p. 1.

not much they could do: *The Tate, a History,* Frances Spaulding, p. 62.

"which would in itself rank . . .": *The Tate, a History,* Frances Spaulding, p. 62.

a colostomy: *Artful Partners,* p. 222.

a life-insurance policy: November 20, 1927, DA.

"I recall a phrase . . .": July 27, 1929, DA.

313 just a game: May 4, 1928, DA.

"One room was . . .": *Merchants of Art,* Germain Seligman, p. 172.

314 allowed to make his first transaction: *Russian Art and American Money,* Robert C. Williams, p. 161.

316 ". . . too little and too late": *Russian Art and American Money,* Robert C. Williams, p. 169.

headed by Duveen: *Russian Art and American Money,* Robert C. Williams, pp. 157–158.

just how specific: July 21, 1930, DA.

varying accounts: *New York American,* August 12, 1930.

317 FEEL CONFIDENT . . .: September 16, 1930, DA.

still standing there: Boggis to Sir Joseph Duveen, September 17, 1930, DA.

318 in Duveen's hands: September 18, 1930, DA.

"I made considerable . . .": deposition, Mellon tax case, 7524–6, DA.

". . . the entire Hermitage . . .": Armand Lowengard to Sir Joseph Duveen, September 29, 1930, DA.

Chapter Seventeen / A PROPER ENGLISH GENTLEMAN

319 had to show sculpture: *Self Portrait with Donors,* John Walker, p. 129.

"the Dreyfus Collection . . .": David Finley, oral history, National Gallery of Art, p. 8.

"a gentle, blond boy": GIM, p. 142.

320 "I had, I think, months . . .": Edward Fowles oral history, Archives of American Art, p. 7.

a very big price: July 10, 1930.

". . . never seen him depressed": November 4, 1929, DA.

321 dollar itself was devalued: ECON, p. 209.

was disdainful when pushed: May 9, 1935, DA.

He had to pay up: *New York Times,* March 19, 1936. Duveen paid $214,034 in back taxes.

a very bad idea: April 14, 1933, DA.

321 ". . . the Wall Street princes . . .": Apollo, VII, 1930.
"I don't believe . . .": GIM, pp. 397–398.

322 "it bores me to death . . .": January 24, 1929, DA.
"I now seriously . . .": letter, July 12, 1929, DA.
"If you can trust . . .": *Bernard Berenson, The Making of a Legend,* Ernest Samuels, p. 365.
". . . chain of sausages . . .": April 1, 1928, DA.
deserved the credit: February 10, 1929, DA.

323 owed Duveen $4 million: Edward Fowles, oral history, Archives of American Art.
less financially embarrassed: October 10, 1929, DA.
two visitors from the Prado: April 28, 1930, DA.

324 could he not sell?: March 9, 1931, DA.
"You will all have to realize . . .": letter to Paris, December 6, 1931, DA.
"It is perhaps the weakest . . .": letter, July 25, 1928, DA.

325 another £12,000 to £15,000: August 14, 1929, DA.
worth £25,000 at most: August 27, 1928, DA.
Giovanelli sold his painting: January 9, 1930, DA.

326 Duveen refused to pay: March 17, 1930, DA.
". . . excessive demands . . .": March 20, 1930, DA.
had been housed: *Giorgione,* Jaynie Anderson, p. 253.
almost mad: February 2, 1923, DA.

327 "Italian dealers are all spies": May 27, 1922, DA.
unwilling to invest: November 25, 1930, DA.
they sold the painting: February 22, 1932, DA.
"I assure you . . .": letter, January 24, 1929, DA.

328 No one else there: July 12, 1929, DA.
invited to a party: April 23, 1933, DA.
formally inducted: June 14, 1933, DA.
reappeared shortly after: *New York Times,* June 15, 1933.
his first country house: January 28, 1931.

329 "was so confident of his charm . . .": *Another Part of the Wood,* Kenneth Clark, p. 68.
"the greatest sculpture gallery . . .": London *Times,* June 30, 1937.
actually brightly colored: *Lord Elgin and the Marbles,* William St. Clair, p. 51.

330 A nice white finish: *Lord Elgin and the Marbles,* William St. Clair, p. 51.

331 sketched the ceremony: on March 31, 1933.

332 "two solid flagstones . . .": *Thirty Years of British Art,* Sir Joseph Duveen, p. 113.

333 "a wicked risk . . .": *Another Part of the Wood,* Kenneth Clark, p. 177.
"a ridiculous figure . . .": *Another Part of the Wood,* Kenneth Clark, p. 181.
arrived nine days later: *The Ephemeral Museum,* Francis Haskell, p. 110.

334 "the strong-room of the ship . . .": *Another Part of the Wood,* Kenneth Clark, p. 182.
SERIOUS DISASTER: letter, March 2, 1929, DA.
"puerile": *Another Part of the Wood,* Kenneth Clark, p. 182.

335 The best idea was to wait: January 28, 1930, DA.

336 "a remarkably lifelike . . .": Behrman manuscript, I-37, National Gallery of Art Archives.
passed them around: December 29, 1935, DA.

"Something of a gourmet . . .": BEH, p. 211, National Gallery of Art Archives.

some sort of bug: letter, February 24, 1934, DA.

underwent an operation: November 25, 1934, DA.

A cable to Paris: January 6, 1935, DA.

337 ". . . he had a Holbein . . .": David Finley oral history, National Gallery of Art.

"He bought directly . . .": interview with author.

the willingness of the Kaiser Friedrich: November 1933, DA.

"the Berlin business": December 29, 1936, DA.

338 to negotiate a price: Ian Locke, interview with author.

"It was the beginning . . .": *The House of Rothschild,* Niall Ferguson, p. 472.

339 "In this case . . .": February 24, 1931, DA.

they should stay on the alert: April 24, 1931, DA.

"the art treasures in Spain . . .": *New York Times,* October 6, 1936.

send a wish list: January 11, 1937, DA.

about twenty pictures: January 12, 1937, DA.

340 WHATEVER GOVERNMENT SUCCEEDS . . .": cable, January 18, 1937, DA.

"a member of that notable . . .": *Art Treasures and Intrigue,* James Henry Duveen, p. 5.

Jack was bankrupt: April 25, 1936, DA.

341 "We all make . . .": BBB, p. 379.

343 The portrait reappeared: June 5, 1935, DA.

Knoedler's had become the enemy: *New York Times,* July 15, 1936.

344 SIMPLY MARVELLOUS . . .: February 5, 1931, DA.

The *New York Times:* February 21, 1936; A.C.R. Carter of the *Daily Telegraph:* March 2, 1936.

NONE OF YOU MUST . . .: March 3, 1936, DA.

could only be helpful: March 10, 1936, DA.

345 "God did not place . . .": *America's National Gallery of Art,* Philip Kopper, p. 106.

346 "But Mr. Mellon thought . . .": *News-Week,* quoted in *America's National Gallery of Art,* Philip Kopper, p. 106.

". . . They are not a commodity . . .": from the trial transcript.

". . . a beautiful clash . . .": Marquis Childs, oral history, National Gallery of Art.

did his star turn: May 9, 1935, DA.

"You kept your . . .": letter, May 15, 1935, DA.

347 had finally triumphed: telegrams, July 22 and 27, 1936, DA.

Chapter Eighteen / RAIN ON THE LAWN

348 The recollection by Richard Kingzett of a dinner party with Sir Joseph Duveen is based on a letter to the author of August 13, 2000, and an interview.

350 ". . . those Jewish noses . . .": GIM, p. 38.

THERE IS A RUMOR . . .: telegram, April 10, 1938, DA.

351 divorced his wife for Dolly: interview with Roger Jenkins.

"tall, elegant, and charming": Anneta Duveen to author.

352 ". . . not as bad as all that": Brian Masters, interview with author.

"I'm quite interested . . .": Lord Skidelsky, interview with author.

354 "... that's quite unusual": interview with author.

"... build up your collection": David Finley, oral history, National Gallery of Art.

Finley said it was his idea: David Finley, oral history, National Gallery of Art.

356 "... looking at the Van Dyck ...": David Finley, oral history, National Gallery of Art.

"... lock, stock and barrel!": BEH, p. 196.

a total of $21 million: BEH, p. 196.

had to pay Duveen in securities: BEH, p. 196.

357 "... as scattered as sheep ...": *Self Portrait with Donors,* John Walker, p. 139.

"... The Wideners were not pleased ...": Agnes Mongan, oral history, National Gallery of Art.

a tidy profit: BEH, p. 213.

359 "In his good looks ...": *Self Portrait with Donors,* John Walker, p. 134.

"the only major buyer ...": Marco Grassi, interview with author.

"For many years B.B. ...": Lord Clark, interview with author.

"Heavy tables ...": *Self Portrait with Donors,* John Walker, p. 137.

360 Boggis, following him: undated correspondence, DA.

the latter was hospitalized: March 20, 1930, DA.

"very fine pictures ...": August 3, 1932, DA.

dates would not coincide: August 7, 1932, DA.

Duveen was willing: August 9, 1932, DA.

impossible to approach: November 3, 1932, DA.

361 selling at a loss: assembled from interoffice correspondence, DA.

to avoid paying: June 26, 1934, DA.

eleven paintings: May 16, 1936, DA.

an even larger batch: March 9, 1937, DA.

he knew his man: June 21, 1938, DA.

362 "the greatest buyer ...": *Bernard Berenson, The Making of a Legend,* Ernest Samuels, p. 425.

the dwindling rewards: *Bernard Berenson, The Making of a Legend,* Ernest Samuels, p. 425.

"bragging and blustering ...": *Bernard Berenson, The Making of a Legend,* Ernest Samuels, p. 425.

363 "... weird sort of family ...": Edward Fowles, oral history, Archives of American Art.

364 a secret plan: *Artful Partners,* Colin Simpson, p. 255.

he was disbarred: *New York Times,* August 5, 1952.

a four-man syndicate: *Artful Partners,* Colin Simpson, p. 256.

transferred his hopes: bought in 1938.

By then Duveen Brothers Inc.: April 23, 1938, DA.

365 His former right-hand man: May 3, 1938, DA.

"... attack of pleurisy ...": June 25, 1938, DA.

it *is* a Giorgione: Kenneth Clark to author, April 23, 1976.

did not like it much: September 15, 1931, DA.

"... in a proper light ...": July 19, 1937, DA.

consider himself insulted: September 7, 1937, DA.

"If Duveen abetted . . .": *Sunset and Twilight,* Bernard Berenson, p. 264.

367 ". . . sparkling with jewels . . .": *Chips, the Diaries of Sir Henry Channon,* pp. 125–126.

quietly acquired the work: *Another Part of the Wood,* Kenneth Clark, p. 139.

". . . 'No good deed . . .' ": *Another Part of the Wood,* Kenneth Clark, p. 266.

368 "a man of battle . . .": March 5, 1951, DA.

an "odd case": GIM, p. 160.

wanted an appraisal: July 18, 1927, DA.

369 a promotional tool: October 2, 1927, DA.

he was luckier: May 8, 1929, DA.

370 "There were those . . .": *New York World,* May 9, 1929.

all about the clever ways: in-house memo, May 21, 1929, DA.

he filed suit: *New York Times,* July 9, 1935.

371 "an Ioni fake": *Artful Partners,* Colin Simpson, pp. 201–202.

372 ". . . Don't answer that . . .": May 9, 1936, p. 235.

"He has answered . . .": May 8, 1936, p. 127.

"and never paid me . . .": May 8, 1936, p. 209.

". . . Can any man do more . . .": May 8, 1936, p. 214.

373 He urged both: April 19, 1938, DA.

Hamilton was dropping his suit: September 22, 1938, DA.

". . . I am tired": May 8, 1936, p. 204.

". . . a great weakness for a crook": interview with author, January 6, 1977.

a room was being planned: John Allen, January 22, 1939, DA.

374 he had completed his plans: oral history, National Gallery of Art.

The rest were hidden: *Daily Herald,* May 26, 1939.

cover for counterespionage: *MI6: British Secret Intelligence Service Operations,* Nigel West, p. 69.

the opening of the new . . . wing: William St. Clair to author, July 9, 2002.

375 ". . . the reverence of love . . .": London *Times,* May 26, 1939.

has found no indication: Dr. Dyfri Williams, letter to author, May 14, 2003.

"I suppose he has destroyed . . .": *Lord Elgin and the Marbles,* William St. Clair, pp. 294–295.

one did not tamper: William St. Clair to author, July 9, 2002.

such an influence on the cleaning: *Lord Elgin and the Marbles,* William St. Clair, p. 298.

376 whiter than white: *Lord Elgin and the Marbles,* William St. Clair, p. 298.

unauthorized use: November 21, 1938, DA.

". . . the villain of the piece . . .": "The Elgin Marbles: Questions of Stewardship and Accountability," William St. Clair, *International Journal of Cultural Property,* vol. 8 (1999), no. 2, p. 487.

. . . YOUR NAME DOESN'T APPEAR . . .: telegram, March 25, 1939, DA.

377 holding hands: *Evening Standard,* May 25, 1939.

no formal opening: April 6, 1939, DA.

offered the paneling: letter, J. H. Allen, August 23, 1939, DA.

a wonderful idea: August 31, 1939, DA.

turned the offer down: November 10, 1939, DA.

irreparable damage: *Daily Mail,* March 25, 1939.

378 The museum began to close ranks: *Daily Telegraph,* T.W. Earp, May 23, 1939.
"... very much to heart ...": *Daily Telegraph,* May 26, 1939.
too ill to visit: *Daily Telegraph,* May 26, 1939.
he took issue: London *Times,* May 25, 1939.

379 "... life-enhancing energies ...": September 24, 1935, DA.

380 "... 'I have had a wonderful life' ...": London *Times,* May 26, 1939.

Paintings, Sculpture, and Objects Sold or Donated by Joseph Duveen, 1900–1939: A Partial List

Although Duveen Brothers was in business for almost a century, records of its art dealings before World War I are spotty and mostly confined to the abbreviated references listed in the Duveen stock books, making a work's previous sales history almost impossible to determine. The firm reserved most of its art history for the two volumes of paintings and sculpture that had entered public collections in the United States by 1940, a year after Duveen's death. Although an enormous amount of important research has been done since by scholars, the museums themselves, and the ongoing Provenance Index that has been prepared by the Getty Research Institute in Los Angeles, much work still remains to be done. Certain archives have been lost forever. Senator William A. Clark, for instance, who left between seven hundred and eight hundred objects to the Corcoran Gallery of Art in Washington, D.C., destroyed all the supporting correspondence, making the story of which objects came from where an impossible guessing game. The National Gallery of Art in Washington is one of the few museums that have made buying histories of their collections available on the Internet. The Huntington has published a complete history of its holdings of British art, but only that. Federico Zeri has published a complete history of Italian Renaissance holdings at the Metropolitan Museum of Art, but other holdings have been pieced together from a variety of sources.

These are the public holdings. No one knows what happened to the paintings, sculpture, and objets bought by private collectors, unless they were subsequently given to museums. There is a reference in the Duveen Archive and then the object disappears. One of the major works of art scholarship still remaining is a complete list of all the objects that went through Duveen Brothers during its spectacular rise and fall. The following list can only give an approximation of that mighty assemblage.

A Note on Attributions

The reader will be aware that a number of paintings bought from Duveen bearing attributions to famous artists have been demoted in recent years, particularly if the works have entered public collections. The change in attribution from a famous to a lesser, and less valuable, name is fairly straightforward. The problem arises principally in the case of the hundreds of early Italian and Italian Renaissance works, in large part bought with certificates of authenticity from Bernard Berenson. Since these works are anonymous, any attribution to a master hand has to be a matter of speculation, however clearly evidence and tradition seem to point to that conclusion.

To state categorically that this is the only hand at work may make the painting worth ten times its value but is the kind of happy certainty that tends to exist only when the painting is for sale. Subsequent scholarship has raised doubts in innumerable cases. These doubts, as the late Carter Brown, former director of the National Gallery of Art in Washington, once observed, reflect "degrees of uncertainty."

So you have such labels as "attributed to," one roughly analogous to such real-estate terms as "*asking* $1½ million." The unwary will be fooled; the cognoscenti will nod knowingly. Further doubts are expressed by such labels as "G. Bellini and assistant," "G. Bellini and workshop," as well as "style of G. Bellini," meaning that it looks like a Bellini but, on the other hand . . . Then there are such labels as "studio of," "circle of," "workshop of," and "follower of," taking the painting successive notches down the certainty ladder. "Copy after" is self-explanatory, and more than one collector has been fooled by a convincing facsimile. "Imitator of" is a polite way of saying a fake. Then there are the "Master of" attributions, in which Berenson specialized. What this label means is that no one knows who painted the most famous work, usually an altarpiece, such as the "Master of the Castello Nativity." Experts have nevertheless decided that whoever painted this also painted the work in question—perhaps the most speculative of all such critical leaps of faith.

Note that attributions given are those at the time of a sale. Subsequent changes are noted.

ALLEGRETTO NUZI   *Madonna Enthroned with Saints,* 1354, triptych, wood, center panel 42¾ × 23⅜"
Provenance: Joseph Henry Russell Bailey, second Baron Glanusk, Glanusk Park, Crickhowell, Wales; Walter Dowdeswell, 9196; Carl W. Hamilton, New York (1922–1926); Duveen; Andrew W. Mellon; National Gallery of Art, Washington, D.C.
Note: Additional subjects are, on the left wing, the Angel of Annunciation, and on the right wing, the Virgin Annunciate. John Walker attributes the work to the "Master of the Fabriano Altarpiece and Allegretto Nuzi." Present attribution: "Puccio di Simone (and Allegretto di Nuzio)."

AMERICAN SILVER   Silver caster, 5¼ × 2⅛, and silver caster cover, 5⅜ × 2", by Benjamin Burt, American (1729–1805)
Provenance: Duveen; Gibbs-William Fund; Detroit Institute of Arts.

AMBROGIO DE PREDIS   *Portrait of a Girl Crowned with Flowers*
Provenance: Ferencz Szarvady, Budapest; Gustave Dreyfus, Paris; Duveen; Samuel H. Kress; North Carolina Museum of Art, Raleigh.
Note: Now "Giovanni Antonio Boltraffio."

ANDREA DEL CASTAGNO   *The Youthful David,* c. 1450, on leather, 45½ × 30¼"
Provenance: Drury-Lowe, Locko Park, England; Duveen; Widener Collection; National Gallery of Art, Washington, D.C.

ANDREA DEL CASTAGNO   *The Resurrection,* c. 1445–50, tempera on poplar panel, 11¼ × 13¼″
Provenance: Senor Funghini, Perugia; C. Fairfax-Murray, London; Dr. Werner Weisbach, Berlin; Duveen, 1930; Frick Collection, New York, 1939.
Note: Exhibited at the 1930 Exhibition of Italian Art at the Royal Academy with an attribution to Castagno by Bernard Berenson. Now attributed to Castagno. Frick catalogue: "At some time before the panel entered the Frick Collection it was reduced to a thickness of ⅜″."

ANDREA DEL CASTAGNO   *Portrait of a Man,* c. 1417–19, on wood, 20½ × 15¼″
Provenance: Baron Cerbone del Nero, Florence; the Torrigiani family, Florence; Rodolphe Kann, Paris; Duveen; J. Pierpont Morgan, New York, 1907; Andrew Mellon, 1935; National Gallery of Art, Washington, D.C.
Note: Kay Silberfeld, head of painting conservation at the National Gallery, noted in 1980 that the painting had marked abrasion of the face and hair. The dark line of the profile was almost all repaint, and she found similar reinforced lines on the nose, eyebrows, and ears.

ANDREA DEL SARTO   *Madonna and Child with Infant St. John,* c. 1528, tondo, diameter 26¾″
Provenance: G. W. Taylor, London; Princess Woronzow, Florence; Robert and Evelyn Benson Collection; Duveen, 1927; William Randolph Hearst; Samuel H. Kress Collection; National Gallery of Art, Washington, D.C.; Lowe Art Gallery, University of Miami.
Note: Now "Follower of."

ANDREA DEL SARTO   *Portrait of a Man,* fifteenth/sixteenth century, oil on panel, 22¾ × 19½″
Provenance: Palazzo Panciatichi, Florence, until c. 1902; Robert and Evelyn Benson, until 1924; Duveen; Detroit Institute of Arts, gift of Joseph Duveen.
Note: Work now attributed to Franciabigio, a fifteenth-century Florentine painter; attributions to Tommaso di Stefano, Francesco Salviati, and an obscure painter working in the manner of Andrea del Sarto and his circle have also been suggested.

FRA ANGELICO   *The Entombment,* c. 1450–1455, tempera on panel, 35⅝ × 22¼″
Provenance: Stefano Bardini, Florence; Duveen (in association with Agnew's and Sulley); Henry Goldman, New York, 1923–4; Duveen; Samuel H. Kress Collection, 1936.
Note: Now "Attributed to Fra Angelico."

FRA ANGELICO   *The Annunciation,* 2 panels, 14 × 10″ each
Provenance: Sold to Carl Hamilton by Duveen in 1917 and one of two paintings over which he sued Joseph Duveen. Went to Edsel Ford of Detroit in 1938 for £37,400.
Note: An "Ioni" fake: Colin Simpson, *Artful Partners* [194].

FRA ANGELICO   *Madonna and Child,* n.d., tempera and gold leaf on panel, 18⅛ × 15″
Provenance: Convento dei Padri Crocoferi, Messina, Sicily; Lazzari family, Messina; Marchese Giovanni Palermo di Messina; Duveen; Norton Simon Museum, Pasadena, CA.

FRA ANGELICO   *Madonna and Child with Angels*
Provenance: Unknown.
Note: Supposedly "sold" to Carl Hamilton by Duveen in 1919.

FRA ANGELICO   *Madonna and Child,* 18½ × 15"
Provenance: Henry Reinhardt; afterwards Mrs. Thaw of New York.
Note: Speaking of another Fra Angelico Madonna owned by Henckel in Wiesbaden, Edward Fowles and Armand Lowengard wrote that faces and hands were entirely abraded. "Unfortunately would be impossible to restore face; consequently picture will always be weak like the Madonna and Child sold to Mrs. Thaw."

ANTONELLO DA MESSINA   *Christ Crowned with Thorns,* c. 1470, oil on wood, 16¾ × 12"
Provenance: Baron Arthur de Schickler, Martinvast, Manche (by 1908); Countess Hubert de Pourtalès, Martinvast, Manche (until 1920); Carl Hamilton; Duveen, 1920–7; Dr. Hans Wendland, Lugano, 1927; Michael Friedsam, New York; Metropolitan Museum of Art, New York, 1931.

ANTONELLO DA MESSINA   *Madonna and Child,* c. 1475, 23¼ × 17¼"
Provenance: William Graham, London; Robert H. Benson; Duveen, 1927; Clarence Mackay, by 1929; Duveen; Mellon, by 1936–7; National Gallery of Art, Washington, D.C.
Note: Thought to have been by an obscure artist, Marcello Fogolino, when bought by collector Robert Benson in London for £40. In 1913, subject of a long article in the *Gazette des Beaux Arts* by Berenson, who decided it was the work of Antonello. In the Benson catalogue of 1914 by that name. Kenneth Clark doubted it authentic; called it a very poor work. A painting conservator at the National Gallery said that it is now in storage because it "bothers everyone."

ANTONELLO DA MESSINA   *Portrait of a Man,* c. 1500, on wood, 12¾ × 9⅜"; also called *Portrait of a Young Man*
Provenance: Prince Alberto Giovanelli, 1928; Duveen, bought for Jules Bache, 1928–30, but not sold to him; Andrew W. Mellon; National Gallery of Art, Washington, D.C.
Note: Mussolini extracted a stiff export price for the painting in 1935; Duveen paid £26,000 for the work. Sir Ellis Waterhouse (notebooks) remarked that the painting was in remarkably good condition but that he did not believe it was by Antonello.

ANTONIAZZO ROMANO   *Madonna and Child with Two Cherubim,* on panel, 18¼ × 14"
Provenance: Charles Butler, London; Warren Wood, Hatfield, Hertford; Robert and Evelyn Benson; Julius H. Haass, Detroit; Duveen; Norton Simon Museum, Pasadena, CA.

ANTONIO DA MONZA   *The Flagellation of Christ*
Provenance: Rodolphe Kann, Paris; Arabella D. Huntington, New York; Duveen; Norton Simon Museum, Pasadena, CA.

ALESSO BALDOVINETTI   *Madonna and Child,* 29½ × 21½"
Provenance: I. F. Ioni; Signor Arnoldo Corsi, Milan; Bernard Berenson, 1910(?); Duveen, 1919; William Salomon, New York; Duveen; Clarence H. Mackay, New York; Duveen; Samuel H. Kress; National Gallery of Art, Washington, D.C.

Note: In *Artful Partners,* Colin Simpson writes that the painting was bought from Ioni for $5,000 in 1910 and sold to Salomon for $62,500 [184]. Writing to Mackay, Berenson called the painting a "very characteristic work" of Baldovinetti's middle years (March 28, 1924). Kenneth Clark believed Berenson had been deceived and that the painting had been "doctored up" early in the century. Duveen, to Arabella Huntington, called the painting "very good, but unfortunately it is in rather bad condition and therefore will not suit you" (January 10, 1923). Painting is now attributed to Pier Francesco Fiorentino and is in storage.

THOMAS BARKER OF BATH   *Landscape near Bath,* oil on canvas
Provenance: Presented by Duveen to the Tate Gallery, 1926.

BARNA DA SIENA   *Christ Bearing the Cross, with a Dominican Friar,* c. 1350–60, on panel, 10 × 14″
Provenance: Lord Leighton; Robert and Evelyn Benson; Duveen; Helen C. Frick; Frick Collection, New York.

BARNA DA SIENA   *Christ Bearing the Cross, with a Dominican Friar,* c. 1350–60; 13¾ × 9¾″
Provenance: Lord Leighton; Robert and Evelyn Benson; Duveen; Frick Collection, New York.

BARNA DA SIENA   *Saint Mary Magdalene,* tempera on panel, 17 1/16 × 10¾″
Provenance: Sir Philip Burne-Jones, London; Duveen; Philip Lehman, New York; Robert Lehman, New York; Metropolitan Museum of Art, New York.
Note: Now "Follower of."

BARONZIO DA RIMINI   *Adoration of the Magi,* on wood, left wing of a triptych
Provenance: Monastero degli Angeli, Rimini; G. A. Hoskins; Robert Langdon Douglas, London; Otto H. Kahn, New York; Duveen; Samuel H. Kress; National Gallery of Art, Washington, D.C.; Lowe Art Museum, University of Miami, Coral Gables, FL (Kress Collection).
Note: Painting has also been attributed to Segna di Buonaventura and is now attributed to "the Master of the Blessed Clare."

BARONZIO DA RIMINI   *Madonna and Child with Angels,* c. 1330–40, on wood, 39⅝ × 18⅞″
Provenance: Prince Léon Ouroussoff, Vienna; Duveen, by 1924; Otto H. Kahn, New York; Duveen; Samuel H. Kress, New York; National Gallery of Art, Washington, D.C.
Note: Now "Master of the Life of Saint John the Baptist."

BARTOLO DELLA GATTA   *Lucretia,* 17 × 11¾″
Provenance: Duveen; William Salomon; Duveen; Kleinberger.
Note: Duveen (to Arabella Huntington) called it "a dreadful work" (January 10, 1923).

BARTOLO DI FREDI   *Madonna and Child with Angels,* on wood
Provenance: Baron Arthur de Schickler, Martinvast, Manche; Countess Hubert de Pourtalès, Paris; Duveen; Samuel H. Kress, New York; National Gallery of Art, Washing-

ton, D.C.; Nelson-Atkins Museum of Art, Kansas City, MO; University of Arizona Museum of Art, Tucson, AZ (Kress Collection).
Note: Painting has been cut down from a larger *Enthroned Madonna.* It entered the National Gallery of Art collection as a Luca di Tomme and is now attributed to Niccolò di Ser Sozzo Tegliacci.

BARTOLO DI FREDI   *Madonna and Child*
Provenance: Supposedly, Duveen, 1919; Carl Hamilton, New York; Duveen, 1924; Samuel H. Kress, 1937.

BARTOLOMEO BELLANO   *Marsyas Playing the Flute,* bronze statuette, h. 13¾″
Provenance: Henry J. Pfungst, London; J. Pierpont Morgan, New York; Duveen; Henry Clay Frick, New York; Frick Collection, New York.
Note: Now "Style of Antonio Pollaiuolo."

BARTOLOMEO BELLANO   *David with the Head of Goliath,* bronze statuette, h. 9⅞″
Provenance: Henry J. Pfungst, London; J. Pierpont Morgan, New York; Duveen; Henry Clay Frick, New York; Frick Collection, New York.
Note: Now "After Bellano."

BARTOLOMEO BELLANO   *Queen Thomyris with the Head of Cyprus,* bronze statuette, h. 12″
Provenance: Chigi-Saracini family, Sienna; Alphonse Kann, Paris; Duveen; J. Pierpont Morgan, New York; Duveen; Henry Clay Frick, New York; Frick Collection, New York.
Note: Now Severo da Ravenna.

BARTOLOMEO BULGARINI   *Nativity*
Provenance: Duveen; Henry Goldman, New York; Fogg Art Museum, Cambridge, MA.

BARTOLOMEO VENETO   *Portrait of a Gentleman,* c. 1520, 30¼ × 23″; also called *Portrait of Massimiliano Sforza (Presumed)*
Provenance: ? Castello Sforzesco, Milan; Agostino Perego, Milan; Commendatore Crespi, Milan; Henry Goldman, New York; Duveen; Kress Collection, New York; National Gallery of Art, Washington, D.C.

BARTOLOMEO VENETO   *Portrait of a Man, a Knight of the Order of St. Paul,* c. 1537, oil on panel, 20⅝ × 15⅝″
Provenance: Baron Michele Lazzaroni, Rome; Duveen; Norton Simon Museum, Pasadena, CA.

BARTOLOMEO VIVARINI   *The Death of the Virgin,* tempera-on-wood altarpiece with arched top, 74¾ × 59
Provenance: Charles Butler, London; Charles Fairfax Murray, London, 1911; Duveen; Philip Lehman, New York, 1929; Robert Lehman, New York; Metropolitan Museum of Art, New York.

BARTOLOMEO VIVARINI   *Virgin and Child,* 28½ × 19″
Provenance: Duveen; Arthur Lehman, New York.

JACOPO BASSANO   *Portrait of a Lady,* c. 1570, oil on canvas, 31 × 25¾″
Provenance: Edward Cheney, Badger Hall, Shropshire; Robert and Evelyn Benson, London; Duveen; Norton Simon Museum, Pasadena, CA.

GIOVANNI BELLINI   *Madonna and Child,* c. 1455–60, tempera and oil on panel, 21¼ × 15¾″
Provenance: Prince Potenziani, Villa San Mauro, Rieti, 1911; Luigi Grassi; Duveen; Philip Lehman, 1916; Metropolitan Museum of Art, New York.
Note: Sir John Pope-Hennessy notes that the paint surface is much abraded and shows signs of extensive retouching.

GIOVANNI BELLINI   *A Portrait of a Young Man,* tempera and oil on wood, 10¼ × 8¼″
Provenance: Baron Arthur de Schickler; Count Hubert de Pourtalès; William Salomon, New York; Duveen; Andrew Mellon; Duveen; Jules Bache; Metropolitan Museum of Art, New York.
Note: Listed in the Duveen Archive's Berenson "X Book" as by Bellini/Vivarini. Sold to Mellon, who returned it, and it went to Bache. Now considered to be by Jacometto Veneziano.

GIOVANNI BELLINI   *Virgin and Child,* oil on panel, 33¾ × 26¾″
Provenance: Hapsburg Imperial Collection, Vienna; Duveen; Norton Simon Museum, Pasadena, CA.

GIOVANNI BELLINI   *Madonna and Child in a Landscape,* oil on panel, 26⅞ × 18¾″
Provenance: Charles Loeser, Florence; Charles Dowdeswell, London; Duveen; Norton Simon Museum, Pasadena, CA.

GIOVANNI BELLINI   *Virgin and Child,* ("The Willys Madonna")
Provenance: Duveen, c. 1915; John North Willys, Toledo; Museu de Arte de Sao Paulo, Brazil.
Note: Willys bought this Bellini at the same time that he bought Fragonard's *The Fountain of Love,* now at the J. Paul Getty Museum.

GIOVANNI BELLINI   *The Madonna and Child,* tempera and oil on wood, 13⅜ × 10⅞″
Provenance: Dukes of Hamilton, Hamilton Palace, Lanark; Sir Michael Robert Shaw-Stewart, Ardgowan, Freenock; Walter Richard Shaw-Stewart, Fonthill Abbey, Tisbury, Wiltshire; Duveen Brothers; Jules Bache, New York; Metropolitan Museum of Art, New York.
Note: Now considered "Workshop of."

GIOVANNI BELLINI   *The Madonna and Child with Saints,* or *The Oblong Madonna,* c. 1490, tempera and oil on wood, 38¼ × 60½″
Provenance: Wynn Ellis, London; William Graham, London; Robert and Evelyn Benson, London; Duveen; Jules Bache, New York; Metropolitan Museum of Art, New York.

Note: When the painting was shown at the New Gallery in 1895, Berenson thought it was by Marco Basaiti. He repeated the verdict in 1901. In 1916, he amended that to "Studio of Bellini." Painting sold by Duveen as a Bellini. Now attributed to "Bellini and Workshop."

GIOVANNI BELLINI   *Portrait of a Senator* or *Portrait of a Man,* or *Portrait of Bartolomeo Colleoni,* now *Portrait of Giovanni Emo,* c. 1475–1480, oil on panel transferred to canvas, 9⅜ × 7½"
Provenance: The Earls Brownlow, Ashridge, Berkhamsted; Duveen, 1937; Kress Collection, New York; National Gallery of Art, Washington, D.C.
Note: Now "Alvise Vivarini."

GIOVANNI BELLINI   *Flight into Egypt,* c. 1500, oil on panel, 29⅝ × 44"
Provenance: Kaiser Friedrich Museum, Berlin; Charles Albert de Burlet, Berlin; Conte Luigi Grassi, Rome; Arthur Sulley, London; Otto H. Kahn, New York; Duveen; Andrew Mellon; National Gallery of Art, Washington, D.C.
Note: Sold through Sulley to Kahn in 1927 with assurance from Berenson that the work was an autograph Bellini; subsequently bought by Mellon, 1937, as by Bellini. Berenson, 1932 and 1936, published as Bellini. Painting a reject from the Kaiser Friedrich and largely repainted by Luigi Grassi (according to Sir Ellis Waterhouse). Now Carpaccio.

GIOVANNI BELLINI   *St. Jerome Reading,* c. 1480–90, 19 × 15"
Provenance: Baron Monson, Gatton Park, Surrey; Charles Butler, London; Robert and Evelyn Benson; Duveen; Clarence H. Mackay, Roslyn, NY, 1929; Duveen; Kress Collection, New York; National Gallery of Art, Washington, D.C.

GIOVANNI BELLINI   *The Madonna and Child,* or *Madonna and Child in a Landscape,* c. 1500, 30⅛ × 23½"
Provenance: Otto von Wesendonck, Berlin; M. Lempertz, Cologne; Duveen; Kress Collection, New York; National Gallery of Art, Washington, D.C.
Note: Painting was exhibited for many years in the Gemalde Galerie, Provinzial Museum, Bonn, and bought in the Bessing sale by M. Lempertz, Cologne. Sold to Duveen, 4/12/37, for £421 18 s. Restored by William Suhr for $1,600. Berenson had considered the painting a studio copy and promoted it to "a late autograph work" after the painting was bought by Duveen.

GIOVANNI BELLINI   *The Infant Bacchus,* c. 1505–10, oil on panel transferred to panel, 18⅞ × 14½"
Provenance: Frederick Richards Leyland, London; Robert and Evelyn Benson; Duveen; Kress Collection, New York; National Gallery of Art, Washington, D.C.

GIOVANNI BELLINI   *Portrait of a Young Man in Red,* c. 1480, oil on panel, 12½ × 10¼"
Provenance: Gallery of Andrea Vendramin, Venice; Manfred, Count of Ingenheim, Ober-Rengersdorf, near Dresden; Duveen; Andrew Mellon; National Gallery of Art, Washington, D.C.

GIOVANNI BELLINI   *Madonna and Child with Saints,* c. 1490, oil on panel, 29¼ × 20"
Provenance: Walter Wysard, Pangbourne, Buckinghamshire; John R. Thompson, Lake

Forest, IL; Duveen; Kress Collection, New York; National Gallery of Art, Washington, D.C.
Note: Now "After Bellini."

GIOVANNI BELLINI   *Orpheus,* c. 1515, transferred from wood to canvas, 18⅝ × 32″
Provenance: Stefano Bardini; Ugo Bardini; Duveen; Widener Collection; National Gallery of Art, Washington, D.C.
Note: In her oral history Edith Standen said that when Widener owned it, "they called it a Giorgione."

GIOVANNI BELLINI   *Virgin and Child in a Landscape,* oil on panel, 27 × 19″
Provenance: Charles Loeser, Florence; Walter Dowdeswell; Duveen; present whereabouts unknown.
Note: Duveen Archives show that the company was looking for the painting for years and did not realize they already owned it. They paid £1,200 for it.

GIOVANNI BELLINI   *Saint Sebastian,* 25¼ × 21¾″
Provenance: Kaiser Friedrich Museum, Berlin; Duveen; present whereabouts unknown.

GIOVANNI BELLINI   *Madonna and Child with Green Curtain*
Provenance: Lord Northbrook; Duveen; Ralph Booth, Detroit; Duveen; Kress Collection, New York; National Gallery of Art, Washington, D.C.; High Museum of Art, Atlanta, GA.
Note: Now "Giovanni Bellini and Assistant." Duveen records show that Duveen sold the painting to Booth for $7,000 and bought it back for $40,000.

GIOVANNI BELLINI   *Madonna and Child,* 30 × 21″
Provenance: Duveen; William Salomon; Duveen; present whereabouts unknown.

GIOVANNI BELLINI   *Madonna and Child,* c. 1475, oil on panel, 20⁹⁄₁₆ × 16⁵⁄₁₆″
Provenance: Niccolo d'Attimis, Conte Maniago, Spilimbergo; Duveen, by 1921; Kress Foundation; National Gallery of Art, Washington, D.C.
Note: One of the paintings briefly held by Carl Hamilton but not paid for. Now "Bellini and Assistant."

GIOVANNI BELLINI   *Madonna and Child,* 20½ × 16″
Provenance: Arthur Ruck, London; Duveen; Earl of Harewood.

GIOVANNI BELLINI   *Madonna and Child,* c. 1480, 29 × 22½″
Provenance: Baron Michele Lazzaroni, Paris; Duveen; The Huntington, San Marino, CA.
Note: Much abraded and repainted.

JACOPO BELLINI   *Madonna and Child*
Provenance: Archduke Leopold of Austria; Hapsburg family of Vienna; Duveen, by 1926; present whereabouts unknown.

JACOPO BELLINI   *Profile Portrait of a Boy,* c. 1400–70/71, tempera and oil on panel, 9⅞ × 7″

Provenance: Otto Mündler, Paris; Gustave Dreyfus, Paris; Duveen, by 1930; Kress Foundation; National Gallery of Art, Washington, D.C.
Note: In 1907, when it was in the Dreyfus Collection, Berenson thought the painting was by Boltraffio. After it was bought by Duveen, it was sold to Kress as a Jacopo Bellini (1937). Now "Attributed to Jacopo Bellini."

BENEDETTO DA MAIANO   *The Virgin Annunciate,* c. 1492, sculpture, polychrome terra-cotta, h. 41″
Provenance: Conte Rasponi Spinelli, Borgo San Sepolcro; Duveen; Benjamin Altman, New York; Metropolitan Museum of Art, New York.

BENEDETTO DA MAIANO   *A Florentine Statesman,* c. 1490, terra-cotta bust, 22 × 26″
Provenance: Ginori Family, Florence; Liechtenstein Gallery, Vienna; Clarence Mackay, Roslyn, NY; Duveen; Kress Collection, New York; National Gallery of Art, Washington, D.C.

BENEDETTO DA MAIANO   *The Madonna and Child,* c. 1491, white marble tondo, diameter 26½″
Provenance: Max Lyon, Paris; Duveen; Kress Collection, New York; National Gallery of Art, Washington, D.C.

BENOZZO DI LESE DI SANDRO   *St. Ursula with Angels and Donor*
Provenance: Herzöge von Sachsen-Meiningen, Schloss Meiningen, Thuringen; Duveen; Samuel H. Kress; National Gallery of Art, Washington, D.C.

BENVENUTO DI GIOVANNI   *Madonna and Child,* c. 1470, tempera on panel, 27¹¹⁄₁₆ × 18⅛″
Provenance: Ernest Odiot, Paris; Chabrières-Arlès, Oullin; Duveen; Philip Lehman, 1916; Metropolitan Museum of Art, New York.

BENVENUTO DI GIOVANNI   *Nativity*
Provenance: Sir Philip Burne-Jones, Sussex; Samuel Untermyer; Jean Paul Getty, Malibu, CA; J. Paul Getty Museum, Los Angeles; deaccessioned, 1992.

BENVENUTO DI GIOVANNI   *Madonna and Child with Two Angels,* c. 1500, arched panel, 25½ × 18½″
Provenance: Bertram, 5th Earl of Ashburnham; Lady Ashburnham, Battle, Sussex; Robert Langton Douglas, Dublin; Duveen; Detroit Institute of Arts.
Note: One of the paintings briefly held by Carl Hamilton. Sold to the Detroit Institute in 1924 for $6,827.

BERNARDINO DI CONTI   *Portrait of Beatrice d'Este,* on panel
Provenance: Duveen; Carl Hamilton; present whereabouts unknown.
Note: Hamilton was trying to sell the painting for $300,000 in 1924.

BERNARDINO DI CONTI   *Portrait of a Woman,* or *Portrait of a Lady,* 31 × 22¼″
Provenance: Duveen Archives note "Ex Weber." Went to Arabella Huntington.

GIOVANNI LORENZO BERNINI   *Bust of Louis XIV,* c. 1665, bronze bust, h. 41½"
Provenance: Philippe, Duke of Orléans, Château de Saint-Cloud; E. Williamson, Paris; Sir Stuart Samuel, London; Duveen; George J. Gould, Lakewood, NJ; Kress Collection, New York; National Gallery of Art, Washington, D.C.

BERTOLDO DI GIOVANNI   *Heraldic Figure of a Man,* or *Heraldic Wild Man,* c. 1475–8, bronze statuette, h. 8¾"
Provenance: Charles Loeser, Florence; J. Pierpont Morgan, New York; Duveen; Frick Collection, New York.

BERTOLDO DI GIOVANNI   *Hercules,* or *Hercules in Repose,* c. 1483–5, bronze statuette, h. 8½"
Provenance: Ferencz Aurel von Pulszky; J. Pierpont Morgan; Duveen; Frick Collection, New York.
Note: Present attribution: "Florentine, early sixteenth century."

ROBERT BEVAN   *The Cab Horse*
Provenance: Duveen Paintings Fund; Tate Gallery, London.

ABRAHAM HENRICKSZ VAN BEYEREN   *Still-Life with a Silver Wine-Jar and a Reflected Portrait of the Artist*
Provenance: William Frederick le Poer, 5th Earl of Clancarty, Downs House, Plumpton, Sussex; Charles Sedelmeyer, Paris; Rodolphe Kann, Paris; Duveen; G. von Hollitscher; W. E. Duits, London; Van Diemen Galleries, Berlin; J. and S. Goldschmidt, Berlin; Mr. and Mrs. T. W. H. Ward, London; Ashmolean Museum of Art and Archaeology, Oxford.

FRANCESCO BISSOLO   *The Annunciation,* oil on panel, transferred to canvas, 43¾ × 39½"
Provenance: Conte Manfrini; Robert and Evelyn Benson; Duveen; Norton Simon Museum, Pasadena, CA; Los Angeles County Museum of Art.

BEATRICE BLAND   *The Almond Tree,* oil on board
Provenance: Duveen Paintings Fund, 1926; presented to the Ferens Art Gallery, Hull, England, by the executors of the Duveen estate in 1949.

GIOVANNI BOLOGNA   *Mercury,* c. 1603–13, bronze sculpture, 69⅝ × 19 × 37¼"
Provenance: Duveen; Andrew W. Mellon; National Gallery of Art, Washington, D.C.
Note: Now "Attributed to Adriaen de Vries."

GIOVANNI BOLOGNA   *Virtue Subduing Vice,* or *Virtue Triumphant Over Vice,* c. 1567–70, bronze group, h. 11½"
Provenance: Charles Mannheim, Paris; J. Pierpont Morgan, New York; Duveen; Henry Clay Frick, New York; Frick Collection, New York.
Note: Now Massimiliano Soldani.

GIOVANNI BOLOGNA   *Virtue Subduing Vice,* c. 1567–70, white marble high relief, 24½ × 14"

Provenance: Sir George Donaldson, Hove, Sussex; Duveen; Benjamin Altman, New York; Metropolitan Museum of Art, New York.

GIOVANNI BOLOGNA   *Nessus and Dejanira,* c. 1580–90, bronze group, h. 19¼"
Provenance: Duke of Marlborough, Blenheim Palace; J. Pierpont Morgan, New York; Duveen; Henry E. Huntington, San Marino, CA; The Huntington, San Marino, CA.

GIOVANNI BOLOGNA   *Hercules and the Boar of Erymanthus,* c. 1590, bronze statuette, h. 17½"
Provenance: Sir George Donaldson, Hove, Sussex; P. A. B. and Joseph E. Widener, Elkins Park, PA; National Gallery of Art, Washington, D.C.

GIOVANNI ANTONIO BOLTRAFFIO   *Portrait of a Youth,* c. 1500, on wood, 18⅜ × 13¾"
Provenance: Baron Gustave Salomon de Rothschild, Paris; Edward Albert Sassoon, 2nd Bart., London; Sir Philip Albert Gustave Sassoon, 3rd Bart., London; Duveen; Mr. and Mrs. Ralph Harman Booth, Detroit; National Gallery of Art, Washington, D.C.

DAVID BOMBERG   *Jerusalem,* oil on canvas
Provenance: Duveen Paintings Fund, 1926; presented to the Ferens Art Gallery, Hull, England, by the executors of the Duveen estate in 1949.

BENEDETTO BONFIGLI   *Madonna and Child with Saints,* 31½ × 21"
Provenance: Baron Michele Lazzaroni; Mrs. Otto H. Kahn; Duveen; present whereabouts unknown.
Note: Extensively repainted by Lazzaroni.

SANDRO BOTTICELLI   *Madonna and Child,* c. 1470, tempera on panel, 29⁵⁄₁₆ × 21⁷⁄₁₆"
Provenance: Prince Bartolomeo Corsini, Villa di Mezzomonte, near Florence; Prince Tommaso Corsini; Prince Andrea Corsini; Prince Tommaso Corsini, Palazzo Corsini, Florence; Beatrice Corsini Pandolfini; Duveen; Andrew W. Mellon; National Gallery of Art, Washington, D.C.

SANDRO BOTTICELLI   *The Last Communion of St. Jerome,* tempera on wood, 13½ × 10"
Provenance: Francesco di Filippo del Pugliese, Florence; Niccolo di Piero del Pugliese, Florence; Marchese Gino Capponi, Palazzo Capponi, Florence; Marchese Farinola, Palazzo Capponi, Florence; Duveen; Benjamin Altman, 1912–3; Metropolitan Museum of Art, New York.

SANDRO BOTTICELLI   *The Coronation of the Virgin,* tempera on canvas, transferred from wood, 39½ × 60¼"
Provenance: Sir Edward Burne-Jones, London; Prince Charles-Max von Lichnowsky, Kuchelna, Prussian Silesia; Duveen, 1927; Jules Bache, New York; Metropolitan Museum of Art, New York.
Note: Now "Follower of Botticelli."

SANDRO BOTTICELLI   *Madonna and Child with Adoring Angels,* tempera on panel
Provenance: Mrs. John F. Austen; Duveen; Norton Simon Museum, Pasadena, CA.

SANDRO BOTTICELLI   *Portrait of a Youth,* early 1480s, tempera on panel, 16¼ × 12½″
Provenance: Louis, Count of Pourtalès-Gorgier, Paris; Baron Arthur de Schickler, Martin-vast, Manche; Countess Hubert de Pourtalès; Duveen; Clarence H. Mackay, Roslyn, NY; Duveen; Andrew Mellon, 1936; National Gallery of Art, Washington, D.C.
Note: Although Berenson, in a letter to Mackay, called this painting a quintessentially characteristic work of Botticelli, opinion has always been divided. When it was in the collection of Pourtalès-Gorgier, it was considered a Masaccio. Duveen's staff thought it was by the less important Florentine Antonio del Pollaiuolo and wrote that it was generally believed to be a school picture (3/23/23). It is accepted by the National Gallery as a work of the master's hand.

SANDRO BOTTICELLI   *Head of the Risen Christ,* or *The Resurrected Christ,* c. 1483–4, 18 × 11¾″
Provenance: Emile Gavet, Paris; Mrs. Oliver H. P. Belmont, Newport, RI; Duveen; Dr. W. R. Valentiner, Detroit; Detroit Institute of Arts.
Note: Some experts, citing the work's lack of detail, believe it to be a school or workshop piece. Detroit conservators note that the painting was at some point transferred to a new panel and probably cut down on at least three sides.

SANDRO BOTTICELLI   *Virgin and Child with St. John,* 18 × 14½″
Provenance: Mrs. John F. Austen, Kent; Duveen, 1928; John D. Rockefeller; present whereabouts unknown.
Note: Duveen bought the painting at a Christie's auction, 12/12/28, for $60,000.

SANDRO BOTTICELLI   *Madonna and Child with Angels,* c. 1470–1476, oil and tempera on panel, 35⅛ × 23⅝″
Provenance: Charles Sedelmeyer, Paris; sold to P. A. B. Widener before World War I and returned; Duveen, by 1926; Mrs. William J. Babington Macaulay, Manhasset, NY; Duveen, 1939; Samuel H. Kress; National Gallery of Art, Washington, D.C.
Note: Painting was considered as by Fra Filippo Lippi when owned by Widener. After Duveen acquired it, Berenson believed he saw an early Botticelli beneath the extensive repaint. Now "Attributed to Botticelli."

SANDRO BOTTICELLI   *Portrait of a Man in a Red Vest*
Provenance: M. Trotti, Paris; Duveen; present whereabouts unknown.
Note: Bought by Duveen in November 1923 for £700.

SANDRO BOTTICELLI   *Adoration,* or *The Nativity,* fresco transferred to canvas, 63½ × 54″
Provenance: Kaiser Friedrich Museum; Julius Bohler; Sir William Abdy; Duveen, 1937 (for approximately £2,000); Columbia Museum of Art, Columbia, SC.
Note: The painting has been heavily restored; present labeling is "Attributed to Botticelli."

SANDRO BOTTICELLI   *Portrait of Giuliano de' Medici,* tempera on panel, 21½ × 14⅛″
Provenance: Count Procolo Isolani, Bologna; Baron Michele Lazzaroni; Duveen; Mrs. Otto Kahn, by 1914; Countess Battyany, Castagnola; present whereabouts unknown.
Note: Opinion on the painting was divided when Duveen bought it just before World War I, some considering it a modern fake.

SANDRO BOTTICELLI   *Virgin and Child,* tondo
Provenance: Lord d'Abernon; Count Alessandro Contini-Bonacossi; Marco Grassi; Duveen; present whereabouts unknown.
Note: Berenson considered it only a school work when queried in 1929, shortly after it was acquired. One of the paintings Duveen could not get out of Italy because of heavy export duties.

SANDRO BOTTICELLI   *Virgin and Child,* c. 1500–5, tondo, diameter 33″
Provenance: Count de Sarty, Paris; Baron de Vandeuvre, Paris; F. Kleinberger; Duveen; El Paso Museum of Art, El Paso, TX.
Note: When Duveen bought the painting in 1924 it had a black background. This was removed by Madame Helfer, his Paris conservator, revealing Botticelliesque architectural detail.

FRANCESCO BOTTICINI   *Madonna and Child,* circular panel, diameter 42¼″
Provenance: Palazzo Panciatichi, Florence; Robert and Evelyn Benson; Duveen; Cincinnati Art Museum.

FRANCESCO BOTTICINI   *Madonna Adoring Child*
Provenance: ? Hengel; Duveen; present whereabouts unknown.
Note: One of the paintings Carl Hamilton contracted to buy in November 1919.

FRANCESCO BOTTICINI   *Virgin and Child with Four Angels and Two Cherubim,* tempera on panel, 25¾ × 19¼″
Provenance: Martin Henry Colnaghi, London; Robert and Evelyn Benson; Duveen; Norton Simon Museum, Pasadena, CA.

FRANÇOIS BOUCHER   *The Seasons,* four painted panels
Provenance: Marquise de Pompadour; Marquis de Marigny et de Menars; Nicolas Beaujon, Paris; Madame Ridgway; Eugene Fischhof; E. R. Bacon, New York; Duveen; Frick Collection, New York.

FRANÇOIS BOUCHER   *The Arts and Sciences,* eight painted panels
Provenance: Marquise de Pompadour, Château de Crécy (?); Robert, Lord Pembroke; Alexander Barker; Samson Wertheimer; Sedelmeyer, Paris; Maurice Kann; Duveen; Frick Collection, New York.

FRANÇOIS BOUCHER   *La Fontaine d'Amour* and *La Pipée aux Oiseaux,* two companion pieces
Provenance: First Baron Michelham; Aimée Geraldine Bradshaw Stern, Baroness Michelham; Duveen, buying through Captain Jefferson Davis Cohn; Anna Thomson Dodge, Detroit; J. Paul Getty Museum, Los Angeles, 1971.

DIRK BOUTS   *The Madonna and Child,* panel, 11½ × 8¼″
Provenance: Gabriel J. P. Weyer; Prince Karl von Hohenzollern; Royal Museum, Sigmaringen; Duveen; Jules Bache; Metropolitan Museum of Art, New York.
Note: Now "Workshop of Dirk Bouts."

DIRK BOUTS *Moses Before the Burning Bush,* 17⅛ × 13⅝"
Provenance: T. Lloyd Roberts, London; Henry Willett, Brighton; Charles Sedelmeyer, Paris; Rodolphe Kann, Paris; Duveen; John G. Johnson, Philadelphia.

ADRIAEN BROUWER *The Brawl,* oil on wood, 9⅝ × 7½"
Provenance: Etienne Martin, Baron de Beurnonville, Paris; A. Febvre, Paris; Rodolphe Kann, Paris; Duveen; Michael Friedsam, New York; Metropolitan Museum of Art, New York.
Note: Now "Copy after Adriaen Brouwer, seventeenth century."

FREDERICK BROWN *Self-Portrait,* oil on canvas
Provenance: Duveen Paintings Fund, 1926; presented to the Ferens Art Gallery, Hull, England, by the executors of Lord Duveen in 1949.

BRUSSELS TAPESTRIES Four anonymous tapestries, c. 1500–10; *Charity,* 150 × 250"; *Pride,* 148 × 264"; *Courage,* 152 × 260"; and *Wrath,* 150 × 264"
Provenance: Count Hunolstein; Duveen, 1922; Detroit Institute of Arts.

PIER JACOPO BUONACCOLSI, "IL ANTICO" *Apollo, Defender of Delphi,* bronze statuette, c. 1485–90, h. 15⅜"
Provenance: Ferencz Aurel von Pulszky, Budapest; George von Rath, Budapest; J. Pierpont Morgan, New York; Duveen; Henry E. Huntington, San Marino, CA; The Huntington, San Marino, CA.
Note: Now "Italian, c. 1500, circle of Tullio Lombardo."

SIR EDWARD BURNE-JONES *Head of Miss M. Benson, Medusa, The Pilgrim,* and *Andromeda*
Provenance: Four paintings given to the Tate Gallery, London, by Joseph Duveen.

BYZANTINE, THIRTEENTH CENTURY *Madonna and Child on a Curved Throne,* or *Enthroned Madonna and Child*
Provenance: ? Weissberger, Madrid; Emile Pares, Paris; G. W. Arnold; Duveen; Mrs. Otto Kahn; National Gallery of Art, Washington, D.C., 1949.
Note: According to a National Gallery conservator, the painting has been massively restored.

GIOVANNI ANTONIO CANAL, OR CANALETTO *Capriccio: Piazza San Marco Looking South and West*
Provenance: Mrs. John Ashley; Duveen; Dr. Benjamin Borow, Bound Brook, NJ; Nehmad, Milan; Dino Fabri, Zurich; Harari and Johns Ltd., London; Ahmanson Foundation, Los Angeles; Los Angeles County Museum of Art, 1983.

ELIA CANDIDO *Hermes with the Head of Argus,* or *Mercury with the Head of Argus,* c. 1570, bronze statuette, h. 21¼"
Provenance: Stefano Bardini; Oscar Hainauer, Berlin; Duveen; Henry Clay Frick; Frick Collection, New York.
Note: Now "Florentine, third quarter of the sixteenth century."

ANTONIO CANOVA   *The Hope Venus,* marble statue, c. 1817–8, h. 70", with pedestal by Thomas Hope, h. 42"
Provenance: Thomas Hope, London and The Deepdene, near Dorking, Surrey; Henrietta Adela Hope; Duveen; Senator William Andrews Clark; Corcoran Gallery of Art, Washington, D.C.
Note: One of several versions of Canova's *Venus Italica* designed for the Vatican Museum and now at the Hearst San Simeon State Historical Monument, CA, that the artist completed himself.

GIOVANNI CARIANI   *Portrait of a Gentleman,* or *Portrait of a Man with a Sword,* 30 × 29"
Provenance: Robert and Evelyn Benson, London; Duveen; Acquavella Galleries, New York; Giuseppe Bellini, Florence; J. Paul Getty Museum, Los Angeles. Deaccessioned in 1992; present whereabouts unknown.

RAFFAELLO CARLI   *The Mass of Saint Gregory,* on wood, transferred to canvas in 1891, 76½ × 74½"
Provenance: Collections of S. Woodburn and Sir John Ramsden; Robert and Evelyn Benson, London; Duveen; John Ringling, Sarasota, FL; the Ringling Museum of Art, Sarasota, FL.
Note: Mark Leonard, conservator at the Getty, found the painting severely damaged and totally repainted. "The picture was quite literally falling apart." He cited a letter in which Duveen noted Ringling was assembling a collection for a museum and that now was the moment for the firm to unload large numbers of pictures they did not want, including "Benson rubbish." Present attribution: Raffaellino del Garbo.

VITTORE CARPACCIO   *Portrait of a Venetian Nobleman,* c. 1510, oil on panel, 14 × 10¾"
Provenance: W. E. Gladstone, London; William Graham, London; John P. Carrington, London; Robert Langton Douglas, London; Martin Henry Colnaghi, London; Mortimer L. Schiff, New York; John Mortimer Schiff, New York; Duveen; Norton Simon Museum, Pasadena, CA.
Note: Now "Attributed to."

VITTORE CARPACCIO   *A Saint Reading,* or *The Virgin Reading,* c. 1505, on wood, transferred to canvas, 30¾ × 20"
Provenance: William Alleyne Cecil, 3rd Marquess of Exeter, Burghley House, Northamptonshire; Robert and Evelyn Benson, Buckhurst Park, Sussex; Duveen; Samuel H. Kress; National Gallery of Art, Washington, D.C.

VITTORE CARPACCIO   *The Flight into Egypt,* c. 1500, oil on panel, 28¼ × 43⅞"
Provenance: Duveen; Andrew Mellon; National Gallery of Art, Washington, D.C.

JEAN-BAPTISTE CARPEAUX   *Neapolitan Fisherman* and *Neapolitan Fisherboy,* marble, 36¼ × 16½ × 18⅜"
Provenance: Duveen; Samuel H. Kress; National Gallery of Art, Washington, D.C.
Note: Signed and dated 1861.

EUGÈNE CARRIÈRE   *Portrait*, or *Man Writing*, oil on academy board, 12½ × 13⅜″
Provenance: Armand Lowengard; Duveen; Detroit Institute of Arts.
Note: Sometimes thought to be a portrait of Paul Verlaine.

ANDREA DEL CASTAGNO   Predella
Provenance: ? Fungini, Perugia; Charles Fairfax Murray; Duveen; present whereabouts unknown.
Note: One of three paintings Van Marle was about to publish as a fake. Duveen subsequently wrote (4/18/30) that the painting was shown at the Italian Exhibition at Burlington House in 1930 and that he sold it to an American collector for a large sum.

VINCENZO DI BIAGIO CATENA   *Madonna and Child with St. Peter and St. Catherine of Alexandria*
Provenance: William Salomon, New York; P. A. B. Widener, Elkins Park, PA; Duveen; Norton Simon Museum, Pasadena, CA.

VINCENZO DI BIAGIO CATENA   *Rest on the Flight to Egypt,* oil on panel
Provenance: Sir John Stuart Hepburn-Forbes, Pitsligo, Aberdeenshire; Sir John Northwick, 2nd Baron, Thirlestane House, Cheltenham, Gloucestershire; J. C. W. Sawbridge-Erle-Drax, Olantigh Towers, Wye, Kent; Duveen; Norton Simon Museum, Pasadena, CA.

DANESE CATTANEO   *Titian,* or *Bust of a Jurist,* bronze bust, life size, h. 27½″
Provenance: Madame Louis Stern, Paris; Duveen; Henry Clay Frick, New York; Frick Collection, New York.

PIETRO CAVALLINI   *Madonna and Child*
Provenance: Duveen; Carl Hamilton, New York; present whereabouts unknown.
Note: Hamilton undertook to buy this painting from Duveen (letter, 11/3/19) for $65,000. Duveen sold it to Mellon in 1936 for $120,000.

BENVENUTO CELLINI   *Triton and Dolphins,* or *Triton Blowing a Trumpet,* c. 1552–4, bronze statuette, h. 17¼″
Provenance: Earl of Bessborough, London; J. Pierpont Morgan, New York; Duveen; Henry Clay Frick, New York; Frick Collection, New York.
Note: Now "Attributed to Battista Lorenzi."

BENVENUTO CELLINI   *Ganymede,* c. 1547–50, bronze group, h. 14″
Provenance: J. Pierpont Morgan; Duveen; Henry Clay Frick, New York; Frick Collection, New York.
Note: Now "After Benvenuto Cellini."

BENVENUTO CELLINI   *Virtue Triumphant Over Vice,* or *Virtue Overcoming Vice,* sixteenth century (first half), bronze group, h. 9½″
Provenance: Lady Amelius Beauclerk, London; J. Pierpont Morgan, New York; Duveen; Henry Clay Frick, New York; Frick Collection, New York.
Note: Now "Roman, late sixteenth century."

BENVENUTO CELLINI *Virtue Triumphant Over Vice,* sixteenth century (first half), bronze group, h. 10¼″
Provenance: John Edward Taylor, London; P. A. B. Widener, Elkins Park, PA; Joseph E. Widener; National Gallery of Art, Washington, D.C.

CENTRAL ITALIAN, THIRTEENTH CENTURY *Madonna and Child with Angels*
Provenance: Duveen; Samuel H. Kress; National Gallery of Art, Washington, D.C.; Fogg Art Museum, Cambridge, MA.
Note: Painting was attacked by Richard Offner as a fake when it was displayed at the National Gallery of Art in 1941; it is now in the study collection at the Fogg, where it is considered a modern pastiche in the style of Marcovaldo di Coppo.

PAUL CÉZANNE *The Bathers*
Provenance: Gift to the Tate Gallery, London, by Joseph Duveen.

JEAN BAPTISTE SIMÉON CHARDIN *Interior, with Mother and Child*
Provenance: Lord Leconfield, Petworth House; Duveen; present whereabouts unknown.

PETRUS CHRISTUS *The Annunciation*
Provenance: Duveen, 1926; Philip Lehman; present whereabouts unknown.

PETRUS CHRISTUS *The Nativity,* or *Adoration of the Child,* c. 1450, oil on panel, 51¼ × 38¼″
Provenance: Prince Manuel Yturbe, Madrid; Duchess of Parcent, Madrid; Duveen; Andrew W. Mellon; National Gallery of Art, Washington, D.C.

CIMA DA CONEGLIANO *St. Jerome in the Wilderness,* c. 1495, oil on panel, 19 × 15¾″
Provenance: Duveen; Samuel H. Kress; National Gallery of Art, Washington, D.C.

CIMA DA CONEGLIANO *Madonna and Child with St. Francis and St. Clare,* tempera on wood, 8 × 10½″
Provenance: Etienne Martin, Baron de Beurnonville, Paris; Oscar Hainauer, Berlin; Duveen, 1906; George and Florence Blumenthal, New York; Metropolitan Museum of Art, New York.

CIMA DA CONEGLIANO *Madonna and Child with St. Jerome and St. John the Baptist,* c. 1500, oil on panel
Provenance: Baron Carlo Marochetti, Paris; Jacques Seligmann, Paris; 1st Viscount D'Abernon, Esher Place, Surrey; Duveen; Andrew W. Mellon, Pittsburgh; National Gallery of Art, Washington, D.C.

CIMABUE (CENNI DI PEPO) *Christ Between St. Peter and St. James Major,* late thirteenth century, tempera on panel, triptych
Provenance: Alexis-François Artaud de Montor, Paris; Julien Gréau, Paris; Countess Bertrand de Brousillon, Paris; Duveen, 1919; Carl W. Hamilton, New York, on credit; Duveen; Andrew W. Mellon, Pittsburgh; National Gallery of Art, Washington, D.C.
Note: Hamilton undertook to buy the painting for $150,000 but never did buy it. Duveen sold to Mellon for $325,000 in December 1936. Now "Follower of Cimabue."

JOHN CONSTABLE   *View on the Stour near Dedham,* 1822, canvas, 51 × 74"
Provenance: John Arrowsmith, Paris; Louis-Joseph-Auguste Coutan, Paris, 1824; William Carpenter, Keeper of Prints and Drawings, British Museum, 1845; Thomas Preston Miller; Thomas Horrocks Miller of Poulton-le-Fylde, Lancashire, 1860; Duveen, 1925; Henry E. Huntington; The Huntington, San Marino, CA.

JEAN BAPTISTE CAMILLE COROT   *The Fisherman*
Provenance: Bought by Henry Duveen at the Yerkes sale in New York in 1910 for $80,500; present whereabouts unknown.

ANTONIO CORREGGIO   *Christ's Farewell to His Mother,* or *Christ Taking Leave of His Mother,* oil on canvas, 33½ × 29½"
Provenance: D. Antonio Rossi, Milan; Eugenia Crippa Parlatore, Florence; Vitale de Tivoli, London; Charles Fairfax Murray, London; Robert and Evelyn Benson; Duveen, 1927; National Gallery, London, 1927, gift of Sir Joseph Duveen.

ANTONIO CORREGGIO   *The Mystic Marriage of St. Catherine,* c. 1510–4, on panel, 53⅝ × 48½"
Provenance: Dukes of Mantua; King Charles I of England; Remigius van Leemput, London; Prince Wenzel Anton von Kaunitz, Vienna; Andreas Ritter von Reisinger, Vienna; Camillo Castiglioni, Vienna, 1920; Duveen, 1925; Mrs. Anna Scripps Whitcomb, New York; Detroit Institute of Arts.

FRANCESCO DEL COSSA   *Portrait of Giovanni Bentivoglio,* c. 1480, tempera on panel, 21¼ × 15"
Provenance: Louis Charles Timbal, Paris; Gustave Dreyfus, Paris; Duveen, 1930; Samuel H. Kress; National Gallery of Art, Washington, D.C.
Note: Now "Ercole de' Roberti."

FRANCESCO DEL COSSA   *Portrait of Ginevra Bentivoglio,* c. 1470, tempera on panel, 21¼ × 15"
Provenance: Louis Charles Timbal, Paris; Gustave Dreyfus, Paris; Duveen, 1930; Samuel H. Kress; National Gallery of Art, Washington, D.C.
Note: Companion piece to *Portrait of Giovanni Bentivoglio.* Now "Ercole de' Roberti."

FRANCESCO DEL COSSA   *St. Liberalis,* or *St. Florian,* c. 1473, tempera on panel, 31¼ × 21⅝"
Provenance: Count Ugo Beni, Gubbio, by 1858; Joseph Spiridon, Paris; Duveen, 1929; Samuel H. Kress; National Gallery of Art, Washington, D.C.
Note: From a polyptych, commissioned by Floriano Griffoni as an altarpiece for a family chapel in the church of San Petronio, Bologna.

FRANCESCO DEL COSSA   *St. Lucy,* c. 1473, tempera on panel, 31¼ × 21⅝"
Provenance: Count Ugo Beni, Gubbio, by 1858; Joseph Spiridon, Paris; Duveen, by 1932; Samuel H. Kress; National Gallery of Art, Washington, D.C.
Note: Companion piece to *St. Florian* and possible companion piece to similar works by Cossa in London's National Gallery, the Brera in Milan, and the Pinacoteca Vaticana in Rome.

LORENZO COSTA   *Portrait of a Man*
Note: Duveen Archive records show that the painting was invoiced to London in March of
1927. Further information is that the sale to Carl Hamilton was canceled and the painting
returned by him. It was subsequently bought by A. J. Fisher as a Ghirlandaio. Present
whereabouts unknown.

JOHN SELL COTMAN   *Crowland Abbey*
Provenance: Gift to Tate Gallery, London, by Joseph Duveen.

ANTONIO COYSEVOX   *Bust of Louis XIV,* bronze
Note: Duveen Archive records show that this bronze by the chief sculptor to Louis XIV was
sold to Arabella Huntington in 1908 for 30,000 francs.

CARLO CRIVELLI   *Pieta,* or *The Deposition of Christ,* or *Lamentation,* c. 1470, lunette
panel, 16½ × 45″
Provenance: Alexander Barker, London (by 1854); Earl of Dudley, London; Thomas Brock-
lebank, Wateringbury Place, Kent; Duveen, 1917; Carl Hamilton; Duveen, 1925; Detroit
Institute of Arts, 1925.
Note: Part of a polyptych from San Fermo, Ascoli. One of the few paintings for which Carl
Hamilton actually paid ($75,000). It later went to Detroit for $15,500.

CARLO CRIVELLI   *Madonna and Child,* c. 1490, tempera on panel, 15⅜ × 12⅛″
Provenance: Eugen Miller von Aichholz, Vienna; Camillo Castiglioni, by 1924; E. ten Cate,
Enschede, Netherlands; Duveen, 1930; Samuel H. Kress, 1937; National Gallery of Art,
Washington, D.C.

CARLO CRIVELLI   *Madonna and Child Enthroned,* tempera on panel, 55½ × 23⅜″
Provenance: Baron Michele Lazzaroni, Paris; Duveen; Philip Lehman, 1912; Metropolitan
Museum of Art, New York.
Note: Sir John Pope-Hennessy, in *Italian Paintings,* notes that few aspects of this former
altarpiece have remained untouched and that "the figures of the Virgin and Child are in all
essentials false" [228]. Now labeled "Attributed to Carlo Crivelli."

CARLO CRIVELLI   *The Madonna and Child,* tempera and gold on wood, 14⅞ × 10″
Provenance: Casa Lenti, Ascoli; Walter Jones; the Earls of Northbrook; Duveen; Jules
Bache, New York; Metropolitan Museum of Art, New York.
Note: In his catalogue of Italian paintings at the Metropolitan Museum, Federico Zeri
called the painting "one of Crivelli's most important and characteristic works" [24].

CARLO CRIVELLI   *Madonna and Child,* c. 1472, 38 × 17″
Provenance: Marland and Graham Collections; Robert and Evelyn Benson; Duveen, 1927;
Metropolitan Museum of Art, New York, bequest of Jack Linsky, 1982.
Note: In 1952, the painting was for sale for $12,000.

CHARLES CUNDALL   *The Artist's Mother,* oil on canvas
Provenance: Duveen Paintings Fund, 1926; presented to the Ferens Art Gallery, Hull, England, by the executors of Lord Duveen's estate, 1949.

ALBERT CUYP   *The River Maas at Dordrecht,* or *The Maas at Dordrecht,* c. 1650, oil on canvas, 46 × 57½"
Provenance: Alexis de La Hante, London; Sir Abraham Hume; Viscount Alford; Earl Brownlow, Ashridge Park, Berkhampstead, Hertfordshire; Duveen; Andrew Mellon; National Gallery of Art, Washington, D.C.
Note: Duveen bought the painting at Christie's in May 1923 for 17,000 guineas (about $92,000) and seems to have had trouble disposing of this wonderful work. At one time he was asked if he would sell the painting at a loss; he declined. Mellon bought it in 1937.

BERNARDO DADDI   *Madonna and Child Enthroned with Saints and Angels,* central panel of a triptych, 21½ × 12"
Provenance: Charles Butler, London; Herbert Henry Spender Clay, Ford Manor, Lingford, Surrey; Henry Charles Somers Somerset, Reigate Priory, Surrey; Duveen, by 1925; Henry Goldman, New York; Duveen; Samuel H. Kress, New York; National Gallery of Art, Washington, D.C.; Nelson-Atkins Museum of Art, Kansas City, MO.
Note: Now "Bernardo Daddi and Assistant."

VINCENZO DANTI   *The Descent from the Cross,* c. 1560, bronze relief, 17½ × 18½"
Provenance: Stefano Bardini, Florence; Oscar Hainauer, Berlin; P. A. B. Widener and Joseph E. Widener, Elkins Park, PA; National Gallery of Art, Washington, D.C.

GERARD DAVID   *The Rest on the Flight into Egypt,* c. 1510, on wood, 17¾ × 17½"
Provenance: Rev. Montague Taylor, London; Rodolphe Kann, Paris; Duveen; J. Pierpont Morgan, London and New York; Andrew W. Mellon, Pittsburgh; National Gallery of Art, Washington, D.C.

GERARD DAVID   *The Coronation of the Virgin,* c. 1515, oil on panel, 27⅞ × 21¼"
Provenance: Prince Juan de Bourbon, Madrid; Duveen; Norton Simon Museum, Pasadena, CA.

GERARD DAVID   *Christ Taking Leave of His Mother,* oil on wood, arched top, 6⅛ × 4¾"
Provenance: Otto H. Kahn, New York; Duveen; Benjamin Altman, New York; Metropolitan Museum of Art, New York.

GERARD DAVID   *Madonna and Child,* or *Rest on the Flight into Egypt,* oil on panel, 20 × 17"
Provenance: W. Mansell MacCulloch, Touillets, Guernsey, until 1902; Frank Stoop, London, by 1906; Duveen; Jules S. Bache, New York, 1928; Metropolitan Museum of Art, New York.

GERARD DAVID   *The Nativity, with Saints and Donors,* oil on panel triptych, 36 × 53"
Provenance: Ramon F. Urrutia, Madrid; Duveen; Jules S. Bache, New York; Metropolitan Museum of Art, New York.

GERARD DAVID *Virgin and Child,* c. 1520, oil on wood, 10 × 8¼″
Provenance: Claramonte family, counts of La Bisbal, Madrid; R. Traumann, Madrid; Duveen; Michael Friedsam, New York; Metropolitan Museum of Art, New York.
Note: Now "Attributed to Simon Bening."

GERARD DAVID *Christ Carrying the Cross, with the Crucifixion* and *The Resurrection, with the Pilgrims of Emmaus,* two wings of a triptych, oil on oak panel
Provenance: Fourth Earl of Ashburnham, Ashburnham Place; Henry Willett, Brighton; Rodolphe Kann, Paris; Duveen; Philip Lehman, New York, 1912; Metropolitan Museum of Art, New York.

DESIDERIO DA SETTIGNANO *Madonna and Child,* marble, 37¾ × 29¾ × 8¼″
Provenance: Charles Timbal; Gustave Dreyfus; Duveen, 1930; Andrew W. Mellon, Pittsburgh; National Gallery of Art, Washington, D.C.
Note: Bronze is now attributed to "Florentine, nineteenth century," and tentatively dated 1860.

DESIDERIO DA SETTIGNANO *Bust of Manfredi,* or *Astorgio Manfredi,* marble bust, 20¼ × 21¼ × 10⅞″
Provenance: Baron Arthur de Schickler, Paris; Duveen; P. A. B. and Joseph E. Widener, Elkins Park, PA; National Gallery of Art, Washington, D.C.
Note: Mino da Fiesole.

DESIDERIO DA SETTIGNANO *A Young Woman,* stone bust, 26⅛ × 19⅜ × 5⅞″
Provenance: Charles Timbal, Paris; Baron Arthur de Schickler, Martinvast, Manche; Duveen; Detroit Institute of Arts.
Note: Now "Anonymous Italian, mid-nineteenth century," i.e., a forgery.

DESIDERIO DA SETTIGNANO *The Infant Christ,* c. 1455–60, white marble bust, 12 × 10⅜ × 6⅜″
Provenance: Oratory of San Francesco dei Vanchetoni, Florence; Duveen; Samuel H. Kress, New York; National Gallery of Art, Washington, D.C.

DESIDERIO DA SETTIGNANO *Bust of a Boy,* or *Bust of a Little Boy,* c. 1455–60; white marble bust, 10⅜ × 9¾ × 5⅞″
Provenance: Eugène Piot, Paris; Paul van Cuyck, Paris; Louis Charles Timbal, Paris; Gustave Dreyfus, Paris; Duveen; Andrew W. Mellon, Pittsburgh; National Gallery of Art, Washington, D.C.

DESIDERIO DA SETTIGNANO *Saint Cecilia,* c. 1458–60, gray stone plaque, 22½ × 15″
Provenance: Palazzo Brunaccini-Compagni, Florence; Samuel Woodburn, London; Earls of Wemyss, Gosford House, Edinburgh; Edward Drummond Libbey, Toledo, OH; Museum of Art, Toledo, OH.

DESIDERIO DA SETTIGNANO *A Florentine Lady,* polychrome wood and gesso bust, 20¾ × 21¼″

Provenance: Louis Charles Timbal, Paris; Gustave Dreyfus, Paris; Duveen; Andrew W. Mellon, Pittsburgh; National Gallery of Art, Washington, D.C.

DESIDERIO DA SETTIGNANO   *Isotta da Rimini* (Presumed), c. 1460, white marble bust, 20¾ × 19⅜"
Provenance: Alessandro Castellani, Rome; Baron Arthur de Schickler, Martinvast, Manche; Count Hubert de Pourtalès, Paris; Clarence H. Mackay, Roslyn, NY; Samuel H. Kress, New York; National Gallery of Art, Washington, D.C.

DESIDERIO DA SETTIGNANO   *Marietta degli Strozzi,* c. 1464, white marble bust, 22 × 20"
Provenance: Strozzi family, Florence; Prof. G. Magherini Graziani, Città di Castello; Prof. Luigi Grassi, Florence; Duveen; P. A. B. Widener and Joseph Widener, Elkins Park, PA; National Gallery of Art, Washington, D.C.

DESIDERIO DA SETTIGNANO   *The Young Christ and St. John,* c. 1450–60, purple-veined white marble plaque, 15¾ × 15¾"
Provenance: Louis Charles Timbal, Paris; Gustave Dreyfus, Paris; Duveen; Andrew W. Mellon; National Gallery of Art, Washington, D.C.
Note: Now "Imitator of."

DESIDERIO DA SETTIGNANO AND LUCA DELLA ROBBIA   *Bust of a Girl (Portrait of Marietta Strozzi),* terra-cotta bust
Provenance: Duveen; Isabella Stewart Gardner Museum, Boston.
Note: The bust was sold to Mrs. Gardner for $19,500 in 1909 as a bust of Marietta Strozzi glazed by Luca della Robbia. Berenson urged her to buy it on November 20, 1909, because the bust was "a beauty." It is now considered a nineteenth-century pastiche of an Antonio Rossellino portrait bust in the Staatliche Museum, Berlin.

FRANCIS DODD   *Miss Isabel Dacre,* oil on canvas on plywood
Provenance: Duveen Paintings Fund, 1926; presented to the Ferens Art Gallery, Hull, England, by the executors of Lord Duveen's estate, 1949.

DOMENICO DI BARTOLO   *Madonna and Child Enthroned with St. Peter and St. Paul,* c. 1430, tempera on panel
Provenance: Earl of Ashburnham, Ashburnham Place, Sussex; Duveen, 1919; Samuel H. Kress; National Gallery of Art, Washington, D.C.

DOMENICO BRUSASORCI   *Portrait of a Lady*
Provenance: Duveen; Museum of Art, Rhode Island School of Design, Providence.

DOMENICO VENEZIANO   *Portrait of Giovanni Olivieri* or *Portrait of Matteo Olivieri,* c. 1430–40, wood transferred to canvas, 19 × 13¼"
Provenance: Stefano Bardini, Florence; Duveen; Andrew W. Mellon; National Gallery of Art, Washington, D.C.
Note: Now "Italian, Florentine, fifteenth century?"

DOMENICO VENEZIANO   *The Virgin and Child with Floral Background,* or *Madonna and Child,* c. 1445, on wood, 32½ × 22¼″
Provenance: Edgeworth family, Edgeworthstown House, Longford, Ireland; Julius Bohler, Munich; Duveen, 1935; Samuel H. Kress, New York; National Gallery of Art, Washington, D.C.

DOMENICO VENEZIANO   *Profile Portrait of a Lady,* or *A Profile Portrait of a Girl,*
c. 1450, tempera on canvas, transferred from wood, 15¾ × 10¾″
Provenance: Robert S. Holford; Sir George Lindsay Holford, Westonbirt, Gloucestershire; Duveen; Jules S. Bache, New York; Metropolitan Museum of Art, New York.
Note: Now "Master of the Castello Nativity."

DOMENICO VENEZIANO   *Virgin and Child with Saints,* triptych
Provenance: Present whereabouts unknown.

DONATELLO   *Mother and Child,* c. 1425, polychrome terra-cotta, 47½ × 18½ × 13⅛″
Provenance: Pazzi family, Florence; Conte Giacomo Michelozzi, Florence; Henry Goldman, New York; Duveen; Andrew W. Mellon, Pittsburgh; National Gallery of Art, Washington, D.C.
Note: Now "Florentine School."

DONATELLO   *Roman Emperor Bust*
Provenance: Maurice Kann, Paris; Duveen; present whereabouts unknown.

DONATELLO   *The Laughing Cupid,* c. 1432–5, bronze bust, h. 14¾″
Provenance: Duke of Westminster, Grosvenor House, London; Duveen; P. A. B. Widener and Joseph Widener, Elkins Park, PA; National Gallery of Art, Washington, D.C.

DONATELLO   *Saint John the Baptist,* c. 1425–30, terra-cotta bust, 18½ × 15″
Provenance: Emile Gavet, Paris; William K. Vanderbilt, Newport, RI; Mrs. Oliver H. P. Belmont, Newport; Duveen; Samuel H. Kress, New York; National Gallery of Art, Washington, D.C.

DONATELLO   *St. John the Baptist,* or *The Young St. John,* c. 1430, stucco plaque,
28¾ × 11½″
Provenance: Martelli family, Florence; Marchese Diego Martelli; Maurice Kann, Paris; Edouard Kann, Paris; Duveen; Benjamin Altman, New York; Metropolitan Museum of Art, New York.

DONATELLO   *The Madonna and Child,* c. 1445, polychrome and gilt terra-cotta high relief, 53 × 38″
Provenance: Rodolphe Kann, Paris; Duveen; Benjamin Altman, New York; Metropolitan Museum of Art, New York.

DONATELLO   *Saint John the Baptist,* c. 1440, polychrome terra-cotta bust, 19½ × 20½″
Provenance: Eugène Piot, Paris; Louis Charles Timbal, Paris; Gustave Dreyfus, Paris; Andrew W. Mellon, Pittsburgh, PA; National Gallery of Art, Washington, D.C.

DOSSO DOSSI   *Circe and Her Lovers in a Landscape,* c. 1525, oil on canvas, 39⅝ × 53½″
Provenance: William Graham, London; Robert and Evelyn Benson, London; Duveen, 1927; Samuel H. Kress, New York; National Gallery of Art, Washington, D.C.

FRANCOIS-HUBERT DROUAIS   *Group Portrait,* 1756, on canvas, 96 × 76⅝″
Provenance: Samuel Cunliffe-Lister, 2nd Baron Masham, Swinton Park, Masham, Yorkshire; John Cunliffe-Lister, 3rd Baron Masham; Lady Mary Constance Boynton Masham; Duveen, 1937; Samuel H. Kress, New York; National Gallery of Art, Washington, D.C.

DUCCIO DI BUONINSEGNA   *The Temptation of Christ on the Mountain,* c. 1308–11, tempera on poplar panel, 17 × 18⅛″
Provenance: Giuseppe and Marziale Dini, Colle Alto, Val d'Elsa, Siena; Charles Fairfax Murray, London; Robert and Evelyn Benson, London; Duveen, 1927; Frick Collection, New York.
Note: From the rear side of the predella of Duccio's *Maestà* in the Duomo, Siena. There are companion pieces, as below, as well as other fragments in Washington's National Gallery and the National Gallery, London.

DUCCIO DI BUONINSEGNA   *The Nativity, with the Prophets Isaiah and Ezekiel,* c. 1308–11, tempera on poplar panel, 17¼ × 30½″
Provenance: Kaiser Friedrich Museum, Berlin; Duveen, 1937; Andrew W. Mellon, Pittsburgh, PA; National Gallery of Art, Washington, D.C.
Note: From the front predella of the *Maestà* in the Duomo, Siena.

DUCCIO DI BUONINSEGNA   *The Calling of the Apostles Peter and Andrew,* c. 1308–11, tempera on poplar panel, 16¾ × 17¾″
Provenance: Giuseppe and Marziale Dini, Colle Alto, Val d'Elsa, Siena; Charles Fairfax Murray, London; Robert and Evelyn Benson, London; Duveen; Clarence H. Mackay, Roslyn, NY; Duveen; Samuel H. Kress, New York; National Gallery of Art, Washington, D.C.
Note: From the back predella of the *Maestà* in the Duomo, Siena.

DUCCIO DI BUONINSEGNA   *Christ and the Woman of Samaria,* c. 1308–11, tempera on poplar panel, 17 × 18⅛″
Provenance: Giuseppe and Marziale Dini, Colle Alto, Val d'Elsa, Siena; Charles Fairfax Murray, London; Robert and Evelyn Benson, London; Duveen; John D. Rockefeller Jr., New York; Baron Thyssen.
Nots: From the *Maestà.*

DUCCIO DI BUONINSEGNA   *The Raising of Lazarus,* c. 1308–11, tempera on poplar panel, 17 × 18⅛″
Provenance: Giuseppe and Marziale Dini, Colle Alto, Val d'Elsa, Siena; Charles Fairfax Murray, London; Robert and Evelyn Benson, London; Duveen; John D. Rockefeller Jr., New York; Kimball Museum, Fort Worth, TX.
Note: From the *Maestà* in the Duomo, Siena.

ALBRECHT DÜRER   *A Portrait of a Lady,* or *Portrait of a Venetian Lady,* 1506, oil on panel, 17¾ × 13¾″

Provenance: Kings of Württemberg; Duke of Urach; Duveen; Jules S. Bache, New York; Metropolitan Museum of Art, New York.
Note: Heavily restored. Now "Style of Dürer."

ALBRECHT DÜRER   *Virgin and Child with St. Anne,* 1519, tempera and oil on canvas, 23⅝ × 19⅝"
Provenance: Royal Gallery, Schleissheim, Bavaria; Josephy Otto Entres, Munich; Marshal Ivan Izaklevitch de Kuriss, Odessa; Mme Loubov de Kurissova, Odessa; Duveen; Benjamin Altman, New York; Metropolitan Museum of Art, New York.
Note: Heavily restored in 1855.

SIR ANTHONY VAN DYCK   *Robert Rich, Earl of Warwick,* c. 1632–5, oil on canvas, 81⅞ × 50⅜"
Provenance: 2nd Marquess and 5th Earl of Breadalbane, Taymouth Castle, Aberfeldy, Perthshire; Lady Elizabeth Pringle; Mrs. Robert Baillie-Hamilton, Langton, Duns; Lady Bateson Harvey; Thomas George Breadalbane Morgan-Grenville-Gavin, Langton, Duns; Duveen, 1925; Jules S. Bache, New York; Metropolitan Museum of Art, New York.

SIR ANTHONY VAN DYCK   *Portrait of a Lady, called the Marchesa Durazzo,* c. 1621–7, oil on canvas, 44⅝ × 37¾"
Provenance: Marchese (?) Gropallo, Genoa; Rodolphe Kann, Paris; Duveen; Benjamin Altman, 1908; Metropolitan Museum of Art, New York.

SIR ANTHONY VAN DYCK   *Portrait of a Man, Possibly Lucas van Uffele,* oil on canvas, 49 × 39⅝"
Provenance: Landgraves of Hessen-Kassel; Napoleon Bonaparte; Dukes of Sutherland; Duveen, 1908; Benjamin Altman, New York; Metropolitan Museum of Art, New York.

SIR ANTHONY VAN DYCK   *A Self-Portrait of the Artist,* or *Self-Portrait as a Young Man,* c. 1621, oil on canvas, 47⅛ × 34⅝"
Provenance: Earl of Arlington; Dukes of Grafton; Duveen; Jules S. Bache, New York; Metropolitan Museum of Art, New York.

SIR ANTHONY VAN DYCK   *A Genoese Lady,* c. 1625–7, oil on canvas, 42 × 32½"
Provenance: Charles Sedelmeyer, Paris; Dr. James Simon, Berlin; Camillo Castiglioni, Vienna; Duveen; Detroit Institute of Arts.
Note: Formerly considered to be a portrait of the Marchesa Spinola and reattributed by Julius Held.

SIR ANTHONY VAN DYCK   *Queen Henrietta Maria,* c. 1637, oil on canvas, 42 × 33½"
Provenance: Lord Ailesbury, Savernake, Marlborough, Wiltshire; Duveen; Ernst Rosenfeld, New York; Fine Arts Gallery, San Diego, CA.

SIR ANTHONY VAN DYCK   *Frederick Henry, Prince of Orange,* 1628, oil on canvas, 45 × 38"
Provenance: Dukes of Anhalt, Schloss Dessau; Duveen; Mrs. Henry Barton Jacobs, Baltimore; Baltimore Museum of Art.

SIR ANTHONY VAN DYCK   *Portrait of the Marchesa Balbi,* or *Marchesa Balbi,* c. 1622–7, oil on canvas, 50 × 41½″
Provenance: Balbi family, Genoa; Baron Heath, British consul, Genoa; Robert Stayner Holford, Dorchester House, London; Sir George Lindsay Holford, London; Duveen; Andrew W. Mellon; National Gallery of Art, Washington, D.C.

SIR ANTHONY VAN DYCK   *Queen Henrietta Maria with Her Dwarf,* probably 1633, oil on canvas, 86¼ × 53⅛″
Provenance: Earls of Bradford; Earl of Mountrath; Earl of Dorchester; Earl of Portarlington; Lord Northbrook; Duveen; William Randolph Hearst; Samuel H. Kress, New York; National Gallery of Art, Washington, D.C.

SIR ANTHONY VAN DYCK   *Anton Triest, Burgomaster of Ghent,* oil on canvas
Provenance: Brownlow; Duveen; Calouste Gulbenkian.

SIR ANTHONY VAN DYCK   *Portrait of the Earl of Newport,* oil on canvas
Provenance: Lord Northbrook; Duveen; present whereabouts unknown.

SIR ANTHONY VAN DYCK   *Portrait of the Princess of Orange,* oil on canvas
Provenance: Duveen, 1935; present whereabouts unknown.

SIR ANTHONY VAN DYCK   *Portrait of Anne Carr, Countess of Bedford,* oil on canvas
Provenance: The Spencers; Duveen, 1935; present whereabouts unknown.

SIR ANTHONY VAN DYCK   *Sir John Suckling,* oil on canvas
Provenance: Duveen; present whereabouts unknown.

SIR ANTHONY VAN DYCK   *Daedalus and Icarus,* oil on canvas
Provenance: The Spencers; Duveen, 1925; present whereabouts unknown.

SIR ANTHONY VAN DYCK   *Countess of Dorset,* oil on canvas, h. 75″
Provenance: Lord Sackville, Knole Park; Duveen, 1930; present whereabouts unknown.

OLD-ENGLISH MINIATURES   Eighteenth-century portraits by Richard Cosway, George Engleheart, Andrew Plimer, and others
Provenance: Duveen, 1926; The Huntington, San Marino, CA.
Note: There are 78 miniatures in this group.

ETIENNE-MAURICE FALCONET   *Venus Chastising Cupid with a Bunch of Roses,* marble sculpture
Provenance: J. Pierpont Morgan, New York; Duveen; Judge Elbert H. Gary, New York; present whereabouts unknown.

FIORENZO DI LORENZO   *Madonna and Child*
Provenance: "Ex [Joseph] Spiridon"; Carl Hamilton, New York; Duveen, 1919; present whereabouts unknown.

FIORENZO DI LORENZO   *The Madonna and Child with St. Jerome,* c. 1500–5, on wood, 20¼ × 15″
Provenance: Signor? Bacchettoni, Rome; Duveen, 1920; Mrs. Walter Scott Fitz, Boston; Boston Museum of Fine Arts.

FRANÇOIS FLAMENG   *Portrait of Lady Duveen,* oil on canvas
Provenance: Commissioned by Joseph Duveen and given to the Ferens Art Gallery, Hull, England, by the executors of the estate of Lady Duveen, 1963.

FLORENTINE SCHOOL, SIXTEENTH CENTURY   *A Faun with a Flute,* bronze statuette, h. 17¾″
Provenance: Sir Henry Hope Edwards, Wooton Hall, Ashbourne, Derbyshire; H. Sternberg, Paris; J. Pierpont Morgan, New York; Duveen; The Huntington, San Marino, CA.

GIROLAMO FORABOSCO   *Lacemaker,* or *Portrait of Eleonora Guadagni,* n.d., oil on canvas, 32½ × 26″
Provenance: Sir William Richard Drake, Oatlands Lodge, Weybridge, Surrey; Robert and Evelyn Benson, London; Duveen, 1927; Norton Simon Museum, Pasadena, CA.

JEAN FOUQUET   *Portrait of an Ecclesiastic,* head-and-shoulders silverpoint drawing
Provenance: "Ex Oppenheimer"; Duveen; present whereabouts unknown.
Note: Duveen bought this at Christie's, 7/14/36, for 10,002 guineas.

JEAN-HONORÉ FRAGONARD   *The Swing*
Provenance: Rodolphe Kann, Paris; Duveen, 1901; Count Jean de Béarn, 1907; family of the Marquis of Ganay.
Note: Duveen paid £3,000 for the painting and sold it to Countess de Bearn six years later for £22,000. The painting exists in two versions; the other version is in the Wallace Collection, London.

JEAN-HONORÉ FRAGONARD   *Romans d'Amour et de la Jeunesse,* or *The Progress of Love,* 1771–3 and 1790–1, panels
Provenance: Alexandre Maubert, Grasse; J. Pierpont Morgan, London; Duveen, 1915; Henry Clay Frick, New York; Frick Collection, New York.
Notes: The panels were sold by Agnew's to Morgan in 1898 for £64,000. Duveen sold them to Frick for £205,500 pounds, or over £20,000 pounds a panel. Four of the canvases were originally commissioned by Madame Du Barry, the mistress of Louis XV, for a new pavilion in the garden of her chateau at Louveciennes. When she rejected them, the painter had them installed in his cousin's house, adding two additional large panels, four overdoors, and four slender panels of hollyhocks. These masterpieces of the French rococo can now be seen in the Fragonard Room at the Frick.

JEAN-HONORÉ FRAGONARD   *The Fountain of Love,* c. 1785, oil on canvas, 23³⁄₁₆ × 20⅝″
Provenance: Charles-Nicolas Duclos-Dufresnoy, Paris; Geoffroy Villeminot, Paris; Lady Holland, Stanmore Castle; J. R. Holland; Christie's, 1913; Agnew's, 1913; Duveen; John

North Willys, Toledo, OH; Mr. and Mrs. Lucom, 1935; Christie's, 1999; Simon Dickinson, 1999; J. Paul Getty Museum, Los Angeles, 1999.
Note: The painting was always thought to be a copy of a similar painting in the Wallace Collection but is now considered an autograph Fragonard.

JEAN-HONORÉ FRAGONARD   *Scenes of Country Life,* c. 1754–5, four panels, oil on canvas, three panels 58 × 37″ and the fourth 58 × 33½″
Provenance: Baron Roger Pourtalis, Paris; Eugen Kraemer, Paris; Judge Elbert H. Gary, New York; Duveen; Anna Thomson Dodge, Grosse Pointe Farms, MI, 1935; Detroit Institute of Arts.

FRANCESCO DA SANT'AGATA(?)   *A Dancing Faun,* c. 1525, bronze statuette, h. 9¼″
Provenance: Rodolphe Kann, Paris; Duveen; P. A. B. Widener and Joseph E. Widener, Elkins Park, PA; National Gallery of Art, Washington, D.C.

FRANCESCO DA SANT'AGATA   *Hercules Strangling Antaeus,* or *Hercules and Antaeus,* bronze statuette, 15 × 4¾ × 10½″
Provenance: Madame Louis Stern, Paris; Duveen; P. A. B. and Joseph E. Widener, Elkins Park, PA; National Gallery of Art, Washington, D.C.

FRANCESCO DA SANT'AGATA   *Ilioneus, Son of Niobe,* c. 1530, bronze statuette, h. 9⅞″
Provenance: Henry J. Pfungst, London; J. Pierpont Morgan, New York; Duveen; Henry Clay Frick, New York; Frick Collection, New York.
Note: Now "Venetian, early sixteenth century."

FRANCESCO DA SANT'AGATA   *A Flute-Playing Satyr,* c. 1525, bronze statuette, h. 13⅜″
Provenance: J. Pierpont Morgan, New York; Duveen; Henry Clay Frick, 1916; Frick Collection, New York.
Note: Now "Camelio."

FRANCESCO DI ANTONIO DI BARTOLOMEO   *The Virgin Annunciate,* c. 1420–30, tempera and gold leaf on octagonal panel, 13 × 10¼″
Provenance: Dr. Paulette Gauthier-Villars, Paris; Claude Lafontaine, Paris; Duveen; Norton Simon Museum, Pasadena, CA.
Note: One of two panels originally forming the pinnacles of an altarpiece by Masolino.

FRANCESCO DI ANTONIO DI BARTOLOMEO   *The Archangel Gabriel,* c. 1420–30, tempera and gold leaf on panel, 13 × 10¼″
Provenance: Dr. Paulette Gauthier-Villars, Paris; Claude Lafontaine, Paris; Duveen; Norton Simon Museum, Pasadena, CA.
Note: Companion piece to *The Virgin Annunciate.*

FRANCESCO DI GIORGIO MARTINI   *The Goddess of Chaste Love,* or *The Triumph of Diana,* c. 1470, fragment of a cassone panel, 16⅛ × 17⅞″
Provenance: Alphonse Kann, Paris; Duveen, 1917; Metropolitan Museum of Art, New York.
Note: A companion piece to another fragment in the Edigio Tosatti collection, Genoa.

FRANCESCO DI GIORGIO MARTINI   *Fidelity,* c. 1485, fresco transferred to canvas, 49½ × 29¾"
Provenance: Duveen; Norton Simon Museum, Pasadena, CA.

FRANCESCO DI GIORGIO MARTINI   *God the Father Surrounded by Angels and Cherubim,* c. 1470, oval, on wood, 14⅜ × 20⅜"
Provenance: Alphonse Kann, Paris; Duveen, 1917; Philip Lehman, New York; Samuel H. Kress, New York; National Gallery of Art, Washington, D.C.

FRANCESCO DI GIORGIO MARTINI   *David with the Head of Goliath,* or *David,* c. 1475–80, bronze statuette, h. 29½"
Provenance: Edouard Aynard, Lyons; J. Pierpont Morgan, New York; Duveen; Henry Clay Frick, New York, 1916; Frick Collection, New York.
Note: Now Baccio de Montelupo?

FRANCESCO FRANCIA   *Madonna and Child with St. Jerome and St. Francis,* c. 1450–1517/8, oil on panel, 24¾ × 18⅝"
Provenance: Francesco Coghetti, Rome; T. Frankland Lewis, London; William Salomon, New York; Duveen; Norton Simon Museum, Pasadena, CA.

FRANCESCO FRANCIA   *Virgin and Child with Saints,* 54 × 24"
Provenance: Ex Stogdon; Duveen; The Huntington, San Marino, CA.

FRANCESCO FRANCIA   *Portrait of a Young Man*
Provenance: Ex Hengel; Duveen; Carl Hamilton, New York; present whereabouts unknown.
Note: Identified from a letter of intent to buy, Hamilton to Duveen, 11/4/19; no price given.

FRANCESCO FRANCIA   *Madonna and Child with St. Joseph and Mary Magdalen*
Provenance: Duveen; Carl Hamilton, New York; present whereabouts unknown.
Note: In June of 1924, Hamilton was trying to sell this painting for $100,000 (6/7/24).

FRANCESCO FRANCIA   *San Roch on a Mountain*
Provenance: Duveen; Carl Hamilton, New York; present whereabouts unknown.
Note: In June of 1924, Hamilton was trying to sell this painting for $250,000 (6/7/24).

FRANCESCO FRANCIA   *Virgin and Child*
Provenance: William Salomon, New York; Duveen; present whereabouts unknown.
Note: Duveen offered the painting to Arabella Huntington (1/10/23) but added, "You already have one much finer."

FRANCESCO FRANCIA   *The Crucifixion*
Provenance: Duveen; Carl Hamilton, New York; present whereabouts unknown.
Note: The painting brought $375,000 at auction in 1929. In a subsequent legal suit, Hamilton claimed that he had bought the painting from Duveen for $650,000.

FRANCESCO FRANCIA   *Virgin and Child with Saints,* 23½ × 19¾"

Provenance: Clarence Mackay, New York; bought back by Duveen; present whereabouts unknown.

FRANCESCO FRANCIA   *Federigo Gonzaga,* c. 1510, tempera on wood, 18⅞ × 14″
Provenance: Isabella d'Este, Mantua; Gianfrancesco Zaninello, Ferrara; Prince Jerome Bonaparte, Palais Royal, Paris; Alexander Barker, London; Edward Aldam Leatham, Miserden Park, Cirencester, Gloucestershire; Arthur William Leatham, Miserden Park; Duveen, 1911; Benjamin Altman, New York; Metropolitan Museum of Art, New York.

FRANCESCO FRANCIA   *Madonna and Child with Sts. Francis and Jerome,* oil on panel, 29⁷⁄₁₆ × 22½″
Provenance: Elia Volpi, Florence; Henry Goldman, New York; Duveen; John R. Thompson, Chicago; Robert Lehman, New York; Metropolitan Museum of Art, New York.

BARNETT FREEDMAN   *Sunday Morning,* pen-and-ink and wash on paper
Provenance: Duveen Paintings Fund, 1929; Presented to the Ferens Art Gallery, Hull, England, by the executors of the estate of Lord Duveen, 1949.

FRENCH, FOURTEENTH CENTURY   Ivory Casket, second half of the fourteenth century
Provenance: Rev. J. Bowle, England; G. Brander; F. Spitzer; Oscar Hainauer, Berlin; Duveen; Henry Walters; Walters Art Museum, Baltimore, MD.

FRENCH, FIFTEENTH CENTURY   *A Tournament Scene* and *A Royal Banquet Scene,* tempera on vellum, both 13¼ × 8¼″
Provenance: Rodolphe Kann, Paris; Duveen; Norton Simon Museum, Pasadena, CA.
Note: Companion pieces, which Duveen did not sell during his lifetime and which entered the Norton Simon collection in 1965 when that collector bought Duveen Brothers.

FRENCH, EIGHTEENTH CENTURY   Combination Writing and Work Table, c. 1770, of fir, oak, and poplar, 28½ × 18⅜ × 14⅛″
Provenance: Mme de Fournières, Paris; Duveen; Anna Thomson Dodge, Detroit, 1932; Detroit Institute of Arts.
Note: Top and shelf inlaid with various woods, veneered with amaranth, *bois satine rubanne,* holly and sycamore maple, and ivory and with a leather writing surface. Trellis and rosette pattern on kingwood and harewood grounds, the sides with bouquets of mixed flowers in panels. Gilt-bronze mounts.

FRENCH, EIGHTEENTH CENTURY   Pair of Candelabra, c. 1766, by Jean Louis Prieur, gilt bronze, 26 × 14″
Provenance: Prince Frodrow (or Feodrov), St. Petersburg; Duveen, 1932; Anna Thomson Dodge, Detroit; Detroit Institute of Arts.
Note: The candelabra closely resemble a set in the Royal Palace in Warsaw from an original set of six, and may in fact be part of that set.

FRENCH, EIGHTEENTH CENTURY   Old French Large Commode, 35 × 56 × 22″

Provenance: Marquis of Hertford; Sir Richard Wallace; Mrs. Frances Gould; Duveen; Marjorie Merriweather Post; Hillwood Museum and Gardens, Washington, D.C.
Note: With corner masks, ormolu frieze and mounts; marqueterie on diamond pattern with conventional floral center, two long drawers and three small ones; signed Jean-Henri Riesener (1734–1806).

FRENCH, EIGHTEENTH CENTURY　　Writing Table
Provenance: Countess of Shannon; Duveen; Marjorie Merriweather Post; Hillwood Museum and Gardens, Washington, D.C.
Note: On fluted legs, with richly chased ormolu mounts and six drawers.

FRENCH, EIGHTEENTH CENTURY　　Gobelin Tapestry Suite
Provenance: Duke de Choiseul; Duveen; Marjorie Merriweather Post; Hillwood Museum and Gardens, Washington, D.C.
Note: Two sofas, six armchairs, and two bergères, covered with tapestry by Neilson, after designs of François Boucher; children in rustic scenes and sporting animals.

FRENCH, EIGHTEENTH CENTURY　　Beauvais Tapestry Panel, *Bacchus and Ariadne*
Provenance: Casimir-Perrier Collection; Duveen; Marjorie Merriweather Post; Hillwood Museum and Gardens, Washington, D.C.
Note: After the famous cartoon by François Boucher.

FRENCH, EIGHTEENTH CENTURY　　Beauvais Tapestry Panel, *Nymphs and Satyrs*
Provenance: Casimir-Perrier Collection; Duveen; Marjorie Merriweather Post; Hillwood Museum and Gardens, Washington, D.C.
Note: Pendant to *Bacchus and Ariadne.*

FRENCH, EIGHTEENTH CENTURY　　Beauvais Tapestry Panel, *L'Opérateur, ou la Curiosité,* 1738, 10′8″ × 19′2″
Provenance: Duveen; Marjorie Merriweather Post; Hillwood Museum and Gardens, Washington, D.C.
Note: The tapestry is one in a series of fourteen representing *Les Fêtes Italiennes,* after cartoons by François Boucher.

FRENCH, LOUIS XV　　Combination Writing and Work Table, c. 1775, by Gaspard Feilt, oak veneered with tulipwood, amaranth, and *bois satiné,* 28⅞ × 25¾ × 17¼″
Provenance: Chilton House, Wiltshire; Count de Gramont, Paris; Duveen, 1934; Anna Thomson Dodge, 1935; Detroit Institute of Arts.

FRENCH, LOUIS XV　　Louis XV Table, signed M. Carlin, ME
Provenance: Baron Alfred de Rothschild Collection; Duveen; Marjorie Merriweather Post; Dina Merrill, Paris.
Note: Inlaid in kingwood, with casket above. Numerous Sèvres porcelain plaques with turquoise blue oeil-de-perdrix ground, on which is painted garlands of flowers and trophies in panels. Rich corner mounts of ormolu masks and oak leaves.

FRENCH, LOUIS XV   Lady's Writing and Dressing Table, c. 1760, 28 × 31 × 14"
Provenance: Marie Antoinette, Paris; Rev. Grey Egerton; Sir Philip Grey Egerton, Oulton
Park, Cheshire; Duveen; Marjorie Merriweather Post; Dina Merrill, Paris.
Note: Inlaid with tulip and other ornamental woods. The top has a brilliant green back-
ground with birds, flowers, and trophies. A center writing slope stamped "L.U.C.Y." with
fleurs-de-lys. Attributed to Oeben.

FRENCH, LOUIS XV   Occasional Table with Sliding Top
Provenance: Duveen; Marjorie Merriweather Post; Hillwood Museum and Gardens, Wash-
ington, D.C.
Note: Marqueterie of city with river background and ormolu mounted.

FRENCH, LOUIS XV/LOUIS XVI   Jewel Cabinet, Jewel Coffer, oak veneered with
tulipwood, holly, ebony, and amaranth, 37⅜ × 20⅝ × 13⅝"
Provenance: Frederike Sophie Dorothea, Duchess of Württemberg; Maria Feodorovna,
Empress of Russia, Palace of Pavlovsk; Grand Duke Mikhail Pavlovich; Grand Duke Constantin Nikolaievich; Grand Duchess Alexandra Iosifovna; Grand Duke Constantin Con-
stantinovich; Duveen; Anna Thomson Dodge, Detroit, 1932; Detroit Institute of Arts.
Note: The cabinet is decorated with thirteen Sèvres porcelain plaques and gilt-bronze
mounts. The soft-paste porcelain plaques have a *bleu celeste* border and are painted with
sprays of pink roses. The gilt-bronze corner mounts on the cabinet legs are in the form of
bearded masks and oak foliage.

FRENCH, LOUIS XVI   Combination Gaming and Writing Table, c. 1775, by Claude-
Charles Saunier, 28 × 44⅝ × 33½"
Provenance: Henry M. W. Oppenheim, London; Duveen, 1913; Mrs. George D. Widener
(?); Anna Thomson Dodge, Detroit, 1932; Detroit Institute of Arts.
Note: Table has a stamped brown leather detachable top with a green felt-lined reverse
enclosing a backgammon board. It is inlaid with tulipwood and kingwood. Its frieze is
inset with panels of arabesque foliage mounted with ormolu borders.

FRENCH, LOUIS XVI   Writing Table, c. 1755, by Roger Vandercruse, called Lacroix,
28½ × 25⅜ × 18"
Provenance: Mrs. Walter Burns, North Mymms Park, Hatfield; Duveen, 1930; Anna
Thomson Dodge, Detroit, 1932; Detroit Institute of Arts.
Note: A writing cabinet shaped with a folding top and rising cabinet at the back containing
five small drawers, and fitted at one side with another small drawer. The oakwood base is
inlaid with tulipwood, kingwood, and other woods, has ormolu mounts chased with
foliage, cabriole legs, and sprays of flowers with a ribboned border.

FRENCH, LOUIS XVI   Inlaid Oval Table
Provenance: Duveen; Marjorie Merriweather Post; Hillwood Museum and Gardens, Wash-
ington, D.C.
Note: Marqueterie of flowers, the top with figures in a ruined landscape.

FRENCH SCHOOL   *Portrait of a Lady,* n.d., pastel on paper, 22½ × 18"
Provenance: Duveen; Norton Simon Museum, Pasadena, CA.

FRENCH SCHOOL   *St. Anthony,* c. 1335–45, fresco transferred to panel, 39¼ × 33½"
Provenance: Duveen; Norton Simon Museum, Pasadena, CA.

AGNOLO GADDI   *The Marriage of the Virgin,* on panel, 14½ × 9"
Provenance: Bohn Collection; Robert and Evelyn Benson, London; Duveen; Fogg Art Museum, Cambridge, MA.

AGNOLO GADDI   *Madonna and Child Enthroned with Saints and Angels,* c. 1380–90, triptych on wood with gabled tops, 80⅝ × 96⅝"
Provenance: Fifth Earl of Ashburnham, Ashburnham Place, Sussex; Lady Mary Catherine Charlotte Ashburnham; Robert Langton Douglas, London; Duveen, 1933; Andrew W. Mellon, Pittsburgh; National Gallery of Art, Washington, D.C.

THOMAS GAINSBOROUGH   *The Painter's Daughters Chasing a Butterfly,* c. 1756, oil on canvas, 44¾ × 41¼"
Provenance: Duveen; National Gallery, London.
Note: In *The Economics of Taste,* Gerald Reitlinger observes that the painting's great value was hardly noticed and that it was sold for the trifling sum of £3,349 in 1923 [191].

THOMAS GAINSBOROUGH   *Lady Mulgrave,* miniature bust portrait, 7½ × 6"
Provenance: George Gould; Duveen; Jules S. Bache, New York; Metropolitan Museum of Art, New York.

THOMAS GAINSBOROUGH   *Miss Catherine Tatton,* 1786, oil on canvas, 29⅞ × 25¼"
Provenance: James Drake-Brockman; Drake-Brockman family, Beechborough, Kent; Duveen, 1908; Herbert Stern, 1st Baron Michelham, London; Aimee Geraldine Bradshaw Stern, Baroness Michelham, Paris; Duveen; Andrew W. Mellon, Pittsburgh, 1927; National Gallery of Art, Washington, D.C.

THOMAS GAINSBOROUGH   *Master John Heathcote,* 1771–2, oil on canvas, 50 × 39⅞"
Provenance: Heathcote family; Duveen, 1913; Herbert Stern, 1st Baron Michelham, London; Aimee Geraldine Bradshaw Stern, Baroness Michelham, Paris; Duveen; Alvan Tufts Fuller, Boston, MA; National Gallery of Art, Washington, D.C.

THOMAS GAINSBOROUGH   *Georgiana, Duchess of Devonshire,* c. 1783, oil on canvas, 92¾ × 57⅞"
Provenance: The Earls Spencer, Althorp, Northamptonshire; Duveen, 1924; Andrew W. Mellon, Pittsburgh; National Gallery of Art, Washington, D.C.

THOMAS GAINSBOROUGH   *Mrs. Richard Brinsley Sheridan,* c. 1785–7, oil on canvas, 86⅝ × 60⅝"
Provenance: Richard Brinsley Sheridan; Harriot Fawkener Bouverie, Delapré Abbey, Northampton; Edward Bouverie; Everard William Bouverie; Baron Lionel Nathan de Rothschild, Gunnersbury, Middlesex; Baron Nathan Mayer Rothschild, Tring, Hertfordshire; Baron Lionel Walter Rothschild; Baron Nathaniel Mayer Victor Rothschild; Duveen; Andrew W. Mellon, Pittsburgh; National Gallery of Art, Washington, D.C.

THOMAS GAINSBOROUGH   *Mountain Landscape with Bridge,* c. 1783–4, oil on canvas, 44½ × 52½"
Provenance: Mrs. Thomas Gainsborough, London; 1st Baron de Tabley, Tabley House, Cheshire; Asher Wertheimer, London; Lady Lindsay, Sir Edgar Vincent D'Abernon, Esher Place, Surrey; Duveen, 1926; Andrew W. Mellon, Pittsburgh; National Gallery of Art, Washington, D.C.

THOMAS GAINSBOROUGH   *The Blue Boy,* 1770, oil on canvas, 70⅝ × 48¾"
Provenance: Jonathan Buttall; John Nesbitt, London; John Hoppner; Robert, 2nd Earl of Grosvenor, 1st Marquess of Westminster; Hugh, 2nd Duke of Westminster; Duveen, 1921; Henry E. Huntington; The Huntington, San Marino, CA.
Note: Edward Fowles said late in life that Huntington did not pay cash at this record-breaking sale but in six-month bills and that Duveen's actual profit was small (Oral History, Archives of American Art).

THOMAS GAINSBOROUGH   *Karl Friedrich Abel,* c. 1777, oil on canvas, 88¾ × 59½"
Provenance: George Francis, 3rd Earl of Egremont, Petworth; Charles John Wertheimer; Lord Ronald Sutherland Gower; Duveen, 1909; George J. Gould, New York, 1914; Duveen, 1925; Henry E. Huntington, 1925; The Huntington, San Marino, CA.

THOMAS GAINSBOROUGH   *Penelope [Pitt], Viscountess Ligonier,* 1770, oil on canvas, 94½ × 61¾"
Provenance: The sitter's father, George Pitt, 1st Baron Rivers, Stratfield-Say, Hampshire; General Pitt-Rivers, Rushmore, Salisbury; A. C. Rivers; W. Pitt Rivers; Charles John Wertheimer, London; Duveen, 1911; Henry E. Huntington, 1911; The Huntington, San Marino, CA.

THOMAS GAINSBOROUGH   *Juliana [Howard], Baroness Petre,* 1788, oil on canvas, 88¾ × 57¼"
Provenance: By descent to William Joseph, 13th Baron Petre; Charles John Wertheimer, London; Duveen, 1911; Henry E. Huntington, 1911; The Huntington, San Marino, CA.

THOMAS GAINSBOROUGH   *Henrietta Read, later Henrietta Meares,* c. 1777, oil on canvas, 89½ × 56⅜"
Provenance: Henry Truman Villebois; Henry Villebois; Alfred Charles de Rothschild, London; Almina, Countess of Carnarvon; Duveen, 1924; Henry E. Huntington, 1924; The Huntington, San Marino, CA.

THOMAS GAINSBOROUGH   *Edward, Viscount (later, Earl) Ligonier,* 1770, oil on canvas, 94 × 62"
Provenance: The sitter's father-in-law, George Pitt, 1st Baron Rivers, Stratfield Saye, Hampshire; General Pitt-Rivers, Rushmore, Salisbury; A. C. Rivers; W. Pitt Rivers; Charles John Wertheimer, London; Duveen, 1911; Henry E. Huntington, 1911; The Huntington, San Marino, CA.

THOMAS GAINSBOROUGH   *The Hon. Anne (Batson) Fane,* c. 1782, oil on canvas, 35½ × 27⅝"

Provenance: By descent to Anne, second wife of Lieutenant General John Michel of Dewlish and Kingston Russell; Field Marshal Sir John Michel; Alfred Charles de Rothschild, London; Ernest Lewis Raphael; Duveen, 1926; Henry E. Huntington, 1926; The Huntington, San Marino, CA.

THOMAS GAINSBOROUGH   *Anne (Luttrell), Duchess of Cumberland,* c. 1777, oil on canvas, 36 × 28¼"
Provenance: By bequest to Sarah Bettina Lawley; Beilby Richard Lawley, 2nd Baron Wenlock; Beilby Lawley, 3rd Baron Wenlock; Charles John Wertheimer, London; Duveen, 1911; Henry E. Huntington, 1912; The Huntington, San Marino, CA.

THOMAS GAINSBOROUGH   *Elizabeth (Jenks) Beaufoy, later Elizabeth Pycroft,* c. 1780, oil on canvas, 91 × 60"
Provenance: By descent to John Hanbury Beaufoy, Grosvenor Place, London; Sir William Heathcote, Hursley Park, Winchester, Hampshire; Alfred Charles de Rothschild, London; Almina, Countess of Carnarvon; Duveen, 1924; Henry E. Huntington; The Huntington, San Marino, CA.

THOMAS GAINSBOROUGH   *The Cottage Door,* c. 1780, oil on canvas, 58¼ × 47¼"
Provenance: Thomas Harvey, Catton House, Norfolk; Daniel Coppin, Norwich; Sir John Leicester, Bart., later 1st Baron de Tabley; Robert, 1st Earl Grosvenor, later 2nd Marquess of Westminster; Hugh, 2nd Duke of Westminster; Duveen, 1921; Henry E. Huntington; The Huntington, San Marino, CA.

THOMAS GAINSBOROUGH   *Lady Anne Hamilton, later Duchess of Donegall,* c. 1777–80, oil on canvas, 92¼ × 60⅝"
Provenance: Arthur Chichester, first Marquess of Donegall; by descent to Arthur Claud Spencer Chichester, 4th Baron Templemore; Duveen, c. 1925; Anna Thomson Dodge, 1935; Detroit Institute of Arts.

THOMAS GAINSBOROUGH   *Richard Savage Nassau de Zuylestein,* c. 1778–80, oil on canvas, 94 × 61"
Provenance: Arthur Chichester, first Marquess of Donegall; by descent to Arthur Claud Spencer Chichester, 4th Baron Templemore; Duveen, c. 1925; Anna Thomson Dodge, 1935; Detroit Institute of Arts.

THOMAS GAINSBOROUGH   *Lady Anna Horatia Waldegrave,* c. 1783, oil on canvas, 30 × 25"
Provenance: By descent to Lord Hugh F. Seymour, Potterells, Hatfield, Hertfordshire; Duveen, 1928; Mr. and Mrs. Edsel B. Ford, Detroit; Detroit Institute of Arts.
Note: The canvas, originally oval and 28 × 24", was enlarged to a rectangle. Duveen paid £20,000 for it.

THOMAS GAINSBOROUGH   *The Mall in St. James's Park,* c. 1783, oil on canvas, 47½ × 57⅞"
Provenance: Algernon William Neeld, 2nd Bart., Grittleton House, Wiltshire, by 1891; Mrs. C. Hanbury; Duveen, 1916; Henry Clay Frick, New York; Frick Collection, New York.

THOMAS GAINSBOROUGH   *Mrs. Peter William Baker,* 1781, oil on canvas, 89⅝ × 59¾″
Provenance: Rev. Sir Talbot Hastings Baker, 3rd Bart., Ranston, Dorset, by 1877; Sir Randolf Littlehales Baker, 4th Bart; Duveen, 1917; Henry Clay Frick, New York; Frick Collection, New York.

THOMAS GAINSBOROUGH   *The Honorable Frances Duncombe,* c. 1777, oil on canvas, 92¼ × 61⅛″
Provenance: Henry Graves, London; Ferdinand and Lionel de Rothschild; Charles J. Wertheimer, London; Duveen, 1911; Henry Clay Frick, New York; Frick Collection, New York.

THOMAS GAINSBOROUGH   *Grace Dalrymple Elliott,* oil on canvas, 30 × 25″
Provenance: Lord William Charles Augustus Bentinck; 5th Duke of Portland, Welbeck Abbey, Nottinghamshire; William John Arthur Charles James, 6th Duke of Portland; Duveen, 1936; Frick Collection, New York.

THOMAS GAINSBOROUGH   *Richard Paul Jodrell,* 1770s, oil on canvas, 30¼ × 25⅛″
Provenance: Joseph Ruston, Monk's Manor, Lincolnshire; George Harland-Peck, London; Arthur J. Sulley and Duveen, 1920; Harold Palmer, Manchester, MA; Duveen; Frick Collection, New York.

THOMAS GAINSBOROUGH   *General Honeywood,* 1764, oil on canvas, 112½ × 115½″
Provenance: Ex D'Abernon Collection; Duveen; John and Mable Ringling Museum, Sarasota, FL.

THOMAS GAINSBOROUGH   *Portrait of Captain Thomas Cornwall,* oil on canvas
Provenance: Duveen (purchased jointly with Scott and Fowles of New York), January 1920; present whereabouts unknown.

THOMAS GAINSBOROUGH   *The Cruttenden Sisters,* or *The Cruttenden Girls,* oil on canvas
Provenance: Kennedy-Purvis Collection; Duveen (for £28,000), November 1928; present whereabouts unknown.

THOMAS GAINSBOROUGH   *Miss Sarah Buxton,* oil on canvas
Provenance: Ex Charles Dumbleton; Duveen; Judge Elbert H. Gary, New York (for $156,250), 1917; present whereabouts unknown.

THOMAS GAINSBOROUGH   *Portrait of Mrs. Lowndes-Stone-Norton,* oil on canvas
Provenance: Duveen; Calouste Gulbenkian.

THOMAS GAINSBOROUGH   *The Harvest Waggon,* oil on canvas
Provenance: Mrs. Fitzherbert (gift of the Prince of Wales); Mrs. Dawson Damer; John Gibbons; Sir Lionel Phillips; Duveen; Judge Elbert H. Gary, New York; Duveen; Frank P. Wood, Toronto; Art Gallery of Ontario, Toronto.
Note: Judge Gary bought the painting from Duveen for $165,000, and to keep up the prices, Duveen bought the painting back from his estate in 1928–9 for $360,000. He sold

it to Frank Wood for $450,000. The painting is confusingly named: There is another *Harvest Wagon* at the Barber Institute of Fine Arts, University of Birmingham, England.

THOMAS GAINSBOROUGH   *The Watering Place,* oil on canvas, 40 × 50″
Provenance: Sir Ellis Waterhouse said in 1960 that the painting was bought by Duveen and inherited by his wife after his death; present whereabouts unknown.
Note: The National Gallery, London, owns a Gainsborough *The Watering Place,* dimensions 58 × 71″.

PAUL GAUGUIN   *Faa Iheihe,* 1898, oil on canvas
Provenance: Duveen; gift to the Tate Gallery, London.

MARCUS GEERAERTS THE YOUNGER   *Portrait of Lady Arabella Stuart,* n.d., oil on canvas, 71 × 39″
Provenance: Duveen; Norton Simon Museum, Pasadena, CA.

GENTILE DA FABRIANO   *Madonna and Child,* c. 1422, on wood, 37¾ × 22¼″
Provenance: Alexander Barker, London; E. J. Sartoris, Paris; Henry Goldman, New York; Duveen; Samuel H. Kress, New York; National Gallery of Art, Washington, D.C.

GENTILE DA FABRIANO   *Coronation of the Virgin*
Provenance: Ex Hengel; Duveen; cited by Carl Hamilton in a letter of intent to buy, November 4, 1919.

HUBERT GERHARD (ATTRIBUTED TO)   *Triton and Nereid,* sculpture
Provenance: Duveen; Frick Collection, New York.

GERMAN OR DUTCH BRONZE, EIGHTEENTH CENTURY   Equestrian Figure, Prince Eugene of Savoy, h. 16″
Provenance: Ex Goldschmidt?; Duveen.
Note: On wooden base veneered with tortoiseshell and engraved brass.

LORENZO GHIBERTI   *Madonna and Child,* c. 1430–50, polychrome and gilt stucco relief, 40⅛ × 22¾″
Provenance: Dr. Eduard Simon, Berlin; Duveen; Clarence Mackay, NY; Samuel H. Kress, New York.
Note: Now "Florentine School, fifteenth century."

DOMENICO GHIRLANDAIO   *Young Man,* oil on panel, 13 × 9″
Provenance: Baron Arthur de Schickler, Martinvast, Manche; Baron Hubert de Pourtalès, Paris; Duveen, 1923; Alfred J. Fisher, Detroit, c. 1931.

DOMENICO GHIRLANDAIO   *Madonna and Child,* c. 1470, transferred from wood to hardboard, 28⅞ × 20″
Provenance: Duveen; Samuel H. Kress; National Gallery of Art, Washington, D.C.
Note: In 1977 the late John Walker told the author: "Berenson was very enthusiastic about it. It was called Verrocchio at one time. I never really questioned its attribution because of

B.B., which was rather unfortunate. I would prefer it if the painting were labeled 'Florentine school.' " The painting is still attributed to Ghirlandaio.

DOMENICO GHIRLANDAIO   *Madonna and Child,* tondo
Provenance: Robert and Evelyn Benson, London; Duveen; for sale 3/25/52 for $55,000 to Bob Jones Jr., of Bob Jones University, Greenville, SC.

DOMENICO GHIRLANDAIO   *Francesco Sassetti and his Son Teodoro,* c. 1478–89, on panel, 29½ × 20½"
Provenance: William Graham; Robert and Evelyn Benson, London; Duveen; Jules Bache, New York; Metropolitan Museum of Art, New York.

DOMENICO GHIRLANDAIO   *Lucrezia Tornabuoni,* c. 1475, on wood, 21 × 15¾"
Provenance: Duveen; Samuel H. Kress, New York; National Gallery of Art, Washington, D.C.
Note: John Walker told the author in 1977 that he got "no joy or pleasure" from this picture.

DOMENICO GHIRLANDAIO   *Portrait of Giovanna Tornabuoni*
Provenance: "Ex Rodolphe Kann"; J. P. Morgan, New York.
Note: Duveen's uncle Henry arranged the sale to Morgan, according to James Henry Duveen in *The Rise of the House of Duveen* [231].

DOMENICO GHIRLANDAIO   *Giovanna degli Albizzi Tornabuoni*
Provenance: Ex Rodolphe Kann; ex Willett of Brighton; Duveen; Museo Thyssen-Bornemisza, Madrid.
Note: May be the same painting as *Portrait of Giovanna Tornabuoni.*

GIAMPETRINO   *Madonna and Child with St. John the Baptist,* on panel, 20½ × 16¼"
Provenance: Charles Butler, London; Robert and Evelyn Benson, London; Duveen; Count Alessandro Contini-Bonacossi, Florence; Samuel H. Kress, New York; Seattle Art Museum, WA.
Note: Previously exhibited as by Marco d'Oggiono (in 1894) and Albertino Piazza da Lodi (in 1898). Now "Attributed to Giampetrino."

GIORGIONE (GIORGIO DA CASTELFRANCO)   *The Holy Family,* c. 1500, transferred from wood to hardboard, 14⅝ × 17⅞"
Provenance: Henry Willett, Brighton; Robert and Evelyn Benson, London; Duveen; Samuel H. Kress, New York; National Gallery of Art, Washington, D.C.
Note: According to the memoir *Let Me Tell You* by A. C. R. Carter, the painting came from a curiosity shop in Brighton and was afterwards bought by Willett for £20, who exchanged it for another painting owned by the Bensons [64]. In *Giorgione,* Jaynie Anderson notes that the painting was in bad condition when bought by Duveen and substantially overpainted by the restorer William Suhr in 1936; nevertheless, she accepts an attribution to Giorgione. John Walker's catalogue of painting and sculpture at the National Gallery also gives the painting to Giorgione.

GIORGIONE   *Courtesan,* or *Bust of a Young Woman,* or *Bust Portrait of a Courtesan,*
c. 1477–1510, oil on panel
Provenance: James Howard Harris, 3rd Earl of Malmesbury, London; William Graham,
London; Prince Karl Max von Lichnowsky, London; Sir Alexander Henderson, Buscot
Park, Faringdon, Berkshire; Alfred Moritz Mond, 1st Baron Melchett, Southampton,
Hampshire; Henry Ludwig Mond, 2nd Baron Melchett; Duveen; Norton Simon
Museum, Pasadena, CA.
Note: Opinion has varied widely on this painting. Some experts consider it to be an
undoubted work of Titian, but in 1971 Sir John Pope-Hennessy maintained that the paint
surface was largely new and the work unattributable (Anderson, 335).

GIORGIONE   *Adoration of the Shepherds,* or *The Allendale Nativity,* c. 1505–10, on wood,
35¾ × 43½″
Provenance: Cardinal Joseph Fesch, Rome; Claudius Tarral, Paris; Thomas Wentworth-
Beaumont, Bretton Hall, Yorkshire; Wentworth Blackett Beaumont, first Lord Allendale;
the Viscounts Allendale, London; Duveen; Samuel H. Kress, New York; National Gallery
of Art, Washington, D.C.
Note: This is the famous painting that Berenson refused to authenticate as a Giorgione,
giving it to Titian. Kenneth Clark, to author, 4/23/76: "Why I genuinely don't know. He
[Berenson] was looking for a pretext and it's a very poor one, because it is a Giorgione."
Duveen bought the painting from Allendale for £63,000 and paid a further $5,000 to the
dealer Charles Ruck. It was sold to Kress for $400,000.

GIORGIONE   *Portrait of a Man,* oil on canvas, 19¾ × 17¾″
Provenance: Grimani Collection (?), Venice; Walter Landor, Florence; Countess of
Turenne, Florence; Duveen; Benjamin S. Altman, New York; Metropolitan Museum of
Art, New York.
Note: The painting is now considered to be by a "Giorgionesque painter." Harold E.
Wethey in *The Paintings of Titian* notes, "The condition of the picture is such that an attri-
bution to either Giorgione or Titian is altogether hypothetical" [186].

GIORGIONE   *Portrait of a Lady, "La Schiavona"*
Provenance: Duveen; H. L. Cook, 1928; Sir Francis Cook; National Gallery, London, 1942.
Note: Bought by Cook as a Giorgione, now at the National Gallery as a Titian.

GIORGIONE/TITIAN   *Portrait of Caterina Cornaro*
Provenance: Duveen; present whereabouts unknown.

GIOTTO   *Madonna and Child with Angels*
Provenance: Duveen; supposedly sold to Carl Hamilton, 11/4/19, for $150,000; present
whereabouts unknown.

GIOTTO   *St. Paul,* 1333, 92 × 35⅛″
Provenance: Stefano Bardini, Florence; Elia Volpi, Palazzo Davanzati, Florence; Stephane
Bourgeois, Cologne; Duveen; Andrew W. Mellon; National Gallery of Art, Washing-
ton, D.C.
Note: Now "Bernardo Daddi."

GIOTTO   *Virgin and Child,* or *Madonna and Child,* c. 1320–30, on wood, 33⅝ × 24⅜″
Provenance: Edouard-Alexandre Max, Paris; Duveen; Henry Goldman, New York; Duveen; Samuel H. Kress, New York; National Gallery of Art, Washington, D.C.
Note: Central panel of a polyptych. Companion paintings are *St. Stephen,* Horne Museum, Florence, and *St. John the Evangelist* and *St. Lawrence,* both at the Musée Jacquemart-André, Châalis.

AMICO DI GIOTTO   Four Panels
Provenance: Ex Spiridon; apparent sale by Duveen to Carl Hamilton, 11/10/19.

GIOVANNI ANTONIO AMADEO   *A Singing Boy,* fifteenth-century marble sculpture
Provenance: Chabrières-Arlès collection; Duveen, 1918; Clarence Mackay, New York.
Note: Sold to Mackay for $58,000.

GIOVANNI ANTONIO AMADEO   *Filippo Maria Visconti,* c. 1480–90, white marble portrait plaque, 20 × 14½″
Provenance: Emile Signol, Paris; Gustave Dreyfus, Paris; Duveen; Samuel H. Kress, New York; National Gallery of Art, Washington, D.C.

GIOVANNI ANTONIO AMADEO   *Gian Galeazzo Sforza, 6th Duke of Milan,* c. 1489–90, white marble portrait medallion, diameter 24⅜″
Provenance: Sir John Charles Robinson, London; Louis Charles Timbal, Paris; Gustave Dreyfus, Paris; Duveen; Andrew W. Mellon; National Gallery of Art, Washington, D.C.

GIOVANNI DI FRANCESCO DA ROVEZZANO   *Madonna and Child and Saints Bridget and Michael,* triptych on wood with arched tops
Provenance: Charles Fairfax Murray, Florence; Giorgio Sangiorgi, Rome; Duveen, 1917; Hugh Satterlee, New York; J. Paul Getty Museum, Los Angeles.

GIOVANNI DI PAOLO DI GRAZIA   *Madonna and Child with Saints,* polyptych on wood
Provenance: Count Luigi Tommasi-Aleotti, Cortona; Elia Volpi, Florence; Duveen, 1916; Michael Friedsam, New York; Metropolitan Museum of Art, New York.

GIOVANNI DI PAOLO DI GRAZIA   *Four Saints: Catherine of Alexandria, Barbara, Agatha, and Margaret,* four panels on wood
Provenance: Alphonse Kann, Paris; Duveen; Michael Friedsam, New York; Metropolitan Museum of Art, New York.

GIOVANNI DI PAOLO DI GRAZIA   *The Annunciation,* c. 1445, on wood, 15¾ × 18¼″
Provenance: Sir William John Farrer, London; Sir John Robinson, London; Charles Fairfax Murray, London; Robert and Evelyn Benson; Duveen; Samuel H. Kress, New York; National Gallery of Art, Washington, D.C.

GIOVANNI DI PAOLO DI GRAZIA   *The Adoration of the Magi,* c. 1450, on wood, 10¼ × 17¾″
Provenance: John Rushout, 2nd Baron Northwick, Northwick Park, Worcestershire;

William Fuller-Maitland, Stansted House, Stansted, Essex; Robert Langton Douglas, London; Dr. Eduard Simon, Berlin; Andrew W. Mellon, Pittsburgh; National Gallery of Art, Washington, D.C.

GIROLAMO DI BENVENUTO   *Portrait of a Lady,* or *Portrait of a Young Woman,* c. 1505, on wood, 23⅝ × 17⅞"
Provenance: George Salting, London; Arthur Sanderson, Edinburgh; Robert and Evelyn Benson, London; Duveen; Samuel H. Kress, New York; National Gallery of Art, Washington, D.C.

FRANCISCO JOSE DE GOYA Y LUCIENTES   *Don Manuel Osorio de Zúñiga,* or *The Red Boy,* 1784, oil on canvas, 50 × 40"
Provenance: Don Manuel Osorio de Zuñiga; Mme Henri Bernstein; Duveen; Jules Bache, New York; Metropolitan Museum of Art, New York.

FRANCISCO JOSE DE GOYA Y LUCIENTES   *Señora Sabasa García,* c. 1806, on canvas, 28 × 23"
Provenance: Don José Juan Herrera, Madrid; Dr. James Simon, Berlin; Count Paalen, Berlin; Heinrich Sklarz, Berlin; Duveen; Andrew W. Mellon, Pittsburgh; National Gallery of Art, Washington, D.C.

BENOZZO GOZZOLI   *Virgin and Child with Angels,* c. 1460, gold leaf and tempera on wood, 25¾ × 19⅞"
Provenance: Baron von Tucher, Vienna; Duveen, 1930; Mr. and Mrs. Edsel Ford, Detroit; Detroit Institute of Arts.

BENOZZO GOZZOLI   *A Miracle of St. Zenobius,* predella panel
Provenance: Ex Rodolphe Kann, Paris; Duveen; Kaiser Friedrich Museum, Berlin.
Note: Berenson tried unsuccessfully to persuade Isabella Stewart Gardner to buy the painting in 1907 for £6,500.

FRANCESCO GRANACCI   *Portrait of a Lady*
Provenance: Ex Spiridon.
Note: One of the paintings Carl Hamilton contracted to buy from Duveen in 1919.

JEAN-BAPTISTE GREUZE   *Ange-Laurent de Lalive de Jully,* c. 1759, on canvas, 46 × 34⅞"
Provenance: Louise de La Live, Countess de Montesquiou-Fezensac, Paris; Raymond Aimery de Montesquiou, Duke of Montesquiou-Fezensac; Oriane Henriette de Montesquiou, Goyon; Vicomtesse Alexandre, Count de la Borde; Duveen; Samuel H. Kress, New York; National Gallery of Art, Washington, D.C.

GUIDO DA SIENA   *Madonna and Child*
Provenance: Duveen; another of the paintings which Carl Hamilton contracted to buy in 1919, this one for $60,000. He returned it in 1924 and Duveen sold it to Mr. Gualino in 1927 for $19,520. Duveen had paid $20,000 for it.

FRANS HALS   *Balthasar Coymans,* or *Willem Coymans,* 1645, on canvas, 30¼ × 25″
Provenance: Coymans family, Haarlem; Mrs. Frederick Wollaston, London; Rodolphe
Kann, Paris; Duveen; Mrs. Collis P. Huntington, New York; Archer M. Huntington, New
York; Duveen; Andrew W. Mellon, Pittsburgh; National Gallery of Art, Washington, D.C.

FRANS HALS   *Portrait of an Elderly Lady,* 1633, on canvas, 40¼ × 34″
Provenance: Simon James, Berlin; Duveen, 1919; Andrew W. Mellon, Pittsburgh; National
Gallery of Art, Washington, D.C.

FRANS HALS   *Portrait of Claes Duyst van Voorhout,* c. 1636, on canvas, 31¾ × 26″
Provenance: Earls of Egremont; Col. Egremont Wyndham; Lord Leconfield; Duveen; Jules
Bache, New York; Metropolitan Museum of Art, New York.

FRANS HALS   *Portrait of a Painter (Jan van de Cappele?),* 1650–1655, oil on canvas
Provenance: Rodolphe Kann, Paris; Duveen; Arthur Grenfell, London; George Eastman,
New York; Duveen; J. M. Stettenheim, New York; Norton Simon Museum, Pasadena, CA.

FRANS HALS   *The Laughing Mandolin Player*
Provenance: A. Veil-Picard, Paris; Duveen; John R. Thompson, Chicago; present whereabouts unknown.
Note: Considered the most important sale since Gainsborough's *Blue Boy* when it was sold
to Thompson in February 1924 for $250,000.

FRANS HALS   *The Fisherman*
Provenance: Ex Northbrook; Duveen; present whereabouts unknown.
Note: Duveen valued the work at £7,000.

FRANS HALS   *Portrait of a Young Woman*
Provenance: Duveen; present whereabouts unknown
Note: Mentioned in correspondence of March 1, 1921. Restorer charged Duveen £450.

FRANS HALS   *Portrait of Dorothea Berck,* 1644, 31 × 27″
Provenance: Mrs. Frederick Wollaston, London; Rodolphe Kann, Paris; Duveen; Mrs. Col-
lis P. Huntington, New York; Archer M. Huntington, New York; Mrs. Henry Barton
Jacobs, Baltimore, MD; Baltimore Museum of Art.

FRANS HALS   *Portrait of Self, Wife, and Child*
Provenance: Duveen, 1914; present whereabouts unknown.
Note: According to a *New York Times* article of February 7, 1914, Duveen paid $400,000 for
the painting.

FRANS HALS   *A Young Cavalier*
Provenance: Judge Elbert H. Gary, New York; John Grosberg; Duveen, 1928; present
whereabouts unknown.
Note: Sales price was $85,000, and the painting was sent to Mme. Helfer in Paris for
cleaning.

FRANS HALS   *Portrait of an Elderly Man,* c. 1627–30, oil on canvas (lined), 45½ × 36″
Provenance: Lord Arundell, Wardour Castle, Wiltshire; C. Wertheimer; C. Sedelmeyer; Maurice Kann, Paris; Duveen; Henry Clay Frick, New York; Frick Collection, New York.

FRANS HALS   *Portrait of a Man,* c. 1660, 45 × 32½″
Provenance: 4th Earl Spencer, Althorp, Northamptonshire; Duveen, by 1917; Henry Clay Frick, New York; Frick Collection, New York.

FRANS HALS   *Portrait of a Man*
Provenance: Duveen; Archer M. Huntington, New York; The Huntington, San Marino, CA.

FRANS HALS   *Portrait of a Man*
Provenance: Ex Count Maurice Zamoyski; Duveen; John McCormack; present whereabouts unknown.
Notes: McCormack paid $150,000 for the painting on November 12, 1921.

FRANS HALS   *Portrait of a Man Seated*
Provenance: 5th Earl Spencer, Althorp, Northamptonshire; Duveen, by 1925; Frank P. Wood of Toronto; present whereabouts unknown.

MEINDERT HOBBEMA   *A View on a High Road,* 1665, oil on canvas, 36¾ × 50½″
Provenance: Welbore Felix and Emmanuel Felix Agar; 1st Marquess of Westminster, London; Baron Alfred Charles de Rothschild, Halton, Hertfordshire; Countess Almina Victoria Carnarvon, Highclere Castle, Hampshire; Duveen, 1924; Andrew W. Mellon, Pittsburgh; National Gallery of Art, Washington, D.C.

WILLIAM HOGARTH   *The Graham Children*
Provenance: Duveen; gift to the Tate Gallery, London.

HANS HOLBEIN THE YOUNGER   *Portrait of a Young Girl (with a Squirrel)*
Provenance: Lady Sybil Cholmondeley, sister of Sir Philip Sassoon, sold the painting to Duveen in 1924 but after the latter discovered it to be a Holbein, she, on a pretext, returned the check and took the painting back.

HANS HOLBEIN THE YOUNGER   *A Lady of the Court of Henry VIII,* on panel, 11¾ × 9¾″
Provenance: Count Lanckoronski, Vienna; Duveen; Jules S. Bache; Metropolitan Museum of Art, New York.
Note: Katharine Baetjer, 1980, considers the work to be by the workshop of the master, but in a dissenting opinion John Rowlands considers the work "a clever pastiche" (*Holbein: The Paintings of Hans Holbein the Younger,* 238).

HANS HOLBEIN THE YOUNGER   *Portrait of Lady Lee,* tempera and oil on wood, 16¾ × 12⅞″
Provenance: Major Charles Palmer, Dorney Court, Windsor; Capt. H. R. Moseley, Buildas Park, Shropshire; Duveen; Benjamin Altman, New York; Metropolitan Museum of Art, New York.
Note: The painting is now considered to be a competent copy by a follower of Holbein.

HANS HOLBEIN THE YOUNGER *Portrait of Lady Rich,* tempera and oil on wood, 17½ × 13⅜″
Provenance: Rt. Rev. Herbert Croft, Bishop of Hereford, Croft Castle, Hertfordshire; Sir Archer Croft; W. Michael Moseley; Capt. H. R. Moseley, Buildas Park, Shropshire; Duveen; Benjamin Altman, New York; Metropolitan Museum of Art, New York.
Note: The museum now considers the painting to be a copy after Holbein the Younger; John Rowlands doubts that such a painting by Holbein ever existed.

HANS HOLBEIN THE YOUNGER *Portrait of Dirk Berck of Cologne,* 1536, transferred from panel to canvas, 21 × 16¾″
Provenance: The Earls of Egremont; Colonel Egremont Wyndham; Lord Leconfield; Duveen; Jules Bache, New York; Metropolitan Museum of Art, New York.
Note: John Rowlands remarks that the transfer of the painting from panel to canvas by Duveen has caused irreparable damage (*Holbein,* 143). It is still considered to be a handsome example of Holbein's style.

HANS HOLBEIN THE YOUNGER *Portrait of a Man,* 1535, on panel, diameter 12″
Provenance: Arthur W. and Alice Sachs; Duveen; Jules Bache, New York; Metropolitan Museum of Art, New York.
Note: John Rowlands considers the portrait to have been painted by an immediate follower of Holbein, possibly someone who worked in his studio. The museum still considers the painting to be a Holbein.

HANS HOLBEIN THE YOUNGER *Edward VI, When Prince of Wales,* on panel, diameter 12¾″
Provenance: Viscount Lee of Fareham; Duveen; Jules Bache, New York; Metropolitan Museum of Art, New York.
Note: John Rowlands gives the work to a follower of Holbein; the museum still considers the portrait to be by Holbein.

HANS HOLBEIN THE YOUNGER *Portrait of Hermann Wedigh,* 1532, on panel, 12 × 16″
Provenance: The Grafen von Schönborn, Vienna; Graf Friedrich Karl von Schönborn-Buchheim, Vienna; Duveen; Frank D. Stout, Chicago; Edward S. Harkness, New York; Metropolitan Museum of Art, New York.
Note: Duveen paid $100,000 for the painting.

HANS HOLBEIN THE YOUNGER *A Woman,* c. 1532–4, tempera and oil on oak panel, 9⅛ × 7½″
Provenance: Earl of Lonsdale, Lowther Castle; Duveen, 1930; Mr. and Mrs. Edsel Ford, Detroit; Detroit Institute of Arts.

HANS HOLBEIN THE YOUNGER *Portrait of a Man,* 1538, oil on panel, 19½ × 15⅜″
Provenance: Royal Polish Picture Gallery; Duveen, 1925; Dr. A. Hamilton Rice, New York; Charles Payson; Yale University Art Gallery.

HANS HOLBEIN THE YOUNGER *Portrait of Sir Brian Tuke,* c. 1527, oil on panel, 19½ × 15¼″

Provenance: Viscount Robert Sydney; Hugh Blaker, London; Duveen, 1921–3; Elisabeth Severance Prentiss, Cleveland; Cleveland Museum of Art; Duveen; Norton Simon Museum, Pasadena, CA.
Note: Now "Attributed to Holbein."

HANS HOLBEIN THE YOUNGER   *Portrait of Mrs. Pemberton,* miniature
Provenance: Duveen, 1901, to J. P. Morgan; Duveen, 1935; present whereabouts unknown.
Note: Duveen sold the miniature to Morgan for $14,264 and bought it back in 1935 as part of Morgan's $2,500,000 miniature collection.

NATHANIEL HONE   *Charlotte Augusta Matilda,* c. 1776, oil on canvas 30¼ × 24¼"
Provenance: Duveen; Norton Simon Museum, Pasadena, CA.

NATHANIEL HONE   *William Henry,* 1776, oil on canvas, 30 × 25"
Provenance: Duveen; Norton Simon Museum, Pasadena, CA.

PIETER DE HOOCH   *A Dutch Courtyard,* c. 1660, on canvas, 26¾ × 23"
Provenance: Baron Lionel Nathan de Rothschild; Alfred Charles de Rothschild; Countess of Carnarvon, Newbury; Duveen; Andrew W. Mellon, Pittsburgh; National Gallery of Art, Washington, D.C.
Note: In his book on the National Gallery of Art, John Walker notes that a similar version of this painting is in the Mauritshuis, The Hague.

JOHN HOPPNER   *Miss Charlotte Papendiek as a Child*
Provenance: Mrs. Vernon Delves Boughton; Louis Breitmeyer, London; Duveen, 1930; William Randolph Hearst, Los Angeles; Marion Davies, Los Angeles; Los Angeles County Museum of Art.

JOHN HOPPNER   *Portrait of Lady Beauchamp*
Note: Just after Duveen bought the portrait in September 1924, René Gimpel described having seen it in his diary: "A marvelous Hoppner, the portrait of Lady Beauchamp; her hat has a ribbon of so lovely a blue that it casts upon her face an azure haze which fills her eyes with love" (*Diary of an Art Dealer,* 273).

JOHN HOPPNER   *Portrait of Lady Georgina Buckley*
Provenance: Major Cornwallis-West; Duveen; present whereabouts unknown.
Note: Duveen paid $14,073 for the painting in 1930. It was shipped in a frame to New York in 1935 and arrived in very bad condition.

JOHN HOPPNER   *Master John Granville,* c. 1790–95, oil on canvas, 30 × 24¾"
Provenance: Col. Bernard Granville, Chadley, Wellesbourne, Warwickshire; Duveen; Mr. and Mrs. Edsel Ford, 1928; Detroit Institute of Arts.
Note: When the painting arrived in New York in May 1928, Duveen was ecstatic; he called it one of the most beautiful Hoppners he had ever seen and vowed not to sell it for less than $110,000, perhaps $150,000. How much the Fords paid is not known.

JOHN HOPPNER   *Susannah Edith, Lady Rowley,* c. 1785, oil on canvas, 30 × 25"

Provenance: Sir George Dashwood, Kirtlington Park, nr. Woodstock, Oxfordshire; Captain George Astley Charles Dashwood, Wherstead Park, Ipswich; Lieutenant Charles Edmund Dashwood; Baron Eugen de Rothschild, Paris; Duveen; Anna Thomson Dodge, Grosse Point, MI; Detroit Institute of Arts.

JOHN HOPPNER *Isabella, Marchioness of Hertford,* 1784, on canvas, 29½ × 24½"
Provenance: Henry Meynell; Georgina Meynell Ingram; John Charles Francis Ramsden, Willinghurst; Frederick William Ramsden; Duveen, 1924; Henry E. Huntington; The Huntington, San Marino, CA.

JOHN HOPPNER *Mrs. Bedford and Son,* or *Frances (Woodis) Borlase, later Frances Grenfell, and Pascoe George Norman Grenfell,* c. 1804, on canvas, 93⅞ × 58"
Provenance: William Grenfell, Holland; Dora Grenfell der Jonchere; J. J. M. Chabot, Wassenaar, Holland; Duveen, 1919; Henry E. Huntington; The Huntington, San Marino, CA.
Note: The painting was traditionally considered to be by either Sir Charles Lee or Martin Archer Shee. Duveen gave the attribution to Hoppner. It is now considered to be by Shee.

JOHN HOPPNER *Portrait of Miss Selina Beresford*
Provenance: One of two Hoppners owned by Mrs. Trevelyan Martin, who sold the painting to Duveen in 1923 on condition that the dealer arrange for a copy. The painting was shipped to New York from London in September 1935; present whereabouts unknown.

JOHN HOPPNER *Duke and Duchess of York,* 1791, a pair of full-length portraits
Provenance: Unknown. The two portraits were sold to Sir George Cooper by Duveen in 1908 for 56,000 guineas.

JOHN HOPPNER *Lady Louisa Manners,* on canvas, 52 × 40"
Provenance: Lady Laura Tollemache; Maria, wife of Charles, 2nd Earl and 1st Marquis of Ailesbury; Lord Charles William Pruce, M.P.; Duveen; Lord Michelham; Duveen, Nov. 23, 1926, for $38,900; present whereabouts unknown.

JEAN-ANTOINE HOUDON *Diana,* or *Diana the Huntress,* sculpture
Provenance: Duveen paid $51,000 for the work at the Yerkes sale in 1910 and subsequently sold to Henry Clay Frick, New York; now in the Frick Collection, New York.

JEAN-ANTOINE HOUDON *Bust of His Baby Daughter, Sabine*
Provenance: Ex Jacques Doucet, Paris. Duveen bought the work in 1912 for $96,000 and sold it to Judge Elbert H. Gary for $110,000. It was next sold to Knoedlers at the Gary sale in 1928 for $245,000, going to Mrs. Edward S. Harkness. It is now at the Metropolitan Museum of Art, New York.

ADRIAEN ISENBRANDT *Young Man with a Rosary,* oil on canvas, transferred to panel, 16¾ × 12½"
Provenance: Duveen; Norton Simon Museum, Pasadena, CA.

ITALIAN Cassone, sixteenth century, carved and inlaid walnut, 27 × 72½ × 26"
Provenance: Gift of Duveen to the Detroit Institute of Arts.

ITALIAN, FOURTEENTH-CENTURY VENETIAN   *Fifteen Scenes in the Life of Christ with Patron Saints,* on wood, c. 1300
Provenance: Prince Leon Ouroussoff, Paris; Duveen; Norton Simon Museum, Pasadena, CA.

ITALIAN, SIXTEENTH-CENTURY (ROMAN OR PADUAN)   Equestrian statuette of Marcus Aurelius
Provenance: Duveen; Walters Art Museum, Baltimore, MD.
Note: The statuette was hollow-cast. It has a natural olive-brown patina with remnants of dark-brown lacquer patina, areas of gilding, and a cloak set with a small garnet at the shoulder. The marble base has Latin inscriptions. It is a copy of the life-size antique statue on the Capitoline Hill, Rome.

JACOMETTO   *Portrait of a Young Man,* on wood
Provenance: Baron Arthur de Schickler, Château de Martinvast, Manche; Comtesse Marguerite de Pourtalès, Château de Martinvast; Duveen, 1919; William Salomon, New York; Duveen, 1922; Andrew W. Mellon, Pittsburgh; Duveen; Jules Bache, New York; Metropolitan Museum of Art, New York.

JACOPINO DEL CONTE   *Portrait of a Papal Notary,* c. 1535, on canvas, 33 × 27″
Provenance: Sir W. Drake; Robert and Evelyn Benson, London; Duveen, 1927; gift to the Fitzwilliam Museum, Cambridge, 1933.

JACOPO DEL SELLAIO   *Portrait of a Man with a Red Cap*
Provenance: William Salomon, New York; Duveen; present whereabouts unknown.
Note: Duveen was trying to get Arabella Huntington to buy this painting in January 1923.

AUGUSTUS JOHN   *Madame Suggia,* 1923
Provenance: William P. Clyde Jr.; Duveen; gift to the Tate Gallery, London.

GWEN JOHN   *Dorelia,* oil on canvas
Provenance: Duveen Paintings Fund; the Tate Gallery, London.

FOLLOWER OF THE MASTER OF THE KARLSRUHE PASSION   *The Procession to Calvary,* c. 1490, oil on panel, 19⅜ × 14″
Provenance: Duveen; Norton Simon Museum, Pasadena, CA.

SIR GODFREY KNELLER   *Marguerite Sawyer, Countess of Pembroke*
Provenance: Bought by Duveen at the Stotesbury sale in 1914 and sold at cost for $2,100; present whereabouts unknown.

SIR GODFREY KNELLER   *Lady Dobden*
Provenance: Bought by Duveen at the Stotesbury sale in 1914 and sold at cost for $3,000; present whereabouts unknown.

CHARLES KNIGHT   *Llangollen,* oil on canvas
Provenance: Duveen Paintings Fund, 1926; presented to the Ferens Art Gallery, Hull, by the executors of Duveen's estate in 1949.

JACQUES DE LAJOUE   *Fête Champêtre,* seven decorative panels on canvas on the themes of music, the picnic, bird-nesting, the musician, the pet goat, the luncheon, and picking flowers
Provenance: 1st Viscount d'Abernon, Esher Place, Surrey; Duveen; Norton Simon Museum, Pasadena, CA.

JACQUES DE LAJOUE   Seven decorative panels now mounted on a folding screen on the themes of a mother nursing her child, a shepherdess, a shepherdess asleep, a youth with a spade, a girl with a spear, the shepherd's song, and a girl with cupid
Provenance: Madame du Sommerard, Paris; J. Pierpont Morgan Jr.; Duveen, 1916; Henry Clay Frick, New York; Frick Collection, New York.
Note: Now labeled "Attributed to."

NICOLAS LANCRET   *The Camargo Dancing,* c. 1730, on canvas, 30 × 42″
Provenance: Deutscher Kaiser Wilhelm II, Berlin; Duveen; Andrew W. Mellon, Pittsburgh; National Gallery of Art, Washington, D.C.

NICOLAS DE LARGILLIÈRE   *Portrait of the Marquis d'Havrincourt,* oil on canvas, 32 × 25½″
Provenance: Marquis Alphonse Pierre de Cardevac d'Havrincourt, Château Havrincourt, Pas-de-Calais; Duveen; Norton Simon Museum, Pasadena, CA.

NICOLAS DE LARGILLIÈRE   *Portrait of Pierre Lepautre, Sculptor,* 1689, oil on canvas, 64¼ × 50¾″
Provenance: William Howard Taft, Cincinnati, OH; Joseph Levey, New York; Duveen; Norton Simon Museum, Pasadena, CA.

FRANCESCO DA LAURANA   *Ippolita Maria Sforza, Duchess of Aragon,* or *Bust of a Lady,* c. 1472, white marble bust, 18½ × 18″
Provenance: Marquise de Mailly-Nesle, Château de la Roche-Mailly, Requeil, Sarthe; Duveen; Henry Clay Frick, New York; Frick Collection, New York.

FRANCESCO DA LAURANA   *Ippolita Maria Sforza, Duchess of Aragon,* or *A Princess of the House of Aragon,* c. 1472, white marble bust, 18½ × 18″
Provenance: Alessandro Castellani, Rome; Stefano Bardini, Florence; Thomas Fortune Ryan, New York; Duveen; Andrew W. Mellon, Pittsburgh; National Gallery of Art, Washington, D.C.

SIR JOHN LAVERY   *The Golf Course, North Berwick*
Provenance: Gift to the Tate Gallery, London, by Duveen.

SIR JOHN LAVERY   *The Family of Lord Duveen*
Provenance: Commissioned by Joseph Duveen and given to the Ferens Art Gallery by Lady Duveen in 1939 in memory of her husband.

THOMAS LAWRENCE   *Lady Templeton and Her Son Henry,* c. 1801, oil on canvas, 84¾ × 58⅝″

Provenance: Henry Edward Montagu Dorington Clotworthy Upton, 4th Viscount Templeton, Castle Upton, Co. Antrim, Northern Ireland; Baron Alfred Charles de Rothschild, Halton, nr. Tring, Hertfordshire; Countess Almina Victoria Marie Alexandra Carnarvon, Highclere Castle, Hampshire; Duveen; Andrew W. Mellon, Pittsburgh; National Gallery of Art, Washington, D.C.

THOMAS LAWRENCE   *Hon. Emma (Crave) Cunliffe, later Emma Cunliffe-Offley,*
c. 1809, oil on canvas, 49½ × 39½″
Provenance: Robert Offley Crewe-Milnes, Marquess of Crewe, Crewe Hall, Cheshire; Duveen; Henry E. Huntington, 1917; Huntington Library, Art Collections and Botannical Gardens, San Marino, CA.

THOMAS LAWRENCE   *Emily Anderson, Little Red Riding Hood,* c. 1821, oil on canvas,
63¾ × 45″
Provenance: Rev. A Anderson; Mrs. Augusta Gordon Watson; Lieutenant Frank A. Anderson; Duveen; Henry E. Huntington, 1918; The Huntington, San Marino, CA.

THOMAS LAWRENCE   *Sarah Goodin Barrett Moulton: "Pinkie,"* 1794, oil on canvas,
58¼ × 40¼″
Provenance: Charles John Moulton-Barrett; Elizabeth Moulton-Barrett, London; Duveen; 1st Baron Michelham, Hellingly, Sussex; Lady Aimee Geraldine Michelham; Duveen; Henry E. Huntington, 1927; The Huntington, San Marino, CA.

THOMAS LAWRENCE   *Portrait of Arthur Atherley as an Etonian,* c. 1790–91, oil on
canvas, 49½ × 39½″
Provenance: Arthur Atherley, Southampton, Hampshire; Atherley family; Mrs. William McGowan and Mrs. Arthur Smith-Bingham; Duveen, 1928; William Randolph Hearst, Los Angeles; Los Angeles County Museum of Art.
Note: Duveen sold the painting to Hearst for $140,000.

THOMAS LAWRENCE   *Portrait of Mrs. Hemmington,* 30 × 25″
Provenance: Duveen; present whereabouts unknown.
Note: Consular invoices for November 12, 1920, note that it crossed on the *Aquitania* with the restorer, W. A. Holder.

THOMAS LAWRENCE   *The Fludyer Children*
Provenance: Duveen; bought by Agnew's; present whereabouts unknown.
Note: Consular invoices for April 9, 1921, note that it was shipped from Paris and bought by Agnew's in February 1928.

THOMAS LAWRENCE   *Mrs. John Allnutt*
Provenance: Duveen paid $45,000 for it in the Judge Elbert H. Gary sale, April 20, 1928; present whereabouts unknown.

NICOLAS & JEAN DE SAINT-PRIEST LECLERC   *Anne of Britany, Wife of Louis XII,*
c. 1499/1500, gilt bronze
Provenance: Duveen; National Gallery of Art, Washington, D.C.

NICOLAS & JEAN DE SAINT-PRIEST LECLERC   *Louis XII, King of France,*
c. 1499/1500, gilt bronze
Provenance: Duveen; National Gallery of Art, Washington, D.C.

SIR PETER LELY   *Lady Derby*
Provenance: Sold by Duveen to E. T. Stotesbury, Philadelphia, in 1914 for $2,750; present
whereabouts unknown.

SIR PETER LELY   *Countess of Cork*
Provenance: Sold by Duveen to E. T. Stotesbury, Philadelphia, in 1914 for $1,875; present
whereabouts unknown.

SIR PETER LELY   *Henrietta Marie*
Provenance: Sold by Duveen to E. T. Stotesbury, Philadelphia, in 1914 for $1,620; present
whereabouts unknown.

SIR PETER LELY   *Anne Bayning, Daughter of First Viscount Boyning*
Provenance: Sold by Duveen to E. T. Stotesbury, Philadelphia, in 1914 for $2,500; present
whereabouts unknown.

SIR PETER LELY   *Sarah, First Lady Bunbury*
Provenance: Sold by Duveen to E. T. Stotesbury, Philadelphia, in 1914 for $2,750; present
whereabouts unknown.

JEAN-LOUIS LEMOYNE   *A Companion of Diana,* marble
Provenance: Duveen; National Gallery of Art, Washington, D.C.

LEONARDO DA VINCI   *Portrait of a Young Lady,* transferred from wood to hardboard,
18⅝ × 13½"
Provenance: Conte di Castel-Pizzuto, Milan; Cesare Canessa, Naples; Duveen, 1916;
William Salomon, New York; Duveen; Samuel H. Kress, New York; National Gallery of
Art, Washington, D.C.
Note: Now variously referred to as "studio of" and "follower of."

LEONARDO DA VINCI   *Madonna and Child with a Pomegranate*
Provenance: John Watkins Brett, London; Charles Timbal; Dreyfus Collection; Samuel
Kress; Kress Collection, New York.
Note: Now "Attributed to."

LEONARDO DA VINCI   *"A Bust"*
Provenance: Gustave Dreyfus Collection; Duveen; Andrew W. Mellon, Washington, D.C.
After questions were raised about the work's authenticity in September 1937, Mellon
appears to have returned it to Duveen Brothers and its present whereabouts are unknown.

LEONARDO DA VINCI   *Beatrice d'Este*
Provenance: Duveen; William Salomon, New York. Present whereabouts unknown.
Note: The painting was at one time attributed to Bernardo di Conti.

LEONE LEONI   *Hope with Hands Raised in Prayer,* bronze
Provenance: Duveen; National Gallery of Art, Washington, D.C.

LEONE LEONI   *Maarten de Hane, Flemish Merchant,* bronze
Provenance: Duveen; National Gallery of Art, Washington, D.C.

LEONE LEONI   *Giovanni Capponi,* c. 1585, white marble bust, h. 22″
Provenance: Oscar Hainauer, Berlin; Duveen; Samuel H. Kress, New York; National Gallery of Art, Washington, D.C.

NEVILLE LEWIS   *Head of a Child (Catherine),* oil on panel
Provenance: Duveen Paintings Fund, 1927; presented to the Ferens Art Gallery, Hull, by the executors of Duveen's estate in 1949.

FILIPPINO LIPPI   *The Madonna and Child,* c. 1487, tempera and oil on wood, 32 × 23½″
Provenance: Possibly Strozzi, Florence; Don Marcello Massarenti, Rome; Dr. Götz Martius, Kiel; Duveen, 1923; Jules S. Bache, New York; Metropolitan Museum of Art, New York.

FILIPPINO LIPPI   *The Madonna and Child with St. Joseph and an Angel,* on wood, 22 × 15″
Provenance: Madame A. de Couriss, Dresden; Duveen, 1911; Benjamin Altman, New York; Metropolitan Museum of Art, New York.
Note: Formerly attributed to "workshop of" Filippino and now attributed to Raffaellino del Garbo.

FILIPPINO LIPPI   *The Madonna Adoring the Child with an Angel,* c. 1480, 32½ × 22½″
Provenance: Grand Ducal House of Saxe-Meiningen; Duveen; Andrew W. Mellon, Washington, D.C.; National Gallery of Art, Washington, D.C.

FILIPPINO LIPPI   *The Coronation of the Virgin,* c. 1480, tempera on wood, lunette, 35½ × 87½″
Provenance: Marquess of Lothian, Newbattle Abbey, Scotland; Duveen, 1937; Samuel H. Kress, New York; National Gallery of Art, Washington, D.C.

FILIPPINO LIPPI   *Tobias and the Archangel,* c. 1480, 13½ × 10″
Provenance: Robert and Evelyn Benson, London; Duveen, 1927; Samuel H. Kress, New York; National Gallery of Art, Washington, D.C.

FILIPPINO LIPPI   *Pieta,* on wood, central panel of a predella
Provenance: Robert and Evelyn Benson, London; Duveen, 1927; Frederick Housman, New York; Samuel H. Kress, New York; National Gallery of Art, Washington, D.C.

FILIPPINO LIPPI   *The Adoration of the Child,* c. 1485, 32 × 28¾″
Provenance: Charles Timbal, Paris; Gustave Dreyfus, Paris; Duveen; Edward Drummond Libbey, Toledo, OH; Museum of Art, Toledo, OH.

FRA FILIPPO LIPPI   *The Madonna and Child,* tempera on wood, 17¾ × 14¼″
Provenance: Charles Butler, London; Oscar Hainauer, Berlin; Duveen, 1906; George and Florence Blumenthal, New York; Metropolitan Museum of Art, New York.
Note: Federico Zeri notes that the painting is a fragment from a larger composition and believes it to be one of the earliest surviving works by the Master of San Miniato (*Italian Paintings,* 116).

FRA FILIPPO LIPPI   *The Madonna with Two Angels,* or *The Madonna and Child Enthroned with Two Angels,* tempera, with gold haloes, on wood, transferred from original panel, arched top, 48¼ × 24¾″
Provenance: Franziska Clavé von Bouhaben, Koln; Ludwig Mond, London; Dr. Adolphe Schaeffer, Frankfurt-am-Main; Duveen, 1921; Jules Bache, New York; Metropolitan Museum of Art, New York.
Note: Central panel of what was originally a triptych, the wings of which are in the Accademia Albertina in Turin. The painting was mentioned in Carl Hamilton's lawsuit against Duveen.

FRA FILIPPO LIPPI   *Saint Lawrence Enthroned with Saints and Donors,* tryptych, tempera on wood, 47¾ × 45½″; *Saint Benedict,* 28½ × 15⅜″; and *Saint Anthony Abbot,* 28½ × 15½″
Provenance: Alessandri family, Palazzo Alessandri, Borgo degli Albizzi, Florence; Luigi Grassi, Florence (1912?); Duveen, 1912; J. P. Morgan, New York; Metropolitan Museum of Art, New York.
Note: The paintings formed the altarpiece of the church of the Villa Alessandri, Vincigliata, Fiesole, and according to experts have been much altered since they were removed.

FRA FILIPPO LIPPI   *The Annunciation,* c. 1445–50, tempera on panel, 40½ × 64″
Provenance: Dr. Achillito Chiesa, Milan; Duveen; Percy S. Straus, New York; Samuel H. Kress, New York; National Gallery of Art, Washington, D.C.

FRA FILIPPO LIPPI   *Madonna and Child,* c. 1440–45, on wood, 31⅜ × 20⅛″
Provenance: Edward Solly, London; Frederick William III, King of Prussia; the Kaiser Friedrich Museum, Berlin; Duveen; Samuel H. Kress, New York; National Gallery of Art, Washington, D.C.

FRA FILIPPO LIPPI   *Head of the Madonna,* c. 1452, 16⅜ × 13⅛″
Provenance: Eugène Piot, Paris; Louis Charles Timbal, Paris; Gustave Dreyfus, Paris; Duveen; Samuel H. Kress, New York; National Gallery of Art, Washington, D.C.
Note: Now listed as a modern copy and no longer at the National Gallery.

FRA FILIPPO LIPPI   *The Madonna,* 45¾ × 30½″
Provenance: Duveen; Mrs. Arabella Huntington.
Note: Reattributed by Berenson as "Master of the Castello Nativity," presumably after the sale.

FRA FILIPPO LIPPI   *Madonna and Child*
Provenance: Corsini Collection, Florence; Duveen; present whereabouts unknown.

Note: This is one of the paintings Duveen left in Italy for several years because of punitive export taxes being exacted by Mussolini.

FRA FILIPPO LIPPI   *Madonna and Child,* 32½ × 24½"
Provenance: Duveen; Carl Hamilton; Duveen; Mrs. Leon Schinasi, New York.
Note: This is the painting Hamilton supposedly "bought" from Duveen for $65,000 and which fetched $125,000 at the 1929 auction. The painting supposedly came from the monastery of the Carmine Brethren. Colin Simpson calls it "a Ioni fake."

LIPPO MEMMI   *The Madonna and Child with Saints and Angels,* additional subjects, from left, male martyr, Saints Clare, Lawrence, Peter, Louis of Toulouse, Catherine of Alexandria and Cecilia, predella, on wood, gabled top.
Provenance: Richard Norton, Boston; Duveen, 1919; Carl W. Hamilton; Duveen; Maitland Fuller Griggs, New York; Metropolitan Museum of Art, New York.

LIPPO MEMMI   *Madonna and Child with Donor,* c. 1335, on wood, 22¼ × 9½"
Provenance: Robert and Evelyn Benson, London; Duveen, 1927; Andrew W. Mellon, Pittsburgh; National Gallery of Art, Washington, D.C.

LIPPO MEMMI   *St. John the Baptist,* c. 1325, on wood, pointed arched top, tempera on panel
Provenance: Jacques Goudstikker, Amsterdam; Duveen, 1938; Samuel H. Kress, New York; National Gallery of Art, Washington, D.C.

PIETRO LONGHI   *Blind Man's Buff*
Provenance: Duveen; Samuel H. Kress, New York; Kress Collection, New York.

AMBROGIO LORENZETTI   *The Crucifixion,* on wood, 15½ × 10½"
Provenance: Augustus Stevens, London; Henry George Bohn, London; Charles Butler, London; Robert and Evelyn Benson, London; Duveen, 1927; Mr. and Mrs. John D. Rockefeller Jr., New York; Metropolitan Museum of Art, New York.
Note: Now "Master of the Codex of Saint George."

PIETRO LORENZETTI   *St. Catherine of Alexandria,* on wood, arched top, pointed, 29 × 16½"
Provenance: Giulio Sterbini, Rome; Julius Böhler, Munich; Godefroy Brauer, Nice; Duveen; Samuel H. Kress, New York; National Gallery of Art, Washington, D.C.

PIETRO LORENZETTI   *Madonna and Child,* or *Large Nativity,* or *The Holy Family*
Provenance: Ex Prince Ouroussoff; Duveen, 1918, for $20,000; "sold" to Carl Hamilton in 1919 for $35,000; taken back and sold July 1928 to Abegg of Turin for $24,250; present whereabouts unknown.

LORENZO DI CREDI   *Portrait of a Lady,* tempera on wood, 23⅛ × 15¾"
Provenance: The Marchesi Pucci, Palazzo Pucci, Florence; Marchese Emilio Pucci, Florence; Duveen, 1920; Andrew W. Mellon, Pittsburgh, 1922; Duveen, 1924; Richard de Wolfe Brixey, New York; Metropolitan Museum of Art, New York.

LORENZO DI CREDI   *Ascension of St. Louis,* c. 1520, tondo, diameter 23″
Provenance: Ex Corbelli; Gaspard Bourgeois, Cologne; Charles Sedelmeyer, Paris; Eduard
F. Weber, Hamburg; Charles Davis, London; Duveen; Arabella Huntington; The Hunt-
ington, San Marino, CA.

LORENZO DI CREDI   *Self-portrait,* c. 1488, transferred from wood to canvas, 18 × 12¾″
Provenance: Duveen; P. A. B. Widener; National Gallery of Art, Washington, D.C.

LORENZO DI CREDI   *Madonna and Child with Two Angels,* on wood, tondo
Provenance: Rev. W. G. Beardmore, London; Lord Elliot, Rackheath Park, Norwich;
Duveen; Stanley Mortimer; Princeton University Art Museum, Princeton, NJ.
Note: Now "School of."

LORENZO DI CREDI   *Madonna and Child with Infant St. John,* on wood, tondo
Provenance: Ex Alexander Barker; Duveen; Mrs. Ludig, 1910, for $17,500; present where-
abouts unknown.

LORENZO LOTTO   *Madonna and Child with Two Donors,* on canvas, 35 × 45″
Provenance: Robert and Evelyn Benson, London; Duveen, 1927; William Randolph
Hearst; Nicholas de Koenigsberg, Buenos Aires; J. Paul Getty Museum, Los Angeles.

THOMAS LOWINSKY   *Sappho,* oil on canvas
Provenance: Duveen Paintings Fund, 1927; presented to the Ferens Art Gallery, Hull, by
the executors of Duveen's estate in 1949.

L. S. LOWRY   *Coming out of School*
Provenance: Duveen Paintings Fund; the Tate Gallery, London.

BERNARDINO LUINI   *Virgin and Child with St. Catherine,* on wood
Provenance: Michele Cavaleri, Milan; Henri Cernuschi, Paris; Jules Féral, Paris; Charles
Wakefield Mori, Monte Carlo; Duveen; Norton Simon Museum, Pasadena, CA.

BERNARDINO LUINI   *The Nativity,* or *The Adoration of the Child,* c. 1525, wood
transferred to canvas, 70 × 47¼″
Provenance: Charles Butler, London; Robert and Evelyn Benson, London; Duveen;
Samuel H. Kress, New York; National Gallery of Art, Washington, D.C.; Kress Collection,
New York; New Orleans Museum of Art.

BERNARDINO LUINI   *Portrait of a Lady,* c. 1515, on wood, 30¼ × 22½″
Provenance: Frederick Richards Leyland, Liverpool; Charles Fairfax Murray, London;
Robert and Evelyn Benson, London; Duveen, 1927; Andrew W. Mellon, Pittsburgh;
National Gallery of Art, Washington, D.C.
Note: The painting sold in 1928 for $290,000.

BERNARDINO LUINI   *Madonna and Child with St. Jerome*
Provenance: Ex William Salomon; Duveen; present whereabouts unknown.

BERNARDINO LUINI   *Virgin and Child with St. John*
Provenance: Duveen; John McGrath; Duveen; Mrs. Nicholas F. Brady; present where-abouts unknown.

BERNARDINO LUINI   *Madonna and Child*
Provenance: Duveen sold the painting to Mrs. Frank Prentice of Cleveland, Ohio, for $140,000; present whereabouts unknown.

BERNARDINO LUINI   Series of nine frescoes depicting Ovid's *Metamorphoses.*
Provenance: Michele Cavaleri, Milan; Enrico Cernuschi, Paris; Rodolphe Kann, Paris; Duveen, 1907; Samuel H. Kress, New York; National Gallery of Art, Washington, D.C.

BERNARDINO LUINI   Series of seven panels from the Torriani Altarpiece, on wood, 24⅝ × 13½"
Provenance: Conte Giovan Battista Lucini Passalacqua, Milan; Charles Butler, London; Robert and Evelyn Benson, London; Duveen, 1927; Norton Simon Museum, Pasadena, CA.
Note: Several other of the original twelve panels are in private collections and the Philadelphia Museum, the Johnson Collection.

STEFANO MADERNO   *Hercules and Antaeus,* c. 1621–22, bronze group, h. 29¾"
Provenance: Sir Bache Edward Cunard, London; Emerald, Lady Cunard, London; Duveen; Henry E. Huntington, San Marino, CA; The Huntington, San Marino, CA.

SEBASTIANO DI BARTOLO MAINARDI   *Madonna and Child with Angels,* tempera on canvas, transferred from wood, tondo, diameter 38¾"
Provenance: Baron Michele Lazzaroni, Paris; Duveen, 1911; Benjamin Altman, New York; Metropolitan Museum of Art, New York.

SEBASTIANO DI BARTOLO MAINARDI   *Portrait of a Lady,* oil on canvas, transferred to panel, 23⁵⁄₁₆ × 12¾"
Provenance: Duveen; Andrew W. Mellon, Pittsburgh; Duveen; Norton Simon Museum, Pasadena, CA.

SEBASTIANO DI BARTOLO MAINARDI   *Portrait of a Young Man,* c. 1475–1500, 17 × 13"
Provenance: Marchese Gherardi, Florence; William Drury Lowe, Locko Park, England; Duveen; The Huntington, San Marino, CA.

SEBASTIANO DI BARTOLO MAINARDI   *Portrait of a Lady,* c. 1475–1500, 17 × 13"
Provenance: Marchese Gherardi, Florence; William Drury Lowe, Locko Park, England; Duveen; The Huntington, San Marino, CA.

SEBASTIANO DI BARTOLO MAINARDI   *Madonna and Child,* on wood, 31½ × 22½"
Provenance: Duveen; Arabella Huntington; the Huntington, San Marino, CA.

ANDREA MANTEGNA   *St. Jerome in the Wilderness,* on wood, 31¾ × 21⅝"
Provenance: Earls of Pembroke, Wilton House, Wiltshire; Duveen, 1917; Carl W. Hamil-

ton; Duveen, 1921; Joseph E. Widener, Elkins Park, PA; National Gallery of Art, Washington, D.C.
Note: Now listed as "Italian, Paduan-Ferrarese, fifteenth century, c. 1450–75."

ANDREA MANTEGNA *Judith and Holofernes,* c. 1495, on wood, 11⅞ × 7⅛"
Provenance: Charles I of England; the Earls of Pembroke; Duveen; Carl Hamilton, New York; Duveen; Joseph E. Widener, Elkins Park, PA; National Gallery of Art, Washington, D.C.

ANDREA MANTEGNA *The Madonna and Child,* c. 1500, 22⅛ × 16⅛"
Provenance: James Hugh Smith Barry, Cheshire; Lord Barrymore, Marbury Hall, Northwick, Cheshire; Duveen; Samuel H. Kress, New York; National Gallery of Art, Washington, D.C.
Note: Now considered to be "Circle of Andrea Mantegna (possibly Correggio)."

ANDREA MANTEGNA *The Adoration of the Shepherds,* c. 1460, tempera on canvas, transferred from wood, 15¾ × 21⅞"
Provenance: Palazzo Estense, Ferrara; Villa Aldobrandini, Rome; Alexander Day, London; A. Rouse Boughton-Knight, Downton Castle, Herefordshire; Duveen, 1924–25; Clarence H. Mackay, Roslyn, NY; Metropolitan Museum of Art, New York.

ANDREA MANTEGNA *Tarquin and the Cumaean Sibyl,* c. 1495, 22⅛ × 19⅛"
Provenance: Duke of Buccleuch, Montague House, London; Duveen; Cincinnati Art Museum.

ANDREA MANTEGNA *The Holy Family*
Provenance: Weber sale, Berlin; Duveen, 1913; present whereabouts unknown.
Note: When he died, Benjamin Altman had been prepared to pay Duveen £103,000 for this large Mantegna that Duveen had bought at auction for £29,500.

MANTUAN, FIFTEENTH CENTURY *Gianfrancesco Gonzaga di Rodigo, Lord of Sabbioneta,* 1479, bronze bust
Provenance: Duveen; National Gallery of Art, Washington, D.C.

MANTUAN, FIFTEENTH CENTURY *House Between Two Hills,* bronze
Provenance: Duveen; National Gallery of Art, Washington, D.C.

MANTUAN, SIXTEENTH CENTURY *A Triumph, with Hunting Scenes,* bronze
Provenance: Duveen; National Gallery of Art, Washington, D.C.

MARGARITONE D'AREZZO *Madonna and Child*
Provenance: Duveen; Carl Hamilton, New York, who contracted to buy the painting in 1919 for $70,000 and who returned the painting to Duveen in 1924: in 1938, the painting was still unsold; present whereabouts unknown.

SIMONE MARTINI *Saint John the Baptist,* c. 1315–20, on wood, 37¼ × 18"
Provenance: Comte Oriola, Florence; Jacques Goudstikker, Amsterdam; Duveen; Samuel H. Kress, New York, 1937; National Gallery of Art, Washington, D.C.

TOMMASO GUIDI MASACCIO   *Profile Portrait of a Young Man,* c. 1425–27, 16¾ × 12¾″
Provenance: Chevalier Alexis-François Artaud de Montor, Paris; Duveen, 1936; Andrew W.
Mellon, Pittsburgh; National Gallery of Art, Washington, D.C.
Note: John Walker told the author in 1977 that the painting was "very doubtful." It is now
attributed: "Italian, Florentine, Fifteenth Century."

TOMMASO GUIDI MASACCIO   *The Madonna of Humility,* c. 1425, 41⅜ × 21⅛″
Provenance: Princesse de Croy-Dullman, Gmünden; Carl, Count Lonyay, Vienna;
Duveen; Andrew W. Mellon, Pittsburgh; National Gallery of Art, Washington, D.C.

MASOLINO DA PANICALE   *The Annunciation,* c. 1423–26, on wood, 58¼ × 45¼″
Provenance: Earls of Wemyss, Gosford House, Lothian, Scotland; Robert Langton Doug-
las, London; Henry Goldman, New York; Duveen, 1937; Andrew W. Mellon, Pittsburgh;
National Gallery of Art, Washington, D.C.

MASOLINO DA PANICALE   *The Archangel Gabriel,* c. 1432, on wood, 30 × 22½″
Provenance: Graf von Ingenheim, Munich; Duveen, 1935; Samuel H. Kress, New York;
National Gallery of Art, Washington, D.C.

MASOLINO DA PANICALE   *The Virgin Annunciate,* c. 1432, on wood, 30 × 22½″
Provenance: Graf von Ingenheim, Munich; Duveen, 1935; Samuel H. Kress, New York;
National Gallery of Art, Washington, D.C.
Note: Companion piece to *The Archangel Gabriel.* Thought to be from a polyptych, or pos-
sibly cut down from a single panel. The pair sold for $70,000 in 1936.

QUENTIN MASSYS   *The Adoration of the Magi,* 1526, oil on wood, 40½ × 31½″
Provenance: Hugh Robert Hughes, Kimmel, Abergele, North Wales; Rodolphe Kann,
Paris; Duveen; Metropolitan Museum of Art, New York.

MASTER OF THE BARBERINI PANELS   *The Annunciation,* c. 1450, on wood,
34½ × 24¾″
Provenance: Strozzi Collection, Florence; Louis Charles Timbal, Paris; Gustave Dreyfus,
Paris; Duveen, 1930; Samuel H. Kress, New York; National Gallery of Art, Washington, D.C.

MASTER OF THE CASTELLO NATIVITY   *Madonna Adoring the Child,* or *Madonna
and the Child with Saint John,* 43¾ × 30½″
Provenance: Ex Brownlow; Duveen; Arabella Huntington; The Huntington, San Marino,
CA.

MASTER OF THE SAINT GEORGE CODEX   *Crucifixion,* tempera on wood panel,
18⅞ × 10″
Provenance: Capparoni Collection, Rome; R. Langton Douglas, London; Duveen, 1936;
Detroit Institute of Arts.
Note: Now attributed to the "Master of the Capella Medici Polyptych."

MATTEO CIVITALE   *Saint Sebastian,* c. 1475, polychrome terra-cotta statuette, 25½ × 7″
Provenance: Eugène Piot, Paris; Louis Charles Timbal, Paris; Gustave Dreyfus, Paris; Duveen, 1930; Samuel H. Kress, New York; National Gallery of Art, Washington, D.C.

MATTEO CIVITALE   *The Madonna Adoring the Child,* c. 1490, terra-cotta statue group, 47½ × 42¼″
Provenance: Commendatore Elia Volpi, Palazzo Davanzati, Florence; Duveen; Samuel H. Kress, New York; National Gallery of Art, Washington, D.C.

MATTEO DI GIOVANNI DI BARTOLO   *The Adoration of the Magi,* c. 1470, tempera and possibly oil on panel, 71¾ × 54⅛″
Provenance: Duveen; Andrew Mellon, New York; National Gallery of Art, Washington, D.C.
Note: Another of the paintings Carl Hamilton undertook to buy, for $90,000, and which was returned. Duveen sold to Mellon in 1936 for $100,000. Now attributed to Benvenuto di Giovanni.

MATTEO DI GIOVANNI DI BARTOLO   *Madonna and Child with Angels and Cherubim,* c. 1470, tempera (?) on panel, 27⁷⁄₁₆ × 19½″
Provenance: Earls of Ashburnham, Ashburnham Place, Battle, Sussex; Robert Langton Douglas, London, by 1919; Duveen, c. 1932; Andrew W. Mellon, Pittsburgh; National Gallery of Art, Washington, D.C.

MATTEO DI GIOVANNI DI BARTOLO   *Madonna and Child with Saints and Angels,* c. 1470, tempera (?) on panel, 26 × 17⁵⁄₁₆″
Provenance: Earls of Ashburnham, Ashburnham Place, Battle, Sussex; Robert Langton Douglas, London, by 1919; Duveen; Clarence H. Mackay, Roslyn, NY, by 1924; returned to Duveen, 1930; Samuel H. Kress, New York; National Gallery of Art, Washington, D.C.

MATTEO DI GIOVANNI DI BARTOLO   *Madonna and Child with Angels,* tempera on canvas, 27½ × 19¾″
Provenance: Charles Fairfax Murray, London; Chester Ralph Brocklebank, Haughton Hall, Tarporley, England; Duveen; Mr. and Mrs. James S. Holden, Detroit, by 1924; Detroit Institute of Arts.

MATTEO DI GIOVANNI DI BARTOLO   *Madonna and Child with Saint Catherine and Saint Anthony of Padua, and Angels,* c. 1480, tempera on wood panel, 25⅞ × 18½″
Provenance: Sir Philip Burne-Jones, London; Duveen, 1925; Mrs. Horace E. Dodge, Detroit; Detroit Institute of Arts.

MEDICI PORCELAIN FACTORY   Flask, c. 1575/1587, imitation porcelain (a version of soft-paste porcelain)
Provenance: Duveen; National Gallery of Art, Washington, D.C.

MEISTER WILHELM   *Adoration of the Magi, St. Severus and St. Walburga, St. James & St. Philip,* c. 1410, oil and gilding on oak panel, 31¾ × 38″

Provenance: Not established; bought at auction in Amsterdam by Duveen in 1925; sold to Detroit Institute of Arts in 1926.
Note: Present attribution: "Anonymous."

HANS MEMLING   *The Annunciation,* c. 1480–89, oil on canvas, transferred from wood, 30⅛ × 21½"
Provenance: Prince Michael Radziwill; Prince Anton Radziwill, Berlin; Prince Wilhelm Radziwill, Berlin; Prince George Radziwill, Berlin; Marie Branicka, Princess Radziwill, Berlin; Duveen, 1920; Philip Lehman, New York; Metropolitan Museum of Art, New York.

HANS MEMLING   *The Madonna and Child,* on panel, 9½ × 7"
Provenance: Dr. Carvalho, Paris; René della Faille de Waerloos, Antwerp; Caspar Bourgeois, Cologne; Richard von Kaufmann, Berlin; Duveen; Jules S. Bache, New York; Metropolitan Museum of Art, New York.
Note: The attribution to Memling has been questioned for decades and is now considered "workshop of," painted by a second-rate follower.

HANS MEMLING   *Madonna and Child with Angels,* c. 1480, on wood, 23⅛ × 18⅞"
Provenance: Fritz Mannheimer, Amsterdam; Duveen, 1927; Andrew W. Mellon, Pittsburgh; National Gallery of Art, Washington, D.C.

HANS MEMLING   *The Blessed Christ,* 1478, oil on panel
Provenance: Manoel II, King of Portugal; Duveen, 1910; Dr. and Mrs. A. Hamilton Rice, New York; Norton Simon, Los Angeles; Norton Simon Museum, Pasadena, CA.

LIPPO MEMMI   *Madonna and Child*
Provenance: Identified from a letter by Carl Hamilton to Duveen, November 1919, in which he is promising to buy the painting for $20,000; he returned it in the spring of 1924. Duveen subsequently sold it to M. Griggs for $8,000.

LIPPO MEMMI   *The Madonna and Child with Saints and Angels,* tempera on wood, 26¼ × 13"
Provenance: Capt. Francis Nicholas Smith, Wingfield Park, Ambergate, Derby; Richard Norton, Boston; Duveen, 1919; Carl W. Hamilton, New York; Duveen, 1924; Maitland Fuller Griggs, New York; Metropolitan Museum of Art, New York.

IVAN MEŠTROVIČ *Girl with a Guitar*
Provenance: Duveen; gift to the Tate Gallery, London.

GABRIEL METSU   *Visit to the Nursery,* or *The Visit to the Lying-in Chamber,* 1661, oil on canvas, 30½ × 32"
Provenance: John Jacobsz Hinloopen; Jan de Wolf, The Hague; David Ietswaart, Amsterdam; Gerret Braamcamp, Amsterdam; Duc de Morny, Paris; C. Sedelmeyer, Paris; Rodolphe Kann, Paris; J. Pierpont Morgan, New York; Metropolitan Museum of Art, New York.

GABRIEL METSU   *The Intruder,* c. 1660, 26¼ × 23½"
Provenance: Sir Gregory Holman B. Way, Denham Place, Buckinghamshire; John Smith, London; 5th Lord Vernon, Sudbury Hall, Derby; Sir Charles Bagot, London; Baron Ver-

stolk van Soelen, The Hague; Sir Thomas Baring; Sir Francis Baring, Baron Northbrook; Earl of Northbrook, Stratton, Micheldever, Hampshire; Duveen; Andrew W. Mellon, Pittsburgh; National Gallery of Art, Washington, D.C.

MICHELANGELO BUONARROTI (AFTER)   *Pieta,* c. 1500, bronze group, h. 14½″
Provenance: J. Pierpont Morgan, New York; Duveen; Henry Clay Frick, New York; Frick Collection, New York.

MINO DA FIESOLE   *Astorgio Manfredi II of Faenza,* 1455, white marble bust, 19½ × 14″
Provenance: Louis Charles Timbal, Paris; Baron Arthur de Schickler, Martinvast, Normandy; Comtesse Hubert de Pourtalès, Paris; Duveen; P. A. B. Widener and Joseph E. Widener, Elkins Park, PA; National Gallery of Art, Washington, D.C.

MINO DA FIESOLE   *The Youthful St. John,* c. 1455, white marble bust, h. 14½″
Provenance: Conte Rasponi Spinelli, Florence; Raoul Heilbronner, Paris; Duveen; Benjamin Altman, New York; Metropolitan Museum of Art, New York.

MINO DA FIESOLE   *Cardinal Guillaume d'Estouteville,* c. 1463–64, white marble bust, 14⅛ × 13″
Provenance: Oscar Hainauer, Berlin; Duveen; Benjamin Altman, New York; Metropolitan Museum of Art, New York.

MINO DA FIESOLE   *The Madonna and Child,* c. 1470–80, white marble low-relief, 16¼ × 11¾″
Provenance: Louis Charles Timbal, Paris; Gustave Dreyfus, Paris; Duveen; Andrew W. Mellon, Pittsburgh; National Gallery of Art, Washington, D.C.

MINO DA FIESOLE   *Charity,* c. 1460–80, white marble high-relief, 49¾ × 17″
Provenance: Louis Charles Timbal, Paris; Gustave Dreyfus, Paris; Duveen; Clarence Mackay, Roslyn, NY; Duveen; Andrew W. Mellon, Pittsburgh; National Gallery of Art, Washington, D.C.

MINO DA FIESOLE   *Faith,* c. 1460–80, white marble high-relief, 49¾ × 17″
Provenance: Louis Charles Timbal, Paris; Gustave Dreyfus, Paris; Duveen; Clarence Mackay, Roslyn, NY; Duveen; Andrew W. Mellon, Pittsburgh; National Gallery of Art, Washington, D.C.

MINO DA FIESOLE   *The Virgin Annunciate,* c. 1480, white marble bust, 20 × 14½″
Provenance: Conte Antonio Palmierinuti, Siena; Duveen; Clarence Mackay, Roslyn, NY; Duveen; Samuel H. Kress, New York; National Gallery of Art, Washington, D.C.

MINO DA FIESOLE   *Conte Rinaldo della Luna,* c. 1461, stucco bust, 18¼ × 18¼″
Provenance: Ugo Jandolo, Rome; Duveen; Samuel H. Kress, New York; National Gallery of Art, Washington, D.C.
Notes: Now considered a late-nineteenth-century forgery and made of cement.

MINO DA FIESOLE   *Large White Marble Bust of a Lady*
Provenance: As described among a group of sculpture, furniture, paintings, and objets
bought from Brauer in 1924; present whereabouts unknown.

MINO DA FIESOLE   *Bust of St. Catherine*
Provenance: Duveen; bought by Clarence Mackay, Roslyn, NY; and then Samuel H. Kress,
New York; present whereabouts unknown.

CLAUDE MONET   *La Japonaise* (*Camille Monet in Japanese Costume*), on canvas
Provenance: Philip Lehman, New York, by 1921; Duveen; Museum of Fine Arts, Boston,
1956.

BARTOLOMMEO MONTAGNA   *Saint Justina of Padua,* tempera on wood, 19½ × 15⅛″
Provenance: Robert Graham, London; William Graham, London; Charles Fairfax Murray,
London; Oscar Hainauer, Berlin; Duveen, 1906; Benjamin Altman, 1907; Metropolitan
Museum of Art, New York.

FRA ANTONIO DA MONZA   *The Flagellation of Christ,* tempera on vellum, miniature
painting from an antiphonary, 17½ × 13½″
Provenance: Duveen; Norton Simon Museum, Pasadena, CA.

ANTHONIS MOR   *Portrait of a Gentleman,* c. 1517–77, signed and dated 1569, trans-
ferred from wood to canvas, 47⅛ × 34¾″
Provenance: The Earls of Spencer, Althorp House, Northamptonshire; Duveen, 1930;
Andrew W. Mellon, Pittsburgh; National Gallery of Art, Washington, D.C.

GIOVANNI BATTISTA MORONI   *Titian's Schoolmaster,* c. 1575, on canvas, 38⅛ × 29¼″
Provenance: Dukes of Sutherland, Dunrobin Castle, Highland, Scotland; Duveen, c. 1908;
P. A. B. Widener, Elkins Park, PA; National Gallery of Art, Washington, D.C.

BARTOLOMÉ MURILLO   *The Holy Family with St. John,* c. 1668–75, 46½ × 43½″
Provenance: Admiral Sir Eliab Harvey, Rolls Park, Chigwell, Essex; Lady Louisa Nugent;
Sir William Eustace; Richard Foster, Clewer Manor, Berkshire; Alfred Beit, London; Mau-
rice Kann, Paris; Sir Ernest Kassel, London; Mrs. Herbert Asquith, Countess of Oxford
and Asquith, London; Duveen; Aaron and Nettie G. Naumburg, New York; Fogg Art
Museum, Harvard University, Cambridge, MA.

DANIEL MYTENS THE ELDER   *Portrait of a Young Nobleman*
Provenance: Duveen; Norton Simon Museum, Pasadena, CA.

NARDO DI CIONE   *Madonna and Child with St. Peter and St. John the Evangelist,*
triptych, with gabled center panel, on wood
Provenance: Count Gustav Adolf Wilhelm von Ingenheim, Schloss Reisewitz, Silesia;
Henry Goldman, New York; Duveen, 1937; Samuel H. Kress, New York; National Gallery
of Art, Washington, D.C.

JEAN-MARC NATTIER   *Madame Bonier de la Mosson as Diana,* on canvas
Provenance: Henry Edwards Huntington, New York, 1911; Duveen; Edward Julius
Berwind, New York; Mrs. Sosthenes Behn, New York; J. Paul Getty Museum, Los Angeles.

JEAN-MARC NATTIER   *Portrait of Mme. la Comtesse de Brac as Aurora,* on canvas
Provenance: L. Goldschmidt, Paris; Comtesse André de Pastre, Paris; Duveen; Norton
Simon Museum, Pasadena, CA.

JEAN-MARC NATTIER   *Portrait of the Duc de Penthièvre,* on canvas
Provenance: Ex Bischoffsheim; bought at Christie's by Duveen in May 1926 for Gulbenkian
for £13,000.

JEAN-MARC NATTIER   *Portrait of the Comtesse de Clermont,* on canvas
Provenance: Ex the Comte de Marvis; Duveen; sold to Eugène Fischoff in May, 1908 for
60,000 francs; present whereabouts unknown.

JEAN-MARC NATTIER   *Portrait of a Lady,* oil on canvas, 46½ × 35½"
Provenance: Bought by Duveen from Christie's, July 1901; Morris K. Jesup, New York;
Metropolitan Museum of Art, New York.
Note: Now "Follower of Nattier."

JEAN-MARC NATTIER   *Madame de la Porte,* oil on canvas
Provenance: According to Edward Fowles in *Memories of Duveen Brothers,* this painting was
bought at auction in the nineteen thirties for Calouste Gulbenkian [180].

NEROCCIO DI LANDI   *Claudia Quinta, Roman Heroine,* or *Claudia Quinta,* c. 1494,
tempera on panel, 41⁵⁄₁₆ × 18⅛"
Provenance: Louis Charles Timbal, Florence; Gustave Dreyfus, Paris; Duveen, 1930;
Andrew W. Mellon, Pittsburgh; National Gallery of Art, Washington, D.C.
Note: Credit for the authorship of the painting is now divided between Neroccio and the
"Master of the Griselda Legend."

NEROCCIO DI LANDI   *The Madonna and Child with Saints,* or *The Madonna and
Child with St. Jerome and St. Mary Magdalen,* c. 1490, tempera on wood, 24⅜ × 17¾"
Provenance: Dukes of Saxe-Meiningen, Castle of Meiningen, Thuringia; R. Langton Doug-
las, Dublin; Duveen; Samuel H. Kress, New York; National Gallery of Art, Washington,
D.C.; Kress Foundation, New York; to the Metropolitan Museum of Art, 1961, by
exchange.
Note: Duveen stockbook records note that the painting was bought from Langton Douglas
in February 1929 and sold to Kress in June 1934, for $117,400.

NEROCCIO DI LANDI   *Madonna and Child,* on wood, 35¾ × 24¾"
Provenance: Bought from Prince Ouroussoff in 1918 and sold to Philip Lehman, along with
a Sassetta, for $11,000; present whereabouts unknown.

NEROCCIO DI LANDI   *Madonna and Child,* tempera and gold leaf on panel, 18⅛ × 12"
Provenance: Duveen; Norton Simon Museum, Pasadena, CA.

NEROCCIO DI LANDI   *Madonna and Child with Sts. John the Baptist and Catherine of Alexandria,* tempera and gold leaf on panel, 29½ × 24⅜"
Provenance: Duveen; Norton Simon Museum, Pasadena, CA.

NEROCCIO DI LANDI   *Madonna and Child with Sts. Mary Magdalen and Sebastian,* tempera and gold leaf on wood, with arched top, 39⅛ × 24½"
Provenance: Carlo Angeli, Florence, 1914; Duveen; Philip Lehman, 1915; Metropolitan Museum of Art, New York.
Note: The Museum has documented that the painting was forged by I. F. Ioni in 1913.

CHRISTOPHER R. W. NEVINSON   *Asters,* oil on canvas
Provenance: Duveen Paintings Fund, c. 1928; presented to the Ferens by the executors of Lord Duveen in 1949.

NICOLA DA URBINO   *Panel with Adoration of the Magi,* c. 1525, tin-glazed earthenware, 8¾ × 6⅝"
Provenance: Maurice Kann, Paris; Duveen; P. A. B. Widener, Elkins Park, PA, 1910; National Gallery of Art, Washington, D.C.

NORTH ITALIAN, SIXTEENTH CENTURY   *Figure of a Gazelle,* bronze statuette, h. 11¼"
Provenance: Rodolphe Kann, Paris; Duveen; J. Pierpont Morgan, New York; Henry Clay Frick, New York; Frick Collection, New York.
Note: Now "Unidentified, nineteenth century," i.e., a fake.

ALLEGRETTO NUZI   Triptych
Provenance: Duveen; Carl Hamilton, 1919, for $40,000, on credit; Duveen; Andrew Mellon, New York, 1936, for $150,000.

ORCAGNA OR NARDO DI CIONE   *Madonna and Child with Two Saints,* triptych
Provenance: Henry Goldman, New York; Duveen, 1937; present whereabouts unknown.

JEAN-BAPTISTE OUDRY   *The Duchesse de Choiseul as Diana,* c. 1704, oil on canvas, 54½ × 42¼"
Provenance: Duveen; Norton Simon Museum, Pasadena, CA.

PADUAN SCHOOL   *Equestrian Figure,* or *Warrior on Horseback,* c. 1505–20, bronze group, 14¼ × 9⁹⁄₁₆"
Provenance: Émile Gavet, Paris; Martin Heckscher, Vienna; Caspar Jongens, Cologne; Charles Stein, Paris; J. Pierpont Morgan, New York; Duveen; Henry Clay Frick, New York; Frick Collection, New York.
Note: Now "Workshop of Riccio."

PADUAN SCHOOL   *Infant Satyr,* or *An Infant Faun,* c. 1505/1520, bronze statuette, h. 17"
Provenance: Sir Henry Hope Edwardes, Wooton Hall, Ashbourne, Derbyshire; J. Pierpont Morgan, New York; Duveen; Henry Clay Frick, New York; Frick Collection, New York.
Note: Now Caspar Gras.

PADUAN SCHOOL, EARLY SIXTEENTH CENTURY   *Figure of a Horse,* or *Cantering Horse,* c. 1505/1520, bronze statuette, h. 9¼"
Provenance: Baron C. A. de Cosson, Chertsey, Surrey; J. Pierpont Morgan, New York; Duveen; Henry Clay Frick, New York; Frick Collection, New York.
Note: Now "Paduan School."

PALMA VECCHIO   *Annunciation,* 60½ × 32"
Provenance: Duveen; William Salomon, 1913; Duveen, 1922; Mrs. Duke, Newport.
Note: Duveen offered the painting to Arabella Huntington in January 1923, telling her it "would look marvellously well in the passage opposite the staircase," but she was not enthusiastic.

PALMA VECCHIO   *Madonna and Saints,* 45¼ × 39¼"
Provenance: Duveen; Kleinberger; James F. Bell, Minneapolis, MN; Minneapolis Museum of Art.

JUAN PANTOJA DE LA CRUZ   *Portrait of Don Diego Gómez de Sandoval y Rojas, Count of Saldana,* oil on canvas, 73 × 41⅛"
Provenance: Duveen; Norton Simon Museum, Pasadena, CA.

PAOLO DI GIOVANNI FEI   *The Assumption of the Virgin*
Provenance: Luigi Grassi, Florence; Duveen, 1929; Samuel H. Kress, New York; Kress Collection, New York.

PAOLO DI GIOVANNI FEI   *Madonna and Child Enthroned with Saints,* tempera on panel, 27⅞ × 17¼"
Provenance: Chigi-Saracini Collection, Siena; Luigi Grassi, Florence; Duveen; Mr. and Mrs. A. E. Goodheart, New York, by 1924; Robert Lehman, 1952; Metropolitan Museum of Art, New York.

PAOLO VENEZIANO   *The Madonna and Child Enthroned,* on wood, central panel of polyptych
Provenance: Carl Anton Reichel, Grossgmain, Austria; Giuseppe Grassi, Rome; Duveen; Edward Fowles, New York; Metropolitan Museum of Art, New York, Fowles Bequest.

JEAN-BAPTISTE PATER   *The Fair at Bezons,* c. 1733, oil on canvas, 42 × 56"
Provenance: Alfred Charles de Rothschild; Almina, Lady Carnarvon; Duveen; Jules Bache, New York; Metropolitan Museum of Art, New York.

JEAN-BAPTISTE PATER   *Procession of Italian Comedians,* on canvas
Provenance: Sidney Herbert, 14th Earl of Pembroke, Wilton House, Wiltshire; Duveen; Henry Clay Frick, New York; Frick Collection, New York.

JEAN-BAPTISTE PATER   *The Village Orchestra,* on canvas
Provenance: Companion piece to *Italian Comedians,* with same provenance.

JEAN-BAPTISTE PATER OR WATTEAU   *Fête Champêtre,* on canvas
Provenance: Kaiser Friedrich Museum, Berlin; bought by Duveen as a Pater in 1927 but referred to interchangeably as "the small Watteau"; present whereabouts unknown.

JOACHIM PATINIR   *St. Jerome in a Rocky Landscape,* on wood
Provenance: Rodolphe Kann, Paris; Duveen, 1907; Mrs. Henry Oppenheimer, London; National Gallery of Art, London.
Note: Now "Attributed to."

PIETRO PERUGINO   *Madonna and Child,* c. 1500, tempera on panel, 31¾ × 25½"
Provenance: King Ludwig I of Bavaria; Alte Pinakothek, Munich; Duveen, 1925; John D. Rockefeller Jr.; Duveen, 1930; Mr. and Mrs. Edsel B. Ford; Detroit Institute of Arts.

PIETRO PERUGINO   *Madonna and Child,* on wood, 27¾ × 19½"
Provenance: Marquès de la Romana, Madrid; Marquès de Villamayor, Madrid; Duveen; Clarence Mackay, New York; Samuel H. Kress, New York; National Gallery of Art, Washington, D.C.

PIETRO PERUGINO   *The Annunciation,* on wood, 15⅞ × 14⅛"
Provenance: Duveen; Samuel H. Kress, New York; National Gallery of Art, Washington, D.C.
Note: Now "Giannicolo di Paolo."

PIETRO PERUGINO   *Virgin and Child with Saint John*
Provenance: Duveen; William Salomon, New York; Duveen; J. R. Thompson, Chicago; present whereabouts unknown.

FRANCESCO PESELLINO   *Madonna and Child with Angels,* on wood
Provenance: Gustave Dreyfus, Paris; Duveen; Godfrey Locker-Lampson, London; Count Alessandro Contini-Bonacossi, Florence; Samuel H. Kress, New York; National Gallery of Art, Washington, D.C.; Samuel H. Kress, New York; Berea College Museums, Art Department Galleries, Berea, KY.
Note: Now "follower of" and also "Virgil Master."

FRANCESCO PESELLINO   *Fragment of an Altarpiece*
Provenance: Duveen; gift to the National Gallery, London.

FRANCESCO PESELLINO   *Madonna and Child with a Goldfinch*
Provenance: Oscar Hainauer Collection; Duveen; Edward Drummond Libbey, Toledo, OH; Museum of Art, Toledo, OH.

PIER FRANCESCO FIORENTINO   *The Madonna and Child with the Infant Saint John the Baptist and Angels,* tempera and gold on wood, 33⅜ × 23¾"
Provenance: Sir George Donaldson, London; Duveen; Michael Friedsam, New York; Metropolitan Museum of Art, New York.

Note: The attribution to Pier Francesco, a modest fifteenth-century Florentine artist, was given by Berenson to a group of works that seemed to have borrowed heavily from Filippo Lippi and Francesco Pesellino. Recent scholarship has demonstrated that this and a group of other works was, in fact, concocted by a group of craftsmen in a Florentine workshop that produced the pastiches by the dozen. This one is now termed "Pseudo Pier Francesco Fiorentino"; in other words, a fake.

PIER FRANCESCO FIORENTINO   *Madonna and Child,* wood, transferred to canvas
Provenance: Arnaldo Corsi, Florence; Duveen, by 1919; William Salomon, New York; Duveen, 1923; Clarence H. Mackay, New York, by 1925; Duveen, by 1936; Samuel H. Kress, New York; National Gallery of Art, Washington, D.C.

PIERINO DA VINCI   *Samson Slaying the Philistines,* or *Samson and Two Philistines,* c. 1552, bronze statuette group, h. 14⅜"
Provenance: Stefano Bardini, Florence; J. Pierpont Morgan, New York; Duveen; Henry Clay Frick, New York; Frick Collection, New York.
Note: Now "After Michelangelo Buonarotti."

PIERO DELLA FRANCESCA   *Crucifixion,* 16 × 14¾"
Provenance: The painting supposedly came from the collection of Marco Antonio Colonna and was, according to Edward Fowles, smuggled out of Italy in 1915 and one of the few paintings Carl Hamilton actually paid for, for $65,000. In 1924, Hamilton was trying to sell the painting for $200,000. It was bought back by Duveen in 1929 for $375,000 and sold to J. D. Rockefeller for the same price. It is now at the Fogg Museum, Harvard University, on loan from the Frick Collection.
Note: Now "Piero della Francesca or Workshop."

PIERO DI COSIMO   *The Visitation with Saint Nicholas and Saint Anthony Abbot,* c. 1490, oil on panel, 72½ × 74¼"
Provenance: Cappella di Gino Capponi, San Spirito, Florence; Marchese Capponi, Legnaja, Florence; Hon. Mrs. Frederick West, Chirk Castle, Denbigh; Frederick Richard West, Ruthin Castle, Denbigh; Colonel W. Cornwallis West, Newlands Manor, Hampshire; Duveen; Samuel H. Kress, New York; National Gallery of Art, Washington, D.C.

PIERO DI COSIMO   *The Madonna Adoring the Child,* c. 1490, tondo, diameter 63"
Provenance: Metzger Collection, Florence; Alexander Barker, London; Duveen; Edward Drummond Libbey, Toledo, OH; Museum of Art, Toledo, OH.

PIERO DI COSIMO   *The Finding of Vulcan,* or *Hylas and the Nymphs,* c. 1485–90, 61 × 58⅝"
Provenance: William Graham, London; Robert and Evelyn Benson, London; Duveen, 1927; Wadsworth Atheneum, Hartford, CT.

PIETRO LOMBARDO DA CARONA   *A Singing Angel,* white marble statue, 34 × 11"
Provenance: Collections of Max Chabrière-Arlès, Lyon; Duveen; Clarence Mackay, New York; Samuel H. Kress, New York; National Gallery of Art, Washington, D.C.

ROBERT EDGE PINE   *David Garrick,* c. 1775, on canvas, 27 × 22⅛"
Provenance: Elias Dexter, London; Thomas B. Clarke; Duveen, 1919; Henry E. Huntington, 1919; The Huntington, San Marino, CA.
Note: Now catalogued as by an unknown artist.

BERNARDINO PINTURICCHIO   *Portrait of a Youth,* c. 1505, oil on panel transferred to canvas, 20¼ × 13⅜"
Provenance: Onnes van Nijenrode, Château de Nijenrode, the Netherlands; Duveen; Ernst Rosenfield, New York; Duveen, 1933; Samuel H. Kress, New York; National Gallery of Art, Washington, D.C.
Note: Now "Master of Santo Spirito."

BERNARDINO PINTURICCHIO   *Virgin and Child,* 19½ × 15"
Provenance: Duveen; William Salomon, New York; Duveen; J. R. Thompson, Chicago; present whereabouts unknown.

BERNARDINO PINTURICCHIO   *Virgin and Child,* 10¾ × 14¾"
Provenance: Ex Baron Lazzaroni; Duveen; Arabella Huntington; The Huntington, San Marino, CA.

ANTONIO PISANO PISANELLO   *Profile Portrait of a Lady,* c. 1410–20, on wood, 20½ × 14¾"
Provenance: Henry Valentine Stafford-Jerningham, 9th Baron Stafford, Costessy Hall, Norfolk; James Gurney; M. de Villeroy, Paris; Paul Jonas; Duveen, 1922; Clarence Mackay, New York; Duveen; Andrew W. Mellon, Pittsburgh; National Gallery of Art, Washington, D.C.
Note: This painting is a famous example of an attribution that baffled experts for decades. At one time it was considered "School of Verona," and the attribution to Pisanello was made by Berenson. In 1965 Perry B. Cott, chief curator at the National Gallery of Art, rebaptized the painting under its new attribution, one that has remained in place. It is now called "Franco-Flemish, Fifteenth Century."

OROVIDA PISSARRO   *The Hunter Prince,* or *The Huntsman,* watercolor, bodycolor, and gold paint on silk
Provenance: Duveen Paintings Fund, 1927; presented to the Ferens by the executors of Lord Duveen in 1949.

DOMENICO POGGINI (?)   *A Warrior,* bronze statuette, h. 20¾"
Provenance: Henry J. Pfungst, London; J. Pierpont Morgan, New York; Duveen; Henry E. Huntington; San Marino, CA.; The Huntington, San Marino, CA.

DOMENICO POGGINI (?)   *A Man Carrying a Child,* bronze group, h. 9½"
Provenance: J. Pierpont Morgan, New York; Duveen; Henry E. Huntington, San Marino; The Huntington, San Marino, CA.

DOMENICO POGGINI (?)   *A Gladiator,* bronze statuette, h. 8¼"
Provenance: King Charles I of England; Henry J. Pfungst, London; J. Pierpont Morgan,

New York; Duveen; Henry E. Huntington, San Marino, CA; The Huntington, San Marino, CA.

POLIDORO LANZANI   *Madonna and Child and the Infant Saint John in a Landscape,* 1540–50, oil on canvas
Provenance: Duveen; National Gallery of Art, Washington, D.C.

ANTONIO POLLAIUOLO   *Virginio Orsini, Lord of Monterotondo,* or *Bust of a Warrior,* c. 1495, terra-cotta bust, 22½ × 20½″
Provenance: Louis Charles Timbal, Paris; Count Edmond de Pourtalès; Baron Arthur de Schickler, Martinvast, Normandy; Duveen; Clarence H. Mackay, New York; Duveen; Samuel H. Kress, New York; National Gallery of Art, Washington, D.C.
Note: Now considered an "imitator" of Antonio Pollaiuolo, i.e. a fake.

ANTONIO POLLAIUOLO   *Hercules, Captor of the Cretan Bull,* or *Hercules,* c. 1485–90, bronze statuette, h. 17½″
Provenance: Marchese Niccolini, Florence; Stefano Bardini, Florence; J. Pierpont Morgan, New York; Duveen; Henry Clay Frick, New York; Frick Collection, New York.

ANTONIO POLLAIUOLO   *Marsyas Astonished by Athena,* or *Naked Youth with Raised Left Arm,* c. 1485–90, bronze statuette, h. 21″
Provenance: J. Pierpont Morgan, New York; Duveen; Henry Clay Frick, New York; Frick Collection, New York.
Note: Now "Riccio," with a question mark.

ANTONIO POLLAIUOLO   *Paris with the Apple of Eris,* or *Paris,* c. 1485–90, bronze statuette, h. 10⅞″
Provenance: Charles Mannheim, Paris; J. Pierpont Morgan, New York; Duveen; Henry Clay Frick, New York; Frick Collection, New York.
Note: Now "Nuremberg, first half of sixteenth century."

ANTONIO POLLAIUOLO   *A Woman in Green and Crimson*
Provenance: Stefano Bardini, Florence; Ernest Odiot, Paris; Oscar Hainauer, Berlin; Duveen, 1907; Bernard Berenson, Florence; Isabella Stewart Gardner, Boston; Isabella Stewart Gardner Museum, Boston.
Note: Antonio Pollaiuolo, Piero's older brother, has always been considered the more accomplished artist, hence the original attribution to him. The painting is now considered to be by Piero.

SCHOOL OF ANTONIO POLLAIUOLO   *A Young Man in Armour,* c. 1480, polychrome terra-cotta, 24½ × 18″
Provenance: Oscar Hainauer, Berlin; Duveen; P. A. B. Widener, Elkins Park, PA; Joseph E. Widener; National Gallery of Art, Washington, D.C.

PIERO DEL POLLAIUOLO   *Portrait of a Man,* c. 1450, on wood, 21¼ × 15⅞″
Provenance: Duveen; Andrew W. Mellon, Pittsburgh; National Gallery of Art, Washington, D.C.

Note: The attribution was Berenson's; it was changed to that of Andrea del Castagno in 1960.

PIERO POLLAIUOLO *Portrait of a Lady,* 18 × 13″
Provenance: Duveen; William Salomon, New York; Duveen; Nils B. Hersloff, New York, 1922; present whereabouts unknown.

GIOVANNI AMBROGIO DA PREDIS *Profile of a Lady,* tempera on sheepskin on panel, 23³⁄₁₆ × 22½″
Provenance: Charles Timbal, Paris; Gustave Dreyfus, Paris; Duveen; Norton Simon Museum, Pasadena, CA.

PUCCIO DI SIMONE *Madonna and Child with Angels,* tempera on panel, 38 × 22½″
Provenance: Simon Thomas Scrope, Earl of Wiltes, Danby-on-Yore, Bedale, Yorkshire; Robert Langton Douglas, London; Duveen; Philip Lehman, New York; Norton Simon Museum, Pasadena, CA.

SIR HENRY RAEBURN *Mrs. Hay*
Provenance: According to Gerald Reitlinger in *The Economics of Taste,* [194], the painting was bought by Duveen in 1912 for £22,260, an inflated price, and the Raeburn market was at least partly supported by American sales from then on; it was sold to E. T. Stotesbury of Philadelphia; present whereabouts unknown.

SIR HENRY RAEBURN *William Scott-Elliot of Arkleton,* on canvas, 47 × 36″
Provenance: William Scott-Elliot; Duveen; Jules Bache, New York; Metropolitan Museum of Art, New York.

SIR HENRY RAEBURN *William Blair,* c. 1814, on canvas, 30 × 25″
Provenance: Col. David Milne Home, Wedderburn, 1901; Helen Milne Home, 1918; Duveen, 1922; Henry E. Huntington, 1922; The Huntington, San Marino, CA.
Note: The painting is believed to be Raeburn's own copy of a slightly earlier version of the same portrait.

SIR HENRY RAEBURN *Mrs. Irvine J. Boswell,* or *Mrs. James Irvine Boswell,* or *Margaret Christie,* c. 1820, oil on canvas, 30 × 25″
Provenance: J. Ervine Fortescue; Col. Walter Brown, Renfrew; Duveen; Mr. and Mrs. Edsel Ford, Grosse Pointe; Detroit Institute of Arts.

SIR HENRY RAEBURN *Captain Patrick Miller,* 1788–1789, oil on canvas
Provenance: Sir Edgar Vincent, 1st Viscount d'Abernon, London; Duveen, by 1917; Mr. and Mrs. Charles H. Sabin, Southampton, New York; National Gallery of Art, Washington, D.C.

RAPHAEL *Bindo Altoviti,* c. 1515, on wood, 23½ × 17¼″
Provenance: Palazzo Altoviti, Rome; Crown Prince Ludwig of Bavaria; Alte Pinakothek, Munich; Duveen, late 1930s; Samuel H. Kress, New York; National Gallery of Art, Washington, D.C.

Note: One of Duveen's final great triumphant sales, this one accomplished by an exchange with the Nazi régime. John Walker, former director, told the author, "The Führer's fanatical passion for Teutonic art led to an arrangement with Lord Duveen whereby 'Bindo Altoviti' came to America in exchange for several skillfully repainted German pictures from the unsold stock of Duveen Brothers."

RAPHAEL   *The Small Cowper Madonna,* c. 1505, on wood, 23⅜ × 17⅜"
Provenance: The Earls Cowper, Panshanger, Hertford, until 1913; Ethel Anne Priscilla Fane Grenfell, Lady Desborough, Panshanger; Duveen; P. A. B. Widener, Elkins Park, PA; National Gallery of Art, Washington, D.C.
Note: Berenson tried to buy this painting for Isabella Stewart Gardner in 1898 for $60,000. Duveen bought it in November 1913, for $700,000.

RAPHAEL   *The Niccolini-Cowper Madonna,* 1508, on wood, 31¾ × 22⅝"
Provenance: The Earls Cowper, Panshanger, Hertford, until 1913; Ethel Anne Priscilla Fane Grenfell, Lady Desborough, Panshanger; Duveen; Andrew W. Mellon, Pittsburgh; National Gallery of Art, Washington, D.C.

RAPHAEL   *St. George and the Dragon,* c. 1504–06, on wood, 11⅛ × 8⅜"
Provenance: Charles I of England; Charles d'Escoubleau, Marquis de Sourdis, Paris; Laurent de Tessier de Montarsy; Pierre Crozat; Louis-François Crozat, Marquis de Châtel; Louis-Antoine Crozat, Baron de Thiers; Empress Catherine II of Russia; Hermitage, Leningrad; Duveen; Andrew W. Mellon, Pittsburgh; National Gallery of Art, Washington, D.C.
Note: Duveen sold the painting to Mellon in 1929 for $747,500.

RAPHAEL   *The Agony in the Garden,* c. 1504–05, tempera and oil on wood, 9½ × 11⅜"
Provenance: Queen Christina of Sweden; Cardinal Azzolini, Rome; Prince Odescalchi, Rome; the Dukes of Orleans, Paris; Lord Eldin, Edinburgh; Samuel Rogers, London; Baroness Burdett-Coutts, London; Clarence H. Mackay, New York; Metropolitan Museum of Art, New York.

RAPHAEL   *Giuliano de' Medici, Duke of Nemours,* 1514–15, on canvas, 32¾ × 26"
Provenance: Ottaviano de' Medici; the Baldovinetti family; Professor Brini; Grand Duchess Marie of Russia; Prince Sciarra-Colonna; Oscar Huldschinsky, Berlin; Duveen; Jules S. Bache, New York; Metropolitan Museum of Art, New York.
Note: This spectacular work is now considered a sixteenth-century copy after Raphael.

REMBRANDT   *Hendrickje Stoffels, Rembrandt's wife,* oil on canvas, 33⅛ × 24½"
Provenance: "Bought through" Von Bode in 1910 and sold to Benjamin Altman in 1910 for £28,000 ($140,000); Metropolitan Museum of Art, New York.
Note: The painting is now attributed to Fabritius Barent.

REMBRANDT   *Portrait of Hendrickje Stoffels,* 1660, oil on canvas, 30⅞ × 27⅛"
Provenance: Marquesa de la Cenia, Madrid; Rodolphe Kann, Paris; Duveen; Arabella Huntington, New York; Archer M. Huntington, New York; Metropolitan Museum of Art, New York.

REMBRANDT   *Aristotle with a Bust of Homer,* or *Aristotle Contemplating the Bust of Homer,* 1653, oil on canvas, 56½ × 53¾"
Provenance: Sir A. Hume; Lord Brownlow; Rodolphe Kann, Paris; Duveen; Arabella Huntington, New York; Archer M. Huntington, New York; Duveen; Alfred W. Erickson, New York; Duveen; Alfred W. Erickson, New York; Metropolitan Museum of Art, New York.

REMBRANDT   *Old Woman in an Armchair,* 1634?, oil on canvas, 50⅛ × 39⅛"
Provenance: Comte de Morny, Paris; Arthur Sanderson, Edinburgh; Duveen; Benjamin Altman, New York; Metropolitan Museum of Art, New York.
Note: Present scholarship favors an attribution to Jacob Backer.

REMBRANDT   *Titus,* 1655, oil on canvas, 31⅛ × 23¼"
Provenance: Count Podstatzky, Bohemia; E. Secretan, Paris; Charles Sedelmeyer, Paris; Rodolphe Kann, Paris; Duveen, Benjamin Altman, New York; Metropolitan Museum of Art, New York.
Note: Present attribution is "Style of Rembrandt."

REMBRANDT   *Flora,* c. 1656–58, oil on canvas, 39⅜ × 36⅛"
Provenance: Earls Spencer, Althorp House, Northamptonshire; Duveen; Arabella Huntington, New York; Archer M. Huntington, New York; Metropolitan Museum of Art, New York.

REMBRANDT   *Old Woman Cutting Her Nails,* c. 1648, oil on canvas, 50 × 40"
Provenance: Ingham Foster, London; Serge Boboloff. St. Petersburg; Nikolaj Mossoloff, Moscow; Rodolphe Kann, Paris; Duveen; Benjamin Altman, New York; Metropolitan Museum of Art, New York.
Note: Now "Follower of Rembrandt."

REMBRANDT   *Pilate Washing His Hands,* oil on canvas, 51¼ × 65¾"
Provenance: Barnett Hollander in *The International Law of Art* writes [224] that Altman bought the painting from Duveen for £58,000 ($280,000); Altman deeded it to the Metropolitan Museum of Art, New York.
Note: Now "Rembrandt, Style of" and "Dutch, late seventeenth century."

REMBRANDT   *Portrait of a Young Man (The Auctioneer),* 1658, oil on canvas, 42¾ × 34"
Provenance: Barnett Hollander in *International Law of Art* [224] writes that Altman bought the painting from Duveen for $262,000; Altman deeded it to the Metropolitan Museum of Art, New York.
Note: Now "Follower of."

REMBRANDT   *Christ with a Pilgrim's Staff,* 1661, oil on canvas, 37½ × 32½"
Provenance: Sir C. Bethel Codrington; Charles J. Nieuwenhuys, Baron von Mecklenburg, Count Eduward Raczynski; Duveen; Jules Bache, New York; Metropolitan Museum of Art, New York.
Note: Now "Follower of."

REMBRANDT   *The Standard Bearer,* 1654, oil on canvas, 55 × 34½″
Provenance: Sir Joshua Reynolds; the Earl of Warwick; George J. Gould; Duveen; Jules
Bache, New York; Metropolitan Museum of Art, New York.

REMBRANDT   Pair of portraits: *Man with a Magnifying Glass* and *Lady with a Pink,*
c. 1662, oil on canvas, each 36 × 29″
Provenance: Comte Ferdinand d'Oultremont, Brussels; Charles Sedelmeyer, Paris; Maurice
Kann, Paris; Edouard Kann, Paris; Duveen; Benjamin Altman, New York; Metropolitan
Museum of Art, New York.
Note: According to Hollander, Duveen paid $625,000 for the pair in 1909.

REMBRANDT   *Portrait of a Young Man,* or *A Youth with a Black Cap,* 1666, oil on
canvas, 29 × 24″
Provenance: Lord Leconfield, Petworth House, Sussex; Duveen; Art Institute, Kansas
City, MO.
Note: Duveen hung the painting at Mellon's in 1927 but failed to persuade him to buy it.

REMBRANDT   *An Old Lady with a Bible,* or *An Old Lady with a Book,* the "Montger-
mont Rembrandt," $647, oil on canvas, 43 × 36″
Provenance: Johan van der Marck, Amsterdam; M. Thélusson, Paris; Julien Folliot, Paris;
Marquis de Montesquiou-Fezensac, Paris; Charles A. de Calonne, Paris; John Alnutt, Lon-
don; François Nieuwenhuys, Brussels; Louis Lebeuf de Montgermont, Paris; Prince Louis
de Broglie, Paris; Andrew W. Mellon, Pittsburgh; National Gallery of Art, Washington.
Note: Fowles bought the work in 1920 for 400,000 francs and the sale caused a sensation.
Matisse came to see it. It was one of the first paintings Mellon bought from Duveen.

REMBRANDT   *A Young Man Seated at a Table,* 1662–63, oil on canvas, 43¼ × 35¼″
Provenance: Count Gustave Sparre, Stockholm; Count de la Gardie, Helsingborg; Count
de Geer, Stockholm; Count Wachmeister; Duveen; Andrew W. Mellon, Pittsburgh;
National Gallery of Art, Washington, D.C.
Note: Bought in 1926 for $169,000.

REMBRANDT   *Head of an Aged Woman*
Provenance: Rodolphe Kann, Paris; Duveen; P. A. B. Widener, Elkins Park, PA; National
Gallery of Art, Washington, D.C.
Note: Now "Follower of."

REMBRANDT   *Head of St. Matthew*
Provenance: Rodolphe Kann, Paris; Duveen; Leo Nardus, New York; P. A. B. Widener,
Elkins Park, PA; National Gallery of Art, Washington, D.C.
Note: Now "Follower of."

REMBRANDT   *Titus, the Artist's Son*
Provenance: Duke of Rutland; James Stillman, New York; Dr. Henry B. Jacobs, Baltimore;
Museum of Art, Baltimore.

REMBRANDT   *The Toilet of Bathsheba,* 1643, oil on wood
Provenance: Baron Steengracht, The Hague; Duveen; Benjamin Altman, 1913; Metropolitan Museum of Art, New York.
Note: A new record was set when Duveen paid £40,000 for the painting at auction, June 9, 1913 (Haskell).

REMBRANDT   *Minerva,* 1635, oil on canvas
Provenance: The Lords Somerville; Duveen, 1924; Marczell von Nemes, Munich; Dr. Axel Wenner-Gren, Stockholm; Baron Bich, Paris; on loan to the Bridgestone Museum, Tokyo; Otto Naumann, Ltd., New York. In 2001 it was on sale for £28.5 million.

REMBRANDT   *Hendrickje Stoffels*
Provenance: Formerly in the Huldschensky Collection, Berlin, the painting was bought by Duveen in September 1928 and sold to Lord Melchett for $200,000. Three years later the picture was bought back by Duveens for $130,000 and still owned by the company in 1953 when the director general of the Rijksmuseum asked to see it but declined to buy on the grounds that it was probably not entirely by Rembrandt. The painting was sold to Norton Simon in 1956 for $200,000.

REMBRANDT   *Jewish Philosopher*
Provenance: Michel Van Loo, 1772; Kappel. Bought in 1925 amid doubts. W. R. Valentiner said he thought the painting was a copy; Von Bode was of the opposite opinion. It seems to have been bought for $60,000 plus 3 percent commission and was not sold until October 1956, to Norton Simon.

REMBRANDT   *Head of Christ,* c. 1660, oil on canvas, 24⅜ × 19¼″
Provenance: Ex Van Diemen. Bought by Armand Lowengard in 1925 for £7,350, described as a "bust portrait"; sold to Lord Melchett in 1929 for £19,000; present whereabouts unknown.

REMBRANDT   *Saskia,* 1633, oval, oil on canvas
Provenance: Ex Lord Elgin; Duveen paid £7,000 for it in 1926 and was not enchanted by it; sold to a Dutchman for $35,000 in 1932; subsequently bought back and sold again; present whereabouts unknown.

REMBRANDT   *Self Portrait*
Provenance: Anthony Reyre; Duveen thought the painting genuine and bought it for £5,000 ($20,000) in London in June 1925; present whereabouts unknown.

REMBRANDT   *Saint Bartholomew*
Provenance: Bought jointly by Duveen and Agnews in May 1916; present whereabouts unknown.

SIR JOSHUA REYNOLDS   *Mrs. Siddons as the Tragic Muse,* c. 1783–84, oil on canvas, 94¼ × 58⅛″
Provenance: The Dukes of Westminster; Duveen; Henry E. Huntington, 1921; The Huntington, San Marino, CA.

SIR JOSHUA REYNOLDS *The Hon. Theresa Parker, later the Hon. Theresa Villiers,* 1787, oil on canvas, 30 × 25"
Provenance: The Earls of Morley; Duveen, 1925; Henry E. Huntington, 1926; The Huntington, San Marino, CA.

SIR JOSHUA REYNOLDS *Anne (Barry) Irwin,* 1761, oil on canvas, 30⅝ × 25⅛"
Provenance: Sold to Henry E. Huntington, 1911, given to Arabella Huntington, whom he later married; exchanged with Duveen in partial payment for another painting, November 1926; sold to Mildred Browning Green and Honorable Lucius Peyton Green, Los Angeles, 1950; by bequest to The Huntington, San Marino, CA.

SIR JOSHUA REYNOLDS *Jane Fleming, later Countess of Harrington,* 1778–79, oil on canvas, 94¼ × 58⁵⁄₁₆"
Provenance: Charles, 8th Earl of Harrington, Elvaston Castle, Derbyshire; Duveen, 1912; Henry E. Huntington, 1913; The Huntington, San Marino, CA.

SIR JOSHUA REYNOLDS *Diana (Sackville), Viscountess Crosbie,* 1777, on canvas, 94¾ × 58"
Provenance: Sir Charles Tennant; Christopher Tennant, 2nd Baron Glenconner; Duveen; Henry E. Huntington, 1923; The Huntington, San Marino, CA.

SIR JOSHUA REYNOLDS *Lord Henry Spencer and Lady Charlotte Spencer, later Charlotte Nares: The Young Fortune Teller,* c. 1774–75, oil on canvas, 56¼ × 44¾"
Provenance: Dukes of Marlborough; Sir Charles Tennant; Christopher Tennant, 2nd Baron Glenconner; Duveen; Henry E. Huntington, 1923; The Huntington, San Marino, CA.

SIR JOSHUA REYNOLDS *Frances Molesworth, later Marchioness Camden,* 1777, oil on canvas, 55¾ × 45"
Provenance: Earls Spencer; Duveen, 1924; Henry E. Huntington, 1924; The Huntington, San Marino, CA.

SIR JOSHUA REYNOLDS *Georgiana (Spencer) Cavendish, Duchess of Devonshire,* 1775–76, oil on canvas, 94¼ × 58¹⁄₁₆"
Provenance: Charles Robert, 6th Earl Spencer; Duveen, 1924; Henry E. Huntington, 1925; The Huntington, San Marino, CA.

SIR JOSHUA REYNOLDS *Lavinia (Bingham), Countess Spencer, and John Charles Spencer, Viscount Althorp, later Earl Spencer,* 1783–84, oil on canvas, 58 × 43¼"
Provenance: The Earls Spencer; Duveen, 1924; Henry E. Huntington, 1924; The Huntington, San Marino, CA.

SIR JOSHUA REYNOLDS *Lavinia (Bingham), Countess Spencer,* c. 1787, oil on canvas, 30⅛ × 25⅛"
Provenance: By descent to Henrietta, Countess of Bessborough; Vere Brabazon, 9th Earl of Bessborough, Stanstead Park, Emsworth, Surrey; Duveen; Henry E. Huntington, 1926; The Huntington, San Marino, CA.
Note: Now "After Joshua Reynolds."

SIR JOSHUA REYNOLDS   *Lady Elizabeth Delmé and Her Children,* 1777–79, oil on canvas, 94⅛ × 58⅛″
Provenance: Delmé family, Cams Hall, Hampshire; Charles J. Wertheimer, London; J. Pierpont Morgan, London; Mrs. Herbert L. Satterlee; Duveen, c. 1930; Andrew W. Mellon, Pittsburgh; National Gallery of Art, Washington, D.C.

SIR JOSHUA REYNOLDS   *Lady Caroline Howard,* 1778, oil on canvas, 56¼ × 44½″
Provenance: Earls of Carlisle, Castle Howard, North Yorkshire; Duveen; Andrew W. Mellon, Pittsburgh; National Gallery of Art, Washington, D.C.

SIR JOSHUA REYNOLDS   *Lady Elizabeth Taylor,* c. 1780, oil on canvas, 50⅛ × 40¼″
Provenance: Charles J. Wertheimer, London; Charles Sedelmeyer, Paris; Maurice Kann, Paris; Duveen, c. 1908; Henry Clay Frick, New York; Frick Collection, New York.

SIR JOSHUA REYNOLDS   *Mrs. Richard Paul Jodrell,* 1774–75, oil on canvas, 30 × 25″
Provenance: Sir Edward Repps Jodrell, Holt, Norfolk; Duveen; Mr. and Mrs. Edsel Ford, Detroit, 1930; Detroit Institute of Arts.
Note: Edsell Ford paid $260,000 for the painting in January 1930.

SIR JOSHUA REYNOLDS   *Felina with a Kitten*
Provenance: Duveen; Anna Dodge Dilman, Grosse Pointe, MI; Detroit Institute of Arts.

SIR JOSHUA REYNOLDS   *The Strawberry Girl*
Provenance: Lady George Gordon; Colonel Copley Wray; George Jay Gould, Lakewood, NJ; Duveen, c. 1900; Elisabeth Severance Prentiss, Cleveland, OH; Allen Memorial Art Museum, Oberlin College, Oberlin, OH.

SIR JOSHUA REYNOLDS   *Mrs. Otway and Child*
Provenance: Henry Oppenheim, Clewer Mead, Windsor; Duveen, 1911; William Evarts Benjamin, a dealer, New York, 1915; present whereabouts unknown.
Note: The painting was slightly damaged in a fire on board the *Mississippi,* in 1914.

JUSEPE DE RIBERA (LO SPAGNOLETTO)   *Sense of Touch,* c. 1615–16, oil on canvas, 45⅝ × 34¾″
Provenance: Prince F. F. Youssoupov, Moscow; Duveen; Norton Simon Museum, Pasadena, CA.

JUSEPE DE RIBERA   *Portrait of a Franciscan Monk*
Provenance: Identified from a letter between Carl Hamilton of New York and Duveen dated June 7, 1924, when Hamilton was trying to sell the painting for $100,000; present whereabouts unknown.

ANDREA RICCIO (ANDREA BRIOSCO)   *Suzanna,* or *Naked Female Figure,* bronze statuette, h. 10¾″
Provenance: Comte Jacques de Bryas, Paris; J. Pierpont Morgan, New York; Henry Clay Frick, New York; Frick Collection, New York.
Note: Now "Attributed to Andrea Riccio."

ANDREA RICCIO *Seated Satyr,* or *Seated Satyr with Inkstand and Candlestick,* bronze lamp and inkwell, h. 11¾"
Provenance: J. Pierpont Morgan, New York; Henry Clay Frick, New York; Frick Collection, New York.
Note: Now "Attributed to Andrea Riccio."

ANDREA RICCIO *Seated Satyr,* or *Seated Satyr with Inkstand and Candlestick,* bronze lamp and inkstand, h. 8⅜"
Provenance: J. Pierpont Morgan, New York; Henry Clay Frick, New York; Frick Collection, New York.
Note: Now "Attributed to Andrea Riccio."

ANDREA RICCIO *Female Satyr and Young Faun,* or *Satyr Mother and a Child,* bronze lamp and inkstand, h. 10⅜"
Provenance: Henry J. Pfungst, London; J. Pierpont Morgan, New York; Henry Clay Frick, New York; Frick Collection, New York.
Note: Now "Nuremberg, last quarter of sixteenth century."

HYACINTHE RIGAUD *Portrait of Antoine Paris, Conseiller d'État,* 1724, oil on canvas, 58½ × 45"
Provenance: Duveen; Norton Simon Museum, Pasadena, CA.

ANDREA DELLA ROBBIA *The Adoration of the Child,* or *Madonna and Child with Cherubim,* c. 1480, glazed terra-cotta bas relief, 50⅜ × 30½"
Provenance: Duveen; Samuel H. Kress Collection, New York; National Gallery of Art, Washington, D.C.

GIOVANNI DELLA ROBBIA *The Young Christ,* c. 1500–10, unglazed terra-cotta, 14½ × 14½"
Provenance: Infanta Beatrice of Spain, Palacio Real, Madrid; Duveen; Samuel H. Kress, New York; National Gallery of Art, Washington, D.C.

LUCA DELLA ROBBIA *The Madonna and Child,* glazed terra-cotta high relief, 31½ × 22⅝"
Provenance: Marchese Viviani della Robbia, Piazza d'Azeglio, Florence; Conte Lionello di Nobili, Florence; Duveen; Benjamin Altman, New York; Metropolitan Museum of Art, New York.

LUCA DELLA ROBBIA *The Madonna and Child,* polychrome glazed terra-cotta high relief, 28¾ × 19"
Provenance: Marchese Viviani della Robbia, Piazza d'Azeglio, Florence; Anatoli, Prince Demidoff, Florence; Theodore Finet, Brussels; Duveen; Edward Drummond Libbey, Toledo, OH; Museum of Art, Toledo, OH.

LUCA DELLA ROBBIA *The Singing Boy,* c. 1431–38, white marble high relief, 9½ × 7¾"
Provenance: Eugène Piot, Paris; Louis Charles Timbal, Paris; Gustave Dreyfus, Paris; Duveen; Museum of Art, Cleveland, OH.

LUCA DELLA ROBBIA   *David, Conqueror of Goliath,* c. 1445, bronze statuette, h. 13″
Provenance: Saracini family, Siena; Chigi-Saracini family, Sienna; Count Piccolomini della Triana, Siena; Godefroi Brauer, Nice; Duveen; Jules S. Bache, New York; Metropolitan Museum of Art, New York.

LUCA DELLA ROBBIA   *Madonna and Child,* or *Madonna of the Lilies,* c. 1460–70, polychrome glazed terra-cotta relief, 19¼ × 15¾″
Provenance: Julius Böhler, Lucerne; Duveen; P. A. B. and Joseph E. Widener, Elkins Park, PA; National Gallery of Art, Washington, D.C.

LUCA DELLA ROBBIA   *The Madonna and Child with Cherubim,* c. 1470, polychrome glazed terra-cotta tondo, diameter 21″
Provenance: M. de Nolivos, Paris; Gustave Dreyfus, Paris; Duveen; Andrew W. Mellon, Pittsburgh; National Gallery of Art, Washington, D.C.

LUCA DELLA ROBBIA   *The Madonna and Child with God the Father and Cherubim,* c. 1471, polychrome glazed terra-cotta high relief, 35½ × 19″
Provenance: Louis Charles Timbal, Paris; Gustave Dreyfus, Paris; Duveen; Andrew W. Mellon, Pittsburgh; National Gallery of Art, Washington, D.C.

LUCA DELLA ROBBIA   *The Adoration of the Child,* c. 1477–79, unglazed terra-cotta high relief, 30¼ × 16¼″
Provenance: Louis Charles Timbal, Paris; Gustave Dreyfus, Paris; Duveen; Andrew W. Mellon, Pittsburgh; National Gallery of Art, Washington, D.C.

LUCA DELLA ROBBIA   *Bust of St. John*
Provenance: Sold by Duveen, c. 1913, with an attribution from Von Bode; present whereabouts unknown.

HUBERT ROBERT   *The Fountain,* c. 1775, oil on canvas, 26 × 20″
Provenance: Duveen; Norton Simon Museum, Pasadena, CA.

RODRIGO DE OSONA (THE ELDER)   *The Adoration of the Magi*
Provenance: Lionel Harris, London; Duveen; Samuel H. Kress, New York; M. H. de Young Memorial Museum, San Francisco.

ROMAN SCHOOL, FIFTEENTH CENTURY   *The Wolf of the Capitol,* or *Symbolic She-Wolf,* c. 1450, bronze statuette, h. 6½″
Provenance: J. Pierpont Morgan, New York; Duveen; Henry Clay Frick, New York; Frick Collection, New York.
Note: Now "Paduan (?), early sixteenth century."

ANTONIAZZO ROMANO   *Madonna and Child with Infant Saint John the Baptist,* c. 1480, oil and gold leaf on panel, 18¾ × 13⅛″
Provenance: Duveen; Norman Simon Museum, Pasadena, CA.

ANTONIAZZO ROMANO   *Madonna and Child with Two Cherubim,* tempera on panel, 21 × 16½"
Provenance: Said to have been bought in the Via Babuino by Charles Butler, London; Robert and Evelyn Benson, London; Duveen, 1927; Norton Simon; Los Angeles County Museum, on loan.

ANTONIAZZO ROMANO   *Madonna and Child*
Provenance: Ex Spiridon; identified from a letter of November 1919 between Carl Hamilton, New York, and Duveen; present whereabouts unknown.

GEORGE ROMNEY   *Miss Penelope Lee-Acton,* 1791, on canvas, 93¼ × 58¼"
Provenance: By descent to Hon. Victor Saumarez of Shrubland Park; Duveen, 1914; Henry E. Huntington, 1916; The Huntington, San Marino, CA.

GEORGE ROMNEY   *Mrs. Susannah (Miller) Lee Acton,* 1786–87, on canvas, 50¼ × 40⅛"
Provenance: By descent to Hon. Victor Saumarez of Shrubland Park; Duveen; Henry E. Huntington, 1917; The Huntington, San Marino, CA.

GEORGE ROMNEY   *Mrs. Catherine (Brouncker) Adye, later Catherine Willett,* 1784–85, on canvas, 30 × 25"
Provenance: By descent to Frederick, Earl de Grey, later 2nd Marquess of Ripon, Studley Royal, nr. Ripon, Yorkshire, by 1894; Duveen, c. 1917; Henry E. Huntington, 1922; The Huntington, San Marino, CA.

GEORGE ROMNEY   *Mary (Palmer), Lady Beauchamp-Proctor,* 1782–88(?); on canvas, 94⅝ × 58½"
Provenance: By descent to Sir Reginald Proctor-Beauchamp, 5th Bart., of Ebley Court, Stroud, Gloucestershire, by 1878; Michael Bass, 1st Lord Burton, of Rangemore Park, Burton-on-Trent, by 1888; Ernest L. Raphael, by 1904; Duveen, 1924; Henry E. Huntington, 1926; The Huntington, San Marino, CA.

GEORGE ROMNEY   *Margaret Beckford, later Margaret Orde, and Susan Euphemia Beckford, later Duchess of Hamilton: the Beckford Children,* or *The Misses Beckford,* 1789–91, on canvas, 60 × 48⅜"
Provenance: By descent to Alfred Douglas, Douglas-Hamilton, 13th Duke of Hamilton; Hamilton Palace Sale, Christie's, 1919; Duveen; Henry E. Huntington, 1920; The Huntington, San Marino, CA.

GEORGE ROMNEY   *Mrs. Catherine (Halhead) Burton,* 1789, on canvas, 36¹¹⁄₁₆ × 28½"
Provenance: By descent to G. G. Maitland; C. W. Mansel Lewis, by 1885; Duveen; Henry E. Huntington, 1925; The Huntington, San Marino, CA.

GEORGE ROMNEY   *Lady Caroline Spencer, later Viscountess Clifden and her Sister, Lady Elizabeth Spencer,* 1786–92, on canvas, 57¼ × 73⅛"
Provenance: By descent to Leopold, 5th Viscount Clifden; Charles John Wertheimer, 1896; Duveen, 1911; Henry E. Huntington, 1911; The Huntington, San Marino, CA.

GEORGE ROMNEY   *Mrs. Rose (Gardiner) Milles,* 1780–83, on canvas, 94 × 58⅜″
Provenance: By descent to Sir Francis Beilby Alston; Alexander Rowland Alston of The Tofte, Sharnbrook, Bedfordshire; Duveen; Henry E. Huntington, 1914; The Huntington, San Marino, CA.

GEORGE ROMNEY   *Emma Hart, later Lady Hamilton, in a Straw Hat,* c. 1782–84, on canvas, 30 × 25″
Provenance: Alfred de Rothschild of Seamore Place, by 1902; by descent to Almina, Countess of Carnarvon, 1918; Duveen; Henry E. Huntington, 1924; The Huntington, San Marino, CA.

GEORGE ROMNEY   *Emma Hart, later Lady Hamilton, in a White Turban,* c. 1791, on canvas, 32 × 25¾″
Provenance: By descent to Sir William Bromley-Davenport; Duveen, 1926; Henry E. Huntington, 1926; The Huntington, San Marino, CA.

GEORGE ROMNEY   *Lady Hamilton as Medea,* c. 1786, on canvas, 29¼ × 25¼″
Provenance: Anonymous collection, Livorno, Italy; O'Cluse, Frankfurt-am-Main, Germany; Duveen; Norton Simon Museum, Pasadena, CA.

GEORGE ROMNEY   *Lady Hamilton as Ambassadress,* or *Emma Hart on Her Wedding Day*
Provenance: Bought by Cohn at the Michelham sale of 1926 for 40,000 guineas; Duveen; Jack G. Taylor.

GEORGE ROMNEY   *Lady Hamilton as Mirth*
Provenance: Bought in 1925 for $35,000; reduced to $25,000 during the Depression; present whereabouts unknown.

GEORGE ROMNEY   *Lady Hamilton as Bacchante*
Provenance: Lord Leconfield, Petworth; Duveen, 1935; present whereabouts unknown.

GEORGE ROMNEY   *Lady Hamilton,* oil on canvas.
Provenance: Bought at auction in Paris for £13,000 in 1926; Duveen described it as "a sketch"; present whereabouts unknown.

GEORGE ROMNEY   *Anne, Lady de la Pole,* c. 1786–99, oil on canvas
Provenance: By descent to Frederick Arundel de la Pole, 11th Bart., Shute House, nr. Axminster, Devonshire; Duveen, 1913; Herbert Stern, 1st Baron Michelham, London, 1919; Baroness Aimée Geraldine Michelham, 1919; Alvan Tufts Fuller, 1926; Museum of Fine Arts, Boston, MA.

GEORGE ROMNEY   *Portrait of Mrs. Davenport,* or *Mrs. Davies Davenport,* 1782–84, oil on canvas, 30⅛ × 25⅛″
Provenance: By descent to Sir William Bromley-Davenport, Capesthorne Hall, nr. Macclesfield, Cheshire; Duveen, 1926; Andrew W. Mellon, Pittsburgh, 1928; National Gallery of Art, Washington, D.C.

GEORGE ROMNEY   *Charlotte, Lady Milnes,* c. 1788–92, on canvas, 94 × 58"
Provenance: Lady Milnes, Tunbridge Wells, Kent; Monckton Milnes, Lord Houghton; the Earl of Crewe, Fryston Hall, Cheshire; Duveen, Henry Clay Frick; Frick Collection, New York.

GEORGE ROMNEY   *Mrs. Bryan Cooke,* c. 1787–89, oil on canvas, 49 × 39"
Provenance: By descent to Philip Bryan Davies-Cooke; J. Davies-Cooke, Gwysaney, Mold, Flintshire, Wales; Duveen; Jules Bache; Metropolitan Museum of Art, New York.

GEORGE ROMNEY   *Lady Lemon,* 1788, oil on canvas, 50 × 40"
Provenance: By descent to Lieutenant Colonel Arthur Tremayne; Duveen; Edward T. Stotesbury, Philadelphia, by 1932; Robert Lehman, 1944; Metropolitan Museum of Art, New York.
Note: The painting is one of a pair; that of Sir William Lemon is of an identical size and both works crossed on the *Aquitania* to New York, accompanied by the restorer, W. A. Holder, in 1932; present whereabouts unknown.

GEORGE ROMNEY   *Mrs. Charles Frederick,* oil on canvas, 30 × 25"
Provenance: Sir Charles Frederick; Duveen; Jules Bache, by 1926; present whereabouts unknown.

GEORGE ROMNEY   *Captain Little's Children,* or *The Children of Captain Little,* oil on canvas, 57½ × 42¾"
Provenance: Samuel Hartley, Lansdown Priory, nr. Bath; Major J. H. Little; Arthur Sanderson; Otto H. Kahn; Duveen; Lord Michelham; Edward F. Fisher, Detroit; Detroit Institute of Arts.

GEORGE ROMNEY   *William Beckford as a Boy*
Provenance: Duveen, 1921; identified from consular invoices when the painting was shipped from Paris, 4/9/21.

GEORGE ROMNEY   *Mrs. Bracebridge and Child,* oil on canvas, 62 × 48½"
Provenance: Duveen, 1920; identified from consular invoices when the painting crossed the Atlantic on the *Aquitania* with W. A. Holder, 11/12/20.

GEORGE ROMNEY   *Hon. Mrs. Lowther*
Provenance: Duveen, 1920; identified from consular invoices when the painting crossed the Atlantic on the *Aquitania* with W. A. Holder, 11/12/20.

GEORGE ROMNEY   *Captain Stubbs*
Provenance: Duveen, half share with Agnew's, 1921; shipped from Paris, 4/9/21; present whereabouts unknown.

GEORGE ROMNEY   *The Hon. Francis North*
Provenance: Duveen, half share with Agnew's, 1919–21; Holder charges £45. 10s. to restore; present whereabouts unknown.

GEORGE ROMNEY   *James Clitherow*
Provenance: Duveen, 1922; identified from a London invoice, 12/20/22.

GEORGE ROMNEY   *The Little Artist*
Provenance: Duveen, 1922; identified from a London invoice, 12/20/22; present whereabouts unknown.

GEORGE ROMNEY   *Master J. W. Tempest*
Provenance: Duveen, 1922; identified from a London invoice, 12/20/22; present whereabouts unknown.

GEORGE ROMNEY   *Captain Stables*
Provenance: Duveen, half share with Agnews, 1921; identified from consular invoices, 5/21/21; apparent value at that time was £5,000; present whereabouts unknown.

GEORGE ROMNEY   *Lord Courtenay*
Provenance: Ex Duke of Hamilton sale in 1919; Eward Fowles reports that Duveens paid 16,000 guineas for the painting; present whereabouts unknown.

GEORGE ROMNEY   *Anne, Marchioness of Townsend*
Provenance: Ex Townsend collection; Duveen bought the painting in 1926 for the trifling sum of £2,500 and then Holder did extensive restoration prior to the resale; present whereabouts unknown.

GEORGE ROMNEY   *Lady Elizabeth Forbes*
Provenance: Michelham sale of 1926; bought through Cohn for £24,000 and sold three years later for $50,000, though to whom sold is not stated; present whereabouts unknown.

GEORGE ROMNEY   *William, 3rd Viscount Courtenay, 9th Earl of Devon*
Provenance: Ex Duke of Hamilton; Christie's; Duveen, 1919; present whereabouts unknown.

COSIMO ROSSELLI   *The Madonna and Child,* c. 1480–90, on wood, 31 × 23″
Provenance: James Stirling Dyce, Edinburgh; Sir George Donaldson, London; James G. Mann, Castlecraig, Dolphinton, Strathclyde; Leopold Davis, Duveen, by 1932; Samuel H. Kress, 1937; National Gallery of Art, Washington, D.C.; Kress Collection, New York; Birmingham Museum of Art, AL, as "workshop of Domenico Ghirlandaio," 1952.
Note: Now "Master of San Spirito."

COSIMO ROSSELLI   *The Madonna and Child with Saints,* or *Madonna Adoring the Child,* c. 1490–1500, on wood, 21¼ × 14¾″
Provenance: Victor de Cock, Paris; Frederick Lewisohn, New York; Duveen, by 1938; Samuel H. Kress, New York; National Gallery of Art, Washington, D.C.; Kress Collection, New York; Philbrook Art Center, Tulsa, OK.

COSIMO ROSSELLI   *Portrait of a Man*
Provenance: Ex Spiridon collection; Duveen; Carl Hamilton, 1919; returned to Duveen; present whereabouts unknown.

COSIMO ROSSELLI   *Virgin and Child with St. John and Saints,* tondo, diameter 38"
Provenance: Duveen; burnt at sea.

ANTONIO ROSSELLINO   *The Madonna and Child with Angels,* c. 1469–70, stucco high
relief, 28¼ × 23"
Provenance: Louis Charles Timbal, Paris; Gustave Dreyfus, Paris; Duveen; Samuel H.
Kress, New York; National Gallery of Art, Washington, D.C.
Note: Now "After Antonio Rossellino."

ANTONIO ROSSELLINO   *The Madonna and Child,* c. 1470, terra-cotta high relief,
38½ × 21"
Provenance: Conte Cosimo Alessandri, Florence; Oscar Hainauer, Berlin; Duveen; Edward
Drummond Libbey, Toledo, OH; Museum of Art, Toledo, OH.
Notes: This was another in the long list of items Carl Hamilton contracted to buy in 1919
but did not pay for. The price quoted to him then was $90,000. After it was returned to
Duveen, Libbey bought it for $112,500 in 1933.

ANTONIO ROSSELLINO   *The Madonna and Child,* c. 1475, polychrome and gilt white
marble high relief, 28¾ × 20¼"
Provenance: Conte Cosimo Alessandri, Florence; Oscar Hainauer, Berlin; Duveen; Benjamin Altman, New York; Metropolitan Museum of Art, New York.

ANTONIO ROSSELLINO   *The Madonna and Child,* c. 1475, terra-cotta statuette,
18¼ × 10⅜"
Provenance: Gustave Dreyfus, Paris; Duveen; Andrew Mellon, Washington, D.C.;
National Gallery of Art, Washington, D.C.

ANTONIO ROSSELLINO   *The Madonna and Child,* c. 1475–78, white marble high relief,
33 × 22"
Provenance: Duveen; Clarence H. Mackay, Roslyn, NY; Duveen; Samuel H. Kress, New
York; National Gallery of Art, Washington, D.C.

ANTONIO ROSSELLINO   *The Young Saint John the Baptist,* c. 1475–79, white marble
bust, 12¾"
Provenance: Church of San Francesco dei Vanchetoni, Florence; Duveen; Samuel H. Kress,
New York; National Gallery of Art, Washington, D.C.

PETER PAUL RUBENS   *Portrait of Anne of Austria, Queen of France,* c. 1622–25, on
canvas, 47¼ × 38⅛"
Provenance: King Friedrich Wilhelm II of Prussia; Kaiser Wilhelm II, by 1933; Duveen,
1933; Norton Simon Museum, Pasadena, CA.
Note: Now "Peter Paul Rubens and Studio."

PETER PAUL RUBENS   *Louis XIII, King of France,* c. 1622–25, on canvas, 46½ × 38"
Provenance: By descent from King Friedrich Wilhelm II of Prussia; Kaiser Wilhelm II;
Duveen, 1928; Norton Simon Museum, Pasadena, CA.
Note: Except for Burckhard, none of Duveen's experts thought the work to be by Rubens.
The work is a companion piece to *Anne of Austria.*

PETER PAUL RUBENS   *Marchesa Brigida Spinola Doria,* 1606, oil on canvas, 60 × 38⅞"
Provenance: Charles J. Wertheimer, London; Bertram Wodehouse Currie, Minley Manor, Hampshire, and by descent to Bertram George Francis Currie, Dingley Hall, Leicester; Duveen, by 1953–57; Samuel H. Kress, 1957; National Gallery of Art, Washington, D.C.
Note: The painting is said to have been exchanged for a Leonardo da Vinci, acquired earlier and not otherwise identified, that the Gallery decided was not by Leonardo (Modestini).

PETER PAUL RUBENS   *Atalanta and Meleager,* c. 1616, oil on wood, 52½ × 42"
Provenance: Dukes of Marlborough, Blenheim Palace, Oxfordshire; by descent until sold at Christie's, 1886; Hon. George Augustus Frederick Cavendish-Bentinck, London; Rodolphe Kann, Paris; Duveen, 1907; Henry Goldman, New York; Duveen, 1939; Fletcher Fund, 1944; Metropolitan Museum of Art, New York.

PETER PAUL RUBENS   *The Holy Family*
Provenance: Ex Dukes of Sutherland; Duveen; sold to Arabella Huntington, July 21, 1908, and she returned it in 1909; present whereabouts unknown.

JACOB VAN RUISDAEL   *Quay at Amsterdam,* c. 1670, oil on canvas, 20⅜ × 25⅞"
Provenance: Baron de Beuronville, 1881; Charles Sedelmeyer, Paris; Maurice Kann, Paris; Duveen; Henry Clay Frick, New York; Frick Collection, New York.

ALBERT D. RUTHERSTON   *Portrait of the Artist,* oil on canvas
Provenance: Leicester Galleries, Duveen Paintings Fund, 1926; presented to the Ferens by the executors of Lord Duveen, 1949.

FRANCESCO DA SAN GALLO   *St. John the Baptist,* or *St. John Baptizing,* c. 1528, bronze statuette, h. 21"
Provenance: Stefano Bardini, Florence; Oscar Hainauer, Berlin; Duveen; J. Pierpont Morgan, New York; Duveen; Henry Clay Frick, New York; Frick Collection, New York.

SANO DI PIETRO   *Virgin and Child with Sain Bernardino, Saint Jerome and Two Angels,* tempera on wood panel, 25 × 16¾"
Provenance: R. Langton Douglas; Duveen, 1923; given by Duveen to the Detroit Institute of Arts in 1924.

ANDREA SANSOVINO   *Madonna and Child with Saints,* bronze
Provenance: Duveen; National Gallery of Art, Washington, D.C.
Note: Now considered "Style of."

ANDREA SANSOVINO   *St. John the Baptist,* bronze statuette
Provenance: Duveen to Clarence H. Mackay in 1918; sold for $15,000; present whereabouts unknown.

JACOPO SANSOVINO   *Antonio San Gallo,* or *Antonio Galli,* c. 1520, bronze bust, h. 23⅝"
Provenance: Baron Achille Seillière, Château de Mello, Oise; Baron Adolphe de Rothschild; Baron Maurice de Rothschild, Paris; Duveen; Henry Clay Frick, New York; Frick Collection, New York.
Note: Now given to Federico Brandani.

JACOPO SANSOVINO   *Bacchus and a Young Faun,* c. 1530, bronze statue, 71¼ × 18½"
Provenance: Napoléon Bonaparte; the French National Collections; Prince Napoléon, Palais Royal, Paris; Marquis de Ganay, Paris; Duveen; Andrew W. Mellon, Pittsburgh; National Gallery of Art, Washington, D.C.

JACOPO SANSOVINO   *Venus Anadyomene,* c. 1530, bronze statue, 65½ × 17¼"
Provenance: Napoléon Bonaparte; the French National Collections; Prince Napoléon, Palais Royal, Paris; Sir George Faudel-Phillips, London; Duveen; George Jay Gould, Lakewood, NJ; Andrew W. Mellon, Pittsburgh; National Gallery of Art, Washington, D.C.

JACOPO SANSOVINO   Two bronze statues, both titled *The Madonna of the Rosary,* mid sixteenth century
Provenance: Duveen; National Gallery of Art, Washington, D.C.
Note: Now "Style of."

STEFANO DI GIOVANNI DI CONSOLO SASSETTA   *The Meeting of St. Anthony and St. Paul,* c. 1440, on wood, 18¾ × 13⅜"
Provenance: 2nd Viscount Allendale, Bretton Hall, Yorkshire, by 1923; Duveen, 1937; Samuel H. Kress, New York; National Gallery of Art, Washington, D.C.
Note: Walker now attributes the painting to "Sassetta and assistant," and the Getty Provenance Index, "Sassetta and workshop."

SASSETTA   *Saint Anthony in the Wilderness,* tempera and gold on wood, from a polyptych, 18⅝ × 13½"
Provenance: Prince Léon Ouroussoff, Vienna; Duveen; Philip Lehman, before 1924; Metropolitan Museum of Art, New York.
Note: Now "The Osservanza Master."

SASSETTA   *The Procession to Calvary,* c. 1437–44, tempera on wood panel, 19¼ × 25"
Provenance: Northwick collections, by inheritance to W. E. S. Erle Drax; R. Langdon Douglas, London; Duveen; Carl Hamilton, New York; Duveen; Detroit Institute of Arts.

SASSETTA   *Scenes from the life of St. Francis,* seven small paintings, 37½ × 22"
Provenance: Always called the "Mackay Sassettas," these small paintings were once part of a large composition painted for the high altarpiece of the Church of San Francesco in San Sepolcro. Berenson owned the central panel, of St. Francis. Duveen probably bought them for £30,000. He spent £4,270 in a botched restoration and sold them to Clarence H. Mackay of New York for £100,000, or $500,000. But then it transpired that Mackay had not paid for them. Kenneth Clark, director of London's National Gallery, reportedly offered £35,000 for them. Now at the National Gallery, London.

MARTIN SCHAFFNER OR BARTHEL BEHAM   *Portrait of a Woman (A Schad von Mittelbiberach),* on wood
Provenance: Schad von Mittelbiberach family (?); Graf von Leutrum Ertingen, Stuttgart; Professor H. Freiherr von Haberman, Munich; Rodolphe Kann, Paris; Duveen; Samuel H. Kress, New York; Denver Art Museum, Denver, CO.

MARTIN SCHONGAUER *Madonna and Child with Two Angels*
Provenance: Ex Mrs. Rabbits; Christie's, 1923; Duveen; present whereabouts unknown.
Note: The painting was bought for 145 guineas and sold to a German collector a year later for £1,000.

SEBASTIANO DEL PIOMBO *Anton Francesco degli Albizzi,* wood transferred to canvas
Provenance: By descent to William John Monson, Viscount Oxenbridge, Burton Hall, Lincolnshire; Robert Henry and Evelyn Benson, London; Duveen; Samuel H. Kress, New York; Museum of Fine Arts, Houston, TX.

SEGNA DI BUONAVENTURA *Madonna and Child,* 1500–50, tempera on wood panel, 29 × 18¾"
Provenance: Prince Léon Ouroussoff; Duveen; Carl Hamilton, New York; Duveen; Detroit Institute of Arts.
Note: The painting was also attributed to Ugolino di Neri and Duccio before being attributed to the Master of Citta di Castello by Berenson in 1932. The Berenson attribution has been accepted by the Institute.

SEVERO DA RAVENNA *Neptune Riding a Sea Monster,* or *Neptune on a Sea Monster,* bronze statuette, 13½ × 11¼"
Provenance: Frederic Spitzer, Paris; Oscar Hainauer, Berlin; Duveen; J. Pierpont Morgan, New York; Duveen; Henry Clay Frick, New York; Frick Collection, New York.

SCHOOL OF SIENA *A She-Wolf,* bronze statuette, h. 7¾"
Provenance: J. Pierpont Morgan, New York; Duveen; Henry Clay Frick, New York; Frick Collection, New York.
Note: Now labeled "Italian, first half of the sixteenth century."

LUCA SIGNORELLI *The Resurrected Christ Appearing to St. Magdalen,* c. 1514, tempera and oil on wood panel, 7⅜ × 16¹¹⁄₁₆"
Provenance: Mancini Collection, Cortona; Elia Volpi, Villa Pia, Florence; W. S. Greening; Duveen; Walter Pach; Detroit Institute of Arts.
Note: Modern strips were added to all four sides and the restorer William Suhr transferred the painting to a new panel in 1929. The Institute also owns a companion work, *The Resurrected Christ Appearing to His Disciples,* also tempera and oil on wood panel, and approximately the same size: 7⁵⁄₁₆ × 16¾".

LUCA SIGNORELLI *The Madonna and Child,* on panel, 20¼ × 18½"
Provenance: Robert H. and Evelyn Benson, London; Duveen; Jules S. Bache, New York; Metropolitan Museum of Art, New York.

HENRY SILK *The Hat on the Floor,* pencil and watercolor on paper
Provenance: Duveen Paintings Fund, c. 1928; presented to the Ferens by the executors of Duveen's estate in 1949.

SODOMA   *St. George and the Dragon,* c. 1518, on wood, 55½ × 38⅜"
Provenance: Earls of Shrewsbury, Alton Towers, Straffordshire; Cook, Doughty House, Richmond, Surrey; Duveen; Samuel H. Kress, New York; National Gallery of Art, Washington, D.C.

GERARD SOEST   *Cecil Calvert, Second Lord Baltimore,* oil on canvas, 85 × 60"
Provenance: Sir Timothy Calvert Eden; Duveen; William Randolph Hearst; Enoch Pratt Free Library, Baltimore, MD.

CRISTOFORO SOLARI (IL GOBBO)   *The Resurrection,* c. 1510, white marble high relief, 11½ × 10"
Provenance: Louis Charles Timbal, Paris; Gustave Dreyfus, Paris; Duveen; Samuel H. Kress, New York; National Gallery of Art, Washington, D.C.

CRISTOFORO SOLARI (IL GOBBO)   *Madonna and Child,* c. 1489, marble statue, 22 × 22⅜ × 6½"
Provenance: Otto H. Kahn, New York; Duveen; Kress Collection, New York; National Gallery of Art, Washington, D.C.

STANLEY SPENCER   *The Resurrection, Cookham*
Provenance: Duveen; gift to the Tate Gallery, London.

STANLEY SPENCER   *The Red House,* oil on canvas
Provenance: Bought from the Goupil Gallery in 1926 by the Duveen Paintings Fund for £55. Presented to the Ferens by the executors of Lord Duveen's estate in 1949.

ARETINO SPINELLO   *Saint Christopher with the Child and Sts. Anthony, Catherine and Lucy,* tempera and gold leaf on panel, 8 × 13¼"
Provenance: Duveen; Norton Simon Museum, Pasadena, CA.

GHERARDO STARNINA   *The Madonna Enthroned with Angels,* c. 1380, triptych, 80⅝ × 96⅝"
Provenance: Bertram, 5th Earl of Ashburnham; Mary Catherine, Lady Ashburnham, Battle, Sussex; R. Langton Douglas, Dublin; Duveen; Andrew W. Mellon; National Gallery of Art, Washington, D.C.
Note: Carl Hamilton undertook to buy the painting in 1919 for $90,000. After no money changed hands, the altarpiece was returned to Duveen and sold to Mellon in 1936 for $170,000.

JAN STEEN   *The Doctor*
Provenance: Ex Northbrook; Duveen, 1927; present whereabouts unknown.

JAN STEEN   *Portrait of Man with a Mandolin,* or *Portrait of the Artist* (?)
Provenance: Ex Northbrook; Duveen, 1927; sold to the "Castle Rohoncz"; present whereabouts unknown.
Note: Duveen valued the painting at £6,000 and sold it for £10,000. It was exhibited in the Dutch Exhibition in London in 1929.

PHILIP WILSON STEER   *Farmyard*
Provenance: Duveen; gift to the Tate Gallery, London.

EDWARD STOTT   *The Good Samaritan,* oil on canvas
Provenance: Bought from the artist by Duveen in 1910 and presented to the city of Hull in memory of his father.

EDWARD STOTT   *Folding Time,* oil on canvas
Provenance: Duveen; gift to the Ferens Art Gallery, Hull, 1927.

EDWARD STOTT   *Study for Rescued Man in "The Good Samaritan,"* chalk on brown paper
Provenance: Duveen; gift to the Ferens Art Gallery, Hull, 1918.

EDWARD STOTT   *Study for the Samaritan's Head,* chalk and pencil on paper
Provenance: Duveen; gift to the Ferens Art Gallery, Hull, 1918.

BERNHARD STRIGEL   *St. Mary Cleophas and Her Family,* c. 1520–28, oil on panel, 49 × 24¾"
Provenance: Rodolphe Kann, Paris; Duveen; Mr. and Mrs. Martin Bromberg, Hamburg; Dr. and Mrs. Jacob Emden, Hamburg; Samuel H. Kress, New York; National Gallery of Art, Washington, D.C.

BERNHARD STRIGEL   *St. Mary Salome and Her Family,* c. 1520–28, oil on panel, 49⅜ × 25⅞"
Provenance: Rodolphe Kann, Paris; Duveen; Mr. and Mrs. Martin Bromberg, Hamburg; Dr. and Mrs. Jacob Emden, Hamburg; Samuel H. Kress, New York; National Gallery of Art, Washington, D.C.

GILBERT STUART   *George Washington,* on canvas
Provenance: Earls of Haldane-Duncan, Camperdown House, Tayside, Scotland; Duveen, 1919; Henry Clay Frick, New York; Frick Collection, New York.
Note: This is an early copy by the artist of his celebrated portrait of George Washington as president for John Vaughan of Philadelphia.

TADDEO DI BARTOLO   *The Coronation of the Virgin*
Provenance: Duveen; the Kress Collection, New York.

GERARD TER BORCH   *The Suitor's Visit,* c. 1658, on canvas, 31½ × 29⅝"
Provenance: Charles-Auguste-Louis-Joseph, Duc de Morny, Paris; Marqués de Salamanca, Madrid; Adolphe de Rothschild, Paris; Maurice de Rothschild, Paris; Duveen; Andrew W. Mellon; National Gallery of Art, Washington, D.C.

GERARD TER BORCH   *Curiosity,* on canvas, 29 × 32"
Provenance: Baron Goldschmidt de Rothschild; Duveen; Jules Bache, New York; Metropolitan Museum of Art, New York.

THIRTEENTH CENTURY   *Virgin and Child* group, in ivory
Provenance: Ex Rodolphe Kann, Paris; ex Larcade; shipped on the liner *La Savoie,* 1/15/21; present whereabouts unknown.

GIOVANNI DOMENICO TIEPOLO   *Deposition from the Cross,* on canvas
Provenance: Rodolphe Kann, Paris; Duveen; Emilie Yznaga, Paris; National Gallery, London.

TIEPOLO   *Head of a Philosopher,* on canvas
Provenance: Rodolphe Kann, Paris; Duveen; Minneapolis Institute of Arts, Minneapolis, MN.

JACOPO TINTORETTO   *Portrait of N. Priuli,* or *Portrait of a Venetian Procurator,* 44½ × 35″
Provenance: Dukes of Abercorn; Duveen; Henry Clay Frick; Frick Collection, New York.
Note: Now considered "Circle of."

JACOPO TINTORETTO   *Portrait of a Venetian Senator,* c. 1565–1570, 44¼ × 35″
Provenance: Dukes of Abercorn; Duveen; George Eastman, Rochester, NY; Memorial Art Gallery, University of Rochester, NY.

TITIAN   *The Madonna and Child,* c. 1510, on panel, 18 × 22″
Provenance: Earl of Exeter; Robert and Evelyn Benson, London; Duveen; Andrew W. Mellon; Duveen; Jules S. Bache, New York; Metropolitan Museum of Art, New York.
Note: Present opinion is that the painting has suffered from damage and extensive restoration and the attribution to Titian is doubtful. It is still considered a Titian by the museum.

TITIAN   *Portrait of a Venetian Nobleman,* c. 1550–55, on canvas, 47½ × 36½″
Provenance: Prince Alberto Giovanelli; Duveen; Frank P. Wood, Toronto; Jules Bache Collection, New York; Metropolitan Museum of Art, New York.
Note: The work is now considered to be by Lambert Sustris.

TITIAN   *Venus and the Lute Player,* 1562–65, oil on canvas, 65 × 82½″
Provenance: Prince Pio, Rome; Thomas William Coke, Holkham, Norfolk; the Earls of Leicester, Holkham; Duveen; Munsey Fund, 1936; Metropolitan Museum of Art, New York.
Note: The painting was sold to the Met for a reported $400,000.

TITIAN   *Filippo Archinto, Archbishop of Milan,* c. 1554–56, oil on canvas, 46½ × 37″
Provenance: The Archinto family, Milan; Duveen; Benjamin Altman, New York; Metropolitan Museum of Art, New York.
Note: Now attributed to "Workshop of Titian or Leandro Bassano."

TITIAN   *Portrait of a Venetian Gentleman,* c. 1510, on canvas, 30 × 25″
Provenance: Robert P. Nichols, London; William Graham, London; Henry Doetsch, London; Lord Rochdale, Beechwood Hall, Lancashire; Duveen; Henry Goldman, New York; Duveen; Samuel H. Kress, New York; National Gallery of Art, Washington, D.C.
Note: Opinion has vacillated for years between an attribution to Titian and present belief that the painting is a joint venture between Titian and Giorgione.

TITIAN   *Portrait of Andrea dei Franceschi,* c. 1532, on canvas, 31¼ × 25″
Provenance: King Frederick the Great of Prussia; Louis Viardot, Paris; Duveen, 1928; Mr. and Mrs. Edgar B. Whitcomb, Detroit; Detroit Institute of Arts.

TITIAN   *A Lady and Children in a Beautiful Landscape*
Provenance: Philip II of Spain; Duc d'Orléans; Earl of Ellesmere, Bridgewater House; Duveen; present whereabouts unknown.
Note: Duveen tried to sell the painting to Arabella Huntington in July 1916, calling it "one of the greatest Titians in the world," but she did not succumb.

TITIAN   *Andrea Navagero,* or *Portrait of a Bearded Man,* c. 1515, 31¾ × 27¾″
Provenance: By descent to Viscount Alford Hume, Ashbridge Park, Herts.; Duveen, 1926; Mr. and Mrs. Edsel Ford; Detroit Institute of Arts.
Note: Now "School of."

TITIAN   *Virgin and Child with St. John,* oil on canvas, 38¼ × 32¼″
Provenance: Hermitage Museum, St. Petersburg; Rumianzoff Museum, Moscow; Duveen; Norton Simon Museum, Pasadena, CA.

TITIAN   *Portrait of Giorgio Cornaro,* or *The Man with a Falcon,* oil on canvas, 43 × 38″
Provenance: James Simon of Berlin; Angus Brothers, London; Duveen, 1921; present whereabouts unknown.

TITIAN   *Portrait of a Man,* oil on canvas, 38 × 23″
Provenance: Duveen; Norton Simon Museum, Pasadena, CA.

TITIAN   *Alfonso d'Este and Laura Dianti (Presumed),* or *Allegory (Possibly Alfonso d'Este and Laura Dianti),* on canvas, 36 × 32¼″
Provenance: Benacossi family, Ferrara, Conte Leopoldo Cicognara, Ferrara; Lord Stewart, 3rd Marquess of Londonderry; Louis, Comte de Pourtalès-Gorgier, Paris; Baron Michele Lazzaroni, Paris; Duveen; Henry Goldman, New York; Duveen; Samuel H. Kress, New York; National Gallery of Art, Washington, D.C.
Note: The painting is now listed "Follower of Titian."

TITIAN   *Venetian Girl,* or *Portrait of Giulia di Gonzaga-Colonna (Presumed),* or *Portrait of a Lady,* c. 1542–55, on canvas, 38½ × 29⅛″
Provenance: Major Hugh Edward Wilbraham, Delamere House, Northwick, Cheshire; Duveen; Samuel H. Kress, New York; National Gallery of Art, Washington, D.C.

TITIAN   *Portrait of Emilia di Spilimbergo,* c. 1560, on canvas, 48 × 42″
Provenance: Conte Niccolo d'Attimis Maniago, Spilimbergo, Lombardy; Duveen; Joseph P. Widener, Philadelphia; National Gallery of Art, Washington, D.C.
Note: Now "Follower of Titian."

TITIAN   *Portrait of Irene di Spilimbergo,* c. 1560, on canvas, 48 × 42″
Provenance: Conte Niccolo d'Attimis Maniago, Spilimbergo, Lombardy; Duveen; Joseph P. Widener, Philadelphia; National Gallery of Art, Washington, D.C.
Note: Now: "Follower of Titian."

TITIAN   *Madonna and Child and the Infant Saint John in a Landscape,* on canvas
Provenance: Col. Henry Edward Burney, London; Duveen, 1930; Andrew W. Mellon, Pittsburgh; National Gallery of Art, Washington, D.C.
Note: The painting is now attributed to Polidoro da Lanciano.

TITIAN   *Portrait of a Man,* oil on canvas, 38 × 32"
Provenance: Duveen; Norton Simon Museum, Pasadena, CA.

TITIAN   *Salome with the Head of John the Baptist,* oil on canvas, 34 × 29"
Provenance: Duveen; Norton Simon Museum, Pasadena, CA.

TITIAN   *Venetian Nobleman, Portrait of a Senator* (*Giacomo Delfino*), oil on canvas, 42½ × 36"
Provenance: Duveen; Norton Simon Museum, Pasadena, CA.

WALTER TITTLE   *Portrait of Lord Duveen, 1933* (?)
Provenance: Commissioned by Joseph Duveen and given to the Guildhall Collection of the City of Hull.

CONSTANT TROYON   *Going to Market*
Provenance: C. T. Yerkes, New York; Duveen; present whereabouts unknown.
Note: The painting was bought by Uncle Henry for $60,500.

COSIMO TURA   *Portrait of a Man,* 1475–85 tempera on panel, 14⁹⁄₁₆ × 10⅝"
Provenance: Duveen, by 1933; Samuel H. Kress, New York; National Gallery of Art, Washington, D.C.
Note: Now "Attributed to."

COSIMO TURA   *A Member of the Este Family,* or *Portrait of a Ferrarese Nobleman,* tempera on wood, 11⅞ × 8½"
Provenance: By descent to Lt. Col. William Drury Drury-Lowe, Locko Park, Derbyshire; Duveen, 1912; Benjamin Altman, New York; Metropolitan Museum of Art, New York.
Note: One expert has called the National Gallery portrait a characteristic work of Marco Zoppo. This would make the Metropolitan portrait the only independent portrait by Tura to have survived.

COSIMO TURA   *The Flight into Egypt,* on panel, tondo, diameter 15"
Provenance: William Graham; Robert H. and Evelyn Benson, London; Duveen; Jules Bache, New York; Metropolitan Museum of Art, New York.

J. M. W. TURNER   *View of Venice: Ducal Palace, Dogana, with Part of San Giorgio,* on canvas
Provenance: Thomas Horrocks Miller, Singleton Park, Poulton-le-Fylde, Lancashire; Duveen, 1925; Elisabeth Severance Prentiss, Cleveland, OH; Allen Memorial Art Museum, Oberlin College, Oberlin, OH.

J. M. W. TURNER   *Rockets and Blue Lights,* on canvas
Provenance: C. T. Yerkes, New York; Duveen; present whereabouts unknown.

Note: This was another of the paintings Uncle Henry bought at the Yerkes sale, for $129,000.

J. M. W. TURNER   *The Grand Canal: Scene—A Street in Venice,* c. 1837, on canvas, 59¼ × 44¼"
Provenance: Ralph Brocklebank, a Haughton Hall, Taporley, Cheshire; Duveen, 1922; Henry E. Huntington, San Marino, CA; The Huntington, San Marino, CA.

GIOVANNI BATTISTA UTILI   *The Adoration of the Child with Saints and Donors,* on wood, from a polyptych, 74 × 71¾"
Provenance: Rev William Stogdon, Harrow-on-the-Hill, Middlesex; Duveen; Carl Hamilton, New York; Duveen; Samuel H. Kress, New York; National Gallery of Art, Washington, D.C.; Kress Collection, New York; Philbrook Art Center, Tulsa, OK.
Note: Now "Biagio d'Antonio da Firenze."

GIOVANNI BATTISTA UTILI   *Nativity,* 45 × 27½"
Provenance: Duveen; Carl W. Hamilton, New York; Duveen; Samuel H. Kress, New York.

AELBERT VAN OUTWATER   *Crucifixion,* c. 1485, oil on oak panel, 56½ × 40⅜"
Provenance: Collection Crombez, Paris; Harriman collection, New York; Mrs. Mary Harriman Rumsey, New York; Duveen; Mr. and Mrs. Edgar B. Whitcomb; Detroit Institute of Arts.
Notes: Now "Master of the Tiburtine Sibyl."

ADRIAEN VAN UTRECHT   *Still Life with Game, Vegetables, Fruit and a Cockatoo*
Provenance: Duveen; J. Paul Getty Museum.

LORENZO VECCHIETTA   "The Resurrection," 1472, bronze plaque, 21¼ × 16¼"
Provenance: Prince Chigi, Rome; Rodolphe Kann, Paris; J. Pierpont Morgan, New York; Henry Clay Frick, New York; Frick Collection.

DIEGO VELÁZQUEZ   *Cardinal Borja y Velasco,* on canvas
Provenance: 1st Baron Labouchère, Bridgewater, Somerset; Captain E. A. V. Stanley, Quantock Lodge, Somerset; Duveen; Samuel H. Kress, New York; Metropolitan Museum of Art, New York; Kress Collection, New York; Museo de Arte de Ponce, Puerto Rico, study collection.
Note: Now "follower of."

DIEGO VELÁZQUEZ   *Count Duke of Olivares*
Provenance: Doña Antonia de Ypeñarrieta; Corral family, Zaraus; Duchess of Villahermosa, Madrid; Duke of Luna, Madrid; Duveen; Benjamin Altman; Duveen; Lord Cowdray; M. Chateaubriand, Paris; Museu de Arte, São Paulo, Brazil.

DIEGO VELÁZQUEZ   *Philip IV, King of Spain,* c. 1623 oil on canvas, 78¾ × 40½"
Provenance: José Cañaveral Manuel de Villena, Seville; Viuda de Garzón, Seville; Manuel de Soto, Zurich; Duveen; Benjamin Altman, New York; Metropolitan Museum of Art, New York.

DIEGO VELÁZQUEZ   *Philip IV, King of Spain,* c. 1650–55, oil on canvas, 24 × 20"
Provenance: Maréchal-Général Nicolas Soult, Duc de Dalmatie; Mrs. Emery; Cincinnati
Art Museum, Cincinnati, OH.

DIEGO VELÁZQUEZ   *Count Duke of Olivares,* on canvas, 79½ × 41¼"
Provenance: Col. Hugh D. Baillie, London; Charles Scarisbrick, Lancashire; Holford Collection, London; Duveen; Mrs. Arabella Huntington; Hispanic Society of America, New York.

DIEGO VELÁZQUEZ   *The Infanta Maria Theresa,* on canvas, 17½ × 15¾"
Provenance: Philippe Ledieu, Paris; Colonel Payne Bingham, New York; Duveen, 1918;
Jules S. Bache, New York, 1928; Metropolitan Museum of Art, New York.
Note: The painting is generally held to be a fragment from a much larger canvas.

DIEGO VELÁZQUEZ   *A Self-Portrait of the Artist,* on canvas, 27 × 21¾"
Provenance: David Bernhard Hausmann; King George of Hanover; Duke of Brunswick-Luneburg; Duke of Cumberland; Duveen; Jules S. Bache; Metropolitan Museum of Art,
New York.
Note: The painting is now titled *Portrait of a Gentleman* and called "Workshop of
Velázquez."

DIEGO VELÁZQUEZ   *Portrait of a Young Man,* on canvas, 23¼ × 18⅞"
Provenance: Alois Thomas Raymund Harrach, Vienna; Duveen; Andrew W. Mellon;
National Gallery of Art, Washington, D.C.
Note: Now "Circle of Velázquez."

DIEGO VELÁZQUEZ   *Portrait of a Young Girl,* c. 1642–45, on canvas, 20¼ × 16"
Provenance: Sir William Knighton, London; Arthur Sanderson, Edinburgh; Rodolphe
Kann, Paris; Duveen; Arabella Huntington, New York; Archer M. Huntington, New York;
Hispanic Society of America, New York.

DIEGO VELÁZQUEZ   *Man with a Wine Glass,* c. 1623, on canvas, 30 × 25"
Provenance: Sir G. Prior Goldney, Derriads, Chippenham, Wiltshire; Captain R. Langton
Douglas, Dublin; Duveen; Edward Drummond Libbey, Toledo, OH; Museum of Art,
Toledo, OH.

VENETIAN SCHOOL   *Scenes in the Life of Christ with Patron Saints,* c. 1300, tempera
and gold leaf on panel, 16⅜ × 15⅝"
Provenance: Duveen; Norton Simon Museum, Pasadena, CA.

VENETIAN SCHOOL   *Bust of an Old Woman,* bronze, life size, h. 20½"
Provenance: Frederic Spitzer, Paris; Oscar Hainauer, Berlin; Duveen; P. A. B. Widener,
Joseph E. Widener, Elkins Park, PA; National Gallery of Art, Washington, D.C.

VENETIAN SCHOOL   *Figure of an Infant,* c. 1500, bronze statuette, h. 9"
Provenance: Madame d'Yvon, Paris; Sir Thomas Gibson-Carmichael, Castle Craig, N.B.;
J. Pierpont Morgan, New York; Duveen; Henry Clay Frick, New York; Frick Collection,
New York.
Note: Now listed as "Italian, nineteenth century," i.e., a fake.

JAN VERMEER   *The Head of a Young Boy,* oil on canvas, 23¼ × 19¾"
Provenance: Anton W. M. Mensing; Yves Perdoux; Duveen; Jules S. Bache, New York;
Metropolitan Museum of Art, New York.
Note: The painting is now considered to be a French work of the second half of the seven-
teenth century, i.e., a fake.

JAN VERMEER   *A Girl Asleep,* oil on canvas, 34½ × 30⅛"
Provenance: Rodolphe Kann, Paris; Duveen; Benjamin Altman, New York; Metropolitan
Museum of Art, New York.

JAN VERMEER   *A Mistress and Her Maid,* oil on canvas
Provenance: James Simon, Berlin; Duveen; Henry Clay Frick, New York; Frick Collection,
New York.

JAN VERMEER   *The Smiling Girl,* oil on canvas, 16⅛ × 12½"
Provenance: Walter Kurt Rohde, Berlin; Duveen; Andrew W. Mellon, Pittsburgh; National
Gallery of Art, Washington, D.C.
Note: The painting was one in a group of forgeries floated on the Vermeer market in the
1920s and 1930s. It is now dated as c. 1925 and called "Imitator of Johannes Vermeer."

JAN VERMEER   *The Lacemaker,* oil on canvas, 17½ × 15¾"
Provenance: Captain Harold R. Wright, London; Duveen, 1927; Andrew W. Mellon, Pitts-
burgh; National Gallery of Art, Washington, D.C.
Note: See note above. Now dated c. 1925 and labeled "Imitator of Johannes Vermeer."

CLAUDE-JOSEPH VERNET   *Bay of Naples (the Bay of Posilipo),* 1762, oil on canvas,
28½ × 38"
Provenance: Duveen; Norton Simon Museum, Pasadena, CA.

ANDREA DEL VERROCCHIO   *Lorenzo de' Medici,* c. 1478/1621, painted terra-cotta,
25⅞ × 12⅞"
Provenance: Emilio Santarelli, Florence; Edward Nicholls Dennys, London; Henry
Labouchere, 1st baron Taunton, Somersetshire; by inheritance to Edward Arthur Vesey
Stanley, Bridgewater, Somersetshire; Clarence H. Mackay, Roslyn, NY, 1925; Duveen;
Samuel H. Kress Foundation; National Gallery of Art, Washington, D.C.
Note: Now considered "Florentine, fifteenth or sixteenth century, probably after a model
by Andrea del Verrocchio and Orsino Benintendi."

ANDREA DEL VERROCCHIO   *Madonna and Child,* on wood
Provenance: Schickler-Pourtales Collection, Paris; Duveen, 1918–19; to Carl Hamilton,
New York, 1919; Duveen; Clarence H. Mackay, Roslyn, NY; Duveen; Samuel H. Kress,
New York; National Gallery of Art, Washington, D.C.
Note: The painting is now considered "Style of."

ANDREA DEL VERROCCHIO   *Madonna and Child with a Pomegranate,* c. 1470/1475, oil
on panel, 6½ × 5¼"
Provenance: Gustave Dreyfus, Paris; Duveen; Samuel H. Kress, New York; National
Gallery of Art, Washington, D.C.

Note: The painting is now considered a workshop picture with a tentative attribution to Leonardo da Vinci.

ANDREA DEL VERROCCHIO *Madonna and Child,* tempera on canvas, transferred from wood, 26 × 19″
Provenance: Rev. Walter Davenport Bromley, Ashbourne, Derbyshire; Sir Walter R. Farquhar, London; Charles Butler, Hatfield, Herts.; Duveen, 1912; Benjamin Altman, New York; Metropolitan Museum of Art, New York.
Note: The painting is now considered to be a workshop picture.

ANDREA DEL VERROCCHIO *Giuliano de' Medici,* c. 1475, terra-cotta bust, 24 × 26″
Provenance: Eugène Piot, Paris; Louis Charles Timbal, Paris; Gustave Dreyfus, Paris; Duveen, Andrew W. Mellon, Washington, D.C.; National Gallery of Art, Washington, D.C.

ANDREA DEL VERROCCHIO *A Putto Poised on a Globe,* c. 1480–85, terra-cotta statuette, h. 29½″
Provenance: Louis Charles Timbal, Paris; Gustave Dreyfus, Paris; Duveen; Andrew W. Mellon, Pittsburgh; National Gallery of Art, Washington, D.C.

ANDREA DEL VERROCCHIO *David, Conqueror of Goliath,* c. 1472, terra-cotta statuette, h. 19½″
Provenance: Louis Charles Timbal, Paris; Gustave Dreyfus, Paris; Duveen; Samuel H. Kress, New York; National Gallery of Art, Washington, D.C.

JAN CORNELISZ VERSPRONCK *Portrait of a Man in Black,* on canvas
Provenance: Rodolphe Kann, Paris; Duveen; Robert Dawson Evans, Boston; Misses Abby and Belle Hunt, Boston; Museum of Fine Arts, Boston.

ANTOINE VESTIER *The Comtesse d'Estrades,* oil on canvas, 39 × 29¼″
Provenance: Duveen; Norton Simon Museum, Pasadena, CA.

ELIZABETH VIGÉE-LEBRUN *Madame du Barry*
Provenance: According to an edition of the *Illustrated London News* cited in a 1972 British edition of S. N. Behrman's book, *Duveen,* the painting was said to have been in Duveen's own collection for some time; present whereabouts are unknown.

PETER VISCHER *Self Portrait* (?), bronze statue
Provenance: Bought by Duveen from Von Benda of Vienna in 1927; present whereabouts unknown.

ALESSANDRO VITTORIA *Jacopo Contarini,* c. 1580, terra-cotta bust, h. 28⅜″
Provenance: Clarence H. Mackay, Roslyn, NY; Duveen; Samuel H. Kress, New York; National Gallery of Art, Washington, D.C.

ALESSANDRO VITTORIA *Simone Contarini,* terra-cotta bust
Provenance: Duveen; bought for the Metropolitan Museum of Art in New York in 1911; dated from a ledger folio.

ALVISE VIVARINI   *Portrait of a Man*
Provenance: Duveen; acquired by Carl Hamilton in 1919 with promise to pay $75,000; returned and sold to Samuel H. Kress, New York, in 1937 for $60,000.

JEAN-ANTOINE WATTEAU   *The French Comedians,* on canvas, 22½ × 28¾"
Provenance: Jean de Julienne, Paris; Frederick the Great; Emperor William II of Germany; Duveen; Jules S. Bache, New York; Metropolitan Museum of Art, New York.

JEAN-ANTOINE WATTEAU   *Embarquement pour Cythère*
Provenance: Mentioned as having been bought by Duveen from the Kaiser Friedrich Museum in a cable dated February 4, 1929.

ROGIER VAN DER WEYDEN   *Christ Appearing to His Mother,* tempera and oil on wood, right wing of a triptych, 25 × 15"
Provenance: Isabella the Catholic, Queen of Castile and Leon; Capilla Real, Granada; Mariano, duke of Osuna, Madrid; Duveen, by 1912; Michael Dreicer, New York; Metropolitan Museum of Art, New York.
Note: Now considered a copy after the original.

ROGIER VAN DER WEYDEN   *Christ Appearing to the Virgin,* or *Christ Appearing to His Mother,* c. 1460, on wood, 64 × 36⅝"
Provenance: Marqués de Salamanca y Mayol, Madrid; Duveen, by 1912; Andrew W. Mellon, Pittsburgh; National Gallery of Art, Washington, D.C.
Note: Now "Follower of."

ROGIER VAN DER WEYDEN   *A Man with a Turban,* on panel, 11 × 7¾"
Provenance: Duveen; Jules S. Bache, New York; Metropolitan Museum of Art, New York.
Note: "Attributed" to Rogier van der Weyden.

ROGIER VAN DER WEYDEN   *Portrait of a Lady,* c. 1455, on wood, 14½ × 10¾"
Provenance: Duke of Anhalt-Dessau, Gptisches Haus, Worlitz; Duveen, 1926; Andrew W. Mellon, Pittsburgh; National Gallery of Art, Washington, D.C.

ROGIER VAN DER WEYDEN   *The Annunciation,* tempera on wood, left wing of an altarpiece, 74¼ × 45¼"
Provenance: Earls of Ashburnham, Battle, Sussex; Rodolphe Kann, Paris; Duveen; J. Pierpont Morgan, New York; Metropolitan Museum of Art, New York.
Note: Now labeled "Workshop of / possibly Hans Memling."

ROGIER VAN DER WEYDEN   *The Madonna and Child,* c. 1460, 19½ × 12½"
Provenance: Henry Willett, Brighton; Rodolphe Kann, Paris; Duveen; Arabella Huntington, San Marino, CA; The Huntington, San Marino, CA.

ROGIER VAN DER WEYDEN   *Portrait of Jehan de Gros,* c. 1460, 15 × 11"
Provenance: Dr. de Meyer, Bruges; Rodolphe Kann, Paris; Duveen; Martin A. Ryerson, Chicago; Art Institute of Chicago.

Index

A Note on the Type

This book was set in Adobe Garamond. Designed for the Adobe Corporation by Robert Slimbach, the fonts are based on types first cut by Claude Garamond (1480–1561). Garamond was a pupil of Geoffroy Tory and is believed to have followed the Venetian models, although he introduced a number of important differences, and it is to him that we owe the letter we now know as "old style." He gave to his letters a certain elegance and feeling of movement that won their creator an immediate reputation and the patronage of Francis I of France.

Composed by North Market Street Graphics,
Lancaster, Pennsylvania
Printed and bound by Berryville Graphics,
Berryville, Virginia